Skills

For

Effective

Management

Of

Nonprofit

Organizations

Edited by

Richard L. Edwards
John A. Yankey
Mary A. Altpeter

NASW PRESS

National Association of Social Workers
Washington, DC

Josephine A. V. Allen, PhD, ACSW, *President*
Josephine Nieves, MSW, PhD, *Executive Director*

Jane Browning, *Director of Member Services and Publications*
Paula Delo, *Executive Editor*
Christina A. Davis, *Senior Editor*
Fran Pflieger, Maben Publications, *Project Manager*
Annette Hansen, *Copy Editor*
Ida Audeh, *Copy Editor*
Beth Gyorgy, *Proofreader*
Bernice Eisen, *Indexer*
Chanté Lampton, *Acquisitions Associate*
Heather Peters, *Editorial Secretary*

Library of Congress Cataloging-in-Publication Data

Skills for effective management of nonprofit organizations / edited by
    Richard L. Edwards, John A. Yankey, and Mary A. Altpeter.
        p.   cm.
    Rev. and expanded ed. of: Skills for effective human services
management / Richard L. Edwards and John A. Yankey, editors. c1991.
    Includes bibliographical references (p.   ) and index.
    ISBN 0-87101-290-1 (alk. paper)
    1. Human services—Management. 2. Human services—United States—
Management. 3. Nonprofit organizations—Management. 4. Nonprofit
organizations—United States—Management.   I. Edwards, Richard L.
II. Yankey, John A.   III. Altpeter, Mary A.   IV. Skills for
effective human services management.
    HV41.S564   1998   98-14804
    658'.048—dc21   CIP

Printed in the United States of America

We are delighted to dedicate this book
to our grandchildren:
Tyler Eric Huskey and Joshua Michael Lakota;
and Jennifer, Jordan, Jacob, Jillian, Jaron, and Jessica Yankey.

They bring so much joy to our lives.

We hope they and others of their generation grow to adulthood in a world
marked by civility, peace, and social justice.

R.L.E., J.A.Y., and M.A.A.

Contents

Acknowledgments

In every edited book project, many individuals contribute to the final product. We wish first to thank the authors of the individual chapters. Their efforts were critical to making this book possible. We also want to thank Linda Beebe and Nancy Winchester, formerly of the NASW Press, who were involved in the early stages of the process. We also are grateful to others currently at the NASW Press, particularly Chanté Lampton, Acquisitions Associate, and Christina A. Davis, Senior Book Editor. Without their efforts overseeing the coordination and editing processes, the book would not have been completed in such a timely manner. Special thanks go to Fran Pflieger of Maben Publications and to Annette Hansen and Ida Audeh, who were responsible for copy editing.

Others who deserve special thanks include Mark Litzler, who contributed the cartoons included in the book, and Professors Robert E. Quinn and John Rohrbaugh, who originally conceived of the competing values approach to organizational effectiveness. Quinn later developed the competing values approach to leadership effectiveness, which serves as the framework for this book.

We especially want to thank Sylvia B. Yankey for her support and wise counsel. Finally, we thank all of our students, colleagues, and mentors. Over the years they have taught so many valuable lessons about management. For our managerial strengths and successes, we give them full credit; for our shortcomings, we take responsibility.

R.L.E., J.A.Y, and M.A.A.

Introduction

If there is one constant in nonprofit management today, it is the need to deal with change. Contributing to this environment are changing conditions, such as increased demands for services provided by nonprofits; evolving service technologies; and reduced government appropriations for human services, the arts, and the humanities. However, also contributing to this environment are developments in management in the for-profit arena.

In the early 1980s, traditional approaches to American management began to be questioned. The characteristics of successful businesses and managers were identified, and questions were raised about whether management education programs were adequately preparing leaders for the realities of contemporary management. A major business school curriculum study (Porter & McKibbon, 1988) suggested that management education programs needed to place greater emphasis on human skills. Quinn, Faerman, Thompson, and McGrath (1990) noted that

> What is now available in management education is necessary but insufficient. All . . . modern organizations, as never before, and even at the lowest levels, are in need of competent managerial leaders. They want technical ability, but they also want more. They want people who can survive and help organizations prosper in a world of constant change and intense competition. This means both technical competence and interpersonal excellence. (p. v)

Numerous books have been written about what makes for excellence, high productivity, and overall success (for example, Blake, Mouton, & Allen, 1987; Kanter, 1983; Lawler, 1986; Ouchi, 1981; Peters & Waterman, 1982). The management of nonprofit organizations is influenced greatly by what is happening in the for-profit or business sector. Today in for-profit organizations there is increasing stress on excellence, leadership, and accountability, as well as on human relations skills. Nonprofit managers must identify and acquire the technical, human relations, and conceptual skills and the various competencies needed to successfully lead nonprofit organizations in the years ahead.

Nonprofit managers often experience some difficulty using texts and training materials that were developed for the for-profit sector. This book addresses the particular needs of nonprofit managers. The content is aimed primarily at mid- and upper-level managers who can benefit from it directly as they strive daily to attain excellence, as well as indirectly as they help those they supervise do a better job of managing. Although this book is directed mostly to managers, it is also useful to students who are studying nonprofit or public management.

ORGANIZING FRAMEWORK

The organizing framework for this book is a metatheoretical model of organizational and managerial effectiveness called the "competing values framework" (Edwards, 1987, 1990; Edwards, Faerman, & McGrath, 1986; Edwards & Yankey, 1991; Faerman, Quinn, & Thompson, 1987; Quinn, 1984, 1988; Quinn et al., 1990; Quinn & Rohrbaugh, 1981, 1983). This model, which is described more fully in chapter 1, serves to integrate four contrasting sets of management skills: boundary-spanning skills, human relations skills, coordinating skills, and directing skills. Each set has two inherent roles that managers must play to be successful in that particular sphere of organizational activity. The eight roles are those of broker, innovator, mentor, facilitator, monitor, coordinator, producer, and director.

The competing values framework helps explicate that managers must function in a world of competing values in which their daily activities usually do not represent a choice between something "good" and something "bad." Rather, most choices that managers must make are between two or more "goods" or values. As used in this book, the competing values framework helps managers consider the complexity and multiplicity of their roles within their organizations and stresses that the performance of a management role is rarely an either–or situation.

The first section of the book provides overviews of the competing values framework. The remaining chapters are organized into five sections. The first four sections relate to the four major sets of skills and the eight managerial roles identified in the competing values framework. The final section deals with the issue of managing for quality. Also included is an appendix that contains Web sites that may be of interest to nonprofit managers.

The validity and importance of the eight roles have been demonstrated in several empirical studies. One study (Quinn, Denison, & Hooijberg, 1989) of more than 700 managers revealed that the measures of the eight roles met standard validity tests and that the roles appear in the four indicated quadrants. Another study (Pauchant, Nilles, Sawy, & Mohrman, 1989) involving more than 900 managers also found support for the eight roles and indicated that of 36 possible roles, these eight were considered the most important ones to be performed by managers. Still another study (Quinn, 1988) found that managers who did not perform these eight roles well were considered ineffective, whereas those who did perform these roles well were considered very effective.

LEARNING APPROACH

This book is designed to be used in a number of ways. It can be used as an individualized learning tool, as a primary text for management-training programs or academic courses, or as a supplement to other texts. The chapters are organized in a way that facilitates the development of competencies needed to perform the various managerial roles identified in the book. The structure of the chapters represents a variation of a learning model developed by Whetten and Cameron (1984), which involves assessment, learning, analysis, practice, and application. The first chapter includes an assessment instrument that enables readers to gain insight into their relative strengths and weaknesses in relation to eight management roles. Each chapter contains a narrative section that provides information about particular topics and one or more skills-application exercises that provide opportunities to apply the material to realistic job situations.

This book is a revision and expansion of an earlier book, *Skills for Effective Human Services Management* (Edwards & Yankey, 1991). The topics addressed in the earlier version and the present edition were identified as a result of the editors' experiences as hands-on managers, consultants, trainers, and educators. The array of topics covers many competencies that are not typically found in a single management book but that are vitally important in the real world of nonprofit management. The authors are a diverse group in terms of gender, race, and ethnicity and have a wealth of real-world management experience.

Finally, the editors believe that effective management requires, in addition to a wide range of technical and human relations skills, a healthy sense of humor. Thus, a number of cartoons have been included in the book.

REFERENCES

Blake, R., Mouton, J., & Allen, R. (1987). *Spectacular teamwork: What it is, how to recognize it, how to bring it about.* New York: John Wiley & Sons.

Edwards, R. L. (1987). The competing values approach as an integrating framework for the management curriculum. *Administration in Social Work, 11*(1), 1–13.

Edwards, R. L. (1990). Organizational effectiveness. In L. Ginsberg (Ed.), *Encyclopedia of social work* (18th ed., 1990 Suppl., pp. 244–255). Silver Spring, MD: NASW Press.

Edwards, R. L., Faerman, S. R., & McGrath, M. R. (1986). The competing values approach to organizational effectiveness: A tool for agency administrators. *Administration in Social Work, 10*(4), 1–14.

Edwards, R. L., & Yankey, J. A. (1991). *Skills for effective human services management.* Washington, DC: NASW Press.

Faerman, S. R., Quinn, R. E., & Thompson, M. P. (1987). Bridging management practice and theory. *Public Administration Review, 47*(3), 311–319.

Kanter, R. M. (1983). *The change masters: Innovation for productivity in the American corporation.* New York: Simon & Schuster.

Lawler, E. E. III. (1986). *High-involvement management: Participative strategies for improving organizational performance.* San Francisco: Jossey-Bass.

Ouchi, W. G. (1981). *Theory Z: How American business can meet the Japanese challenge.* Reading, MA: Addison-Wesley.

Pauchant, T. C., Nilles, J., Sawy, O. E., & Mohrman, A. M. (1989). *Toward a paradoxical theory of organizational effectiveness: An empirical study of the competing values model* (Working Paper). Quebec City, Canada: Laval University, Department of Administrative Sciences.

Peters, T. J., & Waterman, R. H., Jr. (1982). *In search of excellence.* New York: Harper & Row.

Porter, L. W., & McKibbon, L. E. (1988). *Management education and development: Drift or thrust into the 21st century?* New York: McGraw-Hill.

Quinn, R. E. (1984). Applying the competing values approach to leadership: Toward an integrative framework. In J. G. Hunt, D. Hosking, C. Schriescheim, & R. Stewart (Eds.), *Leaders and managers: International perspectives on managerial behavior and leadership.* Elmsford, NY: Pergamon Press.

Quinn, R. E. (1988). *Beyond rational management: Mastering the paradoxes and competing demands of high performance.* San Francisco: Jossey-Bass.

Quinn, R. E., Denison, D., & Hooijberg, R. (1989). *An empirical assessment of the competing values leadership instrument* (Working Paper). Ann Arbor: University of Michigan, School of Business.

Quinn, R. E., Faerman, S. R., Thompson, M. P., & McGrath, M. R. (1990). *Becoming a master manager: A competency framework.* New York: John Wiley & Sons.

Quinn, R. E., & Rohrbaugh, J. A. (1981). A competing values approach to organizational effectiveness. *Public Productivity Review, 5,* 122–140.

Quinn, R. E., & Rohrbaugh, J. A. (1983). A spatial model of effectiveness criteria: Toward a competing values approach to organizational analysis. *Management Science, 29*(3), 363–377.

Whetten, D. A., & Cameron, K. S. (1984). *Developing management skills.* Glenview, IL: Scott, Foresman.

PART ONE

THE
ORGANIZING
FRAMEWORK

THE ORGANIZING FRAMEWORK

The organizing theme for this book is an approach to organizational and leadership effectiveness known as the "competing values framework." In the first chapter, Richard L. Edwards, David M. Austin, and Mary A. Altpeter provide an overview of the roles that managers must perform, comparing and contrasting the roles of managers in the for-profit, public, and nonprofit sectors. They then identify three broad types of skills that managers must have, suggesting that the desired mix of these skills will vary depending on the level that a manager occupies in the organizational hierarchy. Next they discuss the competing values framework, which organizes the roles that managers must play within four distinct sets of skills. Eight specific roles, two related to each of the skills sets, are discussed. The chapter concludes with a self-assessment instrument that enables individuals to develop a graphic profile of their strengths and weaknesses in relation to each of the eight managerial roles. The graphic profile can help managers identify areas of content in this book that may be particularly useful in helping them build skills in areas that need strengthening.

CHAPTER I

Managing Effectively in an Environment of Competing Values

Richard L. Edwards, David M. Austin, and Mary A. Altpeter

We live in an era in which organizational life is characterized by shifting priorities, changing patterns in the allocation of resources, and competing demands. As nonprofit managers, we often must function in an environment of heightened demands for our organizations' services, higher expectations for accountability, and increased competition for funding, all the while being buffeted by change. Indeed, it seems that the only constant in management today is change.

As contemporary managers, we must be equipped with a broad range of knowledge, skills, and abilities to perform in a competent, effective manner. Beginning with a comparison of the executive management role within for-profit, public-sector, and nonprofit organizational contexts, this chapter provides an overview of how you can be an effective manager in an ever-changing environment of competing demands and values. The chapter then provides an overview of managerial skills needed at different levels of the organizational hierarchy, explains a multidimensional model of organizational and management performance, and considers the nature of managerial decision making.

EXECUTIVE MANAGEMENT ROLE

The role that top-level managers in nonprofit organizations must perform is similar to and yet distinct from the roles performed by their counterparts in for-profit and public organizations (Austin, 1989). In the for-profit corporate sector, the simplest version of the role of chief executive officer (CEO) combines policymaking and implementation. In the corporate or industry model, the CEO serves as a member of the corporation's board of directors as well as its senior administrator. The ultimate yardstick for measuring the effectiveness of the executive's performance is the level of financial return to the shareholders. In the public administration model, the traditional role of the CEO has been the implementation of policy but not its formulation. Elected legislative bodies make policy for public-sector managers to carry out (Wilson, 1978). Several yardsticks are used to measure effectiveness, including the consistency of implementation with legislative intent, continuity of the government organization, and break-even financial management—that is, operating within the limits of available financial resources (Austin, 1989).

The nonprofit manager's role is shaped, in part, by organizational characteristics that nonprofit organizations share with other types of formal organizations (Austin, 1988). Nonprofit managers, like their counterparts in the for-profit world, are becoming active participants in the formation, as well as in the implementation, of policy. It is often the top-level manager, or CEO, who brings most policy issues and recommendations to the nonprofit organization's policy board, board of trustees, or board of directors. Like their counterparts in the world of public administration, nonprofit managers are concerned with such issues as the extent to which implementation efforts are congruent with policy, the ongoing health of their organizations, and break-even performance. Also like their public administration counterparts, nonprofit managers have no direct personal economic stake in their organizations' financial performance. Their salaries do not increase in proportion to the size of their organizations' budgets, nor do they get year-end bonuses that are based on financial performance.

Despite these similarities, the role of the nonprofit manager also differs from the roles of the for-profit corporate executive and the traditional public administrator and, in many ways, is more complex (Austin, 1983). Perhaps the most significant difference is the criteria used to determine success. In the nonprofit sector, the most important yardstick for judging the manager's performance is the quality of the services provided by the organization (Patti, 1987).

MANAGERIAL SKILLS IN THE ORGANIZATIONAL HIERARCHY

To be a successful nonprofit manager, you must be prepared to be interactive, adaptive, and able to formulate contingency plans that take into account the operational characteristics of your particular organization and your organization's environmental context. You must be proactive. However, the typical nonprofit manager is invariably confronted by a series of competing values or demands that are likely to pull him or her in many directions at once. This situation was captured in part by Perlmutter (1990), who pointed out that "not only is it necessary to keep the shop running smoothly and efficiently today to meet current needs, but it is also necessary to have a vision of and anticipate what is possible and necessary for tomorrow" (p. 5). Thus, to be a successful nonprofit manager, you must be skilled at both tactical and strategic management.

Managerial performance within any type of organization occurs in a context of organizational change (Cooke, Reid, & Edwards, 1997; Edwards, Cooke, & Reid, 1996). Like human beings, organizations are not static, but go through a variety of phases and life cycles. Hence, different stages in the organizational life cycle may require you to use different types of skills (Quinn & Cameron, 1983). Likewise, organizations that perform similar work but exist in different types of environments may require a different mix of managerial skills. For example, arts organizations may target different client groups and compete for different resources than do human services or grassroots advocacy organizations, and these differences affect which management styles and skills are needed. Individuals may also shape the specific elements of their managerial positions in different ways on the basis of their personalities, training, and experience, as well as their perceptions of the needs of their organizations at a given point in time.

Furthermore, the level of your management position within your organizational hierarchy often shapes the skills you will need (Figure 1-1). According to Katz (1974), management skills may be broadly categorized as technical, interpersonal and human relations, and decision-making and

Figure 1-1. Management Skills Required at Different Levels

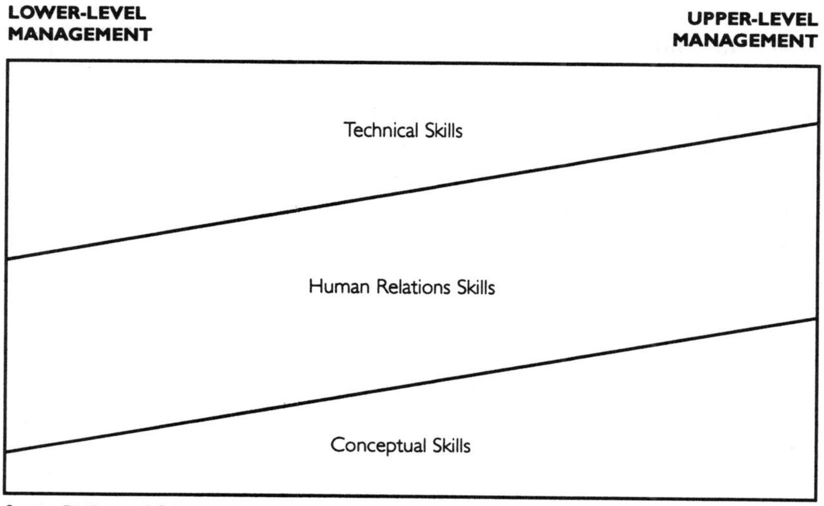

SOURCE: D. Whetten, K. Cameron, A. Shriberg, & C. Lloyd, *Developing management skills*, 3rd edition, Instructor's manual & transparency masters (transparency no. 8). © 1995 Addison Wesley Longman. Reprinted by permission of Addison Wesley Longman.

conceptual skills. In entry-level managerial positions, technical skills tend to be very important. However, the relative importance of technical skills tends to diminish as managers move up the organizational structure. At upper-management levels, the need for decision-making and conceptual skills increases in importance. For top-level managers, conceptual skills are essential, but the nature of their jobs does not require the use of technical skills to the same extent as lower-level managerial positions. On the other hand, interpersonal and human relations skills are equally important for managers at all levels of the organizational hierarchy (Katz, 1974; Whetten & Cameron, 1984).

In nonprofit organizations, individuals who are competent direct-service practitioners in human services or health organizations are sometimes promoted to supervisory or entry-level managerial positions. They may perform effectively in their new roles because their positions require good technical and interpersonal skills. As these individuals gradually move up the managerial hierarchy into positions that require greater conceptual skills, they may continue to be successful. However, they may also begin to display deficiencies and become unsuccessful and ineffective, thereby fulfilling the Peter Principle of being promoted to positions that are beyond their level of competence (Peter & Hull, 1969). Thus, as you move up the organizational management hierarchy, you must attain the additional competencies necessary to be effective.

COMPETING VALUES FRAMEWORK

There is no one best style of management performance. However, there is an inclusive, multidimensional model of organizational and management performance, the competing values approach (Quinn, 1984, 1988), which can help you understand the criteria that are used to judge the effectiveness of organizations and the various roles managers perform (Edwards, Faerman, & McGrath, 1986). The competing values model is an analytic framework built around two dimensions representing competing orientations or values in the organizational context (Figure 1-2). These dimensions are flexibility–control and internal–external. The combination of these two dimensions distinguishes four sectors of organizational activity, each of which embodies distinctive criteria of organizational effectiveness (Edwards, 1987, 1990; Quinn & Rohrbaugh, 1981, 1983). In combination, the four sectors identified in the model deal with two major criteria for assessing organizational outcomes: the quality of services provided and the continuity of the organization (Austin, 1989).

For an organization to perform well with respect to the various criteria of effectiveness, managers must use these different and sometimes conflicting sets

Figure 1-2. Competing Values Framework: Effectiveness

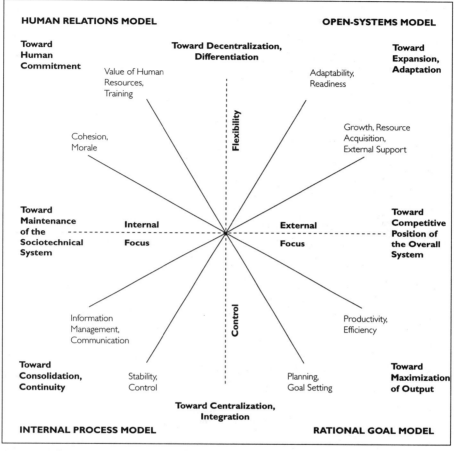

of skills: boundary-spanning skills, human relations skills, coordinating skills, and directing skills. Of course, no single managerial position involves an equal emphasis on all four of these sectors. In any given organization, the top-level manager may be involved primarily in activities that require the use of certain types of skills, whereas other people who are part of the executive component, or management team, may carry major responsibilities for activities in other sectors that require other types of skills. Yet, the CEO or top-level manager bears ultimate responsibility for the effectiveness of the organization's performance in all four sectors. Some of the key concepts associated with each sector of organizational performance and the relevant managerial roles are summarized in Figure 1-3.

Figure 1-3. Competing Values Framework: Leadership Roles

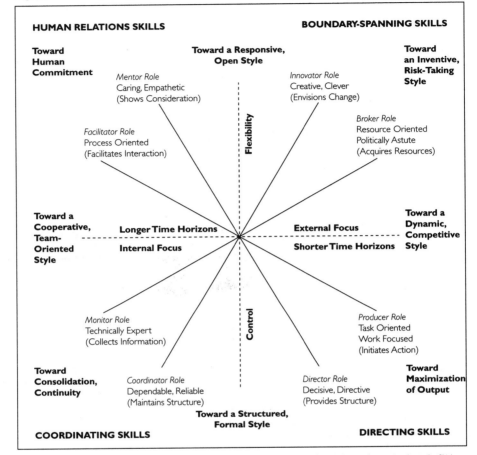

Boundary-Spanning Skills

Each quadrant depicted in Figure 1-3 relates to a different set of skills, and each set of skills includes managerial traits, behaviors, and patterns of influence inherent within it. To perform the roles in the upper right-hand quadrant, the manager is called on to use boundary-spanning skills. Because nonprofit organizations are highly dependent on their environments, the manager is constantly involved in activities that cross the formal boundaries of the organization. These activities include obtaining financial resources, establishing and maintaining the organization's legitimacy, adapting organizational programs in response to environmental changes, managing external requirements for reporting and accountability, negotiating formal and informal interorganiza-tional agreements, participating in action coalitions, and positioning the orga-nization to take advantage of new opportunities.

In the competing values model, this sector is defined by the flexibility and external dimensions. That is, if you were the manager performing the roles in this sector, you would need to be adaptable and flexible, because you would be participating in activities that involve dealing with individuals and organi-zations that are not under your direct control and that are external to the formal boundaries of your organization.

Quinn (1984, 1988) identified two managerial roles that are relevant to this sector: the innovator and the broker. To effectively perform the role of inno-vator, you would need to be creative and clever. These traits require that you have good conceptual skills and constantly be on the lookout for unusual opportunities. The behavior associated with the performance of this role is directed toward envisioning and facilitating change. Hence, to perform this role well you must be the type of individual who seeks new opportunities, encourages and considers new ideas, and is tolerant of ambiguity and risk.

To perform the role of broker effectively, you must be resource oriented and politically astute. These traits require that you be aware of and sensitive to external conditions, especially those related to your organization's legitimacy, influence, and acquisition of resources. The behavior associated with the per-formance of the broker role is directed toward acquiring resources, so you also must be skilled in developing interpersonal contacts, monitoring the organi-zation's environment, amassing power and influence, maintaining the external image of the organization, and obtaining resources (Quinn, 1984, 1988). Nonprofit managers must also be skilled in fundraising (Edwards, Benefield, Edwards, & Yankey, 1997) and adept at navigating the political arena (Gummer & Edwards, 1995).

The boundary-spanning-skills sector involves the political or open-system dimension of organizational performance that is least subject to technical skills and computerization. As a manager functioning in this sector, you need political or negotiating skills and an understanding of the nature of power relationships in the task environment in which your management skills are practiced. Boundary-spanning skills may also require you to perform short-term contingency decision making, in contrast to the systematic and long-term participatory internal decision-making processes that may be important in the mobilization and motivation of human resources. This sector of activ-ity is perhaps the least likely to be fully delegated to other members of an executive management team. However, it may also be the sector that policy-makers, such as volunteers who serve on the organization's board, define as their particular area of activity and in which explicit limits are placed on the scope of the manager's activities.

The effectiveness of the process of contingency decision making, or strategic adaptation, whether carried out by policymakers, you as the manager, or both, may be severely constrained by considerations involving other sectors in which policymakers and managers perform. For example, successful "opportunity-seizing" initiatives involving responses to short-term funding opportunities, such as responding to various requests for funding proposals, may be inconsistent with the organization's overall goals, may require substantial expenditures for the development of new technical production procedures, and may disrupt the cohesiveness and morale of the staff.

Human Relations Skills

The second major sector of executive responsibility, shown in the upper left-hand quadrant of Figure 1-3, involves the use of human relations skills. In performing the roles in this sector, you are responsible for ensuring that your organization has a competent workforce. Because many of the services provided by nonprofit organizations are produced and delivered through person-to-person interactions, these organizations can be called labor intensive. As a consequence, human relations activities constitute a particularly important component in the life of such organizations.

In the competing values model, this sector is defined by the internal and flexibility dimensions. In the role of the manager, you will be dealing with individuals and groups who are internal to the organization and who, as autonomous individuals or groups with the skills required to produce services, represent decentralized centers of authority and influence that cannot be directly controlled by you. Quinn (1984, 1988) identified two specific managerial roles in this sector: the mentor and the facilitator.

In the role of the mentor you need to be a caring and empathic individual. Those who possess these traits tend to view organizational members as valued resources and are alert to the members' individual problems and needs. They operate in a manner that is perceived as fair and objective. You must also be a skilled listener and try to facilitate the development of individuals (Quinn, 1984, 1988). Your behavior is directed toward showing concern about and support for your staff members.

To be an effective group facilitator, you need to be process oriented, diplomatic, and tactful. You must have excellent interpersonal skills and be good at facilitating interaction among individuals and groups in the workplace. You should also be adept at fostering cohesion, building consensus, and bringing about compromises. Your ultimate aim is to foster a cooperative, team-oriented style that permeates your organization.

In performing the roles of mentor and facilitator, your goal is to secure, retain, and motivate a qualified, competent, and committed work force. The human resources—the people—of an organization should have the knowledge, skills, and abilities to perform their jobs effectively. However, achieving the goal of a well-qualified, competent, team-oriented work force is not easy, because your staff often includes members of one or more professions as well as a variety of volunteers who are involved in both the delivery of services and policymaking. In addition, the work force includes both men and women as well as people from a variety of racial and ethnic groups. Furthermore, services users may be a critical element in mobilizing and motivating staff. Because of the composition and the competing needs and interests of the human resources component of the organization, you must be concerned with the organizational culture, which includes symbols and traditions, and the definition of organizational values, which together may be significantly related to staff motivation (Austin, 1989).

Coordinating Skills

The lower left-hand quadrant of Figure 1–3 identifies the coordinating-skills sector, which is defined by the internal and control dimensions. Quinn (1984, 1988) identified the roles of the monitor and the coordinator in this sector. The activities related to this sector are focused primarily on matters that are internal to the organization and that are involved in maintaining the organizational structure. The technical areas in this sector include budgeting and fiscal controls, scheduling procedures, information and communication systems, personnel administration systems, technical training programs, reporting systems, evaluation and quality control measures, and management of technical equipment and physical facilities (Austin, 1989).

To perform the role of monitor effectively, you must be technically competent and well prepared. These traits suggest that you need to be well informed and knowledgeable about the work of the people in your organization and have a high degree of technical expertise. Your role is directed toward collecting and distributing information that is necessary for the smooth functioning of the organization as well as for the orderly flow of work. To perform well in the role of coordinator, you must be dependable and reliable. Those who have such traits are likely to be consistent, predictable people who seek continuity and equilibrium in their work units (Quinn, 1984, 1988). Your focus should be on maintaining structure, organizational stability, and work flow and using your skills in scheduling, coordinating, problem solving, and ensuring that rules and standards are understood and met. This is also the sector of organizational life in which systematic and rational procedures often have their widest application (Austin, 1989).

Because nonprofit organizations are typically so labor intensive, the systematic organization of personnel activities and the monitoring of service production activities assume great importance and become major elements in the managerial or executive position. In a small organization, it may be possible for the manager to carry out many of these tasks directly. However, in larger organizations, these types of managerial tasks, especially personnel administration, financial management, and the maintenance of computing systems, most likely involve technical staff specialists and sometimes entire staffing units.

The use of computers in all kinds of organizations, including nonprofits, has become widespread. It is in the coordinating-skills sector that computers are particularly valuable because the activities involved often represent structured decision-making choices among known alternatives. For example, issues such as the impact of different combinations of direct salary and fringe benefits on staff compensation; the effects of different combinations of staff work schedules; and the patterns of service use by clients, procedures for handling organizational funds, and the tracking of clients or patrons all lend themselves to the use of computers. And these activities and others like them are areas in which consistent, centrally controlled decisions seem to be highly correlated with efficiency and effectiveness.

Directing Skills

The lower right-hand quadrant of Figure 1-3 identifies the directing-skills sector. This sector is defined by the external and control dimensions. Thus, the focus in this sector tends to be on activities that are external to the organization and that are relatively structured and formalized. In the management role in this sector, you will be dealing with the interface between the products or output of your organization and its external environment. The technical activities involved include both tactical and strategic planning, goal setting, and activity monitoring. Quinn (1984, 1988) identified the roles of the producer and the director in this sector.

The thrust of your managerial activity in this sector is the goal-oriented process, which is aimed at improving your organization's efficiency and effectiveness, as well as enhancing your organization's relative position within its environment. This sector involves activities in which the manager plays a pivotal role, such as the improvement of productivity and goal setting (Austin, 1989).

In performing the role of director effectively, you must be decisive and comfortable in guiding the work of others. Those who have these traits tend to be conclusive individuals who can plan work appropriately and provide direction. Your activities will include setting goals and objectives, clarifying roles, monitoring progress, providing feedback, and establishing clear expectations (Quinn, 1984, 1988). In using directing skills, you need to know how

"Faced with the two of you, I'm forced to ask, 'Who's holier-than-thou?'"

to stimulate individual and collective achievement. Thus, you must be comfortable with the use of authority and skilled at delegation, planning, and goal-setting technologies (Faerman, Quinn, & Thompson, 1987).

To perform the role of producer well, you must be task oriented and work focused. Those who exhibit these traits tend to be action-oriented individuals who are highly generative. You must be the kind of individual who is willing to invest large amounts of energy and who derives a great deal of satisfaction from productive work. Your efforts will be directed at stimulating the performance of staff members.

Because nonprofit organizations are established to accomplish particular societal objectives, the process of defining goals is essential. Nonprofit organizations are dependent, to a great extent, on their external environments. As a manager, you must be cognizant of environmental developments and trends, including those that affect your organization's users or clients, financial and personnel resources, technology and, ultimately, legitimacy in political terms. Furthermore, organizational continuity assumes relatively great importance for nonprofit organizations because the costs involved in setting up such an organization and the goodwill represented in its legitimation by the community cannot be turned into financial resources that can be used for other purposes (Austin, 1989).

When confronted by the often difficult choices that are inherent in the competing values environment of nonprofit management, you can use your organization's mission as a kind of litmus test for your decisions. That is, consider how a particular decision will help or hinder your organization to achieve its mission. Thus, you should view your organization's mission as a kind of North Star that can guide you through the wilderness of competing values and demands.

When you occupy a managerial position, you must possess and use many types of skills and must perform many roles. The demands of these roles may shift over time as your organization moves through different phases in its life cycle. In small organizations, the top-level manager role may encompass many skills and roles, whereas in larger organizations, the top-level manager may delegate certain roles to others on the management team.

NATURE OF MANAGERIAL DECISION MAKING

Because organizational life is characterized by an environment of competing values, managerial decision-making requirements are complex. The choices that confront managers daily are rarely choices between something that is good and something that is bad. If this were the case, your job as manager would be relatively easy. Instead, management most often involves choosing between two or more things that are positive or valued. This type of choice makes your job much more difficult. For example, you may be confronted with shrinking resources and thus not be able to hire additional staff or provide opportunities for staff development. At the same time, you may be confronted with a growing demand for services from clients. Because the size of the workforce cannot be enlarged, the increased demand for services may cause you to take steps to increase the caseloads of your existing staff. Such an approach may result in greater efficiency, that is, more clients seen without an increase in staff. However, the approach may also have a negative impact on the morale of your staff, which could lead to increased stress, burnout, and turnover. Thus, your organization may lose some of its experienced staff, which may result in added expenses for recruiting, hiring, and orienting new staff. There is also likely to be some loss related to the time it takes new staff to become fully productive.

Understanding that you are likely to experience pulls from many directions may help you identify the possible consequences of your decisions and enable you to take appropriate steps to minimize negative consequences. Viewing organizations from the competing values perspective can help you assess your particular areas of strength. No one individual will be equally adept at performing all the roles identified in Figure 1-3. Managers who are secure about their abilities are likely to surround themselves with subordinates whose strengths complement their own, whereas managers who are less secure tend to surround themselves with individuals whose strengths mirror their own, which may result in some of the organization's needs being inadequately addressed.

As a nonprofit manager, you must possess a range of knowledge, skills, and abilities and must perform many roles. The particular balance of technical, interpersonal and human relations, and conceptual and decision-making skills required of you will vary, depending on your position in the managerial structure. Each category of skills involves the performance of different managerial roles, which are related to different criteria of organizational effectiveness and which create an environment of competing values. In this environment, your managerial decisions most often represent a trade-off between two values or goods rather than a choice between something that is good versus something that is bad. By understanding the multiple role demands and competing values of your job, you may be better able to guide your organization toward effective performance.

SKILLS-ASSESSMENT EXERCISE

The following instrument will enable you to develop a profile of how you rate on each of the managerial roles identified in the competing values framework. Please complete the Competing Values Management Practices Survey and then transfer your ratings to the Computational Worksheet for Self-Assessment. Place the score or rating you give each item on the survey next to the number of that item on the worksheet. Note that where the symbol (R) appears on the worksheet, you should reverse your score; thus, if you rated the item 1 you will reverse your score and record it as 7, 2 becomes 6, and 3 becomes 5. If your rating was 4, then place 4 on the worksheet. Next, total your scores in each category and then divide the total by the number of items in that category. This sum will give you a score to enter on the Competing Values Skills-Assessment Leadership Role Profile. When transferring your scores to the role profile, place a dot at the point on the spoke that reflects your score for that role, keeping in mind that the center of the figure is 0 and the hash mark farthest from the center is 7. When you have entered your scores on all eight spokes of the diagram, draw lines to connect them. The result will be a profile that will help you identify your areas of relative strength as well as those in which you may not be as strong. This information may be useful to you as you review other chapters in this book.

Competing Values Management Practices Survey

Listed below are some statements that describe managerial practices. Indicate how often you engage in the behaviors, using the scale below to respond to each statement. Please place a number from 1 to 7 in the space beside each question.

ALMOST NEVER   1   2   3   4   5   6   7   ALMOST ALWAYS

As a manager, how often would you

_____   1.   Come up with inventive ideas.

_____   2.   Exert upward influence in the organization.

_____   3.   Ignore the need to achieve unit goals.

_____   4.   Continually clarify the unit's purpose.

_____   5.   Search for innovations and potential improvements.

_____   6.   Make the unit's role very clear.

_____   7.   Maintain tight logistical control.

_____   8.   Keep track of what goes on inside the unit.

_____   9.   Develop consensual resolution of openly expressed differences.

_____ 10.   Listen to the personal problems of subordinates.

_____ 11.   Maintain a highly coordinated, well-organized unit.

_____ 12.   Hold open discussion of conflicting opinions in groups.

_____ 13.   Push the unit to meet objectives.

_____ 14.   Surface key differences among group members, then work participatively to resolve them.

_____ 15.   Monitor compliance with the rules.

_____ 16.   Treat each individual in a sensitive, caring way.

_____ 17.   Experiment with new concepts and procedures.

_____ 18.   Show empathy and concern in dealing with subordinates.

_____ 19.   Seek to improve the work group's technical capacity.

_____ 20.   Get access to people at higher levels.

_____ 21.   Encourage participative decision making in the group.

_____ 22.   Compare records, reports, and so on to detect discrepancies.

_____ 23.   Solve scheduling problems in the unit.

_____ 24.   Get the unit to meet expected goals.

_____ 25.   Do problem solving in creative, clear ways.

_____ 26.   Anticipate workflow problems, avoid crises.

_____ 27.   Check for errors and mistakes.

_____ 28.   Persuasively sell new ideas to higher-ups.

_____ 29.   See that the unit delivers on state goals.

_____ 30.   Facilitate consensus building in the work unit.

_____ 31.   Clarify the unit's priorities and direction.

_____ 32.   Show concern for the needs of subordinates.

_____ 33.   Maintain a "results" orientation in the unit.

_____ 34.   Influence decisions made at higher levels.

_____ 35.   Regularly clarify the objectives of the unit.

_____ 36.   Bring a sense of order and coordination into the unit.

Computational Worksheet for Self-Assessment

Facilitator		**Mentor**	
9 ____		10 ____	
12 ____		16 ____	
14 ____		18 ____	
21 ____		32 ____	
30 ____		Total ____ ÷ 4 = ____	
Total ____ ÷ 5 = ____			

Innovator

I ____	
5 ____	
17 ____	
25 ____	
Total ____ ÷ 4 = ____	

Broker

2 ____	
20 ____	
28 ____	
34 ____	
Total ____ ÷ 4 = ____	

Producer

3 ____ (R)	
13 ____	
19 ____	
29 ____	
33 ____	
Total ____ ÷ 5 = ____	

Director

4 ____	
6 ____	
24 ____	
31 ____	
35 ____	
Total ____ ÷ 5 = ____	

Coordinator

7 ____	
II ____	
23 ____	
26 ____	
36 ____	
Total ____ ÷ 5 = ____	

Monitor

8 ____	
15 ____	
22 ____	
27 ____	
Total ____ ÷ 4 = ____	

Discussion Questions

The following questions may assist you in developing your managerial skills:

1. What is your reaction to the personal skills profile revealed on the role profile diagram? Do the results meet your expectations? Were there any surprises?

2. On the basis of your profile, what areas of managerial skills appear to be the highest priority for further development? What strategies can you use to assist you in developing your skills?

3. Identify where your organization is in terms of its life cycle. What managerial skills are needed at this point in your organization's history? What skills are likely to be needed in the next year? In the next three years?

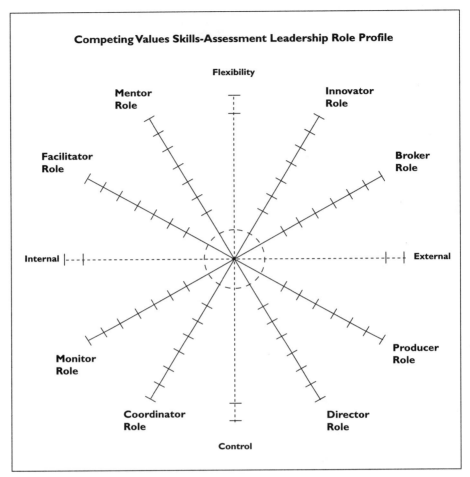

Copyright © Robert E. Quinn. Used by permission.

REFERENCES

Austin, D. M. (1983). Administrative practice in human services: Future directions for curriculum development. *Journal of Applied Behavioral Science, 19,* 143–151.

Austin, D. M. (1988). *The political economy of human service programs.* Greenwich, CT: JAI Press.

Austin, D. M. (1989). The human service executive. *Administration in Social Work, 13*(3/4),
13–36.

Cooke, P. W., Reid, P. N., & Edwards, R. L. (1997). Management: New developments and directions. In R. L. Edwards (Ed.-in-Chief), *Encyclopedia of social work* (19th ed., 1997 Suppl., pp.
229–242). Washington, DC: NASW Press.

Edwards, R. L. (1987). The competing values approach as an integrating framework for the
management curriculum. *Administration in Social Work, 11*(1), 1–13.

Edwards, R. L. (1990). Organizational effectiveness. In L. Ginsberg et al. (Eds.), *Encyclopedia of social work* (18th ed., 1990 Suppl., pp. 244–255). Silver Spring, MD: National Association of Social Workers.

Edwards, R. L., Benefield, E. A. S., Edwards, J. A., & Yankey, J. A. (1997). *Building a strong foundation: Fundraising for nonprofits.* Washington, DC: NASW Press.

Edwards, R. L., Cooke, P. W., & Reid, P. N. (1996). Social work management in an era of diminishing federal responsibility. *Social Work, 41,* 468–479.

Edwards, R. L., Faerman, S. R., & McGrath, M. R. (1986). The competing values approach to organizational effectiveness: A tool for agency administrators. *Administration in Social Work, 10*(4), 1–14.

Faerman, S. R., Quinn, R. E., & Thompson, M. P. (1987). Bridging management practice and theory: New York State's public service training program. *Public Administration Review, 47*(3), 311–319.

Gummer, B., & Edwards, R. L. (1995). The politics of human services administration. In L. Ginsberg & P. R. Keys (Eds.), *New management in human services* (pp. 57–71). Washington, DC: NASW Press.

Katz, R. L. (1974). Skills of an effective administrator. *Harvard Business Review, 51,* 90–102.

Patti, R. J. (1987). Managing for service effectiveness in social welfare: Toward a performance model. *Administration in Social Work, 11*(3/4), 25–37.

Perlmutter, F. D. (1990). *Changing hats: From social work practice to administration.* Silver Spring, MD: National Association of Social Workers.

Peter, L., & Hull, R. (1969). *The Peter Principle: Why things go wrong.* New York: William Morrow.

Quinn, R. E. (1984). Applying the competing values approach to leadership: Toward an integrative framework. In J. G. Hunt, D. Hosking, C. Schreisheim, & R. Stewart (Eds.), *Leaders and managers: International perspectives on managerial behavior and leadership.* Elmsford, NY: Pergamon Press.

Quinn, R. E. (1988). *Beyond rational management: Mastering the paradoxes and competing demands of high performance.* San Francisco: Jossey-Bass.

Quinn, R. E., & Cameron, K. S. (1983). Organizational life cycles and shifting criteria of effectiveness: Some preliminary evidence. *Management Science, 29,* 33–51.

Quinn, R. E., & Rohrbaugh, J. A. (1981). A competing values approach to organizational effectiveness. *Public Productivity Review, 5,* 122–140.

Quinn, R. E., & Rohrbaugh, J. A. (1983). A spatial model of effectiveness criteria: Toward a competing values approach to organizational analysis. *Management Science, 29,* 363–377.

Whetten, D. A., & Cameron, K. S. (1984). *Developing management skills.* Glenview, IL: Scott, Foresman.

Wilson, W. (1978). The study of administration. In J. M. Shafritz & A. C. Hyde (Eds.), *Classics of public administration.* Oak Park, IL: Moore.

PART TWO

BOUNDARY-
SPANNING
SKILLS

BOUNDARY-SPANNING SKILLS

Managerial boundary-spanning skills encompass two major roles—innovator and broker. Competencies for the innovator role include creative thinking and living with and managing change. Competencies for the broker role include building and maintaining a power base, negotiating agreement and commitment, and presenting ideas. The chapters in this section are related to these roles and competencies in terms of the challenges confronting nonprofit managers.

In chapter 2, Douglas C. Eadie discusses the changing environment confronting managers and underscores the need for developing competencies related to creatively leading and managing innovation. He identifies the characteristics of an effective change leadership and management process and cautions against trying to deal with change through a "quick-fix" approach. Instead, Eadie recommends that managers focus on building in themselves and their organizations the capacity to lead, innovate, and implement. He stresses the importance of strategic planning and management to better position organizations to deal with their ever-changing environments.

In chapter 3, Christine E. Henry focuses on the proposal-writing skills required of nonprofit managers in effectively performing the broker role. She provides an overview of different types of foundations, suggesting ways that nonprofit managers can learn about funding opportunities. Henry also identifies the components typically included in funding proposals and provides some guidance about writing such proposals.

Elizabeth A. S. Benefield and Richard L. Edwards in chapter 4 point out that nonprofit managers are spending increasingly large amounts of time in fundraising activities. They urge managers to plan, develop, and implement broad-based, multifaceted fundraising strategies. Benefield and Edwards provide information about a range of activities, including annual giving and major gift work based on sound prospect research, planning, cultivation, and public relations efforts.

Recognizing that many nonprofit organizations are becoming more involved in delivering services under purchase-of-service contracts with government agencies, Ronald K. Green in chapter 5 considers ways that nonprofit managers can maximize the use of performance contracts. He discusses the nature and types of contracts and considers their advantages and disadvantages for nonprofit organizations. Green concludes with recommendations for maximizing the use of such contracts.

In chapter 6, Todd Cohen provides some valuable tips for developing mass media relationships, which are critical for favorably positioning nonprofit organizations in the public eye. While recognizing the difficult challenge that the development of positive media relationships presents for nonprofit managers, Cohen urges that nonprofit managers develop a media strategy for their organizations and provides concrete suggestions for doing so. He also provides helpful information about writing news releases and getting your story in print or on the air. In addition, Cohen provides tips on handling interviews, setting up press conferences, and dealing with crises. He concludes with a discussion of marketing your organization.

Emily D. Pelton and Richard E. Baznik in chapter 7 offer information about dealing with the legislative and executive branches of government to secure resources and favorable policy decisions. The competencies involved in building and maintaining power bases are considered, as well as the importance of nonprofit managers' ability to present ideas, negotiate agreement and commitment, and be creative in their approach to solving problems.

CHAPTER 2

Building the Capacity to Lead Innovation

Douglas C. Eadie

Change is nothing new in the world. Indeed, life and change go naturally together, and history is replete with tales of humans struggling to cope with powerful forces beyond their control. But nobody questions that these are uniquely challenging times for all of us, including economic development professionals. O'Toole observed in *Leading Change* (1995) that "there is reason to believe that in fact the depth of the alterations experienced today is more profound than ever before" (p. xii). And in *Riding the Waves of Change*, Morgan (1988) described change these days as "a sea . . . that can twist and turn with all the power of the ocean" and as having a "degree of flux that often challenges the fundamental assumptions on which organizations and their managers have learned to operate" (p. 1).

Without doubt, the world around us is not only changing at a dizzying speed, but change is also growing in both complexity and magnitude. No wonder many of us are occasionally tempted to remove ourselves from the race altogether, retreating to our own private Walden Pond. The nonprofit and public sectors are no more immune from the impact of the sweeping changes swirling around us than the business sector. Phenomenal technological change—in communications, information processing, medicine, and many other areas—has generated new products, new businesses, and new tools for managing.

The increasingly global economy has steadily eroded the capacity of individual nations, states, and communities to manage and develop their own economies in isolation. Inexorable federal government downsizing since the mid-1970s has forced public and nonprofit professionals to explore new

---

NOTE: A modified version of this chapter was originally published in 1997 as "Building the Capacity for Innovation." In D. C. Eadie, *Changing by design: A practical approach to innovation in nonprofit organizations* (pp. 20–38). San Francisco: Jossey-Bass. Revised and reprinted with the permission of Jossey-Bass Publishers.

revenue streams and to sharpen entrepreneurial skills (Edwards, Cooke, & Reid, 1996). Corporate downsizing, along with the two-career family, has radically reduced the amount of volunteer time to serve on nonprofit boards, committees, and task forces. The list goes on and on, a familiar litany to everyone involved in leading and managing nonprofit organizations.

In a calm and stable world blessed with a high degree of predictability, being a board member, chief executive officer, or manager of a nonprofit organization would be a tough enough job. But in today's topsy-turvy world, the task of leading organizations can seem overwhelming at times. One thing is dramatically clear: The only viable response to the change going on around us and our organizations is to take command of our own individual and organizational innovation and to guide and direct that innovation to capitalize on opportunities to grow and to counter threats to well-being. Merely standing pat, or circling the wagons for a battle, would be a disastrous course.

The fact that the only sensible course in today's world is to lead and manage innovation creatively is not news to the great majority of nonprofit leaders, particularly chief executives. Indeed, the term "change management" has nearly achieved buzzword status. What is news, however, is the rapidly accumulating knowledge about leading innovation and the more powerful innovation management tools that have been developed and tested recently. For one thing, we have become more knowledgeable about the very natural, deep-seated resistance of most human beings to change, regardless of what they might say about thriving on change. We now know that the beloved traditional model of chief executive leadership—the broad shoulders, macho rhetoric ("The buck stops here!"), administrative focus, and control fetish—does not suffice in a world that is always challenging and frequently threatening—a world that demands flexibility, creativity, and the expansion of human capability. Fortunately, a new chief executive model has emerged that consists of key skills and attributes for successfully leading in tumultuous times. And we have learned a considerable amount about ways to build a positive, productive, and close partnership between the board and the chief executive, which is indispensable for successful change leadership. We have also learned ways to move beyond the traditional control bias of planning and to make planning a more powerful innovation engine for economic development organizations.

TRAVELING THE CHANGE PATH

Three tall barriers stand in the way of a nonprofit undertaking the journey of self-determined, consciously directed innovation: (1) failure to see the need to change, (2) fear of changing, and (3) the relentless grind of day-to-day operations. The reader who has embarked on his or her own personal growth journey knows how daunting these challenges can be. Changing one's own life can be a monumental task; moving a whole organization in new directions is more so. Well-traveled paths may offer little in the way of excitement, but at least they feel comfortable and far safer than meandering around unknown terrain, where who knows what terrors await us. And doggedly working toward the never-seen bottom of the constantly filling in-basket day after day may feel productive and virtuous, but it leaves little time and energy to pick up signals from the wider world that change is needed, much less to begin to plot a new journey.

So as individuals and as organizations we often wait for major crises— a heart attack, separation or divorce, a precipitous drop in membership or revenue, an anticipated budget deficit, an exposé in the local press that threatens a stellar reputation—to jolt us out of our complacency and force us to embark in new directions. Fortunately, even major crises, while inevitably painful and costly, are seldom fatal, and as goads to needed action they can be seen as blessings, albeit often well disguised. Crises don't force most nonprofits to close up shop, turn off the lights, and lock the doors. There are second chances: Lessons can be learned and put to good use in the future, budgets can be balanced eventually, and good reputations can be restored. However, the cost of waiting for a crisis to spur action can be appallingly high in dollars, in pain and suffering, in eroded public credibility, in the consumption of precious energy, and in declining internal morale. Indeed, being anticipatory and proactive is cost-effectiveness at its most powerful.

For example, concerned by the sea of gray heads at every concert, a symphony business manager and board might take action—such as giving concerts in various neighborhoods, initiating a children's concert series, and direct-mail marketing to new audiences—to deal with what appears to be an ominous trend before many empty seats show up in the hall. And a health product sales association might take the initiative by redefining its basic markets and aggressively seeking merger opportunities with other associations in the field. Any alert and aggressive organization can decide, before the crisis hits, to take a leading role in its own change.

But in doing so, the board, chief executive, and management team should understand that the journey of self-determined and guided change is seldom smooth, and failure is not uncommon in the world of large-scale organizational change. As De Pree (1989) pointed out, "Anything truly creative results in change, and if there is one thing a well-run bureaucracy or institution or major corporation finds difficult to handle, it is change" (p. 33). No matter how capable, courageous, and disciplined its people, an organization can fail in managing change for one or more of a number of important reasons: weak board and chief executive leadership; absence of a clear strategic framework;

an unsystematic, skewed approach to change; a quick-fix mentality; uncreative thinking and narrowly circumscribed strategy formulation; unrealistic implementation planning; inadequate implementation management; and staff resistance. The approach to leading and managing change that is described in this chapter is intended to deal with all of these major spoilers that have limited the effectiveness of nonprofit efforts to lead and manage change in the past.

EFFECTIVE CHANGE LEADERSHIP AND MANAGEMENT PROCESS

Nonprofit board members, chief executives, and managers who are committed to taking command of their own organizational innovation and change should insist that, as a result of using a particular change process, their organizations are able to put their resources to the best feasible use in capitalizing on environmental opportunities and in coping with environmental threats.

Clear, Detailed Strategic Framework

Strategic framework means the values that the nonprofit most cherishes and that comprise its most important do's and don'ts; its vision for the future in terms of what it aspires to be and the role it aspires to play; and its mission in terms of its services and products, its customers and clients, and its key roles and functions. Without a well-defined framework addressing overall purposes, aspirations, and boundaries, organizational change will not, by definition, have any rhyme or reason, and it will be just as apt to produce bad results as good. The values that govern a nonprofit's change should serve as an ethical framework and, as such, should include the small number of what O'Toole (1995) called the "moral absolutes," which include "only a few moral principles based on natural law. Though most of the major issues in social life are subjective and relative, not all are. There are, in short, some moral absolutes that are not contingent on circumstances" (p. 105).

Rational Priorities

Rational priorities means that the change initiatives that an organization selects should tackle first things first in terms of organizational opportunities and needs. There is only so much time, money, and energy that can be devoted to changing things in an organization while also continuing to manage day-to-day operations, so careful selection of targets is imperative if resources are not to be frittered away on lesser matters while problems threaten organizational existence or one-time opportunities are lost forever.

Humane Expectations

Implementing change, whether personal or organizational, is taxing enough without adding to the pain by making unrealistic demands on the people who must translate change targets into practice. A humane approach will take into account both the feelings and the capabilities of an organization's employees and will never demand the impossible. On the other hand, the adage "no pain, no gain" applies in any serious change process, and so no participant should expect a pain-free experience.

Comprehensive and Balanced Approach

As much attention should be given to the what of change—its content—as to the how—its implementation. All of the forms that change can take should be comprehensively considered in determining exactly what change should be undertaken in any given year. There is outward-looking change, such as in revenue sources, customers and clients, and stakeholder relationships, and there is more internally focused change, such as in planning and management systems. The creative challenge is to choose the mix that best meets an organization's needs in the context of the changing world around it (Tichy, 1983).

Creative and Innovative Responses

Creativity is at the heart of innovation, which is basically the process of bringing the new into being. In a complex, rapidly changing world, merely projecting conventional wisdom into the future would be a high-risk course of action. Being creative means to see what has not yet occurred, to envision responses that are not being made, and to have a more open and questioning process so that practical innovations will yield important benefits (Boden, 1991; Csikszentmihalyi, 1996; Gardner, 1993).

Realistic Expectations

Shooting high and falling short is a surefire recipe for disappointment, lost credibility, frayed tempers, cynicism, and even organizational chaos when the failure is dramatic enough. The point is to implement fully the changes that have been planned and to do so on time, within budget, and without unnecessary pain and suffering (Eadie, 1996).

Self-Sustainable Process

Any process for leading and managing change will ultimately prove too expensive if a nonprofit board, chief executive, and management team cannot use it on an ongoing basis without endless consulting assistance. And only if it becomes one of the nonprofit's mainline planning and management process-es can it yield a powerful return on the investment of time and energy.

QUICK FIXES

Trying to figure out what is happening in a rambunctious world that at times defies understanding and attempting to fashion initiatives for organizational change that will make sense in that environment are part of a complex process that flies in the face of an apparent widespread appetite for quick-fix solutions and low-cost panaceas. The more complex and ambitious the changes being attempted, the less the likelihood of immediate, visible results, and so patience and the willingness to bear costs for some time before reaping benefits are requisites for successful change leadership. Unfortunately, they are often in short supply, especially when things are not going smoothly.

Over the years, many nonprofits have lurched from one half-understood and inadequately implemented management innovation to another, inevitably finding the fault in the innovation rather than in their taste for the costless and painless solution. Management by objectives, program budgeting, strate-gic planning, participatory management, total quality—these have all been tried and abandoned when the costs became clear, the pain was felt, and immediate results failed to materialize.

The instant gratification approach to change not only fails to achieve the desired affects, but it also misuses and abuses the people in an organization while damaging morale. For example, a task force was preparing for a two-day strategic planning retreat. The specific assignment for this group of smart, hardworking managers was to assess internal capabilities, and one of the issues they focused on was how to assess the agency's experience in managing change and how to convey that assessment to the assembled management team at the retreat.

The day of the retreat, the room rocked with laughter when the slide the task force had designed appeared on the screen. The slide depicted a grave-yard crowded with stones. Each stone named a management innovation that had been attempted and abandoned and stated its years on this earth. The average life span was 18 months. The next slide analyzed the reasons for so many premature deaths among such a large population of innovation projects and estimated the hours and dollars wasted over the years. It did not take long for sadness, then anger, to replace humor, as the assembled managers thought about the better uses to which their time and money might have been put (Kemp, Funk, & Eadie, 1993).

"Welcome aboard, and I think I speak for all of us when I say that we expect fresh, different, and innovative ideas from you. . . . Not just more of the same old thing, right guys?"

BEYOND QUICK FIXES: THE THREE-CAPACITY APPROACH

Three broad organizational capacities are essential for successful nonprofit leadership and management of change: (1) the capacity to lead, (2) the capacity to innovate, and (3) the capacity to implement. These closely related and mutually reinforcing capacities are a kind of internal infrastructure that supports the efforts of boards, chief executives, and management teams to determine and direct their organizations' change.

Capacity to Lead

The pre-eminent leadership team of a nonprofit consists of its chief executive and its governing board, and the success of a nonprofit's change efforts depend heavily on how well the respective leadership roles are played and on how effectively the two parties work together (Carver, 1990; Eadie, 1994;

Houle, 1989). A nonprofit's chief executive is without question the prime mover in any large-scale organizational change effort (Bennis, 1989; Gardner, 1990). No other person in the organization is in a better position to make or break the change process. No one else possesses comparable authority, influence, and resources (not even the board, contrary to theory). No other person's words and actions are listened to and observed as closely. And experience has taught that unless the chief executive has a deep understanding of the process of change and is strongly committed to developing his or her organization's capacity to change, little important change is likely to take place.

Chief executives can promote self-determined and managed change by articulating a clear vision that inspires employees; by building a culture that is change friendly; by ensuring that planning and management systems promote and support change; and by ensuring that the resources, primarily money and time, required to implement change initiatives are committed.

Boards can be a precious resource in the change leadership and management process, basically by contributing knowledge and experience to the process of creating a nonprofit's strategic framework—its values, vision, and mission—by helping generate financial and political resources and by supporting the chief executive in carrying out change.

All too often, this top leadership team does not function well (Carver, 1990; Eadie, 1993, 1994). Many nonprofit boards play only the most perfunctory role in blessing vision and mission statements prepared by staff or in signing off on plans that have already been written, edited, and bound. Such boards, involved only at the end of the planning process, naturally feel little ownership of planned change initiatives or accountability for the successful implementation of change. As a passive audience, they have the luxury of sitting back with crossed arms to judge the chief executive and staff, and they cannot be depended on to back the chief executive when the going gets rough.

There are plenty of boards at the other end of the spectrum, too, that can become the enemy of planned change by dabbling in details that are obviously operational and having an ego investment in current operations. For example, membership organizations that are heavily volunteer driven, such as civic clubs, often treat board service as the top rung of the volunteer "career ladder." Having worked their way up the ladder by rolling up their sleeves and getting their hands dirty with the details of running programs, these volunteers-become-board-members can become wedded to these programs and be quite resistant to changing them. Board members with strong emotional attachments to particular organizational methodologies can also become enemies of creative change. For example, recovering alcoholic members on the board of a chemical dependency treatment center would not allow any alternatives to the Alcoholics Anonymous Twelve Step approach to be considered because of their passionate commitment to a treatment process that had literally, in their minds, saved their lives.

Many nonprofit chief executives are ill prepared technically and emotionally to provide strong, creative leadership for a change process that actively involves both board and staff members. They have frequently ascended the professional ladder by demonstrating technical and programmatic virtuosity in specific programs or functions, but these skills do not provide a comprehensive picture of the organization they now lead. In addition, the very competitiveness, drive, decisiveness, and rat-a-tat style that got them where they are now poorly equips them to lead a creative change process.

Perhaps the most serious professional limitation among nonprofit chief executives is a strong need to be in control, which can stifle openness, limit organizational creativity, overly constrain planning, and impede meaningful involvement and partnership. Argyris (1993) wrote about "espoused theory" and "theory in practice," observing that it is not uncommon to find a person espousing one theory while contradicting it in practice, without recognizing the inconsistency. Some chief executives may preach participatory management while at the same time, with apparent unconscious motivation, employing the Louis XIV style of participatory management—I pronounce, you listen and obey.

It is unrealistic to expect that every chief executive, no matter how smart and competent, can grow psychologically to the extent required to lead the change process effectively. Years of training in traditional management, with its control orientation, mitigate against easy transformation. One very bright and capable chief executive was handed an evaluation that his board had just completed. Every technical category was marked A+. He was judged top-notch over the entire management spectrum, from planning and budgeting to financial management and supervision of staff. But the evaluation concluded with the recommendation that he seek other employment because his clear need to be right in every instance, his combativeness in proving his points, and his defensiveness when challenged made him too difficult to work with. Despite advice and encouragement to deal with an obvious character problem that was deep seated, he was not able to rehabilitate himself. Not long after this incident, he lost his job, and eventually two others for basically the same reason, and he has now left the field of nonprofit management.

Another example involves the struggles of the managing director of a nonprofit theater. She was bright, talented, committed to artistic quality, and incredibly hardworking, but her deep-seated need to be in command was so strong that despite her publicly announced and apparently sincere intent to involve the board and staff creatively in setting directions, she could not relinquish control enough to allow meaningful partnerships to develop. As a consequence, the one-woman show was perpetuated, and the theater's slow and steady decline continued.

A new model of chief executive leadership that is suited to the demands of leading and managing change in turbulent times is emerging. This model sees the job as being far more than the boss at whose desk the proverbial buck stops, the program expert who understands the operational dynamics and cannot be snowed by his or her managers, or the technocrat who makes sure the support systems run. The chief executive as effective change leader must be a visionary, not only capable of thinking of the organization in terms of long-run purposes and ends, he or she must also be strongly committed to a collaborative approach to fashioning the vision that creatively draws on the knowledge, expertise, and experience of board and staff members. In this new model, the chief executive must also be an architect and designer, eschewing the old-time command approach to leadership. He or she concentrates on design, putting together all of the complex pieces of the organizational puzzle: board and management team roles, systems such as strategic planning and performance management, programs to enhance individual creative capacity, and more. Only through conscious organizational design can a modern chief executive ensure that creativity is transformed into innovation, that systems are compatible and integrated, and that one or more of the quick-fix solutions being peddled these days is not bought. The chief executive must also play the role of facilitator and coach, helping board and staff members perform their respective functions more effectively and grow in capability. This requires that the chief executive not only be supportive of capability-building efforts, but also that he or she teach by doing rather than by preaching, by visibly engaging in growth strategies even though this will pierce the shield of chief executive infallibility. The chief executive must also be an active partner with his or her board, welcoming its substantive contribution and creative involvement and being committed to developing the board's leadership capacity. This means embracing a nontraditional model of board leadership that sees the board as both a precious asset that needs, for the sake of the organization, to be fully utilized and as a company within the nonprofit corporation that generates essential products. This type of new leadership is secure, nondefensive, and open. It welcomes and encourages wide-ranging questions and new ideas, even if they challenge official positions.

Chief executives who aspire to build their organization's capacity to lead and manage change must be courageous in two major respects. First, they must develop their own creative capacity, which means taking what mythologist Campbell (1968) called the interior "hero's journey" themselves, looking inward and becoming more self-aware by venturing into the subconscious sphere of the mind. Chief executives cannot lead the innovation process effectively without this deeply personal, psychological exploration of their creative capacity. Second, they must be willing to promote the psychological growth of their employees, being "lead psychologists" in the face of almost certain skepticism and even opposition. Talking about the self and the subconscious does not follow traditional macho management rhetoric, and the chief executive who dares to lead in creative capacity building must steel himself or herself against accusations of flakiness or even dementia from traditionalists.

A new approach to board leadership that goes well beyond the traditional board-as-passive-audience is also being successfully tested around the country (Eadie, 1994). In active partnership with the chief executive, the board of the future will function as a kind of business within the nonprofit corporation, guided by a clear leadership mission and focused on producing bottom-line outcomes for the nonprofit. For example, an activist nonprofit board might hold a retreat with the chief executive and management team every year to revisit the vision and mission statements, identify new issues facing the organization (opportunities as well as challenges), and reach agreement on major change initiatives for the coming year.

The board of the future will be accountable for the quality of its membership and for its performance, setting detailed performance standards and regularly monitoring board operations. The board's precise leadership roles and responsibilities will be a matter of ongoing discussion, guided by the needs and circumstances of the nonprofit at any given phase of its development. The division of labor between the board and chief executive will go beyond the old-fashioned policy–administration dichotomy. For example, a small young organization may want its board to play a hands-on role in securing the financial resources to fund growth by making telephone calls to donors and visiting foundations. A more removed stance, involving monitoring rather than doing, may make sense when the nonprofit is securely established and revenue streams are secure.

Capacity to Innovate

The second critical capacity in successful leadership is innovation. The concepts and techniques comprising what is popularly known as "change management" are for the most part aimed at deciding how to implement change, with lots of attention to securing the buy-in of participants who must do much of the work of changing. Deciding how to implement change is, however, distinctly subordinate to the fundamental question that ultimately determines success or failure: What will the content of the change be? Determining the what of change, rather than merely the how to, inevitably leads a nonprofit into the realm of innovation, which is the process of putting something new into practice, whether a service, product, relationship, or management system. In a complex, rapidly changing environment, systematic innovation is a survival tool rather than a luxury, and the greater the complexity and faster the external change, the more pressing the need for innovation.

Innovation means going beyond the tried and true and transcending conventional wisdom in responding to challenges. Innovative solutions are not conveyed in slogans or on bumper stickers. Being innovative requires openness, careful listening, and learning; it means recognizing complexities and subtle distinctions and taking them into account when fashioning effective solutions. Being innovative means seeing through the shell game of no-cost solutions to complex challenges and having the courage to bear the costs.

Innovation is a challenging process; innovative solutions to complex problems can be difficult to explain and sell to the man and woman on the street who elect our public officials and more or less provide the resources to implement solutions. Simplicity can be seductive; sound bites, if not ultimately nourishing, are easily chewed; stereotypes save time and demons are fun to hate.

But no matter how stiff the challenge, true innovative leadership demands more than appeasing anger and pandering to an appetite for no-cost, no-brainer solutions. It means asking second, third, and even fourth questions and seeing beyond the immediate outcomes. Innovative nonprofits do not merely train unemployed people for jobs that do not exist or will quickly become outmoded or place their clients in minimum-wage jobs with no future merely to meet the immediate performance standards of the Department of Labor. Nor do they buy into the notion that the complex issue of violent crime can be solved through three-strikes-and-you're-out sentencing or filling jails to capacity. They know enough to distrust gut reactions and simplistic solutions.

The innovation capacity consists of two major subcapacities: (1) creativity, which generates the ideas, the possibilities for change, and (2) planning, which selects from possibilities and eventually translates them into concrete change projects or initiatives that can then be implemented. They are an inseparable team. Lots of creativity without a well-developed planning capacity is a recipe for unrealized potential, frustration, and little important change. A well-developed planning process run by people with little opportunity to build or express their creative capacity will severely limit the possibilities for innovative action.

Creativity

Think innovation, and creativity comes immediately to mind; the two concepts go hand in hand. Although they are frequently treated as the same thing, it makes sense to view creativity as the capacity that undergirds and enriches the innovation process. Creativity is the supplier of the newness that the innovation process translates into practice. An ill-defined concept having as much mystery as science about it, creativity involves seeing in the mind patterns that have not been seen before. It means going beyond the tried and true and transcending conventional wisdom in thinking about possible responses to environmental challenges. Creativity is the capacity to generate mental possibilities which, through innovation, are put into practice in the real world (Boden, 1991; Csikszentmihalyi, 1996; Gardner, 1993).

Developing the creative capacity that is at the heart of a nonprofit's capability to innovate is a matter of developing the creative capacity of the individual human beings comprising the organization. Individuals, not the systems that support decision making, are more or less creative, and no planning process, no matter how sophisticated its design, can fully compensate for inadequate individual capability.

Planning

Planning, especially of the strategic variety, can be the innovation machine that transforms creative ideas into practical innovations in a nonprofit organization; therefore, it is potentially one of the pre-eminent drivers of nonprofit change. Unfortunately, since the 1970s strategic planning has earned a reputation for generating more paper than action (see chapter 21 for a more comprehensive discussion of planning). This is by no means a bum rap. In actual practice, if not in theory, strategic or long-range planning has tended to be focused on control rather than innovation, basically taking what an organization is already doing and merely projecting it forward three, five, or more years into the future. Of course, since the wider world refuses to oblige us by remaining static or by changing in a nice, neat fashion, such mammoth globs of paper have quickly become outdated and have routinely ended up on dusty shelves, seldom if ever consulted (Bryson, 1995; Eadie, 1993).

It may have been professional planners, with their penchant for order, who created the three-, five-, and 10-year planning cycles. These surely correspond to no natural cycle in human affairs, nor have they ever delivered the world they promised. If the benefits of formal planning have been scant, the costs have been high. For one thing, the illusion of control that bloated documents can create has lulled many nonprofits into a false sense of being secure and in control of their destinies, thereby actually making them more vulnerable than if they had never done formal planning. For another, the time spent writing, editing, printing, and binding such formal plans might have been better spent gathering information on environmental trends and conditions and focusing on specific change targets. In addition, going through the planning motions for no useful purpose has bred understandable cynicism among managers, making it more difficult to build support for serious planning.

Just because strategic planning has been misused as a tool does not mean that it cannot produce powerful results. In reaction to traditional wheel-spinning in pursuit of the illusion of control, serious planning reforms have revitalized the process since the mid-1980s. Indeed, a significant new variation on the strategic planning theme, typically known as "strategic management," has been successfully tested in hundreds of organizations, including a number of nonprofits (Bryson, 1995; Eadie, 1994, 1997; Mintzberg, 1994).

A strategic management process that is seriously applied results in the identification of "change challenges"—strategic issues in the form of opportunities to move closer to an organization's vision or barriers blocking progress toward the vision, the selection of the challenges or issues to be addressed now, and the development of change initiatives to address the selected issues. Taken together, the change initiatives at any given time comprise a kind of organizational change portfolio or agenda, which must be managed separately from day-to-day operations if it is not to be overwhelmed.

The annual process of operational planning and budget preparation can also be a source of systematic organizational innovation, although on a smaller scale than in strategic management and within established boundaries. Because operational planning is by its nature control focused and is a long-surviving, hearty tool without much glamour, its innovative potential has received less attention than it deserves.

Capacity to Implement

The third critical task in successful leadership is implementation. The gap between intent and practice, between plans and action, is frequently not successfully bridged. The following case demonstrates this gap.

> The two days could not have gone better for the board and staff of the Center for Family Services. Millhaven was a superb facility, offering spacious, well-equipped conference rooms, a sylvan setting, and numerous recreational opportunities. The facilitator did a great job of steering the group through a complex process of visioning, assessing external conditions and trends, and identifying several issues that appeared to deserve closer attention. The group narrowed the issues down to four that everyone agreed should be explored in greater detail in the coming weeks and turned into concrete change strategies: (1) an expected cut of 30 percent in the next year's United Way subsidy, (2) a proposed merger with the Children's Services Agency, (3) the need for an aggressive financial development program, and (4) eroding board enthusiasm, as evidenced by several resignations and the cancellation of two board meetings for failure to attract a quorum. Loud applause greeted the chair's closing comments, the meeting ended on a high note, and everyone drove home anticipating the positive changes on the horizon.
>
> Days, weeks, and months went by. Copiers and faxes spewed out paper, staff were up to their eyeballs with just getting through the day-to-day operations

without major mishaps, board members occasionally asked about follow-up to the retreat, which was well on its way to becoming a hazy memory. Things went along pretty much as usual. Fortunately, some last-minute lobbying resulted in a smaller than expected cut in the United Way allocation, and so only a couple of positions had to be eliminated. Filling three board vacancies made achieving quorums easier, but enthusiasm was still lacking.

This downbeat scenario probably sounds depressingly familiar because examples of breakdown between verbal intentions and actual practice are everywhere around us. Planned change is frequently not implemented for three major reasons: (1) unrealistic implementation planning, (2) inadequate implementation structure and process, and (3) a milieu that is unfriendly to change (Dalziel & Schoonover, 1988; Kanter, 1989; Tichy, 1983).

Through detailed implementation planning, an organization determines for each change initiative or project precisely what steps must be taken to carry out the initiative, who is accountable for seeing that each step is accomplished, the timetable that will be followed, and the resources required to implement the plan. A truly realistic plan will pay close attention to the required resources, looking not just at the obvious cost in dollars but also looking at staff skills that may have to be upgraded to ensure full implementation. For example, there may be no point in moving forward with an image-building strategy if a part-time person is not hired to handle media relations.

Change initiatives or projects can easily be overwhelmed by the press of day-to-day events. A change structure and implementation process that is kept separate from the day-to-day management process can provide the protection, nurturing, and oversight required to keep change initiatives alive and well. Many organizations have created special change programs, with a steering committee composed of management team members who meet regularly for the sole purpose of overseeing the implementation of change initiatives or projects, a team member serving as the coordinator of change projects and as the quality control officer, and staff task forces accountable for seeing to the many details involved in implementing the projects. Everyone involved wears only the "change hat" when participating in the program, which is kept well away from normal operations. So, for example, change matters never become the last item on a crowded Monday morning staff meeting agenda.

A nonprofit's internal milieu is another factor with substantial influence on the implementation of change. An organization's milieu is in large measure its culture. Schein (1985) defined *culture* as a "pattern of basic assumptions— invented, discovered, or developed by a given group as it learns to cope with its problems of external adaptation and internal integration—that has worked well enough to be considered valid and, therefore, to be taught to new members as the correct way to perceive, think, and feel in relation to those problems" (p. 9). The organizational milieu also consists of the current climate, including the feelings and attitudes of the staff. Obviously, an organization lurching from one crisis to another over a period of weeks or months, with a fatigued, nervous staff, will have a harder time concentrating on the implementation of change than one with a more secure and peaceful climate. Furthermore, a staff that has been negatively affected on a number of occasions by abrupt, seemingly irrational changes of course by the chief executive is likely to hold back both commitment and energy when asked to participate in a change process.

CHANGING TO GET READY FOR CHANGE

Developing the essential capacities to lead, innovate, and implement, thereby building a foundation for continuous self-generated and guided change, will in itself involve organizational change. Therefore, most nonprofits will be well advised to tackle capacity building early on, even while concurrently responding to change signals from the external world by fashioning new strategic directions, programs, and services. This will require virtuoso juggling among a plethora of competing values, because while a nonprofit works on capacity building to enhance its capability to respond to the changing world, it will have no choice but to respond to specific external opportunities or threats when the stakes are high enough.

In a practical example, in a recent management team meeting a nonprofit nursing home without a contemporary strategic management process has taken note of growing consumer demand for one-stop retirement living, or continuum of care, that offers a full range of accommodations and services without having to leave a core campus. As they live longer and healthier lives, senior citizens want to begin at one end of the spectrum with truly independent living in detached cottages and then move through a range of living styles until they arrive at skilled-nursing care in a traditional nursing home setting at the other end of the spectrum. The strength of the demand dictates that the organization begin to explore strategies for expansion from its current traditional home to a wider range of facilities and services. At the same time, the team has decided that it must take a more systematic approach to identifying and acting on strategic issues in the future, so it has also decided to create a task force to design a new strategic management process for this purpose.

It would not be feasible to ignore the changing outside world while focusing exclusively on building the internal change leadership and management infrastructure. The key is to create an overall change agenda or portfolio that balances the need to respond to external events with the internal capacity-building need, making sure that first things are put first. For example, strengthening the leadership of a board that is not fully involved in setting strategic directions but that is not malfunctioning in any important way would obviously take second place to dealing with the imminent loss of a grant supplying one-third of the budget. However, a board that is upset about its role and mad enough to consider firing the chief executive would merit concerted attention before considering possible diversification options as part of a long-term growth strategy.

A nonprofit's board, chief executive, and management team must work together closely to keep the change agenda or portfolio balanced from year to year, ensuring that it responds effectively to external challenges and opportunities while continuously strengthening the essential capabilities on which effective change leadership and management depend. Their choice of change initiatives should be based on a realistic assessment of what is at stake for their organization in dealing with particular initiatives, and their responsibility is to create a mix of initiatives that promises the greatest benefit possible, including loss reduction, at an affordable cost.

SKILLS-APPLICATION EXERCISES

- Describe the overall experience of your organization, or of an organization you are familiar with, or of your own personal experience, in leading and managing innovation. What change initiatives or planned innovations have been implemented? What change initiatives have fallen by the wayside? Why do you think these have not been successful?

- Assess the strengths and weaknesses of the chief executive's leadership of change in your organization, or in an organization you are familiar with, or your own personal leadership of change in your life. What skills and attributes need to be strengthened to lead change more effectively?

- Assess the strengths and weaknesses of your board's leadership of change, or of a board you are familiar with. What aspects of the board's leadership process and structure might need to be strengthened to enhance its change leadership?

- Does the planning process in your organization, or an organization you know, or your own personal planning, actually produce practical change initiatives consciously aimed at significant innovation? If not, why not? What features of the planning process need to be changed, and how?

- What is the experience of your organization, or an organization you know, or your own personal experience, in implementing change initiatives? What might you do in terms of implementation structure and process to strengthen the implementation process?

REFERENCES

Argyris, C. (1993). *Knowledge for action: A guide to overcoming barriers to organizational change*. San Francisco: Jossey-Bass.

Bennis, W. (1989). *Why leaders can't lead: The unconscious conspiracy continues*. San Francisco: Jossey-Bass.

Boden, M. A. (1991). *The creative mind: Myths and mechanisms*. New York: Basic Books.

Bryson, J. M. (1995). *Strategic planning for public and nonprofit organizations: A guide to strengthening and sustaining organizational achievement*. San Francisco: Jossey-Bass.

Campbell, J. (1968). *The hero with a thousand faces* (2nd ed.). Princeton, NJ: Princeton University Press.

Carver, J. (1990). *Boards that make a difference: A new design for leadership in nonprofit and public organizations*. San Francisco: Jossey-Bass.

Csikszentmihalyi, M. (1996). *Creativity: Flow and the psychology of discovery and invention*. New York: HarperCollins.

Dalziel, M. M., & Schoonover, S. C. (1988). *Changing ways: A practical tool for implementing change within organizations*. New York: AMACOM.

De Pree, M. (1989). *Leadership is an art*. New York: Dell.

Eadie, D. C. (1993). *Beyond strategic planning: How to involve nonprofit boards in growth and change*. Washington, DC: National Center for Nonprofit Boards.

Eadie, D. C. (1994). *Boards that work: A practical guide for building effective association boards*. Washington, DC: American Society of Association Executives.

Eadie, D. C. (1996). Leading and managing strategic change. In J. L. Perry (Ed.), *Handbook of public administration* (2nd ed.). San Francisco: Jossey-Bass.

Eadie, D. C. (1997). *Meeting the change challenge*. Washington, DC: American Society of Association Executives.

Edwards, R. L., Cooke, P. W., & Reid, P. N. (1996). Social work management in an era of diminishing federal responsibility. *Social Work, 41*, 468–479.

Gardner, H. (1993). *Creating minds*. New York: Basic Books.

Gardner, J. (1990). *On leadership*. New York: Free Press.

Houle, C. O. (1989). *Governing boards: Their nature and nurture*. San Francisco: Jossey-Bass.

Kanter, R. M. (1989). *When giants learn to dance*. New York: Simon & Schuster.

Kemp, E. J., Funk, R. J., & Eadie, D. C. (1993). Change in chewable bites: Applying strategic management at EEOC. *Public Administration Review, 53,* 129–134.

Mintzberg, H. (1994, January/February). The rise and fall of strategic planning. *Harvard Business Review*, pp. 102–114.

Morgan, G. (1988). *Riding the waves of change*. San Francisco: Jossey-Bass.

O'Toole, J. (1995). *Leading change: Overcoming the ideology of comfort and the tyranny of custom*. San Francisco: Jossey-Bass.

Schein, E. H. (1985). *Organizational culture and leadership*. San Francisco: Jossey-Bass.

Tichy, N. M. (1983). *Managing strategic change*. New York: John Wiley & Sons.

CHAPTER 3

Effective Proposal Writing

Christine E. Henry

As described in chapter 1, nonprofit managers must be skilled at performing the broker role. As a nonprofit manager, you must be engaged in acquiring resources and relate effectively to your organization's external environment. You will need good boundary-spanning skills to serve as the interface between your organization and others in its environment. You will also need to be knowledgeable about funding sources and adept at preparing funding proposals. This chapter provides information about how to identify potential funding sources and how to develop effective proposals to secure foundation and government funding.

The challenge confronting you is that the competition for dollars and recognition is fierce, particularly as the pressure grows to fill in gaps left by cuts in government funding. The ability to meet these challenges involves constant attention to social trends and the demands for organizational and client service, and the ability to work together with government and business to meet changing needs. A successful nonprofit organization must have a healthy mix of funding sources. A fundraising strategy that includes government funds, direct mail solicitation, foundation grants, individual major gifts, and special events is most successful in the long run (Edwards, Benefield, Edwards, & Yankey, 1997).

The economy of the United States generally includes the government, business, and nonprofit sectors. There are now more than 1 million nonprofit organizations in the United States, and the number grows daily (Independent Sector, 1997). The nonprofit sector is quickly coming into its own as a viable field of study for academicians as well as practitioners. The sector is recognized as a social, economic, and political influence on the way we work, learn, serve others, and enjoy leisure time. A significant source of employment, nonprofits in the United States account for at least 6 percent of the gross domestic product and employ about 7 percent of the total work force (Independent Sector, 1997). Although the majority of nonprofits have annual revenues of less than $500,000, as a group they spend more than $340 billion each year (Independent Sector, 1997). Management expert Peter Drucker refers to the nonprofit sector as America's largest employer—the combined labor pool of paid staff and volunteers in the United States amounts to around 90 million people each year (Independent Sector, 1997).

Only about 12 percent of the revenue from private sources to nonprofits is from foundations. The vast majority of private funds comes from individuals, either from direct gifts or bequests (Carlson, 1995). Nevertheless, grants from foundations are an important part of a nonprofit's funding plan. More than 38,000 foundations in the United States make annual grants to nonprofit organizations totaling more than $12 billion (Geever & McNeill, 1997). Foundations play a powerful role in soliciting support (through challenge and matching grants), permitting new initiatives, furthering causes, servicing trends, and shaping evaluations.

DEVELOPING THE CONCEPT

The first thing to do before investigating foundations or submitting a proposal is to be absolutely clear about your organization's mission, qualifying status, and the specific purpose for your proposal. Develop the who, what, why, where, when, and how of the proposal, whether it be to support general operations or to fund a special project. The following questions will help you clarify and develop your proposal:

- Are your organization's mission and purpose clear? Does the project truly support your mission, or are you tailoring an idea to a funder's interests?
- Do you have your nonprofit tax designation from the Internal Revenue Service (IRS), or do you have a qualified agency that can serve as your fiscal agent?
- Have you carefully assessed the need and population you intend to address, taking into account other agencies or programs that offer similar services? How is your proposal unique? What gap does it fill?
- Do you have a concrete plan that addresses a need that is important to society?
- Can you provide measurable goals and objectives and a reasonable time frame?
- Is your organization capable of implementing the project?
- Have you carefully developed the financial components and made plans for continued funding?

Put the answers to these questions into written form to serve as a rough draft for your proposal. This first step of clarifying your purpose will also help you focus your investigation on those foundations that are well matched to your interests. Most foundations are relatively clear about what they want to fund. For example, some foundations fund only mental health or environmental projects, whereas others are interested in scholarships or the arts. Many have geographic restrictions, and some do not respond to unsolicited proposals. They may specify that they do not contribute to general operations, respond to annual appeals, or fund capital projects.

INVESTIGATING THE POSSIBILITIES

Between 80 percent and 95 percent of all proposals are declined (Golden, 1997). The reasons for rejection include limited foundation dollars, a proposal that is outside the foundation guidelines, an unclear project, costs that are too high, or an idea that is not compelling. The chances of your proposal being funded are increased significantly if you carefully research the types of foundations and their interest areas, guidelines, and limitations. Foundation representatives spend a great deal of time and effort acquiring new information about their areas of interest and learning about the needs in their communities. They often gather at conferences and forums to discuss ways to meet community needs through targeted funding and collaborative measures. Some foundation representatives get very involved in the projects they fund.

Foundations usually publish their interest areas and funding guidelines in an annual report, grant guidelines, or an application form, all of which can be obtained through a letter or telephone call to the foundation. These publications are very specific about the format, deadlines, and limitations the grant seeker should follow in submitting a proposal. It is very important to get this information and do your homework about a foundation's areas of interest and its limitations before you submit a proposal. A preliminary letter of inquiry or a telephone call (the guidelines often say which) is often the best way to get a feel for a possible match.

Also, pay attention to the differences from foundation to foundation, and personalize the proposal as much as possible. Developing relationships with foundation representatives is important, especially if the foundation is one that gives operating support to the same organizations over a long period of time. The foundation is primarily interested in the scope and general application of a project and in how it advances the foundation's philanthropic interests (Brewer, Achilles, & Fuhriman, 1995).

TYPES OF FOUNDATIONS

There are many kinds of foundations. *Independent* or *family foundations*, referred to as "private foundations" by the IRS, are established by individuals or families and are usually funded through inherited wealth or wealth accumulated through a business activity. Many of these foundations are established through a substantial bequest upon the death of the founder, who may have left specific instructions about what program areas the foundation will fund. Foundation funds may later be augmented by contributions from other family members. Family members often become very involved in the awarding of grants, although the majority of the foundation's giving is consistent with the interests of the original donor. Some of these foundations are quite large and powerful, employ several executives and program officers, and wield a good deal of influence in their areas of interest. Some examples are the Charles Stuart Mott Foundation (microenterprise and low-income entrepreneurship), the Ewing Marion Kauffman Foundation (public policy), and the Annie E. Casey Foundation (children and youths). Most foundations, however, are small, and the grants they make are handled by trustees, lawyers, or family members.

Corporate foundations are funded by major national and international corporations such as Sony, Kellogg, and Ford, as well as smaller local corporations. Their annual contributions vary with the company's profits. The foundation executive is usually a company employee who may have other responsibilities in public or community relations. Corporate giving is strongly linked to the company's business interests. Grants and contributions are given to nonprofits that are within the geographic interests of company operations, to community organizations in which company employees are actively involved, or to program areas that are consistent with company products. For example, computer companies tend to give to nonprofits that request funds for projects that use computers, and companies that produce children's products tend to support programs for children. Often corporate foundations will be more interested in in-kind contributions, such as furniture, equipment, publicity, technical assistance, or employee volunteers, rather than cash awards. Requests to corporate foundations often need not be as lengthy and detailed as other foundation proposals; often a letter may suffice. Although there are corporate giving directories, many corporations do not publish their giving programs. Telephone calls to corporations and talking with other nonprofits who have received corporate support is the best way to gather information.

Community foundations, such as the Cleveland Foundation, the New York Community Trust, and the Community Foundation for Southeastern Michigan, are funded by contributions from numerous individuals and families in a given community. They limit their grants to nonprofits within a narrowly defined geographic area such as a city or region. Although grants are approved by the foundation board or its distribution committee, many donors retain a degree of discretion over grants made from the funds they contribute. Large community foundations may employ several professional staff, including specialists in various areas, and may be leaders in developing giving patterns in their communities.

Operating foundations are private foundations that use their resources to conduct research or provide a direct service. The Smith Foundation for Restorative Neurology, the Mariton Wildlife Sanctuary and Wilderness Trust, the Breckenridge Aviation Museum, and the World Peace Fund are operating foundations. Although some are listed in foundation directories, they do not make grants to the general nonprofit community.

Most individual, family, and community foundations invest the contributions they receive from donors and use only the interest or earnings as the primary source of grant dollars. Whether the earnings are high or low, however, these foundations are required by law to give away a minimum of 5 percent of their assets annually to charitable organizations.

The range of categories that foundations may fund includes capital support, general operations, endowments, scholarships, matching or challenge grants, program support, research, start-up funds, bridge funding to ease cash flow problems, technical assistance, emergency funding, and program-related investments.

GOVERNMENT SOURCES

Government agencies whose primary purpose is to make grants are funded by public contributions, generally through annual legislative appropriations. Examples are the National Science Foundation, the U.S. Department of Housing and Urban Development, the National Endowment for the Arts, and the U.S. Department of Health and Human Services (HHS). Typically, these agencies are professionally managed and take some of their direction from advisory boards. Government agencies at local, state, and regional levels also operate ad hoc grant programs as mandated by current legislation. For instance, some grants are targeted to issues such as job development related to welfare reform or child support enforcement initiatives.

Federal grants are usually given in the form of special project funds and often go to a state agency to be distributed to nonprofits within that state. For example, the HHS has special project funds for AIDS prevention that are given to state governments, which in turn award them to local organizations that seek funding to perform services (Carlson, 1995).

There is also federal block grant money that is given to cities to distribute to nonprofits for capital projects and programs considered to be of major significance to the welfare of the community, such as the rehabilitation of neglected urban housing or commercial areas or the development of inner-city recreation sites. Information about this type of grant may be obtained through the mayor's office from the person who deals with Community Development Block Grants.

Government grant funds are declining, but some funds are still available. Learn which government agencies might be interested in your program and what their application requirements and deadlines are. Get to know the influential people in the government agencies, and stay in close contact with them. The application process may be detailed and lengthy and may entail site visits and presentations to the decision makers to justify the need for the funds. Many government agencies use score sheets and assign points to different components of the proposal. Request a copy to refer to as you develop your proposal (Kiritz, 1988).

Federal agencies regularly issue requests for proposals that call for specific program ideas and contain detailed guidelines regarding proposal preparation. Information about government grants can be obtained from the *Catalogue of Federal Domestic Assistance*, published annually by the General Services Administration (GSA) of the U.S. Office of Management and Budget (www.gsa.gov/fdac). The catalog is a compendium of federal programs, projects, services, and activities that provide assistance or benefits to the public. In addition to the hard-copy catalog data, program and grant information is available on machine-readable magnetic tape, high-density floppy diskettes, and CD-ROM, which may be purchased from the GSA or may be available for use at larger libraries.

RESEARCHING FOUNDATIONS AND CORPORATE FUNDERS

Parallel to the national database of federal funders, the Foundation Center is the pre-eminent source of information on foundation and corporate funders. The center's database on CD-ROM, print directories, foundation annual reports, guidelines, and many other resources are available in a national collection located in New York City and Washington, DC, and in regional collections in Atlanta, Cleveland, and San Francisco. The center also has local collections in 190 community libraries throughout the United States. Free orientation and proposal-writing programs are available at the national and regional Foundation Center libraries, and center staff members often visit local collections to conduct these programs. All Foundation Center collections have written materials that outline the research process and suggest places to start.

The Foundation Center's major publications and computer services are the *Foundation Directory, Foundation Grants Index, Foundation Center National Data Book*, Comsearch printout, and Sourcebook profiles. Individual directories list foundations by type, location, geographic focus, fields of interest, type of support, recipient type, total assets, total giving, and so on.

The Foundation Center's database is now available on the CD-ROM FC Search. It covers 40,000 U.S. foundations and corporate givers; includes descriptions of nearly 200,000 grants; and lists more than 180,000 trustees, officers, and donors. Information is also available through direct online search services such as DIALOG, Data Times, and Nexis and through commercial online services such as Compuserve, America Online, and Microsoft Network. The Foundation Center maintains a Web site: www.fdncenter.org. The site is a gateway to a wide range of philanthropic information services.

You can also obtain information on smaller or newer foundations by contacting the local office of the IRS or the nearest Foundation Center Library for the Form 990 PF that small foundations must submit to the IRS each year. This form contains details of the foundation's finances, its grantees, its funding interests and limitations, and its application guidelines and deadlines.

WRITING THE PROPOSAL

After you have specified the purpose of your proposal and identified which government agency or foundation to apply to, determine who will actually write the proposal. This is a time-consuming process that should be considered as important as the design and implementation of the project. For many grant seekers, the proposal is the only opportunity to educate the funder about their organizations and the proposed projects. Thus, the proposal must generate a positive overall organizational image (Geever & McNeill, 1997). The proposal need not be slick, but it must convey all the important ideas in a clear, concise, and compelling manner. The proposal must answer six basic questions: who, what, why, where, when, and how (Frost, 1993). When deciding whether to have a staff member, volunteer, or consultant write the proposal, ask to see writing samples. The writer should spend a great deal of time talking with those close to the project and developing the form, style, and content of the document. Often the foundation representative who receives the proposal must condense it into a brief summary format for the other board or committee members. Hence, the key ideas should appear in the very beginning of the proposal and should be expressed briefly, positively, and in simple but compelling language.

Some foundations ask that proposals follow their guidelines in the order they are written. Typical components of proposals are the cover letter, executive summary, organizational overview, project description, budget, post-project plans, and appendixes.

Cover Letter

Addressed to a specific person at the foundation or government agency, the cover letter should identify your organization, briefly describe the project, reference the connection between your proposed project and the funding entity's interests, state the amount requested, designate a contact person in your agency, and express gratitude for the opportunity to present the proposal. The letter should welcome a visit from or meeting with the grant maker. It should be signed by the board president, which indicates the board's involvement and support, and the executive director. The cover letter should be no longer than one page.

Executive Summary

This first page of the proposal is the most important section of the entire document, because it specifies the importance of your proposed project. The opening of the proposal serves as a sales presentation to convince the reader that the project is worthy of the government agency's or foundation's support (Geever & McNeill, 1997). It is not unusual for a proposal to be rejected because the grant maker lacked interest in this summary. To capture the reader's attention, the summary should include a brief description of the problem or need, the proposed solutions, the overall goals for the proposed project, the funds that you have already committed to the project and what additional funding is needed, and a brief reference to how the project furthers your organization's mission.

Organizational Overview

This section introduces your organization to the funder. It should include when, why, and how the organization was started; the mission statement, purpose, goals, and guiding philosophy; significant historical events; current activities; accomplishments and impact; description of your constituency; funding sources; board, staff, and volunteer make-up; notable accreditations and affiliations; and plans for the future. Include important facts, but do not overload the organizational description with unnecessary details about your organization's structure and philosophy. Focus on your credibility in the area in which you seek support. If other organizations are involved, provide evidence of their credibility as well as their support of your proposed project.

Project Description

The project description is the heart of the proposal. It should provide the details that flesh out the summary statements made in the beginning of the proposal. The project description should answer several questions: What is the need or problem to be addressed, and how was this need determined? What target population will benefit from this project, how many people, and in what way? What are the specific goals and objectives? What methods (activities, procedures) will be used to implement the project? How will progress be measured, evaluated, and reported? What is the project's time frame? Who is responsible for implementation, and what are his or her qualifications? Will other organizations be involved? Is the project clearly related to the purpose and goals of your organization? Does the project have reasonable dimensions?

Each of these topics should be addressed individually and completely but as briefly as possible. The description of each topic should flow logically into the next, and explanations and rationales for choosing certain approaches should be presented. Describe what you are going to do in terms of specific ways you will serve clients or constituents rather than discussing broadly conceptualized problems and needs. Whereas some foundations and government agencies specify page lengths for this part of the proposal, this section is usually not more than six to eight pages.

Budget

A good budget is a plan of action and a powerful tool for exercising managerial control. Your proposal should include a project budget as well as the most current audited financial statements of the organization itself. Different funders require different degrees of detail in the budget. Government agencies require extensive detail and often provide forms and instructions. Foundations and corporations are less structured but require a clear and complete budget. A good budget and budget narrative will relate directly to the objectives and activities of the project and will be consistent with the proposal narrative. For example, if specific staff or staff positions are named in the project description as having a role in the proposed activities, and you are seeking at least part or whole support for their salaries, then these names and positions should be listed in the personnel section of the budget. Similarly, if you named a product such as agency brochures as a proposed materials development activity for which you are seeking funding, then the

"You know, I think we had that grant request approved right up to the point when she counted the zeros on the funding amount."

budget should clearly name and reflect the costs of producing such brochures.

There are two broad categories of expenses: direct and indirect. Direct costs are expenses related to salaries, rent, utilities, telephone, equipment, printing, supplies, postage, insurance, and travel. Indirect costs, also known as "overhead," reflect a host organization's administrative costs to operate several funded projects. Typical indirect costs include the cost of operating and maintaining buildings, grounds, and equipment; depreciation; and general and departmental administrative salaries and expenses. Sometimes indirect costs are calculated as a percentage of the total organizational direct costs, of the personnel costs, or of the salary and wage items alone (Geever & McNeill, 1997). Some foundations do not fund indirect costs, or they cap the indirect percentage rate. Determine if the foundation to which you are applying has a policy about including indirect costs. A revenue statement, if requested, should list anticipated or committed grant funds; income from fees, publications, and services; and earned interest and income from fundraising activities.

Post-Project Plans

A concluding paragraph or two should summarize the future of the project, outline follow-up activities, and discuss ways you plan to acquire future funding. Briefly reiterate what your organization wants to do and why it is important. This is also your last chance to make your appeal (Geever & McNeill, 1997).

Appendixes

The appendixes serve as a reference section. This section should include information not already presented in other parts of the proposal, such as the operating budget and other financial information; the list of board members; your IRS tax exemption letter; your annual report; news articles about your agency and its accomplishments or the problem you hope to work on; and letters of support.

Packaging the Proposal

Different funders have different requirements for packaging the proposal, and some ask for multiple copies whereas others ask for only one. Customize each proposal. Don't bother with binding or fancy folders, as these are usually removed. If possible, send the proposal so that it arrives at the funder's office at least several days before the final deadline to allow time for any necessary follow-up on either end. If the proposal is not there by the submission deadline, it will not be considered.

Follow-Up

If your proposal is funded, send a personalized thank-you letter. Often, at the same time you receive the written notice of award announcement, the funder will include the reporting requirements. Some funders require periodic progress reports and budget statements in addition to a final activity report and final expense report. Be sure to comply with these requirements. Even if the reporting requirements are minimal, it is important to keep the funder informally updated about the project's activities and progress. If the proposal is declined, send a note thanking the funder for reviewing the proposal. Call at another time to find out why the proposal was not accepted.

COMMENTS FROM THE FIELD

Following are some thoughts and ideas from funders and grant seekers who have a great deal of experience in soliciting funds through proposals.

From the Funders

- Do your homework. Every funder is different. One success does not lead to others. The main reason proposals are declined is because they do not fit the guidelines.
- Do not assume the reader knows your field, but do not go on and on about what is common knowledge.
- Relate your idea to current and important theories in your field or in some area of human behavior relating to motivation, communication, or change.
- Initiate innovation. Suggest a creative funding package or idea, or initiate a collaboration.
- Make the proposal brief, easy to read, free of jargon, and written in a positive, energetic style. It should not sound desperate or preachy. Write with excitement, eagerness, and confidence about the organization and the project.
- Know that foundations view their grants as investments and expect good returns on them.
- Know that the real test of a project's success is a reduction of the need that precipitated the project (Brewer et al., 1995).
- Know that the most critical issues in funding relationships are trust and credibility.

From the Grant Seekers

- The foundation culture varies in different communities. In some areas funders are very competitive, and in others there is a great deal of collaboration. Find out where the sensitivities are, especially on the corporate side.
- Many foundations are not receptive to helping or even calling back. Larger, staffed foundations were the most accessible and responsive.
- Some grants came easy; others might have come easier if we had done more homework. Personal contact made a big difference in the positive responses.
- Government grants are tough—it is easier to get renewals than to get new funding.
- Expect to modify the proposal for each potential funder based on that funder's interests and guidelines.

- It will show in your proposal if you are fudging the activity just to fit the foundation's wants and likes. Do not get caught up in the latest funding fads.
- Foundations have a lot of influence. They often are the only evaluators of how an organization or project is doing.
- Securing grants combines many skills. You have to be resource oriented, clever, politically astute, creative, a negotiator, a risk taker, and a good presenter.

SKILLS-APPLICATION EXERCISE

Each funder has priorities, restrictions, and guidelines that govern its grant making. Using the funder's specific criteria, review a proposal that has been submitted to a private foundation, a corporate giving program, or a government agency. Copies or samples of proposals can be found in library materials about grant writing. Grant seekers may be willing to share "old" proposals. Based on the information provided by the proposal, answer the following questions.

1. *Screening and eligibility.* Has the organization provided IRS and basic financial information? Does the executive summary allow you to determine the proposal's eligibility for consideration? Does the request meet the foundation's requirements and interests?

2. *Organization strength.* Is this a credible organization in the program area for which it is seeking funds? What is its mission, its professional standing, its track record? Who is served? Are there similar services in the same area? Is there community support? What are the distinctive merits of the organization?

3. *People.* Do key personnel have the qualifications to undertake the proposed project? Who provides the vision and leadership of the organization? Does the board composition reflect an appropriate diversity of skills and backgrounds?

4. *Financial condition.* How does the organization finance day-to-day operations? Is there a broad base of support? Does the project budget match the narrative? Does it seem reasonable?

5. *Problem or need to be addressed.* Has an important issue of workable dimensions been presented? Has data been given to substantiate the problem? Have the people who will be affected been involved in the needs assessment and solution process?

6. *Program objectives.* What will the proposed funding accomplish? Are the objectives clear, realistic, and measurable? Do they relate to the need? How does the project compare to similar programs?

7. *Methods.* Are the plans sufficiently detailed? Is it evident how the methods will bring about the expected results? Is the timetable realistic? Is there adequate and capable staff to carry out the project?

8. *Evaluation.* Is there a procedure to measure, evaluate, and report the project's progress? For new, pilot, or model projects, are there plans to share the results and findings with funders and other organizations?

9. *Future funding.* What other funding sources have been identified? If the project is to continue beyond the grant period, is there a plan for ongoing financial support?

10. *Language and form.* Is the proposal clear and logically presented? Are assumptions and facts supported? Is there extensive, unacceptable use of jargon and verbiage?

REFERENCES

Brewer, E. W., Achilles, C. M., & Fuhriman, J. R. (1995). *Finding funding* (2nd ed.). Thousand Oaks, CA: Corwin Press.

Carlson, M. (1995). *Winning grants step by step.* San Francisco: Jossey-Bass.

Edwards, R. L., Benefield, E.A.S., Edwards, J. A., & Yankey, J. A. (1997). *Building a strong foundation: Fundraising for nonprofits.* Washington, DC: NASW Press.

Frost, G. J. (1993). *Winning grant proposals.* Rockville, MD: Fund Raising Institute.

Geever, J. C., & McNeill, P. (1997). *Guide to proposal writing.* Washington, DC: Foundation Center.

Golden, S. L. (1997). *Secrets of successful grantsmanship: A guerilla guide to raising money.* San Francisco: Jossey-Bass.

Independent Sector. (1997, July). *What you should know about nonprofits.* Available online from www.indepsec.org.

Kiritz, N. J. (1988). *Program planning and proposal writing.* Los Angeles: Grantsmanship Center.

The author acknowledges and thanks the following foundation and nonprofit professionals for sharing their comments and insights into the proposal-writing process: Dorothy Weiss, executive director, Grantmakers Forum, Cleveland; K. C. Bergman, executive director, Therapeutic Riding Center, Bainbridge, OH; Carol Zett, grants manager, Kelvin and Eleanor Smith Foundation, Cleveland; Kelly Sweeney McShane, executive director, Hannah House, Washington, DC; William J. O'Neill, Jr., and members of the Grantmaking Committee, William J. and Dorothy K. O'Neill Foundation, Cleveland.

CHAPTER 4

Fundraising

Elizabeth A. S. Benefield and Richard L. Edwards

A major function of nonprofit managers, particularly those who occupy chief exectuve officer (CEO) positions, is securing resources for their organizations (see chapter 1). As a nonprofit manager, this means you must be prepared to spend a significant portion of your time fundraising. And the higher your position in the managerial hierarchy, the more you will need to devote increasingly larger portions of your time to the business of raising money.

The next millennium promises challenges as well as opportunities for nonprofit organizations. Government support for many kinds of nonprofit activities, particularly those related to the arts and humanities, is under attack. In the human services, the welfare reform legislation signed into law by President Clinton in 1996 contained a number of funding cuts, including a major reduction in funding for the Food Stamp program (Kaplan, 1997). These cuts will likely result in increased demands for services by many nonprofit human services organizations. On the other hand, the federal government's shifting of responsibilities to the states is likely to mean an increase in state and local government funding through increased use of purchase-of-service contracts for the provision of certain kinds of programs and services by nonprofit organizations (Edwards, Cooke, & Reid, 1996; see also chapter 5).

Because of the changing nature of government funding initiatives, many nonprofit organizations have learned that it is a risky business to become too dependent on public funding. Thus, it is prudent for nonprofit organizations to give significant attention to generating financial support from private, nongovernment sources.

Fortunately, despite the increasing competition among nonprofit organizations for charitable dollars, the fundraising prospects for many nonprofit organizations appear to be quite good, as long as they are prepared and positioned to take advantage of the opportunities that lie ahead. Over the next decade we can expect an unprecedented transfer of wealth in this country, with as much as $11.4 trillion being passed from one generation to another

(Hamilton, 1994; Panas, 1996). In the years ahead, the baby boom generation will reach its peak giving age, women and members of racial and ethnic minority groups are expected to become key players in charitable giving activities, and America's reliance on and trust in the nonprofit sector is expected to remain high. These and other economic and demographic factors will no doubt produce a dynamic and lucrative philanthropic environment.

To thrive in this changing environment, nonprofit organizations and managers must take bold and creative steps to ensure that their planning, management, and fundraising activities are keeping step with the times. No longer can your nonprofit organization rely on one or two funding sources for its operational needs. The key to long-term financial stability for your nonprofit organization is development of a sustaining and diverse funding base that includes individual, foundation, government, and corporate donors. Furthermore, your fundraising program should be multifaceted and include annual fund and major gift solicitations based on sound prospect research, planned giving activities, and a strong public relations component. The most successful nonprofits in the years ahead will be those best able to adjust to a philanthropic environment that is highly market driven and competitive (Firstenberg, 1996).

If your organization is to be effective at fundraising, you cannot rely solely on the goodwill of benefactors. In today's competitive environment, you and your organization must earn the support of donors by clearly and assertively demonstrating the value of your products or services. This requires that you approach fundraising in a disciplined way that uses the management techniques of analysis, planning, and execution (Firstenberg, 1996).

With more than 1 million organizations currently constituting the nonprofit sector, competition for the charitable dollar is intense. Giving patterns show, however, that nonprofits as a group are faring relatively well. In 1996, private-sector giving to nonprofits exceeded $150 billion (Kaplan, 1997). Private or voluntary contributions in 1996 from individuals, foundations, and corporations provided approximately 20 percent of the total revenue for all nonprofits combined (Kaplan, 1996). An analysis of giving trends points to the need to focus fundraising efforts on the cultivation of individual rather than foundation or corporate donors, and dramatic demographic shifts suggest that wealth holders are increasingly female and members of minority groups (Panas, 1996). Therefore, to maximize chances for success, your organization should pursue fundraising strategies that emphasize the cultivation of individual donors and pay particular attention to the needs and interests of nontraditional donors. This approach will enhance your chances for success and place you ahead of your peer organizations.

For those who have little experience in fundraising, it may be helpful to keep in mind that fundraising is largely an art rather than a science. And,

although no specific formula will work for all nonprofits, this chapter addresses some time-tested strategies and tools that can help you get started. In addition, the chapter considers the multiple components and strategies that make
up a good fundraising program, including prospect research and tracking,
annual fund activities, and major gift cultivation. Issues to consider when
launching a major campaign, such as internal and external readiness, are also
considered.

FUNDRAISING FUNDAMENTALS

Many nonprofit organizations lack the experience, expertise, and resources to
build or fund an effective and comprehensive fundraising program. Most lack
the financial capital needed to launch new or to sustain tried-and-true efforts.
Consequently, uninformed or piecemeal efforts to raise funds are commonplace and often result in poor financial returns. At worst, such efforts cause
loss of revenues and organizational credibility. Failed fundraising attempts can
be devastating to organizational morale and cause nearly irreversible damage.

Fundraising for nonprofits must be approached in a planned, strategic manner that places long-term benefit over short-term gain. It is best viewed as a
multifaceted process that should result in building a solid and lasting foundation for your organization. A successful fundraising program will not only
generate significant revenues, it will increase your organization's visibility and
credibility and enhance broad-based community support for your cause.

A key goal of any good fundraising program is to identify and cultivate a
diverse network of government, individual, foundation, and corporate donors
(Edwards, Benefield, Edwards, & Yankey, 1997; Seltzer, 1987). Gone is the era
when nonprofits could rely on one or two funders to sustain operations or
meet funding objectives. Additionally, many nonprofits make the mistake of
relying on a single strategy—a direct mail appeal or special event—to meet
their funding needs. Successful fundraising requires that multiple activities
take place within each 12-month period, ideally including both annual giving activities and major gift work. At the same time you identify and retain a
base of donors who make annual gifts, you must engage in the cultivation of
major gifts tailored to the unique characteristics of diverse donor groups.
Finally, you must recognize the important role that a strong public relations
program can play in enhancing your organization's fundraising success
(Harrison, 1991). A focused, strategic, and multifaceted approach to spreading
the word about the importance and success of your products or services can
dramatically enhance your fundraising activities. A good fundraising program
will maintain a strong base of annual donors through timely and frequent
asks, steadily increase the giving level of annual donors, regularly bring in new

Figure 4-1. Donor Giving Triangle

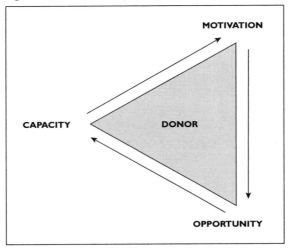

SOURCE: Edwards, R. L., Benefield, E.A.S., Edwards, J. A., & Yankey, J. A. (1997) *Building a strong foundation: Fundraising for nonprofits* (p. 7). Washington, DC: NASW Press.

donors from diverse donor groups, support active and highly personal cultivation of major gift donors, and promote a positive public image of your organization.

Figure 4-1 captures, in a simple way, the essence of fundraising. You must identify prospective donors who have the capacity to give; find ways to motivate them to give to your organization or cause; and then provide them with an opportunity to give, that is, you need to ask them in an appropriate manner to contribute.

Success in fundraising requires time, persistence, and the capacity to juggle both internal and external demands. It also requires that organizations make a tangible and multiyear commitment of staff and funding resources to adequately support fundraising activities. Balancing the needs and interests of donors with those of your nonprofit is not easy and requires the involvement of top staff and volunteer leadership. Every organization is unique in the amount of time and resources it can allocate to raise funds. Because many if not most nonprofits do not have the resources to hire a professional fundraiser, the CEO and other senior managers often must assume the fundraising role in addition to their other management responsibilities. Although this arrangement works well for some organizations, for others it creates an environment of competing values, roles, tasks, and time demands.

Whether your nonprofit allocates a percentage of a staff person's time to raise money or hires a full- or part-time development professional, the key to successful fundraising is that a clear commitment of resources is made. And although your fundraising activities may be heavily dependent upon volunteers, it is essential that staff time be clearly allocated for this purpose. Volunteers, particularly board members, are often eager to help with fundraising but understandably may lack important knowledge and skills. It is critical, therefore, for your organization to designate a point person who at all times has the big picture in mind, can readily respond to volunteers' concerns and questions, and promptly provide material and other types of support.

Fundraising success requires a commitment to the highest level of integrity and professionalism. The National Society of Fundraising Executives and the National Charities Information Bureau have established sets of ethical guidelines for fundraising. These organizations also offer valuable guidelines to nonprofit organizations on everything from Internal Revenue Service (IRS) requirements for appropriate gift acknowledgments to the ethical rights of donors. They also provide tips to prospective donors about issues to consider as they contemplate making a gift (see the list of organizations at the end of this chapter).

STRATEGIES FOR SUCCESS

Many nonprofits still seek to meet their funding needs by using a single fundraising strategy. This often takes the shape of a direct mail appeal, a membership drive, or an annual special event, such as a black tie gala, golf outing, or benefit concert. Nonprofits often believe that simply doing more of the same, for example, sending mail appeals to more prospects or bolstering the invitation list to an annual event, will result in increased revenues. It is true that success breeds success, and the establishment of regular and predictable giving opportunities will likely produce an increase in donors and funds over time. However, it is highly unlikely that a single fundraising strategy will enable your nonprofit organization to make significant progress over time in generating support. Worse, reliance on a single strategy may place your organization in an extremely vulnerable financial position. The funding problems encountered by United Way of America and its affiliates after the scandal involving William Aramony, its former CEO, demonstrate that public sentiment and support for an organization or cause can literally change overnight (Dundjerski, 1995). An unforeseen weather occurrence can wipe out an evening gala after months of work, an economic downturn can dramatically affect a year-end funding appeal or, as we saw with the issue of domestic violence during and following the O. J. Simpson trials, an issue can instantly become hot or cold based on a single, unexpected public event (Edwards et al., 1997).

It is helpful to think of fundraising as a multifaceted process that involves engaging in numerous activities simultaneously. Minimally, these activities include annual fund appeals, major gift cultivation, and planned giving efforts. The way these components fit together is analagous to a bicycle. Annual fund appeals are like the front wheel of the bike, whereas major gift cultivation is like the rear wheel. Planned giving strategies, although not addressed in this chapter, are increasingly important to fundraising programs. Using the bicycle analogy, planned giving may be thought of as the training wheels. Fundraising programs will succeed, or the bike will move smoothly ahead, only if organizations simultaneously engage in all three efforts and if all the wheels are turning in the same direction at the same time. Too often, nonprofits rely on one "wheel" to meet funding objectives, or use strategies that serve only to increase the size or speed of a single wheel. History has repeatedly shown that this practice does not work in the long run.

To complete the picture, add to this analogy the practice of good prospect research and tracking, perhaps best represented by the frame of the bicycle. Thorough and detailed prospect research and efficient tracking of prospect activities are essential to successful fundraising. Like the bicycle frame, the functions of research and tracking undergird all other activities. Without these functions, nonprofits will lack essential donor information to make thoughtful asks at the donor's giving capacity level, and they will have no system to record important steps (thus leaving no legacy for future efforts), which will diminish their overall fundraising potential.

Fundraising success requires the skills of a master juggler. The practice has little room for shortcuts. With every thoughtful and patient step of planning and execution, your nonprofit is building a strong and lasting foundation of support.

ANNUAL FUND APPEALS AND CREATING A CULTURE OF GIVING

Annual fund activities are the bread and butter of a nonprofit organization's fundraising strategy. Most often taking the form of direct mail appeals, annual events, telethons, or membership drives, annual appeals should

- establish a donor base that produces predictable annual income
- provide unrestricted cash support
- regularly generate new donors
- encourage the development of a culture of giving.

Annual gifts typically result from a single ask, often range between $5 and $50, and are usually given as cash. Direct mail campaigns are by far the most common annual fund appeal method used by nonprofits. Klein (1994) suggested that "direct mail remains the least expensive way an organization can reach the most people with a message they can hold in their hands and examine at their leisure" (p. 58). Response rates and giving levels will vary based on the strength of the association and involvement of the donors with your nonprofit.

Annual fund success will be enhanced by efforts to personalize your methods. For example, telethons will typically produce much higher participation and giving rates than direct mail, and highly personalized appeals targeting your board or key volunteers will likely show an even greater return. Most households are barraged daily or weekly by direct mail requests and telephone solicitations. Therefore, your creativity and thoughtfulness in approaching donors even for smaller gifts will be enormously appreciated. Above all, personalize your approach as much as possible, carefully assessing the needs and interests of your donors, and express genuine appreciation for giving at all levels.

Success in annual fund efforts will be greatly enhanced by your organization's ability to establish a tangible culture of giving. Churches, in particular, do an excellent job of creating such a culture (Klein, 1994). Many factors come into play. Most importantly, churches ask, and they do so on a regular and frequent basis. Individuals are often brought up "passing the plate," a ritual that instills at a very young age the importance of giving. Giving is expected, membership usually goes hand in hand with a financial pledge, and it is highly valued. Churches have long known that good stewardship and accountability for expenditure of charitable dollars are critical to their fundraising success. It should come as no surprise that more than 45 percent of all charitable dollars are given to religious organizations (Kaplan, 1997).

A nonprofit organization can create a culture of giving by heeding such lessons. Donors will tend to give, and give more generously, if they feel part of a culture in which giving is expressly valued, is an important membership expectation, and rewarded with assurances of worth and accountability. Giving will be encouraged by your organization's credibility and success; donors want to feel that their giving is a sound investment. Gone are the days when giving was thought to be motivated solely by goodwill or charitable intent. Donors typically want to support a credible organization. At the same time, high-level donors claim they most often give to express a belief in a specific cause or organizational mission, and they clearly express interest in supporting organizations that are financially stable (Panas, 1996). Studies that consider giving motivations have revealed that although donors continue to demonstrate altruistic intent in their giving, they increasingly value strong staff and board leadership and are concerned with issues of community respect and organizational credibility (Panas, 1996).

A successful annual fund program will not only ensure your nonprofit a strong base of operational support, it will be the foundation on which you build major gift support for capital and other needs. Annual appeals will help your organization identify potential major donors and pave the way for more intensive involvement between the donor and the organization. One of the major challenges you face is to keep annual fund support strong at the same time you garner major gift support.

CULTIVATION OF THE MAJOR GIFT

Much has been written about cultivating major gifts and the importance of focusing energy and resources on donors with high giving potential and probability or a high motivation to give to your particular organization or cause. Even in noncampaign periods, securing major gifts is a critical, ongoing component of all good fundraising programs (Goettler, 1996).

Major gift cultivation is best viewed as a series of thoughtful steps that begin with the identification of a potential donor and verification of that donor's giving capacity. This process applies to individual as well as foundation and corporate prospects. To ensure that time and energy are well spent on prospects who have clear giving capacity, fundraising programs must include a strong prospect research component (Edwards et al., 1997). Prospect research can be as simple as seeking direct input from your volunteers and board members about the giving habits of their neighbors and peers to using highly sophisticated data software designed to paint a picture of a person's wealth status. Numerous reference books such as the *Who's Who* series by Marquis and publications such as *The Chronicle of Philanthropy* can be useful. Print resources with extensive information about foundation and corporate prospects are available through the Foundation Center. Based in New York City, the Foundation Center has library collections in New York City and Washington, DC, as well as field offices in San Francisco, Cleveland, and Atlanta (see organizations list for address information) and can be reached on the World Wide Web at http://www.fdncenter.org. With access to the Internet, you can gain extensive information from company and foundation home pages, as well as information from a range of entities that can be useful resources for nonprofits. Companies even electronically file annual reports and other financial, employee, and trustee information (Edwards et al., 1997; Heller, 1996). Quick access to this information via the Internet can translate into an enormous time savings for nonprofits.

You need not be intimidated by the continuous advancements in prospect research practice and technology. While commonplace for most higher education fundraising shops, sophisticated prospect research practices are not part of the culture for the majority of nonprofits. Most nonprofits in a noncampaign period can gain sufficient prospect information by following closely local and state charitable news and major business transactions and happenings. Many major newspapers now include regular columns devoted exclusively to local philanthropic activity, and many consulting firms publish state and local giving directories to assist nonprofits. Many states have resource organizations to assist nonprofits, and there are statewide publications that focus on philanthropy, such as the *North Carolina Journal of Philanthropy*. Local foundations may also offer resource libraries to assist nonprofits in their fundraising efforts. Most importantly, knowledge about income and asset wealth can often best be gathered through direct contact and involvement with the prospective donor. No generic publication can match the knowledge you can gain from personal contacts.

The relatively simple process of identifying and qualifying wealthy people in your community will not bring about fundraising success. Once the giving capacity of potential donors is established, nonprofits must do the hard work of determining if a potential interest exists and if this interest can be turned into tangible support. This process of turning suspects into viable prospects can in part be accomplished through good prospect research and major gift cultivation.

Successful major gift work requires intensive and highly personal contacts with potential donors over a long period of time, often over many years. In contrast to unrestricted annual giving, high-level or major giving is usually designated to support a particular need or program and often represents commitments of assets rather than income. At the center of successful major gift work is a well-nurtured relationship that is beneficial to both the donor and the recipient organization. The key to such meaningful relationships is developing and implementing highly personalized cultivation plans. Such plans should include frequent, meaningful opportunities for the prospect to learn about your organization and for your organization to learn about the potential donor. Find out about hobbies and talents, arrange for fun and educational exchanges, and seek advice on their areas of expertise. In major gift cultivation, it is important to consider each meeting with a prospect an opportunity for meaningful cultivation and acknowledgment (Sturtevant, 1996). As part of a cultivation plan, fundraisers might (Edwards et al., 1997)

- arrange a personal visit from the executive director or board president
- send a stewardship report on the impact of past giving
- seek advice from the prospect on his or her area of expertise
- involve the prospect in cultivating others
- honor the prospect with awards and special recognition
- send personal congratulations on birthdays, anniversaries, and promotions
- seek input on developing your organization's case for support
- recruit the prospect to serve in a key role at a special event

- invite the prospect to do a workshop for your staff on a subject about which he or she has special expertise
- invite the prospect to serve on your board of trustees or an advisory board or committee
- communicate regularly with annual reports, brochures, and speech reprints
- send frequent personal notes about items and events of interest.

It is critically important to consider cultivation moves as part of a clear plan that has specific goals. In fundraising, you must always have in mind the next step (Wood, 1991). It is often useful to discuss with your prospective donor in advance of a meeting or cultivation move your goal for this contact. It is perfectly acceptable, and often helpful, to say directly that you will not be asking for a gift at this time but rather are seeking advice or involvement in another capacity. Donors will appreciate knowing your intentions and will likely be more willing to participate in a multitude of activities. Ideally, your cultivation plans will be so carefully constructed that you and your prospects will always know what comes next. Before leaving a visit with a potential donor, discuss what follow-up steps are needed and agree upon a clear time line. Then, as important to your nonprofit as the cultivation move itself, you must document all donor activities and progress. This step should be part of a consistent and detailed system of prospect tracking.

It is essential that nonprofits establish clear procedures to document all prospect-related activities and contacts. Failure to keep adequate records is a common problem for nonprofits. This can result not only in a poor transfer of knowledge, but also in a loss of funds. Although many software programs exist to manage donor information, most nonprofits can get by with a paper system that uses two simple forms and a good tickler file. First, you should use a form that enables you to maintain a continually updated record of basic biographical information on each of your prospects that includes such categories as home and work addresses and telephone numbers, family make-up, church affiliation, hobbies and special interests, and community service activities. The form should also include information on the nature of the prospect's association with your organization, information on past giving to your nonprofit and others, estimated income level and known assets, anticipated giving level, a section to note such items as preferences on how and when to contact, and important peer relationships. Second, you should use a form to document actual contacts. The type of contact, who made the contact, what was discussed, the outcome of the contact, and next steps to be taken should all be carefully recorded. Finally, you should institute a tickler file system to alert you to birthdays, special occasions, and other significant dates in relation to your major gift prospects and donors. Of course, you should also maintain

"ST. MARY'S COLLEGE FOR WOMEN"

REVENUE

"I say we add an NCAA Division I football program."

files of all original correspondence received as well as copies of everything sent to prospects or donors.

Remember that it takes time for your nonprofit to become an important giving priority for a prospect. It is often a good strategy to ask potential donors directly what it would take for your organization to become one of their top charitable priorities. Take cues from your donors. Like most relationships, much of major gift cultivation is intuitive in nature.

If your cultivation plans are effective, making the major gift ask can be the easy part. It is usually important to ask for a specific amount for a specific program or need. It may be useful to start with a gift range and a couple of program options. However, if donor capacity, giving intent, and interest in your organization is well established, it is often better to ask for a specific amount. The major gift ask is typically done by the staff member or volunteer with the closest relationship to the donor. Often, involvement by a peer or high-level staff or board member is essential. With individual prospects, the solicitation is almost always done face-to-face, with a supplementary written proposal available. Corporate and foundation solicitations will vary widely according to proposal guidelines, but more often tend to require written requests or proposals. Because major gifts often come in the form of a pledge that is paid out over a period of years, it is a good idea to prepare a simple pledge letter or letter of intent with a blank space for a signature, gift amount, and pay-out wishes. If possible, you should attempt to close the gift during your face-to-face meeting, that is, get the commitment in writing on the day of the solicitation. If this is not possible, a pledge letter sent immediately following your visit may suffice.

What do you do when a prospect says no? The best way to handle an objection or an unwillingness to make a commitment is to determine the nature of the problem. Have you determined an appropriate ask level? Is your timing right? Have you arranged for an appropriate environment in which to make the ask, or are there distractions? Is the nature of the objection a result of simple misunderstanding? By all means, attempt to get to the root of the objection, and address any issues or problems directly and honestly. You may discover that the objection can be easily resolved or that you need follow-up steps. Or, you may need to settle for a gift amount that is less than what you had hoped. In any case, remember that all gifts at all levels are important, that all prospects and donors should be valued and respected, and that everything you do lays the groundwork for the next potential gift.

Two schools of thought exist about closing gifts that are less than what you believe the donor is capable of giving. One position is that it is important to take small steps, to close gifts early in the cultivation process, and to settle for gift levels that are less than your prospect's capacity. The theory is that giving encourages more giving, and as a result, your prospect will develop a stronger connection with your organization and continue to give and give at higher levels as she or he increases involvement. The second school of thought is that you cannot leap a canyon by taking baby steps. That is, cultivate, cultivate, cultivate until your prospect is motivated and likely to give at capacity level. This theory requires patience and operates on the belief that smaller-level gifts solicited during the cultivation process may discourage the prospect from ultimately making a much larger one.

A good fundraiser is keenly aware of both scenarios and will tailor solicitation decisions based on the individual characteristics of each potential donor. It is often important to solicit early and lower-level gifts from major prospects to create momentum, encourage others, and cement interest. Giving begets giving, and you will rarely, if ever, diminish your overall fundraising potential by making multiple asks. On the other hand, it is important to always maintain a focus on capacity giving and work to raise the giving sights of your prospects by making it clear that you are counting on them to be leaders. Strategic and goal-oriented cultivation is essential to instill such a level of commitment and participation.

Good major gift work requires that you take appropriate steps to identify potential donors, gather useful information about giving capacity, establish that a viable interest in your organization exists, and engage the prospect in meaningful involvement over a period of time. The process then requires thoughtful and timely solicitation with the goal of long-term potential benefits. This process is the central component to any good and comprehensive fundraising program.

Major gift work can be as tiring as it is exhilarating and as frustrating as it is rewarding. The dynamic and personal nature of major gift cultivation makes it challenging for even the seasoned professional to set aside personal feelings. For example, it is difficult not to feel personally rejected when a request is declined or to feel personally responsible for an unhappiness expressed by a donor with whom you have had a long-term relationship. Because of the intensely personal nature of the donor relationship, sincere and lasting friendships often result. For a fundraiser who has adhered without fail to the highest standards of integrity and professional behavior, this can be major gift work's greatest reward.

LAUNCHING A CAPITAL CAMPAIGN

One of the most important decisions a nonprofit organization will make is whether or not to embark on a major campaign. It seems today that every nonprofit is in the business of either planning, executing, or closing a campaign effort. Successful major campaigns can generate significant resources and in some cases produce the added benefit of bringing unprecedented attention to an issue or cause. However, you should not be fooled by the perception that everyone is doing it and doing it well. Nonprofits often embark on campaigns with little planning or with no hands-on experience or expertise. They fail to recognize the importance of considering many readiness factors that are both internal and external to the organization. Poorly conceived and organized campaign efforts can be devastating to staff and board morale. Worse, they can cause loss of organizational stability and credibility. Campaign planning and execution is tough work and requires special skills and knowledge.

As a first step, consider the extent to which your organization is internally prepared to launch a campaign. Is your current board composition adequate to support a significant campaign effort? The importance of having in place a strong and active board cannot be overstated. Ideally, your board should include members who represent three Ws—wisdom, wealth, and workers. In other words, you need wise people, you need people with some financial resources, and you need people who are willing to pitch in and do the hard work necessary for successful governance and effective fundraising.

You will be fortunate if you have individuals who embody all three Ws; realistically, you more often may find that your board and volunteer leaders embody one or two of these characteristics. To increase your chances for success, consider the following steps in advance of a major campaign (Edwards et al., 1997):

- Recruit at least one attorney and one accountant to your board to provide guidance on charitable tax law issues, deferred giving, and the appropriate handling of gifts other than cash, such as securities and property.
- Be sure that your board includes at least one representative from the local business community.
- If possible, recruit at least one "famous" individual to your board (for example, someone who is highly recognizable and widely esteemed, such as a top-level business executive, local television or radio personality, or athlete).
- Be certain that you have several "worker bees" on your board, individuals who are willing to do the hard and sometimes not-so-glamorous work of fundraising, such as making telephone calls and visits, hosting gatherings, and stuffing envelopes.
- If possible, recruit at least a few individuals to your board who have wealth, can identify a peer group of other wealthy individuals whom they would be willing to contact, and who would be willing to go "public" with their giving.
- Include on your board someone connected to the print or broadcast media, such as an editor, reporter or feature writer, television reporter or anchor, or someone strong in public relations.
- Make sure your board is reflective of the community you serve in terms of gender, race, ethnicity, and socioeconomic status.

A second important step in preparing your nonprofit for a major campaign is to create a leadership structure that extends beyond your staff and board. Many organizations form a time-limited fundraising advisory or steering committee. Another option is to organize your board and other volunteer leaders into committees or task forces around specific subcampaign objectives. For example, one group may be responsible for cultivating and closing leadership gifts and another group for the continuing success of annual fund activities. Another may address the publications, public relations, and media needs of your nonprofit during the campaign period. The key to success in developing new leadership structures is recruiting individuals who are knowledgeable about fundraising, highly committed to your organization and cause, and willing to work. Also key is establishing clear and highly specific objectives for volunteers. It is important to set volunteers up for success.

A major campaign effort can be strengthened by the short-term involvement of individuals who are considered high-level business and community leaders and are peers to your major gift prospects and donors. Do not ask these individuals to be your worker bees. Rather, ask for their guidance and participation in learning about and contacting major gift prospects. Very busy individuals may agree to serve in name only to enhance your nonprofit's credibility and visibility; others may be willing to chair a special event, accompany staff on prospect calls, or sign a solicitation letter. Provide a specified time line to achieve campaign objectives and stick to it. Respecting the multitude of demands on such individuals will have enormous payoffs. A creative option to involve individuals who wish to support the campaign but cannot commit their time is to formulate a document of endorsement and secure their signatures. This document can be an invaluable addition to a case statement or funding proposal.

Before launching a major campaign, it is essential that your staff, volunteers, board members, and other constituents agree about funding needs and strategies. Nothing is more deadly to a campaign than disparate goals and solicitation attempts. Good campaign planning requires that your organization review its mission, take stock of personnel strengths and weaknesses (both staff and volunteer), and clearly determine the community impact of a campaign both in terms of service and possible detriments. Major campaigns, like fundraising activities in general, are generally very labor intensive and can lead to staff and volunteer burnout. On the other hand, they can serve to invigorate your organization and dramatically increase community awareness and support. Your nonprofit organization will be well positioned to succeed if you begin a fundraising campaign with a healthy internal environment, that is, an environment marked by staff and board cohesion, fundraising knowledge, a clear sense of mission and goals, a clear division of labor, and enthusiasm.

In determining the readiness of your organization to launch a campaign, it is also advisable to assess whether the external environment is likely to be conducive. In examining the external environment, consider the following questions:

- What is the current climate of giving in your community and state?
- What other similar organizations are embarking on major campaigns, and with what success?
- Does your nonprofit represent a hot or cold issue?
- Will the current political and economic environment support or hinder your campaign?
- What is the public image of your organization?
- Have you identified and determined a sufficient interest level of an adequate prospect base?

• What are the consequences, both internally and externally, if your organization undertakes a fundraising campaign and fails to meet its goals?

Assessing the external environment for successful fundraising can sometimes be difficult, particularly if your nonprofit has little or no campaign experience. That is why experts now suggest that a strong public relations program accompany fundraising efforts (Harrison, 1991). Research shows that people respond to issues and not organizations and that issue-oriented public relations will strengthen fundraising potential. According to Harrison (1991), "Positioning an organization as an authority on an issue, and as an important part of the solution to the problem, can build tremendous credibility for the organization" (p. 22). Increasing your organization's public visibility, its success in attracting positive media coverage, and its capacity to position itself as part of the solution are essential elements in enhancing fundraising success and preparing for a campaign.

GOAL SETTING AND THE CAMPAIGN PROCESS

Setting an ambitious yet realistic goal for a major campaign is an important task. Your organization will be much better positioned to determine such a goal if the top-level management staff and your board have completed a comprehensive planning process that considers issues of internal and external readiness and establishes clear procedures and personnel structures to cover campaign duties.

Determining a major campaign goal requires some homework. Take a close look at past and current donors, particularly major gift donors, and assess the level of support that is likely to be secured from this group of known supporters. Begin to develop expanded prospect lists using good prospect research strategies, keeping in mind that this list should include a broad base of individual as well as corporate, government, and foundation prospects. It may be helpful to establish a simple rating system that considers both giving capacity and the level of giving that will likely be secured.

The most useful tool in determining a feasible goal is the widely accepted gift pyramid. Based on fundraising's rule of thirds, the gift pyramid suggests that at least one-third of your goal will come from your top 10 to 15 gifts; another one-third of your goal will come from the next 25 or so gifts; and the remaining one-third will come from all other gifts. Using the rule of thirds, a gift pyramid with a goal of $50,000 might look something like Figure 4-2.

It has been shown repeatedly that simple numbers reasoning—that is, "if we can just get 100 people to give us $1,000 each"—does not work. Such

Figure 4-2. Giving Pyramid for $50,000 Goal Based on the Rule of Thirds

	GIFT LEVEL	GIFTS NEEDED	PROSPECTS NEEDED[a]	TOTAL DOLLARS
Top Third	5,000	2	6	10,000
	2,500	3	9	7,500
	1,000	5	15	5,000
				22,500
Middle Third	750	9	27	6,750
	500	12	36	6,000
	250	15	45	3,750
				16,500
Bottom Third	100	75	numerous	7,500
	gifts below 100	numerous		3,500
				11,000
			Grand Total	**$50,000**

NOTE: It is generally true that at least one-third of your goal, and in many cases up to one-half, will come from your top 10 to 15 gifts; the second third of your goal will come from the next 25 gifts or so; and the remaining third will come from all other gifts.

[a] The number of prospects needed is based on the widespread belief that about one of three prospects will make a gift at their capacity level if they have been appropriately cultivated and asked.

reasoning actually depresses overall giving by flattening giving levels, and it falsely assumes that a single strategy or ask level will appeal to all donors. The gift pyramid reminds us of the critical importance of directing time and energy at securing leadership gifts. Success in securing your top 10 gifts will likely determine the overall success of your campaign.

Gift pyramids are especially useful for organizations that have no past campaign experience. The exercise of developing a pyramid and identifying and qualifying actual prospects is extremely useful in determining the feasibility of a campaign goal. Gift pyramids also serve to remind us that campaign fundraising should follow a specific sequence of activities. All thoughtfully executed campaigns will begin with a quiet phase that focuses on closing leadership gifts, those in the top one-third of the pyramid. This is a nonpublic phase that typically helps to validate campaign objectives and protects an organization from the embarrassment of failing to meet a publicized goal. As a general rule, it is advisable not to go public with your campaign until you have received commitments for 50 percent or more of the total goal.

The campaign process should begin with and focus on the cultivation of leadership gifts, and over time it should move toward the closure of lower-level gifts. Experience shows that securing leadership gifts is absolutely essential to campaign success. Do that first and do it well. Success will also be dependent upon the diversity and appropriateness of cultivation and solicitation strategies for all levels of donors, the effectiveness of your organization's staff and volunteers, and the capacity to generate strong public interest and support. Do not sacrifice annual giving activities and fund solicitations during a campaign. The momentum and positive public relations that can be generated from a campaign often have a positive impact on annual giving.

Major, time-limited campaigns can significantly boost resources for your nonprofit, but it is important to keep in mind the necessity to build long-term major gift capacity. Major campaigns can be effective stepping stones to building stronger annual giving programs, and they can help your organization's donors develop fundraising habits that lead to sustained higher levels of support. Building a strong and lasting foundation of support requires that nonprofit managers place a high priority on long-term benefits that can accrue to an organization from a well-planned, multifaceted fundraising strategy.

SKILLS-APPLICATION EXERCISES

- Considering your organization or another nonprofit you are familiar with, set a goal for a campaign, and then create a gift pyramid related to that goal. How many upper-level donors will you need? Is that goal realistic for your particular organization at this time?

- Analyze the culture of giving in your organization or another nonprofit you are familiar with. How would you create or enhance the organization's culture of giving?

- Develop a cultivation plan for two or three major gift prospects.

REFERENCES

Dundjerski, M. (1995, September 7). United Way: 1% increase in gifts. *Chronicle of Philanthropy*, pp. 27–29.

Edwards, R. L., Benefield, E.A S., Edwards, J. A., & Yankey, J. A. (1997). *Building a strong foundation: Fundraising for nonprofits.* Washington, DC: NASW Press.

Edwards, R. L., Cooke, P. W., & Reid, P. N. (1996). Social work management in an era of diminishing federal responsibility. *Social Work, 41,* 468–479.

Firstenberg, P. B. (1996). *The 21st century nonprofit: Remaking the organization in the post-government era.* New York: Foundation Center.

Goettler, R. H. (1996, April). Announcing the "four Ws" of major gift solicitation. *Fund Raising Management*, pp. 40–43.

Hamilton, C. H. (1994, May/June). The coming boom in giving: How you can benefit. *Nonprofit World*, pp. 8–12.

Harrison, T. A. (1991, March/April). Six PR trends that will shape your future. *Nonprofit World*, pp. 21–23.

Heller, J. (1996, June). Get the real story from SEC filings for free. *SmartMoney*, *5*(6), 38–40.

Kaplan, A. E. (Ed.). (1996). *Giving USA—1996*. New York: American Association of Fundraising Counsel Trust for Philanthropy.

Kaplan, A. E. (Ed.). (1997). *Giving USA—1997*. New York: American Association of Fundraising Counsel Trust for Philanthropy.

Klein, K. (1994). *Fundraising for social change* (3rd ed.). Inverness, CA: Chardon Press.

Panas, J. (1996, August). The sky is falling: But don't worry, it could be philanthropy raining down. *Contributions*, pp. 1, 15–16, 19, 29, 31.

Seltzer, M. (1987). *Securing your organization's future: A complete guide to fundraising strategies*. New York: Foundation Center.

Sturtevant, W. T. (1996, April). The artful journey: Seeking the major gift. *Fund Raising Management*, p. 33.

Wood, E. W. (1991, June). *The six key concepts of major gift fund-raising. The skill and art of major gift fund-raising*. Workshop presented by the Office of Development, University of North Carolina at Chapel Hill.

ORGANIZATIONS

The Chronicle of Philanthropy, 1255 23rd Street, NW, Washington, DC 20037 (1-800-842-7817). www.philanthropy.com

The Foundation Center, 79 Fifth Avenue, New York, NY 10003-3076 (212-620-4230). www.fdncenter.org

Marquis Who's Who, Division of Reed Elsevier, 121 Chanlon Road, New Providence, NJ 07974 (1-800-323-3288). www.marquiswhoswho.com

National Charities Information Bureau, 19 Union Square West, New York, NY 10003 (1-800-501-6242). www.give.org

National Endowment for the Arts, 1100 Pennsylvania Avenue, NW, Washington, DC 20506 (202-682-5400). www.arts.endow.gov

National Society of Fundraising Executives, 1101 King Street, Suite 700, Alexandria, VA 22314 (703-684-0410).

CHAPTER 5

Maximizing the Use of Performance Contracts

Ronald K. Green

Among the externally focused, boundary-spanning skills required by nonprofit agency managers are those related to carrying out the broker role (see chapter 1). A key element of this role is the acquisition of needed resources to support the mission of the agency. Top-level managers of nonprofit organizations often secure fiscal support for organizational services from public sources in exchange for providing services to people whom public organizations have an ultimate duty to serve. Most often, the mechanism for this exchange of resources involves purchase-of-service contracts (POSCs) (Eggers & Ng, 1993; Kettner & Martin, 1994). Frequently, the type of POSC used is a performance contract (Kettner & Martin, 1994), making it incumbent on nonprofit managers to fully understand the nature of performance contracting, its advantages, its disadvantages, how to avoid pitfalls, and how to maximize its full potential.

TYPES OF PEFORMANCE CONTRACTS

To begin to gain an understanding of performance contracting, you must have an appreciation of the full range of POSC types and where the performance contract fits into that range. Kettner and Martin (1993) posed a systems view that suggests that different types of contracts tend to focus on different aspects of an organization's total service system. If the contract deals with design specifications involved with either inputs (personnel, facilities, clients, other resources) or throughputs (processes, tasks, methodologies), then it is a process contract. On the other hand, if the contract deals with outputs (measures of service volume) or outcomes (measures of client or consumer impact), then it is a performance contract.

Process Contracts

Process contracts generally involve either cost contracts or fixed-price contracts. The most common cost contract is a cost-reimbursable contract that involves payment based on actual allowable expenditures (or a percentage of actual expenditures) after the fact. Normally, a cost–reimbursable contract will have a maximum total amount set in the contract. A variant of this occurs when an agreed-upon flat amount is provided before the fact and then accounted for by actual allowable costs.

One of the ongoing concerns with these contracts is that public bodies often try to maximize their contract funds by negotiating cost contracts that end up covering only a percentage of the actual allowable costs. Nonprofit managers must always have a clear understanding as to what costs will be reimbursed under the contract, as well as a full appreciation of the real cost of delivering a certain type of service. Another problem often encountered with the use of cost-reimbursable contracts is the tendency for the contracting agency to attempt to micromanage the nonprofit. Because all costs are being reviewed, the contracting agency can challenge the appropriateness of any expenditure even if it is normally allowable. For example, if the nonprofit is capable of providing staff with merit increases above the cost of living, a contracting agency that was not able to do that might question that human resource decision. On the other hand, this type of contract does limit the financial exposure of the nonprofit.

A second form of process contract is the fixed-price contract. In this type of contract the contracting agency agrees to pay a fixed amount to support a given program. The nonprofit is taking all the fiscal risk. The organization is expected to deliver the program even if it ends up costing more than the contract amount. On the other hand, if it can deliver an acceptable program for less than the contracted amount, the nonprofit can use the surplus to help support other aspects of its activities. This type of contract is not used frequently in the human services arena because service demand often cannot be estimated clearly. In addition, contracting agencies may perceive that a service provider might trim the quality of services to maximize the surplus from this type of contract.

Performance Contracts

In the nonprofit and public arenas, the term "performance contract" is used to cover contracts that focus on outputs, such as units of service (foster care days, counseling hours, clients or consumers served), and outcomes such as a child being returned to a birth parent or a welfare client placed in a paying job, and to cover contracts that add fiscal incentives for exceeding some performance standard (output or outcome) (Kettner & Martin, 1993, 1995; Riemer, 1968).

A variant of the performance contract is the accommodation purchase contract (Commonwealth of Massachusetts, 1997), which uses a unit-of-service approach but with payment based on service capacity rather than actual performance. This approach is used when a public agency requires stand-by capacity such as emergency shelter beds, and it contracts with a non-profit organization to guarantee that a specific number of beds will always be available for clients of the public agency. But in this type of contract a unit payment per bed is paid even if the total number of protected beds is not used.

The common factor in these types of contracts is that payment is based on some measured unit. The parties negotiate what payment will be made for each unit meeting some standard that is delivered, and if fiscal incentives are involved, what threshold or benchmark standard must be met to earn the incentive payments. Understanding and affecting how these performance measures are defined and how payments are set for a given unit becomes one critical task of a nonprofit manager.

Performance Measures

The types of performance measures can be categorized according to when the measured item occurs in the service life cycle. Output measures can relate either to activities that occur while the client or consumer is engaged in the service process, or can be a measure of a state at service completion. Outcome measures can relate to a state at service completion or to some later post-service date. Graphically, it would look like this:

	Service in process	*End of service*	*After service*
Output measures	x	x	
Outcome measures		x	x

Performance contracts with nonprofits commonly use output measures for service in process. These are units measured either in terms of a unit of service time, a service episode, or a material unit (Kettner & Martin, 1993). Examples of units of service time include a counseling hour, a foster care or residential treatment day, or a training day. Examples of a service episode include a home health care visit, a teenage crisis hotline information and referral call, a class presentation by a museum staff member, a public concert by a symphony orchestra, or a psychological examination. Examples of a material service include a hot meal, a module of training materials, a survey data collection instrument, or a suit of clothes for a homeless person.

The price for a given service unit is either negotiated individually with a nonprofit or may be a standard unit price established for any organization that contracts to provide a certain type of service. Many public agencies that purchase services from a number of nonprofit organizations develop component prices. The Commonwealth of Massachusetts (1997), for example, develops a standard market-based unit price list for various service components when there are services common to a number of providers. Associations or other collectives of nonprofit providers often play a role in negotiating the common price list on behalf of nonprofit member organizations.

Output measures used at the end of service relate to a service completion by the client (Kettner & Martin, 1993). The standard often used is whether the client finished all the expectations outlined in the case plan—if so, the case would be considered a successful service completion. In a foster care case with reunification as the case goal, the attendance of the birth parents in parenting classes and the subsequent replacement of the child with the birth parents would be counted as a successful end-of-service output. Many public child welfare programs have used this type of measure because of the emphasis of the Adoption Assistance and Child Welfare Act of 1980 (P.L. 96-272) on issues of process and output. The problem presented is that this type of measure does not account for whether the parents' parenting capacity has been enhanced and the child is at less risk at reunification than when he or she was placed in foster care (Tracy, Green, & Bremseth, 1993). To account for actual changes in the originating conditions, one must use outcome measures.

Outcomes in general have been defined as an increase in some desirable trait or condition, a decrease in some undesirable trait or condition, or the stabilization of a trait or condition that would otherwise get worse (Kettner & Martin, 1993). Outcomes can be measured either at the end of service (discharge) or at some later date. Examples of end-of-service outcome measures include a client in a welfare-to-work program securing a job, the return of a child to its birth parents with a reduced state of risk in a child protective services case, or the return home of an emotionally disturbed child with an increased level of social–emotional functioning. The Texas State Comptroller (1996) suggested that in mental health or mental retardation cases, outcome measures such as attainment of personal goals, ability to choose living and work settings, extent of integration into the community, success in developing personal relationships, and stability of living and economic resources should be used.

Although in each of these examples the outcome suggested is positive, the question remains about the longer-term effect of the intervention. In cases in which a contract for services is over a sufficiently long time period, it is possible to base part or all of the compensation on whether the desirable outcome is maintained for a given time after the end of service. In this case payment for job placement services might be made only if the client maintains the job for six months. Or in a reunification case, payment would be made if the child remains with the birth parents for one year without a new report of abuse or neglect. Because of the realities of cash flow for the nonprofit, it is more likely that these types of contracts would be crafted to provide for incentive payments over and above a base rate if post-discharge outcomes exceeded some agreed-upon level.

USE OF PERFORMANCE CONTRACTS

Historical Development

The concept of performance contracting in the human services is not a new concept. In the 15th century at the University of Bologna, a professor was required to teach the contents of an entire book or forfeit part of his or her funds, and in 1862 the British Committee of the Privy Council for Education instituted a system of payment to individual schools based on student grades in reading, writing, and arithmetic (Campbell & Lorion, 1972). In the United States the first major use of outcome performance contracting in the human services came in the late 1960s and early 1970s when the federal Office of Economic Opportunity (OEO) attempted to use Department of Defense procurement procedures to secure educational services for students from low-income families. With the winding down of the Vietnam conflict, a number of defense contractors saw this as a way to convert to a peacetime economy while still securing major government contracts (Blaschke, 1972).

The OEO's interest in this approach was spurred by the experience of the Texarkana, Arkansas, school districts of contracting with a private firm to raise the reading level of students one grade level with 80 hours of instruction. The company was paid its actual estimated cost if the improvement was achieved at the end of 80 hours, received a bonus if this level was achieved faster, and was paid less than costs if it took longer. There were no limits put on the educational process, and the firm was allowed to use any educational technology it wished (Gramlich & Koshel, 1975). The American Association of School Administrators (1972) saw this as a boon for school districts—a way to increase efficiency and productivity at extremely low risk to the school district. The reality was that because of the way these contracts were drawn, almost all the risk was carried by the contractor. The result was that most private companies lost a great deal of money on these contracts and quit by the mid-1970s (Gramlich & Koshel, 1975).

Output performance contracts with nonprofits in the mental health and child welfare arena have been used for decades. In California in the 1960s county mental health and juvenile probation agencies purchased residential treatment services from nonprofit group care agencies using a unit-of-service approach. In San Diego in the late 1960s, the United Way was using a unit-of-service approach for families who needed services from the San Diego Children's Center. In the 1980s, the State of Washington used performance contracts with foster parents that provided payments over and above the basic care rates to provide special services such as working with birth parents or participating in training classes (Barsh, Moore, & Hamerlynck, 1983). In mental health, both Colorado and Oklahoma used performance output contracts starting in the 1980s (Wedel & Colston, 1988).

Current Experience

Since the mid-1970s a number of studies have documented the extensive use of POSCs by public agencies in the human services field. As far back as 1979, approximately 55 percent of services provided by states involved contracting with outside organizations (Eggers & Ng, 1993). A 1982 survey by the International City Management Association found that 12 percent of cities surveyed contracted with nonprofits for the provision of recreational services and 9 percent contracted for the operation and maintenance of recreation facilities (Fixler & Poole, 1987). By 1983, at least $1 billion in public services were provided by nonprofit organizations (Moore, 1987). The American Public Welfare Association's voluntary data system indicated that by 1993 nearly $1.4 billion a year in Title XX funds alone were being used to purchase services from nonpublic sources. The City of New York purchases more than one-third of its child welfare services from outside organizations at a cost of $2.6 billion a year (Kramer, 1994). Much of this POS activity developed before the current emphasis on the devolution of federal provision and control of human services to the state and local level. Edwards, Cooke, and Reid (1996) noted that the current "devolution revolution" will "likely accelerate the trend toward POS contracting by public organizations" (p. 469). A key question is, how much of this contracting involves performance contracts?

Some clarity on this question is provided by two studies by Kettner and Martin (1994, 1995) using data collected by the American Public Welfare Association. One study of contracting activity in 47 states indicated that 69.3 percent of the states used cost reimbursement contracts, 53.5 percent used output performance contracts paying for units of service provided, but only 4 percent used performance contracts based on outcomes of service (Kettner & Martin, 1994). A second study used data from 1990 for 10 states to review contracting procedures involving services in the substance abuse, child day care, employment and training, residential treatment, and specialized transportation areas (Kettner & Martin, 1995). More than 85 percent of the state agencies involved used output performance contracts using service units, whereas almost 10 percent used outcome contracts for employment and training services.

The use of outcome performance contracts in the employment and training arena was no doubt stimulated by the federal Job Opportunities and Basic Skills (JOBS) program and concerns that Aid to Families with Dependent Children recipients involved were going through very expensive training programs but were not getting permanent jobs that paid a living wage. Attempts were made to clarify what an outcome meant in the JOBS program, with a greater emphasis placed on postservice outcomes. Even with this emphasis, a 1995 statewide survey of JOBS programs in New York turned up only two districts using outcome performance contracts (New York

Association of Training and Employment Professionals [NYATEP], 1995). One district used the end-of-service measure of entry into employment and one used a postservice outcome measure of retention in the job for at least 13 weeks.

Although there has been much work done to identify outcome measures in the mental health field, there is not much evidence of the field moving beyond the use of output performance contracts. One exception is New Hampshire, which has initiated a new system of contracting with its 10 non-profit community mental health centers using measures of effectiveness and efficiency aimed at making the centers more responsible for the provision of care for patients who are indigent and severely mentally ill (McGuire, Hodgkin, & Schumway, 1995).

ADVANTAGES OF PERFORMANCE CONTRACTS

A number of advantages exist in the use of performance contracts by nonprofit organizations, including the provision of a clearer and more meaningful focus of accountability, a reduction of micromanagement by the public agency, a greater flexibility in the service process, and an increased capacity for comparison and evaluation.

Clearer Accountability

In a standard cost-reimbursable contract the accountability focus tends to be on whether claims for reimbursement are for expenses allowable under the contract. It becomes primarily an accounting or fiscal auditing function with its requirements for accurate documentation of all expenses claimed. As a result, a great deal of policy and regulatory effort is expended to provide definitions of the categories of allowable costs and the types of activities these costs are allowed to support. This may lead to a reduced focus on the effects these costs have on achieving the ultimate purpose of the service provided. A cost-reimbursable contract is audited by an accountant who has little or no interest in service effectiveness but has a keen interest in the degree to which expenditures can be documented as meeting the regulations, policies, and procedures governing the contract.

This heightened focus on whether expenditures are allowable under a specific set of regulations, policies, and procedures tends to result in the nonprofit's development of a defensive posture in the use of funds claimed under a contract. This posture will include the addition of fiscal staff to deal with contract accounting and monitoring. The fiscal staff will tend to take on greater influence than program staff when it comes to any unusual program expenditures. The result is a tendency to become quite conservative when using claimed funds. Program staff will tend to find a heightened level of bureaucracy when securing expenditure approvals and documenting those expenditures. The net result can be a reduction of focus on client outcomes and an unwillingness to support unusual activities that have cost–claim implications.

In contrast, performance contracting keeps the focus on either the specific service being provided to the client or what effect this service has on the client. The heightened activity by fiscal staff occurs during the precontract period of establishing service unit rates and the compensation rates for meeting certain outcome measures. Once the contract is in place, the contract focus shifts to whether the contract agency actually provided the expected service to the client group and whether the agency met the agreed-upon measures for client outcome. This provides a significant shift in the nature of contract accountability. The contract agency must still be accountable to the Internal Revenue Service standards regarding which expenditures are allowable for a nonprofit and especially a nonprofit charitable organization, but this allows for significantly greater leeway than found under most cost–reimbursable contracts.

The focus of accountability becomes client centered rather than rule centered. The primary emphasis becomes how can one best provide this service or how can one best promote the desirable client outcome? A secondary emphasis becomes how can one provide the service in the most efficient way while maintaining effectiveness? In a performance contract there is an incentive toward efficiency because any contract dollars left over after meeting the service requirements or outcome expectations become discretionary funds for the agency. However, in a cost-reimbursable contract, the incentive is to spend the full amount of the funds allowable under the contract regardless of whether they are needed to provide that particular service. In the current environment of shrinking human services resources, the performance contract has the potential to help keep the emphasis on outputs and outcomes that matter while encouraging efficiency of operation.

Less Micromanagement

Because of the focus of performance contracts on service outputs and client outcomes rather than on how funds are expended, there is less tendency for the public agency to try to micromanage the nonprofit. With the cost-reimbursable contract, the agency purchasing the service normally goes into great detail regarding which expenditures are allowable, which limits the service provider's management discretion about which types of expenditures the agency believes will produce the best service results.

For example, as a nonprofit manager, you may believe that exemplary staff should be given significant merit increases, which will both reward effectiveness and encourage other staff to extend themselves. But the public agency may take the position that you cannot use contract funds to provide staff with an average increase that is more than the state is allowing the public agency. Or, you may believe service effectiveness will be increased if all case managers are provided notebook computers to take into the field. But the public agency may take the position that contract expenditures will not be allowed for what it believes is nonessential equipment. In both cases, your nonprofit conceivably could have the dollars needed to support these expenditures under a current cost-reimbursable contract, but may not be allowed to expend them in this manner. In such instances, the public agency substitutes its management judgment about what is needed to promote the effective provision of service over the management judgment of the contract organization.

In contrast, a performance contract provides an agreed-upon unit rate for a measure of services or client outcomes, and it is within the discretion of the nonprofit organization's managers to use those unit rate revenues to support whatever expenditures they consider necessary to produce the expected services. This system disconnects the revenue budget of the agency from the expenditure budget, which results in the nonprofit organization having to pay as much attention to the generation of organization revenues as it does to containment of expenses. One of the positive factors about this focus is that for every gap between revenues and expenditures, the solution can include trying to generate more revenues and using surplus revenues generated by one service to offset shortfall in another. This type of management discretion is specifically recognized in performance contracts by Massachusetts, which holds the position that if a contracting organization can provide an acceptable level of service at less cost than the established unit rate, then it can keep the surplus (Commonwealth of Massachusetts, 1997). Generally, the response to a shortfall in a program supported only by cost-reimbursable contracts is to reduce expenditures regardless of the impact on the service program.

Greater Flexibility

Because performance contracting uncouples the revenue and expenditure budgets, nonprofit managers have much greater flexibility in supporting programmatic innovations and changes. This is especially true in outcome contracts when no definition of services is provided, and only outcomes are specified. An example of this approach is the early OEO education contracts that specified that grade-level improvements in reading and math were to be obtained, while allowing any educational technology to be used to achieve these improvements. However, although these types of contracts allow for a great deal of innovation, unless one is quite sure the innovation will be effective, significant revenues may be at risk.

In service-unit-output contracts, there is some definition of the nature of service to be provided (residential treatment day, counseling hour, home health visit), but within these definitions there will normally be significant room for flexibility. In some situations, flexibility will be further limited by accreditation standards that may be required in the output performance contract, but most often these contracts allow some room for programmatic discretion in relation to how one goes about meeting these standards. For example, accreditation standards may call for certain roles to be assumed by licensed professionals, but how the nonprofit goes about recruiting, planning client assignments, and compensating these professionals is open to managerial discretion. Finally, even when accreditation standards set clear parameters about which expenditures must be made, with a performance contract the nonprofit manager will never be faced with the situation of having a program need in a budget category that has been spent down, while there is a surplus in another category but the manager is unable to make a line-item transfer because of the limits of a cost-reimbursable contract.

Greater Capacity for Comparison and Evaluation

A final advantage of performance contracts is that they lend themselves to cost comparisons and program evaluation. Because definable service units or outcome measures must be specified in performance contracts, as long as the same units or measures are used in a number of programs, it becomes relatively easy to assess other aspects of the program, holding these measures constant. For example, as long as there is agreement on end-of-service outcome measures, one can compare length and intensity of service provision among organizations providing similar services to similar clients under a service-unit-output contract. If clear client service outcomes have been identified, one can evaluate the effectiveness of various service interventions for particular client types in the case of a performance contract using client outcomes.

This type of comparison or evaluation can be done without having performance contracts, but the nature of performance contracts guarantees that similar measurement units will be used by organizations providing similar services or expecting to produce similar client outcomes. This means that certain types of comparisons and evaluations can be made without having to introduce an added layer of a service assessment system on top of the existing service program. Of course, the validity and reliability of comparison and evaluation assessments depend on the accuracy in defining and collecting performance measures.

DISADVANTAGES OF PERFORMANCE CONTRACTS

Depending on their exact nature, performance contracts may have a number of disadvantages, including problems of measurement, intrusiveness into the lives of clients, uncertainty about the organization's resource base, and an increased cost of contract administration.

Measurement Problems

One of the ongoing issues that limits the growth of outcome performance-based contracts is the difficulties inherent in the development and tracking of outcome measures that actually capture the intent of service outcomes. There is a "tendency to measure what can be most easily measured (which may not be the most important thing to measure) and to use the most easily available, convenient measurement instruments" (Else, Groze, Hornby, Mirr, & Wheelock, 1992, p. 522). For example, in the early 1970s more than 90 percent of all performance contracts used by school districts relied on outcomes related to standardized math and reading scores because the measurement criteria in these two areas were generally agreed upon, even though the goal of general education reached far beyond these two core subjects (Blaschke, 1972).

At the 1972 National Conference on Performance Contracting, those who studied the use of outcome performance contracts in the educational field identified the following four major problem areas related to outcome measures:

1. There was a lack of fit between standardized tests and the actual program being funded.
2. The achievement tests used were subject to large errors and low reliability.
3. Grade-level increases in reading and math were measured by different instruments that were not comparable.
4. The use of criterion reference assessments were subject to manipulation and "teaching to the test" (stimulating instruction aimed only at producing high test scores rather than meeting the broader educational needs of the student) (Levine, 1972).

When one is dealing with postservice outcomes, even when the measures are accurate and do measure the service objective, the issue of how to accurately account for significant intervening variables remains. For example, in the case of employment preparation and placement programs, if "remains employed for a period of six months" is used as a basis of payment, how does one deal with a community where a major plant closes or the general economy takes a major downturn? The measurement development challenge is to create outcome measures that accurately and fully measure the intended outcome of the service, have a high degree of reliability, and are within the control of the service provider to produce.

Intrusiveness on Clients Served

A second disadvantage of outcome performance contracts is that they normally require contract compliance information to be collected from the client both during and after service provision. This involves collecting data that would not necessarily be collected in the normal course of service provision. As a result, outcome performance contracts may cause the service agency or organization to intrude on the client and on others in the client's sphere of living in a way that it would not otherwise. Although a nonprofit organization may, as a matter of quality management, collect outcome data on the clients it serves, that can be done with sampling techniques that do not require the ongoing intrusion into every client's life.

Depending on the outcome measures selected, this intrusiveness may involve the collection of postservice data from a range of sources related to the former client. In the case of a child discharged from residential treatment, this may mean collecting data from the child's current school, the county juvenile justice program, the county department of social services, and the local community mental health center, as well as from family members. In the case of a former client of an employment preparation and placement service, it may mean contacting current and former employers and the state employment service, as well as the client. The effect is that the former client is followed by the service provider after the service episode is completed.

Uncertainty of the Resource Base

The concerns related to a nonprofit organization having to rely on the uncertainty of an outcome-based performance contract go back at least to the late 19th century. By the 1890s, after almost 30 years of paying schools in England based on pupil educational attainment and attendance, this outcome-based performance system was scrapped because it produced great financial insecurity for the local schools. After the major growth in the use of outcome-based performance contracts in the U.S. education system in the late 1960s, even the capitalized private corporations pulled out of the educational contract business because the outcome payment system produced too much financial risk (Gramlich & Koshel, 1975).

Even if a nonprofit organization is confident that it can produce the required outcomes, there is a major issue related to cash flow. If the contract is written so the nonprofit does not get paid until the end of the service

provision period (when a client achieves the desired end-of-service outcome), or even worse, at some point after service discharge, the question arises as to how the organization deals with its current ongoing costs. A for-profit organization may secure up-front capital to deal with this type of cash flow
issue, but most nonprofits do not start with a great deal of capital and most
often do not carry large program surpluses year to year. Although it may be
possible to secure a line of credit from a lending institution based on anticipated contract-related accounts receivables, the very nature of outcome-based
payments may mean the lending institution would not consider this a sufficiently safe lending situation.

Increased Cost of Contract Administration

Although in all POSCs there are additional contract-related administrative
costs created by reporting requirements (Kramer, 1994), the use of performance contracts significantly escalates these contract-related costs. It has been
found that the data-tracking costs related to performance contracts can shift
scarce resources from service provision to contract administration (NYATEP,
1995). In an environment where there has been an increased scrutiny of
administrative costs by policymakers and an increased interest in outcome-
based contracts, the nonprofit organization can get caught in a situation in
which these two foci are not compatible.

In all POSCs, as well as when providing services with United Way funds,
your nonprofit organization will have to maintain an accounting system that
tracks costs by cost objects (see chapter 17 for more information). In the case
of a cost-reimbursable contract, the additional administrative costs relate to
having to track contract costs separately from other costs and to dealing with
issues of allowability and audit trail. Most of these activities will also be
required in the case of performance contracts. Even if cost objects related to
a contract service do not have to be tracked for purposes of reimbursement,
as in the case of an output service unit contract, they do have to be tracked to
know whether the income generated by the unit rate is actually covering costs
and to form the basis for the negotiations related to rate setting. Both of these
elements are also necessary for a nonprofit with an outcome contract. To
determine what level of payment is necessary for a given outcome, the nonprofit must be able to determine the actual cost of producing the outcome.
Therefore, in the case of having to account for costs related to either service
units or outcomes, your nonprofit organization must, over and above tracking
general contract-related costs, also track by specific service unit or outcome.

In addition, in the case of an outcome-based performance contract, your
nonprofit must set up an outcome measurement tracking system that allows
for the collection of outcome data from the client and others both at the end

of service and possibly at a later date. In the case of postservice outcomes, this involves the additional establishment of a system to track former clients and the additional expense of going to the client's location to collect outcome-related data. These two activities will add significantly to the administrative costs of fulfilling the contract.

MAXIMIZING THE USE OF PERFORMANCE CONTRACTS

An understanding of the historical experience with performance contracts and an analysis of their advantages and disadvantages suggest a number of ways that nonprofit managers may be able to maximize the use of this type of purchase-of-service arrangement. It is important to understand when to avoid performance contracts altogether, how to maximize unit rates, and how to shape payment procedures to your nonprofit organization's advantage. Nonprofit managers must also realize the importance of taking the lead in defining service units and outcome measures and understand the critical importance of making sure there is a good fit between the nature of the services offered and the service outcomes expected.

When to Avoid Performance Contracts

A key decision rule to use in deciding whether your nonprofit organization should enter into a performance contract (either output or outcome) is whether there is any historical experience related to the actual costs required to deliver a particular unit of service or to produce a given outcome. If your organization does not have experience in delivering a particular service and there is not good cost data available from similar nonprofit organizations delivering this service, then it is risky for your organization to lock itself into a contract requiring a fixed unit cost. A better approach may be to negotiate a cost-reimbursable contract for one to two years while good cost data can be collected and evaluated. This data can then be considered a sound basis for establishing a given unit cost.

On the other hand, a performance contract clearly has some advantages when your nonprofit has good cost and program experience and when a service product can be clearly defined. Conversely, if the service is new, experimental, or related to research and development, or when key factors affecting costs are in the control of outside forces, then it normally is best to be cautious about entering into a performance contract. Clearly, if you do not have solid data to indicate your nonprofit can consistently produce a given service outcome for a client, it becomes a gamble to enter into a contract when payment is based on producing that outcome.

Maximizing Unit Rates

In any business, whether for-profit or nonprofit, maximizing revenues is an important matter. When dealing with unit rates, whether it is for the sale of a widget, the provision of a day of residential treatment, or for helping someone find a job and keep it for six months, it is critical that the individual unit rate is sufficiently high so that when the income from all the units sold or provided in a given year are totalled they produce enough revenue to cover the organization's net costs of providing that good or service. A seemingly very successful nonprofit that operates all year at full capacity but loses money on each unit of service provided is worse off than an organization that operates at half capacity but at least covers its costs.

The concept of net costs becomes particularly important for many nonprofits because public agencies have a long history of expecting nonprofits to discount the actual cost of a unit of service provided under a POSC. In a recent national study, Kettner and Martin (1996) found that POSCs with nonprofit organizations covered the full cost of providing the service in only 20 percent of the cases studied. The same study found that nonprofits used the following sources, in order of importance, to subsidize the unit cost of services: client fees, charitable gifts, United Way allocations, surpluses from other contracts, grants, volunteer services, and student interns. Even though this practice is ingrained in the public–nonprofit service system, the reliance on discounted rates for units of service is not universally required. In negotiating unit rates, start with an expectation that the public agency will pay your nonprofit for the actual cost of the service in the same way the agency pays for all the services it purchases from the private sector.

In relation to rate setting it is important for your nonprofit to have a realistic understanding of what type of use rate can be expected for a given service during a given time period. For the provision of many services, your core staff and other service-related costs are relatively fixed, regardless of whether your program is operating at full capacity. For example, if you are operating a counseling service or a day care center, you generally must have a full complement of staff on duty whether or not you use 100 percent of the counseling hours available or 100 percent of the available day care slots. As a result, if you set your nonprofit's unit rate based on the assumption of running at 100 percent capacity and end up actually operating only at 90 percent capacity over the course of the year, your total revenues for that service will be nearly 10 percent less than what you had budgeted for expenses. Conceivably, you realize some small savings in variable costs (for example, lunches for day care children, diagnostic instruments for a counseling client, or a job interest assessment instrument for an employment client), but your major costs are likely to be in full-time staff, administration, and the physical plant, which do not tend to go down with a five, 10, or even greater percent reduction in client services.

Therefore, you must be careful to negotiate a unit service rate that takes the use rate into account. If it is known that your organization cannot reasonably expect to run at more than 90 percent capacity and the cost of a unit of service at 100 percent capacity is $100, then the unit rate will need to be negotiated at a rate of $111.11 per unit to produce the same level of revenue at the 90 percent use level. You must be sure that your nonprofit's rate is determined by dividing the realistic estimated number of service units for the year into the total estimated costs (both direct and indirect) related to that service, rather than the total possible number of service units.

In negotiating service unit, or outcome unit rates, your nonprofit normally will be in a stronger position if it can join similar service programs to present a unified front for rate establishment rather than negotiating an individual rate and risking being played off against other organizations providing similar services. Normally, larger programs that can gain from economies of scale will have some advantages over smaller programs. There may be times when smaller nonprofits will want to consider joint program and cost-sharing strategies with other nonprofit organizations as a way to reduce costs in the face of unrealistic unit rates.

Shaping Payment Systems

Because of the long tradition of using cost-reimbursable contracts as the vehicle for purchasing services from nonprofits, there has been a tendency for nonprofits to expect that the public agency will always make payments for services after the fact. But in many contracts for services from the private for-profit sector, the normal expectation is that a percentage of the total contract will be provided up front to cover start-up costs and deal with issues of cash flow. Unless prohibited by procurement policies, your nonprofit should try to take advantage of this flexibility to shape payment systems to its advantage.

This is especially important in the case of outcome contracts. Experience has shown that it is very risky to base the full amount of service revenues on payments based on outcome measures. One reason performance contracting in the educational field fell into disfavor was that the contracts tended to be "all or nothing"—there was no provision to cover any of the organization's real costs if an agreed-upon outcome was not reached. A much more responsible way to approach outcome contracts is to expect some payment to your nonprofit organization up front, to receive at least partial payment in every case service is provided, and to shape payment for meeting or exceeding outcomes as incentive payment. In this way, the focus on achieving client outcomes is maintained and rewarded, but at the same time, the long-term viability of your organization is not put at significant risk. It may not always be possible to negotiate such favorable measures, but they should be your starting point in the negotiation process.

Defining Service Units and Outcome Measures

Your nonprofit must take an active role in developing the definitions of a service unit or a service outcome because they form the basis for what will drive your organization's costs. Although defining a residential treatment day or a day care day may seem straightforward, on deeper investigation you may see that it can become a very complicated matter. The issue has less to do with the amount of time involved than what minimal range of total services will be required to be constituted a unit of service. For example, does the definition of a day of therapeutic foster care include the requirement that the foster parents be trained, that they receive a minimum amount of professional supervision by a given kind of professional, that the child be followed by a professional case manager and, if needed, that the child receive specialized therapeutic services from other professionals? Each of these requirements has important cost implications for the nonprofit, and the organization's leadership must be involved actively in their development.

In some instances, the standards for defining a service will be established by some outside body. In the case of therapeutic foster care, for example, standards may be set by a state licensing board. In such instances, the task is easier, but it is still necessary to clearly understand whether providing the range of services required to meet minimal licensing standards is all that is required or whether there is an expectation that your nonprofit will provide services that go beyond the minimum standards. Obviously, there are significant cost implications in this issue.

One of the things that happened in the ill-fated educational performance outcome contracts in the late 1960s was that the service contractors failed to realize that the total number of hours a child is in school is not the same as the total number of instructional hours (Gramlich & Koshel, 1975). Downtime because of absence, fire drills, assemblies, and class disturbances can greatly lessen the time actually available for instruction. If an outcome is based on achieving a given level of improvement in a fixed amount of time, and the nonprofit service provider has not been involved in making sure the established time limits consider such things as downtime, then meeting that outcome measure becomes highly unlikely and can result in a major fiscal loss. The bottom line is that whether it relates to output unit of service or a service outcome measure, it is important for the nonprofit manager to be involved actively in shaping the definitions that have major cost implications for the program.

Shaping the Fit between the Program and Expected Outcomes

The nonprofit manager has the major role in determining how best to shape the service program to produce the most effective service outcomes. When faced with a performance contract that includes compensation for producing certain client outcomes, it is critical that all the major constituents of your program (management, staff, clients, board) clearly understand the exact nature of the client outcome your nonprofit is expected to produce. The reward systems within your organization must be reviewed to make sure they clearly support behavior and activities that will help produce the relevant client outcomes.

Because of this necessity to shape your total program based on achieving a given outcome or set of outcomes, the way outcomes are defined is critical. If outcomes are accepted that do not adequately capture what your program intends to achieve, the result will likely be conflict, confusion, and the potential for a major displacement of organizational goals.

CONCLUSION

The use of performance contracts to secure support for the provision of non-profit services to specific populations is imbedded firmly in the public–nonprofit partnership experience. This type of contract will most likely continue with the expansion of the privatization of public services through the use of POSCs. Although unit-of-service output contracts provide many advantages for the nonprofit with relatively few disadvantages, the use of client outcome contracts historically has been problematic for nonprofit organizations and must be approached with a great deal of caution. As with any contract situation, the burden is on the nonprofit manager to understand the nature of the advantages and disadvantages of a particular approach to performance contracting and then to become a major actor in shaping the contract to the advantage of the nonprofit organization.

SKILLS-APPLICATION EXERCISE

You are the executive director of a nonprofit human services training and technical assistance organization and have been in discussions with the director of the state agency responsible for oversight of child care programs in the state. She has indicated a willingness to enter into a sole-source contract with your organization for a range of training and evaluation services if you are willing to meet her expectations about program quality, quantity, and effectiveness. She tells you she wants the following services:

- delivery of basic child care service training for new workers, a training course you have been delivering for several years
- development of a new set of training courses to enhance the capacity of child care program managers, based on your having carried out a training needs analysis to determine the scope and length of the training
- delivery of the program management training statewide to all managers
- an evaluation of whether programs in the state are taking appropriate steps to prevent the spread of communicable diseases among children in child care programs.

The director indicates she is committed to effective training and wants to initiate a payment system for the basic child care service training based on the new workers' demonstrated competence in mastering the learning objectives. She also indicates she is willing to use a contract that will pay a fixed amount for each of the major steps in the development and delivery of the management training course. She is unclear as to how best to structure the disease evaluation project. She asks you to outline the basic elements of a contract for the next meeting.

- Outline the key contract elements that you would like to see contained in the contract, including such items as

   — definitions of the units of service to be provided
   — client outcome measures to be used
   — a payment schedule
   — the length of the contract
   — the basis for contract renewal
   — a mechanism for dispute resolution if there is disagreement on whether an outcome has been met.

- Note which of these elements you would require for your organization to proceed with the contract.

- Describe why you made those choices.

REFERENCES

Adoption Assistance and Child Welfare Act of 1980, P.L. 96-272, 94 Stat. 500.

American Association of School Administrators. (1972). *The school executive's guide to performance contracting.* Washington, DC: Author.

Barsh, E. T., Moore, J. A., & Hamerlynck, L. A. (1983). The foster extended family: A support network for handicapped foster children. *Child Welfare, 62,* 349–359.

Blaschke, C. (1972). *Performance contracting: Who profits most?* Bloomington, IN: Phi Delta Kappa Educational Foundation.

Campbell, R. F. & Lorion, J. E. (1972). *Performance contracting in school systems*. Columbus, OH: C. E. Merrill.

Commonwealth of Massachusetts, Department of Procurement and General Services. (1997, October 8). *Purchase of service users handbook*. Available online from www.magnet.state.ma.us/osd/pos/postoc.htm.

Edwards, R. L., Cooke, P. W., & Reid, P. N. (1996). Social work management in an era of diminishing federal responsibility. *Social Work, 41*, 468–479.

Eggers, W. D., & Ng, R. (1993). *Social and health services privatization: A survey of county and state governments*. Los Angeles: Reason Foundation.

Else, J. F., Groze, V., Hornby, H., Mirr, R. K., & Wheelock, J. (1992). Performance-based contracting: The case of residential foster care. *Child Welfare, 71*, 513–516.

Fixler, P. E., Jr., & Poole, R. W., Jr. (1987). Status of state and local privatization. In S. H. Hanke (Ed.), *Prospects for privatization* (pp. 165–178). New York: American Academy of Political Science.

Gramlich, E. M., & Koshel, P. P. (1975). *Educational performance contracting: An evaluation of an experiment*. Washington, DC: Brookings Institution.

Kettner, P. M., & Martin, L. L. (1993). Performance, accountability, and purchase of service contracting. *Administration in Social Work, 17*(1), 61–79.

Kettner, P. M., & Martin, L. L. (1994). Purchase of service at 20: Are we using it well? *Public Welfare, 52*(3), 14–20.

Kettner, P. M., & Martin, L. L. (1995). Performance contracting in the human services: An initial assessment. *Administration in Social Work, 19*(2), 47–61.

Kettner, P. M., & Martin, L. L. (1996). The impact of declining resources and purchase of service contracting on private, nonprofit agencies. *Administration in Social Work, 20*(3), 21–38.

Kramer, R. M. (1994). Voluntary agency and the contract culture: Dream or nightmare? *Social Service Review, 68*, 33–66.

Levine, D. M. (1972). Major problems in performance contracting in education. In D. M. Levine (Ed.), *Performance contracting in education—An appraisal* (pp. 15–34). Englewood Cliffs, NJ: Educational Technology Publications.

McGuire, T. G. , Hodgkin, D., & Schumway, D. (1995). Managing Medicaid mental health costs: The case of New Hampshire. *Administration and Policy in Mental Health, 23*(2), 97–117.

Moore, S. (1987). Contracting out: A painless alternative to the budget cutter's knife. In S. H. Hanke (Ed.), *Prospects for privatization* (pp. 60–73). New York: American Academy of Political Science.

New York Association of Training and Employment Professionals, Welfare Reform Task Force. (1995, June 19). *Jobs/JTPA coordination in New York State, executive summary*. Albany, NY: Author. Available online from www.nyatep.org/jtpajobs.html.

Riemer, W. H. (1968). *Handbook of government contract administration*. Englewood Cliffs, NJ: Prentice Hall.

Texas State Comptroller. (1996, April 22). Contracting and contracting monitoring. In *Special delivery: New models of care* (Comptroller's Texas Performance Review). Austin, TX: Author. Available online from www.cpa.state.tx.us/comtrol/tpr/ch3.html.

Tracy, E. M., Green, R. K., & Bremseth, M. D. (1993). Meeting the environmental needs of abused and neglected children: Implications from a statewide survey of supportive services. *Social Work Research and Abstracts, 29*(2), 21–26.

Wedel, K. R., & Colston, S. W. (1988). Performance contracting for human services: Issues and suggestions. *Administration in Social Work, 12*(1), 73–87.

CHAPTER 6

Media Relationships and Marketing

Todd Cohen

A s a nonprofit manager, you must relate both to your organization's internal constituency and its external environment. The latter often requires that you act as a broker, which involves a variety of behaviors (see chapter 1). These include efforts aimed at acquiring resources, establishing your organization's legitimacy and increasing its influence, and promoting and maintaining its external image. Further, you may be called upon to act as spokesperson for your organization. As a result, you may find that you frequently have contact with the media and are involved in a variety of marketing efforts.

The role the nonprofit sector plays in our communities is one of the best news stories in America. It is also one of the least reported. The news media's failure to report on the work of nonprofit organizations reflects two interconnected problems: The media do not understand the nonprofit sector, and nonprofits do not understand the media.

The media, however, represent a potentially powerful resource for you as a nonprofit manager in carrying out your many responsibilities. And just as you must master each of those responsibilities and figure out how to balance the various roles you play as a manager, you also must develop a strategy for working with the media and integrate that strategy into the functioning of your organization.

This chapter addresses the importance of the media to nonprofit managers and examines strategies and tactics to improve media understanding and coverage of the role your agency plays. It also suggests methods for dealing with crises and critical coverage of your organization and explores ways to cultivate better mutual understanding between nonprofits and the media. Last, the chapter suggests methods to market your organization to various constituencies.

WHY MEDIA?

The nonprofit sector is the heart and soul of America. No community could continue to function without the services nonprofit organizations provide, and no nonprofit could continue to function without the volunteer time and charitable dollars it receives.

Nonprofits are a big part of our economy. Since the mid-1970s, the sector has grown more rapidly than either business or government. The United States has nearly 500,000 charitable organizations whose annual operating expenses account for 8 percent of the economy. Paid employees and volunteers working in the sector account for 11 percent of the U.S. workforce (Hodgkinson, Weitzman, Abrahams, Crutchfield, & Stevenson, 1996). Ninety-three million adults, or nearly half the population, donate more than 20 billion hours a year, with the average volunteer spending more than four hours a week working for a charity (Hodgkinson, Weitzman, Crutchfield, Heffron, & Kirsch, 1996). Charitable giving in the United States grew nearly $10 billion in 1996 to more than $150 billion (Kaplan, 1997).

Nonprofit managers are being challenged as never before. Government is cutting back on services and spending, leaving nonprofits to do more with less (Cooke, Reid, & Edwards, 1997; Edwards, Cooke, & Reid, 1996). Americans are skeptical about the future in general, and because of the nonprofit scandals in recent years they are skeptical about giving money to charity.

The media likewise are crucial to America. If our democracy may be likened to a remarkably complex machine, constructed by millions of citizens and organizations and consisting of gears, pulleys, wheels, and levers, the media are the grease that keeps the mechanism moving. In the same way that the Internal Revenue Code carves out special treatment for nonprofit organizations because of the role they play in society, the First Amendment to the Constitution recognizes the unique role played by the press.

One might reason, then, that nonprofits and the media might find in one another valuable resources. Unfortunately, this generally has not been the case. Few nonprofits understand or make an effort to work with the media. And in the news media—pervaded by cynicism, aggression, and superficiality (Gopnik, 1994)—few mainstream news organizations make even a minimal attempt to report on the work of nonprofits or the nonprofit sector (Cohen, 1996). The media simply do not get it. But that creates opportunities for nonprofit managers.

Faced as they are with shrinking support and rising needs, nonprofits can use all the help they can get, and the media represent a potentially powerful resource. For a nonprofit manager, the media offer a link to a host of constituents—consumers, volunteers, donors, government, other agencies, and the public.

As a nonprofit manager, you have a big enough challenge simply doing your job. The media can be a valuable resource, but learning how to work with the media and then actually doing so poses big challenges. Yet it is in your self-interest to work more closely with the media to help reporters and editors better understand how nonprofit organizations help make our communities better places to live and work.

MEDIA STRATEGY

Your organization should have a communications strategy, and that strategy should be integrated into your organization's overall strategic plan. Communications is a large topic and includes media, marketing, public relations, and communication with a host of constituencies. Most of what we do every day is to communicate. We communicate with staff, board members, volunteers, donors, government, other agencies, the public, and the media.

A media strategy simply is one of many related strategies for communicating. Developing a media strategy need not involve consultants and a lot of jargon. On the contrary, developing a strategy simply offers an opportunity to think about who you want to communicate with through the media, what it is you want to communicate, and how you can communicate most effectively. In other words, how will getting your message into the media help further the mission of your organization?

A simple exercise for thinking about a media strategy might be to list the key tasks assigned to each member of your organization and then to think about the news value of the work your staff does. Ask yourself what your organization is doing that might make a good news story and how getting that story into the media might help your organization. Consider everything your organization does from the perspective of the media and the possible advantages or disadvantages of getting coverage of a particular program, action, or policy.

A key issue here, and one not easily resolved, is what makes a good news story. It's virtually impossible to second guess reporters or editors on what they consider news. Their choices about what is newsworthy can reflect a decision-making process that is bureaucratic or arbitrary, and often both. But a good guideline is to look at how people are affected by the work you do. How does the work of your organization improve the lives of people? That is the news value of your work.

In developing a media strategy, keep your strategic planning simple, practical, and useful. The goal is not to put a sophisticated statement of policy to a board vote and then file it away to gather dust; the goal is to develop a sense of why you want to work with the media and how you plan to tell your story through the media. A media strategy should also spell out who speaks for your organization and should include a game plan for handling announcements, special events, publications such as annual reports, and crises.

CONNECTING

Dealing with reporters and editors is a lot like dealing with prospective funders. Media coverage can be a valuable resource for your organization, but securing that coverage takes a lot of work. The most fundamental principle to remember when dealing with people in the media is to use common sense. In the same way that you conduct research on a prospect before asking for a big contribution, you should get to know the news organization and the reporter, editor, or news director you hope to work with before asking and expecting to get a story published about your organization. If you're targeting a newspaper, for example, study the bylines in the paper. Learn which reporters cover which beats, such as public schools, city hall, and social services. Get to know the type of coverage that the news organization emphasizes. For example, does your local television station emphasize a particular issue, such as children or the environment, in its news coverage and public service promotions?

Larger newspapers have general assignment reporters who cover many topics. Find out who these reporters are and study the types of stories they do; a general assignment reporter may be interested in covering your organization either for a single story or on an ongoing basis. Smaller newspapers employ fewer reporters than larger papers. It may be easier to get to know the managing editor or city editor of a smaller paper in addition to the reporters. Look beyond your local newspaper. Your community may be served by a larger newspaper, and your field of interest may also be covered by a trade publication.

Television and radio news operations typically are short staffed and over worked, and they look for breaking news stories with photo opportunities. It may be tougher to get continuing coverage from television and radio, but they are powerful media, and it is equally important to establish and cultivate relationships with them. Television and radio news stations typically employ only a handful of reporters. The news director or producer is the person you should get to know.

Newspapers and television and radio stations, large or small, are always looking for feature stories. These stories offer a human-interest perspective and focus on an individual or group making a difference in the community.

If you are dealing with a newspaper or television station, it helps if the story has a photo opportunity. Pay attention to the kinds of feature stories your local media run, and then when you have a good story to tell, suggest it to your local news organization.

Keep in mind that many newspapers and television stations, as well as a number of other organizations, produce electronic publications on the World Wide Web. Although these electronic publishers use a medium you may not be familiar with, this emerging medium is powerful and attracts more users every day. As with traditional news media, it is to your benefit to know and understand Web publishing and to use common sense in approaching organizations that publish on the Web.

Making Contact

Once you have a handle on your local news organization and the people who write, edit, or produce the news, make contact with a reporter or editor. Depending on the size of the newsroom, whom you approach may vary. At a small local newspaper, you may want to approach the editor. At a large city newspaper, you may want to talk to a reporter who covers a specialty beat, such as health or social services.

It is a good idea to make contact before you have an item for a news story. But remember that reporters and editors are busy people. They work under the pressure of constant deadlines. For a morning newspaper, and even more so for a television news operation, afternoons are busy and stressful. You might telephone a reporter or editor in the morning and say you would like to stop by to introduce yourself and drop off some materials. Be prepared to be rebuffed, but also be prepared to be politely assertive; at the least, you could drop off your materials at the front desk or simply mail them. Remember, your initial goal is to make contact.

Building Relationships

The next step is to establish and cultivate a relationship with the reporter. After you have made initial contact and dropped off some materials, you might try to meet the reporter for lunch or coffee. Do not pick up the tab for the meal or even for a cup of coffee; reporters prefer to pay their own way so they do not feel compromised.

In offering an invitation for lunch or coffee, explain that you simply would like to share some information about your organization and the issues you face. If the reporter declines the invitation, offer to stop by the news office for 15 minutes to talk. It is important to keep up the initial contact you have made. Do not be frustrated if you are put off; reporters are busy people. Keep your eye on the objective, which is to establish a relationship.

Whether you get a longer face-to-face meeting or not, you should offer your organization as a resource on issues you are involved with. If the reporter is working on a story involving those issues, make it clear that he or she should feel free to call and ask for background or a local angle or quote. If you are aware of an action in Washington, DC, your state capital, or even locally that might, with some background or a quote from your organization, make a good local story, pick up the telephone and call the reporter.

You should also consider the various partnerships your organization may be involved in. Collaboration is increasing among nonprofits, and reporters may be interested in the fact that nonprofit, for-profit, and government organizations and agencies are beginning to work together. The collaboration may be the hook that attracts the interest of the reporter.

A final suggestion for building relationships—If a reporter does a good job on a story, any story, write a short note to that effect. Reporters get a lot of negative feedback but rarely are told they have done a good job.

It is also important to know that reporters, much like fundraisers, tend to move from job to job. Even though you may have invested a lot of time and effort getting to know a reporter and building a relationship, be prepared to start all over again with a new reporter after your contact moves to another job.

WRITING A NEWS RELEASE

When you have news, be prepared to let the media know about it. The most effective way to do that is through a news release—a written statement that summarizes your news and explains its importance. A news release should contain all the information a reporter needs as well as the names and telephone numbers of contacts the reporter can call for additional information.

In deciding what type of information to include in a news release and how to write it, use common sense. What message do you want to send to the reader of the newspaper, the viewer of the television news, or the listener of the radio news? Keep in mind the fundamental principle that the value of your news to the newspaper or television or radio station is your organization's impact on people. A good rule in writing a news release is to stick to the facts and avoid hype and overstatement. Good reporters are trained to answer the following questions in their stories: Who? What? When? Where? Why? How? These are the questions you should address in a news release.

Never forget that your purpose in writing a news release is to convince a reporter or an editor to publish a story about your organization. The immediate target of your news release is the reporter or editor, not the ultimate reader. The news organization typically will use your news release as a starting point for preparing its own story, although some smaller news organizations may reprint your news release word for word.

In deciding how to write a news release, think about how you would explain your organization's news to a friend or family member. In other words, tell the story in plain words and use a conversational style. Think about who will be reading the story that ultimately gets into the newspaper or on television or radio. Who is your ultimate audience? Who is affected by your news? How are are they affected? Why, in other words, are you telling the story?

Get to the point quickly, emphasizing the main points at the beginning. Use details. If money is involved, say how much. Be precise. Avoid jargon and acronyms. If you must use a term common to your profession or field, explain it. It is useful to provide some background about your organization and the issues involved in the subject of your news release, but do not get carried away. A full-blown history is not necessary. It is also helpful to gear your release to the types of issues and coverage emphasized by the news organization you are targeting. And, where possible, link your release to issues that currently are in the news. Include in the news release the names, titles, and telephone numbers (work and home) of individuals the reporter can contact for follow-up questions. Include any pertinent e-mail addresses.

Try to keep your news release to a single page. You should be able to summarize your news on one page, and a one-page release is easy for a reporter or editor to absorb. If your story is important enough to require more space, take another page or two, but remember that reporters and editors may not have time to read your entire news release. The easier and shorter you can make it for them, the better.

At the top of the release, include the words FOR IMMEDIATE RELEASE (in all capital letters), unless you are sending the news release in advance of an official announcement. In that case, include the words EMBARGOED FOR RELEASE UNTIL [the date of the announcement].

If the news you are announcing in the release lends itself to a photo or to some type of artwork the newspaper or television station might use, make that clear in the news release. For example, at the top of the news release you might include the words PHOTO OPPORTUNITY AVAILABLE and then briefly explain what the photo opportunity is. If you can send photos of principals involved in the story, call the news organization ahead of time to find out if they want them.

Writing a news release does not have to be complicated. Keep these simple guidelines in mind as you write your news release:

- Assume nothing.
- Do not get fancy; keep it simple.
- Determine who you are writing for.
- Determine why the release is worth writing.
- Connect the dots. Explain the relationships in the release—involving people, organizations, issues, and causes and effects.

- Tell people what you know in terms they can understand.
- Keep your perspective on the future, and use the past to put into context what is happening now and what is going to happen.
- Know what to omit. You do not have to quote people just because they sit on your board or have important titles.
- Write for the reader and not for yourself, your bosses, or your board.
- Do not use a $64 word when a simple word will do.
- Think about artwork and how to illustrate the release with photos or information graphics. Use your imagination.

GETTING INTO PRINT OR ON THE AIR

Once you have written the news release, your next goal is to get it published or broadcast. The target of your release is an editor or reporter at a news organization, and you want to make it as easy as possible for that person to do his or her job. Before you send a news release, call the reporter or editor to say the release is coming and ask how they would like you to send it—by mail, fax, or e-mail. You can also deliver it by hand. After you send the release, follow up by calling to make sure it was received. If you have included in the news release the names, titles, and telephone numbers of individuals the reporter can call for further information, make sure those individuals will be available if the reporter calls them.

HANDLING INTERVIEWS

Once you have sought coverage, be prepared to get it. If you issue a news release, be prepared to be interviewed. In preparing your organization's media strategy, you should always be prepared to be interviewed even if you have not issued a news release.

In an interview, the best approach is to be direct, honest, and forthcoming. Be prepared both for the question you would most want a reporter to ask and the question you would least want a reporter to ask. Offer to let the reporter call back with any further questions and to let the reporter check facts with you. However, do not ask to see a copy of the article before it runs; reporters are reluctant to let sources see articles in advance.

If a reporter calls you or another individual in your organization without warning and you are not prepared to answer, explain that you are not prepared at the moment to answer questions. Ask the reporter what information he or she needs, and then offer to call back as soon as you can gather the needed information. Ask how soon the reporter needs a response, and be prepared to be told a response is needed within hours or even minutes. Reporters typically call on deadline and are pressed to get something written right away. You will need to return any call from a reporter as soon as possible and certainly the same day. The last thing you should do is stall or stonewall a reporter.

HAVING A NEWS CONFERENCE

Although your first impulse when you believe you have news worth reporting might be to schedule a news conference to announce your news, you should think through whether a news conference truly is the format that will best serve your organization. Reporters tend to look on news conferences as canned events, and they do not like to waste time. If a news release will adequately cover the information you are trying to get to the public, do not call a news conference. But if you have a startling or remarkable announcement to make that will have a big impact on a lot of people, then a news conference might be in order. Another factor to consider is whether you can pull together a number of key individuals who could answer reporters' questions at a news conference. A news conference should not be used simply to make your announcement seem important or because your board or boss believes a news conference best frames your organization's message. When in doubt, call a reporter or two and ask if they believe a news conference would be appropriate.

If you do decide to hold a news conference, give the news organizations you want to reach plenty of notice. Treat the news conference the same as you would a news release: Call in advance, send a release about the news conference, and then call to make sure the release arrived.

The format and content of the news conference will require planning. Who will speak and what will they say? Prepare a release of the news to be announced at the conference and give these to the attendees. Include biographical sketches of the speakers as well as background material on your organization and the program or issues involved in the announcement. Whoever speaks or appears at the news conference should be prepared to answer a slew of questions, including those they may not particularly want to answer. Be prepared for tough questions, and be prepared for follow-up questions later by telephone.

DEALING WITH CRISES

When you have what you perceive to be bad news, do not try to hide it. It is generally better in such a case to make the first move and not to wait for a

"Your crisis management plan should include more than 'four Hail Marys and two Our Fathers.'"

reporter to discover your problem. By avoiding the natural impulse to hide your head in the sand like an ostrich and imagine no one will see you, you will gain several advantages. First, being forthcoming and honest may raise your credibility with the reporter or deepen the level of trust you have built over time. Second, you will avoid a situation in which a reporter uncovers the bad news and then, if you have cultivated a relationship over time, wonders why you did not let him or her know it. Finally, you may be able to get part of your version of the news into the story the reporter writes.

Before calling a reporter with your bad news, however, you must do a lot of planning. Your media strategy should include a plan for dealing with a crisis. That plan should include a checklist of steps to take when a crisis hits. Basic steps might include informing and consulting with the board and key staff; deciding how to respond; deciding which board and staff members should speak for the organization; preparing them to answer media questions; preparing news releases and possibly letters to donors, volunteers, supporters, and other key partners; preparing an opinion column or letter to the editor for local publications; and possibly scheduling a news conference. Your goal is to engage in damage control by acting reasonably, openly, and responsibly and not waiting passively to be discovered.

No matter how hard you try to avoid crises, some actions are beyond your control. A staff member may take money from petty cash, or a major donor may eliminate funding. But for those actions you can control, it is always good to keep in mind a simple exercise: If you are ever in doubt about the ethics of an action, think about whether you would like to see your action reported on the front page of your local newspaper.

DEALING WITH COVERAGE

You can't always get what you want. You may get good coverage, but you also may get bad coverage. You may find that a particular reporter or news organization always seems to cast your organization in a negative light. Or, despite your best efforts, you may never get any coverage. What can you do?

It is generally a good idea to try to meet with the reporter involved and talk about the coverage you have been getting or failing to get. If the reporter refused to meet with you, reported something you believe to be unfair and unreasonable, or unjustly refused to report on your organization, then you should talk to his or her supervisor.

Another option in the face of bad news is to write a letter to the editor or an opinion column for the editorial page. And if all else fails, you can always buy an advertisement and tell your side of the story.

DEALING WITH COMPETITION

Reporters and local news organizations tend to be fiercely competitive. That competitiveness can work to your advantage but, if you are not careful, it can also work to your disadvantage. Unless you have a good reason for doing so, do not play favorites among reporters or news organizations. Reporters love to get the story before a competitor. A good guideline is to be evenhanded in your treatment of reporters when you have news to announce.

It may also be the case that one reporter is more receptive to writing stories about your organization and more aggressive about checking with you to get information. If such a reporter learns something about your organization before the competition does, think carefully about how to handle the matter. Some organizations might want to issue a news release to all the media at the same time. But by doing so, you would be penalizing the reporter who got the scoop. It is a tough call; think about how you would feel if you were the reporter who got the scoop, only to have a source give the story to the competition.

EDUCATING BOARD AND STAFF

Dealing with the media should be an essential part of your job. Yet few boards or agency executives are willing to give you the resources and support you need to develop a comprehensive media strategy. There are steps you can take to increase the awareness of your board or executive about the importance of a media strategy and to secure the resources you need to put a strategy into effect.

Your community probably includes individuals who are savvy about media. They might include a journalism professor at a local college, a public relations professional at a local firm, or a communications director at a local agency. Talk to these professionals about your needs, and invite them to meet with your board or staff. The official purpose of the meeting would be a briefing on media issues; the unofficial agenda would be to raise the awareness of the meeting participants about media issues and cultivate them for support for media initiatives. The cultivation can work on several levels. In addition to cultivating your board, you will also be cultivating the community experts for possible involvement with your organization. Those same professionals you might ask to speak to your organization can also be resources you can ask for advice. If your board or executive cannot supply the money you need to develop and practice a media strategy, look to these local experts to serve as informal advisers to help you find creative ways to raise money, secure materials or services, and recruit volunteers.

EDUCATING THE MEDIA

Reporters, editors, news directors, and producers can always learn some new lessons. With a little creativity and diplomacy, you can help turn the media's lack of awareness about the nonprofit sector to your advantage. One useful strategy is to sponsor media forums to brief news people on issues important to your organization.

You may find it useful to meet with a group of reporters or editors from different news organizations who might be interested in your organization or the issues you deal with. Such a meeting can provide background and perspective for people in the media or simply break the ice and begin an ongoing relationship with them. You may find that a number of nonprofits in your field of interest may want to co-host such a meeting.

Ask some reporters and editors what time of day and type of format they would prefer. Then arrange for a format that lends itself to conversation, with representatives of your nonprofit or group of nonprofits providing insight into the work you do. The goal of such a meeting is to raise the awareness of the reporters and editors about your organization and field of interest. Make the setting and presentation as informal as possible. Distribute written materials, and make it clear that you and other nonprofit representatives are always available as resources for reporters.

Another option is to request a meeting with the reporters and editors of your local newspaper, as well as those who write the editorials. You might ask for such a meeting as a way of making your organization available for questioning by the newspaper staff, particularly if your organization or the issues you deal with are in the news. Or you may simply want to make the meetings a regular part of your year, providing you and the newspaper staff an opportunity to talk about the issues you are involved with. Again, the goal is to build a relationship with the media based on mutual trust.

Another strategy is to work with a local college, university, or some other educational institution on a seminar or workshop to help reporters and editors do a better job of covering the nonprofit sector. Independent Sector is a national trade group for nonprofits in Washington, DC, that has worked with schools of journalism at a number of state universities to sponsor such forums. The School of Journalism and Mass Communication at the University of North Carolina at Chapel Hill sponsored a daylong seminar, funded by Independent Sector, that was attended by newspaper reporters from throughout the state as well as executive directors and communications officers from nonprofit organizations. As a result, news coverage of the nonprofit sector in North Carolina has increased noticeably.

Although reporters and editors can seem set in their ways, resources do exist to help you educate them about the work you do as a nonprofit manager. As in fundraising, achieving success in communicating with reporters and editors requires that you take the time and make the effort to find ways to reach out to them. Independent Sector has a guide for journalists (Morris, 1993) that may help you better understand the media and how to work with reporters and editors.

VOICING YOUR OPINION

Newspapers and radio and television stations offer forums for readers, listeners, and viewers to express their opinions. Take advantage of these options. Newspapers solicit letters to the editor and longer guest opinion columns. Radio and television stations offer opportunities to respond to news coverage. They also offer talk shows and newsmaker shows in which community leaders are interviewed. Such programs offer a golden opportunity to present your case in your own words. The station representatives who schedule guests for these shows typically are grateful for the help they can get finding guests. Do not be shy about offering yourself or a representative of your nonprofit as a guest.

USING OPTIONS BEYOND THE NEWS

The media offer numerous options other than news coverage for you to get your agency's message to the public. Do some research and find the opportunities in your community. Newspapers and television and radio stations typically publish or air community calendars. A calendar is a simple, effective way to publicize events sponsored by your agency. Television and radio stations also air public service announcements (PSAs) that can range from reading a brief news release on the air to broadcasting a television or radio spot you have produced and recorded. To find out about getting your PSA aired, call your local station and ask for the staff member who handles community affairs. Stations can sometimes help you produce your own PSA, but you will have to determine the station's deadline for submitting your request.

You are also likely to have a better chance of getting your message on the air if it is consistent with the types of issues the station supports. Many stations emphasize children's issues or some other cause in their own public service programming, and they are more likely to air your spot or help you produce it if their favorite causes are part of your focus.

If the station will not help you produce a spot but is willing to air it for you, you may be able to get the spot produced with contributed support, either in dollars or the in-kind services of a local company or organization with video production equipment. Be sure, however, that your spot does not become a promotion for whomever is underwriting its production; the local station may not want to air what it considers to be a commercial.

USING ONLINE RESOURCES

The explosion of the Internet and World Wide Web created enormous opportunities for nonprofits. One of the most valuable investments you can make as a nonprofit manager is to spend even a little time familiarizing yourself with information that the Web contains about nonprofits. The Web offers a vast potential for communicating and getting your message to the public. Whether it is news about the nonprofit sector, access to foundations and corporate funders, or classified ads for nonprofit jobs, the Web offers a remarkably diverse set of resources you can put to use (Zeff, 1996).

MARKETING

The news media collectively represent one means of getting your message to the public, but the media are beyond your control. Numerous means of communicating, however, are within your control, and these fall under the area of marketing.

Who are the constituencies you want to reach with your message, and what are the best methods of reaching them? Your nonprofit typically will have many constituencies, including the people you serve, donors, volunteers, board members, other nonprofits, government, business, and your staff and board.

You have numerous opportunities to communicate with those constituents. You can publish a newsletter, use direct mail or targeted mailings, prepare brochures that focus on your entire organization or on specific programs or projects, publish an annual report, or create a site on the World Wide Web.

Keep your materials simple and easy to understand. Keep in mind who your audience is and focus on the message you want to communicate. Take every opportunity to promote your organization and its work, but remember that time is a luxury for everyone, and the more concise your message, the more effective it will be.

You may lack the resources to develop and produce marketing materials yourself. But your community includes individuals and organizations who might be able to help by advising you, by contributing the work, or by helping to fund the work. Use your imagination.

CONCLUSION

Your organization has a good story to tell, and part of your job is to get your message to people who need to know it. By developing a media strategy and integrating it into your organization's strategic plan, you can better ensure your ability to improve your communications with board and staff, with volunteers and donors, with other nonprofits and government, and with the public and media.

When developing and putting into practice your media strategy, use common sense and keep your approach simple. A media strategy and media materials should be written in language that is easy to understand and accessible.

When approaching the media and preparing news releases and other materials, put yourself in the place of the people you are dealing with and try to make their work easier. Cultivate your media contacts and make yourself and your nonprofit available as resources for the media. When seeking media coverage, be prepared to get it by being informed, open, and accessible. And be creative in tapping community resources you can use in preparing a media strategy and media materials. It is in your nonprofit's best interest to be prepared to work with the media and to be persistent and consistent in trying to get your message into print, on the air, and online.

SKILLS-APPLICATION EXERCISE

You are the executive director of a reproductive health agency. You raised $1 million to build a new clinic and have scheduled a news conference to break ground for the clinic. On hand will be local dignitaries, including donors, civic leaders, local government officials, and the congressional representative from your district. Although your agency does not perform abortions, it does make referrals to physicians who do perform abortions, and you are concerned that the groundbreaking event may attract abortion protesters. You are also concerned about whether and how the media will cover the event.

Write a media plan for the event. Explain

- how to deal with reporters in advance of the event

- how to focus your news release announcing the event

- how to focus the news release to be handed out at the event

- how to respond to reporters if protesters are present

- how to respond to any negative coverage stemming from the event.

Also, write a news release annnouncing the event, a news release to be handed out at the event, and an opinion column to run in the local newspaper after the event that focuses on the importance of the new clinic to the community and explains why newspaper coverage of abortion protesters was overblown and out of context.

REFERENCES

Cohen, T. (1996). Don't skip this beat. *Foundation News & Commentary, 37*(5), 43–45.

Cooke, P. W., Reid, P. N., & Edwards, R. L. (1997). Management: New developments and directions. In R. L. Edwards (Ed.-in-chief), *Encyclopedia of social work* (19th ed., 1997 Suppl., pp. 229–242). Washington, DC: NASW Press.

Edwards, R. L., Cooke, P. W., & Reid, P. N. (1996). Social work management in an era of diminishing federal responsibility. *Social Work, 41,* 468–479.

Gopnik, A. (1994, December 12). Read all about it. *New Yorker,* pp. 84–102.

Hodgkinson, V. A., Weitzman, M. S., Abrahams, J. A., Crutchfield, E. A., & Stevenson, D. R. (1996). *Nonprofit almanac 1996–1997, Dimensions of the independent sector.* San Francisco: Jossey-Bass.

Hodgkinson, V. A., Weitzman, M. S., Crutchfield, E. A., Heffron, A. J., & Kirsch, A. D. (1996). *Giving and volunteering in the United States: Findings from a national survey.* Washington, DC: Independent Sector.

Kaplan, A. E. (1997). *Giving USA: The annual report on philanthropy for the year 1996.* New York: American Association of Fund Raising Counsel, AAFRC Trust for Philanthropy.

Morris, R. (1993). *Nonprofit news coverage: A guide for journalists.* Washington, DC: Independent Sector.

Zeff, R. (1996). *The nonprofit guide to the Internet.* New York: John Wiley & Sons.

ADDITIONAL READING

Jones, C. (1983). *How to speak TV: A self-defense manual when you're the news.* Marathon, FL: Video Consultants.

Jones, C. (1991). Developing strategic media relationships. In R. L. Edwards & J. A. Yankey (Eds.), *Skills for effective human services management* (pp. 103–112). Washington, DC: NASW Press.

Philanthropy Journal. Available online from www.pj.org.

Prevent Child Abuse, North Carolina. (1994). *Strategies for a successful public awareness program on child abuse and neglect.* Raleigh: Author.

Strunk, W., & White, E. B. (1959). *The elements of style.* New York: Macmillan.

CHAPTER 7

Managing Public Policy Advocacy and Government Relations

Emily D. Pelton and Richard E. Baznik

Significant cuts in federal spending for human services have led to a reduction in resources available for many government support programs, particularly in health, education, welfare, and the arts. As a result, many nonprofit agencies may see reductions in government financial support and may experience more intense pressure to obtain financial support from nongovernment sources (Edwards, Cooke, & Reid, 1996; Salamon, 1997). In addition, nonprofit organizations are likely to experience a growing demand to serve individuals who were previously served by government organizations.

On the other hand, whereas the demands on nonprofits are increasing in some areas, profit-oriented organizations are moving into traditional areas of nonprofit operations, particularly health care. Although the increasing competitiveness of the health care market may offer benefits to consumers, many people are concerned about the growing privatization of hospitals and the increasing role of the profit motive in health services delivery. Similar concerns are expressed about the move of for-profit organizations into other areas that have traditionally been the domain of public and nonprofit organizations.

As nonprofits struggle with these pressures, they are increasingly expected to justify their funding with measurable, quantitative results. However, the special tax status and other unique aspects of nonprofits have allowed the sector to lag behind in developing financial and program reporting capabilities comparable to those of the for-profit and government sectors. But growing public attention to these factors, along with well-publicized financial scandals, has made accountability a major concern (Gibelman, Gelman, & Pollack, 1997).

In many cases, nonprofit organizations and managers may find it necessary to initiate or support legislative changes that will help make federal policy transitions smoother. As policy changes unfold, lawmakers will be watching for results, and nonprofit managers must be able to articulate what works, what does not, and why. In cases when new policies do not meet public needs, nonprofit leaders will need to help formulate and advocate alternatives. Similarly, when new policies are working, nonprofit leaders may be asked to share information about successful models so that others may follow them. In any event, good advocacy skills will continue to be important in meeting the challenges now facing the nonprofit sector.

PARTICIPATION AND LEADERSHIP IN ADVOCACY

In light of these trends, you must be prepared to participate and exercise leadership in public policy debate. You should be well-informed about your own organization, your organization's position within its sector, and its status with its supporters and opponents. You then must be able to use this knowledge to influence external processes, policies, and individuals with the potential to affect your organization's success.

Participating effectively and providing leadership in public advocacy requires you to apply your skills in two general ways. First, learn your organization's public issues and the political context in which it must operate. Second, be an advocate for your organization's public interests in an appropriate manner.

LAYING THE FOUNDATION

An organization's advocacy objectives can range from general goals such as raising its public profile to defending the very existence of the organization. Some advocacy opportunities will arise in the course of an organization's normal public functions and interactions with government bodies, whereas others may result from major public controversies and debates. Regardless of whether your organization is actively engaged in advocacy, however, you should remain aware of the public environment in which you are operating. Learning about this framework—the people, institutions, and political issues that drive the system—is a basic function that should be integrated into the management of all nonprofits.

For many managers, achieving results may depend just as much on understanding their organization's internal workings as on knowing where it stands with respect to its neighbors, community, supporters, and opponents. As a nonprofit manager entering the advocacy arena, you should begin by taking the following four steps to develop an understanding of relevant public issues and elements of the political system: (1) study the issues, (2) study policy and political processes, (3) study the public players, and (4) study the industry players.

Study the Issues

Identify critical public issues associated with your organization through effective use of research and information resources. As a manager, you have many means of identifying important issues facing your organization, usually including both internal and external resources. If your nonprofit is a small organization with a very specific mission, such as a small shelter for homeless men, you may more easily be able to identify its public policy priorities than if your organization is a larger one with multiple interests, such as the American Red Cross. On the other hand, larger organizations are more likely to have the resources to conduct research and hire public policy professionals to keep abreast of issues that are important to the organization. Thus, an important first step in advocacy is to determine whether your organization's existing information resources are both scaled appropriately to its information needs and effective in helping you and other members of your management team monitor priority issues.

Research and policy analysis capabilities also should suit the size and mission of an organization. Effective advocacy hinges not only on the availability of accurate, timely, and well-organized information, but also access to analysis that puts such information in context and establishes the basis for planning. Typically, research and analysis are required both inside and outside an organization. For example, staff who possess institutional memory can be invaluable in putting issues in historical context, whereas an industry association or the media can provide vital information about an evolving political debate. As with information resources, it is not always necessary to pay for research. The existence of public coalitions may afford you access to reliable information at little or no cost. To make the best use of information, research, and analysis resources, take three steps before proceeding into the advocacy process: (1) assess information resources, (2) conduct internal institutional research, and (3) research and analyze policy issues.

Assess Information Resources

Organizational scale is an important factor here. If your organization is a small, community-based one, information-gathering needs might be met by a single staff person with recent experience in city government who can follow key issues in the local media, monitor industry news bulletins, and informally share information and coordinate activities with other community organizations. However, if your organization is larger, there may be a need to subscribe to professional news services, hire a consulting firm to research certain key issues, or retain a full-time lobbyist to represent the organization in the state capital or in Washington, DC.

Recent advances in technology have made information more accessible and often less expensive to the general public as well as to nonprofit organizations (see chapter 16). Services such as computerized bill tracking, listservs (e-mail distribution lists), and World Wide Web pages can help bridge information gaps for organizations that lack the resources to pay for independent research. Although not all organizations can afford advanced information technology, tax-deductible donations of computers are one way for community-based organizations to obtain technological resources.

Conduct Internal Institutional Research

You should be clear on the mission, goals, and history of your organization before forming or articulating positions on public issues. This type of information is usually available in your organization's mission statement or public information materials. However, major public policy priorities and areas of potential sensitivity often may be better identified in discussions with senior members of your organization who participate in public relations, including members of the board. Assessing the level of consensus within the organization on particular issues may help reveal the amount of staff, volunteer, and constituent support that is likely to be available for advocacy efforts (Gibelman & Kraft, 1996). In this sense, informal conversations about the history of the organization and its members' positions on particular issues can constitute valuable research.

In addition, you can help ensure that your organization is conveying a consistent and focused public message by researching previous public statements made by members of the organization. In preparing annual testimony for a state appropriations committee, for example, you should review not only the preceding year's accomplishments, but also the materials presented in previous years. To avoid public contradictions, you should also try to determine whether other members of your organization have made public statements on the same topics, even if their appearances were not on behalf of the organization. For example, a member of the board may have spoken publicly for her own company. This type of internal research also can help you gather information that strengthens your basis for managing the organization in other ways.

Research and Analyze Policy Issues

Advocacy decisions should rest on an assessment of the general political climate and an examination of relevant political processes and their likely outcomes (Haynes & Mickelson, 1997). However, before deciding to proceed with a certain approach, prepare individual issue analyses that provide relevant background information, describe the issue at hand, and examine the organization's interests. For example, upon learning of a new legislative proposal that might affect your organization's funding, you might request that your staff assemble a policy research paper to answer the following questions:

- What are the key elements and history of the issue?
- What are the concerns and interests of the principal parties involved?
- What are the status and expected outcome of the issue, given the political climate?
- Will the organization's constituency be affected by the outcome? If so, how?
- Does the organization have a position on this issue? If so, what is it?
- What are the positions of the organization's allies and opponents?

Gathering this preliminary information lays the groundwork for further analysis and will be useful in formulating an advocacy strategy, if one is needed.

In the early stages of research, you may prefer to rely on internal resources, particularly when an issue is politically sensitive or when it is not clear whether your organization has a strong stake in the issue. However, as the analysis proceeds, you should also determine whether a regional, industry, or national advocacy organization with centralized resources might also have useful data available. Particularly in social services fields, clearinghouse organizations frequently offer resources such as information on proposed legislation, background information and statistics on specific issues, and legislative action kits to promote participation in national or grassroots lobbying efforts. Obtaining information this way can not only save time and money, but also can provide information about the positions of other organizations and help you gauge the level of effort needed to make a political impact.

Study Policy and Political Processes

Identify the policy and political processes that affect your organization's interests and learn how to influence them. As a nonprofit manager, you should strive to understand the norms, processes, and actors in the political systems in which you will be operating. The process that determines policy outcomes for nonprofit organizations usually will have at least three dimensions: (1) a formal public dimension, which consists of information sharing and government oversight of government–nonprofit agreements (and other administrative and legal requirements); (2) a behind-the-scenes dimension, which consists of nonpublic contacts and events that occur through networks and personal relationships; and (3) an informal public dimension, which consists of how an organization and its members relate to the public and elected officials outside formal mechanisms (typically through the use of media). Each of these dimensions of the policy process is important, and effective advocacy requires an understanding of all three.

The formal public dimension of the policy process is governed by the legal relationship between nonprofit entities and the government, which is typically defined by specific laws, administrative procedures, and other agreements. Frequently, this aspect of government–nonprofit relations focuses on information sharing, compliance with government regulations, or contracts (Union Institute, 1992). Oversight responsibilities for the activities of non-government organizations are designated to public officials by law or are determined by the individual interests of elected officials. These governing authorities conduct policy reviews of the activities of nonprofit organizations and usually define the expectations they must meet in their public service.

A discussion of the formal environment for lobbying by nonprofits should include consideration of the regulations and other legal restrictions on these activities. Nonprofits must abide by the standard rules that govern political activities in the United States, including restrictions on contributions and the public disclosure of certain actions. In addition, charitable institutions are bound by even more stringent limits imposed by the U.S. Tax Code (U.S.C. 26, Sec. 501), which defines a *501(c)(3) organization* as one in which "no substantial part of the activities . . . is carrying on propaganda, or otherwise attempting, to influence legislation (except as otherwise provided in subsection (h)), and which does not participate in, or intervene in (including the publishing or distributing of statements), any political campaign on behalf of (or in opposition to) any candidate for public office." In addition, many states impose specific restrictions on lobbying that nonprofit managers should research and understand before engaging in an advocacy campaign.

The behind-the-scenes dimension is often the least accessible part of the policy-making process, but it is probably the most important. Just as an organization's annual report typically offers a helpful but incomplete picture of how it functions, the formal public review process illustrates only part of the government–nonprofit story. Factors such as personal political alliances and rivalries, organizational politics, competing priorities, and hierarchies within agencies can have a profound impact on public policy decisions, yet they are rarely a part of the public record. To gain access to this information, you must develop personal contacts with decision makers and form networks with individuals and groups who can provide insights into the policy process.

The informal public dimension of policy-making consists of relationships and interactions among an organization, the public, and elected officials, which are often fostered through the media and public interest groups. When possible, you should attempt to determine the relative roles and importance of key public figures and public opinion in particular decision-making processes, as well as the role of the media and interest groups in influencing them. Efforts to affect decision-making processes outside formal government channels can range from petitioning to use of the press (talk radio, op-eds, press releases) to direct involvement in national advocacy efforts or political campaigns.

To learn about the policy-making and political processes that will affect your organization you should explore four areas: (1) oversight authority, (2) policy review processes, (3) politics and the back room, and (4) public discourse and debate.

Oversight Authority

Nonprofit organizations usually fall within the jurisdiction of several government agencies and legislative authorities. These entities will define the procedures an organization is required to fulfill to meet its obligations to the government. In addition, they provide the official venues through which the organization reports to the public. Typically, organizations will interact with both legislative and executive authorities. On the level of local government, organizations will interact with the mayor's office, city council, county board, school board, board of commissioners, citizen advisory boards, and local departments and agencies. In the state government, nonprofits will deal with the governor's office, legislative leaders, legislative committees, state departments and agencies, and state commissions and oversight boards. And in the federal government, nonprofits will interact with members of Congress (especially those representing the local district); key congressional committees; and federal departments, agencies, and commissions.

Learning the identities, functions, and norms of public entities responsible for an organization's oversight is the first step in understanding the formal public decision-making process. However, over time, nonprofits are likely to interact on a variety of issues with many public officials and organizations, not just those who oversee their contractual obligations, funding, or core mission concerns. Thus, nonprofit managers should attempt to be informed about the full range of political issues and the policymakers in their communities.

Policy Review Processes

Oversight and policy development usually involve a review process consisting of activities such as public hearings; submission and consideration of industry testimony, budget requests, or annual reports; and meetings among public officials, agency staff, and contractors. Consideration of new policies, regulations, and bills typically follows a formal procedure that includes opportunities for public comment. Examples of public policy review processes in which nonprofits might wish to (or, in some cases, be required to) participate include

- public hearings pertaining to the organization's mission or interests
- administrative proceedings of oversight agencies

- solicitations of public comments on proposed rules and regulations (such as notices of proposed rule-making in the *Federal Register*)
- government–industry roundtable discussions of new policies or legislation.

Nonprofit managers should be certain they are informed about and prepared to respond on key issues at each point of the formal policy process. Schedules and announcements of these events are usually made available to the public. Responses and presentations at public events should be carefully prepared both to meet the expectations of public officials and to take advantage of opportunities to present information about the organization to the public in a positive light.

Politics and the Back Room

Once you are familiar with the formal public decision-making processes pertaining to your organization and the individuals, organizations, and groups involved, you must learn the inside game that is often played in negotiating public policies. For example, it may be crucial to know that certain members of a legislative committee, such as the chair, wield the most power; that some agencies are more effective than others in obtaining resources from elected officials; and that certain personal relationships among legislators tend to yield unexpected outcomes. Additional considerations, such as election schedules, campaign commitments, demands on politicians from their constituents, and the internal politics of institutions—factors that do not derive from policy considerations—can also affect outcomes.

One aspect of advocacy that can be particularly challenging is accurately identifying which individual or group in the policy mix is most likely to determine the outcome of a particular issue. This uncertainty can make it difficult to prepare an effective advocacy strategy. Gaining the necessary insights often requires participation in the political process over a period of time. However, the following are good questions for you to ask at the outset:

- Which government entity or entities typically exerts the most significant influence on the policy process?
- Who within the organization actually makes decisions (elected officials, staff, others)?
- What are the norms and protocols for interacting with these individuals outside formal public venues?
- When are key decisions made and, if multiple interests are involved, what is the internal review process?
- What internal relationships (oppositions and alliances) exist that may affect the positions taken by key individuals?

With some of this information in hand, you can begin to communicate with decision makers directly or help foster relationships between members of your organization and key decision makers. If direct contact with key decision makers is not possible, you or other members of your organization may be able to work with allies, coalitions, or other surrogates to represent your interests. Frequently, it is the responsibility of the executive director of an organization to provide advocacy leadership by personally participating in the political process (Menefee, 1997):

> Executive directors are highly active in building and using support networks that will provide fiscal, legislative, and community support for their agencies. They cultivate and nurture long-term relationships with potential funding sources, legislative committees, complementary service agencies, referral sources, and private for-profit organizations. They submerge themselves in highly political arenas to gain support and exercise influence over impending decisions that affect their agency. Executive directors work with various groups to advocate for clients, changes in policy, or specific legislation. (p. 4)

Finally, you and your colleagues can gain much information about the political climate simply by paying attention to the political events taking place in the community when an issue is being debated. In addition to traditional media, Internet resources are now available that can enable you to obtain not only background information and policy analyses of issues, but also political analyses (see Attachment 7-1 for a list of the Web sites).

Public Discourse and Debate

Just as advocates sometimes have difficulty identifying the key public decision makers on particular issues, they may struggle to determine the role of public opinion in the policy decision-making process. Consider these questions about the role of public opinion:

- Is the public generally informed about a particular issue? If so, is the public concerned?
- Are members of the public likely to hold their elected officials accountable for decisions on the issue by taking political action?
- What evidence is available that public opinion has been used as leverage on similar issues?
- What role do the media play in shaping public opinion and influencing the actions of public officials?

If public opinion matters, then communications and media relations are likely to be important. If, on the other hand, the public is relatively uninformed or uninterested in an issue, managers must decide whether to attempt to educate the public or to deal directly with legislators and inside players. These are crucial determinants of advocacy strategy.

It is usually not difficult to identify high-profile issues in which public opinion is a major factor in national debate. Controversial issues, such as abortion rights, welfare reform, or school prayer, have been debated in the public

"We could obliterate homelessness with just what it costs to retain good public rela-
tions and lobbying counsel. Of course, dropping them would mean not getting invited
to any more Capitol Hill parties."

arena for many years, and it is generally safe to assume that both members of
the public and elected officials have opinions on such matters. These positions
can often be learned through news coverage, opinion polls, and information
disseminated by public interest groups. Controversy can be valuable in advocacy, because it tends to generate news coverage. However, there is no guarantee that such coverage will be positive, and controversial issues tend to be
cast in emotional terms that make it harder to build a case based on facts.
Thus, such issues should always be handled carefully. With new or untested
issues, however, there may be no means of judging how the public will react.
Use the following preliminary questions to assess the role of public opinion
in debates on particular issues:

• Has the public shown an interest in similar issues in the past? Are opinion
  polls available? If so, what are the prevailing public opinions?

- Have any public interest, political action, or other citizen groups been formed that are concerned with these issues?
- Historically, how responsive have elected officials been to public opinion on such matters?
- Have similar issues been the source of debate in any recent elections?
- Does the community tend to participate in political debate? If so, on what issues?

If public opinion is well formed or seems likely to affect the policy-making process, other issues to consider are the role of the media and your organization's capacity to use the media to influence public opinion. The following are some key questions you will want to explore:

- Do the news media regularly report on similar issues? If so, how? What does this suggest about their interest and orientation on the issue?
- Are there examples of media impact on similar issues (such as investigative reporting or editorials directed at elected officials on similar issues)?
- What resources does the organization have available for media communications? Is this an area of strength?
- Does the organization have an existing relationship with members of the media? Is it a positive one?

Public discourse and debate can inform and influence the actions of elected officials outside officially established government structures. In many instances, nonprofits may be able to exert political influence on decision makers through the actions of their members, through public education and advocacy campaigns, or through direct political action that is intended to influence the outcome of elections. Small, grassroots organizations may wish to undertake activities such as soliciting signatures for petitions or enlisting constituents to make public appearances to advocate positions on behalf of the organization. Other approaches include writing letters, running newspaper ads, submitting opinion pieces to newspapers, and coordinating grassroots campaign support for candidates (but keep in mind that there are restrictions on participation in partisan campaigns by nonprofits). In deciding how to influence public officials, nonprofits should consider not only their own capacity to conduct these activities, but also the political consequences of doing so.

The increasing availability of communications technology may lead nonprofits to increase advocacy efforts via electronic media. However, bringing issues into the public realm can sometimes have considerable drawbacks. What might be accomplished easily through an informal political contact by one of your organization's board members could be far more difficult to achieve through a public relations campaign and could actually be harmful to your organization's long-term interests because it might put an otherwise supportive elected official in an awkward position. Because most organizations have lasting relationships with public officials, public confrontations are likely to cause effects that go beyond the issue of the day. Thus, you and other members of your management team should carefully consider the advantages and risks of initiating public information campaigns, debates with elected officials, and media coverage on issues as you develop advocacy strategies.

Study the Public Players

Learn the identities, positions, and capabilities of key decision makers and public groups with interests common to or opposing those of your organization. Because the interests and positions of key public officials are major determinants of policy and political decision making, you should gather general background information about decision makers, as well as factors that are likely to influence their positions such as concurrent public debates, their previous votes, their constituencies, and the identity of campaign contributors. If possible, obtain this information for each individual within the body that controls the decision-making process.

Public interest groups and organizations and coalitions with similar or opposing interests are another important constituency in the public arena. In general, policy debates evolve over a period of time with input from a variety of groups. Understanding the role that other organizations play in the political process can help you anticipate and interpret events and identify potential allies as they attempt to influence policy debates.

The Decision Makers

In researching decision makers involved in particular issues, you may want to start with known quantities, such as governing bodies that typically review your organization's activities or budget. If a relationship already exists between a government official and your organization, it may be relatively simple to assess such factors as the official's positions on various policies and his or her general level of support of your organization and its mission. However, before deciding whether to request the official's political support on specific matters, you might also wish to research these additional factors:

- What are the official's political ambitions, and what is his or her political affiliation and role within the political party? How might these factors influence the official's public stances?
- Who are the official's constituents (including political donors), and how would their interests be affected by proposed policies or issues under consideration?

- What is the official's voting record on similar measures?
- What other responsibilities or political factors, such as sitting on multiple committees within a legislature, might influence the official's position?

When public officials involved are unknown to you and your organization, further research is required, and the role of personal networks becomes paramount. Before preparing to approach unfamiliar individuals, you will want to learn about their reputations and modes of public interaction by asking the following questions:

- Does the official make time to meet with public groups? If so, does he or she prefer to be approached directly, through staff, or through surrogates?
- Is the official likely to request a campaign contribution? Is this problematic? Keep in mind legal restrictions and other constraints.
- Is the official well-informed, interested, or generally sympathetic to the type of work performed by your organization?
- What are the other key issues with which the official is publicly associated? How do they relate to the ones at hand?

In conducting background research on a public official, it is important to evaluate his or her relative impact and effectiveness. A politician with a powerful title might fail to deliver on a political objective if he or she is not in good standing within his or her party, whereas little-known legislators may wield considerable influence if they are expected to cast the swing vote on a contentious issue. It is also important not to focus solely on the majority party or the most powerful figures in a decision-making body, because many issues are not determined along strict party lines, and back room negotiations can lead to unexpected outcomes. Thus, research should focus on determining not only the positions and interests of individual officials, but also whether and how they can be expected to influence the votes of their colleagues on key issues.

Although it is natural to focus first on potential allies and supporters in the political process, advocacy also requires contact with officials who are opposed to the interests of your organization. You should research the public record, constituencies, and backgrounds of officials expected to oppose your organization's position just as you would research your likely supporters. You should also consider these issues:

- How effective are the officials likely to oppose an issue, versus those who may support it?
- What public groups are likely to support the opposition's stand?
- Might opponents take retaliatory measures against your organization, either on the issue at hand or in other ways?

- How committed are opponents to their positions? Does it appear possible to achieve a closer alignment of their positions with those of your organization?

Information resources can be useful in learning about the public record, but perhaps the best means of learning about public figures is through personal networking. Staff, board members, and colleagues within and outside your organization can usually help shed light on the reputations, personalities, and political interests of government officials. Lateral contacts, such as government program officers, legislative staff, or others who interact regularly with your organization, can offer useful insights about the leaders of their organizations and how they are likely to respond to certain ideas.

Other Public Players

It is necessary to identify coalitions and organizations with similar or opposing interests, both as a general practice and in the context of lobbying specific issues. Often, industry groups will be involved and can be counted as allies when advocacy issues arise. This may not always be the case, however, because the interests of specific organizations will vary from issue to issue.

In general, one might expect organizations in the same sector to take similar positions on legislation. However, the provisions of individual legislative proposals can sometimes divide a community, such as when resources must be split among organizations. Moreover, specific proposals can sometimes generate unusual coalitions. Groups that might normally oppose one another may learn that their interests are temporarily in alignment and join forces in a coalition to defeat a particular bill or advocate specific political positions. Thus, it is important to research the profiles and positions of groups in each public debate in which your organization is involved.

You also should make informed judgments about your strategic alliances in advocacy. In some instances, participation in coalitions may enable your organization to help promote stronger measures (Alexander, 1991), whereas in others your positions may be watered down by the need to meet multiple interests. When joining forces with another organization or entering a coalition, you should assess the reliability, public legitimacy, and public interests of the organization; the political influence, access, and sophistication of the organization; and the extent to which the organization's interests and expectations are aligned with yours.

Just as you should research your opposition within decision-making bodies, you must identify organizations and groups that are likely to oppose measures supported by your organization, or to promote alternatives that are objectionable. Although the existence of opponents should not deter organizations from advocating their interests, the strength and resources of the opposition should help guide decisions about selecting battles to be fought and may suggest the chances of prevailing in the political process. Use the following questions to assess opposition groups:

- What are the interests of opposing groups, and who are their supporters and constituents?
- How well-known, politically connected, and respected are opposition groups?
- What kinds of tactics are these groups likely to use? Could these pose long-term threats to the organization beyond the outcome of the debate on one issue?
- How committed are these groups to their positions? Is it possible to achieve a closer alignment of their positions and those of the organization?

Although it is not always possible to know about the existence and behavior of opposing groups at the beginning of an advocacy effort, you can monitor the political process to identify such groups through the media, the public records of events (hearings and testimony), and personal networking. The more information that is available in advance about potential opposition, the better you can plan your advocacy strategies.

Study the Industry Players

Learn the identities, positions, and capabilities of other organizations in the same industry (including similar organizations, coalitions, and opponents). Public issues do not arise in a vacuum, and nonprofit managers will rarely find themselves to be the sole advocates or opponents of any particular issue. Large-scale national issues such as welfare reform, gun control, or school vouchers evolve over many years and involve literally hundreds of organizations. Even local issues, such as zoning laws, county budget expenditures, or environmental disputes, can be complex and are likely to involve multiple organizations or coalitions. In many cases, organizations join together to advocate a position or hire an individual or organization to coordinate their advocacy efforts.

Even more important than understanding the perceptions of a particular organization or its public policy concerns is your ability to understand the industry in which your organization operates. Some managers may be uncomfortable with the use of the word "industry" to refer collectively to the entire range of organizations engaged in providing similar services or pursuing related objectives. Yet it is in this context, whether the word is used or not, that policymakers may be best able to understand the capabilities and needs of individual organizations. This is especially true for political officials asked to consider requests by organizations not located in their own districts: They are most likely to try to compare the requesting organization with similar entities in their own districts.

The skills involved in understanding your own organization as part of an industry are primarily those of envisioning and environmental scanning. You will find it useful to consider the following aspects of an issue or situation to know how important it is to position your organization in the context of its industry:

- How broad is the impact of the issue among similar organizations or client groups? Is it more understandable when presented as affecting many groups?
- Although the issue may be crucial to your own organization, does it have enough scale independent of its impact on other groups to capture the attention of policymakers whose actions are needed to address it?
- Will presenting an issue on behalf of a large group of organizations reduce the likelihood that opponents will blame the problem on the performance of one organization?
- Are there jurisdictional aspects to the issue, or to its legislative solution, that are more easily managed by involving organizations from several regions?

There are other situations when it is impossible or impractical to pursue any version of an industry-based approach to a public policy issue. The affected groups may be unwilling to cooperate in this fashion, for example, or the affected programs may be small components of larger organizations that are otherwise very dissimilar or even antagonistic. In this case, an alternative strategy is the coalition—a collaborative effort among organizations or groups that may have little in common other than their shared position on a particular set of issues. Observers of European governments will be familiar with the coalition style, because it has produced some of the most stable, yet flexible, political leadership for these nations. Within the United States, coalitions have occasionally been formed by disparate groups to accomplish shared objectives, as shown in the following news report ("Groups Unite," 1995):

Groups Unite to Slash Wasteful Spending

In February 1995, an unusual coalition of taxpayer and environmentalist groups released *The Green Scissors Report*, which recommends cutting $33 billion in wasteful and environmentally harmful federal spending and subsidies. The 34 programs targeted by the report include water projects, highways, energy R&D, public land subsidies, foreign aid projects, agriculture programs and federal flood and disaster insurance. The report cites the price tag for each program and describes the environmental damage.

Led by the National Taxpayers Union Foundation (NTUF) and Friends of the Earth (FOE), the Green Scissors campaign involves more than 20 other progressive and conservative organizations. The activists are launching a year-long campaign to carry out the report's recommendations. NTUF was founded in

1977 and works to cut federal spending and taxes. Founded in 1969, FOE works to protect the environment and has affiliates in 52 countries. Both NTUF and FOE are membership organizations headquartered in Washington, D.C. (p. 50)

As may be assumed from this example, coalitions often have short lives. Whitaker (1982) offered this observation:

> It is possible to imagine a permanent coalition, but few social action coalitions last longer than a year or two without transformation into organizations with a life of their own; they then cease to operate as genuine coalitions of independent organizations. The relatively brief duration of social action coalitions reflects their typical creation for single-issue campaigns that are won or lost in limited periods of time. (p. 146).

As a manager, you should prepare yourself for public policy situations in which industry-based approaches or coalitions are appropriate by becoming familiar with the positions of the organizations within your industry. In the research stage, learn the positions of other groups. Keeping an open mind is crucial, particularly at the beginning, because other organizations may have interpreted an issue quite differently. Assess the ability of other groups to make an impact on an issue. But guard against elitism in making this assessment: The largest and most successful organizations in an industry group may not be the most credible in presenting an issue to policymakers. Then identify existing and emerging coalitions and their positions. Compare them with those of your own organization. When positions are aligned, use coalitions and partnerships with other organizations. This can reduce expenditures of time and resources and can lead to more effective interactions with policymakers.

PUBLIC ADVOCACY

The best way to prepare your organization for effective advocacy is to ensure that its public interests and objectives are well-defined and that its management is well-informed about the political environment. After following the steps described above, you should have a well-developed understanding of your organization's public interests, as well as the public issues, political context, and policy processes that can affect them. The following road map suggests how to use this information to develop and use advocacy strategies.

Carpe Diem: Seize Opportunities

Be on the lookout for opportunities to affect public policy favorably or to defend the organization's interests when necessary. Develop criteria to decide when advocacy is necessary or desirable. New developments in public policy often occur rapidly, and your organization must be prepared to mobilize when issues arise that are important to it. Your nonprofit organization may also wish to initiate public policy proposals of its own. Information resources and analytical capabilities should be used not only to put issues in historical context, but also to examine current events and evolving public debates. This information can help you and other members of your management team respond quickly to the current political environment and also anticipate future trends and formulate new policy initiatives if necessary (Menefee, 1997).

Nonprofit managers, board members, and staff must watch for opportunities to advance the interests of their organizations. However, it is equally important to determine whether advocacy efforts are necessary or appropriate on a particular issue. Not all public debates lend themselves to an organization's involvement, and in some cases participating in an unsuccessful advocacy effort can be counterproductive for your organization.

The impetus for an organization to engage in advocacy can arise in a variety of ways: through the regular policy review process, through public events and community activities, or through changes in the political landscape that either enable an organization to take new positions or force it to take defensive action. To be aware of these opportunities, you should use your information resources and personal networks to stay informed about the general political climate, to learn about specific new proposals that could affect your organization, to monitor the actions of government agencies that affect your constituents or clients, and to anticipate or follow the actions of other groups involved in the political system.

Advocacy opportunities that are sometimes overlooked occur in the context of regular policy review processes. Preparing reports, testimony, and presentations can involve considerable paperwork and seem tedious to managers. On the other hand, public hearings provide a free and valuable means of portraying your organization's work to decision makers and the public. Informal interactions with public officials can also be effective. For example, after a series of hearings on domestic violence and child abuse, nonprofit organizations operating safe houses for a county might invite members of the county board and their staff to visit their facilities. Such visits can allow officials to ask questions in an informal setting and to see the results of funding decisions from a human perspective. In addition, they enable the organization to thank officials for their interest and to educate them about public needs and challenges associated with the organization's work.

In areas of nonprofit operations in which the public may have a particularly active interest, such as health care, education, community services, and crime prevention, organizations can educate the public by making public service announcements, participating in public events such as state or county fairs, and displaying information in public buildings such as libraries.

In some cases, advocacy objectives may coincide with your organization's fundraising and community relations activities. For example, major charitable events or benefits can provide an excellent opportunity to recruit supporters and to improve your organization's name recognition within a community. Such events can also enable your organization to engender goodwill by inviting volunteers, community leaders, and government officials. Although such methods are not a means of directly influencing votes or legislative actions, they can contribute to public appreciation of your organization, its activities, and policy issues, which can indirectly affect public policies (Edwards, Benefield, Edwards, & Yankey, 1997; see also chapter 4).

External factors that might suggest the need for advocacy include legislative proposals or administrative reforms that would affect your organization's funding, operations, or the interests of your client base, or an election that changes the political orientation of key decision-making bodies. For example, if key members of a predominantly liberal state legislature were replaced by fiscal conservatives who ran on a platform of cutting government spending, nonprofit organizations that receive public funds might expect to see an adverse shift in the political climate. In anticipation of this, they might prepare to defend their publicly funded programs by forming coalitions to oppose spending cuts.

Finally, advocacy does not have to be a purely reactive process. Although nonprofits face many serious challenges and frequently have limited staff and resources, you should be prepared to use the political process to promote new initiatives when appropriate. Nonprofit organizations, particularly those that carry out public functions, often have the firsthand knowledge that legislators need to make informed public policy decisions. This knowledge can be used by nonprofits to promote new or creative approaches to program implementation or policy reforms.

The nature and importance of advocacy will vary considerably among nonprofit organizations according to factors such as size, resources, public interest, and the policy and political systems in which they operate. Thus, various organizations will base their advocacy decisions on different considerations. Organizations sometimes have no choice but to defend their interests or account for their actions to public officials. In these cases, managers may have little room to develop strategies or evaluate their options. When advocacy is pursued as an elective strategy, however, your organization should follow certain criteria to determine whether it is appropriate, especially when an advocacy campaign will require significant resources or is likely to draw public attention. These criteria should also inform strategic questions that must be addressed in developing your advocacy action plan. Individual organizations will want to develop their own questions, but generally you will want to address these four key questions before you attempt to influence policy: (1) What are your organization's interests? (2) What is your organization's capacity to influence the process? (3) What are the potential benefits of advocacy? and (4) What are the risks and potential drawbacks?

Generally speaking, your organization's board members are responsible for making final determinations about the organization's public interests, whereas managers are responsible for helping the board make informed decisions and implementing related programs. Defining your organization's interests can be a relatively simple exercise when there is an internal consensus about the importance of the issue at hand and its relevance to your organization, when the consequences of possible outcomes can be predicted, and when the possible outcomes affect the various parts of your organization and its membership in the same ways.

However, nonprofit organizations rarely have the luxury of making decisions under such conditions. More often, crafting a public position involves making tough choices about how to manage competing values and priorities within an organization, particularly within large organizations with different regions or chapters to satisfy. This can be complicated when the implications of a particular policy are unclear or when a policy could affect various parts of an organization's membership differently. Obtaining accurate information about the issue at hand, the political factors driving it, and other supporting analyses can make this process easier. Managers can help their boards define the organization's interests by consulting with members, clients, and constituents and by conducting consensus-building activities such as internal and external focus group sessions.

Once the interests of your organization have been defined, it is equally important to assess its capacity to influence the decision-making process. Not all advocacy strategies require large budgets and highly paid lobbyists, and you should not be deterred from participating in the political process even if you have limited resources. On the other hand, many factors can limit the ability of an organization to influence public debate or the outcome of issues, and these should be assessed realistically. Before committing to a particular advocacy effort, you should address these critical questions:

- What is the political climate among the general public, decision makers, and other public groups? How powerful are your organization's allies and opponents?
- What resources are available for the effort, both internally (research capability, staff, funding) and externally (organizational allies, coalitions, public interest groups)?

- How strong are your organization's political connections? Historically, how successful have your organization and others like it been at influencing the relevant decision–making process?
- What does your organization have to offer that will enhance efforts already underway to influence the desired policy outcome? How experienced is your organization at operating in venues such as media relations?
- Does your entire organization (staff, management, board members) back the effort, and will they lend their support?

Finally, the potential benefits and drawbacks to a particular advocacy effort should be examined within the context of the long- and short-term interests of your organization.

- What do your organization and its membership stand to gain or lose as a result of the outcome of the issue under consideration? What does this suggest about the level of time, energy, and resources to devote to the effort?
- To what extent might the effort divert needed resources and organizational energy from other areas? Is this acceptable?
- What are the possible drawbacks to entering public debate? Are there long-term repercussions that should be considered, such as political tension with particular groups and decision makers?
- Are there alternatives to the political process for achieving desired objectives?
- Can the probable outcome of the issue be estimated? What are the chances that results will be negative? What does this suggest about the need to act?
- Overall, how likely is your organization to prevail in the political process, given the factors discussed in this section?

Develop an Advocacy Strategy

When an opportunity or need for advocacy arises, develop a strategy with specific goals and milestones, one that maximizes current resources and defines a clear role for your organization. Once your organization has identified an advocacy need or opportunity that satisfies the appropriate criteria, the next step is to develop a strategy. In doing so, you should use the tools, resources, and information obtained through the information-gathering and analytical processes already described. The strategy should include advocacy objectives, an action plan, and milestones and midcourse corrections.

Advocacy Objectives

Establishing advocacy objectives is an extension of identifying advocacy opportunities and needs. The overall goals for the advocacy process must flow logically from your organization's interests. However, in defining what your organization should try to achieve through advocacy, you and other members of your management team must be careful not to engage in wishful thinking that links your organization's interests and ambitions to impossible outcomes. Setting realistic objectives for a particular advocacy effort can be complex given the number of variables influencing policy processes and the effort generally required to achieve an internal consensus on organizational positions. Richan (1996) proposed two rules to aid in this effort: (1) decide between incremental and fundamental change goals and (2) establish clear priorities and develop backup positions.

The first rule, deciding between incremental and fundamental change, is important because public debates often focus not on whether a policy should be altered, but rather on the extent to which change is required. In establishing your organization's position, you should help your board assess whether the current political climate allows for proposals for long-term or fundamental changes. Deciding on a strategy in this area can also be made on a strategic basis. For example, when organizations are fighting undesirable proposals and prefer the status quo, they may advocate incremental change measures as alternative political solutions.

In general, advocacy efforts involve many dimensions and multiple objectives. Except in the most unusual circumstances, organizations should not count on being able to achieve all of their objectives. The nature of the political process demands that participants engage in debate, negotiation, and compromise. Nonprofit organizations should have an internal list of priorities when entering the advocacy process so that staff, management, and trustees can work in concert toward common objectives. Your organization's list should rank the importance of each objective, on both a long- and short-term basis, in terms of the most vital gains to be made or interests to be protected.

Developing such a list can be useful not only for building and maintaining consensus, but also in maneuvering in the political process. For example, political figures sometimes insist that an organization define its top priorities before they will lend their support or negotiate compromises. Having a list of priorities provides organizational representatives with a basis for dealing with such requests and engaging in negotiations when necessary. In addition, a priorities list can help managers and their advocacy teams develop backup positions and strategies if their initial efforts are unsuccessful.

It is worth noting that prioritizing has taken on significant negative connotations since the 1980s, when it was a tactic used occasionally by both public and private funding sources to structure discussions in which requesting organizations were destined to receive less support than they sought. You may find colleagues unwilling to go through the exercise of identifying and ranking priorities, even for strictly internal use, because they fear that outside groups will use such information to justify removing funds for anything but the top few items.

There is no question that an organization that dares to rank any of its activities as other than its highest priority faces certain risks, but it is just as true that no organization can honestly state that every activity is as important as all the others. The burden is on the organization to foster a level of understanding among its constituents that supports rational discussion, one that recognizes the difference between urgency and importance and does not misuse candid communication by turning it against the organization.

Action Plan

Your advocacy strategy should define the specific steps your organization intends to take to achieve its objectives. These steps should be laid out clearly in an action plan that accounts for your organization's capacity to effect change (see Figure 7-1). This assessment should be based on the political climate as well as factors such as your organization's financial and human resources and the strength of its political allies and opponents. The elements of your action plan should also account for relevant political norms and procedures. If an issue requires advocacy within an unfamiliar government body, it is important to check with others outside your organization who may be able to provide insights about the process or the officials involved. Such information should help suggest the most appropriate and effective tactics.

Your action plan should define specific roles for individuals and groups, usually both within and outside your organization. Internally, you should assign advocacy responsibilities to particular staff or yourself and ensure that the efforts will be well-coordinated, particularly when public statements or actions are concerned. This assignment of responsibility can be significant for a variety of reasons, including the respect that may be accorded to managers who are viewed as effective external advocates for the organization's interests and who demonstrate good boundary-spanning skills (Edwards & Austin, 1991; see also chapter 1).

If in-house managers or existing resources are insufficient to meet advocacy needs, professional lobbyists can be hired to strengthen your organization's capacity to influence the policy process. Hiring a professional lobbyist eliminates the problems associated with diverting managers' organizational energy from their regular functions. This may be particularly important in service delivery organizations. In addition, a professional would also offer immediate access to behind-the-scenes information, as well as political access, and eliminates the investments needed to build up internal advocacy capacities. This is particularly relevant when an organization with little political experience conducts what it expects to be a one-time advocacy campaign. However, such services can be costly, and paid professionals may not be viewed as having equal legitimacy with the members, staff, trustees, or management of the organization itself. Officials may give less weight to a message if they believe the source

Figure 7-1. Sample Action Plan

Issue and Interests
- A nonprofit community theater receives a major share of its funding from the local county government. A new member of the county board makes a specific proposal at a public hearing to cut arts funding by one-half to finance public education programs. Internal county budgetary decisions are due to be made within four weeks.

Objectives
- Prevent severe funding cuts that will threaten the existence of the organization.
- Maintain good relations with the county board, including the new member proposing spending cuts, and the education community.

Actions
- Work through a coalition of nonprofit arts groups to develop a statement for the county board on the importance of the arts in the community.
- Set up meetings between board members of the organization and the new county board member, as well as potential arts advocates on the county board.
- Work with the public arts funding agency to influence the decision-making process. Offer to provide support to agency staff who also are opposed to cuts.
- Show that arts programs benefit children. Identify teachers or individuals representing educational interests willing to oppose funding cuts to the county arts program.

Roles
- Executive director leads the nonprofit arts coalition effort, including planning meetings, distributing materials, and drafting and achieving consensus on the statement.
- Staff write materials, gather information, and coordinate with arts agency staff.
- Board president sets up county board meetings to oppose cuts and identify possible supporters.

Milestone
- Budgetary hearing scheduled for two weeks after hearing where initial proposal was made. See if new board member continues to advocate same position or if other board members offer public opposition. Revise strategy if necessary.

Corrections
- Research reveals many arts–education links in the community. Place an op-ed editorial piece signed by arts organizations and a teacher's union in the local newspaper.
- Agency arts staff do not appear to be making headway; focus solely on direct meetings with county board members, emphasizing link between arts and education.
- A strong advocate has been identified on the county board. Provide as much direct assistance to her and her staff as possible.

Result
- An alternative measure is passed specifying that 10 percent of the agency's budget must be restricted to support student programs. The theater company's overall operation will be minimally affected.

is merely a hired gun. In making a decision about whether to hire a lobbyist, managers should ask themselves the following questions (Brown, 1991):

- Does the lobbyist understand your issues? Does he or she have access to the right political leaders? How is he or she regarded by officials who will be lobbied?
- Is he or she experienced in working on your issues? What is his or her track record, and have other organizations been satisfied with his or her work?

- Does he or she have a political affiliation? What other organizations does he or she represent, and how might this reflect on your organization?

The roles of individuals and groups outside the organization may be less defined than those of organizational staff, but it is important to incorporate them into an action plan, particularly when coalitions and other industry organizations are involved. Preliminary meetings with organizational allies should establish roles for each organization as well as expectations for how political coordination will occur. You should discuss the common interests and priorities of the group (or affiliated organizations); which organizations or individuals will lead the advocacy effort; who will serve as the public representative of the group; when and how communication will take place; and what level of resources each organization and coalition member will devote to the effort.

When possible, action plans should consider potential roles for government officials (Smucker, 1991). Although it may not be possible to obtain up-front commitments for political support, organizations can target key public officials or staff to help promote certain positions with their colleagues. This approach to lobbying may be less time consuming, less risky, and more effective than other methods. However, in your role as an advocate for your organization's interests, you should not rely solely on public officials to represent your interests, because monitoring inside developments may be very difficult, and unforeseen political factors may cause even sympathetic elected officials to change their positions.

Milestones and Midcourse Corrections

Finally, an action plan should contain milestones and measures of success to guide implementation of the strategy. You can use these elements of the plan to help determine when changes are needed or at what point advocacy efforts should stop. If advocacy has been successful, your organization may choose to end its efforts or to expand its initial objectives to reflect more favorable political conditions. If, on the other hand, your advocacy objectives are not being met, you may wish to reassess key elements of the strategy and consider midcourse corrections by asking these questions:

- Have sufficient resources been devoted to the action plan? If not, are more available, and how should they be used?
- Has the political environment, including the actions or effectiveness of the opposition, changed? Should current objectives be revised to account for this?
- Have certain tactics failed? Is a different strategic approach necessary? For example, should you use a grassroots campaign as opposed to managerial lobbying of decision makers?

- Are staff and other members of your organization carrying out their responsibilities as expected? Should current roles be reassigned?
- Are external groups carrying out their responsibilities as expected? Should your organization alter its participation in current coalitions or alliances?
- Should your organization revise its objectives to achieve less ambitious results? If so, what should the alternative proposal be? Is the initial backup plan still the best alternative?

Engage in the Political Process

Once you have gathered information through your research activities and have developed an understanding of the political process, individual decision makers, and industry players, you should be well-prepared to engage in the political process. Active advocacy involves at least three steps: (1) recruit supporters, (2) lobby for the organization's positions, and (3) monitor and stay involved in the debate.

Recruit Supporters

Part of defining an action plan is identifying organizations with common interests, cultivating relationships with them, and agreeing on a coordinated approach. However, efforts to recruit supporters should extend even further. Your organization should target public figures and groups, as well as individual decision makers, to support its lobbying efforts. In the Sample Action Plan (Figure 7-1), a community of nonprofit organizations (the arts) reached out to another community (education) that shared at least some of its interests. Although educators might have supported increasing school funding, they also agreed that slashing the county arts budget would be a divisive and untenable means of achieving that end. Convincing nonaffiliated groups to endorse an organization's position can be effective, particularly when the surrogates chosen can lend their legitimacy, credibility, or objectivity to the debate.

A good way to bring others into advocacy efforts is to seek their input in developing advocacy positions. Although it is not always necessary to involve outsiders in the early stages of planning, it is often valuable to circulate proposals outside your organization for comment and endorsement before they are made public. This process can create a sense of ownership among others for the proposal, potentially motivating them to support the cause, and can help you make adjustments that are likely to strengthen support for the measure. Moreover, such a review process adds different perspectives on the issue and can generate new ideas and help avert mistakes by identifying unanticipated problems with the planned advocacy approach. Sharing proposals with certain groups outside your organization's industry can also help you assess how the proposal might be received by the general public.

Beyond reaching out to public groups and supporters, you may also wish to consider sharing your proposals with certain policymakers before taking a public position. For example, you might ask trusted public officials and their staffs to provide private feedback on a preliminary draft position statement by answering these questions:

- What are the strengths and weaknesses of the position? Would you be willing to publicly endorse it or advocate it among your colleagues? If not, what modifications would you wish to see in order to do so?
- How are other members of the policy-making body likely to react to the position? How could it be made more politically palatable?
- What other issues could potentially affect the outcome of this issue (for example, alternative proposals or unrelated politically charged disputes)?
- What strategies are most likely to succeed in lobbying for this position? (This can be a particularly important question to ask staff, who may be able to provide unique insights about the preferences of the governing body as well as the interests of the officials for whom they work.)

Lobby for the Organization's Positions

Choosing the appropriate methods of lobbying can be difficult, particularly when an organization is doing so for the first time. Although the terms "advocacy" and "lobbying" may seem interchangeable, we use "lobbying" to refer to the specific context of communicating with decision makers to influence their positions.

There are many ways to lobby an issue, including coordinating grassroots campaigns, using the media to send a public message, and using informal networks to participate in the inside game of policy negotiations. Perhaps the most direct means of lobbying, however, is to meet or present information to decision makers and their staffs. The norms of the political system and the preferences of influential public officials should inform strategic decisions about the timing of lobbying meetings, the appropriate participants, and meeting objectives. There are several guiding principles you may wish to consider when lobbying public officials.

When preparing for meetings or presenting materials, you should focus on providing information that is appropriate for the intended audiences. One way to ensure this is to learn in advance the extent to which the individual or group is already informed about the issue. The concerns of public officials often hinge on many factors other than the direct implications of a policy decision for one group. So you should remember that your organization and its views are not necessarily the policymaker's main concern. Anticipating how public officials see their responsibilities and the demands of their constituencies can help you prepare good responses for the questions they are likely to ask.

Although it is easy to assume that decision makers will not appreciate being asked for favors, it is often best to be direct in making lobbying requests. Most officials and their staffs are extremely busy and will not have time to read or listen to an extensive background report on an issue. Meetings may be extremely short, and it is important not to waste time discussing tangential matters. In a lobbying meeting, you should inform the official about the issue under consideration by providing a brief and concise analysis. Then present your organization's proposal, explain why it will result in the best outcomes, and offer to answer questions. If the proposal is favorably received, you should make a specific request for endorsement or support, making clear exactly what actions you would like the official to take to affect the outcome of the issue.

When making a request for legislative assistance, it may be wise to offer support to policymakers. For example, public officials and their staffs frequently lack the time and resources to conduct their own research and monitoring activities. Even keeping track of press accounts or internal developments within the decision-making body itself can be time consuming. Supplying useful and reliable information is often an invaluable service that lobbyists provide to public officials. Your organization's advocates should focus on providing the type of information requested by officials and their staff, not merely persuasive materials designed to help build a case. To maintain credibility and trust, it is crucial that information given to policymakers and their staff is accurate.

This points to another crucial point: Never underestimate the role of staff. Although elected and appointed officials are officially responsible for making policy decisions, their staff members often make key determinations that influence the officials' behavior and decisions. Government staff serve important functions, such as presenting information from outside groups, setting priorities for meeting schedules, and making recommendations on policy decisions and political responses. Staff also tend to engage in strategic networking and may have access to considerable information about the inner workings of their institutions. In some cases, actual decisions may be made by staff and merely executed or voiced by public officials.

Although it is often necessary and desirable to meet with elected officials personally, when the objective is to gather inside information rather than to make a request or when an official is uninterested in an issue and may want a staff recommendation before granting a meeting request, you and others advocating for your organization may wish to consider meeting with staff.

Monitor and Stay Involved in the Debate

Once an organization has begun its advocacy efforts, its managers must remain engaged in the political process. Although initial indications may suggest that a successful outcome is likely, the dynamics of most political processes make it difficult to predict results until final decisions are reached. New legislative proposals, backroom deals, and shifting coalitions can change a proposal's prospects overnight. You and other managers in your organization should use their information resources, media, and personal networks to keep informed about the political climate as well as specific developments that occur during the stages of the policy-making process. Milestones contained in the advocacy action plan should suggest key events to monitor.

Finally, staying involved in the process means carefully following up on advocacy activities. For example, if a public official has offered to seek support from other members of his or her committee, has he or she done so, and what were the results of that effort? If a commitment was made to provide information to an official's staff after a meeting, has it been sent, and is more needed? If a coalition member has promised to obtain certain information and report back on his or her results, has this taken place? Internally, you should confirm that your own staff members are carrying out their expected functions and assess the impact of advocacy activities on your organization. Even the activities of board members should be monitored to ensure that your organization's commitments are kept and that all elements of the advocacy strategy remain on track.

Communicate Strategically

Identify an appropriate and practical means for your organization to inform and influence the public, elected officials, and the media, whether an active advocacy campaign is underway or not. Be responsive to information requests and present information in clear and accessible formats. Your management team should be prepared to provide information (to the public, elected officials, or reporters) and to explain information clearly and concisely in the appropriate form, level of detail, and context. The experienced manager will recognize that these are virtually the same skills that he or she uses to develop and maintain effective relationships with staff, trustees, clients, and other internal constituencies. The key steps in this approach are to use media strategically, conduct outreach activities, and develop strong presentation skills.

Use Media Strategically

In the United States and most other Western nations, the press represents an independent voice in society, one that is assumed to have a degree of objectivity unattainable by virtually any other organization. For this reason alone, you should consider how to communicate with editors and reporters about the objectives of your organization's advocacy efforts (see chapter 6). Your organization can build up and refine its media relations capabilities by using these approaches (Cruz, 1997):

- *Develop contacts in the media.* An editor or reporter who already knows your organization's programs and record will be much more responsive to its advocacy.
- *Use technology.* Advanced information technology offers opportunities to get the word out at relatively low cost through faxes and e-mail. For example, building and maintaining a Web page can create a sophisticated link to a growing community of users.
- *Use news releases when needed, but sparingly.* A call or personalized note is often much more effective.
- *Communicate in a timely fashion.* Do not overburden the audience, but make sure that information is provided soon enough to take advantage of an issue's news value.
- *Be consistent and accurate.* Make sure facts are double checked before they are released. Coordinate information within your own organization and among the members of your industry or coalition.
- *Use information strategically, but never misrepresent the facts.* Do not feel obliged to state the opposition's case, but recognize that an incomplete or misleading account will eventually backfire.

Setting up a World Wide Web page can be a strategic means to reach large audiences. Numerous companies design and establish Web sites for organizations, and a variety of publications focus on how best to structure Web pages to meet your organization's objectives (Frenza & Hoffman, 1997). You may be able to locate businesses that will provide such assistance free or at low cost. The Web site can meet multiple objectives at once, such as providing up-to-date news to internal constituencies, publicizing the activities and positions of your organization, and centralizing information-gathering functions (this can be particularly helpful in large organizations with regional chapters and subgroups). By establishing links with other Web sites, publicity can be expanded even further. However, your organization should clearly define the purpose and audience of a Web site before embarking on this process, focusing primarily on content rather than form at the outset. Once established, the site should be updated frequently; a poorly maintained Web site that provides little or inaccurate information to users reflects poorly on your organization.

Conduct Outreach Activities

An organization's audience can only be as supportive as it is informed and engaged in the issues addressed in the advocacy effort. There are a variety of ways to reach audiences, both internal and external. The means chosen should reflect the importance of the issue, the role of the audience to potentially affect policy, available resources, and expected interest in the issue. Examples of outreach mechanisms frequently used by nonprofits include

- *Speakers' bureaus.* Providing an experts list to policymakers, to the media, and to the community demonstrates an organization's connection to its constituents.
- *Events.* You can develop special events for a campaign, but most organizations already schedule many events that would interest policymakers.
- *Newsletters.* They can be helpful, but remember who the audience is. An internal staff newsletter may be boring to an external reader.

Outreach can be conducted on a much broader level through grassroots campaigns (Kahn, 1991). It is beyond the scope of this chapter to discuss grassroots politics and organizing techniques. However, many national organizations offer information about how to carry out grassroots lobbying. Many of these organizations can be found on the Web sites listed in Attachment 7-1 at the end of this chapter.

Develop Strong Presentation Skills

Individuals who are accustomed to receiving carefully produced information through the media are likely to expect a comparable level of performance from spokespersons for its major institutions. Although nonprofits may lack the resources to purchase expensive graphics and presentation materials, effective presentation skills can more than compensate for slick packaging of information. As you prepare a presentation, keep these principles in mind:

- *Create eye-catching materials.* Brief and simple messages are generally most effective. Put extensive quantitative information into graphic or tabular formats.
- *Develop simple, useful formats.* Consider how the information will be used—if the organization has developed a database to support its case, make it available on a diskette or on the World Wide Web so that reporters and legislative staff can use it.
- *Deliver clear messages.* If your organization has not developed a clear position on an issue, its communication campaign is doomed.
- *Be prepared.* Formulate notes, or even a full text, for the person who will be presenting information. Rehearse.
- *Be prepared for trouble.* Bring backup information and equipment—the projector may fail, or the oversight committee may have unexpected questions.

Each of these practices is important for effective communicating. However, the critical encompassing principle is to know one's audience. Having the facts in order is a vital first step for a presentation, and it is easy to focus primarily or even solely on this element. Yet, it is just as crucial to package information in a format that will be easily understood by the audience and useful for decision making. This includes not only written materials, graphics, and presentation charts, but also the language used to address the audience. For example, a presentation full of abbreviations, acronyms, or numerical data in unfamiliar formats may be as incomprehensible as if it were given in a foreign language. Moreover, no audience enjoys feeling condescended to, which is the impression often given by using overly technical terminology or professional jargon. By the same token, it is important to guard against insulting the intelligence of listeners. It may help to visualize the issue from the listeners' perspective.

CONCLUSION

Whether your organization is a small, community-based one or a very large one with a national scope, the practices involved in advocacy and lobbying are important for you as a manager of a nonprofit organization with public policy interests. The steps and process discussed in this chapter are applicable both to the executive and legislative branches of government and to organizations ranging from direct service providers and public watchdog groups to professional societies, colleges and universities, and beyond. Although organizations covering such a wide spectrum seldom gather together to discuss programs and operations, there are actually many commonalities with respect to how they can best affect the outcomes of public policy decisions.

Many coordinated activities are required to achieve results in advocacy, but the skills and capabilities described here do not necessarily require formal training. Often, very effective advocacy campaigns can be run with minimal resources. As a nonprofit manager engaging in advocacy activities, your most important asset is your familiarity with your own organization, the community in which it exists, and the issues it faces. The key to successfully effecting change through advocacy and government relations activities is your ability to clearly articulate your objective, develop and implement a coherent plan, and monitor and revise the plan as necessary.

SKILLS-APPLICATION EXERCISE

Positioned as a measure to stop nonprofit organizations from spending public funds on lobbying activity, and hailed as the end of welfare for lobbyists, legislation under consideration in the U.S. House of Representatives proposes to do the following:

- Prohibit any nonprofit organization from receiving a taxpayer-subsidized federal grant if it received more than one-third of its total income from such grants or exceeded certain limits on lobbying expenses in the previous year.
- Prohibit any nonprofit organization that receives a taxpayer-subsidized federal grant from using grant funds to purchase anything, including membership, from an organization that in the previous year spent more than 15 percent of its total income on political advocacy.

You are the senior manager of a private, nonprofit organization that promotes equal housing opportunity in a major metropolitan area. Your organization's programs include active monitoring of the real estate industry, both sales and rentals, as well as advocacy at the local, state, and federal levels for reducing discriminatory housing practices. Your organization receives private gifts and grants and an annual operating subsidy from the county, which in total account for about one-half of your organization's operating budget. Your organization also seeks and receives major support from the U.S. Department of Housing and Urban Development for private enforcement programming. Your board of trustees and your organization's state and national membership associations have urged you to play a leadership role in developing a regional campaign against this legislation.

- What information do you need to formulate a legislative game plan?

- What are the channels you would use to learn the details of the proposed legislation? How would you get access to these sources of information?

- What do you need to know about your own member of Congress as you plan this effort?

- What are the criteria that would suggest which members of Congress and which advocacy groups would support or oppose this legislation?

- Are there opportunities to build coalitions to support your objectives? What regional mechanisms might you use to identify and coordinate with other groups sharing your position?

- What kind of support should you expect to receive from the regional and national associations to which your organization belongs?

- Suggest roles in the campaign that might be played by your organization's trustees and staff.

- If your campaign will involve expenses, what are the most appropriate and likely sources for these funds?

- Suggest specific advocacy strategies you might use at various points in the legislative life of this bill.

- If you were invited to present testimony on the bill, what are the key points you would make?

REFERENCES

Alexander, C. A. (1991). Creating and using coalitions. In R. L. Edwards & J. A. Yankey (Eds.), *Skills for effective human services management* (pp. 90–102). Washington, DC: NASW Press.

Brown, D. (1991, May). Tracking state legislation. *Association Management*, p. 25.

Cruz, J. (1997). The top ten keys to effective communication. *Nonprofit World, 15*(4), 24–25.

Edwards, R. L., & Austin, D. M. (1991). Managing effectively in an environment of competing values. In R. L. Edwards & J. A. Yankey (Eds.), *Skills for effective human services management* (pp. 5–22). Washington, DC: NASW Press.

Edwards, R. L., Benefield, E. A. S., Edwards, J. A., & Yankey, J. A. (1997). *Building a strong foundation: Fundraising for nonprofits.* Washington, DC: NASW Press.

Edwards, R. L., Cooke, P. W., & Reid, P. N. (1996). Social work management in an era of diminishing federal responsibility. *Social Work, 41*, 468–479.

Frenza, J. P., & Hoffman, L. (1997). So you want a Web site, now what? *Nonprofit World, 15*(5), 21–24.

Gibelman, M., Gelman, S. R., & Pollack, D. (1997). The credibility of nonprofit boards: A view from the 1990s and beyond. *Administration in Social Work, 21*(2), 21–40.

Gibelman, M., & Kraft, S. (1996). Advocacy as a core agency program: Planning considerations for voluntary human service agencies. *Administration in Social Work, 20*(4), 51.

Groups unite to slash wasteful spending. (1995, June 30). *Healthy & Natural Journal*, p. 50.

Haynes, K., & Mickelson, J. (1997). *Affecting change: Social workers in the political arena.* White Plains, NY: Longman.

Kahn, S. (1991). *Organizing: A guide for grassroots leaders* (rev. ed.). Washington, DC: NASW Press.

Menefee, D. (1997). Strategic administration for nonprofit human service organizations: A model for executive success in turbulent times. *Administration in Social Work, 21*(2), 1–19.

Richan, W. C. (1996). *Lobbying for social change* (2nd ed.). Binghamton, NY: Haworth Press.

Salamon, L. M. (1997). *Holding the center: America's nonprofit sector at a crossroads.* New York: Nathan Cummings Foundation.

Smucker, B. (1991). *The nonprofit lobbying guide: Advocating your cause—and getting results.* San Francisco: Jossey-Bass.

Union Institute. (1992, May). *The nonprofit policy agenda: Recommendations for state and local action.* Washington, DC: Union Institute Office for Social Responsibility, Center for Public Policy.

Whitaker, W. H. (1982). Organizing coalitions. In M. Mahaffey & J. W. Hanks (Eds.), *Practical politics: Social work and political responsibility* (pp. 136–158). Silver Spring, MD: National Association of Social Workers.

Attachment 7-1. Helpful World Wide Web Sites

WEB SITE	MAINTAINED BY	CONTENTS
Federal government		
www.house.gov www.senate.gov	U.S. House of Representatives U.S. Senate	Provides information on members, committees, and the legislative process; contains Internet links to the home pages of members, committees, and congressional agencies (Congressional Budget Office, Government Printing Office, General Accounting Office, Library of Congress).
www.thomas.loc.gov	U.S. Library of Congress	Lists ongoing activities of the House and Senate; allows user to search for and download legislative materials such as bills, committee reports, hearing transcripts, and references in the *Congressional Quarterly*.
www.whitehouse.gov	The White House (Executive Office of the President)	Provides links to White House offices, as well as cabinet-level departments, and most federal agencies and commissions.
State and local governments		
www.csg.org	Council of State Governments	Contains issue alerts and state government news; lists national associations of state officials.
www.ncsl.org	National Conference of State Legislatures	Contains press releases, searchable database of public issues, schedules for U.S. state legislatures, and updates on federal–state relations.
www.localgov.org	National League of Cities, National Association of Counties, International City/County Management Association, Public Technology, Inc.	Lists state and local government home pages nationwide; lists links to public policy analysis institutes, nonprofit resource centers, and advocacy groups.
www.governing.com	*Governing* magazine	Lists home pages of U.S. cities and counties and municipal leagues. Contains directory of government officials at all government levels.

Attachment continues

Attachment 7-1 (continued)

WEB SITE	MAINTAINED BY	CONTENTS
www.lib.umich.edu/libhome/Documents.Center	University of Michigan	Extensive database of federal, state, and local government information. Includes links to associations and federations of state agencies and administrators; lists congressional delegations by state.
Nonprofits and advocacy organizations		
www.commoncause.org/special.pisites	Common Cause (public interest group)	Contains links to home pages of media and news services and public interest groups (American Association of Retired Persons, League of Women Voters, Public Citizen)
www.igc.org	Institute for Global Communications	Contains links to nonprofit resources on the Internet. The activist toolkit includes links to a number of electronic magazines, Web-based publications, and legislative directories.
www.fdncenter.org/onlib/linxtoc	The Foundation Center	Provides links to dozens of nonprofit resources and Web sites and a listing of nonprofit resources organized by program area.
www.philanthropy-journal.org/plhome/plmeta	*Journal of Philanthropy*	Contains meta-index of nonprofit organizations and information resources for nonprofit organizations and activists.
www.voxpop.org/jefferson	Stardot Consulting, Ltd. (Internet consulting group)	Online guide to obtaining information about politicians and political issues at the federal, state, and local level. Provides information by party, issue, and region. Identifies watchdog groups.
www.epn.org	*The American Prospect* magazine	Provides information on policy analysis and current affairs in areas such as welfare, education, civic participation, and health policy. Links to members (mainly policy institutes, journals, and watchdog groups).
www.tri-media.com/fmicause/html	Tri-Media Marketing and Publicity, Inc.	Describes cause-related marketing. Provides list of services, marketing tips, and case studies of cause-related marketing.

PART THREE

HUMAN RELATIONS SKILLS

HUMAN RELATIONS SKILLS

Managerial human relations skills encompass the roles of mentor and facilitator. Competencies for the mentor role include an understanding of self and others, interpersonal communication skills, and development of subordinates. Competencies for the facilitator role include team building, participatory decision making, and conflict management. The chapters in this section give attention to these roles in effective managerial performance.

Peter J. Pecora in chapter 8 offers a comprehensive approach to recruiting and selecting employees, suggesting steps and guidelines for implementing a system that is consistent with equal employment opportunity and affirmative action. He pays considerable attention to the processes involved in recruiting, selecting, and placing employees. In a wide-ranging discussion of job descriptions, the public relations aspects of recruitment, and job application forms and tests, he emphasizes the importance of objectivity and fairness. Pecora provides especially useful information about conducting screening interviews and describes two interview strategies. A sound recruiting and selection process, according to Pecora, can help foster an organizational climate that leads to employee commitment, a team orientation, and the personal development of employees.

In chapter 9, Darlyne Bailey provides an overview of past, present, and future approaches to the design and maintenance of effective organizational teams. She presents a developmental theoretical framework for examining stages of team development and the behaviors that are frequently associated with each stage. Bailey emphasizes the importance for managers to understand themselves and others, as well as the need to be skilled at fostering participatory decision making. Further, she suggests that the management of conflict is a pivotal competency. She views consensus building and the involvement of employees as critical aspects of the management role.

Roslyn H. Chernesky in chapter 10 discusses the status of women in management, commenting on the special issues and challenges that women may encounter in pursuing management positions and performing effectively as managers. She considers organizational culture and how it can create a hostile or inhospitable workplace environment for women. Chernesky also includes a series of suggestions for advancing women in the managerial ranks.

The issue of performance appraisal is addressed by Kenneth I. Millar in chapter 11. He points out that an organization's experience with performance appraisal can be either positive or negative, depending on a variety of factors. Millar then identifies a set of "ideal" characteristics of a performance appraisal system, suggesting that the best type of system is one that is nonpunitive and is viewed by employees as fair and appropriate. Millar also provides specific suggestions to aid managers in working collaboratively with their employees to develop a performance appraisal instrument tailored to the needs of the particular organization.

John E. Tropman in chapter 12 suggests that managers can improve the decisions made in their organizations by involving groups in the process. He discusses the following components: the management of the decision process, the management of decision rules, and the management of decision results. Tropman identifies what he calls "meeting masters," managers who are particularly adept at structuring meetings of boards, committees, and the like, so that time is used wisely, and the important decisions are made with maximum input from all concerned.

In chapter 13, Robert F. Rivas contends that dismissal of problem employees is a managerial prerogative but recognizes that unions can influence the process. He provides an overview of the phenomenon of "separating" employees and underscores the importance of good supervision in arriving at a decision to terminate. Offering a typology of supervision, Rivas examines the relationship of supervision to performance. In addition, he strongly emphasizes the importance of performance evaluation and feedback for effective management of the dismissal processes. He urges nonprofit managers and supervisors to assume a proactive approach. To this end, he offers guidelines to prepare for and conduct dismissal interviews with employees being terminated.

Richard L. Edwards, Daniel A. Lebold, and John A. Yankey conclude this section with chapter 14 on managing decline in organizations. As resources diminish, many managers are confronted with the need to restructure their organizations and reduce their work forces. The chapter includes a discussion of the managerial processes for making difficult decisions about downsizing nonprofit organizations. Attention is given to focusing on the "health" of the organization, assessing its strengths and weaknesses, and exploring staff responses to cutbacks. The chapter concludes with recommendations for proactive responses to organizational decline.

CHAPTER 8

Recruiting and Selecting Effective Employees

Peter J. Pecora

I n nonprofit organizations, line staff and supervisors constitute one of the most valuable resources for maximizing organizational productivity and effectiveness. Among the important roles that managers must play are those of mentor and facilitator (see chapter 1). The aim, in part, is to have a workforce that is cohesive, productive, and has high morale. In terms of the mobilization of the organization's human resources, the recruitment and screening of potential staff members is an essential management skill. This chapter presents an overview of some of the important principles for recruiting, screening, and selecting employees, including two exercises that will enable you to test and practice your skills in this area.

The employee selection process requires analytical and interpersonal skills. In terms of analytical skills, the position for which you are recruiting must be defined in task-specific ways. Task-based job descriptions must be developed, and essential competencies of knowledge, skills, abilities, and attitudes must be identified. Interpersonal skills are required for interviewing job candidates in a courteous and professional manner. The selection process also requires knowledge of both affirmative action guidelines and the rules of the Equal Employment Opportunity Commission (EEOC). But keep in mind that beginning in 1997, a number of states such as California were passing legislation to remove the protections and preferences for ethnic minorities and women that are part of affirmative action.

In this chapter, the necessary steps and guidelines for the recruitment and selection of employees are described, including the ways in which affirmative action and EEOC guidelines affect the processes of recruitment, selection, and placement. Recruitment is concerned with providing the organization with an adequate number of qualified applicants. Selection is concerned with reviewing and assessing the qualifications of job applicants to decide who should be offered the positions. Placement involves assigning new employees to the positions and orienting them properly so they can begin working

(Shafritz, Hyde, & Rosenbloom, 1986). This chapter emphasizes the first two components.

STEPS AND GUIDELINES FOR RECRUITING, SCREENING, AND SELECTING STAFF

There are five major steps involved in recruitment and selection:

1. Develop a job description that contains information regarding the primary duties of the position, key job parts, and the minimum prerequisite qualifications for the position in terms of education, experience, and skills.
2. Recruit candidates by advertising and posting announcements of positions.
3. Screen applicants using application forms, reviews of résumés, and tests, if appropriate.
4. Conduct screening interviews and reference checks, if permitted.
5. Select the person, secure a signed letter of hire, and notify other applicants that a decision has been made.

The necessary interpersonal skills include the ability to work collaboratively with organization staff to develop common expectations for the position and a common set of interview questions. Supervisory and other administrative personnel must also be able to interview job applicants in a professional and courteous manner.

The employee selection process should be considered an important investment of your management time. If this process is not carried out properly, supervisory staff and managers will later spend valuable time and energy dealing with the employee's marginal performance, the increased organizational conflict, and the stress involved in transferring or terminating the person (see chapter 13 for a discussion of terminating employees).

Developing a Job Description and Minimum Qualifications

The first step in the employee selection process is to define the job and the types of knowledge, skills, and abilities that are necessary for effective performance (McCormick, 1979; Pecora & Austin, 1987). A task-based job description helps managers develop a clear definition of the job and the type of qualifications necessary to perform it. Your organization can use such job descriptions in the next step of the process, preparing employee recruitment materials.

In preparing job descriptions for recruitment purposes, be sure they contain clear and specific statements of the essential duties of the positions. In addition, the knowledge, skills, abilities, educational degrees, and years of related job experience required must be specified. For ethical and legal reasons, the required minimum qualifications for a job should match the work to be performed. In other words, you must be able to substantiate the connection between the education and experience required and the tasks of the job.

Recruiting Candidates

The next step is to prepare announcements to publicize the availability of the position, describe the tasks of the job, attract a wide range of qualified candidates to improve the pool of candidates and maximize compliance with the legislative intent of both the EEOC and affirmative action, and inform interested people of the minimum qualifications and the process involved in applying for the position. You should be mindful that the recruitment and selection of employees is a form of public relations. The quality of recruitment materials and the respect and professionalism shown to applicants shape the image of your organization, especially to the many applicants who are not selected.

How the recruitment and screening process is carried out may well improve or damage your nonprofit's reputation. For example, if you receive applications from 45 people, interview eight, but select only one, the 44 people not selected are then left with a positive, neutral, or negative impression of your organization. If unsuccessful applicants are treated fairly in a demanding, well-organized professional screening process, they may be disappointed, but their level of respect for your organization will probably increase. Thus, future case referrals or the organization's community image may depend on the people not hired.

This public relations aspect of recruitment has implications for how the other steps in the process are carried out. For example, the announcement of the position should be as detailed as possible to allow potential applicants to determine whether the position fits their qualifications, current interests, and career goals. Communication with applicants and screening interviews should be handled carefully. To meet affirmative action regulations, the job announcement should include the following information (Klingner & Nalbandian, 1985):

- job title, classification, and salary range (although salary ranges in some organizations are listed as open and negotiable)
- location of job (geographic and organizational unit)
- description of duties
- minimum qualifications

- starting date for the position
- application procedures (which materials should be sent to whom)
- closing date for the receipt of applications.

A typical position announcement is shown in Figure 8-1. Most newspaper advertisements are shorter than this example because of their cost. Various forms of this basic announcement can be distributed to a variety of organizations, placed as newspaper advertisements, listed in professional newsletters, and given to potential applicants. Many organizations make special efforts to recruit women or people of color by contacting certain community organizations, churches, university departments and placement centers, minority newspapers, radio shows, and other community groups. These special efforts may also be necessary because of economic or other factors that may affect the labor market and the availability of qualified applicants.

Check to see that the announcement contains the necessary details of the position and is clearly worded. Make sure that the application deadline is realistic given the usual delays in the dissemination of announcements and the response of applicants. For example, does the deadline allow the applicant sufficient time to respond to the announcement? Consider also whether the announcement has been distributed to enough community, professional, or other groups. Both formal and informal networks are useful for publicizing the position. Finally, keep a record of how and where the position was advertised or posted and include your personal recruitment efforts.

Screening Applicants

Application Form

If properly designed, the application form can provide a significant amount of information about the applicant's qualifications. It should gather objective data about the applicant's previous work history. Other aspects of the screening process (reference letters and calls to former employers) focus on how well the applicant performed in his or her preceding jobs. Application forms typically require the following information:

- name, address, and telephone numbers
- educational degrees and related course work
- employment history (positions, places of employment, major duties of employment, reason for leaving, supervisor's name)
- veteran status (this information may be required—some agencies give points for employment tests or special consideration to veterans)
- references

Figure 8-1. Sample Position Announcement

POSITION ANNOUNCEMENT
Family Preservation Service Specialist
Children's Society

Function and Location Provides intensive in-home services to families considering out-of-home placement for one or more members. Is on call 24 hours per day to provide crisis intervention and other family services and problem resolution. Will work out of the Wallingford social services office.

Duties and Responsibilities (Partial List)

1. Provides in-home crisis-oriented treatment and support to families in which one or more family members are at risk of being placed outside the home in foster, group, or institutional care to prevent unnecessary child placement.**

2. Works a 40-hour nonstructured workweek (including evenings and weekends) to be responsive to the needs of families**

3. Provides family education and skills training as part of a goal-oriented treatment plan to prevent the recurrence of or to reduce the harmful effects of the maltreatment of children.**

4. Advocates for family members with schools, courts, and other social service agencies to help family members obtain financial assistance, housing, medical care and other services.**

**Key job parts.

Qualifications: Master's degree in social work, psychology, educational psychology, or psychosocial nursing is required. Graduate degree in social work preferred. Experience in counseling families and children is required. Knowledge of crisis intervention social casework, communication skills, and family therapy techniques is required.Knowledge of cognitive-behavioral interventions, group work, and functional family therapy is desirable. Must have reliable transportation. Required to live in county served. Salary range: $29,000-35,000.

Application Procedures and Deadline An agency application form, resume, and cover letter describing related education and experience must be submitted. Position closes April 25,1998. Starting date is tentatively scheduled for May 25,1998. Please send application materials to

Program Supervisor
Children's Services Society

AN EQUAL OPPORTUNITY EMPLOYER -- ALL QUALIFIED INDIVIDUALS ARE ENCOURAGED TO APPLY

- any disabilities that would interfere with performing the particular job
- adult convictions for a class-A misdemeanor or felony
- affirmative action information, such as ethnic group, sex, age, and any disability (this information is detached from the application and kept on file for affirmative action analysis).

In addition, some agencies require applicants to complete a questionnaire in which they indicate their level of knowledge and skills for major tasks of the job and to provide references of supervisors or instructors who can verify the information. Your organization's application should not contain questions that violate affirmative action guidelines, such as those on marital status or number of children.

Tests

The use of tests to screen and select candidates in nonprofit organizations is limited because of the lack of adequately validated and appropriate tests, the need to validate tests, and recent controversy surrounding such tests (American Psychological Association, 1980). Opponents of testing argue that tests are rarely powerful predictors of job performance and tend to discriminate against certain groups, typically racial and ethnic minorities (Howell & Dipboye, 1982; Zedeck & Cascio, 1984). But given the lack of alternatives for screening a large number of applicants, tests may continue to be used in certain nonprofit organizations.

Many states use licensing examinations, such as those developed by the American Association of State Social Work Boards, that attempt to test qualifications at both the BSW- and MSW-degree levels (Teare, Higgs, Gauthier, & Feild, 1984). These examinations may encourage the development of tests for screening applicants for social services and other nonprofit organization jobs nationwide. In addition, research on psychological testing has shown that certain types of tests (such as those testing cognitive ability) are valid predictors of successful job performance across jobs and settings (Zedeck & Cascio, 1984). Finally, Mufson (1986) reported that scores on certain scales of the California Psychological Inventory were successful in discriminating between the most and least desirable child welfare workers.

Beach (1975) offered the following seven guidelines for using tests as devices to select employees: (1) Tests should be used only as a supplement to other selection devices, not as a substitute for them; (2) Tests are more accurate at predicting failure than success; (3) Tests are more useful in picking a select group of people who are most likely to succeed on the job from among a much larger group; (4) Tests should be validated on one's own organization; (5) Tests can make their greatest contribution in situations when it is difficult to obtain satisfactory employees through other selection methods; (6) Test scores should not be viewed as precise and exact measures of the characteristic being tested; and (7) High test scores are not necessarily better predictors of satisfactory job performance than are slightly lower scores.

Preliminary Screening

Once the application forms and test scores (if any) have been received, a preliminary screening of applications should be conducted by a small committee of administrators, supervisors, and staff to eliminate applications that clearly do not meet the minimum standards and to help select a group of applicants to be interviewed. To facilitate this process, a screening grid may be used (see Figure 8-2). Each application is reviewed in relation to the minimum qualifications and the applicant's competencies or experience in certain areas (such as the amount of training in mental health services, the number of years of direct practice experience in child mental health, or the number of years of supervisory experience). Be sure to include ample space on the screening grid for the special characteristics section. This section allows reviewers to note the applicant's abilities, experiences, or training that may be of special relevance to the position. Alternately, one could list more required competencies and other characteristics using the format presented in Figure 8-3.

The usefulness of the screening grid and the application review process depends, to some extent, on the amount of information provided by the applicant. Clearly, the committee's ability to assess the applicant's qualifications, beyond adherence to minimum qualifications, is dependent upon the application form, résumé, and any other information that is gathered. Therefore, some organizations also ask applicants to supply a detailed cover letter describing how their education, training, and experience qualify them for a particular job. Detailed cover letters and screening grids facilitate the initial screening process, especially when the screening committee may have to consider 10 or more applicants.

In screening applicants, double check to ensure that the job application form provides information that helps you determine whether the applicant has related education, training, and experience. In addition, check that the application form does not contain questions that are illegal according to equal employment opportunity laws. The following information cannot be requested on either an application form or in a job interview: maiden name, type of residence, proof of age, verification of birthplace and citizenship, language and national origin, photographs, physical condition, religion, criminal record, military service, organizational affiliations, and references (Jensen, 1981). But be prepared to encounter many fellow staff members who are not aware of which questions are illegal or improper to use in application forms and interviews. Affirmative action and equal employment opportunity regulations summarize some of the most important guidelines.

Figure 8-2. Applicant Screening Grid for a Child Mental Health Supervisor Position

APPLICANT NAME	MSW OR MAIN ONE OF THE SOCIAL SCIENCES (YES/NO)	YEARS OF EXPERIENCE IN MENTAL HEALTH	SPECIALIZED TRAINING IN CHILD THERAPY	YEARS OF SUPERVISORY EXPERIENCE	SPECIAL CHARACTERISTICS OR QUALIFICATIONS

Figure 8-3. Résumé and Cover Letter Screening Checklist

Instructions: To promote objectivity, make one copy for each reviewer. Keep with résumé and cover letter.

Reviewer Name: _____ Candidate: _____

Minimum Qualifications	Has	Does Not Have
1.	_____	_____
2.	_____	_____
3.	_____	_____
4.	_____	_____
5.	_____	_____
6.	_____	_____

Screened In ❏   Screened Out ❏   Send Letter ❏

	No Info	Meets Expectations	Exceeds Expectations	Notes/Comments:
1. Organization/ priority setting	❏	❏	❏	_____
2. Flexibility	❏	❏	❏	_____
3. Two-way communication	❏	❏	❏	_____
4. Team work	❏	❏	❏	_____
5. Relationship building	❏	❏	❏	_____
6. Valuing diversity	❏	❏	❏	_____
7. Develops self and others	❏	❏	❏	_____
8. Critical thinking and judgment	❏	❏	❏	_____
9. Technical expertise	❏	❏	❏	_____

Other Observations:

_____

_____

_____

Decision: Phone Screen ❏   Hold ❏   Screen Out ❏   Send Letter ❏
             or
             Interview ❏

SOURCE: Casey Family Program. (1997, September). *Competencies recruitment and selection committee executive summary.* Seattle: Author.

Conducting the Screening Interview

Because of the problems associated with testing, many nonprofit organizations have traditionally relied on the employment interview as a screening device. During the interview, you should address four major questions (Attard, 1984). First, does the applicant have the necessary knowledge, skills, and abilities? Second, does the person have the motivation and initiative to do the job well? Third, will the individual be compatible with the other employees in that unit and the organization as a whole? This question requires learning about the applicant's work style and personality through the interview process and later through a check of references, if possible legally. Fourth, can desirable candidates be convinced to leave their jobs to come to work for you?

Purposes of the Interview

Staff members who will participate in interviewing candidates should be aware of the three purposes of the interview (Glueck, 1978):

1. *To aid in screening and selecting applicants who best meet the position requirements.* Data on the application are examined for gaps in time, missing information, and apparent inconsistencies, and any irregularities should be discussed and corrected. Additional information that is not contained in the application is gathered.
2. *To develop good public relations.* An organization may have many applicants for a position. Whether applicants are interviewed, the primary contact with your organization for many is those who interview them. The interviewers, therefore, are your organization's representatives to the professional community and must promote good public relations. Good public relations include prompt action. A hiring decision should be made as quickly as possible so that all applicants, whether interviewed or not, can be informed of their status.
3. *To educate applicants.* The interviewer, or interviewers, must be able to explain aspects of the position that are not readily apparent from the description of the position. Explanations requested may cover anything from a more detailed description of the position to the organization's overall policies. (p. 226)

Predictive Value of Interviews

Many researchers argue that interviews, as typically conducted, are of limited predictive value (Campion & Arvey, 1989; Howell & Dipboye, 1982). Despite the lack of conclusive empirical evidence in this regard, interviews are the most widely used means of selecting personnel. However, there is some evidence that properly conducted interviews may yield information that is valid for predicting an applicant's performance of a job (Eder & Ferris, 1989;

Mayfield, Brown, & Hamstra, 1980). Ross and Hoeltke's (1985) study of a residential child welfare program, in which a structured interview was used to rate applicants in relation to 10 competencies associated with "excellent" staff, tested the ability of the interview to select superior workers by correlating the scores on the interview with four measures of worker performance and found this method to be beneficial. Although this method requires further validation, the results are encouraging.

Furthermore, there is a growing body of practice wisdom (Campbell, 1983) and some research (Eder & Ferris, 1989) that provide useful guidelines for interviewing applicants for jobs. For example, a number of studies have documented the usefulness of training interviewers in the steps of the selection process, in interviewing techniques, and in methods for combining various sources of information to evaluate applicants (Carlson, Thayer, Mayfield, & Peterson, 1971).

The successful interviewing of applicants also involves preparation in a number of areas. Clearly, each member of the selection committee should be familiar with the duties, responsibilities, and qualifications of the job. Interviewers should carefully read the application form, résumé, cover letter, and letters of reference before the interview. They should be prepared to check out inconsistencies or gaps in the interview and possibly later when calling references. Finally, to standardize the areas covered in the interview, the staff should monitor each member of the screening committee to make sure that the same job-related questions are asked of each applicant because applicants may respond differently to the same questions when asked by different interviewers (Robertson, 1982).

Interviewers must gather information to answer the following two basic questions (Goodale, 1989):

1. *Can the applicants do the job?* To assess the applicants' potential to assume specific responsibilities, the interviewers should examine their previous work and nonwork experience, training and education, and actual behavior during the interview.
2. *Will the applicants do the job?* Interviewers may overlook the applicant's willingness to perform key responsibility areas. This part of the information collecting involves examination of applicants' preferences for and interest in the nature of the work to be done, their preferences for conditions of employment (such as salary, hours, travel), and the compatibility between their career goals and the organization's career opportunities. (p. 316)

In general, you should select open-ended questions that cannot be answered with a simple yes or no but require information or explanations. In other words, interviewers should start their questions with the words what, why, where, when, and how—not with the words can, did, or have. Do not hesitate to ask the applicant to provide more details. It is also important to establish a comfortable, confidential, supportive, and nonthreatening atmosphere to reduce the applicant's nervousness or hesitancy to talk. In this regard, you should divert all calls and visitors, avoid interviewing from behind a desk that is stacked high with books and papers, have all the necessary materials (applicant's résumé, application form, note-taking equipment, description of the position) ready, and set aside adequate time for the interview (Robertson, 1982).

Phases of the Interview

These guidelines are designed to maximize the effectiveness and fairness of selection committees. But preparation alone is not sufficient; the interview itself should be conducted in a smooth, directed, professional manner and be led by one spokesperson for the group. There are essentially four phases in an effective interview: (1) opening, (2) information gathering from the applicant, (3) responding to applicant questions, and (4) closing. Each phase is critical for gathering the proper information or for providing applicants with the necessary details of the screening process (Robertson, 1982).

During the opening or introductory phase, the interviewer uses small talk to relax the applicant and to help him or her settle into the interview setting. This phase may last anywhere from two to 10 minutes, depending on the overall length of the interview. The transition from this phase to the information-gathering phase is usually accomplished by an introductory statement that may take the following form: "We're glad you could meet with us today. We will have the next 45 minutes to discuss the position and your qualifications. Members of our committee will be asking you questions and possibly taking some notes. After that, you will have an opportunity to ask questions about the position and our organization."

The lead interviewer may then briefly review the organization and the nature of the position. In the information-gathering phase, the interviewers provide direction without talking too much. Job-related questions and follow-up questions should help the applicant describe his or her qualifications more clearly. It is also important to assess the degree of match between the applicant's career goals and the organization's mission.

To signal the end of this phase and movement into the third phase of answering applicant questions, the lead interviewer might discuss the next steps and time line for recruitment and then say, "Now that we have had the opportunity to discuss your experience, do you have any questions for us?" This statement invites the applicant to ask any questions he or she may have. This is an important part of the interview because superior candidates often have thoughtful or challenging questions about the organization. If questions arise that you cannot answer at that time, offer to call the applicant with the answer (Robertson, 1982).

"I'd say our recruiters did an exceptional job identifying you."

Before closing the interview, the lead interviewer may want to reiterate the timeline for the final selection, along with any further steps that must be taken (contacting references, a possible follow-up interview, the date when the decision will be made, and how the applicant will be notified). Finally, thank the applicant for his or her interest in the position.

During the interview, try to avoid the types of mistakes discussed by Jensen (1981). One serious mistake is to fail to establish rapport by hurrying the interview, allowing frequent interruptions, not using active-listening techniques, or making sarcastic or critical remarks. These problems impede communication by making candidates more uncomfortable. The absence of an interview strategy with preplanned questions can produce incomplete or nonsystematic information about the applicant. A common mistake of many novice interviewers is to dominate the interview with details about the organization, to jump in to fill a pause in the conversation, and not to allow the applicant to present his or her qualifications. A problematic technique is to put the candidate under significant stress. Deliberate or inadvertent stress destroys rapport, causes resentment, inhibits the open disclosure of information, and is not equivalent to stress on the job. However, the use of realistic job-related role-play simulations, although slightly stressful, can help assess an applicant's skills and abilities. Finally, another common mistake is to form a premature judgment about the applicant (based on the applicant's unusual physical appearance or speech mannerisms, for example) that biases the interviewer's acceptance of important information later in the interview.

At the close of the interview, some organizations conduct a tour to familiarize applicants with the organization. These tours provide applicants with a more complete picture of the nature of the organization and the job and may also lead to additional questions or comments from the applicant that can be used in selecting the appropriate candidate. Some agencies reserve these tours for the two to three finalists on the day of the final interview to save staff time.

Two Practical Interviewing Strategies

Two techniques may help you maximize the validity, reliability, and usefulness of the interview process. One technique is the Patterned Behavior Description Interview (PBDI), in which a special set of questions is incorporated into the interview process, allowing the interviewers to move beyond asking general questions to focus on what applicants have actually done in the past regarding certain situations. According to Janz (1989), "The PBDI zeros in on what applicants have accomplished (or failed to accomplish) and how they went about doing it, in situations similar to ones they will face on the job" (p. 159). For example, an interviewer might ask an applicant how he or she responded to a hostile client, what circumstances were involved, and how the applicant handled the situation. The answers to this question reveal the specific choices the applicant made in the past. Long-standing patterns of behavior are highly predictive of future behavior.

A second related technique is the situational interview, which poses hypothetical questions to applicants such as "What would you do if . . . ?" This technique is one of the few approaches to interviewing based on any type of theory—in this case goal-setting theory, which states that intentions or goals are the immediate precursors of a person's behavior (Locke & Latham, 1984). According to Latham (1989), "The purpose of the situational interview is to identify a potential employee's intentions by presenting that person with a series of job-related incidents, and asking what he or she would do in that situation" (p. 171). The technique uses job analysis and performance appraisal analyses to devise ways of scoring an applicant's response to a "what if" question in relation to what interviewers think would result in effective job performance. Interviewers then use the scoring criteria to rate each applicant. Results from a number of recent studies have shown relatively high levels of reliability and validity (see Latham, 1989) for specific guidelines regarding how to use this technique).

Selecting the Person and Notifying Other Applicants

After the final candidates have been interviewed, some organizations may contact references to clarify questions or issues that have arisen during the interview (see Figure 8-4 for some practical guidelines for checking references). Reference checks can be important for obtaining information on how the applicant interacted with his or her fellow employees; exploring questions left unanswered during the interview; and determining work habits, attendance, and other criteria of performance. The most cost-effective approach is to call references, especially if you use open-ended and nondirective questions that seek to confirm the facts of the person's position (such as date of hire, job responsibilities, relationships with colleagues, and rapport with clients being served).

Experienced interviewers keep their approach on the telephone businesslike, and they avoid sounding too eager to hire the person. One of the most important questions to ask is whether the reference would hire this person again. This question may elicit information that is valuable for screening candidates. Do not reveal information obtained in reference checks to the candidate. If the person is not hired, state that the person who was selected most closely met the qualifications of the position. Divulging information from references is a violation of confidentiality, and many organizations are therefore becoming wary of releasing information (Jensen, 1981). Some human services and other nonprofit organizations are being advised to provide only information regarding the duration of the former employee's employment unless the screening organization can provide a signed release of information from the applicant or unless the employee, upon leaving that organization, had signed a release form authorizing the release of performance-related and other reference information.

After contacting references of the highly rated candidates, the selection committee chooses one person by carefully assessing the information collected about his or her job-related qualifications and the degree to which the candidate's career goals, practice skills, and philosophy of work fit the organization and the position. The person selected is usually offered the position over the telephone, and if he or she accepts, is sent a written letter of confirmation

Figure 8-4. Strategies for Checking Applicant References

1. *Choose a method.* Reference checks can be made by letter or by telephone, with telephone checks more detailed, more honest, and less subject to applicant pressure.

2. *Choose a time.* Many employers in the human services require letters of reference from the final group of candidates only as a means of streamlining the screening process and avoiding undue applicant burden. If calling references, many times it is better to do so after the interview as a means of confirming certain qualifications or clarifying questions or inconsistencies in the application or interview (for example, writing ability, performance under stressful conditions).

3. *Obtain at least three references.* Obtain multiple references with telephone numbers and addresses so that you can weigh the comments of at least three people.

4. *Be businesslike and job focused when calling references.* Use nondirective open-ended questions that elicit detailed answers, and don't sound eager to hire the person. Former employers may be reluctant to disappoint you with negative information.

5. *Ask a preplanned series of questions,* such as
    a. What were Mary's dates of employment with you?
    b. What were her duties or responsibilities:
    c. How long did she work for you? In what capacities?
    d. How would you describe her level of performance?
    e. She tells me she earned $1,200 per month with you, is that correct?
    f. How was her attendance record? Punctuality?
    g. How did she get along with fellow workers? With clients? With you?
    h. Would you rehire Mary?

6. *Be sure to ask the rehire question.* This may be the most important question you ask, as it checks the honesty of the preceding questions and provides a "bottom line" assessment of that employer's opinion of the applicant.

7. *Don't reveal reference information to candidates.* This information was provided in confidence to you and should not be disclosed unless you are required to document and defend your hiring decision. Above all, do not tell the nonchosen applicants that they were not hired because of poor references. Instead, rely on the fact that the person selected had better qualifications for the position.

SOURCE: Jensen, J. (1981). How to hire the right person for the job. *The Grantsmanship Center News, 9*(3), 30–31. Reprinted with permission.

(or asked to stop by the organization to confirm his or her acceptance of the offer). Once the acceptance has been received, and the commitment from the candidate is firm, the other applicants should be promptly notified. The letter notifying the other applicants should be reviewed carefully so that it is worded sensitively to ease their disappointment and to thank them for their interest in the position.

Organizational excellence is determined, in large part, by the staff's compatibility with and commitment to the organization's mission. Sound recruitment and screening practices help ensure that effective staff are hired and that a minimum number of people are released during the probationary period. Although this process requires organizational, analytical, and interpersonal skills, it is critical for obtaining high-quality personnel (see Figure 8-5 for a summary).

Figure 8-5. Summary Checklist for Recruiting, Screening, and Selecting Employees

Step 1: Developing a Job Description and Minimum Qualifications

A. Does the job description contain clear and specific task statements that describe the essential duties of this position?

B. Are the knowledge, skills, abilities, educational degrees (if any), and years of related job experience specified anywhere?

C. Do the required minimum qualifications for the job match the work to be performed; that is, can you substantiate the connections between the education and experience required and the tasks of the job?

Step 2: Employee Recruitment

A. Do the job announcements include the necessary details of the position?

B. Are the announcements clearly worded?

C. Is the application deadline realistic, given the usual delays in dissemination and publication; that is, does the deadline allow the applicant sufficient time to respond to the announcement?

D. Have you distributed the announcement to enough community, professional, or other groups? Have you used both formal and informal networks in publicizing the position?

E. Is a record being kept of how and where the position was advertised or posted, including personal recruitment efforts?

Step 3: Screening Job Applicants Using Application Forms and Tests (if Appropriate)

A. Does the application form provide information that helps you determine whether the applicant has related education, training, and experience?

B. Does the application form contain questions that are illegal according to equal employment opportunity laws?

C. Can you structure the application form and process so applicants are asked to submit a cover letter or other summary statements to highlight how their training and experience qualify them for the position?

Step 4: Conducting the Screening Interview

A. Have you trained the interviewers in the basic phases and principles of the selection process?

B. Have you developed a list of standard questions to be asked of each applicant by the same interviewer?

C. Has a quiet place been set aside for the interview, and are telephone or other interruptions prevented?

D. Have you chosen a person to lead the interview through the opening, information-gathering, and closing phases?

E. Have you established a time line for the selection process and informed each applicant of how and when he or she will be notified?

Step 5: Selecting the Person and Notifying the Other Applicants

A. Have you contacted a sufficient number of applicants' references?

B. Has the committee weighed carefully all the information gathered to determine the most qualified and committed applicant?

C. Do you have a firm commitment from the primary candidate before notifying the other applicants?

D. Is your letter notifying the other applicants worded sensitively to ease their disappointment and thank them for their interest in the position?

AFFIRMATIVE ACTION AND
EQUAL EMPLOYMENT OPPORTUNITY

Legislation for affirmative action and equal employment opportunity contin-ues to affect the recruitment, screening, and selection of employees in both for-profit and nonprofit organizations. The distinctive components of EEOC laws are based on Title VII of the 1964 Civil Rights Act and other laws, including the Age Discrimination in Employment Act of 1967; Sections 503 and 504 of the Rehabilitation Act of 1973, as amended; the Vietnam Era Veterans' Readjustment Assistance Act of 1974; and the Equal Pay Act of 1963. As Klingner and Nalbandian (1985) noted,

> With few exceptions, Title VII (EEO) prohibits employers, labor organizations, and employment agencies from making employee or applicant personnel deci-sions based on race, color, religion, sex, or national origin. Although it origi-nally applied only to private employers, the concern of EEO was extended to local and state governments by 1972 amendments to the 1964 Civil Rights Act. (p. 64)

Equal opportunity laws reflect a management approach to reducing dis-crimination against employees by ensuring that equal opportunity is imple-mented in all employment actions. These laws require nondiscrimination, which involves the elimination of all existing discriminatory conditions, whether purposeful or inadvertent. Nonprofit organizations, because of their tax-exempt status and because they may have government contracts, must carefully and systematically examine all their employment policies to be sure they do not operate to the detriment of any people on the grounds of race, color, religion, national origin, sex, age, or status as a person with a disability, disabled veteran, or veteran of the Vietnam era. Managers must also ensure that practices of those who are responsible for matters of employment, includ-ing supervisors, are nondiscriminatory.

In contrast, affirmative action requires that most organizations take steps to ensure proportional recruitment, selection, and promotion of qualified mem-bers of groups, such as members of ethnic minority groups and women, who were formerly excluded. Most employers, unions, and employment agencies are required to plan and document, through written affirmative action pro-grams (AAPs), the steps they are taking to reduce the underrepresentation of various groups. Most public and private organizations that provide goods and services to the federal government and their subcontractors must comply with the affirmative action provisions described in Executive Order No. 11246. Guidelines for working with AAPs are found in Title 41, Part 60-2 (known as "Revised Order No. 4") of the Office of Federal Contract Compliance.

Although both equal employment opportunity and affirmative action seek to eliminate discrimination in employment, the safeguards and improvements mandated by these guidelines in relation to specific practices for recruiting, screening, selecting, and promoting employees vary. For example, a mental health organization may develop a specific campaign to recruit and hire more female supervisors to increase the proportion of female managers in the organization as part of its plan to comply with affirmative action regulations. In contrast, equal employment opportunity organization guidelines cover such areas as the type of questions that can be asked on an employment application or in an interview and emphasize the use of screening or interviewing committees that are composed of a mix of men, women, and people of color.

Knowledge of equal employment opportunity and affirmative action guidelines is essential for designing employment application forms and interviewing protocols that avoid the use of illegal questions. However, recent and ongoing court cases may alter what is permissible under equal employment opportunity and affirmative action guidelines. Government updates and legal consultations are important resources for assessing the adequacy of procedures.

Equal Employment Opportunity, Affirmative Action, and the Classification of Jobs

In addition to banning certain types of questions on applications or in interviews, equal employment opportunity guidelines forbid any selection process for candidates that has an adverse impact on any social, ethnic, or gender group, unless the procedure is validated through the analysis of jobs or research on the selection of employees. Descriptions and notices of positions that delineate knowledge, skill, ability, education, or other prerequisites require a determination of whether the prerequisites are genuinely appropriate for the job. Some requirements (such as years of experience, certificates, diplomas, and educational degrees) may be considered unlawful on the basis of previous court decisions for a particular position. Proscriptions against discrimination in employment demand that any requirement (education or experience) that is used as a standard for decisions about employment must have a manifest relationship to the job in question (Meritt-Haston & Weyley, 1983; Pecora & Austin, 1983).

The use of standards that disqualify women, certain racial or ethnic groups, or other groups at a substantially higher rate than white male applicants would be unlawful unless they could be shown to be significantly related to the successful performance of a job and otherwise necessary to the safe and efficient operation of the job for which they are used. Educational requirements are defined as a test by the federal government and must be validated in accordance with EEOC's testing guidelines. In addition, if an organization validates its selection criteria, equal employment opportunity guidelines require it to demonstrate that no suitable alternative with a lesser adverse impact is available.

When an adverse impact can be demonstrated with regard to a screening instrument or process (a test or structured interview, for example), employers should use alternative measures that are equally valid but produce a less adverse impact. Unfortunately, little progress has been made in identifying and using screening procedures as alternatives to educational and experience qualifications (Zedeck & Cascio, 1984). Nevertheless, your nonprofit organization should carefully analyze its jobs and clearly define their tasks and requisite knowledge, skills, and abilities. This information is essential for establishing minimum qualifications for various positions so qualified individuals can be recruited and selected. Table 8-1 provides a concise summary, based on equal employment opportunity and affirmative action regulations, of what is acceptable and unacceptable to use in application forms and as interview questions. Note that the guidelines for people who have physical disabilities are being revised, and questions must be carefully considered. To check your knowledge of these guidelines, test yourself using the Skills-Application Exercise at the end of this chapter.

Americans with Disabilities Act

The Americans with Disabilities Act (ADA), enacted July 26, 1990, extended broad civil rights protection to an estimated 43 million Americans with disabilities. The act contains four major sections: employment (Title I), state and local government services (Title II), public accommodations provided by private entities (Title III), and telecommunications (Title IV). The ADA is neither pre-emptive nor exclusive; stricter requirements of state or federal law will continue to apply.

The purpose of the act is to

- provide a clear and comprehensive national mandate for the elimination of discrimination against individuals with disabilities
- provide clear, strong, consistent, enforceable standards addressing discrimination against individuals with disabilities
- ensure that the federal government plays a central role in enforcing the standards established in this act on behalf of individuals with disabilities
- invoke the sweep of congressional authority, including the power to enforce the 14th Amendment and to regulate commerce, in order to address the major areas of discrimination faced every day by people with disabilities.

Table 8-1. Guide to Fair Employment Regulations on Pre-Employment Inquiries

SUBJECT	ACCEPTABLE	UNACCEPTABLE
Name	Name. "Have you ever used another name." "Is any additional information relative to change of name, use of an assumed name, or nickname necessary to enable a check on your work and education record? If yes, please explain."	Maiden name.
Place of residence	Statement that hiring is subject to verification that applicant meets legal age requirements. "If hired can you show proof of age?" "Are you over 18?" "If under 18, can you, after employment, submit a work permit?"	Age. Birthdate. Dates of attendance or completion of elementary or high school. Questions that tend to identify applicants over age 40.
Birthplace, citizenship	"Can you, after employment, submit verification of your legal rights to work in the United States." Statement that such proof may be required after employment.	Birthplace or citizenship of applicant, applicant's parents, spouse, or other relatives. "Are you a U.S. citizen?"
National origin	Language applicant speaks, reads, or writes.	Questions as to nationality, lineage, ancestry, national origin, descent, or parentage of applicant, applicant's parents, or spouse. "What is your mother tongue?" Language commonly used by applicant. How applicant acquired ability to read, write, or speak a foreign language.
Sex, marital status, family	Name and address of parent or guardian if applicant is a minor. Statement of company policy regarding work assignment of employees who are related.	Questions that indicate applicant's sex or marital status. Number or ages of children or dependents. Provisions for child care. Questions regarding pregnancy, childbearing, or birth control. Name or address of relative, spouse, or children of adult applicant. "Who do you live with?" "Do you live with your parents?"
Race, color	None.	Questions as to applicants race or color. Questions regarding applicant's complexion or color of skin, eyes, or hair.
Physical description, photograph	Statement that photograph may be required after employment.	Questions about applicant's height or weight. Request for applicant to affix a photograph to application. Request for applicant, at his or her option, to submit a photograph. Request for photograph after the interview but before employment.

Table continues

Table 8-1 (continued)

SUBJECT	ACCEPTABLE	UNACCEPTABLE
Physical condition, disability	Statement that offer may be made contingent on applicant's passing a job-related physical examination. "Do you have any physical condition or handicap that may limit your ability to perform the job applied for? If yes, what can be done to accommodate your limitation?"	Questions regarding applicant's general medical condition, state of health, or illnesses. Questions regarding receipt of workers' compensation. "Do you have any physical disabilities or handicaps?"
Religion	Statement of regular days, hours, or shifts to be worked.	Questions regarding applicant's religion or religious days observed. "Does your religion prevent you from working weekends or holidays?"
Arrest, criminal record	"Have you ever been convicted of a felony or (within specified time period) a misdemeanor that resulted in imprisonment?" Such a statement must be accompanied by a statement that a conviction will not necessarily disqualify the applicant.	Arrest record. "Have you ever been arrested?"
Bonding	Statement that bonding is a condition of hire.	Questions regarding refusal or cancellation of bonding.
Military service	Questions regarding relevant skills acquired during applicant's U.S. military service.	General questions regarding military service, such as dates and type of discharge. Questions regarding service in a foreign military.
Economic status	None.	Questions regarding applicant's current or past assets, liabilities, or credit rating, including bankruptcy or garnishment.
Organizations, activities	"Please list job-related organizations, clubs, professional societies, or other associations to which you belong. You may omit those that indicate your race, religious creed, color, national origin, ancestry, sex, or age."	"List all organizations, clubs, societies, and lodges to which you belong."
References	"By whom were you referred for a position here?" Names of people willing to provide professional or character references for applicant.	Questions of applicant's former employers or acquaintances that elicit information specifying the applicant's race, color, relgious creed, national origin, ancestry, physical disability, medical condition, marital status, age, or sex.
Notification in case of emergency	Name and address of person to be notified in case of accident or emergency.	Name and address of relative to be notified in case of accident or emergency.

SOURCE: Adapted from Jensen, J. (1981). How to hire the right person for the job. *Grantsmanship Center News, 9*(3), 28–29. Copyright © 1981, The Grantsmanship Center. Reprinted with permission.

The effective date for compliance with specific sections of the ADA varies by topic and by the size of the corporation or entity. The employment provisions became effective July 26, 1992, for employers with 25 or more employees; effective July 26, 1994, for employers with 15 to 24 employees. Under the public accommodations provisions the compliance dates are January 26, 1992, for large businesses (more than 25 employees and gross receipts of more than $1 million); July 26, 1992, for medium-sized businesses (25 or fewer employees and gross receipts of less than $1 million); January 26, 1993, for small businesses (10 or fewer employees with less than $500,000 in gross receipts).

The ADA is not an affirmative action law. It is an equal employment opportunity law because it addresses discrimination in hiring, accommodation of a disabled person on the job, and access of people with disabilities to public and private facilities. Even if a person has a disability, he or she still must be qualified under the act. A qualified individual with a disability is one who, with or without reasonable accommodation, can perform the essential functions of the job that the person holds or desires. It is a two-step analysis: (1) What are the essential functions of the job? and (2) Can the individual perform the functions with or without a reasonable accommodation?

First and foremost, job requirements should always be expressed in terms of actual job duties and skill requirements and should never be expressed in terms of an applicant's or employee's limitations. The employer should not focus on whether a candidate or employee has a disability or is protected under the act. Rather, an employer should focus on the essential functions of the position and whether a candidate or employee, with reasonable accommodation, will be able to perform the essential functions of the job. An applicant should not be asked about the existence, nature, or severity of a disability but may be asked whether he or she is able to perform each essential job function.

An employer is still free to hire the most qualified candidate for any particular job. Qualifications of all applicants should be reviewed without regard to the disability of one of the applicants. If the applicant with a disability is the most qualified, then the employer should evaluate whether the disability limits or precludes the performance of an essential function of the job and, if so, whether reasonable accommodation will permit the person to perform the essential functions of the job.

Duty of Reasonable Accommodation

The concept of reasonable accommodation is the new, unique distinguishing characteristic of employment practices under the ADA. However, the concept is not well defined in the act. In simple terms, a reasonable accommodation is an action taken by the employer that assists a person with a disability to perform the essential job functions.

In determining whether a person is qualified for a position, any individual with a disability must be evaluated assuming all reasonable accommodations will be provided. If the individual is then not qualified for the position, he or she may be rejected.

Accommodations Provided by Private Entities

Title III of the ADA prohibits discrimination against individuals with disabilities "in the full and equal enjoyment of goods, services, and facilities, of any place of public accommodation by any person who owns, leases (or leases to) or operates a place of public accommodation." A public accommodation is broadly defined and includes places of lodging (excluding facilities with not more than five rooms for rent that is occupied by the proprietor as his or her residence); restaurants and bars; theaters and stadiums; auditoriums, convention centers, or other places of public gathering; sales or retail establishments such as bakeries, grocery stores, clothing stores, and shopping centers; service establishments such as banks, insurance offices, hospitals, and medical offices; public transportation stations; museums, libraries, and galleries; parks, zoos, amusements parks, or other places of recreation; private educational facilities; social services establishments such as day care centers, homeless shelters, food banks, adoptions agencies, and senior citizens centers; and places of exercise or recreation such as gymnasiums, spas, and golf courses.

The alterations and new construction provisions of the ADA also apply to commercial facilities intended for nonresidential use whose operations affect commerce. These facilities include office buildings (to the extent they are not covered by the public accommodations provisions of the act), factories, and warehouses.

Discrimination

The ADA requires that services be provided to individuals with disabilities in the most integrated setting appropriate to the needs of the individual. It is discriminatory to deny a person with a disability the opportunity to participate in or benefit from the goods, services, facilities, privileges, advantages, or accommodations offered by an entity or to provide such opportunity in a manner that is not equal to that afforded to other individuals. An entity may provide a service that is different or separate from that provided to other individuals only if such action is necessary to provide a service that is as effective as that provided to others.

The ADA identifies certain specific acts or omissions that constitute discrimination.

- The imposition or application of eligibility criteria that screen out or tend to screen out an individual with a disability from fully enjoying any goods, services, or facilities unless the criteria can be shown to be necessary for the provision of the goods, services, or facilities. For example, a bank cannot require a person to have a driver's license to open a checking account, but a rental car agency can require a driver's license.

- Failure to make reasonable modifications in policies, practices, or procedures when such modifications are necessary to afford the goods, services, or facilities unless the entity can demonstrate that making such modifications would fundamentally alter the nature of such goods, services, or facilities.
- Failure to take steps necessary to ensure that no individual with a disability is excluded, denied services, segregated, or otherwise treated differently than other individuals because of the absence of auxiliary aids and services unless the entity can demonstrate that taking such steps would fundamentally alter the nature of the goods, services, or facilities or would result in an undue burden.
- Failure to remove architectural and communication barriers that are structural in nature in existing facilities where such removal is readily achievable. If removal of a structural barrier is not readily achievable, failure to make such goods, services, or facilities available through alternative methods if such methods are readily achievable.

The limitations on the responsibility of a public accommodation to make modifications to procedures and practices is limited in two ways. First, the public accommodation can show that taking such steps would fundamentally alter the nature of the goods, services, or facilities. Second, the public accommodation can show that taking such steps would result in an undue burden—a significant difficulty or expense. In addition, an entity is not required to permit an individual to participate in or benefit from goods, services, and facilities when that individual poses a direct threat to the health or safety of others. The term "direct threat" means a significant risk to the health or safety of others that cannot be eliminated by a modification of policies, practices, or procedures or by the provision of auxiliary aids or services. Legitimate safety requirements, including crime prevention measures, may also be taken into account as long as they are based on actual risks and are necessary for the safe operation of the public accommodation.

SKILLS-APPLICATION EXERCISES

Equal Employment Opportunity Exercise

According to current law and/or EEOC policy:

1. It is permissible for you to keep on file information concerning your employees' race, color, religion, sex, or national origin.

   T____ F____ Don't know____

2. If your department is charged with one form of discrimination and the EEOC's investigation finds the charge to be untrue, the EEOC may find you guilty of another form of discrimination even if you were not charged with it.

    T____ F____ Don't know____

3. You may use the fact that a job applicant has a long arrest record as a reason for not hiring him or her.

    T____ F____ Don't know____

4. You may require a pregnant woman to take a leave of absence at a specified time before her delivery date.

    T____ F____ Don't know____

5. An employer must give a woman who has been off for maternity leave her *same* job and salary and guarantee no loss of seniority when she is ready to return to work.

    T____ F____ Don't know____

6. If a job applicant's religious faith requires that he or she be off on a normal workday, you may refuse to hire him or her.

    T____ F____ Don't know____

7. Even if your department has few or no members of a racial minority group, it is permissible for you to refuse to hire someone from that group because he or she failed an employment test.

    T____ F____ Don't know____

8. This decision is permissible: John is 60. Bill is 38. You choose Bill because he is younger and, therefore, will be able to devote more years to the department before retirement.

    T____ F____ Don't know____

9. You may terminate or refuse to hire a white male because of a conviction record.

    T____ F____ Don't know____

10. You may discharge a male employee for refusing to cut his long hair.

    T____ F____ Don't know____

11. An applicant may be refused employment because of a poor credit rating.

    T____ F____ Don't know____

12. It is permissible to refuse employment to someone without a car.

    T___ F___ Don't know___

13. General questions about high school or college degrees may be asked during an interview even though that educational degree is not necessary to perform the job.

    T___ F___ Don't know___

14. You may ask for an applicant's age or date of birth.

    T___ F___ Don't know___

15. An employer may ask an applicant if he or she is a U.S. citizen or ask for place of birth to avoid violating immigration laws.

    T___ F___ Don't know___

16. It is permissible to ask applicants if they have any mental or physical disabilities that relate to their fitness to perform a particular job.

    T___ F___ Don't know___

17. Applicants may be asked whether they are married.

    T___ F___ Don't know___

SOURCE: *Abstracted from materials developed by Gloria J. Rendon, Training Section, Personnel Administration, University of Utah, Salt Lake City, UT 84112.*

Answers to Equal Opportunity Exercise

NOTE: These answers must be viewed with some caution, as equal opportunity regulations are periodically revised, and local court cases may have implications for employment practices in your organization.

1. *True.* On application forms, this information is separated before the application is screened.

2. *True.*

3. *False.* The person must be *convicted,* and the crime must be job related.

4. *False.* This is generally a decision between a woman and her medical doctor except if the woman is ignoring her doctor's orders. In corrections and other fields with a possibility of physical assault, the employer can require a leave of absence.

5. *False.* The employer could reinstate her in a comparable job.

6. *True.* But the employer is required to make a good-faith effort to adjust the employee's schedule before refusing to hire or terminating.

7. *True.* Provided that the employment test is objective, valid, and job related.

8. *False.* Age discrimination is illegal.

9. *True.* The issue is conviction, not merely arrest. It also depends on the job. If the conviction is not job related or if you hired others with convictions who were not members of racial or ethnic minority groups, you may be violating equal employment opportunity policy.

10. *False.* Generally hair length is not enforceable. But it depends on the job, because a hair net may be required, especially in restaurants and institutional food service. In addition, a police department was upheld in a recent Supreme Court case for mandating short hairstyles because of special circumstances such as a safety factor.

11. *True.* But it applies only in certain cases because it has to be job related (to work at certain bank jobs, you must be bonded with the bonding company, which is contingent upon a good credit rating).

12. *False.* Not owning a car does not mean without transportation. But it may be required in areas without mass transportation where the job requires a personal mode of transportation.

13. *False.* Because an educational degree is not necessary for the job.

14. *True.* Possibly, but only if to work in a liquor store or some other position in which the age requirement is clearly related.

15. *True.* But this policy is controversial and varies according to the way it is asked. Use questions such as the following: Are you a citizen (yes or no)? If not, do you have a visa? Do you have a green card? This is a difficult situation, as sometimes the personnel department performs a visa or green card check before the interview process, but the interviewer does not have this information.

16. *True.* But how the question is asked is important. One appropriate method is, Do you have a physical disability or mental or physical condition that would prevent you from performing this job?

17. *False.*

Interviewing Skills Exercise

Members of a selection committee or a group of graduate students can practice these interviewing skills by dividing into small groups to develop a set of interview questions for a position. One member of each group becomes an "applicant" for the other group, and the other members choose who will lead the interview and who will ask which questions. The applicants from each group switch and are then interviewed by the other group.

After the interview, the applicant and the group debrief by discussing what went well and what aspects of the process could be improved. This interviewing simulation allows members of a selection committee to test a set of interview questions and practice interviewing skills.

REFERENCES

Age Discrimination in Employment Act of 1967, P.L. 90-202, 81 Stat. 602.

American Psychological Association. (1980). *Principles for the validation and use of personnel selection procedures* (2nd ed.). Washington, DC: Author.

Americans with Disabilities Act of 1990, P.L. 101-336, 104 Stat. 327.

Attard, J. (1984). *You can hire the perfect employee.* Westbury, NY: Caddylak.

Beach, D. S. (1975). *Personnel: The management of people at work.* New York: Macmillan.

Campbell, A. (1983). Hiring for results: Interviews that select winners. *Business Quarterly, 48*(4), 57–61.

Campion, S. E., & Arvey, R. D. (1989). Unfair discrimination in the employment interview. In R. W. Eder & G. R. Ferris (Eds.), *The employment interview—Theory, research and practice* (pp. 61–74). Newbury Park, CA: Sage Publications.

Carlson, R. E., Thayer, P. W., Mayfield, E. C., & Peterson, D. A. (1971). Improvements in the selection interview. *Personnel Journal, 50,* 268–275, 317.

Casey Family Program. (1997, September). *Competencies, Recruitment, and Selection Committee executive summary.* Seattle: Author.

Civil Rights Act of 1964, P.L. 88-352, 78 Stat. 24.

Eder, R. W., & Ferris, G. R. (Eds.). (1989). *The employment interview—Theory, research and practice.* Newbury Park, CA: Sage Publications.

Equal Pay Act of 1963, P.L. 88-38, 77 Stat. 56.

Glueck, W. F. (1978). *Personnel: A diagnostic approach* (rev. ed.). Dallas: Business Publications.

Goodale, J. G. (1989). Effective employment interviewing. In R. W. Eder & G. R. Ferris (Eds.), *The employment interview: Theory, research and practice* (pp. 307–324). Newbury Park, CA: Sage Publications.

Howell, W. C., & Dipboye, R. L. (1982). *Essentials of industrial and organizational psychology.* Homewood, IL: Dorsey Press.

Janz, T. (1989). The patterned behavior description interview: The best prophet of the future is the past. In R. W. Eder & G. R. Ferris (Eds.), *The employment interview—Theory, research and practice* (pp. 158–168). Newbury Park, CA: Sage Publications.

Jensen, J. (1981). How to hire the right person for the job. *Grantsmanship Center News, 9*(3), 21–31.

Klingner, D. E., & Nalbandian, J. (1985). *Public personnel management: Contexts and strategies.* Englewood Cliffs, NJ: Prentice Hall.

Latham, G. P. (1989). The reliability, validity, and practicality of the situational interview. In R.

W. Eder & G. R. Ferris (Eds.), *The employment interview—Theory, research and practice* (pp. 169–182). Newbury Park, CA: Sage Publications.

Locke, E. A., & Latham, G. P. (1984). *Goal setting: A motivational technique that works.* Englewood Cliffs, NJ: Prentice Hall.

Mayfield, E. C., Brown, S. H., & Hamstra, B. W. (1980). Selection interviewing in the life insurance industry: An update of research and practice. *Personnel Psychology, 33,* 725–739.

McCormick, E. J. (1979). *Job analysis: Methods and applications.* New York: Amacom.

Meritt-Haston, R., & Weyley, K. N. (1983). Educational requirements: Legality and validity. *Personnel Psychology, 36,* 743–753.

Mufson, D. W. (1986). Selecting child care workers using the California Psychological Inventory. *Child Welfare, 65,* 83–88.

Pecora, P. J., & Austin, M. J. (1983). Declassification of social service jobs: Issues and strategies. *Social Work, 28,* 421–426.

Pecora, P. J., & Austin, M. J. (1987). *Managing human services personnel.* Newbury Park, CA: Sage Publications.

Rehabilitation Act of 1973, P.L. 93-112, 87 Stat. 355.

Robertson, M. A. (1982). *Personnel administration employment interviewing guide for supervisors.* Salt Lake City: University of Utah, Office of Personnel Administration.

Ross, A. R., & Hoeltke, G. (1985). A tool for selecting residential child care work initial report. *Child Welfare, 64,* 46–55.

Shafritz, J. M., Hyde, A. C., & Rosenbloom, D. H. (1986). *Personnel management in government: Politics and process* (3rd ed.). New York: Marcel Dekker.

Teare, R. J., Higgs, C., Gauthier, T. P., & Feild, H. S. (1984). *Classification validation processes for social service positions: Vol. I, Overview.* Silver Spring, MD: National Association of Social Workers.

Vietnam Era Veterans' Readjustment Assistance Act of 1974, P.L. 93-508, 88 Stat. 1578.

Zedeck, S., & Cascio, W. F. (1984). Psychological issues in personnel decisions. *Review of Psychology, 35,* 461–518.

The author thanks Stacy Radley and Gloria Rendon at the University of Utah, Michael J. Austin of the University of California at Berkeley, and members of the Casey Family Program Recruitment and Selection Competencies Work Group for their advice.

CHAPTER 9

Designing and Sustaining Meaningful Organizational Teams

Darlyne Bailey

anagers at all levels of organizations must have good human relations skills. Among the roles that managers must play is that of group
facilitator, which demands skills in team building, fostering participatory decision making, and conflict management. The presence of teams
in the workplace has a long history. However, as the type, amount, and complexity of the demands on America's nonprofit organizations increase, nonprofit managers are rediscovering the productivity of effective teams.

Teams are being used in nonprofits in a wide range of activities, including
researching new programs and services, developing clinical treatment plans for
the improved care of patients, and redesigning the organizational environment. The literature supports this posture. Almost every new book on organizational effectiveness stresses the importance of teamwork (Bolman & Deal,
1997). In a *Fortune 100* survey, more than half of the companies reported
anticipating a heavy reliance on work teams in the future (Schilder, 1992).
However, despite this recognition, a study by Dyer (1987) showed that few
managers actually take the time to understand when and how to develop and
sustain these teams. In interviews with 300 managers from various organizations, Dyer found that less than 25 percent had instituted programs to ensure
the continued success of teams. Moreover, although these managers were on
teams themselves, only 10 percent to 15 percent of their supervisors had
addressed the issue of team success with them.

A lack of information may be the reason for this inattention. Top-level
managers may not realize that effective teams require an environmental context in which the organization's goals and resources support the team's needs,
team members who have the skills necessary to accomplish the task, and a
team leader who can focus on both the task and interpersonal processes using
the most effective motivators.

This chapter explores three issues: (1) the process of team development
(how teams are formed and how they become functional); (2) typical

behaviors of team members during the course of the team's existence; and most important, (3) the requisite motivators and skills that effective team leaders must learn and use (why wanting a team to be productive is just not enough).

The words "team" and "group" are used interchangeably to describe a work unit that "has a particular process of working together, one in which members identify and fully use one another's resources and facilitate their mutual interdependence toward more effective problem solving and task accomplishment" (Hanson & Lubin, 1988, p. 77). More recent definitions of organizational teams underscore this aspect of interdependence. Bulin (1995) defined a team as "a group of people who are interdependent and who recognize that the success of each one of them hinges on the success of the group" (p. 124). Losoncy (1997) suggested seven working principles for effective teams. The first principle is the "Synergy Principle . . . all of us together can do more than each of us can do alone" (p. 3).

Now more than ever, nonprofit organizations need leaders who understand the needs of such organizations, and teams can clearly assess their abilities and ask for help with their limitations. The future of nonprofit organizations may well depend on these abilities.

ORGANIZATIONAL TEAMS: PAST, PRESENT, AND FUTURE

Recognition of the strength of people when they work together in organizations dates back to the 1800s. A number of scholars have made notable contributions in this area.

Late 1800s to Early 1900s

The German sociologist Weber (1930) preached the need for (and potential dangers of) authority and rationality in working with organized groups of people. Le Bon (1903/1960) discovered the powerful effects of this collectivity on the individual group member. Taylor (1911/1978), the subject of the novel and film *Cheaper by the Dozen* (Gilbreth, 1948), studied the process of efficiency and proposed that large systems are most efficient when their organizational members are scientifically managed. During the same period, Mayo (1933) conducted his Hawthorne Western Electric Studies and noted the relationship between group identity and cohesion in informal groups and worker productivity. Contemporaneously, Freud (1922) analyzed the effects of conflict in groups.

Mid-1900s

Lewin (1947), credited as the father of modern group dynamics, explored the phenomena of the formation and development of groups through laboratory and experience-based learning. Maslow (1965) and Rogers (1970) wrote about the almost limitless quality of human potential when fundamental needs are met within a culture of positive regard for self and others. At about the same time, Katz and Kahn (1966), McClelland (1961), McGregor (1966), and Von Bertalanfy (1968), each working separately, generated a collective description of organizations. They viewed organizations as open systems composed of subsystems of people whose level of satisfaction with tasks, coworkers, and authorities played a major role in determining the productivity of organizations.

Late 1900s

Ouchi (1981) and Pascale and Athos (1981) suggested that Americans have much to learn from alternative forms of management, such as those used in some of the highly successful Japanese organizations. One example is the quality circle, a method in which a team of employees actively participates in the resolution of the organization's problems. Although the quality circle, as a variant of team building, continues to receive mixed reviews among American workers, an article in *Business Week* ("Payoff from Teamwork," 1989) helped bring the role of work groups up-to-date.

In some companies, the problem-solving nature of quality circles evolved into special-purpose or project management teams that focused on specific tasks through the collaboration of staff and management. Then, in Norway and throughout Scandinavia, under the guidance of Thorsrud (1977), research began to emerge on autonomous teams. In the 1980s, teams of employees began producing entire products instead of parts of products, such as a whole car instead of just the doors. These autonomous or self-managing teams have also assumed responsibility for some management-level decisions. The literature describes this form of organizational work group as the wave of the future (Courtright, Fairhurst, & Rogers, 1989; Manz & Sims, 1987), and studies continue to explore the dynamics of self-managing teams, such as their cost, benefits, and the role of external leadership.

Senge's (1990) work on learning organizations emphasized the need for teams who model continuous learning in their daily operations. Katzenbach and Smith (1994) built on this idea to suggest that teams are not static entities, but rather are constantly shifting collaborations of individuals who make the work happen. Such an approach to teams requires the crafting of an organizational culture that recognizes that everything is the result of interdependencies. It is only within these cultures that the most successful learning units arise. Such groups, best described by Wheatley and Kellner-Rogers (1996), "no longer seek their security behind the stout walls of exclusion. They learn that by reaching out they become stronger. Their support comes not from unnatural boundaries but from the inherent strength of wholeness" (p. 102). Such is the life of a team unit that has the potential to be organizationally productive as well as meaningful on both the individual and group levels.

MEANINGFUL TEAMS: CREATION AND MOTIVATION

Social scientists have been exploring the what and how of motivation since the 1940s. The what or content approach, as demonstrated by Maslow's (1943) hierarchy of needs, Herzberg's (1968) two-factor theory of motivators and hygiene, and Alderfer's (1972) existence, relatedness, and growth theory, essentially purports that behavior is driven by an individual's attempt to fulfill unsatisfied needs. The how or process perspective, as demonstrated by Vroom's (1964) expectancy theory and the Porter-Lawler model (Porter & Lawler, 1968) in which performance leads to satisfaction, defines motivation as personal choice. Over time we have realized that interweaving both approaches to understanding motivation is the most effective way to support meaningful teams.

Today's top management faces four challenges in working with teams. First, managers must create a team whose membership and leadership best meets the needs of the tasks. Kotter (1996) recommended individuals with necessary degrees of position, power, expertise, credibility, and their own recognized leadership. Second, they must identify the socioemotional needs of the team individually and collectively. Third, they must ensure that the organization provides the team with an array of opportunities to meet those needs. Fourth, managers must make explicit the interdependence between the team members and leaders as well as the interdependence between the team and the rest of the organization. Doing so requires that each member receives the concrete resources necessary to do his or her best work. These steps will prepare the foundation for a meaningful team that is ready to assume an identity as part of, yet distinct from, the organization.

As historians readily tell us, the future carries the thumbprints of the past. The first need for order within groups of people was recognized in the literature of the 1800s. The scientific management of people (often referred to as "Taylorism") was proposed in the early 1900s, only to be ameliorated by the role of social support and the need to manage conflict. The mid-1900s brought recognition of the dynamics of the evolution of groups and how groups are most effective in raising organizational productivity when the members' individual and social needs are met. As we approach the 21st century, organizations worldwide in the for-profit and nonprofit sectors alike are experimenting with innovative designs for organizational teams.

STAGES AND BEHAVIORS OF MEANINGFUL TEAMS

Central to any system's existence are the dynamics of growth: progressive, lateral, and regressive movements. Organizational teams are no different. Given the long-standing and robust history of organizational teams, it is not surprising that there are many models to describe their evolution. Regardless of the differences in specific responsibilities, size, and the necessary degree of internal collaboration among these teams, once formed, all these groups seem to go through similar stages.

Small-group theorists tend to see these models as developmental, with the successful movement through one stage dependent on the satisfactory completion of the stage or stages that preceded it (Bennis & Shepard, 1956; Dunphy, 1974; Katzenbach & Smith, 1994; Moosbruker, 1988; Neilsen, 1972). These models have anywhere from three to seven stages, but one five-stage model is comprehensive, descriptive, and easy to remember (Tuckman & Jensen, 1977). Tuckman and Jensen's model included the stages of forming, storming, norming, performing, and adjourning. Using this model as a guide, one may describe the developmental challenges and skills of the leaders of managerial teams that are necessary to facilitate the team's successful movement through the stages.

Table 9-1 consists of four columns: (1) the developmental stages, (2) the general types of behaviors that team members exhibit at each of these stages, (3) the corresponding motivators (both content and process) for the team leader, and (4) the behavioral skills the leader needs to help the team accomplish its goals in ways that are efficient in terms of time and resources and meaningful to the individuals and the group as a whole.

In the forming stage, people come together to work on a common task. Some of these people may have worked together before on a similar project, but this is the first time that these individuals are uniting to work on this task. Amid questions about the purpose of the group, the role of the leader, and attributions regarding each member's potential power in the group and real influence outside the group, the leader must provide general guidelines for the group and take steps to establish a group culture that fosters and rewards the free exchange of ideas and opinions.

Table 9-1. Stages, Behaviors, Tasks, and Skills of Team Development

STAGES	MEMBERS' BEHAVIORS	LEADER'S TASKS	LEADER'S SKILLS
1. *Forming:* People volunteer or are recruited to work together on a common task.	Questioning the leader about the group's purpose, appropriate behaviors of members, and leader's role Attributing in-team status to members on the basis of outside-of-team information Obeying the leader Discussion patterns are jerky, and there are long periods of silence	Provide structure regarding boundaries of the team (such as the frequency and place of meetings, the organization's reason for forming the team, time lines for achieving the team's task) Offer guidance in setting directions for the accomplishment of the task Solicit each member's opinions and ideas Encourage dialogue	Awareness of a personal leadership style Effective communication Thorough knowledge of the fit between the team's task and organizational goals
2. *Storming:* Individual and subgroup differences of opinions, values, skills, and interests start to surface.	Expressing opinions and disagreements Exploring the degrees of individual power and challenging the leader's role and style Attending to and avoiding the team's task Emergence of cliques and bonds	Discuss the team's decision-making process Model appropriate awareness of self and others Provide the team with the resources necessary to accomplish the task Help the team establish procedures and norms for the resolution of conflict	Management of different values, behaviors, and skills Awareness of personal strengths and limitations Use of process and content

Table continues

Table 9-1 (continued)

STAGES	MEMBERS' BEHAVIORS	LEADER'S TASKS	LEADER'S SKILLS
3. *Norming:* The team focuses on the need for order and guidelines for how to work together.	Stabilizing the team's purpose, authority relationships, individual levels, and types of participation Exhibiting in-group humor Emergence of informal leadership Establishing procedures for the resolution of conflict and the accomplishment of the task	Adhere to the team's established structure and procedures Ensure that the team's actions are in accordance with what the team really wants to do Infuse the team with enthusiasm and energy Reward individual and team efforts Acknowledge and reinforce the informal leadership Protect the team from outside interferences	Mentoring Management of agreement Balancing work with play Buffering the team from ongoing operations
4. *Performing:* The team delivers the completed task.	Producing results: alignment of members' energies and interests with the team's task	Vigilance: attend to the team's need for fine tuning its skills and attitudes Develop mechanisms for the continued monitoring of the team	Visioning Listening with the "third ear" Evaluation
5. *Adjourning:* The original need for the team no longer exists.	Assessing process and product Dissolving the team	Publicly acknowledge the team's accomplishments	Positive regard of self and others

To accomplish these tasks, the leader must have a strong sense of self-awareness and an understanding of the interrelatedness of the team's task and the organization's goals. Moreover, the leader must be able to communicate this personal and professional information in a way that models candor and appropriate self-disclosure and acknowledges the team's value to the effectiveness of the total organization. It is these skills that will help the group members begin to risk sharing their ideas, an activity that will move the group from forming into storming.

In the second stage—storming—individual group members and small subgroups continue to share their different perspectives. As they do this, differences in values, types and levels of skills, and degrees of interest in and commitment to the group's task are a few of the areas that may become reasons for members to be attracted to or repelled by each other. As these differences emerge, members also begin to explore their own leadership abilities, often by challenging the role and style of the designated leader. At this time, the leader must continue to model self-awareness and help the group establish guidelines, yet focus more explicitly on issues of self in the context of others and on procedures for resolving conflicts and making group-level decisions. While ensuring that the team has the concrete resources (time, space, and materials) that are required to accomplish the task, the leader must also demonstrate skills to equip the team members with the necessary intellectual and emotional tools. The leader's ability to recognize and appreciate the differences that arise in this group will serve as a guide for how the members can use these differences to make the team's time together more productive. The leader's knowledge of the difference between the group's process (the methods and procedures the group uses to achieve its goals) and its content (the activities and issues that a group discusses and enacts to achieve its goals) must be used to help the group work effectively in both areas. It is only when the group as a whole agrees on how it will disagree that it is able to move into the third stage of development.

In the third stage—norming—the team must continue its work on establishing codes of conduct for how members will interact. With the abatement of tensions surrounding the issues of individual identity and authority, the bonding of members to the subgroups, the bonding among the subgroups, and a focus on the purpose of the team, informal leaders start to emerge as the group determines exactly how it will complete the task. Amid a strong sense of group identity, the leader motivates the team by continuing to focus on content and process and by helping the group adhere to its procedures. The leader also ensures that the necessary resources are maintained; enthusiastically rewards the efforts of individuals, subgroups, and the team as a whole; and supports the members who assume leadership roles. Moreover, the leader must help the group build on its new process for disagreeing by teaching its

"We had a wonderful group established. Harmonious. Supportive. Even established our own goals and norms. Then our boss came back from her meeting, and we got task oriented very quickly."

members how to avoid the trap of agreeing just to maintain the group's harmony. When the group learns how to balance work with play and agreement with disagreement, it is then able to accomplish the task and moves into the performing stage.

This fourth stage—performing—is the payoff, when the team's energies and interests are focused on completing the task. The leader's role is offstage directing—attending to the fine tuning of the members' skills and feelings of being team players while helping the team develop the skills to monitor the execution of the task. The leader also models visioning skills (communicating a sense of what this team can be like when the task is completed); responds to the individual's and team's needs, desires, and fears; and joins the team in the collective evaluation of the finished product.

In this fifth stage—adjourning—members acknowledge and assess the total process and content of the team as they move toward dissolution. The leader informally and publicly recognizes the team's accomplishments as belonging to the entire team. At this time the leader must show a positive regard for his or her role in this process and for the roles and responsibilities of the other members. The worth of the product is thus a symbol of a job well done by an effectively functioning team.

Although these team behaviors, motivators, and leadership skills are understandable, teams often get stuck in one or more of these stages. It is at this point that a leader's skills are most needed to facilitate the group's development. To understand these leadership skills better, we will consider some key moments in the development of a social services agency's planning team. This group consists of members of the board of trustees and the staff. Although this organization and its personnel are fictitious, the issues and process are true to life.

CASE OF THE EASTSIDE YOUTH CENTER

Because of rapidly shrinking resources, particularly money and appropriately trained personnel, as well as the changing needs of the community and the demand for increased accountability from funding bodies, the Eastside Youth Center (EYC) decided to develop a three-year strategic plan. This process will enable EYC to revisit the agency's mission statement, staffing patterns, and programs and to forecast the changes that are needed in the agency's structure and operations to help it become a multiservice family center.

At a recent monthly meeting, the board unanimously decided to hire a local consultant to outline the strategic planning process and help the organization move through it. Because of limited funds, the consultant agreed to meet with a planning team at the beginning of the process and six months later and to meet periodically with the team leader to answer questions and suggest subsequent steps.

The executive director and members of the board selected a planning team of four board members and three staff members. The president of the board was quickly appointed the team leader for the same reason she had earlier been voted president—a sound background in leadership training.

Forming

At a half-day workshop for the team, the consultant described the major steps and issues of a good strategic plan. The team members asked many questions, and everyone left the meeting feeling comfortable and confident about the pending process. However, two weeks later, at the first real meeting, the members focused more on themselves than on the plan. They began to refer to their community and business status and to position themselves to influence the others.

The group also began to question the expertise of the team leader. Whenever the leader would try to refocus the conversation, the group fell silent. The leader then began to make fewer statements and ask more

questions, such as "Given the fact that the team is to develop a plan to recommend to the board at the end of six months, how frequently do you want
to meet?" And, "What ideas do each of you have about the process as a result
of our workshop with the consultant?" The members slowly began to respond
to the leader's questions, offering their ideas and deciding that the group
would meet for three to four hours every other week.

In the next two meetings, the group began to explore the specifics of the
task more actively, with the leader modeling skills of active listening, asking
open-ended questions, and providing basic information about the mechanics
of the planning process.

Storming

In the fourth meeting, the leader noticed that the members were talking to
her less and arguing more among themselves. A week earlier, she had telephoned the consultant and happily reported the team's progress. The consultant reminded her of the calm before the storm and urged her to remember
her conflict mediation skills. So, when the members began to quarrel about
the superiority of one person's ideas over another's and to imply that the
board members' and staff's intentions were different, the leader pointed out
what they were doing. She noted the benefits of each subgroup's perspective
and asked the entire team to decide the type of process they would use for
appreciating and then using any differences they may identify.

At first, the leader was accused of not being direct enough. Then she was
told that she was too dictatorial. The leader maintained her position and
noticed that the next three meetings were attended by only two board members and two staff members. She began to urge the group to talk about the
content of planning as well as the process they were using to work as a team.

Norming

In the eighth meeting, the members began to talk about wanting more guidelines for the team. A lively discussion ensued about requirements for attendance and procedures to use for resolving disagreements. The leader told the
story of the Abilene paradox (Harvey, 1974), in which a group of people
agreed to do something that was bad for the group and that no one really
wanted to do—a case of mismanaging agreement. Sprinkled throughout this
otherwise serious conversation were quips and jokes about the leader and the
team members. Then there was a general feeling of camaraderie and anticipation as the group reviewed its progress and articulated future steps.

During the next two meetings, the leader noticed that one board member
was taking a leadership role within the group by starting the meetings,

soliciting comments, and then summarizing a seemingly disparate list of ideas. She began to support this man's behavior and met with him twice outside the group to get his ideas about how the group could finish the plan. During a monthly meeting of the entire board when a motion was made to expand the team's responsibilities, this man supported the leader in refusing the additional work. At the leader's suggestion, a party was held for the team members at this man's house—a celebration of all the work that had been done and a rehearsal of the team's recommendations to the rest of the board.

Performing

Just before the team submitted its plan, it met with the consultant to get another perspective on the recommendations. The leader encouraged the team to be creative with its suggestions and then facilitated a discussion about its work as a team. The members were animated about their work together over the past several months and felt as though each had played a significant role in the process. The consultant was satisfied with the results and suggested that the team volunteer to monitor the effectiveness of the plan, pending its ratification by the rest of the board. The group agreed and immediately began to formulate a mechanism for the continued evaluation of both the implementation of the plan and the process of the team.

It is not surprising that when the team presented the three-year strategic plan for the agency, the board and the executive director were pleased. The discussion was animated, creative, and productive. The board voted to continue the team for another six months to oversee the plan and assess future steps, such as installing another monitoring team and rotating members. The team leader publicly thanked her colleagues and distributed framed certificates of appreciation to each member of the team.

Adjourning

Even though the original team was going to stay intact, the tasks and responsibilities were different. The leader encouraged the team to celebrate the ending of the initial work. She shared her perceptions of the team's progress, focusing on both the process and the product. All the members expressed their views and while praising themselves and the leader, began to talk about the first steps to take in their new roles as monitors of the plan.

It is important to keep in mind several factors about team development that apply to Tuckman and Jensen's (1977) model. First, as a team progresses through these stages, it may regress because of a change in the membership, responsibilities or the need to work through the issues presented at an earlier stage.

Second, a team's developmental stage may have nothing to do with its age. Depending on the roles and responsibilities of a team, its relationship to the rest of the organization, and the effectiveness of its leader, a team that has been working together for two years may be stuck in an early stage, such as storming. The team is likely to stay at that stage unless it is helped, whereas a much newer team may rapidly progress through the various stages.

Third, although there are clear benefits to establishing work teams, there are also some costs, or what Schindler-Rainman (1988) called "negative aspects," to using teams. Reasons to avoid forming a team include the incompatibility of the members' commitments, the lack of a sense of purpose and direction, a member who cannot work as part of the team, or the lack of organizational support. Thus, top managers must weigh the costs and benefits of forming work teams before they begin the process.

Fourth, the team does not usually move from one clearly differentiated stage to the next. As with all models, this one represents an ideal type. In reality, the stages tend to be less obvious, and a team may even remain between stages for a time.

The identification of the typical behaviors of members and the motivational skills that the team leader must possess, as well as an analysis of Tuckman and Jensen's (1977) model, all help top managers become aware of the dynamics of work teams. This knowledge, combined with a clear sense of their own abilities and limitations, enables top managers to help their teams and the team's leadership become more productive for the organization and more rewarding for their members. As noted by Katzenbach and Smith (1994), "teams will be the primary building block of performance in the high-performance organization of the future"(p. 239).

Yet as they use this powerful tool to enhance organizational performance, upper-level managers should realize that teams change over time, and recognizing the team's stage of development at any point in time is only part of the challenge. The more important message is that team leaders must be willing to search for and use this information while recognizing and aligning their own abilities with the needs of the group. As leaders, we know that the synergy that comes from effectively operating teams in our organization is limitless. Building teams is an ongoing process, one in which organizational leaders have the most critical role.

SKILLS-APPLICATION EXERCISES

Here are some suggestions for exercises that can be used for experiential learning opportunities:

- You are assigned to lead a work team that has been meeting for several months. After reading the organization's charge to the team, you call a meeting and discover that only one-third of the members have come. They are the same one-third who usually come, and they call themselves the "real workers" on the team. What do you do and say? Why?

- You are hired as a consultant to facilitate the merger of two small nonprofit organizations. As part of the premerger agreement, the management teams of both agencies have been asked to form the leadership of the new organization. How would you get these people to work as a team? What initial problems or issues would you expect to encounter?

- You are asked to write a chapter in a new book about the development of teams, highlighting the major principles and skills that managers need to learn. What do you write about and why?

REFERENCES

Alderfer, C. P. (1972). *Existence, relatedness, and growth.* New York: Free Press.

Bennis, W. G., & Shepard, H. (1956). A theory of group development. *Human Relations, 9,* 415–437.

Bolman, L. G., & Deal, T. E. (1997). *Reframing organizations* (2nd ed.). San Francisco: Jossey-Bass.

Bulin, J. G. (1995). *Supervision: Skills for managing work and leading people.* Boston: Houghton-Mifflin.

Courtright, J. A., Fairhurst, G. T., & Rogers, E. L. (1989). Interaction patterns in organic and mechanistic systems. *Academy of Management Journal, 32,* 773–802.

Dunphy, D. C. (1974). *The primary group: A handbook for analysis and field research.* New York: Appleton-Century-Crofts.

Dyer, W. G. (1987). *Team building: Issues and alternatives* (2nd ed.). Cambridge, MA: Addison-Wesley.

Freud, S. (1922). *Group psychology and the analysis of the ego.* London: Hogarth Press.

Gilbreth, F. B. (1948). *Cheaper by the dozen.* New York: T. Y. Crowell.

Hanson, P. G., & Lubin, B. (1988). Team building as group development. In W. B. Reddy & K. Jamison (Eds.), *Team building: Blueprints for productivity and satisfaction* (pp. 76–87). Washington, DC: NTL Institute for Applied Behavioral Science–University Associates.

Harvey, J. (1974, Summer). Managing agreement in organizations: The Abilene paradox. *Organizational Dynamics,* pp. 63–80.

Herzberg, F. (1968, January–February). One more time: How do you motivate employees? *Harvard Business Review,* pp. 53–62.

Katz, D., & Kahn, R. L. (1966). *The social psychology of organizations.* New York: John Wiley & Sons.

Katzenbach, T. R., & Smith, D. K. (1994). *The wisdom of teams.* New York: Harper Business.

Kotter, J. P. (1996). *Leading change.* Boston: Harvard Business School Press.

Le Bon, G. (1960). *The crowd.* New York: Viking. Original work published 1903.

Lewin, K. (1947). Frontiers in group dynamics: Concept method and reality in social equilibria and social change. *Human Relations, 1*(5), 41.

Losoncy, L. E. (1997). *Best team skills*. Delray Beach, FL: St. Lucie Press.

Manz, C. C., & Sims, H. P., Jr. (1987). Leading workers to lead themselves: The external leadership of self-managing work teams. *Administrative Science Quarterly, 32*(1), 106–129.

Maslow, A. H. (1943, July). A theory of human motivation. *Psychological Review*, pp. 370–396.

Maslow, A. H. (1965). *Eupsychian management: A journal*. Homewood, IL: Irwin-Dorsey.

Mayo, E. (1933). *The human problems of an industrial civilization*. New York: Macmillan.

McClelland, D. C. (1961). *The achieving society*. New York: Van Nostrand Reinhold.

McGregor, D. (1966). *Leadership and motivation*. Cambridge, MA: MIT Press.

Moosbruker, J. (1988). Developing a productivity team: Making groups at work work. In W. B. Reddy & K. Jamison (Eds.), *Team building: Blueprints for productivity and satisfaction* (pp. 88–97). Washington, DC: NTL Institute for Applied Behavioral Science–University Associates.

Neilsen, E. H. (1972). Understanding and managing intergroup conflict. In T. W. Lorsch & P. R. Lawrence (Eds.), *Managing group and intergroup relations* (pp. 329–343). Homewood, IL: Irwin-Dorsey.

Ouchi, W. G. (1981). *Theory Z: How American business can meet the Japanese challenge*. Cambridge, MA: Addison-Wesley.

Pascale, T., & Athos, A. G. (1981). *The art of Japanese management: Applications for American executives*. New York: Wagner Books.

Payoff from teamwork. (1989, July 10). *Business Week*, pp. 56–62.

Porter, L. W., & Lawler, E. E. (1968). *Managerial attitudes and performance*. Homewood, IL: Irwin-Dorsey.

Rogers, C. (1970). *Carl Rogers on encounter groups*. New York: Harper & Row.

Schilder, J. (1992, February). Work teams boost productivity: *Personnel Journal*, p. 68.

Schindler-Rainman, E. (1988). Team building in voluntary organizations. In W. B. Reddy & K. Jamison (Eds.), *Team building: Blueprints for productivity and satisfaction* (pp. 119–123). Washington, DC: NTL Institute for Applied Behavioral Science–University Associates.

Senge, P. M. (1990). *The fifth discipline*. New York: Doubleday.

Taylor, F. (1978). The principles of scientific management. In J. Shafritz & P. Whitbeck (Eds.), *Classics of organizational theory* (pp. 12–19). Oak Park, IL: Moore. Original work published 1911.

Thorsrud, E. (1977). Democracy at work: Norwegian experiences with nonbureaucratic forms of organization. *Journal of Applied Behavioral Science, 13*, 410–421.

Tuckman, B. W., & Jensen, M.A.C. (1977). Stages in small group development revisited. *Group and Organization Studies, 2*, 419–427.

Von Bertalanfy, L. (1968). *General systems theory*. New York: George Braziller.

Vroom, V. (1964). *Work and motivation*. New York: John Wiley & Sons.

Weber, M. (1930). *The Protestant ethic and the spirit of capitalism*. (T. Parsons, trans.). New York: Charles Scribner's Sons.

Wheatley, M. J., & Kellner-Rogers, M. (1996). *A simpler way*. San Francisco: Berrett-Koehler.

CHAPTER 10

Advancing Women
in the Managerial Ranks

Roslyn H. Chernesky

Although women have made great strides into the managerial ranks
since the mid-1970s, their progress conceals a pattern of pervasive
and persistent gender inequality. Earlier explanations of women's
slow move into management and then up led to a number of individual and
organizational strategies for women. However, these strategies did not succeed in shattering the glass ceiling, and women remained stuck in entry-level
and middle-management positions and in certain kinds of jobs, positions, and
organizations.

This chapter reviews the status of women in management as well as several perspectives that may account for the persistent nature of inequality. The
theories and research presented are drawn from the for-profit and public sectors because the nonprofit sector has not given much attention to the phenomenon. This literature provides a context for a presentation of skills, strategies, and methods that nonprofit managers can use as they face the challenge
of assuring women's continued advancement in management. Managers
should be concerned if a segment of the workforce cannot fulfill its potential
because of employment practices that inadvertently discriminate or organizational structures that limit options and mobility. Effective managers will want
to know if gender inequality exists in their organizations and will look toward
rectifying the conditions that create and contribute to the inequality.

WOMEN'S PROGRESS ENTERING MANAGEMENT

Every study and report since 1990 has acknowledged that women have
entered management since the mid-1970s in far greater numbers than ever
before. Their progress has been remarkable, representing a major step toward
occupational integration. Whereas 18.5 percent of executive, administrative,
and managerial positions were held by women in 1970, the percentage had

increased to 30.5 percent a decade later (Blum, Fields, & Goodman, 1994). By 1990, women occupied 48 percent of managerial and professional positions, including vice presidents, office managers, and middle-management titles (Dobrzynski, 1996b). The increase of women in management is found in all employment sectors. In the public sector in 1990, three-fourths of the states hired a higher proportion of women for management jobs than they already had working for them. Women held 31 percent of state officials and administrator positions, an increase of 35 percent from 1980. Women held an even higher percentage of county officials and administrator positions, 40 percent, but only 26 percent of city officials and administrators were women (Center for Women in Government, 1991–1992).

This growth in the number of women managers is especially impressive in the nonprofit sector, where women employees generally outnumber men, except in religious organizations. The percentage of women in nonprofit management positions has almost tripled since the mid-1970s. Women today are much more likely to be in managerial positions in nonprofit organizations than in business or government work. In 1990, more women than men held executive, administrative, and managerial positions. In 1970 women held about 35 percent of nonprofit managerial positions, but in 1990 they held 58 percent of these positions (O'Neill, 1994).

The reasons for the rise in the number of women managers are not altogether clear. Studies have been unable to explain why it became much easier for women to enter management. However, a number of factors have been identified as contributing to this rather sudden and rapid increase. The most important of these factors are listed in Figure 10-1.

Although all of these factors have been found to be important, there is no evidence that any one is necessarily more significant than another. Apparently, multiple and converging forces operating during the 1970s and 1980s made it desirable or advantageous to bring more women into management. Many of these factors were not even among the strategies recommended at the time to remove the internal and external obstacles to women's entry into management (Martin & Chernesky, 1989; Martin, Harrison, & DiNitto, 1983). Nor do they reflect the individual or collective actions toward organizational reform and structural change that were deemed necessary if circumstances were to improve for women. For example, leveling job hierarchies and empowering subordinates are not listed. Improving attitudes toward and changing stereotypes about women managers, on the other hand, had been identified and have shown positive change.

In contrast, the recommended strategies did not foresee that the desirable qualities sought in managers in the 1990s would coincide with those qualities typically associated with women. Who could have predicted that the nurturing, supportive, and empowering leadership style and participatory,

Figure 10-1. Factors Contributing to an Increase in Women Entering Management

- Women were more prepared for management positions.
- Affirmative action activities influenced hiring decisions.
- Organizations grew and new organizations sprang up, expanding the number of management positions
- Jobs already held by women were reclassified and retitled.
- Management job titles expanded.
- Managerial salaries became depressed.
- Female-dominated fields grew, requiring women managers to oversee lower-level women workers.
- Male-dominated jobs shifted to women's jobs.
- Male managers were more difficult to attract and retain.
- Stereotypes of women as not suitable for management declined.
- Organizations became more hospitable to women managers.
- Women were mentored more effectively.
- Women supervisors and managers were perceived less negatively.
- Paths to the top increased in number and variety.
- Greater numbers of women entered the work force in general.
- Women were seen as having desirable qualities as managers.

nonhierarchical organizational structures that are associated with women's approach to management would be on the cutting edge of management technology today (Chernesky, 1995, 1996)? Nor was the proliferation of management positions and titles that accompanied the emergence and expansion of organizations anticipated. This rapid growth in the nonprofit sector from 1960 to 1990, which was dominated by the female-intensive health and human services, opened managerial opportunities for women that were still closed to them in the for-profit sector. Similarly, a disenchantment with government services in the 1980s drove men into the for-profit sector, leaving management positions open for women.

To be sure, what individual women and organizations have done helped increase the number of women managers. Women are more likely to be prepared today for management than in the past and to be making career choices that give them the skills, experiences, and mentors they need for management. And many organizations also took actions designed to bring in more women managers. But it seems that more profound political, cultural, and social forces were primarily responsible for the growing number of women entering management in all employment sectors.

THE CEILING ON WOMEN'S ADVANCEMENT

Despite the increase in the number of women entering management and the significant change in the composition of the managerial workforce, there is increasing evidence that the picture is not so perfect. Women are apparently not moving into management as early or as rapidly as their male colleagues (Gibelman & Schervish, 1993a; Guy, 1993). In her study of the career paths of social services managers, Zunz (1991) found that the men in her sample were promoted into their first managerial positions at a significantly faster pace than were women, even though the men and women did not differ significantly in their training and education, use of mentors, or career aspirations in management.

Women continue to be concentrated in the lower levels of management and in less prestigious positions and do not advance into top management positions. Regardless of the setting, few women are found among chief executive officers (CEOs), executive directors, or corporate executives. Fewer than 5 percent hold senior management positions in the corporate sector. Only 10 percent of the 13,000 corporate officers of the nation's largest 500 companies are women. Among the 2,400 individuals holding titles of chairman, chief executive, vice chairman, president, chief operating officer, or executive vice president in 1995, only 2.4 percent were women (Dobrzynski, 1996b).

Women also continue to be underrepresented in top managerial jobs in state and local government. Although women fill 46 percent of federal white-collar jobs, they hold only 12 percent of senior executive positions and 15 percent of management positions at federal grade levels 13 to 15 (Newman, 1994). They hold 40 percent of senior managerial positions in counties and 26 percent of city officials and administrator positions (Center for Women in Government, 1991–1992).

Women do better in nonprofit organizations. They are much more likely to head the largest nonprofit organizations than they are to head the largest for-profit or government organizations. In 1992, 16 of the nation's largest 100 nonprofits had CEOs who were women, whereas only one *Fortune 500* company was headed by a woman (O'Neill, 1994). In education, women make up only about 5 percent of the nation's superintendents, even though two-thirds of all public school teachers are women. They hold fewer than 350 of the nation's approximately 3,000 college and university presidencies (Hicks, 1991). Among health care managers, virtually all senior health care executives are male except in institutions managed by Catholic orders (Weil & Kimball, 1996). Only 12 percent of hospital administrators are women (Bailis, 1987). In social services, women hold approximately 40 percent of CEO positions in child welfare and family services agencies. And in schools of social work, 42 percent of deans are women (Healy, Havens, & Pine, 1995).

The "in the pipeline" theory claims that all organizations must do is bring women in at entry-level management positions and then they will advance to the top of the organization. But women do not percolate up the ranks, and there is little reason to think that it is simply a matter of time. Instead, women are locked into entry-level management positions that are dead ends or have such short ladders that they remain far below the top. Women are channeled into staff positions, which may have attractive management titles and benefits, but unlike line jobs, provide few chances for upward mobility. They are confined to positions or settings that are not viewed as part of the pool from which top-level managers are drawn. They are concentrated in job titles, fields, and organizations that are dominated by women, which narrows their horizons and mitigates against real options for advancement. A case can even be made that women are crowded into fields with a high proportion of women and are denied access to other fields and opportunities equal to those of men. This results in an oversupply of labor, lower rewards, and suppressed salaries (Shenav & Haberfeld, 1992). Human resource departments, for example, have been female dominated, and director of human resources is likely to be the highest position many women will advance to. Many women fill management positions and job titles that proliferated during better times through grants and contracts but were among the first to be retrenched when government support declined. Moreover, even though the salary gap between men and women managers has narrowed, men are still paid more (Jacobs, 1992).

Labor market studies have been invaluable in furthering an understanding of the persistent nature of gender inequality. Studies on the extent of women's integration and equity in managerial ranks that examine gender stratification, intraoccupational segregation, salary data, and mobility across occupations show women are disproportionately found in and confined to secondary labor market jobs that are out of the mainstream and do not lead to top management (Bielby & Baron, 1986; Jacobs, 1992; Morrison & Von Glinow, 1990; Preston, 1994).

Women's advancement beyond entry-level positions into top management continues to be thwarted by a glass ceiling. The glass ceiling has received considerable attention since it was first introduced to describe "those artificial barriers based on attitudinal or organizational bias that prevent qualified individuals from advancing upward into management level positions" (U.S. Department of Labor, 1991, p. 1). The barriers are so subtle they are virtually transparent and yet so ingrained as to prevent women from advancing. What makes the glass ceiling so invidious is that it is not only a barrier for individual women, but it blocks all women in an organization who wish or attempt to move up the managerial ladder. A gender-based glass ceiling was confirmed in studies of social workers, which found that men were disproportionately represented in the higher-paying supervisory and managerial positions (Gibelman & Schervish, 1993a, 1993b). Similarly, studies of state and federal government, where women have made considerable inroads in securing top administrative posts, showed that barriers continued to limit women's advancement and that the glass ceiling had not been shattered (Bullard & Wright, 1993; Guy, 1993; Naff, 1994).

EXPLAINING GENDER INEQUALITY

A number of theoretical perspectives have been used to explain why so few women make it into top management just as they had been used earlier to explain why women were not moving into management in general (Martin et al., 1983; Morrison & Von Glinow, 1990; Newman, 1994). Both individual-level and organizational-level explanations are used to account for the under-representation of women in upper management.

Individual-Level Explanations

Individual-level explanations claim that women themselves are responsible for their differential treatment and lack of advancement in management. Women's traits, behaviors, and attitudes are perceived as unsuitable for management, and their education and experiences are not considered adequate preparation. This person-centered view may be placed within the context of the human capital theory, which purports that individuals are rewarded in their jobs according to their past investment. Therefore, gender inequality is attributed to women's failure to invest in their future and to acquire the necessary training and experience in top-management skills. The underrepresentation of women at the top is even attributed to the choices they have made to remain at entry-level management positions, perhaps in exchange for other job-related benefits such as greater flexibility to meet family responsibilities. Or, it is explained by women's preference to remain in supervisory jobs in the social services because as supervisors they can generally continue to work directly with clients, which is why they went into social work in the first place.

A lack of commitment to their work and their organizations has long been used to explain women's underrepresentation in upper management. Because it is assumed that women place a greater emphasis on their family roles than men, the expectation that they will also be less committed to their jobs and their careers enters into decisions about promotions and work assignments. Data suggest that even women without children are assumed to be less committed to their careers until they have demonstrated their commitment by remaining in the workforce for several years without having children (Naff, 1994). Findings on gender-related work and actual organizational commitment have been contradictory (Aven, Parker, & McEvoy, 1993; Cohen, 1992), although a recent study suggests that gender differences in commitment result from different workplace experiences and not from family roles (Dodd-McCue & Wright, 1996).

Although there is widespread reliance on this perspective, studies of women in management have generally failed to support it. Insufficient skills, abilities, motivation, and career choice do not explain women's slower progress in advancing (Stroh, Brett, & Reilly, 1992). One study of women in federal service found that women still received fewer promotions than men, even after controlling for education and experience at entry (Naff, 1994). Despite the evidence that women and men in management have similar aspirations, values, and other personality traits as well as job-related skills and behaviors, women's investment in education and experience continues to yield lower returns in terms of promotion and advancement (Morrison & Von Glinow, 1990).

Organizational-Level Explanations

A second theoretical perspective posits that work organizations are fraught with blatant and subtle situations that influence women's experiences and processes that impede women's upward mobility (Chernesky, 1983). They include biases and stereotyping that discriminate against women, as well as organizational cultures and workplace environments that may be inhospitable to women. Women continue to claim they are treated differently and unfairly in their workplace and believe that is why they are unable to break the glass ceiling. In 1992 more than 90 percent of women executives surveyed at major corporations believed a glass ceiling prevented women from reaching the top (Noble, 1992). Fifty percent of the women in a study of state public welfare managers (Odewahn & Ezell, 1992) agreed that women in management "have to work twice as hard and do twice as good a job as their male counterparts to prove themselves worthy of promotion" (p. 52). Similarly, 55 percent of female government workers surveyed agreed that a woman must perform better than a man to be promoted in federal agencies (Naff, 1994). When 461 top corporate women were given a list of barriers to advancement, male stereotyping and preconceptions of women topped their list (Dobrzynski, 1996a). Of the 400 female corporate executives surveyed by *Business Week,* 70 percent saw the male-dominated corporate culture and 56 percent considered the glass ceiling as obstacles to their success (Segal & Zellner, 1992). And, 53 percent of these corporate women did not believe that women have the same chance as equally qualified men to be promoted to senior management positions. A recent study of almost 400 corporate men and women found that the women viewed working conditions as more hostile (Stokes, Riger, & Sullivan, 1995).

Organizational-level explanations also include characteristics of organizations and their external environments that seem to influence the number, percentage, and distribution of women in the overall organization. There is increasing evidence that organizational characteristics determine the place of women in management positions as much as, if not more than, the beliefs and attitudes of individual organization members and the skills and experiences of women themselves. Organizational dimensions may even increase the

Figure 10-2. Organizational-Level Explanations for Gender Inequality in Management

- Hiring decisions are influenced by attitudes that only men make good managers.
- Gender stereotypes influence assessment of individual's readiness for promotion.
- Women are concentrated in jobs that are gender stratified and not necessarily on an organizational ladder.
- Structure and organizational location of certain jobs, filled primarily by women, prevent women from being seen as having managerial potential.
- Hostile or inhospitable workplace environments influence women's performance.
- Male organizational cultures hinder acceptance of women, even if they adapt.
- Poor organizational fit blocks opportunity and advancement.
- Different expectations and standards govern how women must prove themselves worthy of promotion.
- Women's organizational networks tend to reinforce gender inequality.
- Hiring and advancing women is associated with organizations' social-equity orientation.
- Women are not considered to have what organizations need to reduce uncertainty or acquire essential resources.
- Advancing women does not correspond to the expectations of significant actors in the organization's environment.

likelihood that women will be in management positions despite individual preferences or pro-male biases as well as decrease the likelihood of women managers when there may be pro-female biases. A number of organizational-level explanations are presented in Figure 10-2.

Gender Discrimination

Sex-role stereotypes, prejudices, and negative perceptions of women's capacity for managing are said to affect women's promotion and advancement. Studies conducted during the 1980s found that negative attitudes and stereotypes about women as managers were not decreasing, even though more women were entering management at that time (Dubno, 1985; Ezell & Odewahn, 1980; Powell & Butterfield, 1989). A more recent study of state public welfare managers found some improvements in the attitudes toward women managers since 1980 (Odewahn & Ezell, 1992). There is ample evidence that gender stereotypes that suggest women are unsuitable for management are stronger in organizations when men dominate the top (Ely, 1995). In some instances, hiring decisions are influenced by a notion that only men make good managers. This pro-male bias appears to be greater in situations in which those who do the hiring never worked for a female manager themselves (Pazy, 1992).

In other cases, discrimination occurs because evaluations of actual or anticipated behavior and performance are distorted by prejudices or assumptions based on gender. Empirical evidence suggests individuals, consciously or not, contribute to differential treatment of women in management (Morrison & Von Glinow, 1990). Even an initial job assignment or department location, which ultimately affects beginning salaries, working conditions, and career opportunities, may be discriminatory, although not deliberately (Haberfeld, 1992). A more offensive kind of discrimination occurs when the job itself is a gendered concept, although it is perceived as gender neutral. A job that contains a gender-based division of labor is filled by people of that gender. As long as executive management positions are embedded in a male image, it is highly unlikely women will be placed in them. Just as supervisors in nonprofit organizations tend to be women, assistant and associate director titles frequently are gender linked. Whereas women are likely to be assistant directors, whose responsibilities for day-to-day internal operations rarely lead to executive director positions; associate directors, most often men, are generally in training to be executive directors.

Viewing women through a filter of gender stereotypes influences whether they are seen as being committed to their careers, are considered sufficiently skilled or experienced to take on managerial tasks, or are thought to say anything worthwhile. The expectation that employees will object to working for a woman is affected by gender stereotyping. When an assessment of an individual candidate's readiness for promotion or advancement into management is based on generalized assumptions about deficiencies of groups of individuals, stereotyping occurs.

Workplace Environments

Hostile or inhospitable workplace environments represent another kind of gender discrimination (Stokes et al., 1995). Although certain behaviors are neither overt discrimination nor sexual harassment, they nevertheless put women at a disadvantage relative to men (Chernesky, 1983). Many forms of subtle discrimination, either conscious or unconscious, include sexist attitudes and comments and microinequities experienced through humor, remarks, stories, and everyday interactions that reinforce gender stereotypes of women and define gender in terms of male dominance and female devaluation (Laporte, 1991; Leap & Smeltzer, 1984). The ongoing rumor that a top-level woman achieved her position because of a personal relationship with her mentor is one example. Comments such as "What do you expect, she's a woman" or "She was just lucky, in the right place at the right time" demean women. In many organizations such behaviors are condoned. This inappropriate saliency of gender is especially heightened in organizations in which there are few women at top levels of management.

Not only do women have to survive and be effective managers in organizations where they are thought of as the second sex, but they also are expected to stay in their place and handle the discomfort and indiscretions their presence creates. Gherardi (1994) referred to this responsibility as "doing gender."

Organizational Culture

A lens of organizational culture is useful to explain entrenched hostile or inhospitable workplace environments and to further clarify women's organizational experience (Gherardi, 1994). Organizational culture is bound up with attributes associated with male or female as reflected in the physical aspects of the environment, values, language, and symbols. The culture can convey male sagas of conquest and winning or losing campaigns and reflect the traditionally masculine attributes of rationality, aggressiveness, and non-emotionality. Or a culture can reflect the typically female characteristics of caring, nurturing, serving, and including. Cultures also affect organizational roles, activities, and desired competencies. The symbolic order of gender is maintained, reproduced, and culturally transmitted by ceremonial work in which rules are defined by the norms, customs, and etiquette of a particular organizational culture. How women and men are expected to dress, how much they can talk about their children, and which emotions they can demonstrate are all culturally determined. Whether men are secretaries or women repair computers is culturally constructed.

Women and men may work in same- or cross-gendered organizations. In cross-gendered organizations, gender is pronounced. Women moving into organizations, occupations, or positions in which the male culture dominates are caught in the margin between two cultures. Women have traditionally been advised on how to fit into the male management culture. Many women do adapt by changing their attitudes, values, and behaviors to those of the dominant culture. But even if they adapt or are acculturated, few are fully accepted or assimilated (Hood & Koberg, 1994). Women are seldom allowed into senior management.

Organizational Fit

Closely related to organizational culture is the extent of homogeneity or diversity in the types of people in an organization. Studies on the processes by which individuals end up working for a particular organization examine attraction, selection, and attrition and suggest the importance of the fit between men and women and the organizations (Schneider, Taylor, Fleenor, Goldstein, & Smith, 1993). This research offers some additional insights about the advancement of women managers (Lovelace & Rosen, 1996; O'Reilly, Chatman, & Caldwell, 1991). For example, Newman (1994) examined three agency types among Florida state government agencies. Each type had characteristic policies and distinctive administrative structures, features, and work environments. From both quantitative and qualitative data, the findings revealed that agency type was indeed a significant determinant of opportunity structure. Women were most represented when they fit the agency type and were excluded in other agency types because they did not fit the desired mold.

Job performance, satisfaction, and turnover have been shown to be related to an individual's perception of how he or she fits into an organization. It is likely that poor organizational fit may account for blocked mobility. Not surprisingly, top managers in any one organization tend to be more similar to one another than they are to workers at other levels in the organization.

Organizational Characteristics

Variations in the percentage of management positions held by women among organizations seem to suggest that women managers fare better in some organizations than others and that some organizations may be more conducive to women's advancement than others. Possible interagency differences led to studies to determine whether gender inequality was systematically related to an agency's demographic and organizational characteristics. Attention has been given to the age (Baron, Mitman, & Newman, 1991) and technology (Newman, 1994) of organizations as well as their demography, including workforce composition and internal distributions of age, gender, race, management versus nonmanagement positions (Ely, 1995; Shenav & Haberfeld, 1992), and organizational mission (Cornwell & Kellough, 1994). For example, a study of federal government agencies (Cornwell & Kellough, 1994), although not specifically directed toward women in management but rather to women employed, found that increased representation of women (as well as Hispanics and African Americans) had less to do with agency size, rates of new hiring, or union strength than previously thought and more to do with an organization's mission. Organizations with a social–equity orientation attracted women and people of color and were apparently more sensitive to providing equal employment opportunities. Agencies that spend large percentages of their budgets in areas related to the redress of social and economic inequality tend to have more women and people of color in their workforces. Because these organizations also demonstrate greater progress toward further integration, it is likely there will be more women in senior management positions among them.

Organizational Environments

Resource dependence and institutional theories also hold promise in explaining why some organizations hire and advance women managers (Blum et al., 1994). According to resource dependence theory, if women have what an organization needs to reduce uncertainty or acquire essential resources, a higher proportion of women will be placed in management in those organizations. For example, women may be placed in management jobs to improve an organization's ability to attract and retain female workers or clients. Or, if an organization is having difficulty attracting or retaining male managers, it may be willing to substitute women to ensure an adequate supply of qualified personnel. Institutional theory suggests that women will be placed in management if doing so symbolizes legitimacy or corresponds to the expectations of significant actors in the organization's environment. For example, not having one woman among six senior management positions in a nonprofit organization would generally be viewed suspiciously and would compel an organization to hire at least one woman senior manager. If the organization does not do so, it is likely to trumpet its support for affirmative action and the steps it has taken to locate a qualified woman, such as the number of women interviewed, to give the impression it is not discriminating (Rockway, 1996).

A recent study of industrial workplaces in Georgia (Blum et al., 1994) confirmed findings from earlier studies that an increase in the percentage of management jobs filled by women is a strategic response on the part of organizational decision makers. The need for organizations to adapt to market and environmental forces to succeed and survive influences the dispositions of organization members who have the power to hire for and promote into management jobs. In their study, resource needs and institutional tendencies accounted for almost half of the variation in the percentage of management positions filled by women. Both resource dependence theory and institutional theory accounted for organizational differences in the percentage of management positions filled by women. However, although the theories predicted the percentage of women managers overall, they were somewhat less effective in predicting the percentage of women in top management positions.

MANAGERIAL CHALLENGES

The challenge for today's managers is to remove the glass ceiling to enable women to advance in the managerial ranks and thus rectify the persistent underrepresentation of women in upper management. It will be necessary for managers to alter those factors that are within the organization's control and are blocking women's advancement. Strategies and methods to do so emerge from the research and literature on women and management and from efforts of corporations to advance women (Deutsch, 1990; Table 10-1). The strategies also build upon the kind of audits that the U.S. Department of Labor conducts to determine compliance with affirmative action and nondiscrimination mandates (Gibelman & Schervish, 1993a).

To ensure that women advance in managerial ranks, managers must see that it is in their organization's best interest for women to be fully included in management. Changes must begin with those at the top. Factors leading to the underrepresentation of women in middle- and upper-management levels are complex and difficult to change. But there are a number of changes that

Table 10-1. Strategies and Methods for Advancing Women in the Managerial Ranks

STRATEGY	METHODS
Identify gender inequities in the organization.	Institutionalize ongoing self-monitoring of employment data.
	Audit hiring, promotion, and employment practices for gender bias and gender stereotyping.
	Examine the distribution of men and women in jobs, titles, and positions for gender clustering.
	Assess hiring and promotion decisions to determine if gender bias and gender stereotyping influenced decisions.
	Assess the work environment and women's perception of how supportive or hostile it is to them.
	Evaluate all entry-level and mid-level management positions to see if they provide chances for upward mobility.
Give women access to influence and power	Assign women to jobs, tasks, and positions that are sources of organizational power.
	Legitimize the authority in the positions women hold.
	Validate differing interpretations of power and the cultural symbols that represent power.
Provide opportunities for women to showcase their managerial potential.	Formally assign cross-gender mentors.
	Integrate women into natural networks that emerge from jobs, tasks, and roles women hold and in which senior managers participate.
	Assign jobs and tasks that are visible to others in the organization.
	Encourage women to participate in groups and associations outside the organization.
	Distribute work to women that requires participation on committees or task forces that include people from across the organization.
	Provide work in areas where there is discretionary authority as well as opportunities to demonstrate creativity.
	Distribute to women tasks that are critical to organizations to women.
	Expand the amount of discretion and autonomy in jobs given to women.
Create new and alternate paths to the top that are not gender linked.	Expand the options for movement within the organization through lateral transfers, job rotation, and declassification of lock-step progression systems.
	Acknowledge and reward paths that circumvent traditional hiring and promotion patterns such as graduate education, volunteering, and moving back and forth between organizations.
	Work on agency boards, in fundraising, and in political or lobbying campaigns.
	Reconsider criteria necessary for middle- and upper-level management positions.
Dismantle the traditional hierarchical structure.	Establish collegial structures that foster broad representation in problem solving and decision making.
	Introduce a "web of inclusion" (Helgesen, 1995) as an alternative to a hierarchical management structure.
	Encourage group and team work to accomplish assignments.

Table continues

Table 10-3 (continued)

STRATEGY	METHODS
Recognize that women bring to management a particular approach, orientation, or style that is valuable to organizations.	Become familiar with the growing body of literature on how women lead and structure organizations. Encourage women to use the management style they are comfortable with. Support women managers whose approach to management may reflect qualities traditionally associated with caring, sharing, empowering, and collaborating. Do not expect women to adopt the behaviors, language, and the style of the dominant leadership to do well and survive. Be alert to the processes of organizational socialization by which women learn the organization's culture and give messages that counter the organization's claim that it welcomes women as managers.
Cultivate an organizational culture that does not tolerate discrimination or harassment and encourages raising concerns about gender discrimination.	Establish agency policies that women have the right to work in an environment free of discrimination, harassment, stress, interpersonal friction, and inhospitable and offensive behaviors. Foster a climate in which concerns or complaints can be voiced, knowing they will be taken seriously and that there will be no recriminations. Demonstrate and reward behaviors consistent with an organizational culture that is neither hostile nor discriminatory. Penalize managers who do not promote women. Create supportive environments that enable women to express their feelings about discrimination, microinequities, and their responsibility for "doing gender." Create family-sensitive workplace policies and do not stigmatize or penalize women or men who take advantage of them.
Establish organizational mechanisms specifically for the purposes of putting women on the fast track and shattering the glass ceiling.	Make upward mobility for women a primary organizational issue. Set up a task force charged with identifying obstacles to women's advancement and implementing needed changes. Design programs to promote opportunities for the advancement of women. Create broad-based structures in which managers can work together on advancing women, allowing issues to be brought into the open.

SOURCES: Chernesky, R. H. (1996). Women managers are better: No they're not, yes they are! *Affilia, 11,* 356–361; Collingwood, H. (1995, November). Women as managers: Not just different—better. *Working Woman,* p. 14; Helgeson, S. (1995). *The web of inclusion.* New York: Doubleday.

managers can make to improve the position of women in organizations and remove the glass ceiling. Although these changes may not guarantee meaningful gender redistribution or the advancement of women, organizations are likely to benefit from women managers and the qualities and skills they bring. Neither women nor men want to work in organizations that are perceived as hostile or discriminatory (Stokes et al., 1995). Therefore, supporting women in the workplace and increasing the number of women in senior management positions contributes to cohesion and commitment and enables organizations to draw on the positive qualities of both men and women.

SKILLS-APPLICATION EXERCISE

The scale on the next page measures your perception of how supportive or hostile your organization's work environment is for women. Circle the number that corresponds with the rating of each statement as it applies to the actual situation at your workplace (not what you think the situation should be), using the continuum from "Do Not Agree At All" on the left to "Strongly Agree" on the right. The scale itself may appear from 1 to 5 or from 5 to 1.

Variations on the Exercise

- Ask your colleagues to complete the exercise. Compare scores of men and women to assess the amount of agreement shown by workers in your organization. Do women perceive the work environment as more hostile than do men? Compare scores of women in management with other women workers. Do women managers perceive the environment as more hostile than do women workers in general?

- Think about how these results can be used in your organization. Can the results be used to stimulate discussion? Is there a basis here for further study, problem-solving, or planned action to improve the work environment? What kinds of mechanisms and forums can be established in your organization to address the results?

- You may wish to use this exercise as part of exit interviews. The decisions of both men and women to leave an organization may be related to their perception of a supportive or hostile work environment.

- You may wish to repeat this exercise periodically to track the progress of your organization with respect to its environment for women. This would be especially useful after your organization has taken some steps to create a gender-fair workplace.

STATEMENT		DO NOT AGREE AT ALL			STRONGLY AGREE	
1.	High-visibility assignments are assigned without regard to gender (that is, similarly qualified men and women would be equally likely to receive this assignment).	1	2	3	4	5
2.	Compared to men, women in this organization are appointed to less important committees and task forces.	5	4	3	2	1
3.	Workers who raise concerns about balancing family and career usually are supported by upper management.	1	2	3	4	5
4.	People here seem more comfortable socializing with others of the same sex rather than those of the opposite sex.	5	4	3	2	1
5.	Staff who raise issues about the treatment of women in this organization find themselves ignored by other workers.	5	4	3	2	1
6.	Some men in this organization refer to some women here as "honey," "cutie," "sweetheart," or other "endearing" terms.	5	4	3	2	1
7.	In this organization, men are not as comfortable serving as a mentor to a woman as they are to a man.	5	4	3	2	1
8.	In general, this organization is a good place for women to work.	1	2	3	4	5
9.	If a worker in this organization told a joke that was degrading to women, someone would be likely to criticize them.	1	2	3	4	5
10.	Small talk in the organization is geared more to men's interests than to women's interests.	5	4	3	2	1
11.	Promotions are given in this organization without regard to gender (that is, men and women are treated equally if they are equally qualified).	1	2	3	4	5
12.	Men and women are treated differently in this organization.	5	4	3	2	1
13.	In general, supervisors in this organization are understanding when personal or family obligations occasionally take a worker away from work.	1	2	3	4	5
14.	In this organization, staff pays just as much attention when women speak as when men speak.	1	2	3	4	5
15.	The administrators in this organization are serious about treating women and men equally.	1	2	3	4	5

How to score: Total your answers. If your score is higher than 60, you probably perceive your work environment as supportive for women. A score close to 75 would suggest you perceive the work environment as very supportive for women. If your score is below 45, you probably perceive the environment as hostile for women. The closer to a score of 15, the more hostile the environment would be perceived.

SOURCE: Adapted from the short version of the scale used in Stokes, J., Riger, S., & Sullivan, M. (1995). Measuring perceptions of the working environment for women in corporate settings. *Psychology of Women Quarterly, 19*, 533–549. Used with permission. See the article for discussion of the development of the scale, its dimensions, and its use in corporate settings.

REFERENCES

Aven, F. F., Parker, B., & McEvoy, G. M. (1993). Gender and attitudinal commitment to organizations: A meta-analysis. *Journal of Business Research, 26,* 63–73.

Bailis, S. S. (1987). Reflections on a journey. *Social Work in Health Care, 12*(3), 5–15.

Baron, J. N., Mitman, B. S., & Newman, A. E (1991). Targets of opportunity: Organizational and environmental determinants of gender integration within the California civil service, 1979–1985. *American Journal of Sociology, 96,* 1362–1401.

Bielby, W., & Baron, J. (1986). Men and women at work: Sex segregation and statistical discrimination. *American Journal of Sociology, 91,* 759–799.

Blum, T. C., Fields, D. L., & Goodman, J. S. (1994). Organization-level determinants of women in management. *Academy of Management Journal, 37,* 241–268.

Bullard, A. M., & Wright, D. S. (1993). Circumventing the glass ceiling: Women executives in American state governments. *Public Administration Review, 53,* 189–201.

Center for Women in Government, State University of New York at Albany. (Winter 1991–1992). Women face barriers in top management. *Women in Public Service.*

Chernesky, R.H. (1983). The sex dimension of organizational processes: Its impact on women managers. *Administration in Social Work, 7*(3–4), 133–143.

Chernesky, R. H. (1995). Feminist administration: Style, structure, purpose. In N. Van Den Bergh (Ed.), *Feminist practice in the 21st century* (pp. 70–88). Washington, DC: NASW Press.

Chernesky, R. H. (1996). Women managers are better: No they're not, yes they are! *Affilia, 11,* 356–361.

Cohen, A. (1992). Antecedents of organizational commitment across occupational groups: A meta-analysis. *Journal of Organizational Behavior, 13,* 539–558.

Collingwood, H. (1995, November). Women as managers: Not just different—better. *Working Woman,* p. 14.

Cornwell, C., & Kellough, J. E. (1994). Women and minorities in federal government agencies: Examining new evidence from panel data. *Public Administration Review, 54,* 265–270.

Deutsch, C. H. (1990, December 16). Putting women on the fast track. *New York Times,* p. 25.

Dobrzynski, J. H. (1996a, February 28). Viewing the barriers to women's careers. *New York Times,* p. D2.

Dobrzynski, J. H. (1996b, October 18). Study finds few women in 5 highest company jobs. *New York Times,* p. D3.

Dodd-McCue, D., & Wright, G. B. (1996). Men, women, and attitudinal commitment: The effects of workplace experiences and socialization. *Human Relations, 49,* 1065–1091.

Dubno, P. (1985). Attitudes toward women executives: A longitudinal approach. *Academy of Management Journal, 28*(1), 235–239.

Ely, R. J. (1995). The power of demography: Women's social constructions of gender identity at work. *Academy of Management Journal, 38,* 589–634.

Ezell, H. F., & Odewahn, C. A. (1980). An empirical inquiry of variables impacting women in management in public social service organizations. *Administration in Social Work, 4*(4), 53–70.

Gherardi, S. (1994). The gender we think, the gender we do in our everyday organizational lives. *Human Relations, 47,* 591–610.

Gibelman, M., & Schervish, P. H. (1993a). The glass ceiling in social work: Is it shatterproof? *Affilia, 8,* 442–455.

Gibelman, M., & Schervish, P. H. (1993b). *Who we are: A profile of the social work labor force as reflected in the NASW membership.* Washington, DC: NASW Press

Guy, M. E. (1993). Three steps forward, two steps backward: The status of women's integration into public management. *Public Administration Review, 53*(4), 285–292.

Haberfeld, Y. (1992). Employment discrimination: An organizational model. *Academy of Management Journal, 35*(1), 161–180.

Healy, L. M., Havens, C. M., & Pine, B. A. (1995). Women and social work management. In L. Ginsberg & P. Keys (Eds), *New management in human services* (pp. 125–150). Washington, DC: NASW Press.

Helgesen, S. (1995). *The web of inclusion.* New York: Doubleday.

Hicks, J. P. (1991, November 3). Women in waiting. *New York Times*, Section 4a, p. 19.

Hood, J. M., & Koberg, C. S. (1994). Patterns of differential assimilation and acculturation for women in business organizations. *Human Relations, 47*, 159–180.

Jacobs, J. A. (1992). Women's entry into management: Trends in earnings, authority and values among salaried managers. *Administrative Science Quarterly, 3*, 282–301.

Laporte, S. B. (1991, January). The sting of the subtle snub. *Working Woman*, pp. 53, 55.

Leap, T. L., & Smeltzer, L. R. (1984, November–December). Racial remarks in the workplace: Humor or harassment? *Harvard Business Review*, pp. 74–75, 78.

Lovelace, K., & Rosen, B. (1996). Differences in achieving person–organization fit among diverse groups of managers. *Journal of Management, 22*, 703–722.

Martin, P. Y., & Chernesky, R. H. (1989). Women's prospects for leadership in social welfare: A political economy perspective. *Administration in Social Work, 13*(3–4), 117–143.

Martin, P. Y., Harrison, D., & DiNitto, D. (1983). Advancement for women in hierarchical organizations: A multilevel analysis of problems and prospects. *Journal of Applied Behavioral Science, 19*, 19–33.

Morrison, A. M., & Von Glinow, M. A. (1990). Women and minorities in management. *American Psychologist, 45*, 200–208.

Naff, K. C. (1994). Through the glass ceiling: Prospects for the advancement of women in the federal civil service. *Public Administration Review, 54*, 505–514.

Newman, M. A. (1994). Gender and Lowi's thesis: Implications for career advancement. *Public Administration Review, 54*, 277–284.

Noble, B. P. (1992, February 23). Round two on the mommy track. *New York Times*, p. D23.

Odewahn, C. A., & Ezell, H. F. (1992). Attitudes toward women managers in human service agencies: Are they changing? *Administration in Social Work, 16*(2), 45–55.

O'Neill, M. (1994). The paradox of women and power in the nonprofit sector. In T. Odendahl & M. O'Neill (Eds.), *Women and power in the nonprofit sector* (pp. 1–16). San Francisco: Jossey-Bass.

O'Reilly, C. A., Chatman, J., & Caldwell, D. F. (1991). People and organizational culture: A profile comparison approach to assessing person–organization fit. *Academy of Management Journal, 34*, 487–516.

Pazy, A. (1992). Sex-linked bias in promotion decisions. *Psychology of Women Quarterly, 16*, 209–228.

Powell, G. M., & Butterfield, A. D. (1989). The "good manager": Did androgyny fare better in the 1980s? *Group and Organization Studies, 14*, 216–233.

Preston, A. (1994). Women in the nonprofit labor market. In T. Odendahl & M. O'Neill (Eds.), *Women and power in the nonprofit sector* (pp. 39–77). San Francisco: Jossey-Bass.

Rockway, J. (1996). *Women in administration: A cultural view.* Unpublished manuscript, Fordham University Graduate School of Social Service, Bronx, NY.

Schneider, B., Taylor, S., Fleenor, J., Goldstein, H., & Smith, B. (1993). The issue of homogeneity within organizations. *Leadership IS: Issues & Observations, 13*(4), 44–45.

Segal, A. T., & Zellner, W. (1992, June 8). Corporate women. *Business Week,* pp. 74–78.

Shenav, Y., & Haberfeld, Y. (1992). Organizational demography and inequality. *Social Forces, 71,* 123–143.

Stokes, J., Reiger, S., & Sullivan, M. (1995). Measuring perceptions of the working environment for women in corporate settings. *Psychology of Women Quarterly, 19,* 533–549.

Stroh, L. K., Brett, J. M., & Reilly, A. H. (1992). All the right stuff: A comparison of female and male managers' career progression. *Journal of Applied Psychology, 77,* 251–260.

U.S. Department of Labor. (1991). *A report on the glass ceiling initiative.* Washington, DC: Author.

Weil, P. A., & Kimball, P. A. (1996). Gender and compensation in health care management. *Health Care Management Review, 21*(3), 19–33.

Zunz, S. (1991). Gender-related issues in the career development of social work managers. *Affilia, 6*(4), 39–52.

CHAPTER 11

Evaluating Employee Performance

Kenneth I. Millar

rom the perspective of the competing values framework, performance evaluation is lodged in the human relations skills quadrant and deals specifically with the managerial responsibility of ensuring that your organization has a competent workforce. The focus is on retaining, motivating, and developing a committed, qualified, and competent cadre of employees that have the knowledge, abilities, and skills to perform their jobs effectively. As a nonprofit manager charged with performance evaluation responsibilities, you must be skilled at performing the role of mentor and possess such characteristics, traits, and skills as empathy, caring, listening, and alertness to problems and needs (see chapter 1).

The evaluation of employee performance is an annual occurrence in nearly all organizations, whether they are nonprofit or for-profit, and the consequences of this evaluation for the individual being evaluated, the evaluator, and the organization can be profound. On the positive side, a well-conducted performance appraisal may

- increase the person's motivation to perform effectively
- increase the self-esteem of the person being evaluated
- allow new insights for the person or people doing the appraisal
- result in more clarification and better definition of the job of the person being evaluated
- facilitate valuable communication among the individuals taking part
- facilitate among participants a better understanding of themselves and of the kind of development activities that are of value
- clarify organizational goals and facilitate their acceptance
- allow the organization to do better human resource planning, test validation, and development of training programs.

On the other hand, a poorly conducted performance evaluation may

- cause individuals to quit as a result of the way they were treated
- create false and misleading data

- damage the self-esteem of the person being appraised and the person doing the appraising
- waste large amounts of time
- permanently worsen the relationship between the individuals involved
- lower performance motivation
- waste money on forms, training, and a host of support activities
- lead to expensive lawsuits by those who feel unjustly evaluated (Mohrman, Resnick-West, & Lawler, 1989).

All too often, negative results are what organizations get when they try to operate traditional appraisal systems. Frequently, the high hopes associated with a new performance evaluation system are destroyed by the reality of a system that produces more conflicts, problems, and resistance than it does positive results. In many organizations, performance appraisal systems simply become inoperative because of the problems and conflicts they generate. The challenge is to develop and implement a performance evaluation system that eliminates the many negative consequences and produces the important positive ones. Unfortunately, this is not an easy task.

Most people find the performance appraisal process a totally unrewarding, if not unpleasant, experience. Discomfort is often expressed both by supervisors and supervisees because of the event (McGregor, 1972; Wiehe, 1980). Supervisors express anxiety at judging the performance of their supervisees, and the latter experience anxiety about being judged (Wiehe, 1980).

Supervisors frequently balk at the idea of performance appraisals because of an understandable dislike of criticizing a subordinate (and perhaps having to argue about it), a lack of skill needed to handle the performance evaluation interview, and a mistrust of the validity of the appraisal instrument (McGregor, 1972). In addition, supervisors may experience role conflict because of an inability to separate the judgmental–evaluative and educational–developmental components of performance evaluation (Cummings & Schwab, 1973). This difficulty in resolving competing roles at the managerial level reflects the fact that managers must function in an environment of competing values (see chapter 1). Supervisors also frequently lack an overall conceptual model of how appraisal contributes to other personnel functions such as recruitment, selection, placement, training, and utilization.

Despite the inherent difficulties, evaluating performance is something that people do all the time. A great deal of informal evaluation takes place in organizations, just as it does in all sectors of people's lives. The performance of each individual in an organization is constantly being appraised by the individual, as well as by his or her supervisors, peers, and subordinates. Formal appraisal is an inevitable consequence of the way jobs are designed and organizations are structured. The assignment of responsibility to particular individuals for the performance of certain tasks makes the assessment of how an individual performs both possible and necessary: possible because it identifies the results for which the person is responsible and necessary because complex, differentiated organizations need information on how well jobs are performed to operate effectively.

But why is performance appraisal so difficult? On the surface, it appears simple. One individual observes another performing a task and reaches a judgment about how adequately that task has been performed. Such judging occurs regularly throughout all human interactions, but the situation is substantially more complex in organizational environments than it is in most other types of situations. Two characteristics make the appraisal of work performance unique: (1) Frequently, the evaluator has reward power over the evaluatee, and (2) the appraisal occurs in the context of an ongoing relationship.

The difficulties inherent in performance evaluation in nonprofit organizations are, in many cases, further compounded by the lack of hard, objective measures. Performance often goes unobserved by managers because of the nature of the services provided and by the confidential nature of an employee–client relationship. In addition, because the service technologies of nonprofit organizations often are not as clearly specified as those of production organizations, there remains an aura of mystery about what constitutes an effective and efficient service (Ferris, 1982; see also chapter 13).

Because it deals with competence and effectiveness, performance appraisal involves people's sense of who they are and what they can be. In addition, an appraisal is the point at which the sometimes conflicting goals of organizations and individuals can be addressed. Performance appraisal is also an activity that has important legal considerations and can lead to the courtroom. Perhaps most of all, an appraisal is an interaction between two human beings who are often nervous, tense, defensive to some degree, poorly prepared to talk about such important issues, and full of their own misperceptions, biases, hopes, and values.

As Latham and Wexley (1981) observed "performance appraisal systems are a lot like seat belts. Most people believe they are necessary, but they don't like to use them" (p. 2). As a result, evaluation systems are often used reluctantly to satisfy some formal organizational or legal requirement. Despite this prevalent perception about performance evaluation, the evaluation of employee performance is a critically important management responsibility. Performance appraisal is crucial to the effective management of your organization's human resources, and the proper management of human resources is a critical variable that will affect your organization's productivity and effectiveness. In addition, decisions by arbitration boards and the courts emphasize the importance of organizations having well-documented, objective records of employee performance relative to advancement, dismissal, or salary increases (Latham & Wexley, 1981; Wiehe, 1980).

CHARACTERISTICS OF A
PERFORMANCE EVALUATION SYSTEM

A good performance evaluation system should meet three criteria: it should be valid, reliable, and practical. *Validity* refers to the degree to which an instrument is measuring what it is supposed to measure. *Reliability* is the extent to which a measurement gives consistent appraisals of individuals from one time to another or from one evaluation to another. *Practicality* refers to the instrument's acceptability to management and staff, ease of administration and interpretation, and reasonable time required for completion (Baker & Holmgren, 1982; Matheson, Millar, & Van Dyck, 1995; Millar, 1990; Smith, 1976; Wexley & Yukl, 1977).

This chapter delineates and then describes a set of ideal characteristics of performance evaluation that, when present, will enable you to accomplish a number of objectives. First, they ensure that your performance evaluation process and instrument satisfy the validity, reliability, and practicality requirements. Equally important, they provide assurance that your evaluation system will be seen as fair and appropriate by its users. The characteristics of the ideal performance evaluation system also guarantee a sense of responsibility and ownership that can reduce and even eliminate the feelings of anxiety, suspicion, and insecurity that frequently accompany performance evaluation.

Before describing the ideal performance evaluation system, one point must be emphasized. What is described below is premised on the fundamental assumption that the performance evaluation system is positive and nonpunitive in design. Lombardi (1988) understated the issue when he declared that "the common problem with performance appraisal is that there is not a positive purpose to the whole exercise" (p. 147). It often appears that the main intention of performance evaluation is to use the results solely to manage human resources in order to promote the economic and managerial efficiency of the overall operation (Levine, 1986; Rendero, 1980). As a result, the system is frequently seen as nothing more than an inherently punitive control device.

Performance evaluation must communicate a positive message. Unfortunately, all too often the message tends to be a critical appraisal rather than a supportive, conjoint evaluation. Indeed, according to McGregor (1972), performance appraisal can be so negatively perceived that "unless handled with consummate skill and delicacy, constitutes something dangerously close to a violation of the integrity of the personality" (p. 134). To present a positive image, the evaluation must be seen as being driven by an overriding concern for the person being evaluated. A more predictable pattern, however, is that appraisal is done *for* organizations and *to* people, and the average employee takes six months to recover from the effects (Peters, 1985).

A critical point, then, is to orient the process and the instrument toward a positive intention and a constructive process. Whenever possible, your goal should be to reduce the negativism frequently associated with the performance evaluation concept and aim to produce an optimistic outcome. Simply stated, this outcome is to help your employees in ways they would like to be helped as well as in ways others, such as peers and supervisors, would like to see them improve. Both goals are relevant, but the latter one should not be the overriding thrust of the process. The energy of the performance evaluation should be directed toward a genuine responsiveness to the person being evaluated, and it should carry a message that there is something in it for everyone involved.

IDEAL INSTRUMENT AND SYSTEM FOR PERFORMANCE EVALUATION

The ideal performance evaluation system should

- emphasize managerial expectations as well as self-development and professional growth on each dimension by use of a benchmark
- include both generic (core) and job-specific (a la carte) dimensions
- not be associated with pay or increments
- describe and be anchored in real events
- be responsive to both development and diminution in ability over time
- have a goal orientation step as part of closure
- fit all staff
- be able to grow and change with the organization.

Managerial Expectations, Self-Development, and Personal Growth

Keeping a performance evaluation system positive and nonpunitive is a challenging task if you try to direct the instrument and process toward both managerial concerns and self-development and professional growth. Combining judgmental and developmental dimensions on the same instrument is difficult (Cedarblom, 1982) because it is widely held that one of the problems with performance evaluation is that its managerial and developmental objectives are contradictory (Brumback, 1988). However, you can manage this problem by using a benchmark. In such a system, the first few steps on any performance dimension scale deal with managerial concerns, and the benchmark specifies the organization's expected level of performance and the ceiling of managerial expectation. The benchmark usually is point 4 on a seven-point scale, or in other words, the midpoint on the scale. The remainder of the steps beyond the benchmark are oriented toward professional growth and development. This approach to building dimensions with benchmarks for managerial expectations is far better than the more typical performance evaluation scale, which provides a ceiling of perfection. Brumback (1988) remarked that

> placing unreasonably high expectations upon individuals can create a breeding ground for discontent, hypertension, protest, and cutting corners, including ethical and legal ones. True leadership, in our opinion, allows each individual to decide whether to strive beyond reasonable expectations and makes clear the individual will also be held accountable for his or her manner of striving. An organization can be more sure that its expectations are reasonable by keeping them job-related. That is, consistent with each individual's duties and responsibilities. (p. 391)

The more traditional approach invariably leads to one of two outcomes. Either grade inflation occurs as everyone, or nearly everyone, is ranked at or near the top of the scale (a leniency effect), or the scale is seen as punitive and defeatist, particularly by younger or less experienced staff, because it sets unrealistic and unattainable expectations of performance. In either case, the notion of professional growth and development is defeated by the performance evaluation instrument.

Lombardi (1988) concluded that "virtually every attrition study done in the human resources field has found that a major reason for an employee leaving one firm for another is the well-formed impression that the former employer was uninterested in the employee's long-term development" (p. 157). The effort with the benchmark system is to try to respond to this concern by building the two components of managerial expectation and developmental issues together on every dimension of the scale. The two components are linked together but are separated by the benchmark or managerial ceiling where the employee can satisfy organizational demands and still have room to move upward on the professional development range of the scale.

A contentious issue in performance evaluation is addressed through this benchmark distinction between organizational expectation and professional growth and development. This is reflected in the competing values between the monitor role of judging and evaluating and the mentor role of helping and counseling (Edwards & Yankey, 1991; Sashkin, 1981). The benchmark concept eliminates this antagonism by simultaneously addressing both perspectives. This approach provides an opportunity to assess and monitor limitations and weaknesses in expected levels of performance, and for those employees who have already reached your organization's expectation—the benchmark—the approach can facilitate areas of professional growth and development.

Generic (Core) and Job-Specific (a la Carte) Dimensions

Two critical features of any performance evaluation process are that your employees are evaluated according to their actual job descriptions and that the criteria for evaluation are both objective and familiar to them (Latham & Wexley, 1981; MacIntosh, 1988). However, more is typically expected of an employee than what is stated in the job description (Lombardi, 1988). For example, every organization expects its employees to represent it appropriately and to behave with professional integrity in their working roles. These responsibilities are not always articulated within the job description but nevertheless should be a part of any evaluation process (Harkness & Mulinski, 1988; Spano, 1981).

To be comprehensive, a performance evaluation must address all aspects of a job—those that are specifically and clearly outlined in the job description and those that are more generic or core for any individual working in the organization. Each employee should be made aware of these generic aspects of performance expectation as well as those that are more formally outlined in the job description.

This notion of discriminating between generic aspects of work and more specific job description components may be unclear. An example taken from a human services agency may clarify the idea. Few would argue that a job dimension such as "establishing relationships with colleagues" is an appropri-

Figure 11-1. Core Dimension A:
Establishment and Maintenance of Cooperative Relationships with Colleagues

This dimension is associated with work-related activity and not with outside social behavior. It is concerned with how you deal with your colleagues within the employment setting. It is confined to your behavior and is not an attempt to evaluate the way others behave toward you. Try to respond to this dimension in terms of how you relate, at work, to your professional colleagues.

7   This person cooperates with colleagues in a way that continually demonstrates helpful, supportive, and respectful collegial relationships.

6   This person cooperates with colleagues, provides guidance, and demonstrates supportive and respectful relationships.

5   This person cooperates with colleagues and assumes a responsibility for providing professional guidance to these colleagues.

4   This person cooperates with colleagues with respect to their mutual roles and responsibilities.

3   This person can cooperate with colleagues, but his or her behavior may fail to respect their mutual roles and responsibilities.

2   This person has difficulty cooperating with colleagues and fails to respect their mutual roles and responsibilities.

1   This person is unable to cooperate with colleagues and is disrespectful within their mutual roles and responsibilities.

Figure 11-2. A La Carte Dimension M: Identifying and Assessing Client Problems

This dimension considers your ability to identify and assess problems. Are you able to collect information and to prioritize the presenting problems? Can you see how these problems interfere with client functioning?

7   This person has a superior ability to collect data and identify significant client problems. He or she can expertly see how the problems interfere with client functioning.

6   This person has an excellent ability to collect data and identify significant client problems. He or she can skillfully see how the problems interfere with client functioning.

5   This person has advanced ability to collect data and identify significant client problems. He or she can readily see how the problems interfere with client functioning.

4   This person has ability to collect data and identify significant client problems. He or she can see how the problems interfere with client functioning.

3   This person has some ability to collect data and identify client problems. He or she can see, to some extent, how the problems interfere with client functioning.

2   This person has deficiency collecting data and identifying client problems. He or she has difficulty appreciating how the problems interfere with client functioning.

1   This person is unable to collect data and identify client problems. He or she cannot see how the problems interfere with client functioning.

ate universal expectation for individuals in human services work (see Figure 11-1). It is a dimension with generic relevance and importance that applies to everyone, irrespective of their particular job station. However, consider a dimension such as "identifying and assessing client problems" (see Figure 11-2). Not everyone who works within a human services agency is charged with this task. This dimension speaks to a particular job group within a service system, one that deals directly with clients. Hence this task is job specific. Generic job expectations are called "core" dimensions and those specific to a job description are called "a la carte" dimensions.

The performance evaluation instrument should thus be built to reflect the dimensions that address the actual job description as well as those that address the more generic components of expected behavior in the organization. The combination of these elements makes the performance evaluation process and instrument more comprehensive. All of your employees should be evaluated on an agreed-upon set of generic or core dimensions, whereas you select more discriminating job description or a la carte dimensions for particular individuals or job groups. The a la carte job description dimensions can reflect all potential job roles and can continue to be added, amended, or deleted as your organization changes, whereas the core dimensions remain stable across time. In this way, your instrument will be flexible yet all-embracing and universal.

Disassociation with Pay or Increments

The performance evaluation process must be clearly seen by all players as disconnected from any reimbursement and not directly related to pay or financial value to the agency. Because the performance evaluation process must be seen as positive and nonpunitive, it is important that it not be tied to any formal relationship with annual increments, bonuses, or financial incentives (Patten, 1976; Patz, 1975; Rock, 1972; Wiehe, 1980). Performance evaluation and remuneration should occur in different contexts and at different times in the working life of the employee (McGregor, 1972). When you tie the two issues together, you implicitly connect performance evaluation with a management decision about the monetary worth of the staff member. To associate the performance evaluation with a financial consequence also distracts from the true intent of performance evaluation, which is to encourage competence, objective appraisal of skill, and the planning of goals and personal development. In addition, employees may be unwilling to be self-critical if reimbursement issues are contingent upon a successful evaluation. The whole process can become stilted, lacking in genuineness and honesty (Lombardi, 1988). The issues of pay, increments, and bonuses should be dealt with as a separate mechanism in the policy and procedures manual.

Anchored in Real Events

The performance evaluation instrument should confine its content to those dimensions that actually occur in the job. Although this may seem like a statement of the obvious, it is remarkable how frequently items appear in an evaluation instrument that have absolutely nothing to do with a particular job. As Baker and Holmgren (1982) reminded us, the process must be perceived to measure the right things, which frequently are best determined by employees familiar with the job and, as a result, can generate context-specific material for use in building the instrument (Atkin & Conlon, 1978; Ferris, 1982). Encourage employee involvement by openly promoting the value of staff experience, training, and knowledge and by using these qualities in the design of the evaluation process and the construction of the instrument. Lombardi (1988) identified this technique of promoting the situational relevance of evaluation items as one of the 10 traits of a fair and effective review. A further advantage of a performance evaluation instrument and system that is grounded in specific job-related behavioral content is that it is more easily defensible in courts of law. As a manager, you must never lose sight of the fact that an evaluation may be challenged legally.

Responsive to Both Development and Diminution in Ability

The assumption inherent in most performance evaluation instruments is that people always continue to improve. Of course, this is not always an accurate reflection of reality. Some people plateau at a modest level of achievement. Others, during a particular review period, for reasons both personal and professional, perform at lower levels than they did in the past.

An ideal performance evaluation instrument should thus measure both growth and loss of function as well as be able to show whether your employee has hit a plateau. Most instruments are designed to reflect continual upward movement over time, and employees expect that each evaluation will bring improved scores. Hence, many appraisal instruments are constructed so that the bottom step on the rating scale is the lowest level of organizational expectation and the top step is the highest. This managerially driven instrument thus communicates, at least implicitly, that a person starts at the bottom and works his or her way up the scale, somewhat like one does on the pay scale. To stop climbing the scale is akin to failure, and falling on the scale runs the risk of experiencing managerial sanction or penalty. These failings are further amplified if the performance evaluation is tied to raises or bonuses.

Employees should not be expected to grow on every dimension every year. They need to know that not only can they grow and develop, but that they can also stay put. Our goals and aspirations, our commitment to our jobs, and the priorities in our lives all change throughout our careers. There are periods when we question what we are doing, when we feel burned out, when we need to pause for some refueling. For a period of time, we decide to stop working through our lunch hour and instead train for a marathon. Perhaps we decide to pass up weekend seminars and other training activities to coach our daughter's soccer team. A performance evaluation system must have the flexibility to reflect these changes while at the same time setting a minimal, acceptable expectation of performance.

The use of the benchmark concept is critical here. By using the benchmark, your organization's expectations can be made clear. Above the benchmark, the scale is concerned with professional growth and development, and loss of function or plateauing in this area has little impact on organizational expectations.

The ideal instrument allows people to move up and down the scale above the benchmark without having a negative impact on organizational standards or expectations. For example, if an individual's scores fall from step 6 back to step 4 on the professional growth and development steps of the scale, there is no reason for organizational concern because the expected organizational standard or benchmark is still being achieved. Furthermore, if the score remains at the benchmark for several review periods, there is no organizational consequence. This approach communicates to employees that it is acceptable to maintain a steady state once the benchmark has been achieved.

Goal Orientation

Toward the close of the evaluation process, the discussion should focus on the future. At the end of the instrument itself there should be a section to specify goals and objectives for the future (Bechman, 1981). This is an open-ended section that both employee and supervisor respond to. Each party completes the goals and planning section and returns for the joint interview when they share perspectives, try to reach a consensus on the key points, and sign the evaluation document. This process is an important part of any ideal performance evaluation instrument (Burke, Wetzel, & Weir, 1978; Nemeroff & Wexley, 1979). This goal-setting process and the use of a standard criteria for measuring goal achievement enhances the employee's belief in the objectivity of the appraisal results (Dipboye & de Pontbriand, 1981; Landy, Barnes, & Murphy, 1978).

Fits All Staff

An ideal performance appraisal instrument should be usable by all staff, including management (Spano, 1981). The universality of the instrument's application promotes unity as well as a sense of loyalty. Staff know that the executive management team is evaluated on the same core dimensions as they are. A la carte dimensions, on the other hand, are applicable only to specific job groups.

Ability to Grow and Change

The core dimensions of the instrument have the capacity to adapt to the growth or contraction of your organization. Because of this feature, the tool does not have to be rebuilt when new programs are started or when existing programs are discontinued. As your organization develops new programs, all that is necessary is to meet with the job group to review the existing task dimensions of the instrument and select those appropriate for the new roles. Anything absent can be noted and subsequently built and added to the pool of dimensions available within the instrument.

THE PERFORMANCE EVALUATION INSTRUMENT

The ideal performance evaluation instrument should

- use simple, commonly understood language
- have a user's guide

- have high content validity
- be comprised of both semantic and numerical components.

Simple Language

The language of the evaluation instrument must be free of jargon, buzz-words, and generalizations. Here are two examples of the language that often appears in performance evaluation instruments: (1) "Worker can successfully integrate the complementary components of service interface," and (2) "Operates with an understanding of conjoint, client–service provider influence in intervention processes." Clearly, such performance dimensions have little meaning or relevance and do little more than invite cynical comments from employees. Your instrument must also be cleansed of words that are so comprehensive and all-encompassing that they lack specificity. Words that are difficult to define and measure such as "frequently," "continually," "occasionally," "absolutely," and "persistently" come to mind. These language pitfalls should be avoided because they rob the instrument of its credibility, appropriateness, and usefulness. The performance evaluation instrument will have little merit if the tool's language is not understood by your target group.

User's Guide

Ideally, your performance evaluation instrument should include a user's guide. This guide provides details about the evaluation process and the instrument, outlines the scales and how they are designed, describes the dimensions, and tells what the dimensions measure. The guide should dispel any vagueness or confusion about the instrument and provide an opportunity to promote a shared understanding about the evaluation. Additionally, and sometimes more importantly, the guide tells the user what not to do and what not to be concerned about.

Content Validity

Your performance evaluation instrument should stay within its cover. In other words, everything that is relevant or expected through the evaluation is addressed by the instrument itself. The language should reflect the terminology of the work performed, and the dimensions involved should be self-explanatory (Dipboye & de Pontbriand, 1981). Having employees involved in the instrument construction should ensure that the dimensions are relevant and clearly understood (Schwab, Heneman, & DeCotiis, 1975).

Semantic and Numerical Components

An ideal performance evaluation tool requires descriptive features at each scale point. This means that each dimension is anchored with behavioral statements at each point on the scale. These statements must be in clear and concise language that is descriptive of expected behavior. Each of these behavioral statements requires a numeric symbol that serves as shorthand for an individual's location on a scale. Although the supervisor or employee may be required during the evaluation to return to the exact statements on the dimension that led them to a particular score, the numbers provide a way of quickly identifying and reviewing the dimensions. A system of numbers at each point on the scale also enables the supervisor or employee to transfer the ratings to a scoring grid for a view of the overall appraisal. Bechman (1981), as well as Landy and Farr (1983), advocated this combination of numerical ratings and substantiating comments as the most satisfactory performance evaluation design.

PROCESS OF EVALUATION

The ideal performance evaluation system should be

- built with staff participation
- available immediately upon employment as well as throughout an individual's employment
- completed separately in advance by each party
- time framed and repetitive
- future oriented in operation
- fast and efficient
- nonadversarial, allowing for disagreement
- fair
- personalized for each employee.

Staff Participation

Involving your employees in the development of the evaluation instrument ensures it is written in job-relevant language that has meaning to those who will be evaluated by it. A participatory performance evaluation process or instrument also generates staff investment and empowerment. The loyalty and commitment of staff to any evaluation process is virtually impossible without their input and involvement from conception to finished product. Evans and McShane (1988) reported that, with few exceptions, employees have more positive attitudes toward appraisal when they are given the opportunity to participate. Furthermore, the contribution through staff participation is considered a major element in successful appraisal systems, particularly when combined with problem-solving and mutual goal setting (Nemeroff & Wexley, 1979; Wexley, Singh, & Yukl, 1973).

Unfortunately, most performance evaluation tools are not built in this fashion. Too often they are purchased or borrowed and then altered or modified to accommodate the host organization. Lacking employee input, they rely solely on management's knowledge and appreciation of the tasks performed in any job. As Pottinger and Goldsmith (1979) noted, the input of management should not be undervalued, but experience suggests that this expert opinion approach is the least valid method of competency evaluation. The experts may be involved in management or training more than in the actual practice of the profession and thus may emphasize attitudes that are relatively unimportant in actual practice (Kane, 1982).

Availability

When new employees are hired, they should immediately be familiarized with the evaluation instrument. The evaluation process should be a standard part of your organization's orientation for new employees. The new employee and the supervisor should spend time reviewing the instrument and outlining its purpose, features, and strengths, especially its positive, nonpunitive style, professional growth features, and job-specific as well as generic components. Additionally, the new employee should be informed about the first evaluation date and encouraged to try out the instrument and raise any questions before that date. This early introduction to the evaluation process can increase the employee's comfort and reduce the chance that he or she will be surprised on the evaluation date (Rasmussen, 1988; Spano, 1981; Timmreck, 1989).

Independent Component

In the ideal performance evaluation process, the two parties come together and share their respective observations and conclusions. This meeting should occur at a time of mutual convenience in a setting where neither evaluator nor evaluatee will be disturbed. Before this meeting, the employee and the supervisor should have had an opportunity to score the performance evaluation instrument privately and independently. A fair and egalitarian approach to evaluation requires the opportunity for employees to evaluate themselves independently (Lombardi, 1988; MacIntosh, 1988; Rasmussen, 1988). Timmreck (1989) also supported the position that any good evaluation system requires self-assessment as a fundamental component. After this self-assessment process, the parties can then come together with their respective initial reflections to share and discuss results.

Too frequently, this period of self-reflection and independent evaluation does not occur in the performance evaluation process. Instead, the evaluation is one-sided, completed only by the supervisor, and the employee is simply provided with the results. She or he may be then be invited to respond, but even this is not always the case.

Some performance evaluation procedures suggest a jointly performed assessment as a compromise to the sole assessment by superiors. However, joint assessment can instigate duress and subtle pressures to compromise. Furthermore, joint assessment that occurs at the time of review wastes time scoring and marking evaluation forms when it would be better spent in dialogue about consensus or differences.

Time Framed and Repetitive

The performance evaluation system must be communicated to each employee as a process framed in time. Each employee should be evaluated annually and at a time he or she finds easy to remember. Most organizations use the anniversary date of initial employment for subsequent evaluations. Frequently, new employees are reviewed after six months of probationary employment and then at subsequent anniversary dates. Whatever the method for determining review dates, it is most important that the evaluation encompasses only the time period between reviews. It is also important that the performance evaluation not focus solely on recent events or isolated incidents at the expense of the overall pattern of performance throughout the total period of the review.

When a performance evaluation instrument is repeatedly used across evaluation cycles, the instrument should be capable of reflecting patterns of improvement and change. The repetition of the same evaluation process is a key to its success (Landy et al., 1978). Unfortunately, many employees are never evaluated. Others are evaluated, but the evaluation instruments are changed between reviews. As a consequence, ongoing change and development cannot be measured over time.

Future Oriented

Traditional performance evaluation focuses both on the past, on what the employee has done since the last review, and on the present, including the employee's current level of performance. Levinson (1979) suggested that one of the main problems in this approach is that it dwells too long in the past. The consideration of future goals and objectives and the training and education required to reach them should become a featured component of the evaluation system.

By including a future component in the evaluation process, management communicates that it is interested in the long-term professional development of their employees. This is important for a number of reasons. Staff retention is one. Concern about employee retention is of particular importance when professionals are costly to recruit and train. Employees can easily be driven away because of appraisal systems they believe are punitive and pay little attention to their future professional development.

A future-oriented evaluation system also assists management to more accurately and effectively plan educational, training, and other developmental activities for employees. Frequently, managers invest inordinate amounts of time and money on activities they think are important for staff. Managers are then surprised, bitter, cynical, or even angry when employees express or demonstrate little enthusiasm for these programs. The problem, of course, is that these activities often have little relevance to what employees believe are their development needs. A future-oriented evaluation process heightens the likelihood that staff development efforts will be accepted by staff and will be cost effective. A future-oriented focus also allows for career planning with employees and facilitates better decisions and more acceptance of internal promotions and transfers.

Fast and Efficient

No part of the performance evaluation process should require extraordinary lengths of time to complete. No part of the process, from the personal appraisal completed individually to the joint evaluation interview to the sign-off, should require more than one hour of time. Three hours should be all that is required to complete the entire evaluation process. The paperwork and technical assistance required by the traditional appraisal system can place an unreasonable workload on managers (Sashkin, 1981). This can be a deterrent to proceeding with the evaluation and can give the whole function a burdensome tone. Failing to streamline the process can even interfere with organizational effectiveness (Wexley & Yukl, 1977).

Nonadversarial

A good performance evaluation instrument does not demand consensus. The parties need not come to agreement about raw scores on individual performance dimensions of the instrument. In fact, the individuals involved can agree to disagree. The subsequent dialogue about the disagreement can become the substance of the evaluation process. However, consensus and agreement must be reached in the areas of goal setting and planning. Reducing the discussion about scores and permitting individuals to disclose their own opinions allows attention to be focused on a more constructive task—a dialogue about what the instrument scores reflect in terms of their similarity or disparity and goal setting for the future.

Fairness

The ideal performance evaluation system should always appear fair and just to employees. Regardless of the results of the evaluation, the staff member should feel that the process was not suspect and that the instrument reflected accurately and fairly both job-specific duties and generic aspects of the work. Employee attitudes about the system of appraisal and its apparent justice can be as relevant as more traditional considerations of whether the instrument and process were valid or reliable (Bernardin & Beatty, 1984; Caroll & Schneier, 1982). Evans and McShane (1988) posited that "employee acceptance of appraisal decision outcomes depends at least partly upon their belief that observed characteristics of the performance appraisal system are consistent with fair process" (p. 178). Folger and Greenberg (1985) and Greenberg (1986) echoed this sentiment. Such beliefs about the fairness and accuracy of the appraisal system are thought to influence employee motivation and might influence other more subtle outcomes such as organizational commitment and turnover (Demarco & Nigro, 1983).

Personalized Experience

Each employee should have an individualized evaluation experience (Beer, 1981; Spano, 1981). A personalized experience requires that the evaluation not be group based or made in comparison to fellow employees. It also demands that the employee has a chance for self-appraisal and to meet face-to-face to respond to his or her supervisor's ratings. Failure to personalize the evaluation process in this fashion can lead to a loss of confidence in the system and feelings of indifference, cynicism, and even hostility (Wexley & Yukl, 1977).

CONSTRUCTING THE IDEAL PERFORMANCE EVALUATION INSTRUMENT

Instrument Characteristics

The most efficient method for including both textual and numeric components within the evaluation instrument is through the use of behaviorally anchored rating scales (BARS). The development of BARS was prompted largely by dissatisfaction with trait-based rating scales and by the realization that rating scales needed to be clarified for users by anchoring the various scale points with context-specific and job-related statements (Atkin & Conlon, 1978; Ferris, 1982; Schwab et al., 1975). Such scales were first introduced by Smith and Kendall (1963) to evaluate the performance of nurses. The procedures used to develop the scale represented a variation and enhancement of the critical incident technique described by Flanagan (1954):

> The critical incident technique consists of procedures . . . for collecting observed incidents having special significance and meeting systematically defined criteria. . . . By an incident is meant any observable human activity that is sufficiently complete, in and of itself, to permit inferences and predictions to be made about the person performing the act. To be critical, an incident must occur in a situation where its consequences are sufficiently definite to leave little doubt concerning its effects. (p. 327)

Flanagan (1954) emphasized that the technique is comprised of a flexible set of principles rather than a "single, rigid set of rules governing data collecting" (p. 327). Hence, it can be modified for a variety of practical applications.

Unlike the critical incident technique, Smith and Kendall (1963) used "inferences or predictions (of behavior) from observations rather than actual observed behaviors" (p. 151). The format of BARS developed by Smith and Kendall consisted of a set of continuous graphic rating scales arranged vertically on a page. Behavioral descriptions served as anchor points and were placed beside the numbers on the scale. Raters were instructed to check anywhere along the continuum. The rationale for the format was that it was perceived to be a "means of combining the relevance of direct observation of critical incidents and similar techniques with the acceptability to raters of graphic rating scales" (Smith & Kendall, 1963, p. 150). Smith and Kendall noted that because such scales were referenced to behaviors, involved the actual raters or participants who were comparable to the actual raters, and included terminology germane to the raters, valid and conscientious ratings tended to result from their use.

A benchmark level of organizational expectation is central to this performance evaluation system. The benchmark provides the division between the managerial levels of acceptable behavior and the professional development components of the dimensions. On a seven-point scale, there should be a step where the performance expectations, from the employer's perspective, reach a ceiling. Because the instrument is also concerned with professional growth and development, the managerial ceiling of job expectations cannot reach point 7, or there would be no ability to measure professional growth. The instrument must also measure loss of function. This means that the benchmark must be set at a midpoint that has growth and loss on either side of it.

The choice of step 4 on the scale as the highest managerial expectation for performance on any dimension meets this requirement. This allows steps 5 through 7 to be directed solely toward professional growth and development. Additionally, if the behavioral description of step 4 is a neutral statement that reflects the basic performance expectation, then steps 1 through 3 can reflect specific gradations of managerial concerns about loss of function or performance that is not acceptable.

Involving Staff in the Instrument Construction

Employee participation in the instrument construction should begin with a general staff meeting about the purpose of the project. You may need to field questions about BARS scales and the use of the benchmark separation of managerial and professional growth elements. Above all else, what you must communicate is that the intent of management is sincere, and the purposes of the performance evaluation are for both organizational and individual growth. You must also promote a professional attitude toward evaluation and work and emphasize that the process is not to be associated with pay, promotion, or other financial rewards. This is a controversial issue in performance evaluation, and employees may need clarification and reassurance on this point. You should set aside time to reassure skeptical employees that management is serious about disconnecting evaluation from monetary issues. Thus, the primary aim of the general staff meeting is to gain support for the project and to seek employee participation.

Subsequent meetings can then take place in job groups and should begin with a review of the information from the earlier general staff meeting. At this point your efforts should be directed at obtaining employee commitment to begin the process of identifying job dimensions. At this stage, only a general description of the job dimensions is required. However, these dimensions should encompass only those tasks of specific job groups, reflecting their particular role and service in the organization.

After specific job groups have met and identified their discrete job dimensions, these dimensions are pooled across all job groups. Invariably, there will be dimensions in common that, although they may have different titles, describe the same expectations across different jobs, roles, and service responsibilities. In other words, they are generic to work in any capacity within that particular organization. On the other hand, the job groups will also identify dimensions of work that pertain only to them. Consequently, one of the outcomes of this exercise is the production of the identification of both job-specific or a la carte and generic or core expectations required of employees in the organization.

The next task for the job groups is to construct the performance evaluation scale for each a la carte dimension. Each of these scales will consist of seven steps with a behavioral description for each step. Steps 1 through 4 can be derived from the job description, with step 4 as a neutral statement reflecting achievement of the expectation. Steps 5 through 7 are behavioral statements that reflect aspects of professional growth and development that are beyond the basic job description and above the managerial level of performance expectation.

It is not easy to build a performance evaluation scale. It must be nonpunitive and positive and use commonly understood, simple language. The nonpunitive, positive aspect is addressed by the three steps dedicated to professional growth issues. It is exceedingly difficult to avoid jargon and buzzwords associated with the work of the organization. A screening, perhaps by a reviewer outside the job group, is necessary if you wish to build an instrument that is clearly understood and free of the potential for different interpretations or distortion.

The ideal performance evaluation instrument also requires expectations to be anchored in real situations and be readily understood by anyone evaluated on the dimension. This may not be difficult for steps 1 through 4 because each job group can return for guidance to the actual job description. Steps 5 through 7 require more thought and effort and will rely heavily upon the experience and leadership of key people in the job group who can describe the key aspects of professional growth and development with respect to a particular job dimension.

The second set of dimensions, the core dimensions, are considered universal and generic to all employees in the organization. A small cross-section of job group representatives can help define the dimensions, construct the scales, and identify the seven behavioral anchors. As with the a la carte dimensions, each dimension has seven steps, with the steps 1 through 4 grounded in the job description and managerial expectations. Step 4 is a neutral statement of the basic expectation, and steps 5 through 7 are concerned with professional growth and development.

The resulting instrument consists of a set of core dimensions and a set of a la carte dimensions. The orientation of all dimensions should be toward the future and should not be tied to pay, promotion, or merit increases. The number of a la carte scales is virtually unlimited and depends on the number and diversity of programs within a particular organization. A final task for each job group is to reach agreement with management on which a la carte dimensions will be used with their particular group.

The process can be tiring and time consuming. Indeed, a recurring criticism of BARS evaluation instruments is the time and expense involved in instrument construction (Cronbach, 1970; Thorndike & Hagen, 1977).

However, the outcome is well worth the effort. Most of us have learned that it is wise to practice preventive maintenance on the vehicles we drive. In similar fashion, the costs of not having a well-developed performance evaluation system, such as employee turnover, lowered productivity, poor morale, and possible litigation, more than justifies the front-end expense.

PERFORMANCE EVALUATION PROCESS

The evaluation process should be fast and efficient and have an independent component in which both the supervisor and the employee complete rankings of the employee's performance. There must also be opportunity for dialogue and disagreement, and the process must be time framed and occur, usually, on an annual basis.

To illustrate the performance evaluation process in action, assume that an organization has completed the tasks of dimension identification and scale construction. The resulting instrument consists of 10 core dimensions and another 22 a la carte dimensions. Through negotiation and agreement with management, a particular job group has 10 specific a la carte dimensions designated as part of its evaluation. This group, then, will be evaluated by using 20 scales, the 10 core dimensions and the 10 agreed-upon a la carte dimensions.

The evaluation of a particular staff member would begin with two independent processes. The employee would score himself or herself on each seven-point scale, and the supervisor would do likewise. Experience has shown that this task should take no more than one hour for either person to complete. Once this independent component is completed, the next step is a face-to-face meeting between supervisor and staff member. It is important that the performance evaluation not be interrupted. Nothing is more frustrating or vexing for an employee than to have his or her evaluation interrupted by the supervisor taking telephone calls or responding to other diversions. Not only do interruptions detract from the evaluation, they communicate a negative message that the employee's evaluation is not important to the supervisor.

The purpose of this meeting is to share and discuss scores. The need for clear and open communication at this meeting is critical. It should be made clear that disagreement is acceptable. The only criteria that must be respected is that people defend their scoring on the basis of the actual behavioral description contained within the performance evaluation scale. The scores must be based upon that data and not on subjective impressions or personalities, or one or two critical incidents. Although either party can feel free to change scores because of discussion, new information, or clarification, there should be no requirement that consensus must occur. Employee and supervisor can agree to disagree. Because both parties are allowed to retain their own set of scores, pressure toward consensus is reduced, and the employee's sense of justice and fairness about the process can be enhanced.

A second face-to-face meeting is recommended two weeks later. At this meeting, the focus should be on goals and objectives for the coming year. Although the individuals are not required to agree on scores, there should be some consensus about goals and objectives. A summary sheet should include space for comments about the process, a delineation of goals and objectives, and a place for employee and supervisor to sign off on the evaluation. This second meeting provides closure to the evaluation process. At this point, both parties should feel there are no loose ends or unfinished business. Although the duration of the process may vary, the independent scoring, face-to-face meeting about scores, and second meeting about goals and objectives should not exceed three hours.

Once the instrument has been successfully implemented, it should become part of your orientation package for new employees and also an integral part of organizational policy and procedure. Employees should be encouraged to read the user guide and review the instrument, sharing any concerns they have. You should inform new employees about the process, agree upon their evaluation dates, and reach agreement on the a la carte dimensions that will be included in their review. If the position is a new one or is part of a new program, you will need to engage the new employee in scale construction to develop a dimension to be included in the a la carte group of scales. This early introduction of new employees to their responsibility in helping to build the performance evaluation system can foster loyalty and commitment to it.

The construction of the performance appraisal instrument and the implementation of the process is now complete. If the process that has been described here is followed, a performance evaluation system that embodies all the ideal characteristics will result. This process takes time and effort and is labor intensive. However, failure to work through this process invites the common problems and failings of the majority of performance evaluation models.

SKILLS-APPLICATION EXERCISES

- Obtain the performance evaluation instrument from a nonprofit organization you are familiar with and interview the individuals responsible for overseeing performance evaluation, most likely the director of human resource management or the chief executive officer. Learn all you can about the organization's performance evaluation system and process. Using the characteristics of the ideal performance evaluation system, assess the organization's system in terms of its strengths and weaknesses. If you were a consultant to this organization, what steps would you take to bring it more in line with the ideal system?

- Obtain some of the job descriptions from a nonprofit organization you are familiar with. Identify two or three job dimensions associated with each of these positions. Construct a behaviorally anchored rating scale for each of the dimensions using the appropriate characteristics of the ideal instrument, such as that it uses a benchmark, is anchored in real events, uses simple language, has content validity, and uses both semantic and numerical components. If necessary, interview a position incumbent to learn more about the specifics of the job.

REFERENCES

Atkin, R. R., & Conlon, E. G. (1978). Behaviorally anchored rating scales: Some theoretical issues. *Academy of Management Review, 3*, 119–128.

Baker, H. K., & Holmgren, S. R.(1982). Stepping up to supervision: Conducting performance reviews. *Supervisory Management, 27*(4), 20–28.

Bechman, C. W. (1981). Performance appraisal challenges in mental health services. *Journal of Mental Health Administration, 8*(1), 24–26.

Beer, M. (1981). Performance appraisal: Dilemmas and possibilities. *Organizational Dynamics, 9*(3), 24–36.

Bernardin, H. J., & Beatty, R. W. (1984). *Performance appraisal: Assessing human behavior at work.* Boston: Kent.

Brumback, G. B. (1988). Some ideas, issues, and predictions about performance management. *Public Personnel Management, 17*, 387–402.

Burke, R. J., Wetzel, N., & Weir, T. (1978). Characteristics of effective employee performance review and development interviews: Replication and extension. *Personnel Psychology, 31*, 903–919.

Caroll, S. J., & Schneier, C. E. (1982). *Performance appraisal and review systems.* Glenview, IL: Scott, Foresman.

Cedarblom, D. (1982). The performance appraisal interview: A review, implications, and suggestions. *Academy of Management Review, 7*, 219–227.

Cronbach, L. J. (1970). *Essentials of psychological testing* (3rd ed.). New York: Harper & Row.

Cummings, L. L., & Schwab, D. P. (1973). *Performance in organizations: Determinants and appraisal.* Glenview, IL: Scott, Foresman.

Demarco, J. J., & Nigro, L. G. (1983). Using employee attitudes and perceptions to maintain supervisory implementation of CSRA performance appraisal systems. *Public Personnel Management Journal, 12*, 43–51.

Dipboye, R. L., & de Pontbriand, R. (1981). Correlates of employee reactions to performance appraisals and appraisal systems. *Journal of Applied Psychology, 66*, 248–251.

Edwards, R. L., & Yankey, J. A. (1991). *Skills for effective human services management.* Silver Spring, MD: NASW Press.

Evans, E., & McShane, S. L. (1988). Employee perceptions of performance appraisal fairness in two organizations. *Canadian Journal of Behavioral Science, 20*, 177–191.

Ferris, G. R. (1982). The performance evaluation process: Implications of supervisor-subordinate attributional congruency for subordinate work attitudes. *Dissertation Abstracts International, 43*, 862A (University Microfilms No. 82-18, 464).

Flanagan, J. C. (1954). The critical incident technique. *Psychological Bulletin, 51*, 327–358.

Folger, R., & Greenberg, J. (1985). Procedural justice: An interpretive analysis of personnel systems. In K. M. Rowland & G. R. Ferris (Eds.), *Research in personnel and human resource management* (Vol. III, pp. 141–185). Greenwich, CT: JAI Press.

Greenberg, J. (1986). Determinants of perceived fairness of performance evaluation. *Journal of Applied Psychology, 71*, 340–342.

Harkness, L., & Mulinski, P. (1988). Performance standards for social workers. *Social Work, 33*, 339–344.

Kane, M. T. (1982). The validity of licensure examinations. *American Psychologist, 37*, 911–918.

Landy, F. J., Barnes, J. L., & Murphy, K. R. (1978). Correlates of perceived fairness and accuracy of performance evaluation. *Journal of Applied Psychology, 63*, 751–754.

Landy, F. J., & Farr, J. L. (1983). *The measurement of work performance: Methods, theory, and applications.* New York: Academic Press.

Latham, G. P., & Wexley, K. N. (1981). *Increasing productivity through performance appraisal.* Reading, MA: Addison-Wesley.

Levine, H. Z. (1986). Performance appraisal at work. *Personnel, 63*(6), 63–71.

Levinson, H. (1979). Management of what performance? *Harvard Business Review, 57*(5), 120–126.

Lombardi, D. N. (1988). *Handbook of personnel selection and performance evaluation in health care.* San Francisco: Jossey-Bass.

MacIntosh, J. (1988). Staff appraisal. *Physiotherapy, 74*(2), 95-97.

Matheson, W., Millar, K., & Van Dyck, C. (1995). *Performance evaluation in the human services.* New York: Haworth Press.

McGregor, D. (1972). An uneasy look at performance appraisal. *Harvard Business Review, 50*(5), 133–138.

Millar, K. (1990). Performance appraisal of professional social workers. *Administration in Social Work, 14*(1), 65–85.

Mohrman, A. M., Jr., Resnick-West, M., & Lawler, E. E., III. (1989). *Designing performance appraisal systems.* San Francisco: Jossey-Bass.

Nemeroff, W. F., & Wexley, K. N. (1979). An exploration of the relationships between performance feedback interview characteristics and interview outcomes as perceived by managers and subordinates. *Journal of Occupational Psychology, 52*(1), 25–34.

Patten, T. (1976). Linking financial rewards to employee performance: The roles of O.D. and M.B.O. *Human Resource Management, 15*, 2–17.

Patz, A. (1975). Performance appraisal: Useful but still resisted. *Harvard Business Review, 53*(3), 74–80.

Peters, T. (1985). *The no-win world of performance appraisal.* Palo Alto, CA: Tom Peters Group.

Pottinger, P. S., & Goldsmith, N. (1979). *Defining and measuring competencies: New directions for experimental learning.* San Francisco: Jossey-Bass.

Rasmussen, J. (1988). Occupational therapy staff evaluation: A personnel and program management system. In F. S. Cromwell & C. Brollier (Eds.), *The occupational therapy manager's survival handbook* (pp. 23–31). New York: Haworth Press.

Rendero, T. (1980). Performance appraisal practices. *Personnel, 57*(6), 4–12.

Rock, M. (1972). *Handbook of wage and salary administration.* New York: McGraw-Hill.

Sashkin, M. (1981). Appraising appraisal: Ten lessons from research to practice. *Organizational Dynamics, 9*(3), 24–36.

Schwab, D. P., Heneman, H. G., III, & DeCotiis, T. (1975). Behaviorally anchored rating scales: A review of the literature. *Personnel Psychology, 28*, 549–562.

Smith, P. C. (1976). Behaviors, results, and organizational effectiveness: The problem of criteria. In M. D. Dunnette (Ed.), *Handbook of industrial and organizational psychology* (pp. 745–775). Chicago: Rand McNally.

Smith, P. C., & Kendall, L. F. (1963). Retranslation of expectations: An approach to the construction of unambiguous anchors for rating scales. *Journal of Applied Psychology, 47*, 149–155.

Spano, R. M. (1981). Performance appraisal in a hospital social service department. *Social Work in Health Care, 7*(2), 13–37.

Thorndike, R., & Hagen, E. (1977). *Measurement and evaluation in psychology and education* (4th ed.). New York: John Wiley & Sons.

Timmreck, T. C. (1989). Performance appraisal systems in rural western hospitals. *Health Care Management Review, 14*(2), 31–43.

Wexley, K. N., Singh, J. P., & Yukl, G. A. (1973). Subordinate personality as a moderator of the effects of participation in three types of appraisal interviews. *Journal of Applied Psychology, 58*, 54–59.

Wexley, K. N., & Yukl, G. A. (1977). *Organizational behavior and personnel psychology.* Homewood, IL: Richard D. Irwin.

Wiehe, V. (1980). Current practices in performance appraisal. *Administration in Social Work, 4*(3), 1–11.

CHAPTER 12

Effective Group Decision Making

John E. Tropman

Nonprofit managers have many tasks. On the one hand, there are the executive tasks involved in running the organization. Many of these involve the management of human resources, budgets, and capital resources, and in general keeping the organization running. So the very first task of the nonprofit manager or administrator is to keep the organization in the "on" position.

The second task is to develop a high-performance organization, which is different from actually running the organization. In this case, the manager is challenged not only to do the job, but to do it faster, better, and cheaper.

The third task of a nonprofit manager is to transform the organization. Nonprofit organizations need to be periodically reinvented, and it is the mandate of managers to lead those kinds of efforts.

In each of these pieces of the executive enterprise, the management of decisions is crucial. Current language and usage suggest that decisions are "made." It seems that a more effective and accurate description of decision making might be decision "constructing," because it is more true that decisions are built—piece by piece, element by element—very much like a menu for Sunday dinner might be built. One thinks about the main course, one thinks about the vegetables, one thinks about the starch, one thinks about the dessert, and they are assembled piece by piece. And then, once the entire range of possibilities is in place, the chef looks at the overall fit and sees whether or not everything harmonizes with everything else, and some adjustments might be made at that point. We might call that decision "sculpting."

Creative decision management is the management of competing values. There are always at least two points of view, interests, ideas, or perspectives that must be blended, prioritized, selected, and organized as the manager goes about his or her decision-making work. Typically, people have thought of decision making as an individual activity. The top-level manager retreats to some corner of his or her office and "makes" the decision. In the decision-building approach, it is more usual that many parties are involved, and very frequently there are meetings, conferences, and discussions during which the decision construction occurs and through which decision building occurs. Hence, non-profit managers must manage competing values in the decision-making process itself, because by implication, construction occurs over time rather than at a single moment in time.

Second, the manager must manage competing values among decision rules. Decision rules are the norms that make decisions legitimate. Typically, rules conflict with each other. One person–one vote, for example, deals with breadth of preference but not the depth of preference. So that issue must be attended to by the top-level manager or chief executive officer (CEO). And finally, in terms of decisions, one hopes for high-quality results. If decisions are indeed one organizational product, then they can be examined by asking "How good are these decisions?" This question is almost never asked, but it is an important question, especially for the contemporary executive.

This chapter examines the issue of conflicting values in three areas—the management of decision processes, the management of decision rules, and the management of decision results. Useful hints and tips will be provided to help the executive achieve better process, better rule balance, and higher-quality decisions.

GROUP CONTEXT

The myth that it is lonely at the top suggests that CEOs and other managers work alone. A common observation is that "I didn't get any work done today; I spent my whole day in meetings." But that phrase tells us that our culture assumes that "work" is not done in a collective setting. It suggests that the collective setting is something of a waste of time and that real work is done when one is alone in one's office. That idea is not only erroneous but also pernicious, because it devalues the most common setting where a decision construction goes on—the group context or group setting. It devalues work that might be undertaken to improve one's skill as a decision manager within the group context, and it offers stereotypic and negative views of the group context. However, in most nonprofit organizations today, the group context is ubiquitous. We spend a lot of time in meetings. The degree of their formality varies, and they are run using whatever technology the individual in charge has picked up in his or her training. Jokes about meetings abound. For example, someone commented that a camel is a horse assembled in a staff meeting. Someone else commented that a nonprofit board is a group that takes minutes to waste hours. Somehow, negative and hostile humor is an attempt on the part of our culture to either control or make understandable and comprehensible the ubiquity of meetings. But meetings can be viewed as an organizational process, the output of which is a decision stream. What that means for the CEO is that like other organizational processes—the budget process, the capital improvement process, the fund-raising process—meetings must be managed carefully.

Values are enacted in group situations. Hence, if one is to manage competing values, one is most likely to do it in the group context. It is the people sitting around the table who exemplify competing values and whose commitments must be harmonized so forward progress can be made and a high-quality result achieved. When blended, competing values have the ability, like various strands of rope, to add strength to a decision. On the other hand, when ignored, competing values can create stall through their conflict and opposition.

Finally, because of its ubiquity and its centrality in the place where competing values are present, efforts in managing the group decision context is one place where management success can be most telling. The most successful CEOs and top-level managers have had the ability to manage group decision making at the board level, the staff level, the community level, and at the other levels where they sit with colleagues, superiors, subordinates, peers, and citizens and try to create policies that will be a positive force for their community.

CONFLICTING VALUES

Conflicting values have an important place in thinking about the job of the nonprofit manager. A theory of competing values (Tropman, 1989) that emphasized the diversity of values we all entertain talked about the importance of understanding that competing values are not either–or types of situations, but rather both–and types of situations. I was not committed *either* to equality *or* to achievement, but rather I was committed to *both* equality *and* achievement in some mix, the proportions of which may change over time and space.

When packaged or bundled, conflicting values become conflicting cultures. In thinking about decision making and the skills required in decision making, it is often helpful to think about organizations as being characterized by differing and competing subcultures. In the management area, Quinn (1988) perhaps has been the most articulate spokesperson for competing values. Quinn's approach, based on differing positions an organization might take on the dimensions of flexibility and control, yields four organizational subcultures (Figure 12-1). Each organizational subculture has dominant skills.

Figure 12-1. Quinn's Quadrants: Organizational, Cultural Archetypes, and Skills in Relationship to Level of Control and Amount of Flexibility

LEVEL OF CONTROL	AMOUNT OF FLEXIBILITY	
	LOW	HIGH
LOW	**Clan** Facilitating Mentoring *Consensual* *Decision Making*	**Adhocracy** Innovating Brokering *Political* *Decision Making*
HIGH	**Hierarchy** Coordinating Monitoring *Empirical* *Decision Making*	**Market** Producing Directing *Rational (Results)* *Decision Making*

Each quadrant has its own cultural archetype or cultural name. In the upper left is the clan subculture, low on flexibility and formal control. It is culture driven by membership, and the main reward is acceptance into membership. Key skills are facilitating and mentoring.

In the lower left is the hierarchy subculture, low on flexibility and high on formal control. It is driven by adherence to rules and structure, and the reward is promotion. Important skills are coordinating and monitoring.

In the lower right, the market subculture is juxtaposed to the clan subculture. High on flexibility and control, this subculture pays almost no attention to membership (how long you have been with the organization, who you are, who your parents are) and stresses results almost entirely. Control comes through results only. If you produce, you're in; if not, you're out. In the market culture, the question is "What have you done for me lately?" Whereas the clan subculture is more like a sorority, the market subculture is more like an investment bank—you do not care how nice your investment banker is; you want results. Core skills are producing and directing.

Finally, in the upper right, there is the adhocracy juxtaposed to the bureaucracy. Adhocracy is high on flexibility and low on control. Whereas the bureaucracy is focused on rules and structure and the routinization of events, the adhocracy is like a pick-up baseball game or a jazz band. Whoever is around may do what needs to be done. There is an exciting openness, fluidity, and porosity to the adhocratic subculture, but it can also be chaotic and undirectional. Central skills are innovating and brokering.

Each of these subcultures has particular strengths and weaknesses, which will be detailed in a moment. As one might guess, some of these strengths and weakness apply directly to the decision-making process.

COMPETING VALUES: STRENGTHS AND
WEAKNESSES IN THE DECISION-MAKING PROCESS

We might begin by briefly looking at the strengths of the decision-making process that each of the subcultures presents. These are well-illustrated by Quinn, Rohrbaugh, and McGrath (1985) in their perspective chart (Figure 12-2).

Quinn et al. (1985) talked about the decision-making perspectives each of the subcultures offers. The clan subculture uses a consensual perspective. Participation in and commitment to decisions is high. All members of the organization characterized by this subculture would typically be involved and would participate. Members of this subculture feel that if you participated in the process, you must and will support the resulting outcome. But too much participation leads to a poky and sometimes stalled decision process. Commitment to membership means that one member with a different view can hold up the whole process. Nonprofit organizations are heavily represented in the clan quadrant, and the delay in decision making is a common problem.

The strength of the hierarchy subculture is in its empirical perspective—doing it by the numbers. Decision makers here use database processes and explicit decision accountability. Knowing where the buck stops is a hallmark of a hierarchical subculture's decision-making process. But going by the numbers alone can lead to a decline in effective participation and empowerment. As numbers go up, people frequently go down. Database processes are fine, but qualitative perspectives are also important.

In the market subculture, goal attainment and efficiency—results, results, and more results, and fast—become crucial. Decisions are made quickly and rationally, usually by those closest to the possible result rather than by the right official or all of the members. Here again, too much of a good thing becomes a bad thing. Premature decisions are often characteristic of the market culture. Short-run, immediate perspectives are dominant, and a longer-run perspective is driven out by the need for "more for me, sooner."

In the adhocracy subculture, adaptable and stakeholder buy-in elements are strong. Who makes decisions often depends on who is around to do it. But the decision making is less focused on the decision maker than the decision supporters. In thinking politically, the decision maker is more often the decision packager, seeking views from others and putting them into an acceptable package. Hence, who makes the decision is less important than will it fly. Of course getting everyone on board is important. But adhocracies can let leadership shift from the decision-making core to the periphery and suggest only what will pass as opposed to what is right.

Figure 12-2. Perspective Chart

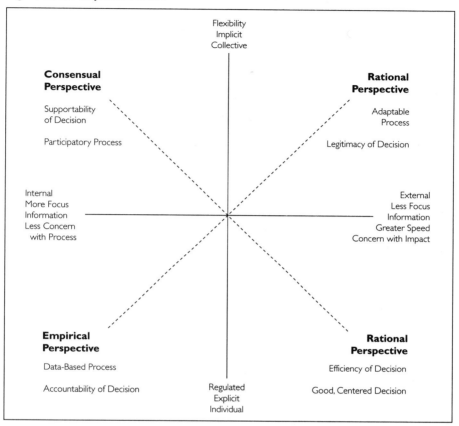

SOURCE: Quinn, R. E., Rohrbaugh, J., & McGrath, M.R. (1985). Automated decision conferencing. *Personnel, 62*(11), 49–55.

Quinn (1988) dealt with this idea of strengths and weaknesses in his concept of positive and negative zones (Figure 12-3). Let us look at the outer circle. Here we see familiar problems of group decision making. When the strengths of a subculture are pushed too far, or overstressed, they pass the utility point and become overdone. Then problems occur.

In the clan subculture, extreme permissiveness and inappropriate participation become key, sprinkled with a good helping of unproductive discussion. In the hierarchy subculture, procedural sterility and trivial rigor become hallmarks (as in the saying "You have erroneously initialed the attached memo; please erase your initials and initial your erasure"). Iron-bound tradition is also common in the hierarchy subculture ("It's the weekly meeting; we have it

Figure 12-3. The Positive and Negative Zones

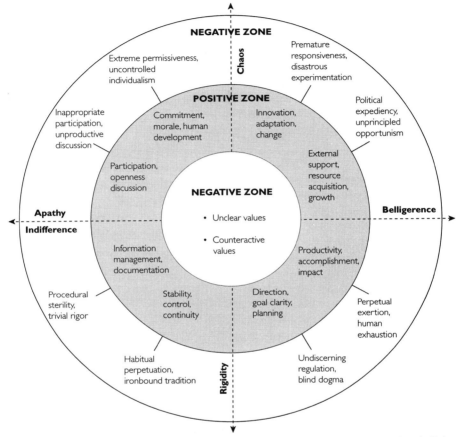

every week; we always have"). In the market subculture, perpetual exertion and human exhaustion can become problems, and in the adhocratic subculture, premature responsiveness and unprincipled opportunism can become difficulties as well.

PUTTING IN THE FIX: CREATING HIGH-QUALITY DECISIONS

What, then, might be the antidote to some of these problems? A common meeting structure that allows the difficulties to be avoided and the strengths to be blended is part of the answer. A research project on the "meeting masters" suggests some things that nonprofit managers might do to manage competing values and eliminate the difficulties of moving to extremes in any one of these four cultural cases (Tropman, 1997). The meeting masters were individuals interviewed and videotaped over the years whose meetings were astonishing because they were so different from all of the other meetings that one might typically experience. They ran terrific meetings—terrific in this case meaning that high-quality decisions were made, and the participants enjoyed themselves.

What did these meeting masters do differently? First, they thought about the decision-making process differently. From their point of view, the decision-making process was something like an orchestra performance or a play. It required preparation and organization. As they met with their boards, staffs, citizen groups, and volunteer groups, those meetings were at the end of a process of preparation rather than at the beginning. They never said "Let's get together and see if there's any reason for having gotten together." They always had some sense of what needed to be done, although they never had a sense of the exact output. Thus, the gatherings they orchestrated were never rubber stamps; instead, they were honest, open, participatory forums, organized within decent, reasonable time frames and with decent and reasonable alternatives available to the participants. Attendees were always alerted ahead of time to the topics and the hoped-for outcomes, whether it was a decision outcome or a brainstorming outcome, so they could prepare intellectually and conceptually before they came. One of the meeting masters told me,

> You know, there are only three things done at meetings. You announce things, you decide things, and you brainstorm about things. The way I organize my meetings is that I gather all of the announcements and put them at the beginning. Then I take the decision-making items and put them in the middle. And finally, when it comes to the brainstorming items, I put those at the end. It works out very well.

This way of organizing meetings can be called the "three-characters rule."

Because the meeting masters felt that the play or drama was an apt metaphor for a meeting, they put less emphasis on the personalities of the participants and more emphasis on the scripts they did or did not have. The meeting masters, through the agenda and other preparatory processes, spent a good deal of energy on providing scripts for the individuals coming to the meeting. This allowed individuals to come prepared, participate authentically and fully, achieve decisions, and have a good time.

The meeting masters followed several rules to enhance the ability of members to fully participate. Among the most important was the rule of halves, under which the masters simply asked the participants, whether it was a board, staff, or volunteer meeting, to hand in agenda items they wanted considered at the next meeting at least halfway between the meeting dates. That

"The first meeting of the coalition 'Groups Organized to Conserve Humorous Acronyms (GOTCHA)' will now come to order."

meant that for a typical staff meeting on Monday, the staff had to turn in items by the previous Tuesday or Wednesday. This gave the meeting master a chance to see what was afoot, organize the material sensibly, and get the necessary information and people set up to attend the meeting. Very little is worse than getting together with colleagues, board, or staff and having an issue come up for which you could have been prepared if you had known about it. None of us likes to look foolish.

Another rule the meeting masters followed is the rule of sixths. This rule was described in the following way by one of the meeting masters:

> When I put my agenda together, I like to think of it this way. About a sixth of the material should be from the past. And if we have more than that, we're simply not moving quickly enough through the material that we have. About four-sixths of the material should be from the here-and-now, and about one-sixth— and this is the fun part, for my board—is from the future. Each meeting, we take time to look ahead and to speculate about what are the issues that are coming down the pike that might or will affect us. We share ideas and feelings, we brainstorm about them, then begin to prepare ourselves intellectually and, I might add, emotionally, for what's just ahead. This process means that my board is never surprised by issues. They've always had a chance to think them through. And I do the same thing with my staff, as well.

This manager used the rule of sixths to create a sense of anticipation, to get a feel for where her board and her staff were in terms of issues of the future.

Having talked with the board and staff, I can also share their reaction. One of the board members remarked,

> This is a great system. We always go through things in about the same way. We finish some leftover matters, usually rather quickly, get to matters at hand, and then wrap up our meeting with brainstorming, anticipating the future, and getting our ideas. I have a really deep sense of participation in this board, and it's more than I can say for the other boards I'm on, let me tell you.

The meeting masters also followed the rule of three-quarters. About three-quarters of the way between meetings, whatever the schedule was, they sent out a package including the agenda, the minutes, and any reports. Although many people do this for boards of directors, it is infrequently done for staff. But the same principle applies. Individuals need a chance to think about the material that is coming up. As one of the masters said,

> It's a little bit like playing a musical instrument. If I were to give you a piece of music and say, "Play this on the piano," we call that sight reading in music. And it has all the squeaks and grunts that a sight-reading rendition frequently has. And how much better we sound if we have a chance to practice a bit. Yet, in meetings, we routinely engage in sight-reading, except we don't recognize all those crazy little bits of participation as a result of the fact that individuals have just gotten the agenda and the materials, are struggling through it, are struggling to understand it, and struggling to make sense of it. It doesn't make any sense to me not to send stuff out a little bit ahead.

The meeting masters also followed the rule of the agenda bell outlined in Figure 12-4. The agenda bell is a system for organizing the agenda itself. It contains seven items. The first item is the minutes for the previous meeting. If you have minutes they should be approved right away. If it is a board meeting and a quorum is not present, my experts said "Approve them anyway, and reapprove them later. It's important to begin on time, and you don't want to wait, punishing those who have shown up on time and rewarding those who, for whatever reason, can't seem to make it." The second item represents announcements. These are short, factual, noncontroversial statements of things that might be of interest. Announcements are not discussed except for a quick factual question, and they should not contain matters that people would logically wish to discuss.

The third, fourth, and fifth items on the agenda bell structure are items for decision. Here the meeting masters did an interesting thing. They divided the items for decision (and they knew which items needed a decision because they had already gotten them under the rule of halves) into three categories—easy ones (3a, 3b, 3c), moderately difficult ones (4a, 4b, 4c), and one really tough item (5). The idea behind this structure is that the group begins by taking action on those items that are fairly easy to deal with but require formal

Figure 12-4. The Agenda Bell

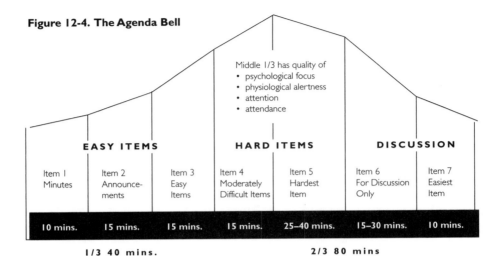

approval. There is a transition into the somewhat more difficult items, and at about the halfway point of the meeting, the group tackles the toughest item. After that item has been dealt with, the group moves to item 6, a category containing the brainstorming items. Finally, an easy item, perhaps a thank you or even a motion for adjournment, is put in as item 7.

One of the meeting masters explained the rationale behind this structure in the following way:

> The way I set up my meetings is a little bit like the way I exercise. There's a get-go period, a heavy work period, and a decompression period. You know, decision making tears at the fabric of the group, so I try to finish up the big decision item about two-thirds of the way through the meeting. This means that we can spend the last part of the meeting working together—because, of course, in many instances, when you're making decisions there's conflict—on items for the future. It really works well.

It also turns out that the division of decision items into an easy group, a somewhat more difficult group, and the toughest group means that individuals are more likely to be buoyed by success on some easy items as they tackle harder items and hopefully are buoyed by success on those when they tackle the toughest item. Thus, the agenda is shaped rather than handled in a random fashion.

These basic processes—getting information ahead of time; shaping and structuring the agenda, including items from the future; sending the agenda and attendant documents out ahead of time; and structuring the actual meeting according to the agenda bell principle—prove immensely helpful in managing conflicting values. Although people might have different perspectives, they will all be singing from the same music. Common structure, although it is not a total antidote to uncommon commitments, serves a useful function. People with a clan orientation can have an adequate chance at appropriate participation, whereas people with a market orientation can see that there is a structure that will probably lead to action. Thus, those two kinds of commitments are balanced. The agenda itself provides a kind of structure, often preferred by those with a hierarchy orientation, whereas the rule of sixths and the brainstorming and speculative material at the end of the meeting provide something that those with an autocracy orientation value and cherish. In this sense, then, a common structure is a tool for managing conflicting cultural orientations.

There were also some practices that the meeting masters avoided or changed from traditional practice. One of these was the no-new-business rule. Using the rationale of the rule of halves, participants were encouraged to present new business in agenda items they submitted before the meeting rather than at the meeting itself. As one of the meeting masters said,

> New business is the worst enemy that a meeting can have, in my opinion. People come in with half-thought-out concerns and worries, no one has had a chance to adequately prepare, and it tends to draw people away from the agenda at hand. We try to get people to think ahead about what they want to discuss at the meeting, and let us know. Then we can have the information and people ready.

Another thing the meeting masters got rid of was the traditional report. One of the masters described the no-more-reports rule:

> Many meetings are just oral newsletters. They go around the room, and people try to put the best face on whatever they're doing. It's a curious mixture of announcements, decisions, and discussions, and nobody knows really when to cut in or how. I've been able to get rid of all of that and have completely reorganized. Now, I ask people to "break up" what would have been their report into an announcement item—and then I put it in the announcements section—or a decision item—and then I put it in the decision section—or a brainstorming item—and then I put it in the brainstorming section. This means that we don't have a finance committee report anymore. If the finance chairperson has a simple announcement, as I said it goes there. If there are items from the finance committee that we need to act on from a decision point of view, they go into the middle section. If the finance committee wants us to brainstorm around some issues, I put that at the end. It works very well.

Naturally, these techniques will not be the full answer to the problem of managing competing or conflicting values in a group decision-making setting.

Figure 12-5. Key Rules from the Meeting Masters

Three-characters rule
Agenda bell rule
	Announcement items first
	Decision items second
	    Easy decision items
	    Then tougher decision items
	    Then the toughest decision items
	Brainstorming discussion items third
	Organizes items according to what must happen with them

Rule of halves	Get upcoming items halfway between meeting times. Then you can organize them and get the information and people you need. *Gets people to think ahead*
Rule of sixths	About one-sixth of the items should be for brainstorming and discussion only and should relate to the future. *Reaches ahead for tough items and dealing with them proactively*
Rule of three-quarters	Send material out about three-quarters of the way between meetings so people can read and think about it. *Invites people to prepare intellectually and psychologically before the meeting*
No-new-business rule	New business is sent in ahead of time so it can be structured into the ongoing flow of the meeting. *Creates the expectation of getting items in early and preparing for them rather than bringing them up at the last minute*
No-more-reports rule	Individuals who might have given reports now divide up that content into three parts that appear at the appropriate place under the rule of the agenda bell. *Reports are gone, replaced by individual items*

But they provide a different kind of answer. Typically, when people think about managing conflicting values, they tend to think about people getting together on the values themselves. The problem is that the structures or processes that we use for these kinds of settings often exacerbate their very differences, leading to worse fissures and cleavages than there were at the beginning. Providing a common structure and an indirect way of managing conflicting values appear to be successful (Figure 12-5).

MANAGING CONFLICTING VALUES IN DECISION RULES

Decision rules are norms that make decisions legitimate. We bring them into our decision-making settings—board meetings, staff meetings, volunteer meetings—from our wider life. In effect, decision rules represent different cultural preferences about how decisions should be made. So managing decision rules is, in effect, managing conflicting cultures.

Our most common decision rule is the extensive decision rule, which says basically that one person has one vote. Everyone has a say, and everyone's say is weighted equally. This rule is preferred by clan culture.

The second decision rule is the intensive decision rule—who cares most? This view says that decisions are driven by intensity. It is a favorite of adhocracy culture because individuals within this culture get deeply and heavily involved in particular projects and tend to think of these projects as most important.

The third decision rule is the involvement rule. Who might have to carry out a particular decision? This rule gives preference to the implementers—the doers—and it is a favorite of the market culture. Market culture is, after all, a can-do culture, and its view is typically "let the person who has to do the job have the most say about it."

A fourth decision rule is the expert rule—what do the lawyers, the doctors, and the scientists have to say about this? Have they signed off? This rule is a favorite of the hierarchy culture, organized in lines and boxes as it tends to be. They have the right experts and officials sign off.

A fifth rule is the power rule, sometimes known as "What does the boss think?" The power rule can reflect individual preferences on the one hand or reflect cultural preferences on the other. If the boss happens to be a clan-oriented person, then the extensive rule might get priority, and so on.

The key element to understand decision rules is that all five operate in almost all groups, and they conflict with each other. In this context, "conflict" means that the distribution of outcomes would be different if only one rule was followed, as opposed to a blending of all five. Two kinds of problem can arise.

The first problem is in the mixed-culture organization, in which all rules are simultaneously operating. This means that the CEO has to continually manage the situation to be sure that breadth, depth, involvement, expertise, and power all have their proper place. The proposals most likely to go forward and reach a decision point in a timely fashion are those that can meet and be shown to meet the interests of most of these decision rules. Formulating and expressing options that are linked to these rules is the process of decision crystallization. For example, suppose we are discussing where to have lunch. There is much talk and among the issues coming up are what most people want to do (the extensive rule), what the vegetarians want to do (the intensive rule), who's going to drive (the involvement rule), whether they have harmful additives at the place we might be thinking of (the expert rule), and what would the boss say (the power rule). A meeting master in this discussion suggested they go to the nearby Chinese restaurant because it would satisfy most of their preferences (the extensive rule addressed). It appealed to the vegetarian colleagues because it had vegetarian dishes (the intensive rule addressed). The meeting master said she would drive (the involvement rule addressed), and that the restaurant did not put monosodium glutamate in their food (the expert rule addressed). Last, she stated that the boss did not care where they spent their lunch money (the power rule addressed).

This was an amazing occurrence, because the group understood that issues of concern to them in decision making, including breadth, depth, involvement, power, and expertise, were addressed. Everyone in the group agreed, and off they went. Although the issue was small, the performance was masterful. And the example is one that managers might wish to keep in mind in mixed cultures when there are conflicting bases people will accept as a reason for a decision being legitimate.

The second problem can occur when one culture is very dominant. In this type of organization (clan, market, hierarchy, or adhocratic), one rule tends to be very dominant over all others. Hence, in the clan culture, the extensive decision rule might be given preference. This means that people who feel strongly—experts, people with power, and people who might have to carry out decisions—are not given the kind of weight that a high-quality decision truly deserves. In these instances, the manager wants to be sure that the other bases of decisions are articulated and brought into play. Obviously agencies will have their preference for decision rules, but the exclusion of appropriate alternative bases will create a weaker, poorer-quality decision than might otherwise be expected.

For example, a task force from a clan-oriented organization was working on a proposal. In this group experts were not well regarded, power was really well regarded, and involvement was not well regarded. Depth of preference was given short shrift. After a considerable amount of time, effort, and work, a proposal was voted upon, to the great satisfaction of the task force, and proudly presented to upper management. The proposal was quickly rejected. The first mistake was that the task force had not considered the wishes of the boss. The second mistake was that they had not considered certain legalities. The third mistake was that the individuals who had to carry out the recommendation had serious questions about it. And the fourth mistake was that the people who felt deeply but differently about the proposal had not been consulted or involved. Hence, if the chairperson had articulated the alternative decision bases and pointed out that these perspectives needed to be included and addressed, there would have been a much better result.

MANAGING CONFLICTING VALUES IN DECISION RESULTS

A good deal of thought has been given to documenting awful decisions or awful types of decisions. Perhaps the most famous kind of bad decision is the group-think decision, a concept developed by Janis (1972). Cohesion of the group is very high, and individual members of the group hesitate to bring up contrary points of view because they do not want to put stress on the cohesion of the group and disturb the peace. Group-think is typically a problem of the clan organization.

A second kind of decision problem is decision randomness, exemplified by what has been called a "garbage can model of organizational choice" (Cohen, March, & Olsen, 1972). Cohen and colleagues argued that for high-quality decisions, four types of people or perspectives are needed in the same room at the same time: (1) the problem knowers (individuals who know the problems the organization faces); (2) solution providers (creative individuals who can solve problems if they know what the problems are, but they often do not); (3) resource controllers (individuals who sign off on the allocation of money and people, and are therefore crucial to implementation); and (4) "decision makers looking for work" (usually the top-level managers who have to bless a decision if it is to go forward). Cohen and colleagues argued that most organizations assemble these individuals at random, as if tossed into a garbage can. This randomness is a feature of the adhocratic culture. A few people get together and do this, then a few more get together and do that, then others get together and do yet a third thing, and there is a huge amount of rework and very little orchestration and organization.

A third decision problem is the do–it, fix–it method, which is characteristic of a group that is so eager to act that it often takes premature action. This could also be called the "fire, ready, aim" group. Although group-think becomes mired in process and the failure to surface authentic alternatives, the do–it, fix–it group grabs the first gold ring that seems reasonable, proceeds with it, and often winds up needing to repair, sometimes very quickly.

The last decision problem is same as last year, a decision type characteristic of hierarchical cultures. Given the rigidities and often ponderous nature of hierarchies, making decisions that are new, different, risky, or odd is very difficult. This method seems to fit with the conservative mentality. After all, hierarchies are very good at doing something on a repeated basis over time and space. In a sense, this method continues that skill or competence into the decision-making area.

Each of these bad decisions occurs because of an overemphasis on the particular strengths of a particular culture and because those strengths get carried over into the decision-making process. For example, the adhocracy subculture tends toward chaos, and so it has a tendency toward randomness in its decision-making process. The clan subculture, with its skills at involving individuals and processing issues and concerns, may never reach a decision or may succumb to group-think.

The antidote to these problems is complex. First, the commonly used decision processes ensure that a certain amount of structure, openness, participation, and promptness will be simultaneously present. Thus, the potential perils of using only one cultural preference as the basis for decision making are reduced. Second, the management of decision rules goes a long way toward creating the balance culturally necessary for a high-quality decision. Third, one can do assessments of the decisions themselves. One way to assess decisions is to go back into the history of a particular group, such as your nonprofit's board. Look at the decisions the board made and ask these questions: Are these decisions good? Why or why not? A discussion about the quality of the decisions can be useful.

The announcement ahead of time that decisions will be evaluated in the future changes the nature of the process itself. People pay more attention when they know they are going to be evaluated. If a man knows he will be weighed at the end of the week by his physician, he will probably be careful, during that week at least, to exercise and watch his diet. Hence, what the physician sees when she looks at the man's weight is a modified weight, not a true weight. Similarly, boards, staff groups, and volunteer groups working on a decision will be more careful and articulate and will participate with more authenticity if they know they are going to be evaluated.

In addition, a no-fault discussion of why certain decisions were good and why certain decisions were not so good helps everyone understand their mission, their task, and their role as a group working together for the organization's good.

CONCLUSION

The management of group decision making is one of the most important tasks that a nonprofit manager can undertake simply because so much of a manager's time is spent in decision-making groups. Many CEOs and other top-level managers spend more than half of their time in meetings. Most of them express mild disbelief to vigorous dislike of this allocation of their time and consider this time largely wasted, ceremonial, useless, and not productive. One can only imagine what it would be like if the decision-making groups we participate in so frequently were to become productive and useful groups we looked forward to attending. And yet, the meeting masters created such groups and sustained enthusiasm in them over considerable periods of time. Their peers, superiors, and subordinates turned to them to undertake difficult tasks and chair difficult task forces, and they almost always did an outstanding job. Their goal was to make high-quality decisions, and the tips and suggestions presented in this chapter will help the nonprofit manager move in that direction.

SKILLS- APPLICATION EXERCISES

• Thinking of the four quadrants, rank your organization according to the dominance of the clan, hierarchy, market, and adhocracy subcultures. Consider whether your organization has the decision-making problems discussed in this chapter. Feel free to add more problems, other problems, and different problems.

• Think specifically of the kinds of problematic decisions discussed in the chapter: group-think; garbage can or randomness; do-it, fix-it; and same as last year. Considering the past six months at your organization, count how many of these decisions your organization has been involved with. Think of one or two really awful decisions. Try to understand what when wrong, and think about some of the ways the material in this chapter (and other chapters) could help you fix it.

• Review Figure 12-5 and then make some plans for your own action at your organization to implement these rules.

• Observe a meeting at your organization (or somewhere else) and see if you can observe the decision rules in action (or more likely, in nonaction). Develop a plan to practice thinking up possible solutions that meet and can be shown to meet most of these rules. It will be a little bumpy at first, but you will be surprised at how quickly you become good at it.

REFERENCES

Cohen, M., March, J., & Olsen, J. (1972, March). A garbage can model of organizational choice. *Administrative Science Quarterly*, pp. 1–25.

Janis, I. (1972). *Victims of groupthink*. Boston: Houghton-Mifflin.

Quinn, R. E. (1988). *Beyond rational management: Mastering the paradoxes and competing demands of high performance*. San Francisco: Jossey-Bass.

Quinn, R. E., Rohrbaugh, J., & McGrath, M. R. (1985). Automated decision conferencing. *Personnel, 62*(11), 49–55.

Tropman, J. E. (1989). *American values and social welfare*. Englewood Cliffs, NJ: Prentice Hall.

Tropman, J. E. (1997). *Successful community leadership: A skills guide for volunteers and professionals*. Washington, DC: NASW Press.

CHAPTER 13

Dismissing Problem Employees

Robert F. Rivas

One of the roles that managers must play is that of mentor. Those who are good mentors tend to be fair, objective, caring, and empathic individuals. Good mentors view employees as valued resources and are cognizant of their employees' needs and aspirations. Good mentors are also concerned, supportive individuals who seek to facilitate the development of those they mentor. However, there are some instances in which, despite your best efforts as a mentor, you may have an employee who just does not work out. In such a situation, you will find yourself pulled in several directions. On the one hand, you may want to be supportive of the employee, not wanting to do something that might cost that individual his or her job. On the other hand, as a manager you have a responsibility to your organization and to the other staff members. Such a situation may result in the need to take steps to dismiss the employee.

This chapter discusses the dismissal of employees as part of an overall management process that requires you to use specific procedures and skills. This discussion of the manager's personnel function emphasizes the categories of job separation and the types of employee problems that result in dismissal. The supervisory process is also explored, and a framework is offered for understanding how the supervision and dismissal of employees is connected to the organizational context. Finally, specific skills and procedures needed to dismiss problem employees are described.

NOTE: This chapter originally was published as Rivas, R. F. (1984). Perspectives on dismissal as a management prerogative in social service organizations. *Administration in Social Work,* 8(4), 77–92. Revised and reprinted with permission of Haworth Press.

DISMISSAL AND HUMAN RESOURCES MANAGEMENT

As a nonprofit manager, you undoubtedly are concerned with the work of your organization and the employees who carry it out. Because nonprofit organizations are labor intensive, they are highly dependent on the quantity and quality of workers who deliver social benefits and services. Thus, the human resources management aspects of the delivery of services are particularly important.

Human resources management may be conceptualized as a continuum of several activities, including recruiting, selecting, inducting, training, supervising, and evaluating employees. Each activity is connected with the dismissal process in two ways: (1) an employee can be dismissed during each of these stages of employment, and (2) the dismissal process often depends on how well each stage has been carried out during the employment process.

Recruitment and selection usually require a number of steps. As Patti (1983) noted, "Some would argue that there are no managerial decisions that so vitally influence the ultimate success of a program than the choice of its personnel. [Recruitment and selection involve] maximizing the fit between the jobs that must be done and the people who will do them" (p. 138). Managers develop job descriptions, advertise, form a pool of applicants, match the qualifications of the applicants with the job descriptions, and select the most appropriate candidates. Organizational policies usually formalize the process, which may also be heavily regulated or influenced by civil service regulations, labor and employment laws, union contracts, affirmative action plans, and professional personnel standards. In this chapter, these influences are discussed more fully in relation to dismissal than to recruitment (see chapter 8 for more information about recruitment and selection).

Induction, training, supervision, and evaluation are also ongoing concerns for managers, although the responsibility for these activities is often delegated to line supervisors. In larger organizations, these functions may be carried out as a staff function of the personnel or human resources department. During induction, managers or supervisors set beginning parameters for workers' functions. Workers seek the structure of the organization's rules and policies for direction in their work (Lewis & Lewis, 1982). Training closely follows induction and may be in a particular field, method, or job function. More specialized training may be offered under the staff development function of the organization.

Supervision in nonprofit organizations is sometimes considered to be within the general scope of management, although supervision can also be viewed as a distinct function or method of management practice. Supervision can provide employees with education, support, feedback on performance, and professional development. Kadushin (1976) suggested that supervision can be conceptualized as administrative, educational, or supportive. However, it is particularly within the structure of administrative supervision that the adequacy of employees' work is evaluated. In this regard, Kadushin (1976) noted that supervisors are responsible "for seeing that the work is done . . . that it is done in accordance with agency policy and procedures and . . . [that] it is being accomplished at a minimally acceptable level" (p. 51). Hence, the process of dismissal can be linked directly to the function of supervision of employees.

Considering the extent to which the literature emphasizes educational or supportive supervision, it is not surprising that supervision is seen as inimical to the control aspect of management or to the ultimate managerial sanction of dismissal. The two concepts represent one of the paradoxes of competing values in the managerial process. The terms "education" and "support" are usually not used in the same context with the term "dismissal" in relation to the overall supervisory function, perhaps because according to Kadushin (1976), "supervision has been primarily sensitive to, and aware of, the human being rather than the organization" (p. 115). Although Kadushin noted that there has been an attempt to accommodate the use of power and authority and the supportive or educational models of supervision, the literature appears to underemphasize those control structures that permit the dismissal of employees.

Although dismissal is rarely conceived of as part of the continuum of human resources activities, it is a valid part of the larger activity of the separation or termination of employees. "Separation" has a neutral connotation and thus may be considered part of the normal cycle of personnel activities for an organization.

Separation

All organizations lose employees for various reasons. The separation of employees, especially resignations and retirement, may be considered the last or final activity in the continuum of personnel functions. Resignation and retirement may be basically healthy actions for both the employee and the organization. Layoffs and downsizing, although usually not desirable from any standpoint, do not necessarily carry negative connotations about the performance of the worker or the organization (see chapter 14). Leaves of various types (vacation, military, educational, sick, parenting and family, jury, and holiday) are other forms of employee separation, albeit temporary and without negative connotations. Layoffs and leaves can legitimately be placed on the end of the continuum, but dismissal does not fit as easily because it is not seen as a normal or desirable outcome of the personnel function. It is, perhaps, treated as taboo. As Strauss and Sayles (1980) noted, dismissal is often viewed by employers and employees as "industrial capital punishment," and thus the strong negative connotation associated with dismissal may have obscured its treatment in the literature.

Dismissal

Dismissal is the discharge of an employee from an organization because of unsatisfactory job performance; violation of a contract; or the commission of acts that violate the policies, personnel standards, or code of ethics recognized by the organization. There is a qualitative difference between unsatisfactory job performance and the other conditions for dismissal. Dismissal resulting from violation of a contract, organizational policy, personnel standards, or ethics constitutes what may be considered "dismissal for cause." Dismissal for cause is more easily applied by managers, particularly when the act of the employee is in clear violation of some prescribed standard of conduct or in gross violation of an organization's rules. Dismissal for unsatisfactory job performance may not be as easily applied, particularly because of difficulties associated with the employee evaluation process.

Evaluation

To dismiss an employee on the basis of unsatisfactory performance, it is first necessary to document and evaluate his or her performance. Kadushin (1976) described evaluations as troublesome processes, noting that they "tend to be avoided if not actively resisted" (p. 277). Some reasons for this phenomenon are that evaluations explicitly call attention to the difference in status between the supervisor and the supervisee, reflect on the supervisor, evoke strong negative feelings, and discourage workers (Kadushin, 1976).

The evaluation of a worker's performance may pose other problems. Managers must exercise judgments about their employees, a process that runs counter to the tenet of being supportive and nonjudgmental. When the performance of employees is inadequate, managers may believe that with additional educational training or supportive supervision, employees can change and improve and that organizations have the responsibility for providing these tools to help employees change.

A host of other difficulties can accompany the evaluations of employees. Many managers and supervisors do not observe their employees' performance because of the nature of the service that is rendered and the confidentiality of the employee–client relationship (Hoshino, 1978). In these circumstances, managers must rely on case recordings, supervisory discussions with employees, and other indirect means of evaluation. Because the service technologies involved in nonprofit organizations may not be as easily specified as those used in industry or certain other professions (medicine or nursing, for example) or the technologies of production (business and factory work, for instance), it can be difficult to determine what constitutes an effective or efficient service (Newman & Turem, 1978). Hence, it may be difficult to evaluate an employee's performance in relation to the service technology used in nonprofit organizations.

If evaluation is fraught with problems, dismissal based on an evaluation is also difficult. Supervisors' reluctance to evaluate employees and their tendency to view employees as resources to be developed through educational and supportive supervision influence organizations to develop, rehabilitate, or remotivate inadequate employees before considering dismissal or an alternative. However, once the line is crossed from this developmental approach to the dismissal approach, a return to development is generally impossible.

Issues Involved in Dismissal

There has been little research on the extent or circumstances of the dismissal of employees in service organizations (Dworaczek, 1983). Yet there is evidence (Patti, 1977) that managers have spent a "majority of their time and energy in relations with subordinates where obtaining compliance and cooperation was, at least implicitly, their principle concern" (p.16). Although the extent of this phenomenon is unclear, some of the factors that influence the use of dismissal can be identified and discussed.

Job Ownership

A range of issues relate to job ownership or tenure in employment. Employees in large bureaucratic organizations, for example, tend to view their employment as tenured. Civil service regulations (for public organizations), grievance procedures, the influence of unions, and the influence of law tend to support employees' views that once they have passed through the probationary period, the organization cannot remove them. The stereotypical view of the employee in a bureaucracy suggests that the employee, rather than the organization, controls the circumstances of employment.

There may be some basis for this position. Given the supportive and educational nature of supervision during the probationary period, the employer may be reluctant to exercise the dismissal option, even though dismissal during probation is far less complicated than it is later. Once the probationary period is over, additional information is required to document an employee's inadequate performance. As time passes, managers may perceive a progressive loss of job ownership to their employees, which makes the evaluation of performance for the purposes of dismissal a progressively time-consuming and problematic activity.

The concept of lifetime employment is increasingly being seen as beneficial for both the organization and the employee. Borrowed from the Japanese, lifetime employment has been instituted in a number of American companies with a view toward treating employees as both investments and assets (Luxenberg, 1983). Although not universally accepted as a practice, this notion can influence the general climate of employment in many organizations and lead employees to believe further in their rights to job ownership.

Management Prerogative

Long experience with legislation and executive orders concerning affirmative action, equal opportunity employment, and antidiscrimination may have eroded the view that dismissal is the first prerogative of management. The influence of labor law has sparked debates about the rights of management and workers. Fisher (1973) noted that "supporters of management rights have urged basically that all rights in the employment relationship not won by contract or forbidden by law belonged to employers, and supporters of worker rights argued that labor possessed some 'inherent' rights quite apart from contracts or laws" (p. 4).

The place of management rights in the employment situation is difficult to understand because of the many influences and restrictions applied to the circumstances of employment. Ewing (1983) suggested, for instance, that the right of management to fire employees is the basis of its authority. However, court decisions reviewed by Ewing were often inconsistent in their findings; some supported management's prerogative to fire, whereas others warned management to exercise its rights carefully and within the limits of legal precedents. The resulting conflict, court decisions, and inconsistencies confuse the issue of wrongful discharge.

Influence of Unions

Although somewhat cyclical, the influence of unions in organizations has also tended to constrain management's use of the dismissal prerogative. Fisher (1973) noted that early labor legislation was passed largely as a supportive statement of workers' rights, particularly the right to organize on their own behalf. The organization of the workforce and the presence of union contracts tend to require managers to exercise due process in disciplinary actions, particularly in cases of dismissal. Dismissal may have been effectively rendered a last resort in dealing with union employees because of the formality of procedures governing any disciplinary action against them.

Antidiscrimination Laws

The federal government restrains organizations from dismissing employees on the basis of discrimination with regard to a number of protected categories. Federal legislation provides for a number of guarantees against discriminatory dismissal by employers. Other laws have enlarged the definition of discrimination to include the categories of age, pregnancy, and disability. These laws cover both public and private employees and are enforced through the Equal Employment Opportunity Commission (EEOC) (Lewis & Lewis, 1983). Since 1972, the EEOC has had the power to take employers to court to enforce the antidiscrimination laws in these categories. In addition to federal legislation, many states have passed similar antidiscrimination laws. Federal employees and employees of organizations under government contract are also protected by executive orders that parallel this federal legislation.

Under antidiscrimination laws the rights of employees have been expanded in a sense. An employee is free to file a complaint with the EEOC if he or she feels that the dismissal was based on discrimination. More recently, court decisions regarding sexual harassment in the workplace have reinforced employees' rights to be free from gender discrimination, sexual harassment, and retaliation from using grievance procedures. In addition, courts have upheld employees' rights to a workplace free from a sexually harassing climate. The issue of sexual harassment further enlarges employee rights by establishing that regardless of the intent of the person who carries out a behavior, it is the recipient of that action who has the right to define it as sexually harassing or not.

A TYPOLOGY OF SUPERVISION

Kadushin (1976) suggested that supervision can be administrative, educational, or supportive. This chapter offers an alternative typology that more clearly specifies the types of supervision provided to an employee in relation to the employee's position with the organization over time. In addition, the typology accounts for the relationship between the type and extent of supervision and the professional employee's need for increased autonomy over time.

The relationship of supervision to autonomy over time is illustrated by Figure 13-1. The upper portion of the figure represents the extent of the organization's use of supervision. The lower portion suggests the level of autonomy exercised by the employee in relation to the organization's use of supervision. As an employee progresses through the probationary period, the extent of supervision decreases, and the employee's level of autonomy increases. Although the figure is only a model, it graphically represents how the supervision and autonomy of employees are related. In the early stages of employment, an employee is subject to a far greater level of supervision than during the later stages.

Figure 13-1 also suggests that differential supervision occurs over time. At the point of hiring, the employee is provided with probationary supervision,

Figure 13-1. Typology of Supervision

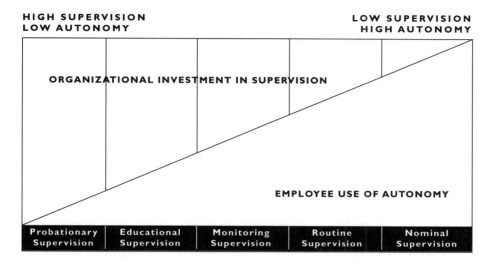

HIGH SUPERVISION
LOW AUTONOMY

LOW SUPERVISION
HIGH AUTONOMY

ORGANIZATIONAL INVESTMENT IN SUPERVISION

EMPLOYEE USE OF AUTONOMY

| Probationary Supervision | Educational Supervision | Monitoring Supervision | Routine Supervision | Nominal Supervision |

which is usually intense and involves a great deal of cost and effort for the supervisor and the organization. During probation, the employee is carefully oriented, inducted, and monitored for minimally acceptable performance. As the employee moves from probationary to permanent status, supervision continues to be intense. The nature of the supervisory relationship appears to take on an educational flavor, with both the organization and the supervisor assuming considerable responsibility for schooling the employee.

At some point, the organization and the supervisor gradually reduce their educational commitment to the employee. The employee is then expected to perform adequately, and the supervisor monitors the performance. Monitoring supervision requires less organizational and supervisory investment than does educational or probationary supervision. As the employee begins to function more effectively, supervision becomes somewhat routine. The organization and the supervisor can expect that as the worker's autonomy increases, the investment in supervision decreases. Finally, supervision becomes nominal, in that little is required for the highly autonomous employee.

Although it is not represented in Figure 13-1, another type of supervision requires a great deal of organizational and supervisory investment. Adversarial supervision occurs when the organization and supervisor determine that an employee cannot maintain his or her performance at an acceptable level or that the organization cannot raise the level in a cost-effective fashion. At this point, the organization prepares for the dismissal of an employee by carefully documenting his or her poor performance. During this time, the relationship between the supervisor and employee may take on an adversarial quality.

Although this typology represents a theoretical version of supervision, it helps to clarify the ideal in terms of the autonomy of employees. It suggests what the organization may expect to invest in supervision and how, over time, the costs of the investment should decrease while the return on the investment—the employee's autonomy—should increase. The typology also suggests that dismissal can be related to performance over time and investment in supervision.

Relationship of Supervision to Performance

The concept of the organization's investment in the supervision of employees is important. It is clearly impossible for an organization to maintain a high level of supervision and an ongoing, intense investment of supervisory resources in employees. Employees' autonomy and performance should increase over time. The ideal relationship of supervision to the performance of employees is illustrated in Figure 13-2.

Theoretically, supervision progresses over time from high to low, whereas performance progresses over time from low to high. In practice, the investment in supervision and the employee's level of performance progress on the basis of the employee's need for supervision and the available organizational resources. There is, however, a point at which the organization cannot

Figure 13-2. The Ideal Relationship of Supervision to Performance

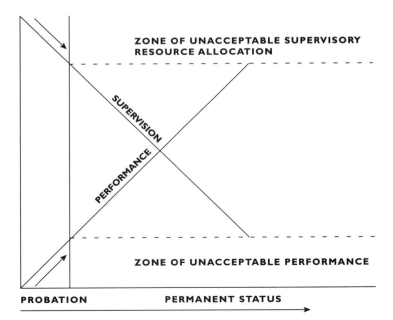

ZONE OF UNACCEPTABLE SUPERVISORY
RESOURCE ALLOCATION

SUPERVISION

PERFORMANCE

ZONE OF UNACCEPTABLE PERFORMANCE

PROBATION   PERMANENT STATUS

Figure 13-3. The Dismissal Decision

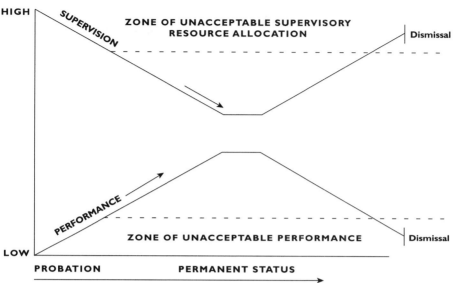

continue to invest a great amount of resources in supervising an employee. During probation, the organization expects to do so, but when the employee attains permanent status, the organization expects not to have a return to the level of its earlier investment. Similarly, the organization expects that once probation is over, the employee will not return to the lower level of performance allowed during this period.

The unacceptable levels of supervision and performance are indicated in Figure 13-2 as the zones of unacceptable supervisory resource allocation and unacceptable performance. These zones signal the organization that the cost of supervision, relative to the employee's level of performance, may be too high to maintain. When an employee falls into the zone of unacceptable performance, dismissal may be in the best interests of the organization on the basis of cost–benefit considerations.

Supervision, Performance, and Dismissal

The process of dismissal is represented in relation to cost–benefit considerations in Figure 13-3. As an employee's performance declines, the investment in supervision increases. Eventually, the employee enters the zone of unacceptable performance, and the organization responds by increasing its supervisory investment. In the absence of an improvement in performance, the

Figure 13-4. Dismissal during Probation

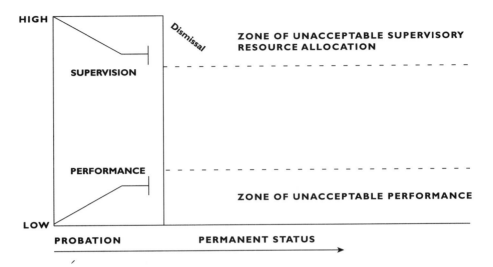

organization may no longer be able to invest resources at that level and may choose to dismiss the employee. A similar decision made on the basis of an employee's failure to reach the zone of acceptable performance by the end of the probationary period is depicted in Figure 13-4.

Dismissal: Practice Perspective

Dismissal remains the ultimate penalty (Strauss & Sayles, 1980). Many practical considerations are involved in using dismissal. The cost of replacing and retraining workers is high. Dismissal may have a negative effect on the morale of the other employees in the organization, and it may create other staff problems. In some instances, however, employees welcome the dismissal of an employee who does not perform to expectations or who violates a policy or ethics. When contemplating dismissal, the organization should consider many factors that are external to the employees's performance.

When considering dismissal, you should distinguish between employees with problems and problem employees. Employees with problems are those whose performance may be impaired by family problems, substance abuse, mental health problems, financial concerns, or other sources of personal stress. It has long been accepted that organizations, especially nonprofits involved in human services, have much to gain by offering such workers help in overcoming their problems through health insurance provisions or employee assistance plans. However, employees who cannot overcome such problems with help from employers eventually may be candidates for dismissal. Problem employees are those who are dismissed for cause—violation of a contract, a policy, personnel standards, or ethics—and employees who are dismissed for their unsatisfactory performance.

When you exercise the dismissal prerogative, you should consider several fundamental principles, some of which vary with the reason for dismissal. In extreme cases of dismissal for cause, an employee should be suspended (with pay, if necessary) until a full investigation of the infraction or violation is carried out. If the violation involves the safety of clients (as in the abuse of clients or the violation of ethics), care should be taken to prevent the employee from having official contact with clients until the investigation is completed. In other situations of dismissal for cause, decisions about suspension depend on the seriousness of the situation, the circumstances under which the violation took place, and the motivations of the employee.

Cases of dismissal for unsatisfactory job performance (including the performance of employees with problems who have failed to respond to rehabilitative efforts) have several practice considerations. Before the dismissal, an employee should receive adequate warning, in writing, about the intention to dismiss (Halloran, 1981). Huberman (1975) described a four-step sequence of fact-finding that should precede dismissal for unsatisfactory performance, including (1) a casual, private warning; (2) a repeat of the warning; (3) a discussion with the employee with other managers present; and (4) a final discussion with a warning that further problems will result in dismissal. Strauss and Sayles (1980) suggested that disciplinary action before dismissal should be immediate, that an employee should be given advance warning, and that an employee should be treated with consistency and without regard for his or her personality.

Dismissal Interview

The dismissal interview is one of the more difficult tasks of organizational life. Anxiety levels are high, negative feelings are present, and relationships may be adversarial. The following are suggestions for overcoming or at least ameliorating some of the difficult feelings and processes in which an employer and a dismissed employee often engage.

Pay Attention to the Evaluation Process

Several questions must be considered before the dismissal interview. Does any documentation lead to conclusions other than imminent termination? Who, if anyone, will be surprised by the dismissal? Has the alleged misconduct been adequately investigated? Does the employee's salary record reflect his or her unsatisfactory performance? Have other employees been treated differently under similar circumstances? (Jensen, 1981). In general, the issue of due process should be considered as well. Has the employee received the benefit of due process in the evaluation and disciplinary process?

Choose the Right Time and Place

Although it has been suggested that Friday afternoon is an ideal time to dismiss an employee, timing is really a function of the circumstances of the dismissal and the good judgment of the manager. In certain types of organizations, such as those involved with human services, other concerns affect the time and place for dismissal. For example, issues of termination from clients, including clients' records and record keeping, must be worked out with the employee in a responsible manner. In addition, care should be taken to ensure privacy and confidentiality for the employee during the dismissal interview. These human concerns and ethical issues should be part of the planning phase of dismissal.

Prepare for the Interview

Planning for a dismissal interview is important, but plan it without trying to write the script. The employee's record should be reviewed and past disciplinary actions noted. Using the skill of tuning in to an employee's situation also may help. Shulman (1979) noted that tuning in is an effective skill that prepares the interviewer to understand the client's situation, a form of preliminary empathy. At this time, finding the right words can be considered. Even the most skilled interviewers have some difficulty choosing words to inform an employee that he or she is being dismissed.

Begin with a Clear Statement of Purpose

This generic skill is useful for all interviews, but its use in the dismissal interview signals to the employee the seriousness of the interview. The clarity of the statement is most important. It should be short, to the point, and framed in clear language, for example, "We are here to discuss your performance on the job" or "I have made some decisions about your job performance."

Clearly and Factually State the Action Being Taken

It is difficult to find just the right words to tell an employee "You're fired" without making the action seem harsh. An effective statement is "I have decided to dismiss you as an employee of the organization" or "As of today, you are being dismissed from employment with us." Avoid euphemisms such as "We are letting you go" or other general statements.

Clearly State the Reasons for the Action

If the dismissal is for cause, clearly indicate this; for example, "The reason for your dismissal is because you violated agency policy, and despite warnings, continued to violate policy." If the dismissal is for performance, indicate the employee's shortcomings and the processes used to evaluate them; for example, "On the basis of our recent performance evaluations, you have not been able to form helping relationships with your clients, nor have you kept adequate records on the clients." Avoid euphemistic expressions such as "You don't seem to be working out" or "You don't seem to be the right person for the job." Be factual and stick to observable, measurable, behavioral criteria. It is also important to use clear, nonverbal cues to accompany the statement of dismissal and the reasons for it. Nonverbal messages, such as body language, posture, gestures, and paralanguage (the vocal quality of the message) should bespeak the assertion of authority that is being exercised. Do not send mixed messages.

Do Not Negotiate

At this point in the dismissal process, the decision has been made. Further evidence, arguments, or considerations should not be entertained. It may be necessary to explain this to the employee and to repeat that the decision is final and not open to further consideration.

Inform the Employee Fully about Appeal or Grievance Procedures

An employee can often make use of the appeal or grievance machinery in the organization if there is such a policy. An employee should be informed of all such rights.

Offer Support When Possible

Although a dismissed employee may find it difficult to accept support from an employer, some effort should be made to acknowledge the difficulty of the situation for the employee and to offer help in other areas. An employer can make suggestions for new employment, further education, behavioral change, or other resources. Although support can be offered, giving the employee another chance should not be implied.

Take Personal Responsibility for the Dismissal

The employee is being dismissed from the organization. The person dismissing him or her is the agent of the organization and should act accordingly. Avoid placing the blame on the organization. Do not contradict the facts or try to ameliorate the situation by speaking for yourself or disagreeing with the dismissal.

CONCLUSION

The dismissal of employees is a troublesome process. The extent to which employers use their prerogative to dismiss is unknown. Dismissal is sometimes shrouded in secrecy and constrained by law, organizational policy, union contract, and other factors. Before an employer dismisses an employee, he or she must have clear evidence of misconduct or evidence of inadequate performance that is based on the processes of supervision and evaluation. Substantial documentation is necessary. The dismissal interview requires advance preparation, the use of assertive behavior, clear messages, empathy, and fairness in dealing with the dismissed employee. Although dismissal is generally an unpleasant process, it is sometimes necessary to protect consumers or to maintain the effectiveness of the organization as a service delivery vehicle. A primary concern of managers must be the quality of the service being provided; sometimes the dismissal of an employee is the only recourse available after other developmental and remedial approaches have failed.

SKILLS-APPLICATION EXERCISE

John is a new employee of the Cosmos Child Care Center, a nonprofit residential treatment center for emotionally disturbed children. He has been employed for the past four months as a member of the direct care staff. His duties include caring for the physical and emotional needs of a group of eight children and seeing to the needs of their daily life in a small group home setting.

John's supervisor Alice has been carefully monitoring John's work as he has progressed through his employment at the center. She has given John two written performance appraisals, one after the first month of employment and another after the third month. John's probationary period is scheduled to last for six months.

John's performance appraisals have been based on Alice's observations of John's behavior with the children in his care. Alice pointed out to John that he seemed distant and discourteous to several of the children. When the children asked him for help with some activity, he would often become silent and not respond. Alice noted that this behavior was difficult for the children to understand. She observed this behavior on four occasions, and after the last two, Alice raised her concerns directly with John when they had a private moment together.

John's reaction to these two encounters was strange. He did not respond to Alice and simply stared at her while apparently trying to control his nonverbal behaviors, particularly his facial expressions. In their last encounter, Alice became personally uncomfortable with John's lack of reaction and blank stares.

Alice decided to have another conference with John to bring up the negative reports by the staff and to ask John's perception of his situation. Upon learning of the negative comments made by his colleagues, John confided to Alice that he had grown up in a residential treatment center for children and felt that he knew what was best for the children in his care. He also asserted that the children did not need a social worker getting involved in their lives. John continued to assert that he knew what was best and that other staff members did not have the same insight he had because of his personal history.

After this conference, Alice reflected on the facts of John's employment as she knew them. John was in the fourth month of his six-month probationary period. He had had two performance appraisals and several supervisory conferences. John's behavior, as observed by Alice and by the staff, was strange and disturbing. The messages his behavior sent were unclear and upsetting to the children in his care. John did not display insight into his behavior when questioned about it. John grew up in a residential treatment center and had some strong opinions about caring for children.

Discussion Questions

1. On the basis of the facts in this case, does Alice have sufficient cause to terminate John's employment?

2. If John's employment is terminated, what reasons will Alice give John for her action?

3. What effect will John's probationary status have on the firing process?

4. How might Alice phrase a final verbal warning to John about his problem behavior with the children?

5. If Alice decides to terminate John's employment, what would constitute a clear, concise statement informing him that he is being fired?

Answer Key

1. Alice probably has sufficient reason to terminate John's employment because of his behavior with the children, his lack of insight into his behavior, and his inability to change his position to conform to the demands of the organization. In addition, the retention of John would require an inordinate allocation of supervisory time, which the agency could not afford.

2. Alice should cite John's behavior with the children and point out that it is confusing to them. She should note that John has shown a pattern of failing to meet the children's needs for assistance. She should cite his past performance appraisals and bring up incidents that she directly observed rather than using the staff's reports.

3. The fact that John is on probation probably makes it easier to dismiss him. Probation is usually considered a time during which an employer can dismiss an employee without a great deal of process. However, ethical,

professional management practice should include due process for all personnel on the employment continuum.

4. A clear statement of the desired outcome should be used, worded in the form of a reachable, behavioral goal. One example might be "John, by the time of our next conference, you must be more attentive to the requests of the children. I will observe you during your shift and will observe your expressions and actions toward the children's requests. If you are unable to be more attentive, I will have to dismiss you from the agency."

5. If she dismisses John, Alice should begin with a clear statement describing the action she is taking. She might begin by saying, "John, based on your job performance, I have decided that effective immediately, I am dismissing you from employment with the organization."

REFERENCES

Dworaczek, M. (1983). *Dismissal of employees: A selected bibliography*. Monticello, IL: Vance Bibliographies.

Ewing, D. (1983). Your right to fire. *Harvard Business Review, 61,* 32–38.

Fisher, R. (1973). When workers are discharged: An overview. *Monthly Labor Review, 96,* 4–17.

Halloran, J. (1981). *Supervision: The art of management*. Englewood Cliffs, NJ: Prentice Hall.

Hoshino, G. (1978). Social services: The problem of accountability. In S. Slavin (Ed.), *Social administration: The management of the social services*. New York: Haworth Press.

Huberman, J. (1975). Discipline without punishment lives. *Harvard Business Review, 53,* 6–8.

Jensen, J. (1981, September–October). Letting go. *Grantsmanship Center News,* pp. 37–43.

Kadushin, A. (1976). *Supervision in social work*. New York: Columbia University Press.

Lewis, H., & Lewis, M. (1982). *The intellectual base of social work practice*. New York: Haworth Press.

Lewis, J., & Lewis, M. (1983). *Management of human service programs*. Monterey, CA: Brooks/Cole.

Luxenberg, S. (1983, April 17). Lifetime employment: U.S. style. *New York Times,* p. 12.

Newman. E., & Turem, J. (1978). The crisis of accountability. In S. Slavin (Ed.), *Social administration: The management of the social services*. New York: Haworth Press.

Patti, R. (1977). Patterns of management activity in social welfare agencies. *Administration in Social Work, 1,* 5–18.

Patti, R. (1983). *Social welfare administration*. Englewood Cliffs, NJ: Prentice Hall.

Rivas. R. F. (1984). Perspectives on dismissal as a management prerogative in social service organizations. *Administration in Social Work, 8*(4), 77–92.

Shulman, L. (1979). *The skills of helping: Individuals and groups*. Itasca, IL: F. E. Peacock.

Strauss, G., & Sayles, L. R. (1980). *Personnel: The human problem of management* (4th ed.). Englewood Cliffs, NJ: Prentice Hall.

CHAPTER 14

Managing Organizational Decline

Richard L. Edwards, Daniel A. Lebold, and John A. Yankey

Reductions in funding frequently have strong negative effects on the delivery of services provided by nonprofit organizations and on the clients or patrons who are served. What is less obvious is the impact of budget cuts on the lives of the people who work in nonprofit organizations. This chapter addresses the potential causes of organizational decline, the impact of budgetary reductions on managers and staff in nonprofit organizations, and strategies that you, as a nonprofit manager, can use when facing a budgetary crisis. The chapter reviews the literature on downsizing, rightsizing, cutback management, and retrenchment and draws on the personal experiences of upper-level managers in organizations that experienced major funding cuts, necessitating significant reductions in programs or workforce.

A NEW ERA OF FISCAL AUSTERITY

During the 1980s, many nonprofit organizations, particularly those involved in the human services arena, entered into a new era characterized by declining economic conditions. This represented a dramatic shift after nearly 50 years of almost uninterrupted growth in government support of social programs. These changes also paralleled a growing sociopolitical revolution that led to a redefinition in the way government responds to social problems at both the federal and local levels (Edwards, Cooke, & Reid, 1996).

For most of the 20th century, government policies regarding funding for social welfare, community development, and the arts and humanities evolved from an activist ideology (Firstenberg, 1996). From Roosevelt's Works Progress Administration initiatives in the 1930s to Johnson's War on Poverty in the mid-1960s, it was popularly accepted that government had both a role and a responsibility for providing solutions to chronic social and economic problems (Firstenberg, 1996; Newland, 1996). This period, which peaked in the 1960s and early 1970s, represented the largest expansion of government support for social initiatives in American history (Cooke, Reid, & Edwards, 1997).

During this time, many nonprofit organizations came to depend heavily on the widely available federal funds for their services, leading some nonprofit managers and board members to assume, falsely, that those dollars would always be available. However, public sentiment toward the federal government began to sour in the 1970s as a result, at least in part, of American involvement in the Vietnam War, the Watergate scandals during the Nixon administration, and a severe economic recession triggered by an international oil embargo. By the time Ronald Reagan assumed the presidency in 1980, antigovernment rhetoric was at an all-time high. Government was no longer viewed as a problem solver but as the cause of many economic and social problems (Firstenberg, 1996; Newland, 1996).

Capitalizing on the antigovernment fervor, Reagan quickly followed through on his campaign pledge to make significant realignments in the priorities of the federal budget. As a result, the nation entered into a first round of federal reductions in spending for social services programs. During fiscal years 1981 and 1982, most programs serving poor people suffered from severe budgetary cuts. Many other community-based programs, including those in the arts, humanities, and education, also came under political pressures that resulted in cuts in federal funding. Reagan, in effect, set into motion what many people now refer to as the postgovernment era, a reversal in the long-standing federal commitment to ensuring support for social services and other community-based initiatives (Firstenberg, 1996).

The initial federal budget reductions affected state and local governments differently. Some states and localities were able to use local resources to buffer the impact of the federal cuts, whereas others immediately had to reduce staffing and services.

During the early years of the Reagan administration, the issue of managing under conditions of decline, or what has been labeled "cutback management," was frequently addressed both in the literature and at a variety of professional conferences (Austin, 1984; Bombyk & Chernesky, 1985; Hirschhorn, 1983; Knighton & Heidelman, 1984; Pawlak, Jeter, & Fink, 1983; Turem & Born, 1983). However, interest in the subject soon waned when the initial impact of the federal budget cuts passed. The subsequent impact was lessened, in part, because although federal funding for some social programs was further reduced in the following years, the reductions were much smaller than the earlier ones, and funding for some social programs even increased slightly. In addition, many states as well as many voluntary or nonprofit-sector organizations were able to absorb part of the burden.

However, by the mid-1980s a second round of federal reductions was initiated as a result of growing public concern over the rapidly increasing federal deficit. Focus on the deficit intensified with the Gramm–Rudman–Hollings Act (Balanced Budget and Emergency Deficit Control Act of 1985). Named after its original cosponsors, it was an important piece of federal legislation because it mandated major reductions in the federal budget deficit each year and a balanced budget by fiscal year 1991. Although the original targets were not met, the legislation represented the first serious attempt by Congress to impose strict reductions in the federal deficit, which had grown from $2.8 billion in 1970 to more than $58.9 billion in 1980. By 1992 the federal deficit reached its peak of $290 billion (Newland, 1996). Given the enormity of the federal deficit, the reduction targets of the act generated vigorous political debates on national priorities. Commenting on the effect of the Gramm–Rudman–Hollings Act, Greenstein (1986) was prophetic when he stated that "In the years ahead, our nation will have to make hard choices on what should be reduced or eliminated, what should be maintained, and what, if anything, should be increased. Decisions must also be faced on whether to raise revenues. The choices made will shape our society for years to come" (p. 1).

By early 1990 it became clear that the targets established by Gramm–Rudman–Hollings would not be met. Although President Bush continued the push for additional deficit reduction legislation, it was not until the Omnibus Budget Reconciliation Act of 1993, under President Clinton, that necessary tax increases and expenditure reductions were instituted, and the federal deficit finally began to drop (Newland, 1996).

By the mid-1990s the United States entered a period of economic prosperity marked by an expanding stock market, low interest rates, and record levels of low unemployment. Nearly all states, contrary to earlier predictions, were experiencing budget surpluses. However, because of the antigovernment trends set into motion during the 1980s, there continued to be a backlash against federal funding for a wide range of community-based programs, including those involved with the arts and humanities, education, and human services. As a result, we have entered into a third round of federal reductions based not on economic pressures but primarily on a philosophical shift in the perception of federal responsibility. Labeled the "devolution revolution," this era was heralded by the 1994 election of a Republican Congress and the Republican Party's Contract with America, a political movement to decentralize social policies and pass more responsibilities down to state and local governments (Cooke et al., 1997; Milward, 1996; Newland, 1996).

Subsequent legislation, such as the Personal Responsibility and Work Opportunity Reconciliation Act of 1996, which ushered in welfare reform, dramatically altered the way nonprofit programs are funded and services are delivered (see chapter 5). This has been especially true for human services organizations. And, even though many sectors of our society are enjoying economic prosperity, the number of families, and particularly children, living at or below the poverty line is actually increasing. Also on the rise are a range of serious social problems such as teenage pregnancy, domestic violence, drug and alcohol addiction, school truancy, and teenage violence associated with gangs.

The resulting dilemma for nonprofit managers is that we are entering an era of increased uncertainty when funding patterns are decreasing or fragmented and demand for services is increasing (Cigler, 1996; Cooke et al., 1997; Firstenberg, 1996; Menefee, 1997; Pappas, 1996). Funding streams are becoming more complex and difficult to predict. Technological advances are becoming necessary for most organizations to remain competitive, but they are extremely expensive to maintain (see chapter 16). And, because of the move toward increased privatization of services, competition for funding at the local level has escalated in recent years, leading many experts to predict that the demand for private dollars will soon exceed available funds (Firstenberg, 1996).

Continued rounds of cutbacks undoubtedly will require some nonprofit organizations to engage in retrenchment or layoffs of staff. As a nonprofit manager, you will be required to use new skills to deal with a rapidly changing environment. All signs point to a new era of fiscal austerity for many nonprofit organizations that will likely persist for many years. However, to prepare for this future, we can learn from the earlier rounds of cutbacks.

AN OVERVIEW OF ORGANIZATIONAL DECLINE

According to Menefee (1997), the primary administrative responsibilities of a nonprofit manager are to identify emerging trends and anticipate their impact, create vision and purpose, and introduce and sustain innovation. Of course, your prevailing responsibility as a nonprofit manager is to ensure that adequate funding is available to support your organization's core programs and staff. However, budget shortfalls sometimes occur that require you to make hard choices that may involve cutting services or staff. As a nonprofit manager, it is therefore important that you recognize and understand the organizational and individual responses that tend to accompany declining resources. Regrettably, however, many nonprofit managers, like our counterparts in other fields, tend to be inadequately prepared to manage effectively under conditions of decline. This tendency is not surprising because most managers have more training for and experience in responding to conditions of growth.

Growth has been viewed as consistent with the ideology and values of our culture, which considers growth and expansion to be primary indicators of effectiveness (Cameron, Sutton, & Whetten, 1988). Most organizations must increase their budgets annually just to keep up with inflation (Firstenberg, 1996). The idea that "bigger" or "more" is better has long been an internalized assumption held by many nonprofit managers and their staffs, particularly those working in the human services arena.

Whetten (1980) noted that our culture views bigness as a highly desirable characteristic. The enhancement of economies of scale, the ability to absorb shocks that accompany environmental changes, and increased productive capacity are among the presumed benefits of largeness. Managers tend to be regarded as successful if they produce more, obtain larger budgets, and expand their organizations, and are regarded as ineffective if they do the reverse. The question is, how big is too big? Most agree that growth is desirable, but there is less agreement on the merits of growth once it has been achieved (Cameron et al., 1988).

Much has been written about organizational decline in recent years as a direct result of the many rounds of cutbacks that were experienced in both the nonprofit and corporate sectors. Throughout the 1970s and 1980s fashionable topics in the literature regarding cutback management included downsizing, deregulation, and devolution. The literature in the 1990s focuses on retrenchment, rightsizing, reinvention, and re-engineering (DuBran, 1996; Newland, 1996). Whatever the terminology, a great deal more attention has been focused on the issues related to organizational decline both in the literature and among nonprofit professionals in the field.

However, management training programs still do not generally focus on developing skills related to managing under conditions of decline. Most current organizational theory is based on assumptions of growth; decline tends to be either ignored or treated as an aberration.

Causes of Organizational Decline

The most common causes of organizational decline include economic shifts in the external environment, mismanagement or overexpansion of program services or staff, and loss of a competitive edge on a particular niche service (Banning, 1990; Cameron et al., 1988). In some cases, shortfalls may be the result of a single event, such as a factory closing that displaces hundreds or thousands of workers and thereby devastates a local United Way campaign. Scandals can also inflict enormous damage on an organization's credibility and cause substantial losses of financial support. Mismanagement or uncontrolled growth in services beyond available resources can also lead to budget shortfalls.

Whetten (1988) discussed whether organizational decline may be a natural process associated with life cycle models of organizational behavior. He pointed out that the four most common stages used in life-cycle models are (1) entrepreneurial (early innovation, niche formation, high creativity), (2) collectivity (high cohesion, commitment), (3) formalization and control (emphasis on stability and institutionalization), and (4) elaboration and structure (domain expansion and decentralization). These four stages roughly mirror the four skills sets—boundary spanning, human relations, coordinating, and directing—identified in the competing values framework discussed in chapter 1.

However, although biological models are frequently used to describe organizational behavior, often focusing on growth stages, they generally fail to include research about the later stages of decline and death. Whetten (1988) pointed out that "This reluctance to concentrate on decline and death stages ignores important finds in the life cycle literature. Research on the effective management of declining organizations has shown that the problems associated with shrinking economic resources and moral support are qualitatively different from problems associated with growth" (p. 29). Determining which stage of the life cycle model your organization is in is important when responding to an organizational crisis.

Most often, a combination of factors ultimately leads to organizational retrenchment or requires cutbacks in programs or staff. Whatever the situation, it is imperative that you carefully examine and fully understand the specific cause or causes of the potential crisis to effectively develop strategies that ensure your organization's ultimate survival.

General Responses to Decline

Avoiding the conditions of decline is a primary objective for any nonprofit manager. However, because the traditional emphasis on organizational growth is being assaulted by the realities of decline, you must be prepared to deal with cutbacks. Regardless of how effective you are as a nonprofit manager, you may someday be faced with a financial crisis that necessitates serious cutbacks in either programs or staff. Unfortunately, most managers find that their knowledge and skills are inadequate for the challenges presented by decline. As a result, the following conditions can be observed in organizations and agencies that are experiencing decline or cutbacks in funding (Cameron, 1983):

- high levels of manager and staff stress
- low trust, secretiveness, and centralization
- increased conflict and decreased morale
- conservatism and aversion to risk
- staff turnover and a self-protection orientation.

Under conditions of growth, the availability of slack resources makes it possible to overcome most of these problems. That is, when there are sufficient resources, people are more likely to be able to get what they want from the organization, and staff feel more secure. Slack resources create conditions in which experimentation and innovation are possible. In addition, slack resources create buffers for your staff and organization. When there are no slack resources, your personal skills as a manager become more critical for the effective management of your organization.

In organizations that are experiencing cutbacks, there is often a mood of meanness because the staff feel insecure. Scapegoating is common, managers are often blamed for the decreased resources, and the staff believe that the manager should have foreseen the problem and taken earlier actions to lessen the impact.

Because managers in organizations that are experiencing cutbacks do not have slack resources, they are less able to neutralize conflicting interest groups and buy internal consensus. Adaptation by addition is no longer possible, and managers must contend with their own high levels of stress as well as the stress of their staff members. This stress often results in a restriction of the flow of communication in the organization, both from the top down and from the bottom up.

Concern for human relationships tends to be substantially reduced in such organizations, and relationships among managers and their staffs tend to become more formalized. Decision making tends to be more centralized as managers begin to feel a need to maintain control.

A feeling of impending crisis often pervades the organization as individual staff members fear they may lose their jobs, and staff turnover rises because those who can leave often do. Those who are unable to leave often become embittered and feel trapped. For the organization, this atmosphere creates a major personnel problem because the staff members who are best able to leave are often the most capable. Consequently, the organization runs the risk of losing its best staff. Managers are aware of this possibility and often guard against it by keeping bad news to themselves, thus intensifying their own stress and the mistrust of their subordinates.

Impact on Staff

The literature on cutback management tends to focus more on the impact of cutbacks on managers and managerial strategies for dealing with declining resources than on other staff members. However, all staff are clearly affected by funding cuts, even when their particular jobs are not lost. Despite staff members' best professional efforts to avoid letting their concerns interfere with their relationships with volunteers, clients, or patrons, it is not reasonable to assume that these stakeholders are not adversely affected. Consequently, it is essential that if your organization is experiencing declining resources you concern yourself with the range of reactions of your staff members.

When the worst does happen and layoffs are required, the consequences for employees and their families can be devastating. DuBran (1996) pointed out that

> While still in shock, [downsized workers] hurriedly put together résumés and send blanket mailings to prospective employers. Stress-related disorders such as migraine headaches, colitis, dermatitis, and cardiac disease escalate. Abuse of family members skyrockets. The suicide rate for laid-off workers is 30 times the national average. In short, the layoffs associated with downsizing create enormous human suffering. (p. 263)

Austin (1984) suggested that employees in organizations that are experiencing declining resources often go through a five-step process that is similar to Kübler-Ross's (1969) stages of death and dying: (1) denial and isolation, (2) anger, (3) bargaining, (4) depression, and (5) acceptance. The first reaction of your staff members to the possibility or reality of funding cuts is often denial and isolation or withdrawal. They initially express the belief that rumors of such cuts are exaggerated or that their particular organization, unit, or program will not be affected, and they often justify this by pointing to the quality of services they provide. Many of your staff members may also react by attempting to withdraw from any discussions of cuts, taking what may be called an "ostrich approach."

As your employees become more aware of the reality of funding cuts, they often react with anger, which is frequently focused toward the organization's managers, who are blamed for the situation. The anger stems from the staff's fear that they may lose their jobs, and local targets are much more accessible than distant policymakers.

As their initial anger subsides, your staff may begin to acknowledge the reality of the situation and bargain for the survival of their particular unit, program, or job. When such bargaining fails, they tend to become depressed. At this point, they may feel helpless and hopeless, believing that the situation is beyond their control. If they are able to work through their depression, they will settle into a state of acceptance.

Unfortunately, not all of your staff members who are affected by cutbacks will be able to work through these stages to the point of acceptance. Many may leave your organization while they are still angry or depressed. Thus, if you are a manager who is involved in an organization that is facing a decline in resources, you must recognize that these stages are normal concomitants of the situation and find ways to help your staff members negotiate through them.

Impact on Management

The literature on cutback management suggests that managers tend to deal with conditions of decline by focusing on internal organizational concerns to the relative exclusion of external concerns. This focus on internal concerns is a common theme identified in the literature, and a number of authors have suggested that the tendency to do so is dysfunctional. Austin (1984), for example, noted that the management of cutbacks requires that administrators play the two major roles of the cheerleader and the strategic planner:

> The cheerleader role involves the . . . capacity to engage in problem finding as well as problem solving, to model the learning process so that staff can participate in organizational and personal renewal, to increase staff involvement in all levels of decision making, and to take care of the "managerial self" to maximize effectiveness. The role of strategic planner includes the ability to develop viable policy and program options for both the agency's governing boards and its staff to consider and debate, to develop and maintain interagency networks for support and collaboration, to acquire skills and resources to market new and existing agency services, to manage computerized information systems, and to plan for staff involvement in seeking organizational excellence. (p. 428)

Weatherley (1984) considered two types of executive leaders that may emerge in organizations faced with cutbacks: the technician and the statesman. The technician views the organization and its staff as a means to an end and when confronted with decline is likely to attempt to maximize organizational efficiency, going to great lengths to avoid having the organization perceived as one that is declining. Furthermore, the technician generally assumes an authoritarian, top-down managerial style and exhibits a short-term perspective. The statesman, on the other hand, views the organization and its staff "as a social entity meeting certain needs of its participants and embodying certain values that emphasize service, however that may be defined" (p. 41). The statesman generally assumes a democratic managerial style and exhibits a long-term perspective. Finally, the statesman is attentive to the informal organizational structure, showing real concern about clients as well as staff at all levels in the hierarchy. Weatherley (1984) concluded that "an organization led by the pragmatic technician concerned primarily with short-term survival may inadvertently and incrementally adopt policies that undermine its long-term viability and subvert its mission" (p. 44). The statesman, Weatherley suggested, must also deal with current crises, but views them in the context of a broader vision that seeks to protect and promote organizational values. Thus, in weighing different policies the statesman will consider their long-range implications for the organization and its staff as well as their immediate impact.

"After the layoffs, no one was left who knew how to fill out purchase requisitions, expense vouchers, or make coffee."

In their discussion of cutback management, Bombyk and Chernesky (1985) identified two leadership models—the alpha style and the beta style—which are similar to the two leadership styles identified by Weatherley. The *alpha style,* they suggest, is a "leadership style that focuses on hierarchical structure, clear definitions of power and authority, and on rewards to promote individual achievement and compliance with the rules [and] . . . is based upon a belief that problems are essentially technical matters and that solutions can be engineered" (p. 49). The *beta style* is characterized more by a concern for people and processes and less by a task orientation. The beta model emphasizes collective problem solving, sharing information, and attention to the needs and feelings of staff members. Bombyk and Chernesky (1985) argued that "the strengths of the beta style for cutback management lie in its fluid conception of power, its empowerment of staff and clients to be co-participants in the decision making process, and its ability to tolerate the chaos and uncertainty of the organization's retrenchment phase" (p. 56).

Certainly, managers and staff members in organizations that are experiencing declining resources often are confronted with navigating through an environment of competing values (see chapter 1). Environmental conditions may dictate that you emphasize certain aspects of organizational life, and this emphasis can have an adverse effect on other aspects. For instance, one of the first actions you might take when confronted with declining resources is to institute a freeze on hiring and to order that positions that become vacant through attrition be left unfilled. You might then develop revised budget projections that take into account the savings you expect by not filling positions that became vacant through retirements or resignations. Turem and Born (1983) noted that, "Superficially, attrition seems a reasonable, conflict-avoiding response to newly imposed fiscal constraints. By combining attrition with hiring freezes, administrators may avoid the bureaucratic, union, and interpersonal hassles related to layoffs and quell the disruption of staff morale (and thus staff performance) that 'RIF' (reduction in force) rumors may have stirred up" (p. 207).

However, Turem and Born (1983) pointed out that attrition is not a good way to deal with budget cuts because at best, attrition represents personnel decision by default; at worst, it is a tactic to avoid confronting issues that should be addressed squarely regardless of their unpleasantness or difficulty. Attrition, like across-the-board reduction, does not require nonprofit managers and staff to undertake the arduous task of defining and setting priorities for specific goals for each service program. Both approaches ignore the possibility that the value of maintaining established staffing patterns in certain areas may more than justify making disproportionate cuts in other areas.

When attrition and hiring freezes are instituted, your staff may have to assume a greater workload. This change may be regarded as a move to make your staff more productive and your organization more efficient. However, over time such a strategy may have an adverse affect on the cohesion and morale of your staff, who may experience higher levels of stress, which may lead to greater absenteeism and increased turnover.

Another common response of managers to declining resources is to attempt to trim the "frills" from the budget by reducing or eliminating various support services, including janitorial, equipment and building maintenance, secretarial, and other services. In addition, such benefits as reimbursement for continuing education or professional development activities are also frequently curtailed or eliminated. Managers do so to protect or shield their professional staff members as long as possible and out of a desire to maintain direct services to clients or patrons.

Over time, however, these actions can also lead to increased stress in your staff and may contribute to staff turnover. Your organization may find itself with a predominantly younger, less experienced staff that is not able to provide the same quality of services that more experienced staff who were with your organization might have been able to provide. The net result is that your organization may experience communication problems, the flow of information may be impeded by not having sufficient support staff, and your organization will be increasingly less stable. These conditions may curtail productivity and the delivery of services, which may have a further adverse affect on funding.

Yet another common strategy that managers use to deal with declining resources is to institute across-the-board cuts. The idea behind this strategy is that the organization will continue to do all it has been doing, albeit on a reduced level. This approach is intuitively appealing because it seems to be an equitable way to share the pain involved in cutting back and "no program, provider, or client constituency can claim to have been singled out to bear the brunt of retrenchment" (Turem & Born, 1983, p. 206).

As a manager, you may find that the across-the-board approach to dealing with declining resources seems to be the least painful. And it may be effective when the reductions in resources are relatively small and are likely to be short term. However, when reductions in resources are major and are likely to persist for a long time, the across-the-board strategy may lessen the effectiveness of all aspects of your organization's programming. In the long run, it may be far better for your organization to do fewer things well than to do many things poorly.

Dealing with Staff

When confronted with the specter of declining resources, you can take a number of actions to help your staff members deal more effectively with the situation. First, however, you must recognize that your own level of stress is likely to increase. Therefore, you must take steps to identify and handle the sources of this stress. Identifying and dealing with stress are likely to involve grappling with a paradox, because managers tend to react to their own increasing stress by withdrawing, keeping information to themselves, and becoming more autocratic in making decisions. However, you must resist these tendencies and make efforts to be more open about sharing information and decision making. In addition, you must attend to your own stress through a variety of stress reduction techniques, from doing more physical exercise to creating and participating in support groups with other managers who are in a similar situation.

Particular attention also must be paid to those in your organization who will have the responsibility and burden of telling others they are being laid off or that their jobs are eliminated. This is an extremely stressful task that often falls on middle managers, and its impact should not be overlooked.

An important component of your managerial activity in dealing with declining resources is the management of rumors (Hirschhorn, 1983). Decisions must be made about what to tell your staff and when to tell it. Rumors not only structure and reduce anxiety, they give the staff a way to make sense of the situation. In other words, rumors often enable staff to gain a sense of control. You and other members of your management team can counteract rumors by recognizing the purposes that rumors serve and by providing alternative mechanisms for your staff to meet their needs for greater control. These mechanisms include helping staff members at all levels in your organization structure their anxiety by engaging them in planning activities as well as by providing them with opportunities to express the negative feelings they have. You can establish planning groups and charge them with developing a range of best case—worst case scenarios with a set of alternative decisions for each scenario.

You may also engage staff planning groups in an examination of your organization's mission and goals to identify the core program. Such identification can be helpful in the subsequent development and structuring of a plan for handling decisions about retrenchment or layoffs. As Hirschhorn (1983) noted, managers must often confront the need to make trade-offs between the issues of fairness and strategy. When layoffs are contemplated, managers generally desire a fair process, yet they often would like to be able to keep those staff members who are most likely to prove valuable to the agency in the future. A consideration of your organization's core program helps identify those individuals within your organization who have the knowledge and skills that make them best able to further the core program.

Of course, union contracts and civil service regulations may set limits on your ability to make staffing decisions under conditions of decline. When such contracts or regulations exist, it is incumbent upon you to be well informed about their requirements and restrictions. When no such contracts or regulations exist, you may have more latitude in making decisions about retrenchment. In either case, decisions about whom to keep and whom to let go should be based on judgments about which staff members can contribute most to your organization's core program and which will best enable your organization to be positioned to take advantage of environmental opportunities that may arise in the future.

When decisions are made to lay off particular staff members, these individuals should be informed as early as possible to afford them the maximum chance to find other jobs. You should provide these individuals with a range of supports or outplacement services. These supports may include providing them with assistance in preparing résumés, ensuring that they will be able to get reference letters that indicate the circumstances under which their employment was terminated, and giving them opportunities to ventilate their feelings about the situation. In addition, you may find it helpful to arrange for a representative of the local unemployment compensation office to meet with your staff to explain how to apply for unemployment compensation, how long it will take for them to receive their first check, how much money they can expect to receive, and how long they may be eligible to collect benefits. This kind of information is essential to staff members who must plan how they will manage their lives in the period immediately after being laid off. Furthermore, every effort should be made to help your staff learn about other employment opportunities.

You and other members of your management team should engage in planning activities aimed at defining the primary functions of your organization and developing strategies for the future. Friesen and Frey (1983) stated that cutbacks "may alter an organization's strategic position in the network, reduce its relative power, and increase its dependency on other organizations" (pp. 36–37). Thus, it is important to consider how your organization will relate to other organizations and whether you will enter coalitions, attempt to keep a monopoly on your services, or look for new markets or opportunities for services.

You also must become actively involved in the development of resources. These activities may range from writing grants, obtaining contracts, and instituting fee-for-service programs to devising strategies for using volunteers and paraprofessionals and building relationships with policymakers (see chapters 3, 4, and 5). Friesen and Frey (1983) observed that managers who are confronting declining resources "need to develop both technical skills (i.e., how to raise new funds) and interactional skills (i.e., how to build a constituency)" (p. 37).

STRATEGIC STEPS IN MANAGING ORGANIZATIONAL DECLINE

Determining the Scope of the Problem

When faced with severe shortfalls in funding, there are a wide range of strategies you can use depending on the nature of the specific crisis. Cutback strategies may differ depending on the sector within which your nonprofit organization functions. For example, art museums may elect to raise ticket prices for admission, whereas homeless shelters that depend solely on community donations may need to rally political support or face imminent staff layoffs. Strategies may also differ depending on how long the shortfall is anticipated to last. Across-the-board cost reductions may be effective for short-term crises but probably will weaken your organization further if implemented as a long-term solution. So, when faced with a funding short-fall, you must carefully evaluate the problem in all its complexity and develop a planned strategic response.

Behn (1988) argued that "the analysis of any managerial problem depends upon the assumptions about its severity." When faced with a funding crisis, Behn suggested that managers consider the three following conditions:

- *Retrenchment is necessary*—Real resources are declining, for whatever reason (tax cut, shifting priorities, a steady budget combined with inflation). Moreover, the agency cannot easily expand by creating new programs with new clients who will supply new resources. The agency will simply have to get along with less.
- *The problem is serious*—It cannot be solved simply by cutting out the fat. The required retrenchment is greater than whatever organizational slack the manager has been able to accumulate.
- *The manager's responsibility is to make the retrenchment work*—Naturally, the temptation is to resist—to make cuts in such a way that the natural forces of politics will restore them. . . . But the other two assumptions preclude this possibility; there will be fewer resources and the manager will simply have to make the agency function as well as possible under this constraint. (p. 348)

Once it is determined that retrenchment is required, Behn (1988) suggested a two-stage process of (1) preparation and announcement and (2) implementation. Behn further stated that throughout the process of retrenchment, your primary responsibilities as a nonprofit manager are to

- Decide what to cut;
- Maintain morale;
- Attract and keep quality people;
- Develop the support of key constituencies (and legislators);
- Create opportunities for innovation;
- Avoid mistakes. (pp. 350–351)

Although many of these responsibilities are the same whether the organization is expanding or contracting, they are especially difficult to carry out during periods of retrenchment.

Selecting a Strategy

Deciding what or whom to cut is one of the most difficult decisions you will make as a nonprofit manager, and the results of your decisions will likely affect many people throughout your organization. As you consider the various options for retrenchment, it is essential that you conduct a strategic assessment of your organization. It is often helpful to establish a special task force composed of managers, staff, and board members to help determine which strategies will be most effective and how to implement them. You must then evaluate the pros and cons of implementing various strategies, including cutting some programs or personnel. You may want to consider hiring an outside management consultant who can help you develop a retrenchment plan as well as provide outplacement services for your staff. The most common strategies used in response to funding cutbacks are cost reductions, political influence, cooperation and mergers, downsizing, refinancing, commercialization and fundraising, and relocation (DuBran, 1996; Palmer, 1997).

Cost reductions are most often used when the source of the cutback is temporary and when their impact will not likely affect the long-term performance of the organization. However, many nonprofit managers mistakenly use across-the-board cutbacks without fully addressing the real budget problems facing their organization. Such overuse of cost reductions often leads to continued funding shortfalls and a further decline in the organization.

Political influence is used as an attempt to reverse externally imposed funding cuts, often when funding is received from government sources. According to Palmer (1997), the three most frequently used techniques of exerting political persuasion include (1) *reasoning*—a rational presentation of the facts and an appeal to personal values, (2) *retribution*—the use of intimidation and coercion, and (3) *reciprocity*—creating exchanges or obligations between two organizations. This strategy usually involves board members, clients, patrons, local citizens, or other stakeholders who may be in positions of power to influence decision makers in your community. For some organizations, political influence may be the most important element for survival. In North Carolina, for example, the Artworks for State Buildings Program was cancelled after the state legislature determined it was politically unpopular to use public monies for state art projects. The program, which operated from 1989 through 1995, allocated one-half of 1 percent of each building's construction budget to commission artwork for that building. Administrators of the program are now attempting to persuade local citizens and other stakeholders to lobby their legislators to reinstate the defunct project. Although political leverage is usually a slow process and will rarely lead to an immediate funding solution, it is an important strategy that is often overlooked.

Cooperative strategies and mergers are frequently used when two or more organizations determine that cost savings can be made by combining elements of their programs or services. Also referred to as "survival sharing" (Jeffri, 1983), these strategies move away from a focus on competition to one of cooperation. This may include sharing materials and supplies, office space, staff, printing, community networks and boards, fundraising, and joint marketing and distribution (Palmer, 1997). Cooperation strategies can also be used among program units within organizations that are particularly large or complex. An extreme form of cooperation is a merger between two independent organizations (see chapter 23). However, although mergers may save money in the long term, they are costly and extremely disruptive and often cause staff turnover or a change in leadership.

Downsizing has been the focus of much concern since the mid-1970s because of the large number of organizations, both for-profit and nonprofit, that have experienced it. Downsizing typically is most often used either when organizations become too large or when substantial budget shortfalls necessitate immediate reductions in staff. According to Cascio (1993), *downsizing* is essentially "the planned elimination of positions or jobs" (p. 96). However, for many organizations, downsizing frequently has been shown not to be a long-term cost-saving strategy. Many organizations that downsized during the 1980s discovered that low employee morale, decreased productivity, and the high cost of rehiring and retraining often lead to even further decline and retrenchment (Perry, 1988). However, depending on the circumstances, you may have no choice but to downsize your workforce. When that is the case, it will probably be one of the most difficult and painful situations you will have to encounter as a nonprofit manager.

If it is determined that staff reductions are necessary, DuBran (1996) suggested the following four steps: (1) eliminate low-value and no-value activities, (2) keep future work requirements in mind, (3) identify the tasks that retained employees will perform, and (4) decide which workers will be let go. He further recommended that once you determine who will be laid off, you should make the cuts as quickly and completely as possible. In the long run, it will be far less disruptive to make a single round of cutbacks quickly than to make several rounds over a protracted period of time. Prolonging cutback decisions only increases staff insecurities and further demoralizes your workforce.

Determining the criteria to use when deciding who to lay off is both complicated and controversial. Decisions are often based on seniority, employment status (part-time and temporary workers), voluntary resignations and early retirements, and performance. All of these options have advantages and disadvantages.

For example, DuBran (1996) noted that although basing layoff decisions on seniority may seem to be the most fair, you lose control over which employees are maintained. However, letting go of senior staff may have serious negative effects on the staff who are left behind and who now fear that loyalty to the firm no longer ensures job security. Similarly, dismissing workers according to function may appear to benefit overall operations but may be interpreted as political on the part of management to get rid of staff they do not like. Laying off temporary or part-time workers may have appeal because it protects job security for permanent employees. However, temporary employees are sometimes hired to carry out highly specialized tasks, and they are usually less expensive than permanent full-time employees. Hence, letting go of temporary workers may have a high negative impact on your general operations but a relatively low impact on your total budget.

Voluntary resignation and early retirement incentive strategies are often used by organizations that have large workforces. Eligible employees are offered early retirement or severance packages that they can take now or risk being laid off later. The obvious disadvantage is that you may lose your most highly skilled workers because you lose control of which employees you retain.

Basing layoff decisions on performance can be one of the most challenging, but more productive, methods of achieving a downsized workforce. Most authors agree that basing layoff decisions on performance both increases employee morale in the long run and minimizes productivity loss (DuBran, 1996; Perry, 1988). Essentially, program managers are asked to assess their staff and make recommendations for termination or dismissal based on individual performance measures. However, DuBran (1996) discouraged the practice of conducting performance appraisals strictly for the purpose of downsizing because they may appear too political.

Throughout the process of downsizing, it is essential that as manager you demonstrate compassion and understanding both for the workers who are laid off and for those who are left behind who may experience survivor guilt. Outplacement services should be provided for displaced workers. It is also important to recognize that although downsizing may be necessary, it will undoubtedly cause a loss in productivity and may prove to be more costly in the long term than other retrenchment strategies.

Refinancing is a strategy often used in the arts and humanities sectors. Many performing arts organizations will borrow money from a bank or lender against anticipated future growth in earned income through ticket sales (Palmer, 1997). Shortfalls result when proceeds are insufficient to cover costs, forcing organizations to then refinance to avoid defaulting on their loan. These types of strategies are used for short-term crises when shortfalls are temporary.

Commercialization and fundraising involve a change in your marketing strategy, usually through raising ticket prices, increasing fees for services, or expanding fundraising activities to raise additional funds for your organization. Fundraising activities, including special events, should be considered and may help attract attention to the needs of your organization, as well as increase the level of financial support from individuals, foundations, and corporations (see chapter 4). Developing innovations or modifying existing programs may also increase revenues or efficiency. Each of these strategies should be pursued throughout the life of your organization, but they are especially important during periods of decline.

Relocations are used when the cost of overhead for an existing facility becomes too expensive. A relocation may help reduce property taxes, involve a merger with another similar organization, or simply be a move to a smaller, less expensive facility. In some cases, relocation parallels a reduction in the overall scope of the services provided. However, there are many costs associated with moving your organization, both in terms of real dollars needed to carry out the move and in the loss in productivity and potential loss of customers or clients who may not know where your new facility is located.

CONCLUSION

Managers of nonprofit organizations are confronting a new era of fiscal austerity prompted by a profound philosophical shift in the perception of federal responsibility and a subsequent reduction in government funding for many community-based programs. As we approach the new millenium, it is clear that we will continue to experience increased demand for services in an environment of shrinking financial resources and increased competition for private dollars.

To be effective as a nonprofit manager, you must be able to recognize your own reactions to stress and find ways to handle it effectively. Having done so, you should involve staff in identifying the organization's core program and delineating the agency's mission, primary functions, and goals. At the same time, you should pursue resource development strategies to increase revenues. If layoffs are necessitated by dwindling resources, they should be handled in a straightforward, honest manner, and outplacement assistance should be provided to staff who are losing their jobs. It is evident that these varied responses to organizational decline will require both technical and interactional skills.

SKILLS-APPLICATION EXERCISE

You are the director of large nonprofit shelter for runaway youths. Your programs include a 24-hour crisis hotline, a 24-hour runaway shelter (which provides meals, individual and group counseling, peer support, and crisis intervention), in-home family unification services, and services to prevent physical and sexual abuse (counseling and public education). Your funding sources include government grants (65 percent), small grants from foundations and corporations (20 percent), fees (10 percent), and individual donations (5 percent). You have been advised that your government funding will be reduced by 20 percent over the next two years.

The board of county commissioners has requested that you submit your plan for dealing with these budgetary cuts. What managerial actions or approaches would you take? Include in your design how you would respond to these questions:

- What activities can the agency stop performing?

- What activities can you get other agencies to do?

- What activities can be performed more effectively?

- How can you reduce the cost of labor?

- How can you increase the agency's revenues?

REFERENCES

Austin, M. J. (1984). Managing cutbacks in the 1980s. *Social Work, 29*, 428–434.

Banning, R. L. (1990, September). The dynamics of downsizing. *Personnel Journal*, pp. 68–75.

Behn, R. D. (1988). The fundamentals of cutback management. In K. S. Cameron, R. I. Sutton, & D. A. Whetton (Eds.), *Readings in organizational decline: Frameworks, research, and prescriptions* (pp. 347–356). Cambridge, MA: Ballinger.

Bombyk, M. J., & Chernesky, R. H. (1985). Conventional cutback leadership and the quality of the workplace: Is beta better? *Administration in Social Work, 9*(3), 47–56.

Cameron, K. S. (1983). Strategic responses to conditions of decline: Higher education and the private sector. *Journal of Higher Education, 54*, pp. 359–380.

Cameron, K. S., Sutton, R. I., & Whetten, D. A. (1988). *Readings in organizational decline: Frameworks, research, and prescriptions*. Cambridge, MA: Ballinger.

Cascio, W. F. (1993). Downsizing: What do we know? What have we learned? *Academy of Management Executive, 7*(1), 95–104.

Cigler, B. A. (1996). Adjusting to changing expectations at the local level. In J. L. Perry (Ed.), *Handbook of public administration* (2nd ed., pp. 60–76). San Francisco: Jossey-Bass.

Cooke, P. W., Reid, P. N., & Edwards, R. L. (1997). Management: New developments and directions. In R. L. Edwards (Ed.-in-Chief), *Encyclopedia of social work* (19th ed., 1997 Suppl., pp. 229–242). Washington, DC: NASW Press.

DuBran, A. J. (1996). *Reengineering survival guide: Managing and succeeding in the changing workplace*. Cincinnati: Thomson Executive Press.

Edwards, R. L., Cooke, P. W., & Reid, P. N. (1996). Social work management in an era of diminishing federal responsibility. *Social Work, 41*, 468–479.

Firstenberg, P. B. (1996). *The 21st century nonprofit: Remaking the organization in the post-government era*. New York: Foundation Center.

Friesen, B., & Frey, G. (1983). Managing organizational decline: Emerging issues for administration. *Administration in Social Work, 7*(3/4), 33–41.

Gramm–Rudman–Hollings Act (Balanced Budget and Emergency Deficit Control Act of 1985), P.L. 99-777, 99 Stat. 1038.

Greenstein, R. (1986). *Hard choices: Federal budget priorities in the Gramm–Rudman–Hollings era.* Washington, DC: Interfaith Action for Economic Justice.

Hirschhorn, L. (Ed.). (1983). *Cutting back: Retrenchment and redevelopment in human and community services.* San Francisco: Jossey-Bass.

Jeffri, J. (1983). *Arts money: Raising it, saving it, earning it.* New York: Schuman.

Knighton, A., & Heidelman, N. (1984). Managing human services organizations with limited resources. *Social Work, 29,* 531–535.

Kübler-Ross, E. (1969). *On death and dying.* New York: Macmillan.

Menefee, D. (1997). Strategic administration of nonprofit service organizations: A model for executive success in turbulent times. *Administration in Social Work, 21*(2), 1–19.

Milward, H. B. (1996). The changing character of the public sector. In J. L. Perry (Ed.), *Handbook of public administration* (2nd ed., pp. 77–91). San Francisco: Jossey-Bass.

Newland, C. A. (1996). The national government in transition. In J. L. Perry (Ed.), *Handbook of public administration* (2nd ed., pp. 19–35). San Francisco: Jossey-Bass.

Omnibus Budget Reconciliation Act of 1993, P.L. 103-66, 107 Stat. 312.

Palmer, I. (1997). Arts management cutback strategies: A cross-sector analysis. *Nonprofit Management and Leadership, 7,* 271–290.

Pappas, A. T. (1996). *Reengineering your nonprofit organization: A guide to strategic transformation.* New York: John Wiley & Sons.

Pawlak, E. J., Jeter, C. S., & Fink, R. L. (1983). The politics of cutback management. *Administration in Social Work, 7*(2), 1–10.

Perry, T. P. (1988). Least-cost alternatives to layoffs in declining industries. In K. S. Cameron, R. I. Sutton, & D. A. Whetton (Eds.), *Readings in organizational decline: Frameworks, research, and prescriptions* (pp. 357–368). Cambridge, MA: Ballinger.

Personal Responsibility and Work Opportunity Reconciliation Act of 1996, P.L. 104-193, 110 Stat. 2105.

Turem, J. S., & Born, C. E. (1983). Doing more with less. *Social Work, 28,* 206–210.

Weatherley, R. (1984). Approaches to cutback management. In F. D. Perlmutter (Ed.), *Human services at risk* (pp. 39–56). Lexington, MA: Lexington Books.

Whetten, D. A. (1980). Sources, responses, and effects of organizational decline. In J. Kimberly & R. Miles (Eds.), *The organizational life cycle* (pp. 342–374). San Francisco: Jossey-Bass.

Whetten, D. A. (1988). The organizational growth and decline process. In K. S. Cameron, R. I. Sutton, & D. A. Whetton (Eds.), *Readings in organizational decline: Frameworks, research, and prescriptions* (pp. 27–44). Cambridge, MA: Ballinger.

ADDITIONAL READING

Bielous, G. (1996, October). Stretch targets: The art of asking for miracles. *Supervision,* pp. 16–18.

Boulding, K. (1975). The management of decline. *Change, 7*(5), 8–9, 64.

Briar, K. H. (1987). Unemployment and underemployment. In A. Minahan (Ed.-in-Chief), *Encyclopedia of social work* (18th ed., Vol. 2, pp. 778–788). Silver Spring, MD: National Association of Social Workers.

Brown, M. J. (1996, September). What can community organizers teach us? *Journal for Quality and Participation*, pp. 78–80.

Cameron, D. B. (1996). Do you need to rebuild your organization to survive the 3rd millennium? *Nonprofit World*, *14*(3), 48–51.

Drucker, P. F. (1996, August). Nonprofit pioneers. *Executive Excellence*, p. 5.

Hernandez, D. G. (1996, December). Advice for the future. *Editor and Publisher*, pp. 6–34.

Ingraham, P. W. (1996). Evolving public service systems. In J. L. Perry (Ed.), *Handbook of public administration*, (2nd ed., pp. 375–391). San Francisco: Jossey-Bass.

Miller, J. R. (1997, March). Transforming for the 21st century. *Management Accounting*, pp. 15–16.

Perry, J. L. (1996). *Handbook of public administration* (2nd ed.). San Francisco: Jossey-Bass.

Tolchin, M. (1991, February 4). Cuts after decade of cuts: Governors grim at meeting. *New York Times*, p. A10.

PART FOUR

COORDINATING

SKILLS

COORDINATING SKILLS

Managerial coordinating skills encompass the roles of monitor and coordinator. Competencies for the role of monitor include receiving and organizing information, evaluating routine information, and responding to routine requests for information. Competencies for the role of coordinator include planning, organizing, and controlling work. The chapters in this section focus on these internal, control-oriented roles and competencies as nonprofit managers seek to create conditions of organizational stability and continuity.

Kathryn Mercer, Mary Kay Kantz, and Peter Ben Friedman, in chapter 15, discuss how to write effectively. They argue that nonprofit managers must "gain control" over their writing so that it works for them, and they focus on the difficulties of getting started, suggesting ways to overcome these start-up barriers. Special attention is paid to the purpose of the written communication and to the audience to whom the communication is directed. The authors suggest that writing skills are important for nonprofit managers in both the monitoring and coordinating roles and that documentation, record keeping, and technical writing, as well as other internal and external communication, contribute to the efficient flow of work.

Computers can aid managers in performing their monitoring and coordinating functions. In chapter 16, Laura I. Zimmerman and Andrew Broughton provide an overview of issues related to computing and information technology. They discuss some of the most recent advances in information technology, with attention to networks and the Internet. Further, they recommend that nonprofit organizations engage in strategic planning for technology and suggest specific management steps that can be taken to plan for technology in your organization.

In chapter 17, James L. Strachan provides a primer on financial management for nonprofit managers. Given that an organization's finances are critical to its effectiveness and even to its survival, nonprofit managers need to be familiar with basic accounting and financial management concepts and practices. Strachan's goal is to enable nonprofit managers to develop familiarity with terms and understanding of basic concepts, not to make them accountants. He includes definitions of many terms and concepts, as well as guidelines that managers can use in selecting an auditor or auditing firm. He also gives attention to the budgeting function in organizations.

Andrea Meier and Charles L. Usher, in chapter 18, describe the changing context of program evaluation in nonprofit organizations, suggesting that the traditional separation of the roles of manager and evaluator have begun to blur in response to increased demands for organizational accountability. They review different types of program evaluation approaches or strategies, and they provide some helpful tools for managers.

In chapter 19, the final chapter in this section, Paul A. Kurzman emphasizes the risks and liabilities that nonprofit organizations encounter and the monitoring and coordinating roles of managers in establishing and overseeing risk management activities. He identifies the most frequently noted risks and discusses recommended responses, including insurance protection, legal counsel, staff training, and internal risk audits. Kurzman provides useful insights into the rationale and practices related to each of these potential responses. He urges nonprofit managers to deal proactively with the risks their organizations face.

CHAPTER 15

Writing Effectively

Kathryn Mercer, Mary Kay Kantz, and Peter Ben Friedman

W e teach law students how to write as lawyers. Of course, in doing so we convey the technicalities of legal writing. Many of our students are shocked to learn, however, that these technicalities are the easy part of legal writing. Far more difficult and important is our emphasis on the lawyer's role as advocate—a person whose words are meant to accomplish the client's goals. Only with experience do our students realize what we already know: Effective legal writing is simply effective writing. The only essential difference is that whereas most writers need to convey clearly and concisely who they are, what they want, and why they should get it, a lawyer needs to convey who the client is, what the client wants, and why the client should get it.

In addition, our students need to understand that there are many reasons not to write. Most of us are overwhelmed with the amounts of paper sitting on our desks waiting to be read. It is not worth writing if your readers are going to be irritated with what you have written (unless, of course, you want to irritate them). Similarly, you may not want to write when the message would be better conveyed in person or by telephone. Writing can be abrupt, harsh, and impersonal. Moreover, it can have a lasting effect on future relationships. Do not write without a good reason.

Keep in mind that whenever you write, you put a little of yourself down on paper to be judged by someone else. Your writing, in fact, is likely to be the principal basis on which someone decides whether you are managing your organization efficiently or whether you have exercised your professional judgment wisely.

Furthermore, although paranoia is among a lawyer's professional skills, there are good reasons for being careful before putting anything in writing. Spoken words are fleeting and memory fallible. Written words, on the other hand, can last years. They survive the context that might give them one meaning rather than another. Once put down on paper, mere suggestions or daily routines become rules and policies. They can even be cited by later authors as a basis for their statements. Written down, one person's (perhaps ill informed) opinion becomes the authoritative word on the subject.

As a manager of a nonprofit organization, you cannot afford to be a poor writer. As discussed in chapter 1, effective management requires good coordinating skills, and one of the roles related to coordination is that of monitor. To be successful in the monitoring role, you must be able to communicate clearly with those within and beyond your organization. If the words you put down on paper are not clear to your reader, they might simply be ignored. Or they might be misinterpreted and provoke action you never intended to provoke. Despite these risks, there is plenty that you must put in writing. For example, you might need to convey your thoughts effectively in writing to obtain funding for a new project or to get approval for additional staffing or to get the go-ahead for new programs and services. If you cannot convey the necessary information clearly, concisely, and persuasively, you do not get what you want. If you cannot write efficiently—if it takes you or a staff member a long time to complete a report or a request for funding—it may no longer matter whether you get what you want.

In this chapter we introduce you to ways of improving your writing to accomplish what you want. We focus on the purpose of and audience for your writing. In addition, we suggest methods we and other writers have found effective for organizing our writing. Finally, we provide examples meant to demonstrate ways these organizational methods can help a writer effectively accomplish his or her purpose. The best writers are those with years of writing experience, but such experience without close attention to purpose and audience creates the obscurity that mars far too much professional writing.

GETTING STARTED

The best way to start is to identify your strengths and weaknesses as a writer in order to develop a program of improvement. In both evaluating your writing and developing a plan to improve it, look at the three distinct components of your writing: content, organization, and style.

Unfortunately, most of us have had our hands slapped often enough, literally or figuratively, over errors in grammar and punctuation that we tend to think only of checking for those kinds of mechanical problems ("style") in dealing with our writing. In fact, content is the most important consideration. The content of writing is its message. So the message, the meaning you wish to convey in your writing, is of prime importance. The organization of content and attention to details of style are separate matters to be dealt with after you have decided on your message. Learning to recognize and deal separately and explicitly with these various components of the writing process enables you to build on your writing strengths and systematically overcome your weaknesses.

EVALUATING AND IMPROVING CONTENT

In reviewing your writing to determine whether your message is clear and complete, always pay attention to your purpose and audience.

Purpose

The purpose of your writing should be your first consideration. You need to be aware of what specifically you are trying to accomplish and how you use your writing to achieve that goal (for example, informing, persuading, or motivating). Think about what you want to do—to get action, to direct, to persuade, to inform, to challenge—and what you want your reader to do—to act, to follow, to agree, to understand, to react.

One way of ensuring that you focus on your purpose is to ensure that your writing clearly conveys who you are, what you want (your purpose), and why your purpose is appropriate. Who you are helps clarify your purpose. Conveying what you want makes it far more likely that your writing accomplishes your purpose, whether it is to inform the reader or to persuade the reader to take certain action. Depending on your audience and your message, who you are and why your purpose is appropriate might be self-evident. Nevertheless, paying attention to these matters in advance ensures that the reader understands them.

It is surprising how often writers do not convey the message they have in mind simply because they have not taken the time to think about why they are setting something down on paper. Instead, they sit down and start to write whatever comes to mind. It may well be that what they write has more to do with their emotional state at the moment or the distractions of the day than with the essence of their message. For instance, a supervisor may write a simple memo announcing the agenda for an upcoming staff meeting. The supervisor's purpose is to see whether anyone has anything to add to the agenda. Unless he or she focuses on the purpose, however, the memo might evolve into an explanation of why the meeting was postponed from the original meeting date, how the current severe weather conditions affect the ability of staff members to make early morning meetings, why the staff meetings have been so long and drawn-out lately, and so on. The supervisor is angry about some of these matters and apologetic about others. Some of them may be worth adding to the agenda so that solutions can be found. In the meantime,

"Quite frankly, Kevin, I'd be hesitant to accept an annual report submitted in green and yellow crayon."

however, these extraneous items have distracted the reader of the memo, who is now less likely to respond to what the supervisor wanted in the first place.

You can avoid this problem by taking a few minutes before drafting a document to list the points you want to make. Later, for purposes of evaluation, try backtracking through several pieces of your writing and list the separate points you made in each. Check to see how many of the points really support your purpose in writing the document. How often did you include irrelevant ideas or comments that may distract the reader or be counterproductive to your purpose?

It is easier to weed out irrelevant points when they stand alone in a list than when they are embedded in a completed text. More important, when you simply list your ideas—without being concerned with constructing well-formed sentences and coherent paragraphs—you allow your thoughts to flow more freely and creatively. Stopping frequently in your initial writing to check the spelling of a word or to decide just how you want to start a paragraph is likely to cause you to lose your train of thought or (even worse) to neglect to pick up on spur-of-the-moment ideas that just may lead to the solution for which you are looking.

In more complex writing tasks, you need more than a quick listing of ideas to keep you on track (some other approaches are discussed later), but the same principle applies. Deal first with the message: your purpose for writing. In doing so, make sure your audience understands who you are and why your purpose is appropriate. If you let yourself fall into the grammar-picker syndrome—proofreading continuously as you write, afraid you missed a mistake in punctuation—you may have trouble producing as creative or as thorough a piece of writing as you would like. Work on developing your thoughts and speaking directly to your audience, knowing that you can correct grammatical problems later.

Audience

Know your audience! You do not communicate with your supervisor in the same way you communicate with your family. Different clients have vastly different ways of understanding the same subject matter. Getting the attention and sympathy of a bored bureaucrat requires a different approach than getting the attention of the grants manager of a philanthropic trust. Although your audience might at times seem a less immediate concern because you are writing for the same audience all the time (such as your staff), in fact you already have a well-developed sense of how to communicate with this group. Staying alert at all times to your audience ensures that your message is crafted effectively. For example, your goal may be to obtain funding from a particular source, which has a tendency to fund only certain activities favored by the predilections of its original benefactor. Your goal, then, is not only to ask for a grant, but to appeal to the interests of the benefactor as seen through the eyes of the fund administrator.

Before you write, find out as much as you can about your audience. If you lack the time or resources to find out what you need to know, then conjure up an audience for your own benefit. Make it as close as possible to the audience you believe you are addressing. Then speak to that audience. How would you convey your message to that audience in person? Try to speak as directly to that audience on paper as you would in person. Sometimes, especially if your writing projects call for creativity, it may be helpful to forget about the audience until you have had time to explore fully your own ideas on the subject you are addressing. Too much focus on your audience too early in the process may stifle creative thought. You may subconsciously supply answers to a problem on the basis of what you believe your audience would like you to think. However, you must deal with the demands of your audience before the writing task is finished.

Another important point to consider in terms of audience is the use of jargon. It is obvious that the use of professional jargon may create problems for a nonprofessional audience. Less obvious are the problems that arise from the overuse or indiscriminate use of such language in writing for members of the "in" group. Whereas some jargon does allow for the precise expression of technical concepts, it often masks imprecise and unclear thinking. The solution is to think through the ideas you wish to express and make sure you have resolved the problem or fully developed your idea or proposal before you try to convey your thoughts to the reader. Even if you are writing for a professional audience, examine any jargon you use very carefully. Could a more prosaic term convey as effectively the meaning of some technical term you are using? If not, is the technical term in fact obscuring some ambiguity or incoherence in your message? Having answered these questions, you can safely resort to technical language if your only audience is conversant with the jargon. Nevertheless, it is a good idea to try to substitute everyday terms for technical jargon wherever doing so does not deprive your writing of necessary meaning.

ORGANIZING THE IDEAS: THE FREE-WRITING MODEL

An audience does not respond to a message unless the message is clear, and the message is not clear unless it is well organized. Your thoughts do not have to be well organized as they tumble from your brain onto the page; usually they are not. The problem is that many people expect that they are and consequently do not make an effort to organize their thoughts.

The process of organization, however, is separate from the idea-generating process, and most people are better at one than the other. In either case, writing tends to go faster and to bring forth more original thought, regarding both solutions to problems and methods of expression, when the process of generating the message precedes the process of organizing it for presentation to a reader.

The traditional approach—the sit-down-and-just-start-writing approach—may still be all you need for brief, routine writing tasks. For more complex or more critical pieces, however, you may find free writing to be of value. This method is based on the concept of dealing separately with the separate components of the writing process. Many writers today use the free-writing approach to overcome writer's block and to get more ideas per minute down on paper. The idea is simply to start writing in whatever form feels comfortable to you. The easiest way is just to list your thoughts and perhaps (for later organizational purposes) to number each separate thought. You should feel free to let your mind wander as you write, jotting down even half-thoughts, tangential ideas, and distractions. Start your pencil moving and keep it moving no matter what, taking no time out to check spelling, to correct punctuation, or to decide how to phrase an opening sentence. You can even interrupt yourself in the middle of a thought.

Free writing can be done as an exercise to loosen up before beginning a writing project—in which case it does not matter what you write about. It also can be done as the initial phase of your real task. At any point in the free-writing process, you can stop jotting down ideas and begin to organize your material. Although idea generating and organizing are two separate processes in free writing, you use them in tandem, moving one or the other to the fore-front as you choose.

Many different organizational patterns can be followed for different writing tasks (some are discussed later in the chapter). In this initial phase—your free-writing session—simply group similar ideas together, nothing fancy or complicated.

For example, suppose you decide to draft a memo proposing that your staff be given some kind of training in writing. You want to come up with some practical suggestions for doing so and you want to be persuasive, but you are not quite sure where to start. A free-writing exercise might look like this:

1. In an office setting it is important to be able to communicate clearly.
2. Many people have trouble finding the time to write.
3. Maybe it's because they put it off because they don't want to do it.
4. Maybe they don't want to do it because they are embarrassed by their writing.
5. A lot of people have negative feelings about writing because teachers in the past have criticized whatever they have written.
6. But now we're not in school.
7. On the other hand, some people have never had any significant help with their writing.
8. Professionally, it is important to appear well on paper. It indicates you have a solid educational background and looks good to others.
9. It helps you get ahead professionally if you can communicate effectively. Speech and writing.
10. What about nonprofit professionals in particular? Who do they have to communicate with?
11. There are many audiences for nonprofit professionals—clients, lawyers, judges, foundations and other sources of support, the general public, co-workers, and supervisors.
12. How can—Maybe the approach should be a series of workshops or seminars by different people, might make it more interesting—how to meet all the different needs?
13. I would like to improve the speed of my writing—getting something into a finished form—different projects have different requirements as far as what "finished" means—getting into a finished form without wasting a lot of time that I need for other things. Same for others?
14. Maybe I should do more writing than I have been doing—just on my own—to get up to speed.
15. But are there helpful techniques for doing this?

At this point you may decide to start organizing these thoughts to see where you are. Let us assume that you look over the list and see four groups of ideas (A, B, C, and D). You run down your list, jotting the appropriate letter in front of each numbered idea: A for ideas 1, 8, and 9; B for ideas 2–7; C for ideas 10, 11, and 13; D for ideas 12, 14, and 15.

Now you are ready to do a quick outline of your material, not worrying about the form, such as the following (the numbers in parentheses are the numbers of your original ideas):

A. Importance of writing in an office setting (1)
      Credibility (8)
      Professional development (9)
B. Why social work professionals would need help with writing
      Many procrastinate (3)
          Why?
              No time (2)
              Embarrassed by lack of skills (4)
                  Why? Baggage from the past (5)
                  But time to let that go (6)
          Others really do lack basic skills (10)
C. What kind of help is needed (10)?
      Audience (10, 11)
      Efficiency (13)
      Purpose (13)
D. Kinds of help available?
      Self-help (14, 15)
      Workshops (12)

From the rough outline that emerges, you can begin to see which topics are worth developing and which points may be omitted. You can begin to firm up your ideas of audience and purpose if those points have not yet been clarified. By expanding the entries in the outline into complete sentences, you can sharpen the focus of your thoughts. Moreover, by eliminating the pressure of producing a finished product on the first try, you have more room for creative problem solving.

To experience the free-writing process and to compare it with the more traditional approach to writing, try these exercises.

FREE-WRITING EXERCISES

Choose one of the following assignments (A–C). Spend about 20 minutes responding to it, following Instruction 1. Then choose a second assignment and spend the same amount of time responding to it according to Instruction 2. Complete just as much of the assignment as you can reasonably do in the allotted time. Then compare the results by answering the questions that follow the assignments.

Instruction 1: Draft the memo, newsletter article, and so forth, in the format in which such a document would actually appear. Remember to start each paragraph with a topic sentence that tells clearly what the paragraph is about and end each paragraph with a conclusion. Make transitions between paragraphs clear. Do your best to avoid errors of grammar, punctuation, spelling, sentence structure, and choice of words.

Instruction 2: List your thoughts and suggestions as they come to you. Number them if you wish. Do not worry about organization, paragraph or sentence structure, grammar, spelling, or punctuation. Write down your thoughts just as they come to you.

Assignments

A. Write a letter aimed at persuading a legislator to endorse proposed public funding of a particular nonprofit organization project.
B. Write an opinion-page article for your local newspaper, encouraging the general public to support a particular nonprofit program.
C. Write a memo to the chairperson of an undergraduate department at your local university, who has asked your advice in designing a program to train and place student interns in nonprofit agencies in your community.

Evaluate Your Work

Compare the writing you did according to Instruction 1 with what you did according to Instruction 2.

1. How many paragraphs did you write in 1?
2. How many different ideas did you express in 1? 2?
3. Did you write anything that surprised you in 1? 2? What was it?
4. How did you feel about each of these writing assignments?
5. Who was your audience, and what was your purpose in 1? 2?

Some experienced writers find that they are skilled enough to write a final draft at the first attempt, and some writers find that for routine tasks they need or want to take the time for only one draft. However, many experienced writers find that some form of free writing helps them develop their writing skills and produce more thoughtful and well-organized written work. Although it is a multistep process, free writing can actually help you become a much more efficient writer—to get more good writing on paper faster— than the writer who tries to do a final draft all at once.

ATTENDING TO MATTERS OF STYLE

Although it is better not to worry about punctuation, grammar, and sentence structure while you are busy defining and organizing your message, you must deal with this aspect of your writing before you are finished. Your credibility suffers if you do not.

It is relatively easy to clean up your prose after you have made the big decisions about the content and arrangement of your message. There is no law that says you have to do it yourself. Sometimes another pair of eyes can be a great help and time-saver when it comes to this stage of writing. Do not be embarrassed or hesitant about asking a colleague to proofread your writing. Your willingness to take this step simply demonstrates your commitment to improving your writing for your own sake and for the benefit of your organization.

In dealing with problems of style, identify (perhaps with the help of the proofreader) several problems that seem to recur in your writing. Browse through some of the many excellent books on writing that you find at your library or bookstore (many are listed at the end of this chapter), and set a little time aside each week to work on one problem at a time. It is not a difficult task, but it requires some dedication. You can truly accomplish on your own what all the knuckle rapping of your elementary school teachers could not achieve. Your computer can also provide some help at this point. Get in the habit of using its spell-checking feature, and investigate the possibility of acquiring grammar-checking software (such as RightWriter). Just remember to use these features thoughtfully. They help you, but they do not do all the work; they respond mechanically to their task and need some input from you.

USING THIS INFORMATION

Nonprofit managers often function as problem solvers. Their clients present dilemmas that have personal, social, and legal implications. The managers are asked to assess the situation, to form an opinion, and to communicate that opinion to an audience. The audience might be a funding source; the government; a board of directors; or the agency's staff, clients, or patrons. Usually there is no single correct view of a given situation. Thus, the reader needs sufficient information to be persuaded or to reach an independent decision. The professional's written opinion serves its purpose if it is based on logically connected arguments that lead to a clearly formulated conclusion. To communicate the logical problem-solving process to another person, a clear organizational plan is needed.

Identifying the Purpose of Your Writing

The first task is to identify your mission in preparing a document. Take a few minutes to think about the role that requires you to write the document, what you need to write, why you need to write it, and to whom you need to write it. A clear summary helps you maintain your focus throughout the writing process.

For example, assume that you are a manager of a nonprofit child protective services (CPS) organization through a purchase-of-services contract with a public agency. You have been requested by the public funding agency to justify your request for additional personnel. Here is the statement of purpose you have drafted:

> As a manager of a nonprofit child welfare agency providing child protective services in a major metropolitan center, my goal is to educate and persuade the state funding agency (the audience) that my agency is understaffed.

Presenting General Information

To begin preparing this report, you make a list of ideas that have led you to believe that the deficiency in staffing poses an immediate problem. You jot down examples, statistics, background material, and major and minor factors. In making this list, you do not worry about the order of the information or how the information will be structured in the report.

Some of the ideas you generate in this information "dump" include the following:

- The number of child abuse reports increased 20 percent in the past year.
- New state and federal legislation requires extensive investigation and documentation.
- Numerous CPS workers have complained about their inability to do the job.
- Workers' caseloads are up 12 percent.
- During the past month, CPS was sued by a parents' group for not making reasonable efforts to reunify families.
- CPS lost 10 workers in the past two months who discussed "burnout" in their termination meetings.

Clustering and Organizing Ideas

Several organizational schemes can be used to convert a rambling list of ideas into a coherent, persuasive report. All schemes have the objectives of putting similar thoughts together in groups, arranging the items within each group in a logical order, and connecting those groups in a coherent fashion.

The six ideas just listed can be separated into three categories:

1. external pressures—legislation and increased reporting
2. internal pressures—increased caseloads, complaints, and burnout
3. danger signals—lawsuits and the attrition of workers.

Grouping and labeling separate ideas give a basic structure to the writing and help the reader absorb the information.

Next, look for a unifying theme and message that connect one group to the next. In this example, the theme that emerges is that the problem—understaffing—is a result of the workers' response to increased external demands on the agency. The problem is evidenced by the lawsuit and increased staff turnover. The persuasive message of the report could be that corrective action is needed before the agency's ability to function disintegrates further.

The writing's theme or message should match the statement of purpose written at the beginning of the process. A theme helps generate an order for the groups and a sequence of information within each group. Some ways to arrange information include chronology, geography, analytical deduction, steps in a process, and comparison or contrast. In the CPS example, you decide to combine two sequencing methods. First, you decide to trace chronologically the sequence of external events that led to the problem of understaffing. Then, you plan to present and interpret data to show the current impact on the agency and to forecast the future inability of the agency to render needed services. Ideally, this analytical process persuades the reader that your proposed solution—increased funding—is imperative.

Drafting the Persuasive Document

Once ideas have been generated, clustered, and organized, you are ready to draft the document.

- *Identify the problem or issue to be addressed.* The reader needs to know the subject of the document at the beginning.
- *Introduce your position in a lead paragraph, and give a road map.* The first paragraph should make clear to the reader in summary form who you (the writer) are, why you are writing the document, and why your purpose is an appropriate one. This "position statement" sets forth concisely the organization and content of the entire memo. It states at the beginning the solution to the problem and summarizes the reasons for your conclusion. The lead paragraph tells the reader where you are going and how you will get there. Never underestimate the effectiveness of repetition; a well-taken point that the reader does not grasp when he or she first encounters it might well come across on the second or even the third encounter.

- **Control the discussion through assertive paragraphs that focus on a single idea.** One method of writing persuasively is to divide the document into ARAC (assertion, rule, analysis, and conclusion) arguments.

    Assertion—For each topic or idea, begin by stating your position on that topic. Write one sentence that directly states your major point. Keep it simple, focused, and direct.

    Rule—Identify the relevant authority that supports your position—a statute, statistics, literature you have consulted, and so forth.

    Analysis—Use the rest of the paragraph to support and explain your position. Use the facts of the situation you are analyzing to demonstrate how you arrived at your position.

    Conclusion—Restate your position, highlighting the main point you presented.

    The first sentence of the next paragraph should be linked to the last paragraph and direct the reader to the next topic or subtopic. Thus, the four-step process begins again.

- **Divide more complex discussions.** If your discussion of a point is lengthy, consider dividing the paragraph into two or three paragraphs, using the parts of ARAC as dividing points. For example, your assertion and rule could be in the first paragraph, and your analysis and conclusion could be in the second paragraph. Remember that readers need visual breaks. It is difficult to maintain attention through an overly long paragraph (note how short the paragraphs are in a newspaper article). On the other hand, too many paragraphs make the writing choppy and may lose your theme and focus. Alternatively, if your paragraphs are too long, you may be trying to say too much at once. Consider if there are subpoints to each topic that could be separated. Each subtopic deserves its own ARAC paragraph. If you are struggling to keep focused on the topic, chances are there are several subtopics (several points you are trying to make) lumped together, thus making the writing more difficult.

- **Use organizational signals.** The reader needs signals so that the direction and flow of the writing are always apparent. The appearance of the prose on the formatted page focuses the reader's attention on your important points and leads the reader to the appropriate conclusions.

    First, use the paragraph to indicate your separate topic organization. Each paragraph should address only a single topic. The break between paragraphs allows the reader to see the topic organization of your writing.

    Second, begin new paragraphs with topic and transitional sentences to give continuity and cohesion to your writing. These sentences provide the reader with a point of view for looking at a paragraph. Transitional sentences explain to the reader how one point leads to the next.

Third, use signposts—that is, periodic indicators of where your argument has been and where it is going. Signposts help redirect the reader back to the larger pattern, placing all the pieces in the larger context. Consider using headings as signposts. These breaks in the writing allow the reader to catch a breath and rejuvenate. They also visually demonstrate the structure of your argument and give the reader a sense of your major points.

- **Conclude your argument.** Confidently restate your position, putting everything into perspective. This conclusion sums up the entire analysis—all the issues and subissues. It may also recommend future action.

APPLYING THE PRINCIPLES IN AN EXERCISE

The following exercise demonstrates the ARAC method for organizing a persuasive memorandum.

You are a supervisor of a CPS agency. The court has asked the agency to assess whether a child is neglected or dependent and to draft recommendations. You are familiar with the state statutes that define dependency and neglect.

Section 51 defines a *neglected child* as any child (A) who lacks proper parental care because of the faults or habits of his or her parents . . ., (B) whose parents neglect or refuse to provide him or her with proper or necessary subsistence, education, medical or surgical care, or other care necessary for his or her health, morals, or well-being. To show neglect, you must show that the parent was at fault. However, the court can find a dependent child when there is no parental fault. Section 52 defines a *dependent child* as any child (A) who lacks proper care or support by reason of the mental or physical condition of his or her parents . . ., (B) whose condition or environment is such as to warrant the state, in the interests of the child, in assuming his or her guardianship.

A CPS investigation revealed the following facts concerning the Dorwins. Is state intervention appropriate in this case? You may classify the child as a dependent child or a neglected child in your recommendation.

CASE STUDY: THE DORWINS

NOTE: *From Katz, S. (1971). When parents fail (pp. 53–54). Boston: Beacon Press. Copyright 1971 by Sanford Katz. Reprinted by permission.*

Mr. and Mrs. Dorwin . . . were reported to a child protective agency in a large metropolitan city. They had moved to the city from a farming community. Mrs. Dorwin, who was 28 years old, had been reared in a poverty-stricken rural area. She had completed six years of formal education. Her family had lived in a shack without electricity or plumbing. Both her father and sister had been hospitalized several times because of mental illness.

Mr. Dorwin was 31 years old; he was raised in an urban area of a predominantly rural state. Because of his mother's mental illness and his father's alcoholism and abusive treatment of his children, Mr. Dorwin and his brothers and sisters lived with and were raised by a relative. Mr. Dorwin completed eight years of formal education. An auto mechanic, he had a criminal record for drunkenness and assault and battery on his wife and children. He seldom worked steadily. The Dorwins were married when Mrs. Dorwin was six months pregnant.

Mr. and Mrs. Dorwin had moved into an attractive, well-kept apartment, later to be evicted for nonpayment of rent and causing damage to the residence. The walls of their present apartment were dirty, with large holes where plaster had been removed. The floors were uncared for; garbage and feces were spread throughout the rooms. The house had a strong urine odor. The five Dorwin children (ages 10, nine, seven, five, and four) were dirty, poorly clothed, and malnourished. Frequently they were seen begging in the streets for scraps of food. Neighbors reported that the children were often left alone at night or with an alcoholic uncle as a babysitter. Often the children slept on sodden mattresses without sheets. Sometimes they all slept in the same bed with their mother. Neighbors said that the parents frequently swore at their children. The children themselves said they were afraid of their father, who often struck them in the head with his fist. The children were also witnesses to physical battles between their parents.

The children were absent from school between 50 and 60 days during the year. When they did attend, they were dirty. Their peers rejected them. They had few playmates. Frequently they were without money for lunch or for recreational activities. Teachers reported they fell asleep in class. Although they exhibited average intelligence on standard psychological tests, they consistently failed in school. David (age seven) was sent home from school after seven days because he, like his sisters Donna (age five) and Sonia (age four), was not toilet trained and could not control himself in the classroom. The three older children had severe visual problems, but the Dorwins never followed through with an ophthalmologist's recommendation for treatment. Nor did the Dorwins cooperate with a physician who was treating Donna for a painful bowel disease that could have been cured by their supervising a simple program of diet and medication for the girl.

The Persuasive Memorandum

Identify the Issue

Is state intervention appropriate on the basis that the Dorwin children are neglected or dependent?

State Who You Are and What Your Position Is

The court has requested that as supervisor of child protective services I assess and draft recommendations as to whether the Dorwin children are neglected or dependent. I have concluded that the Dorwin's five children are neglected under section 51 because (1) they lack proper parental care owing to the faults of their parents and (2) their parents have refused or neglected to provide them with necessary subsistence, education, and medical care necessary for their health and well-being. State intervention is imperative for the safety, health, and welfare of the children.

The statute itself suggests an organization for the persuasive memorandum. Section 51 identifies two ways that children could be neglected: the lack of proper parental care owing to parental fault and parental neglect or refusal to provide necessary care. From the facts, arguments could be made supporting each alternative. Thus, the memo can be separated into two major topics.

Outline Topics and Subtopics to be Discussed, and Create a Road Map for the Reader

The Dorwins have failed to provide for their children in three ways: First, the Dorwins have provided substandard housing and living conditions. Second, the Dorwins have a violent and unloving relationship with their children. Third, the Dorwins have refused to cooperate with a physician's recommendation for treating the visual impairments and physical diseases of their children.

The factual information is clustered around three topics, each of which demonstrates that the children are neglected.

Draft Assertive ARAC Paragraphs

Begin by explaining to the reader the authority on which you rely (in this case the statute's requirements). Then, break the argument down into sub-arguments. Under each argument, demonstrate the application of the statutory requirement by using the facts. Use signposts when they are helpful. When you have finished your arguments, conclude the memo. Here is an example of the remainder of the persuasive memorandum.

Topic paragraph: sets up the analysis and presents the author's position	The court has requested that as supervisor of child protective services I assess and draft recommendations as to whether the Dorwin children are neglected or dependent. I have concluded that the Dorwins are responsible for the neglect of their children. Section 51 indicates that a child is neglected if his or her parents neglect or refuse to provide him or her with proper or necessary subsistence, education, medical or surgical care, or other care necessary for his or her health, morals, or well-being. Thus, the statute requires a demonstration that (1) the child

lacks proper parental care and that (2) this lack of care is the fault of the parents. Under this definition, the Dorwin children are physically, educationally, and medically neglected. The parents have not provided for their children in three ways: (1) the Dorwins have provided substandard housing and living conditions, (2) they have a violent and unloving relationship with their children, and (3) they have refused to cooperate with a physician's recommendation for treating their children's visual impairments and physical diseases.

Topic: Inability to provide necessary subsistence

The Dorwins have neglected their children. [*This is the assertion.*] A parent's failure to provide a suitable living environment, restful sleeping conditions, or warm clothing and sufficient food evidences neglect. [*This is the rule. It is a good idea to use some authority for these statements if there is any. For example, a well-respected author could be quoted.*] The Dorwin apartment where the five children and their parents live is dirty. The walls of their present apartment have large holes where plaster has been removed. The floors are uncared for. On the day of my visit, garbage and feces were spread throughout the rooms. The house had a strong odor of urine. The children sleep on sodden mattresses without sheets. Sometimes they all sleep in the same bed with their mother. The five Dorwin children (ages 10, 9, 7, 5, and 4) were dirty, poorly clothed, and malnourished. Neighbors reported that frequently they were seen begging in the streets for scraps of food. [*In the application section, facts are mustered in support of the paragraph's position. The rule is applied to the current situation.*] Thus, the Dorwins have failed to provide their children with adequate subsistence for their well-being. [*Conclusion: The original assertion is restated.*]

Topic: Lack of proper care

The parents have shown an uncaring attitude toward their children. [*This is the assertion.*] Parental alcoholism that has detrimental impact on the child, and domestic violence is an indicator of neglect. [*This is the rule.*] Mr. Dorwin has a criminal record for drunkenness and assault and battery on his wife and children. Neighbors said that the parents frequently swore at their children. The children themselves said their father often struck them in the head with his fist. The children were also witness to physical battles between their parents. Neighbors reported that the children were often left alone at night or with an alcoholic uncle as a babysitter. [*This is the application.*] Because of Mr. Dorwin's drinking and his violent conduct toward his children and his wife, the children are fearful. State intervention is necessary to protect them from this unloving environment. [*This is the conclusion.*]

Topic: Unattended medical problems

The children are also medically neglected, since the Dorwins have failed to provide medical treatment that would alleviate their children's visual and physical impairments. [*This is the assertion.*] Parents have an obligation to give their children basic medical care for diseases, even those that are not life threatening. [*This is the rule.*] The three older children had severe visual problems, but the Dorwins never followed through with an ophthalmologist's recommendation for treatment. Nor did the Dorwins cooperate with a physician who was treating Donna for a painful bowel disease that could have been cured by their supervising a simple program of diet and medication for the girl. [*This is the application.*] In the latter situation in particular, the Dorwins have no excuse for failing to provide simple medical care that would greatly improve their daughter's health and comfort. [*This is the conclusion.*]

Concluding paragraph: Shows impact of parental neglect on the children

In sum, the Dorwin children have been physically and emotionally neglected by their parents. The children's totally inadequate school performance evidences the detrimental impact that their environment has had. The children were absent from school between 50 and 60 days during the year. When they did attend, they were dirty. Their peers rejected them. They had few playmates. Frequently, they were without money for lunch or for recreational activities. Teachers reported they fell asleep in class. Although the children exhibited average intelligence on standard psychological tests, they consistently failed in school. David (age 7) was sent home from school after seven days because he, like his sisters Donna (age 5) and Sonia (age 4), was not toilet trained and could not control himself in the classroom.

Recommendation: File neglect charges, not dependency charges, because evidence shows parental fault

The state has authority to adjudicate the Dorwin children neglected because Mr. and Mrs. Dorwin are responsible for their children's condition. Section 51 requires a showing of parental fault. Although the parents have had limited formal schooling and a familial background that may have inadequately prepared them for parenthood (which would support a finding of dependency, not neglect), the Dorwins's deliberate refusal to provide the children with basic medical care, their violent behavior, and the presence of feces and urine in the household show neglect.

CONCLUSION

Focusing on the purpose of written communication is the first step in effective writing. Such focus requires making explicit your perspective, what you are trying to accomplish with the document you are writing, and why you are trying to accomplish it. In addition, awareness of the specific audience for whom you are writing is also an essential ingredient. Organizing the message—which is separate from the idea-generating process—constitutes yet another critical task in communicating effectively in the written mode. Finally, proofreading your writing for punctuation, grammar, sentence structure, and other style problems shows your commitment to improving your writing.

The free-writing approach may be used to overcome writer's block and to generate ideas. It is an approach that can be used as an exercise to loosen up before actually beginning a writing task, or it can be the initial phase of your task.

Different approaches to clustering and organizing ideas you have generated have the goals of putting similar thoughts together in groups, arranging the items within each group in a logical order, and connecting those groups in a coherent fashion. Once ideas have been generated, clustered, and organized, you are ready to draft the written document. This draft should identify the problems or issues to be addressed, introduce your position and give a road map, use assertive paragraphs that focus on a single idea, use organizational signals, and conclude your argument.

ADDITIONAL READING

Beebe, L. (Ed.). (1993). *Professional writing for the human services.* Washington, DC: NASW Press.

Boone, L., Kurtz, D., & Block, J. (1997). *Contemporary business communication* (2nd ed.). Englewood Cliffs, NJ: Prentice Hall.

Dumaine, D. (1989). *Write to the top: Writing for corporate success.* New York: Random House.

Elbow, P. (1981). *Writing with power: Techniques for mastering the writing process.* New York: Oxford University Press.

Ettinger, B. (1997). *Communication for the workplace: An integrated language approach.* Englewood Cliffs, NJ: Prentice Hall.

Fowler, H., & Aaron, J. (1989). *The Little Brown handbook* (6th ed.). New York: HarperCollins.

Fruehling, R., & Oldham, N. B. (1988). *Write to the point!: Letters, memos, and reports that get results.* New York: McGraw-Hill.

Goodman, M. (1984). *Write to the point: Effective communications in the workplace.* Englewood Cliffs, NJ: Prentice Hall.

Hill-Miller, K. (1983). *The most common errors in English usage and how to avoid them.* New York: Arco.

Kaye, S. (1989). *Writing under pressure: The quick writing process.* New York: Oxford University Press.

Kilpatrick, J. (1984). *The writer's art.* Kansas City, MO: Andrews & McMeel.

Mack, K., & Skjei, E. (1979). *Overcoming writing blocks.* Los Angeles: J. P. Tarcher.

Munter, M. (1997). *Guide to managerial communication: Effective business writing and speaking* (4th ed). Englewood Cliffs, NJ: Prentice Hall.

Schertzer, M. (1986). *The elements of grammar.* New York: Collier Books.

Shaw, H. (1993). *Spell it right* (4th ed.). New York: Harper Perennial.

Sorenson, R., Kennedy, G., & Ramirez, I. (1997). *Business and management communications: A guide book* (3rd ed., rev.). Englewood Cliffs, NJ: Prentice Hall.

Stott, B. (1991). *Write to the point, and feel better about your writing.* New York: Columbia University Press.

Strunk, W., Jr., & White, E. B. (1979). *The elements of style* (3rd ed.). New York: Macmillan.

Venolia, J. (1987). *Rewrite right: How to revise your way to better writing.* Berkeley, CA: Ten Speed Press.

Williams, J. (1997). *Style: Ten lessons in clarity and grace.* New York: Longman.

Zinsser, W. (1989). *Writing to learn: How to write—and think clearly—about any subject at all.* New York: Harper & Row.

Zinsser, W. (1994). *On writing well: An informal guide to writing nonfiction* (5th ed.). New York: Harper Perennial.

CHAPTER 16

Assessing, Planning, and Managing Information Technology

Laura I. Zimmerman and Andrew Broughton

As a nonprofit manager, you work in a difficult environment in which you simultaneously are pulled in many different directions (see chapter 1). Pressures on you often include shrinking resources, growing service responsibilities, and increasing demands for accountability. In response to this set of circumstances, many organizations have increased their use of automation and technology. Unfortunately, technology has been changing at an increasingly fast pace, which causes many problems for nonprofit organizations. As Heath (1991) pointed out, "Information technologies are changing the way people communicate with each other, where they work, how they earn a living, and how they entertain themselves" (p. 238).

To say that several significant developments have taken place over the past 40 years in terms of the availability and uses of computers and information technology in nonprofit organizations is a gross understatement. Initially, as mainframe computers became more generally available, many larger nonprofit organizations began to make use of them for such administrative tasks as payroll and accounting. Next, as personal computers (PCs) became more widely available, they began to be used to fill in the gaps in mainframe applications and for such office tasks as word processing. (All computer terms are defined in the glossary at the end of this chapter.) Subsequently, local area networks (LANs) began to be used to connect computers together. With LANs people could easily work together on the same tasks and share equipment, such as printers, and software. Currently, nonprofit managers and organizations are confronted with challenges and opportunities presented by the growing presence of the Internet and the World Wide Web (WWW).

Throughout this period, nonprofit managers have had to make many decisions. In the area of technology alone, managers have had to find ways to fund it, manage it, anticipate changes caused by it and, often most daunting, try to anticipate the direction of the next technological advance. This environment required managers to make many difficult choices.

In this chapter, we review some of the most recent advances in computer technology, focusing on networks and the Internet. These developments are likely to have a profound effect on how nonprofit organizations function and how their staff and clients or patrons interact. In addition, we discuss specific management steps you may take in planning for technology in your organization.

CHANGES IN TECHNOLOGY

During the 1990s, computers underwent many innovations and improvements. PCs are now more powerful, easier to use, and more interconnected than ever before. They are also less expensive. Word-processing programs now have the capacity to do what desktop-publishing programs could five years earlier. Databases are more powerful, and a computer user with average skills can make good use of them. Electronic spreadsheets make it possible to do more sophisticated analyses, and they have the charting functionality that only a dedicated graphics program had a few years ago.

Even with these improvements, many of the new versions of software do not require more powerful hardware to be effective. A Pentium-level computer should handle the work that is needed in most nonprofit organizations for the next few years. This section lays out some basic computing needs and changes with which you should be familiar in order to make good use of technology.

Hardware

Recent changes in hardware now allow you to process information faster, view an increased amount of information more clearly on your screen, and make use of new ways to enter information into the computer. All of these functions require changes in the hardware; some also require software additions and changes. We begin our discussion with what are currently considered standards for hardware and then consider some of the changes that are on the horizon.

The central processing unit (CPU) of the computer is the "box" that comes with the monitor and keyboard. This box usually includes a motherboard and random access memory (RAM), hard and floppy-disk drives, compact disks–read only memory (CD-ROMs) for storage, and a power supply with fan. Most computers now require these features. Additional accessories also can be obtained, such as a sound card for speakers and microphones or a network interface card (to connect the computer to a network); a modem (to dial up another computer); or a Zip drive (to increase storage capacity or to move large amounts of data). Such characteristics as speed, hard–disk size, and RAM have changed the most over time. A typical computer today has a 200-megahertz Pentium processor, 16 or more megabytes of RAM, and a 2-gigabyte or larger hard disk.

Monitors have grown in size and capacity as well. Standard monitors have 17-inch screens and at least Super VGA capability. This means they can display more information or display it in a larger format (which is less stressful for the eyes). When set up correctly, the newer monitors are easier on the eyes for those who have to view them all day or for extended periods of time.

Keyboards have undergone few technical changes. A number of companies have changed the size of the keyboard for ergonomic reasons or to fit laptop limitations. The mouse is often incorporated onto the keyboard, especially in laptops. Two main types of mouse are common: One type uses the thumb to move the mouse, and the other uses the pointer in the middle of the keyboard, with the buttons controlled by the thumb. The second type allows the user to keep the hands in place on the keyboard while using the mouse and is very efficient and practical. Some of the newer mice also have a third button or a scroll wheel, although this usually requires special software.

Software

Although hardware is important, it is probably more important to be aware of the potential uses of software. The appropriate use of the following software tools will help maintain an efficient and productive organization. The most common way to buy software is through the purchase of office productivity suites that have come to be the preferred mode for marketing this software. These software packages typically include the four basics: databases, word processors, spreadsheets, and presentation software. Today's word-processing software (such as Microsoft Word, WordPro, and WordPerfect) are still useful for writing letters and memos, newsletters, and reports, and they can also produce much more sophisticated products. Spreadsheet software (such as Lotus 1-2-3, Excel, and Quattro Pro) work well for financial tracking, charting numerical data, and performing many basic statistical analyses. Database software (such as Access, Paradox, Foxpro, and dBase) are useful for tracking client and transaction (service) information. Presentation software (such as PowerPoint, Harvard Graphics, and Freelance) can be used to make sophisticated video (and audio) presentations.

Some basic tasks that are performed in nonprofit organizations nearly every day can be done more efficiently using a computer and a good office software package or suite. Word processors can be used to do a mail merge for any type of mass mailing. (A mail merge allows the sender to personalize a single letter sent to a number of people.) Setting up a mail merge involves writing the letter and setting up another file that contains each individual's unique information, such as mailing address and preferred form of salutation. This process has many advantages both for your organization and the clients or patrons who receive your letters. Using the mail merge capability can save significant time for your organization (depending, of course, on the number of mailings performed). This may also save wear and tear on your copy machines.

Modern word-processing software can also produce sophisticated newsletters. Most allow the inclusion of digitized images to make the newsletter more attractive. The most difficult part of producing your organization's newsletter may be getting the articles written, not putting it together. When the articles are keyed in and edited, basic formatting takes just a little time. Of course, newsletters that are laden with graphics take longer to produce. Some software also can put a newsletter into hypertext markup language (HTML), which is the format for the Web on the Internet, thus making it much easier to publish your newsletter on the Internet.

Many nonprofit managers give presentations or provide training to various groups. Often the presentations are for funders or funding prospects. Presentation software has many advantages for this purpose. Some software provides preset presentations, ordering overheads for you. As the user, you have only to tailor the overheads for your particular topic. For instance, PowerPoint has an autocontent wizard that asks what type of presentation you are making and gives you an attractive background for each slide and a standard outline from which to work. Attractive overheads can be made in little time with a color printer. With a liquid crystal display (LCD) panel or projector, the presentation can be displayed directly from the computer (allowing last-minute changes if necessary).

Budgeting is much more efficiently done with the help of a computer and a spreadsheet program. You can use this type of software for simple or complex budgeting processes. Some software packages allow you to explore the ramifications of different scenarios with regard to income and expenses. Many nonprofit organizations use spreadsheet applications to track simple data on clients, patrons, or consumers. Spreadsheets also provide an excellent vehicle for the graphic display of data. Chart wizards enable you to display data visually for reports and presentations. Some spreadsheet packages can be used to perform sophisticated statistical analyses.

Perhaps the most sweeping change in information technology has come about in the area of communication. Initially, LANs connected computers within offices. Then the networks were connected to each other sometimes to form intranets that are all connected within a single organization. Finally, these became connected to the Internet, that network of networks, which connects computers around the world. This makes the communication possibilities almost limitless.

Whereas the most popular function performed on a PC used to be word processing, now it is electronic mail (e-mail). Through the use of this application, you can communicate with other managers, staff, clients or patrons, board members, funders, or other stakeholders. You can send and receive many kinds of files as attachments to your mail. However, e-mail is not plausible or possible in an organizational setting unless PCs are interconnected.

Groupware

Groupware is a fairly new software category made possible by the increasing use of LANs. LANs make it possible for computers to be interconnected and to share resources within an office or organizational environment. As a result of these networks, office groups can use software that allows them to share files. Such software includes group scheduling packages (such as Schedule+ and Ontime) and workflow applications (such as Lotus Notes). E-mail and personal information managers (PIMs, such as Groupwise and Outlook) are usually included in this category.

This class of software, used in a LAN environment, allows information to be shared, processed, and communicated to a whole organization instead of a single individual. These software applications are used interactively by all computer users in the organization. Although potentially extremely useful to your organization, these packages require more time to manage the network and the software on the network. Thus, resources need to be allocated to provide the necessary staffing, and time needs to be allowed for this administration so all users can take advantage of the tools and work more efficiently. Consequently, although this type of software can be very useful, not all nonprofit organizations may be able to use it.

Group scheduling has many advantages over individual calendars, especially for managers. While we were writing this chapter, people called to make appointments with us. Our secretary (or anyone else in our office) can schedule an appointment for either of us through any computer. When we go to our computerized calendars, each of us is notified about these new appointments. We can accept or reject the appointment. If one of us needs to schedule a meeting with a few people, we can set the time, and the scheduling software tells us whether it conflicts with other people's schedules. If it does, we can either schedule the appointment anyway or change to another time. It is possible to add the meeting to a number of calendars at one time instead of going to each individual's calendar separately.

Groupware packages may include scheduling, mail, and contact management all in one package. This can work well for an organization that has a LAN. Some packages can synchronize the calendar on a desktop computer with that kept on a portable PIM (Pilot or Newton) or a laptop with its own scheduling software. This corrects an earlier problem in which people frequently did not have their schedules with them because they were away from their desktop computers.

Networks and the Internet

Perhaps the most profound change in computer technology in recent years is in the ability to interconnect them. Today, the majority of PCs sold for office use come with network interface cards already installed. When these computers are placed in an office, they can be immediately connected to the building network. This permits the sharing of files and peripheral devices such as printers and also makes possible the use of groupware software. People can now consult others' schedules and work on shared reports without leaving their desks. As networks and Internet connections become more widespread, groupware using the WWW is also becoming readily available. If you use this kind of software, you can use an Internet connection to check your e-mail or your schedule no matter where you are.

This is possible because more and more networks are in turn connected to that international network of networks, the Internet. The Internet connection is important for a number of reasons. First, it makes statewide, nationwide, and even international communication possible. Second, it makes getting and giving information, be it numeric data, case information, or policies and procedures, a simple task. Organization members can seek and send information almost anywhere in the world, and they can see their own information from anywhere in the world.

In a relatively short period of time, vital statistics, program participation information, and even images of documents and pictures are readily available to qualified users over the Internet. In about the same amount of time, sound and video are easily transmitted on the Internet. This makes many kinds of training, client service, and meetings possible at a worker's desktop (Holden, Rosenberg, & Weissman, 1996).

Connections to the Internet also make it possible for workers to share expertise and questions with their peers or even with a distant expert. A popular method for achieving this is to set up a listserv or discussion forum. Through the use of a listserv, people with e-mail can hold an "electronic discussion" about a topic of common interest to them. Thus, a group of people might start a listserv on a topic such as family protective services or funding possibilities for arts programs. People can write e-mail messages about problems and solutions in this area, and everyone on the list would receive each e-mail message. With discussion forums, the conversations can be stored and read on a Web page or an electronic bulletin board at anytime. Each member of the listserv can read and respond to the posting. Either can be an effective vehicle for organizations in rural or geographically isolated areas.

With the advent of video and sound on the Internet, many other uses for an Internet connection are possible. Staff training can be performed using the Internet as the transmission medium. "Phone calls" can be made over the Internet to coworkers or outside experts. Clients can be interviewed at a distance. Paper-and-pencil diagnostic measures can be administered and scored immediately over the Internet. In short, the Internet offers many new opportunities.

How do these changes affect organizations? How can we plan for these changes? How can we be sure to have the money to keep the technology at the most beneficial level possible for our organizations? As a manager, you must have an understanding of these new technologies and be able to assess their viability for your particular organization. Among the things you must consider are the extent to which new technologies result in increased worker efficiency and organizational effectiveness. How do we educate ourselves and our staff for these changes while maintaining workflow? What barriers exist that limit technology in our organizations? The mid-1990s have been financially challenging both for nonprofit and public or governmental organizations and agencies. The need for greater program efficiencies has required many leaders to plunge into technology. The second part of this chapter presents an approach to doing this.

MANAGING TECHNOLOGY

You need to consider six basic components to planning and managing technology. First, assess the current state-of-technology in your organization. A strategic planning process to define goals and to gain a technological vision should follow this. The third and fourth components are personnel and training, which are often overlooked by managers when implementing technology. The fifth component is the place of hardware and software in your technology plan. The last component entails the budgeting strategies and changes to support the technology.

Assessment

To prepare to make some strategic decisions about information technology, you must first assess your organization's current situation in terms of technology. Depending on your organization's goals and objectives, the assessment can take many forms and can be basic or comprehensive. Minimally, the assessment should include an evaluation (inventory) of the current hardware and software in your organization. A machine description should include dimensions of hardware components (such as storage capacity, amount of RAM memory, CPU speed, number of accessory cards in each, the presence of a mouse) and the installed software components with their respective versions (such as DOS 6.0 or Windows 6.0).

Another important part of the assessment phase is to define goals for automation. Goals can be developed for different levels of the organization, and this should be done with input from all levels. Typically, the executive director's goals include a vision of technology for the organization. Direct service providers and supervisors typically focus more on computer tools and training to improve their skills. Both sets of technological needs are important and must be balanced by budget constraints and the efficient use of resources.

A comprehensive assessment should measure the computer skills of employees in relation to the goals of the organization. This information can also be used to determine training needs. For example, a comprehensive assessment of health worker's computer skills (Zimmerman & Broughton, 1996b) helped in the development of a computer training curriculum for the State of North Carolina (Zimmerman & Broughton, 1996a). This assessment found that three levels of training were needed: basic skills, a core curriculum, and advanced skills. Not all employees needed advanced-skills training, and many had already completed basic skills. The core skills included computer skills that all employees needed to perform their jobs.

Strategic Plan

Too often, nonprofit organizations introduce computer technology in an unplanned, haphazard, incremental manner. This can be costly in the long run. Instead, it is advisable to take some time to engage in a strategic planning effort that relates to the organization's technology needs. When this is done, the strategic plan guides the implementation of technology in the organization and should be based on the goals of the organization, the results of the technology skills assessment, and the current technological environment. The technology strategic plan should be reviewed at least yearly and adjusted for changes in technology and business practices. The following sections are designed to help you consider important issues in order to implement better computer technology, including such items as personnel, computing inventories, training, and the budget.

Personnel

Technology support personnel are probably the most important commodity necessary for increasing the use of computer technology in an organization. A single computer used by one person may never need much technical support. As more computers are introduced into an organization, the need for support increases, not so much for the computers as for the computer users. Initially, a more sophisticated computer user in an organization may provide the support for technology. However, with the addition of more computers and users, this role can become a job in itself. The number of people needed to support computers and users depends on the size of the organization, its goals, the software on the computers, and the computer skills of the staff.

When planning for a LAN, you should consider budgeting for at least one staff person to support the network. Whether this responsibility can be handled on a part- or full-time basis depends on a number of factors, including the size of your organization and the magnitude of your planned network. If a vendor installs the LAN for only a few computers, a savvy computer user on your staff may be able to support it, whereas a larger network requires more staff time and more specialized knowledge and skills. As a rule, you can generally figure that at least a half-time position, or one-half the workload of a full-time staff person, should be considered for every 10 to 15 computers in a LAN environment.

The staff person who provides your technological support should have some experience with the type of network installed in your organization and most of the software applications used by your staff. For a smaller group, a generalist who knows something about application software and networks is generally the best choice for this type of position. For larger organizations, where two support people are needed, one should administer the network while the other handles the application software. Both should share information for emergency coverage.

Ideally, your network administrator has prior experience working with the type of network installed in your organization. Although many formal training and certification programs are available, experience is the most important qualification. If the person is not certified (and in most cases nonprofit organizations cannot afford certified network engineers), funds should be put aside for training and outside support for emergencies. Such support can be telephone support, dial-in support, or onsite support. Of these, telephone support is usually the least expensive.

Your support person for applications should know how to use different software applications, assess the work that needs to be done, and recommend appropriate software. This person should know database and spreadsheet programming and other applications used by your organization. If this person does not know how to program, he or she should obtain some formal training at a local community college or other training facility.

Training

Training is an important component that is often overlooked or intentionally excluded in the development of an organizational plan for technology. This may be in part a result of the expense of training staff and the time it takes for them to develop computer skills. We have also found on a number of occasions that without training, the costs of doing work the less efficient, less productive way can be just as high or higher than the cost of training. However, some steps can be taken to reduce the cost of training without reducing the benefits. In our experience, people can learn only so much in a session. We find that short, hands–on experiences are more fruitful than all-day intensive cram sessions. We also find that most people learn best in small classrooms with each learner at a computer. An isolated environment allows close interaction among the learner or trainee, the computer, and the instructor with minimal disturbances. Time for practice is also needed. Because most computer skills are best acquired through hands-on computer training, we recommend the following:

- *Train in small groups.* Hands-on computer training needs to be more intensive than most other types of training. In general, the lower the trainee-to-instructor ratio, the more effective the training.
- *Train for short periods of time.* Usually a two- to four-hour training session with a break gives users time to learn and practice new skills without being overloaded with information.
- *Make sure workers have access to computers and software at their work site before training.* Training should not occur until workers have ready access to computers (preferably on their desks). If employees cannot immediately use what they have learned during a training session, the usefulness of the training may be lost.
- *Make sure workers train on the same software they have on their work computers.* Training workers on the software they use at their office is optimal. This includes training on the same version of the software. It is often difficult to learn how to use software in training that does not apply directly to the work environment.
- *Do not interrupt training with other work.* The training environment should be away from a worker's desk, where the worker is not distracted by other problems and concerns. The best training environment is away from a person's office, and an off-site location is often preferable.
- *Have workers take classes appropriate for their level of competence.* Beginning users are lost in an advanced class. It is better to have workers begin with introductory classes and review techniques rather than have them enter a class that is beyond their current skill level. Often, even in basic classes, the workers with slightly more advanced skills can learn a new or different way to use the software.
- *Give new computer users time to practice their new skills.* New computer skills take time to master. Becoming comfortable using the mouse may take some practice. Workers must also apply their new skills in practical situations

before they completely commit them to memory. At first, using the computer may take longer than processing items by hand, but with practice, users pick up skill and speed, and the automated system eventually becomes a time-saver. Workers need time to process, practice, and implement what they have learned outside the training environment.

- *Use the buddy system for training.* Workers who learn together often help each other outside the training environment. Sometimes two workers pick up two different pieces of information in training that can be shared while they are practicing in the office later.

Having an onsite expert in the organization has some benefits. One method of training that managers may find helpful is to send one person to intensive training and then have that person train or help the less skilled computer users. Another strategy is to send a few people for basic training and then send individuals from this group to more advanced or concentrated training programs that focus on different areas (such as one to word-processing training and another to spreadsheet training). These individuals can then train their colleagues.

Computing

Software and hardware make the computer usable. Hardware includes the things you touch and see: the monitor, keyboard, mouse, and CPU. Software is the "stuff" that makes the computer perform. It is important to understand the difference and the need for both parts. Many managers make the mistake of allocating money for computers without also allocating money for software and training. As a result, many organizations make little use of these brand new pieces of equipment, which tend to become expensive paperweights. It is better for your organization to have fewer computers, with more software and training, than more computers that are not being used efficiently.

When purchasing computers, select a brand and model that can run all the software your staff need to use. Ideally, a computer with power (high CPU speed, large RAM) is able to handle future changes in software and should be useful for a long time. It is important for decisions about purchasing computers to be made on the basis of a fair amount of research. Compare features and prices. The best computer for your organization may not necessarily be the least expensive you can buy, but it may not be the most expensive either.

Budget

Support personnel, hardware, software, and training all require resources. Budgeting for technology resources can be as difficult as learning some of the technical jargon associated with the technology. In most nonprofit organizations, lump-sum budgeting tends to be the norm for computer technology. Lump-sum budgeting is useful to initiate the purchase of computers, software, and training, but it does not help cover the required year-to-year personnel, maintenance, and upgrades for the information technology used in the organization. One organization with which we are familiar obtained a $36,000 grant "for technology." The organization's managers wanted to purchase 12 computers (for $3,000 each). If they had followed this initial plan, they likely would have had 12 expensive paperweights taking up valuable space on small desktops. However, after further discussion with technology support personnel and some careful planning, the organization purchased a LAN and connected five computers to it, purchased some software for the workers and a database system for collecting client data, trained a staff member to become the LAN administrator, and trained workers to use the software. In the final plan for the original $36,000 grant, half of the budget went to purchase computers, a portion to software, and a portion to training personnel. Seven years later, this organization, with over 150 staff, is almost fully automated.

An efficient approach to budgeting for a technology project involves allocating funds among four major categories: software, support personnel, hardware, and training. Your first budget item (which is usually left for last) should be software which, although it may not be your most expensive budget item, is nonetheless the most important. Your software determines what you can do. As part of your strategic plan for technology, you should have defined your goals (such as what you want to do as an organization), so the initial phase of your budget planning should consider those goals. Estimate the cost of the software that best allows your organization to perform the functions you need it to perform. Look for a combination of software, such as an office suite, that is easy to learn and provides these functions. Then take steps to standardize this software application throughout your organization. Otherwise you may have different individuals and staff groups using different word-processing programs or spreadsheet packages, and this greatly complicates your network administration and technical support needs. By standardizing, you create a simpler work environment that is much more cost efficient and effective.

Most software companies give discounts for multiple copies of software (site licenses), so you must also consider in your budget projections whether to secure a license per computer or simultaneous usage licenses, if the latter are available. Simultaneous usage licenses allow you to purchase only the number of licenses you need for the number of people who are using the application at any one time (on a network). Therefore, if you have a large organization, but only three people use a software package at any one time, you need only three licenses even if more people use the software at different times. For very large organizations, some software companies sell site licenses that further reduce the price of software.

The second item to include in your budget plan is technology support personnel. Computers are intricate tools. Just as pencils need sharpening, computers need care and maintenance. When something goes wrong with a computer, it takes time for technology support personnel to figure out what is wrong and whether they can repair it or if they need to send the computer out for repair. The less knowledge your computer users have about their computers, the more technology support personnel time is needed per machine and user. In smaller organizations, technology support personnel often emerge from within the organization, often with little or no time dedicated to these tasks.

The more computers, linkages, software, and so on that your organization has, the more personnel time you need to dedicate to the tasks of supporting computer users and their machines. Generally, you should consider at least one full-time technology support staff person for about every 30 to 40 machines and users in your organization. The primary role of this staff person should be the support, maintenance, and upgrading of the machines, the software, and the LAN. If computer programming is needed, this should be considered a separate task from that of supporting the computer users. Often database development is needed for specialized applications. Do not assume that a person trained in database programming can also support users and the LAN on anything but the database software program itself.

The third component of your technology budget plan is hardware. Computer hardware and software (and related technology) change rapidly. Ideally, your computers have an effective life of at least three years, but some may need to be replaced more frequently, depending on particular software applications. Thus, hardware purchases need to be made with thought about the software to be used, their capacity, the likelihood that the machines can be used for several years, the hardware standards for your organization, and what comes with the hardware. It is a good idea to develop hardware standards, just as it is important to have software standards. As new, more powerful computers come out, you can continue to buy the same type or, in some instances, the same brand of machine, making sure the new machines are fully compatible with your existing hardware and software. This helps you maintain your software licenses with little or no extra cost for software. Depending on which users need new machines, you may circulate the used machines to staff for whom these machines represent an upgrade.

Of course, your budget ultimately defines the types and numbers of machines that you purchase. You may find that you can save money by purchasing equipment through mail-order rather than from local vendors. Nonetheless, it is important to try to adhere to your hardware and software standards as much as possible. This minimizes personnel support time for different machines and older machine upgrades. It also makes it easier to use old parts to keep your older machines running and upgraded.

Some drawbacks to the mail-order approach are worth noting. An organization just beginning to become involved with information technology may need to work with a local vendor to obtain onsite support or technical assistance. Another drawback is that new computers come with newer versions of software. It can be very difficult, if not impossible, for your organization to keep one version of software on multiple machines, let alone have everyone learn every new version. Your choice, then, is between spending more time setting up new computers using a single, older version of software or requiring all of your support personnel to know each new version and the various combinations. Some prefer the latter approach because of the useful tools in newer versions of software, but it is not for the faint of heart.

The fourth budget category is personnel training. Training should be viewed as an ongoing event to accommodate organizational changes. For example, if your organization is planning for a LAN or already has one, the people supporting this LAN need to keep up with the latest changes to the network software. End-users, that is, those personnel who use the computers on their desks, only help the organization by expanding their knowledge of desktop software. Turnover also affects your organization's training needs, because employees often need training on the standard software used in your organization.

Staff training is often more important for nonprofit organizations than for other types of organizations because many nonprofits, particularly smaller ones, cannot afford to pay the salaries of network administrators. In rural, isolated areas, this can be a particular problem. It may be far less costly to train one of your existing staff members who is an astute computer user and who is committed to your organization and geographical area than it is to try to hire someone with the necessary skills. Therefore, where possible, you should consider training one of your own employees to become your network administrator. This approach has worked successfully in a number of organizations, especially smaller nonprofits in rural areas. A great deal of network support can occur through telephone consultation once your network support staff has had some training. For midsize and larger organizations, having two people trained in this capacity is helpful.

Maintaining and Upgrading the Technology

Whether your technology infrastructure is started through donated computers, computers purchased for your organization for a specific task, or large donations of money for this purpose, the technology you obtain eventually becomes old and unreliable. A good computer should be expected to last at least three years; some last longer. Many companies now provide two- or three-year warranties on their computers. Issues of warranty and service availability should be considered when you plan to purchase new computers or upgrade existing ones. With present-day computers, it is generally not necessary to purchase maintenance agreements. Almost all hardware problems occur during the warranty period; most of the problems tend to be related to software, not to the machines. Upgrading software, installing new software on the computer, and turning off the computer without correctly closing programs tend to be the major causes of problems. Your support personnel should be able to help when these problems occur. Training end-users also helps reduce these problems.

When you start building your computer infrastructure, two areas require attention. One is continuing to build and upgrade the infrastructure; the other is maintaining the current level. Both need to be considered but often pose some difficulties for nonprofit managers. A three- or four-year maintenance budget is necessary to maintain a base level of service. If old equipment is replaced with brand new equipment, then a software upgrade for office productivity software should be included.

Finally, you must decide how much of your total budget should focus on information technology. This is up to you as a manager and should be related to the three-year replacement cycle. Many for-profit companies that use high levels of technology spend up to 10 percent of their annual budgets on information technology; nonprofit organizations tend to average less than 5 percent. As a rule, if you want a technology infrastructure that works for you, aim for the 5 percent level.

CONCLUSION

Technology changes at an increasingly rapid rate. Among the roles that managers must perform are those of monitor and coordinator. Clearly, modern computing and information technology provide managers with tools that can greatly aid them in performing these roles. At the same time, managers must engage in thoughtful planning; acquire resources necessary to accomplish their organizations' missions; and ensure that they have an adequately trained, competent workforce. Thus, as pointed out in chapter 1, managers must function in an atmosphere of competing values, which often requires that managers make some hard choices.

To use technology effectively, managers must engage in careful assessment, planning, budgeting, and managerial oversight. Sufficient resources must be allocated for hardware, software, training, and technical support. When these resources are made available, nonprofit organizations and managers can realize the benefits of technology.

GLOSSARY

Browser
: Software used to "surf" the Internet and the World Wide Web. Provides a common interface for users across many computers. The two most popular browsers are Internet Explorer and Netscape Navigator.

CD-ROM
: Compact Disk–Read Only Memory; used to store large programs and great amounts of data.

CPU
: Central processing unit (the "computer" part of the computer); the chip where the computations are done.

Database
: Software used to store, sort, select, and track information of all kinds. These applications are often used to track and report data on clients. Some of the more popular PC-based databases include Access, Paradox, Foxpro, and dBase.

Desktop publishing
: Software used to prepare publications from brochures to books. Some of the more popular PC-based desktop-publishing software includes Pagemaker and Quark XPress.

Discussion forum
: Software that allows people to communicate about a topic. People must post messages to the discussion forum. The software documents the discussion, and participants can interact with any posting.

E-mail
: Electronic mail; allows computer users to send, receive, and store messages.

HTML
: Hypertext markup language; used to present information of all kinds on the World Wide Web.

Internet
: Millions of computers around the world linked together through the use of the Internet Protocol (IP) for communication. Each computer on the Internet must have an IP address to communicate with other computers on the Internet.

Intranet
: An internal Internet system that is limited to the confines of a single organization.

LAN
: Local area network; computers in the same locale linked together for communications and sharing of software and hardware.

LCD
: Liquid crystal display; a method for displaying computer images used mostly in laptops and for projectors.

Listserv
: A computer program that manages e-mail communications to a list of e-mail recipients. By sending a single message to the list address, each member of the list receives the message.

Mainframe
: Large computer usually shared by many users running different programs. Mainframe computers are more massive than PC com-

	puters. The PC computers today are more powerful than many older mainframes.
Modem	Modulator–demodulator; allows computers to communicate over telephone lines. A computer connects to a modem that dials another modem connected to another computer, allowing the two computers to communicate with each other. Software is needed to allow the computers to communicate with the modem.
PC	Personal computer.
PIM	Personal information manager; software that helps organize schedules, telephone numbers, and personal contact information. Some popular PIMs are Outlook, Organizer, Sidekick, and Up-to-Date. Some software can be used in a handheld device to synchronize with information on your computer (such as Newton and Pilot).
RAM	Random access memory; memory used by the computer chip while doing computations. This memory is used only when the computer is turned on. Any information in RAM is deleted when the computer is turned off.
Spreadsheet	Electronic version of an accountant's pad of columns and rows that may contain text, formulas, or numbers. Many software packages allow the user to make charts from data.
Super VGA	Super Video Graphics Array; a video display standard for color monitors.
WWW	World Wide Web; a method for organizing information of all kinds located on the Internet.
Zip drive	A drive that holds a removable disk that can store up to 100 megabytes of data.

SKILLS-APPLICATION EXERCISES

- Obtain a budget for a nonprofit organization and determine the percentage of the total budget that the organization currently expends on information technology.

- Draft a proposal for developing a strategic information technology plan for your organization or another with which you are familiar. Indicate what issues are addressed in the strategic planning effort, who is involved, and how the process must proceed.

- Assess the current state of information technology in your organization or another with which you are familiar, then develop a proposed three-year budget for upgrading computers and computing skills.

REFERENCES

Heath, P. P. (1991). Managing information technology. In R. L. Edwards & J. A. Yankey (Eds.), *Skills for effective human services management* (pp. 238–250). Washington, DC: NASW Press.

Holden, G., Rosenberg, G., & Weissman, A. (1996). World Wide Web accessible resources related to research on social work practice. *Research on Social Work Practice, 6,* 236–262.

Zimmerman, L. I., & Broughton, A. (1996a). *Education plan for local health workers in North Carolina.* Chapel Hill: University of North Carolina, Human Services Smart Agency.

Zimmerman, L. I., & Broughton, A. (1996b). *A survey of staff computer knowledge in local health departments.* Chapel Hill: University of North Carolina, Human Services Smart Agency.

CHAPTER 17

Understanding Nonprofit Financial Management

James L. Strachan

V isualize yourself in a country in which you know neither the language nor the culture. Can you sense how unsettling an experience this would be? Your insecurity and discomfort will not begin to subside unless you take the steps necessary to learn the language and to become familiar with the culture. The same holds true for understanding the realm of nonprofit accounting and financial management. After the initial steps are taken, you are in a position to become much more comfortable with and knowledgeable about accounting and financial topics. By learning the definitions and context of a few terms, you become a much more comfortable participant in the financial process.

This chapter introduces you to accounting and financial management with a particular view to and emphasis on understanding words, concepts, and analysis rather than on learning how to "do accounting" or to prepare reports. The material is intended to be general, useful information to help improve your understanding of the world of financial management in a nonprofit context. The definitions provided are intended to be easily and intuitively understood rather than being entirely, technically correct. Nevertheless, these definitions can be applicable in and helpful to you in many situations.

FINANCIAL STATEMENTS AS COORDINATING TOOLS

Financial statements are used for the differing purposes of reporting how the agency's financial resources were used in the past and how executive management plans to use those resources in the future. When financial statements chronicle and report past actions and accomplishments, they fill the monitoring role inherent in the provision of coordinating skills (see chapter 1). Alternatively, when these same statements are prepared in budgetary form and capture the plans and expectations of the board of directors and executive management for the coming fiscal period, they provide coordinating skills in the form of a coordinating document. The requisite monitoring and coordination converge when actual results are compared to planned results, which comparison requires that historical and budgeted financial statements are prepared in the same format and have the same content.

FINANCIAL REPORTS—
THE FOUNDATION OF FINANCIAL MANAGEMENT

Financial reporting for and management of nonprofit organizations generally centers around three statements—the Statement of Support, Revenues, and Expenses (commonly referred to as the "operating statement"); the Statement of Financial Position (more commonly called the "balance sheet"); and the Statement of Cash, a historical representation of the general movement of cash into and out of the organization. The first two reports, the operating statement and the balance sheet, are examined in detail.

Operating Statement

The objective of the operating statement is to report, in monetary terms, how the organization's resources were used during the time period reported (usually one year). It does so by including the following components: operating revenue, support, expenses, surplus–deficit, gains–losses, and changes in net assets. These components are defined below.

- *Operating Revenue.* Resources generated by the organization through the provision of services or the sale of products.
- *Support.* Resources generated by the organization through public sources for reasons other than the sale of products or the provision of services (such as donations, grants, government and third-party contracts, support provided by outside funding sources such as the United Way and Community Shares, and bequests).
- *Expenses.* Resources consumed by the organization as it conducts its business activities of providing services or selling products.
- *Surplus–Deficit.* The term "surplus" or "excess" is used in situations where the total sources of support and revenue exceed the total expenses. In contrast, the term "deficit" or "deficiency" is used when total expenses exceed total sources of support and revenue.
- *Gains–Losses.* These terms are used to report the results of transactions that are not part of or are incidental to the organization's normal operations of providing services or selling products but that nevertheless affect the

organization's resources. Selling unneeded office equipment is one example. Selling stock purchased as part of the investment activities of an organization is another. If the item is sold for more than the dollar amount carried for that item in the financial records, then only the difference between the two amounts is reported and is reported as a gain. If the item is sold for less than the amount carried in the records, then the difference is reported as a loss. When the sale has been completed, the gain or loss is classified as a realized gain or loss. A difference between the amount carried in the records for stock investments, such as a share of stock being carried at $40 ($60) and its market price being reported in *The Wall Street Journal* at $50 ($35), is reported as an unrealized gain ($10) or an unrealized loss ($25).

- *Changes in Net Assets.* This is the preferred title for the dollar amount that arises when the total of all expenses and losses is subtracted from the total of all sources of support, revenue, gains, and interfund transfers reported for the organization's fiscal period. This amount is also frequently and informally referred to as the "bottom line," "surplus," or "deficiency."

A summary of these statement segments is as follows:

Sources of Support	$100
Sources of Revenue	50
Total Sources of Support and Revenue	150
Minus Expenses	130
Equals Net Operating Excess (or Deficiency)	20
Plus Nonoperating Gains	0
Minus Nonoperating Losses	0
Equals Change in Net Assets (current term)	20
(Surplus or excess if total sources exceed expenses; deficit if expenses exceed total sources)	

In the above example, $150 in resources were generated by the organization, $50 (one-third) of which came from program or activity sources and $100 (two-thirds) of which came from other sources of support such as donations, grants, and third-party contracts. On the minus side, $130 (87 percent) in resources were used up (thus becoming expenses) during the reporting period. The net amount of resources available at the end of the period increased by $20 (13 percent) because more resources were generated than were utilized. If, however, $190 in expenses were incurred, then the resources of the organization would have decreased by $40, and a negative change in net assets (deficit) would have been reported.

The basic terms and concepts just covered will remain unchanged as we proceed. Next, the accountant further defines and distinguishes varying types and sources of resource inflows and resource outflows by placing additional names (adjectives) in front of the basic terms introduced above. What the accountant does is similar to what individuals do when they place additional names in front of a surname to further distinguish themselves from others having that same surname. This expansion and simultaneous segmentation in the operating statement format and structure are now illustrated as the operating statement segments of "unrestricted," "temporarily restricted," and "permanently restricted" are introduced, after which a more inclusive and representational operating statement is presented.

Currently Required Revenue–Expense Classifications

In 1993 the Financial Accounting Standards Board (FASB) issued Statement of Financial Accounting Standards No. 116 entitled *Accounting for Contributions Received and Contributions Made*. Among other things, this position statement specified how pledges made and to be paid over more than one period are to be recorded, the titles to be assigned to categories of revenues frequently received by an organization, and the titles to be assigned to the fund balances arising from those respective revenues. The new types of revenue are called "unrestricted" revenue (replacing the title of "operating"), "temporarily restricted" revenue (adding the term "temporarily" to the previously used "restricted" title), and "permanently restricted" revenue (replacing the more entrenched title of "endowment"). Accordingly, four columns, when applicable, now appear on an organization's Statement of Support, Revenue, and Expenses, with three of the columns reporting the three respective sources and the fourth reporting the total of each statement line.

Accounting guidelines now require that when pledges are made and are to be paid over more than one operating period, the amount of pledges applicable to the current period must be reported in current period's unrestricted revenue. The amount of reliable pledges made for the remaining periods are to be reported as temporarily restricted. The cash received in the current period will increase the balance reported in the cash account, and the amount to be collected in future periods will increase the balance of pledges receivable. For example, assume that a corporation pledged to contribute $300 to the organization over the next three years, giving $100 at that time and committing to pay $100 in the second and the third years. Under the reporting requirements of FASB 116, cash will be increased by $100, the amount of pledges receivable reported will be increased by $200, the amount of unrestricted revenue reported will increase by $100, and the amount reported as temporarily restricted revenue will increase by $200. As a consequence of FASB 116, then, agencies now report an improved financial condition by reporting higher total assets, higher total revenue, and higher fund balances. The operating statement concepts that have been presented are illustrated in Figure 17-1.

Figure 17-1. An Example of a Statement of Support, Revenue, and Expenses

	UNRESTRICTED	TEMPORARILY RESTRICTED	PERMANENTLY RESTRICTED	TOTAL ALL FUNDS
Public Support				
Donations and Bequests	$ 42			
Grants	1			
Government Contracts	8			
Third-Party Contracts	5			
Support—Funding Agencies	19			
Total Public Support	$ 75			
Operating Revenue				
Service Revenue	$ 24			
Miscellaneous Income	3			
Total Operating Revenue	$ 27			
Total Public Support and Operating Revenue	$102			
Operating Expenses (by function or program)				
Salaries and Wages	$ 55			
Employee Benefits	16			
Personnel Development	2			
Repairs and Maintenance	2			
Depreciation Expense	4			
Professional Services	10			
Supplies	3			
Travel	2			
Financial Expenses	5			
Miscellaneous Expenses	1			
Total Expenses	$100			
Operating Excess (Deficiency)	$ 2			
Nonoperating Sources				
Realized Investment Gains (losses)	0			
Unrealized Investment Gains (losses)	0			
Transfers between Funds	0			
Total Nonoperating Sources	0			
Change in Net Assets (Excess or Deficit)	$ 2			

NOTE: Because of space limitations for analytical comments, assumed dollar amounts are intentionally provided in only the unrestricted column.

Revenue and Expense Analysis

Revenue Analysis

Critical to both revenue and expense analysis is the application of percentage analysis and the asking of the "right questions." With respect to percentage analysis, the recommended approach is to divide each revenue source by the total revenue available to the organization for the reporting period. In Figure 17-1, the dollar amounts reported for the respective sources also provide the percentage of the total revenue that that amount represents. Donations and bequests, for example, are reported as $42 which, in turn, represent nearly 42 percent of the $102 reported as total revenue. Figure 17-1 is the basis for asking the following questions.

- What is the distribution of revenue sources relative to the total? Is that distribution satisfactory, or is there a redistribution of sources that would be preferred? In Figure 17-1, a hefty 42 percent of total revenue is generated by donations and bequests, whereas only 5 percent is generated by third-party payers. Do these percentages reflect those desired as specified in the organization's operating budget?
- What amount of revenue is being generated by the client base the organization serves? Does the distribution of fee-paying clients reflect the organization's targeted client base in terms of need and ability to pay? Alternatively, how much revenue is not being collected, and should policies be implemented to reduce that loss? In Figure 17-1 client fees provide 24 percent of the operating revenue. Is this the amount targeted by the organization in the revenue section of its operating budget? A closely related question is whether third-party sources (only 5 percent of the sources) should be targeted to increase the client fee revenue base. Are the percentages of support coming from particular funding sources at desirable levels? Alternatively, is the organization relying too heavily on any particular source of support?
- Are there sources of revenue that are being overlooked? Of equal importance, has the use of grant funding sources, which require the implementation of "new programs" to qualify for continued funding, caused the organization to subtly change its program focus and to move gradually and further away from its mission? In Figure 17-1, grants provide only 1 percent of the organization's funding. This implies that there is no such overreliance and that additional funding through grants could be incorporated into the organization's revenue generation plans.
- How reliable is the revenue base? How much of that base is reliably available, and how much is merely tentatively available (hard versus soft money)? This question cannot be answered from the data given in Figure

17-1 because no information is provided on the characteristics of the sources and the terms established by those sources.

Expense Analysis

Like revenue analysis, basic expense analysis begins with percentage analysis, with each expense item reported in the operating section being divided into one of two reported totals—total operating expenses or total operating revenue. As was the case for the respective revenue percentages, the dollar amounts reported for the expenses also approximate their respective percentages of either total. For example, salaries and wages are reported as being $55 and also as comprising approximately 55 percent of both total revenues and total expenses.

When the relative percentages have been determined, the following questions and issues should be addressed:

- What is the relative distribution of the respective expenses being incurred by the organization?
- Does the distribution of those expenses indicate that the organization's mission and objectives are being served as directed by the board of trustees in the organization's budget?
- What percentage of total employee costs consists of program costs?
- What percentage consists of administrative, general, and other indirect or support costs?
- Is the administration too top heavy, using resources that should be spent on programs and services?

The question of whether the organization is accomplishing its mission and objectives is best addressed by comparing the organization's budgeted amounts against those reported in its historical financial statements. The reason is that the budget is developed and approved under the auspices of the board of trustees and is thus presumed to reflect the board's plan of action, expressed in monetary terms, to achieve the mission and objectives of the organization. Stated another way, the more the actual amounts differ from budgeted amounts, the more executive management is susceptible to scrutiny in terms of whether the organization's mission and goals are being accomplished in the manner and to the extent prescribed by the board.

- What percentage of total expenses is composed of wages, salaries, benefits, and other employee costs? Is this percentage the appropriate percentage? Are the employees being properly compensated? Can the organization support the current levels of pay and benefits? Are the compensation and benefit levels sufficient to retain key personnel and to maintain a positive, constructive work environment?

In Figure 17-1, 55 percent of the total expenses went to salaries and wages, and another 16 percent was incurred for employee benefits such as social security, vacation time, sick leave, and health and other insurance. In total, 71 percent of every dollar spent by the organization went to employee costs, an amount that may not be surprising given that many social services agencies are labor intensive. Only by developing a standard of comparison, such as the amounts specified by the budget or the percentage historically spent in these cost categories, however, can one evaluate whether the amounts spent were too high, too low, or on target. To ensure that another important characteristic is not overlooked, note that the amount spent for employee benefits approximates an additional 29 percent of salary, a percentage that is not uncommon in compensation systems today.

According to Figure 17-1, 10 percent of total costs is paid to outside professionals. Are these costs being incurred for programmatic purposes, such as for licensed social workers who provide counseling during periods of excess demand or outside of business hours? Are the fees being paid for nonprogrammatic personnel? In either case, can the amounts be reduced, or does the amount suggest that it may be time to replace outside expertise by adding one or more trained professionals to the employee base?

- What percentage of organization resources is used to pay interest expense on borrowed funds? Can the organization support its current level of borrowing? Alternatively, is the level of debt too high, thus draining resources from the organization's activities and programs?

The issue here is that dollars spent to cover the interest costs of debt are not available for program needs. Alternatively, the wise use of debt can provide needed funds at an opportune time so that more services than would otherwise be possible can be provided at a particularly critical time. In Figure 17-1, 5 percent of the organization's resources are being used to cover interest costs. Therefore, 5 percent of organization resources are being diverted from program services.

- Are adequate and reasonable repair expenses being reported in the operating statement? The important issue here is to ascertain whether funds are being diverted from making needed repairs to support other cash demands of the organization. Although this may work for a short period of time, over the long run the capital base of the organization will deteriorate.

An example of this problem is found in the recent financial history and status of Central State University located in Wilberforce, Ohio. Central State has been on the verge of bankruptcy for some time and is currently at the mercy of the state government. Among other actions, the university had been diverting cash destined for maintaining university buildings to other operating purposes such that some buildings, particularly dormitories (which are revenue generators, thus exacerbating the problem), had to be closed because they did not meet safety code requirements.

- What is the percentage of costs incurred for fundraising purposes versus the amount of funds raised?

If the organization's reporting system does not directly provide this information, as is the case in Figure 17-1, then the information should be made available in some form. If it is not, and if the matter is deemed important, then it should be requested. Should an organization spend a very high percentage of contributions for fundraising purposes (horror stories of 90 percent and even 100 percent of funds raised being used to cover fundraising costs are, unfortunately, both embarrassing and true), and should that fact become public knowledge, then the fundraising future and the longevity of the organization may be jeopardized.

Balance Sheet

The intent behind the content and format of the balance sheet is to present a picture of where the entity stands with respect to resources and their specific characteristics at a point in time. Three general types of items are reported in a monetary context in this statement: assets, liabilities, and fund balance (now referred to as "net assets").

- *Assets.* Resources that are owned by the organization and that can provide future benefits to the organization.
- *Liabilities.* Debts or obligations for which the organization has assumed the responsibility to repay or to otherwise resolve such as through the provision of services or delivery of products.
- *Net Assets.* Often referred to as "fund balance," the dollar amount derived when total liabilities are subtracted from total assets. An alternative definition is that the balance in Net Assets is the sum of surpluses and deficits that have been reported by the accounting process over the life of the organization.

Although both definitions are technically correct, I believe they are devoid of intuitive meaning. I offer the following definition:

The *operating* (unrestricted) *fund balance* is the amount of services expressed in dollars (as determined by the Generally Accepted Accounting Principles applied by the accountant) that the organization has yet to perform in order to have fulfilled its legal obligations to the Internal Revenue Service (which granted the organization its tax-exempt status), its obligations to the state (which granted corporate status to the organization), and its obligation to the constituency of donors and other sources that provided resources to support the activities of the organization.

To put the three terms into perspective, consider the following example. Assume that you own a house worth $100,000 and that you borrowed $65,000 to purchase it. Now, visualize the way you think about your current status. You own an asset (worth $100,000), you have a debt ($65,000), and you have a residual or equity (ownership) interest in the house in the amount of $35,000 ($100,000 − $65,000 = $35,000). However, no one owns a nonprofit organization. Still, because of the way in which the accountant has definitionally specified the accounting structure, that is, Assets = Liabilities (Debts) + Ownership ($100,000 = $65,000 + $35,000), a substitute for the equity or ownership segment must be made for the accounting system to work. The accountant accomplishes this by interjecting the concept of "net assets" or "fund balance" into the accounting structure: Assets ($100,000) − Debts (Liabilities) = Fund Balance (or Net Assets). For example, assume that a nonprofit organization owns this same structure as a group home. A simplified report format of that organization's balance sheet at the time of purchase is as follows:

Assets	$100,000	Mortgage Debt	$ 65,000
		Fund Balance	$ 35,000
		Total Debt and Fund Balance	$100,000

One requirement for developing a reference base for understanding, overseeing, and evaluating the financial health of an organization, then, begins with an understanding of the three terms—assets, liabilities, and fund balance. Once the contexts of these three account types are intuitively understood, the next step is to become comfortable with their further segmentation within the format of the balance sheet (see Figure 17-2), which reflects the order in which major topics are addressed.

Cash and Near Cash

A single dollar amount for the amount of cash (checking accounts) and near cash investments (cash equivalents) is frequently reported in an organization's balance sheet. If access to invested funds is accomplished with minimum difficulty and the *intent* of organization management is to support the cash needs of the organization rather than to invest for long-term purposes, then the balances in these accounts are viewed as being cash equivalents. As an analogy, think about how you might manage your personal funds. You are presumed to have a checking account balance to cover your day-to-day transactions. Assume that you also have a savings account, which you manage in one of the following two ways. Cash requirements may exceed the amount in the

Figure 17-2. An Example of a Balance Sheet

Assets (presented in order of liquidity, that is, nearness to cash)	Liabilities (presented in order of nearness of maturity or due date)
Current Assets (either cash or expected to be converted into cash within one year or the operating cycle, whichever is longer)	Current Liabilities (expected to be paid in one year or within the operating cycle, whichever is longer)

Cash
  Trading Securities
  Accounts Receivable
  Due From (_____ Fund)
  Prepaid Expenses
	Accounts Payable
	  Accrued Expenses
	  Due To (_____ Fund)
	  Notes Payable

Investment and Funds (Available for Sale Securities)	Deferred Credits
Noncurrent or Long-Term Assets (presented in inverse order of economic life)	Noncurrent or Long-Term Liabilities (those that do not mature within one year or the operating cycle, or that are not expected to require funds classified as current assets)

Land
  Buildings (original cost less depreciation)
  Equipment (original cost less depreciation)
  Furniture and Fixtures (original cost less
    depreciation)	

	Net Assets (Fund Balances)

	Unrestricted
	  Temporarily Restricted
	  Permanently Restricted (Endowment)

NOTE: A completed balance sheet is displayed in the exercise at the end of this chapter.

checking account, thus necessitating that funds be transferred from savings to checking. Under these conditions your savings account is an extension of and intermediary for your checking account, and you are using your savings account as a cash equivalent. Hence, the accountant reports the two types of cash balances as a single dollar amount, simply referred to as "cash."

Instead, now assume you have a savings account into which you deposit funds with the objective of letting the balance build up over time through the earning of interest and not withdrawing funds from the account unless absolutely necessary. Under these circumstances, you are operating this account for long-term investment purposes, the balance of which would be reported in the investments section of your personal balance sheet. If an organization has this same investment intent, then the balance sheet for the organization reports the balance in either the "investment and funds" or "available for sale" sections of its balance sheet rather than in the current assets section.

In summary, "short-term intent" and "easy access" translate into classification as cash. Long-term investment intent or lack of easy access requires classification into the investment and funds or available for sale categories.

Cash Management Issues

Some significant issues concerning cash management are as follows:

- Does the organization have sufficient cash to cover its day-to-day transactions (referred to in financial circles as the "transactions motive for holding cash") as they come due? If the organization can pay its bills, then the organization is said to be "solvent" and, if it cannot, then the organization is said to be "insolvent." Should the organization continue to be insolvent for a period of time and should the creditors want to force the issue, then the next legal step is to force the organization into bankruptcy.
- Beyond the transactional needs of the organization, is there an amount of cash (called the "precautionary motive") that provides a "cushion of comfort?" The purpose of this cushion is to cover unexpected costs and expenses that arise from time to time.
- Furthermore, is a third layer of cash (reflecting the "speculative motive") being held for unexpected opportunities (for example, to purchase some items that the organization will eventually need at an extremely advantageous price, or to temporarily invest at an advantageous rate of return)?
- Are there ways in which the amount of cash available to the organization can be increased?
- Do the size and the timing of the cash flows meet the organization's operating needs?
- Does the organization prepare and monitor cash budgets in managing its cash flows?
- Are policies and procedures in place (internal control) to protect the cash and the other assets of the organization to ensure that the assets are used for their intended purposes?

Receivables

An organization customarily reports at least two types of receivables, which are claims for resources that are owed to the organization. An adjective is then used in the account title to identify the source of the claim. An "account receivable" reflects amounts owed to the organization by its clients because of the sale of products or the provision of services. In contrast, "pledges receivable" arise from the commitment of donors to the organization that have not yet been collected. However, not all claims owed to the organization are collected. Those parties who either do not or cannot pay give rise to uncollectible amounts, referred to as "bad debt." Funds that are not expected to be collected and the impact their noncollection has on the system must be taken into account when planning for the organization or when reporting its results.

Accordingly, then, one of the questions to be asked is whether an allowance has been made within the fiscal system for amounts expected to not be collected. If no such allowance has been made, then the amount of receivables, net assets, and operating surplus will be overstated in the financial statements. Thus, the organization is represented as being in better financial shape (higher assets and operating fund balance) than it actually is.

It is the accountant's objective to reflect this situation by reporting that which is called "net realizable value," the amount expected to be collected. Specifically, the accountant evaluates the receivables in terms of their likelihood of collection, estimates the amount of funds not expected to be collected, and then increases the bad debt expense, which in turn decreases the reported surplus. The accounts receivable balance reported by the organization is reduced by an allowance for the amount predicted to be uncollectible, simultaneously reducing the net realizable value being reported in the balance sheet.

For example, assume that $100 is owed to the organization and that it is projected that $10 will not be collected. The gross amount of the receivables is $100 and the amount expected not to be collected (referred to as the "allowance for uncollectibles") is $10, so the net realizable value is $90. Simultaneously, the total expense of the organization is increased by the amount of the bad debt expense of $10, which in turn reduces the amount of the surplus reported by the organization in the amount of $10.

When an organization is owed funds, two consequences simultaneously occur. The first is that the organization is acting as a lender; the second is that the organization is consuming its own resources, thereby reducing its resource (asset) base. For example, assume that it takes 60 to 90 days or more to receive the cash earned from services rendered. The outflow of cash for rendering those services, particularly for salaries and supplies, occurred at the time of service. Where does the organization get the cash required to carry the organization from the point of outflow (service rendered) to the point of inflow (cash collected)? If the delay in collection is too long or the growth in the provision of services on credit is too rapid, an organization can literally bring about its own demise by being too successful. Alternatively, under less extreme conditions the organization may experience severe cash flow problems that can drain management attention and time from other significant issues.

The following questions regarding receivables should be asked:

- What dollar amount of receivables is the organization carrying? Given this amount, does the organization have the necessary level of cash and cash equivalent resources required to carry this level of receivables until they are collected?

- Has an allowance been made to reflect the likelihood that some amount of the receivables will not be collected? What is that amount? Can and should steps be taken to reduce that amount? Should the client base be changed to reduce the amount of uncollectibles?
- How long is it taking, on average, to collect the organization's receivables? Can the length of that time period be reduced, thus enabling the organization to have quicker access to the resources owed to it?
- What proportion of the receivables is the responsibility of third-party payers? Did these payers negotiate reduced service rates? Can the organization continue to provide services at the reduced rates? What amount of receivables is being lost to contractual disagreements regarding charges for services performed but not approved for reimbursement by the third parties?

Inventory

Overall there are two types of inventory: (1) items held for resale (merchandise inventory) and (2) items purchased to support the activities of the organization (supplies inventory). In the nonprofit arena, merchandise inventory is unique to a limited number of agencies, whereas supplies are common to all. Therefore, only the supplies inventory is discussed here.

The dollar amount invested in supplies (such as letterhead stationery, staples, laser printer cartridges) may not represent material amounts, may not warrant a great amount of management's time and attention, and in fact may not even be reported as an asset in the balance sheet at the end of the reporting period because it was reported as an expense in the operating statement. It is within this context that the following questions should be asked:

- What is the dollar amount of supplies being used to support the activities of the organization? Does this amount seem reasonable given the volume of the organization's activities?
- Is the appropriate amount of inventory being held? Can the level of inventory be reduced without affecting the operations of the organization? Has the inventory been reviewed to ascertain its appropriateness for the changing nature of operations and technology?
- Is the inventory periodically reviewed so that obsolete or deteriorated inventory is removed?

Prepaid Expenses

Commonly used account titles found on balance sheets are "deferred expenses" and "deferred charges." "Prepaid expenses" is a self-explanatory term used in this section. The dollar amount reported as the balance of the account represents the amount of services or benefits to be received in the coming, as opposed to the current, operating period. An excellent example of a prepaid expense is the premium paid for automobile insurance. Assume that the date is November 1, that the organization's reporting period ends on December 31, and that the organization has just paid a six-month auto insurance premium of $600 ($100 per month). On December 31, four months of insurance benefits with the equivalent cost of $400 are available to the organization in the coming fiscal period. This $400 should be reported as a prepaid expense in the balance sheet prepared at the end of the period.

The following questions regarding prepaid expenses should be asked.

- What types of insurance coverage are being carried? Do the policies carried cover the major areas for which the organization is at risk? Does insurance adequately cover the liability risk of the organization, its employees (including executive management), and the board of directors?
- Is business interruption insurance being carried? If not, should it be?
- Should the organization undertake a risk assessment study?

Long-Term Assets

Assets that benefit the organization over a period of years are referred to as "long-term assets," "noncurrent assets," "fixed assets," or "property and equipment." Specific assets found in the sample balance sheet section are land, buildings, equipment, office furniture, and office equipment. Note that each is capable of providing benefits to the organization over more than one year and usually requires a large investment. With the exception of land, all are presumed to be used up by the organization as it conducts its business.

Four terms become part of the accounting and reporting process. First, the accountant brings into the records the asset's cash equivalent cost, referred to as the asset's "book value." Then, as the assets are consumed, a portion of their cost, called "depreciation expense," is subtracted from the cost of the asset. This subtraction process reduces the net amount of the assets carried on the balance sheet, increases total expenses reported by the organization, decreases the reported surplus, and reduces the reported fund balance (net assets) of the organization. Next, the amount of depreciation expense taken each year is summed cumulatively over the asset's life. This accumulated sum is called "accumulated depreciation" and is subtracted from the gross book value of the asset, generating a dollar balance that is the asset's "net book value."

Significant management considerations relating to the management of fixed assets are as follows:

- Does the organization have the right amount and the right mix of property, buildings, and equipment given the amount of services projected to be provided for the immediate and near-term operating periods?
- Does the organization have and is it executing a repair and maintenance plan that maintains the productive capital base of the organization? Stated another way, are resources for repairs and maintenance being diverted to

other uses, a policy that will cause the asset base of the organization to deteriorate over the long run?

- Is a capital replacement–expansion plan in place and being executed such that aging and obsolete assets are replaced and assets needed to support organization growth are purchased?

Liabilities

A liability, or debt, is an obligation for which the organization has accepted the responsibility to pay or otherwise dissolve. A debt has a "maturity date" on which it is due and payable. If no maturity date is specified in the debt agreement, then the debt is due on demand. The base amount of money advanced (loaned) is referred to as the "principal" amount, and charges added for the use of the principal over its lifetime are referred to as "interest." If the organization is unable to meet either the interest or the principal repayment obligations as they come due, then the organization can be said to be insolvent (or in default). Should the position of insolvency persist, then the status of the organization can change to one of bankruptcy, which means that at the extreme the doors of the organization can be forced to close by the creditors. The point to be emphasized is that each dollar of debt carries with it an element of financial risk (that of possible bankruptcy). Furthermore, it is debt that comes due in the near term, today, tomorrow, next week, or next month—not that which is due next year or in five years—which must be paid now and which can draw the organization into insolvency and possible bankruptcy. In recognition of this dichotomy the accountant segments debt outstanding on the balance sheet into two categories: (1) current (due within one year) liabilities and (2) long-term (maturity date is beyond one year) liabilities.

The degree of financial risk and the organization's ability to meet its debt commitments constitute the major issues that organizational oversight must address:

- What is the distribution between current versus long-term debt? Does the amount of current debt represent an immediate payment problem for the organization?
- Does the organization have sufficient liquid (cash and near cash) resources to cover the current debt?
- Can the organization cover the interest and principal payments that are due on the debt?
- How much financial flexibility does the organization have if it is necessary to borrow? For example, what assets are available to pledge as collateral for additional debt?

Deferred Credits

"Deferred credits," or delayed obligations, refer to the cash that has been received without the requisite services having been performed. Thus, there is a timing difference between the receipt of resources and the performance of the contractual commitments. This timing difference sometimes leads to the confusing titles found in financial reports.

Even though the title "deferred credits" is frequently used, referring to the amounts in this category as "deferred revenue" or "support and revenue designated for future periods" may be more appropriate and more self-explanatory. "Deferred" in this context refers to the fact that the amounts reported will be assigned as revenue having been earned in future (hence deferred or delayed) operating statements. In the interim the unearned balances are reported in the liability section of the balance sheet because they represent resources that have been received by the organization but for which the terms of their receipt have not been met. Accordingly, the organization has the obligation (liability) either to perform the services or return the cash.

The following management issues are related to deferred liabilities:
• Management should properly manage the resources received to ensure their availability in the future when the services are performed. It is easy, for example, for the resources to be either intentionally or inadvertently expended because of more immediate and pressing demands on cash.
• Should the organization be unable to meet its contractual commitments or to return the funds, legal problems can arise, the minimum being charges of breach of contract.

SCOPE AND CONTEXT OF THE AUDIT

Stated briefly, the objective of the audit process is to contribute to an organization's fiscal integrity. It does so by providing the users of the organization's financial statements with assurance that those statements are constructed on a consistent basis and present reliable data on which analysis can be conducted and informed decisions made. Although fiscal integrity is presumed, its importance must still be emphasized in the following way. Lose your fiscal integrity and you begin a process that can easily lead to the demise of the organization. Once lost, restoring that fiscal integrity is a monumental task that consumes the energies of all involved for an extended period of time. For this reason, it is strongly recommended that the organization have its statements audited by certified public accountants. In addition to the immediate credibility that audited statements are presumed to possess, the experience and insight that these professionals can bring to evaluating the organization and to recommending changes provide the opportunity to improve operating effectiveness and to assure organization quality.

The following issues should be considered when selecting an auditor:

- How experienced is the accounting firm in conducting audits in the non-profit sector? Specifically, what is the experience level of the firm's personnel who will conduct the organization's audit?
- Who are some of the firm's nonprofit clients? Obtain approval to contact those organizations and get the name of the individual to contact at that organization.
- What will be the scope of the audit and the services provided by the firm conducting the audit?
- What is the estimated date of completion of the audit?
- What fees will be assessed for having the audit performed? What steps can the organization take to maximize the effectiveness of the audit and to minimize its cost?
- What role will your organization's personnel play in supporting the prescribed audit program?

Two documents are created as part of the audit process: (1) a written opinion about the reliability of the data reported in the financial statements and (2) a letter (called the "management letter") submitted to the chairman of the board of trustees recommending changes that the organization should make to improve reporting and fiscal integrity. One of the areas reviewed and evaluated as a part of developing that opinion is the study of two control systems: (1) administrative control and (2) internal or accounting control.

Administrative Control

Administrative control examines established procedures that enhance organizational operating efficiency and effectiveness. Key concepts here include a four-step process that consists of approval, authorization, execution, and recording.

- *Approval* emanates from the proper level of authority within the organization to ensure that the activities undertaken support the mission, goals, and objectives of the organization.
- *Authorization* follows approval by specifying that specific actions are to be taken to achieve the objectives of the organization.
- *Execution* of the authorized activities must occur to accomplish the objectives of the organization.
- *Recording* the execution of the authorized activities—the final step—maintains historical documentation of actions and accomplishments for reporting, review, evaluation, and control purposes.

Internal (Accounting) Control

Internal control may be loosely defined as a process establishing a system to ensure that an organization's assets are used for the purposes for which they were intended. A more limited perspective defines *internal control* as the establishment of a system to ensure that cash and other assets are not diverted for the benefit of parties for whom such benefits were not intended.

At a minimum, internal control attempts to reduce the possibility of diversion by requiring the collusion of two or more individuals. Prevention of collusion is strengthened by implementing a set of procedures known as the "separation of duties" wherein no one individual is responsible for all aspects of a transaction, such as opening the mail; removing, recording, and depositing checks received; recording the reduction of any pledges receivable; and reconciling the bank statements.

Four elements of internal control—personnel, separation of duties, documentation and record keeping, and budget—are discussed below.

Personnel

There are four items to consider for personnel:
1. *Competency* refers to the employee's ability to meet job requirements and includes experience, training, and continuing education.
2. *Trustworthiness* refers to establishing systems to minimize the opportunity to commit dishonest acts (for example, the bonding of key employees with its background checks and confirming the employment and educational histories of potential employees).
3. *Authority* considerations require that clearly established lines of authority be established. The intent here is to enhance the likelihood that actions are taken that support the organization's objectives.
4. *Responsibility* flows from the establishment of lines of authority. Holding personnel responsible and tying that responsibility to that authority plays an important role in keeping them focused on the reasons for the organization's existence.

Separation of Duties

No one party has complete control over a transaction from its point of inception through its being recorded in the accounting system. One reason is to reduce or prevent the opportunity for fraud, but a second, and equally important, reason is to establish checks and balances within the recording system that help improve the reliability inherent in the reported financial data.

Documentation and Record Keeping

Adequate documents and records are necessary to verify data reported by the system. This characteristic is important for substantiating to outside parties,

*"For your convenience we've consolidated all our forms into one, which I'll ask you
to take a few minutes to review."*

such as funding agencies and the Internal Revenue Service, that the organization has fulfilled its nonprofit obligations.

Budget

One normally does not view a budget as an internal control tool, but it is. On the one hand, budgets are administrative control tools to evaluate management efficiency and effectiveness, the use of resources within the context of the organization's mission and purpose. On the other, the comparison of actual against budgeted expenses can provide general checks of how resources were used versus how they were directed to be used by the board when the budget was approved.

PUTTING IT ALL TOGETHER: THE PLANNING, BUDGETING, AND REVIEW PROCESS

Two of the key budgeted statements prepared as part of the planning process are the balance sheet and the operating statement. Budgeted statements should be in the same format and of the same content as the historical statements, the only difference being that the statements prepared at the end of the period contain historical or "actual" amounts, whereas the budgets contain future or predicted amounts. Both statements have a role in the budgeting, planning, review, and approval process. They chronicle and report the past actions and accomplishments for review and evaluation purposes, they capture the plans and expectations for the coming fiscal period, and they are the focus of the annual board meeting, which finally leads to approval in budgetary form.

The concepts and contexts that underlie the planning, budgeting, and review process permeate the day-to-day "business" of the organization (see Figure 17-3, which depicts the major flows and segments of the planning and budgeting process). From Figure 17-3 the following guidelines emerge.

The mission of the organization should be the driving force behind the resource allocation decisions made by the board of trustees. It is the responsibility of the board members to develop a long-term strategy for accomplishing the organization's mission. Included in this strategic plan is the specification of the long-term objectives of the organization. In this context, "objectives" refer to more general levels of achievements to be accomplished. In contrast, "goals" refer to specific levels of accomplishments to be achieved. For example, "provide mental health services to needy people" is an objective; "provide mental health services to 1,000 needy people during the current operating period" is a goal.

When the long-term objectives of the organization have been determined, long-term goals, or targets, to be accomplished over time should be specified. Goals to be achieved during the current fiscal period are then delineated by the board of trustees in consultation (and negotiation) with executive management. These goals should be specific and measurable so they can act as valid standards against which accomplishments are compared at the end of the fiscal period.

At this point the construction of the operating budget for the coming period begins. The various types of revenues should be reviewed in terms of their applicability to the coming year and estimates made as to the amounts expected to be generated. Although the planning and budgeting sequence should begin with the projection of expected revenues, do not be surprised to encounter an organization that first estimates the expenses required to support the targeted level of program activity and then estimates the revenue generated as equal to those expenses, in order to "balance" the budgeted amounts. For example, if a deficit is projected when the desired expenses are compared with projected revenues, executive management may take the stance that revenue sources will, magically but with certainty, appear to cover the deficit. Many budgets are prepared and adopted on this dubious premise.

Figure 17-3. Overview of the Planning and Budgeting Process

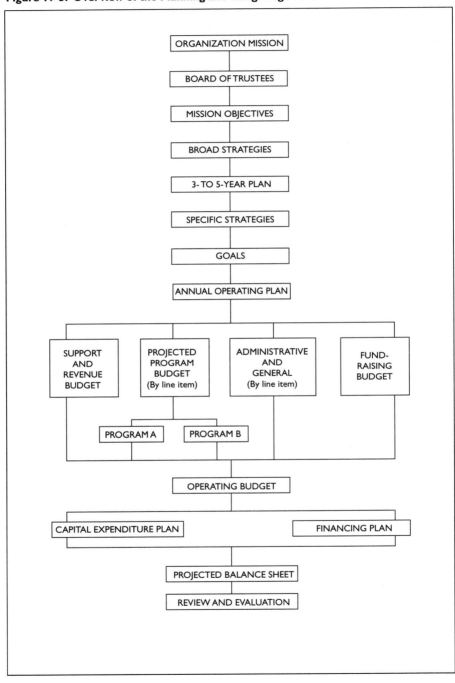

After projecting the resources expected to be available to the organization for the coming period, the next step is to project the amount of expenses to be consumed by providing the projected level of services. The major expense categories are program, management and general, and fundraising. Line-item functional projections frequently are incorporated into the respective budget segments. "Functional" in this context relates to the purpose for which the expenses were incurred, such as salaries and wages, employee benefits, supplies, and postage.

The next area to reviewed and resolved is the amount of resources to be expended for long-term asset replacement, improvement, and expansion purposes. A review and evaluation of the projected cash flows and the pattern of their timing must then be performed. The focus here is to develop a financial plan that addresses the indicated cash flow pattern. Included here could be line of credit issues that arise because of seasonal cash flow patterns, capital campaigns, borrowing strategies for capital asset projects, and an investment plan for excess cash situations.

The overall financial interrelationships are now reviewed and evaluated to discern whether changes are needed to bring the financial plan into harmony with the mission, objectives, goals, and financial concerns. If inconsistencies exist, the process starts anew with changes and tradeoffs being introduced to balance the financial picture.

When the board reaches agreement on the budget, it then formally approves it; the budget now represents executive management's marching orders. The process now moves on to the authorization, execution, and recording phases prescribed by the internal control process.

The process thus ends and begins at the end of the fiscal period: It ends with a review and evaluation of the actual amounts compared against their budget amounts for the period just ended; it begins anew in the form of the new budgeting cycle.

SKILLS-APPLICATION EXERCISES

Presented below are the Statement of Financial Position (balance sheet) and the Statement of Support, Revenue, and Expenses (operating statement), Part A. Review these statements, and try to apply the definitions and concepts introduced in this chapter. Each statement is evaluated and analyzed below.

Statement of Financial Position

The first characteristic to notice is that the organization has $22,900 in cash and near-cash assets (cash = $2,500, trading securities = $7,500, and net

Statement of Financial Position (Balance Sheet)

ASSETS		
Current Assets		
Cash		$ 2,500
Trading (Marketable Securities)		7,500
Accounts Receivable (Gross)	$17,900	
(Less Projected Uncollectibles)	(5,000)	12,900
Supplies Inventory		3,000
Prepaid Insurance		600
Total Current Assets		$26,500
Available for Sale Securities		$5,000
Property, Buildings, and Equipment		
Property		$36,000
Buildings	$52,500	
(Less Accumulated Depreciation)	(48,000)	4,500
Equipment	19,000	
(Less Accumulated Depreciation)	(18,000)	1,000
Total Property, Buildings, and Equipment		$41,500
TOTAL ASSETS		$73,000

LIABILITIES AND NET ASSETS		
Current Liabilities		
Accounts Payable		$ 5,000
Salaries and Benefits Payable		4,000
Payable to Third Parties		7,500
Notes Payable to Bank		5,000
Total Current Liabilities		$21,500
Long-Term Liabilities		
Mortgage Payable on Buildings		$12,500
Program Revenues for Future Periods		5,000
Total Long-Term Liabilities		$17,500
Net Assets (Fund Balances)		
Unrestricted Net Assets		$34,000
Temporarily Restricted Net Assets		0
Permanently Restricted Net Assets		0
Total Net Assets		$34,000
TOTAL LIABILITIES AND NET ASSETS		$73,000

accounts receivable = $12,900). The organization's $21,500 in current liabilities nearly deplete those assets. Thus, it appears that the organization may have to convert its "savings" in the form of the trading securities to cash to pay the impending financial obligations. Steps to ensure the collection of as many dollars of accounts receivable as is possible should be taken while

Statement of Support, Revenue, and Expenses, Part A (Operating Statement)

Support and Revenues			
Grant Revenue		$ 5,000	
Client Fees	$80,000		
(Less Expected Nonpayment)	(16,000)		
Net Client Fees		64,000	
Fundraising Revenue	$52,000		
(Less Fundraising Costs)	(21,000)		
Net Fundraising Revenue		31,000	
Total Support and Revenue			$100,000
Expenses			
Program Salaries and Benefits		$44,000	
Administrative Salaries and Benefits		34,000	
Office Supplies		3,500	
Rent and Utilities		6,000	
Insurance		4,800	
Contract Services		2,500	
Depreciation		3,000	
Repair/Maintenance		4,000	
Miscellaneous Expense		2,200	
Total Expenses			$104,000
Change in Net Assets			($4,000)

simultaneously implementing procedures to maintain or even increase the amount of revenue being generated through client fees, donations, grants, or other means.

The organization owns securities (classified as "Available for Sale Securities"), so presumably the intention is to hold these securities for long-term investment purposes, the reason being that long-term intent is the defining characteristic for this classification. Accordingly, this investment strategy may have to be changed should cash be unexpectedly and quickly needed to cover resource demands.

Approximately 28 percent ($5,000 ÷ $17,900) of the amounts owed to the organization is projected as being uncollectible. On the surface, this percentage suggests that the number of nonpaying clients is high. That may well be the case, but notice the dilemma: The mission of a nonprofit organization is to provide needed services to those who cannot pay, so the issue addresses the core question of what the organization is really about.

The amount of supplies being carried might be reviewed to determine whether the level can be reduced, thereby freeing up resources for other uses. Not much time should be devoted to this question, however, because the potential dollar amount to be saved is rather small. That the amount of prepaid insurance is low suggests that insurance premiums are coming due just beyond the end of the reporting period. Therefore, steps should be taken to ensure that these premiums are paid.

With respect to the organization's long-term assets in the form of property, buildings, and equipment, the statement indicates that the original cost of the property (land) was $36,000. However, the current market value of the property is unknown. This information would provide some insight as to what the property might bring should it have to be sold quickly to generate cash. With respect to the buildings and equipment, these assets may be nearing the end of their useful lives as indicated by the fact that the amount of depreciation taken to date (shown as "accumulated depreciation") is almost equal to the original costs of those assets. Specifically, approximately 91 percent ($48,000 ÷ $52,500) of the cost of the building has been charged to operating periods over time. With respect to the equipment (desks, chairs, computers), the implication is that almost 95 percent ($18,000 ÷ $19,000) of their useful lives have been used. Taken together, the data suggest that an increased level of expenditures may be on the horizon if the assets are in need of replacement, thus indicating that even greater pressures will be exerted on future cash resources.

Of the current (due for payment within the coming year) liabilities, three are commonplace: (1) accounts payable (amounts owned to suppliers), (2) salaries and benefits payable (amounts owed to employees because of timing differences between when wages, salaries, and benefits are earned and when they are paid), and (3) notes (short-term loans) payable to the bank. Payables to third-party payers, however, should at least generate some questions because these amounts represent services rendered to clients that were presumably covered by agreement with an outside (third) party and that were paid for by that party, but that subsequently were determined not to have been covered, thus requiring repayment by the organization. The existence of such a liability suggests that our service providers may be in need of either review or training on the services covered by third-party agreements.

With respect to those debts (liabilities) that are classified as long term (due for payment beyond one year), note that the property and building have a mortgage outstanding. One implication is that should cash be quickly needed by the organization, its ability to use that property as collateral for a loan has, in all likelihood, been greatly impeded.

As for the liability classified as "Program Revenues for Future Periods," the organization is obligated to provide program services for some specified period of time into future operating periods. In reality, this liability should be reported in two components: (1) one in the current liabilities section for those program services to be rendered in the coming fiscal period and (2) the remainder in the long-term section for services to be rendered beyond that time frame. Regardless of how it is reported, however, this type of liability substantiates that the organization has an obligation to consume a portion of its resources in the future to provide those services.

Next, one gets the impression that the operating deficit generated in the current year may be an anomaly. The reason is that the organization has accumulated an operating surplus in the amount of $34,000 since it has been in existence. And finally, the organization has not generated an investment base for the generation of income to support future operations because the balance in the endowment account (entitled "Permanently Restricted Net Assets") is zero.

Statement of Support, Revenue, and Expenses

Perhaps the first financial characteristic to be noticed is that a deficit in the amount of $4,000 is being reported as a summary of the fiscal results for the period. One way of viewing this deficit is that executive management must not have performed in a satisfactory manner or else a deficit would not have been generated. Such a conclusion, however, may not be justified. It may be that a deficit was intentionally budgeted for the period, in which case the actions of executive management reflected the directives of the board of directors. On the other hand, the amount of the deficit is only a small percentage (4 percent) of the total budget, which may be due to nothing more than chance events, particularly in light of the organization's positive operating fund ("Unrestricted Net Assets") balance in the amount of $34,000.

In terms of revenue generation, client fees generated 64 percent of the total budget, and fundraising efforts generated 31 percent of the revenue base, with only 5 percent generated by grants. Whether this is the proper mix of revenue sources can best be addressed by examining their relative amounts in the budget. One should also note that 20 percent ($16,000 ÷ $80,000) billed to clients is projected as being uncollectible. This certainly begs the question as to whether losing $.20 of every dollar billed is in the best interest of the organization. In contrast, approximately $.60 ($30,000 ÷ $52,000) of every dollar generated through fundraising activities becomes available to the organization for operating purposes. Alternatively, $.40 ($21,000 ÷ $52,000) of every dollar raised goes to covering the costs of the various fundraising events. On the surface these proportions appear to be reasonable, but again judgment should not be passed until these percentages are compared against some target. On the subject of increased revenue generation, that the amount of revenue lost to nonpaying customers is so large certainly suggests a premise on which a grant proposal to an outside funding source could be made.

As for expenses, approximately 75 percent ($44,000 + $34,000 ÷ $104,000) of the resources used by the organization cover the cost of personnel. Such a ratio gives the impression of being rather high, but again, there must be some standard for comparison. Perhaps somewhat more disconcerting is that 33 percent ($34,000 ÷ $104,000) of the resources are used to cover the cost of administrative personnel, whereas only 44 percent ($44,000 ÷ $104,000) is being paid out to those providing the program services.

The remaining expenses generate the impression of being reasonable given that neither their respective dollar amounts or percentages are a very large portion of either total revenue or total expenses. The amount of office supplies consumed during the year ($3,500) suggests that almost a year's needs are being carried in inventory ($3,000). The interest-bearing debt of the organization consumes about 4 percent of the organization's annual resources.

Now that you have taken some initial steps to develop your financial vocabulary and your understanding of nonprofit financial statements, the time has come to move on to the next level of financial understanding. Obtain a copy of a nonprofit's balance sheet and operating statement. Review the content and meaning of the statements, classifying the various accounts of the organization as being assets, liabilities, fund balances, revenue, and expenses. Review the different gains and losses that appear on the operating statement and develop an understanding of why they are classified as gains or losses. Next, examine the financial statements from an analytical perspective. Try to develop some perceptions of the financial status of the organization. Then set up an appointment with the organization's treasurer or chief financial officer to discuss the statements.

REFERENCE

Financial Accounting Standards Board. (1993). *Accounting for contributions received and contributions made* (Statement of Financial Accounting Standards No. 116). Stamford, CT: Financial Accounting Foundation.

ADDITIONAL READING

Anthony, R. M., & Young, D. W. (1994). *Management control in nonprofit organizations* (5th ed.). Boston: Irwin.

Bryce, H. J. (1992). *Financial management for nonprofit organizations* (2nd ed.). Englewood Cliffs, NJ: Prentice Hall.

Wildavsky, A. (1992). *The politics of the budgetary process* (2nd ed.). New York: HarperCollins.

Ziebell, M. T., & DeCoster, D. T. (1991). *Management control systems in nonprofit organizations.* New York: Harcourt, Brace, Jovanovich.

CHAPTER 18

New Approaches to Program Evaluation

Andrea Meier and Charles L. Usher

This chapter describes the changing context of program evaluation in nonprofit organizations and considers new approaches to doing evaluation. As the operating environments of nonprofit organizations have changed, so has the role of management. Managers used to be responsible primarily for monitoring and controlling the processes and functions within their organizations. Now they also are called on to act as facilitators and mentors for staff within their organizations, as innovators in program development, and as brokers between their organizations and the surrounding communities. These multiple roles can be mutually enhancing, or they can conflict. Prompted by this progressive expansion of their responsibilities, nonprofit managers are seeking new ways to get feedback on how well they perform their roles and assess their organizations' effectiveness.

As a nonprofit manager, you must be able to function effectively in this environment of competing values and demands (see chapter 1). In addition to your other duties, you also must function as a monitor and coordinator of activity, both within your organization and in relation to your organization's performance relative to its mission and external environment. In this chapter we review how the field of social program evaluation has developed over the past 30 years and describe the changing roles of evaluators, program staff, consumers, and policymakers in the evaluation process.

CHANGING POLITICAL CONTEXT OF HUMAN SERVICES EVALUATION

Although many kinds of nonprofit organizations have begun to incorporate evaluations into their program activities, the strongest demand for accountability has long been within the human services sector. Because of this historical emphasis, we begin this chapter with a summary of how recent changes in human services policy suggest a need for a new system of account-ability in the public and nonprofit human services sector, one that tradition-al approaches to evaluation cannot support.

The mid-1990s saw a clear conservative shift in American politics, most evident in new Republican majorities in Congress and in many state legisla-tures. The legislation that emerged from these bodies resulted in less federal support for human services and a shift in authority and responsibility from the federal government to the states and from the states to local government. Fundamental premises of the social welfare system, such as the entitlement of poor families to support under the Aid to Families with Dependent Children program, were discarded, and states were required to establish new principles of social responsibility.

This shift in power was consistent with the recommendations of liberal social reformers who saw community-based decision making and resource allocation as essential to the renewal of disadvantaged neighborhoods and communities (Nelson, 1994). A key difference, however, was the expectation that federal financial support would continue or possibly even expand in cer-tain areas, such as prevention and early intervention programs (Usher, 1995). Thus, the devolution of power grew out of demands from both ends of the political spectrum, although from two quite different sets of motivations.

The political transformation of the mid-1990s was, of course, the culmi-nation of a conservative shift that began with the election of Ronald Reagan in 1980 and continued through the next decade. During this period, man-agers of nonprofit organizations and public agencies increasingly faced pres-sure to eliminate fraud, waste, and abuse and to control caseload growth in the programs they administered (Terry, 1997). A variety of strategies, such as total quality management (Walters, 1994; see also chapter 25) and results-ori-ented management, were devised to help managers improve the efficiency and effectiveness of their organizations. Moreover, the concept of managed care emerged during this period in an effort to create incentives for cost-effective delivery of services (Usher, in press). Changes in federal funding mechanisms that resulted in the increased use of purchase-of-service agree-ments enabled new nonprofit and for-profit organizations to enter into the service provision "market." To compete effectively with public agencies for resources, newcomer organizations have begun to incorporate these new management strategies to satisfy consumer demand (Edwards, Cooke, & Reid, 1996).

Public and nonprofit human services agencies have not been the only enti-ties affected by these trends. In the 1990s, many state and local arts programs experienced funding cutbacks caused by national campaigns to eliminate the National Endowment for the Arts (Loyacano, 1995). Even less controversial arts programs have been forced to justify the value of their programs to their funders using evaluation techniques to show how their services are culturally enriching to their communities.

In addition to attacks from political conservatives, the federal government also came under criticism from other sources. Some social policy analysts, such as Sar Levitan (1992) and Lisbeth Schorr (1997), charged that federal social experiments had not been useful to policymakers or administrators and were not a worthwhile investment of resources. Indeed, they challenged the very scientific approach on which many programs were based as inconsistent with the premise that the most effective programs are those that are responsive to the particular interests, needs, and resources of given communities as opposed to conforming to a "one-size-fits-all" program model (Usher, 1995). Consistent with these critiques, evaluators began experimenting with and advocating new approaches to program evaluation that they perceived to be more appropriate to a more decentralized political system (for example, Fetterman, Kaftarian, & Wandersman, 1996). The emergence of these new approaches is described below.

Although the program evaluation concepts and methods discussed here are relevant and applicable to public agencies, for-profit, and nonprofit organizations, much of the research in program evaluation has been done to assess the effectiveness of human services programs. The examples of different types of evaluations and the case study presented in this chapter reflect our personal experiences with program evaluations and the richness of this body of research.

CONCEPTUAL ROOTS OF PROGRAM EVALUATION

Contemporary approaches to program evaluation draw on at least two conceptual foundations: policy analysis (for example, Quade, 1979; Wildavsky, 1979) and social psychology and educational assessment (for example, Dugan, 1996). As a result, evaluators differ in the aspects of programs (process, outcome, impact) that are accorded top priority and the research approaches they consider valid and appropriate (for example, qualitative or quantitative). Policy analysts typically draw heavily on political and economic theory and focus on cost-effectiveness and the impact on institutional power relationships. Evaluators trained in educational and psychological theoretical frameworks tend to be more concerned with *social learning*—the developmental processes associated with individual and collective learning. The following discussion describes these different perspectives in more detail.

Policy Analysis and the Rational Decision-Making Model

Policy analysis emerged in the 1970s as an intellectual discipline to help decision makers make choices that produce results that are "systematic, efficient, coordinated and rational" (Wildavsky, 1979, p. 127). From the point of view of the politicians and taxpayers, this means that things are "done well and cheaply" (Quade, 1979, p. 45). The definitions of "done well" and "cheap" vary according to whom is making the judgments. The policy analyst's goal is to promote decision makers' understanding of the costs and benefits of using different strategies to achieve social objectives. Originally, policy analysts labored at "pure planning," generating alternatives without regard to the political contexts in which the decisions were being made (Wildavsky, 1979). Now they attempt more explicitly to take into account the interactions between planning objectives and power relationships (Durning, 1993).

Policy analysts view public agencies and human services programs as tangible responses to conditions that are defined politically as social problems (Wildavsky, 1979). From a social ecological perspective of organizational behavior, each of these organizational systems is a subsystem within a larger institutional political system, within which subsystems compete with each other for scarce resources (Hall, 1991). Whereas each organization or program satisfies a specific set of societal values, the value systems themselves may conflict. Policymakers and program managers routinely face decisions that involve shifting resources from one program or organization to others. Ideally, the best decisions lead to courses of action in which available resources are used to provide the greatest increase in social benefits to the greatest number of people. However, such decisions are never so simple. Often they are driven by political pressures and local crises whose effects unexpectedly spill over into programs that were directed at resolving apparently unrelated problems.

Competing Values Framework and Evaluation Approaches

Organizations are effective to the degree they are able to maintain a dynamic equilibrium between their internal needs and the demands of society (Quinn, 1988). They vary in their internal operational stability, social cohesion, and employee morale. They also differ in the efficiency with which they are able to achieve their institutional missions while adapting to or exploiting changing conditions in their operating environments. Managers play different roles in each of these organizational domains. To be effective, managers must use different and sometimes conflicting sets of skills: boundary-spanning skills, human relations skills, coordinating skills, and directing skills (see chapter 1). Similarly, managers need different types of information to know how well they are performing in each of these skill areas.

Savvy managers assess their information needs and those of key stakeholders in choosing specific evaluation approaches. Managers have typically used conventional outcome evaluation strategies based on rational decision-making principles to determine how effective they have been in directing their programs' progress toward their goals. As changing conditions compel managers to expand their conceptions of their roles, they are looking to new participatory approaches. For example, managers now may use social- and organizational-learning-based evaluation approaches to obtain feedback on their performance of internal coordination functions. In cases in which the growing demand for comprehensive services, interagency collaboration, and greater consumer involvement call for systemic perspectives, managers may be better served by models of participatory evaluation to enable them to determine how effective they have been in using their human relations and boundary-spanning skills in response to systemic changes in their communities, institutional networks, and social policies. Each of these newer forms of evaluation approaches is described in detail in this chapter.

Rational Decision-Making Model in Program Design and Evaluation

Policy analysts use an iterative rational decision-making model to identify and compare various policy alternatives. The rational decision-making cycle includes five interrelated stages. Policy analysts first work with decision makers to define the policy's objectives as explicitly as possible. They gather data to establish base rates for existing conditions. They then try to identify all reasonable alternatives available for those achieving policy objectives and the conditions and constraints under which they are likely to perform. Having identified several alternative strategies, analysts examine each one in terms of its feasibility (legal, economic, technical, and political) and its immediate and long-term positive and negative effects. As part of this exploration, analysts develop conceptual models to link decisions explicitly to outcomes. Because each alternative has positive and negative features, analysts then work with decision makers to develop criteria to be used to decide which alternatives are preferable (Quade, 1979). Human services programs constitute the outcomes of this analytic process, where decision makers have selected one alternative for dealing with a problem over all other options according to some set of criteria.

Program evaluation is used to assess how well the chosen strategy worked to achieve policy objectives. Typically, there have been two main purposes for evaluations. Policymakers draw on evaluations to help them decide whether they should continue to allocate resources to a program. Program managers use the information to improve program operations. More recently, variants of the self-evaluation model of program evaluation have been developed to expand the usefulness of evaluations to a wider range of audiences. These approaches enable recipients of program services and their families and communities—as well as program managers and administrators—to obtain the information they need to shape services so that they are better suited to local conditions (Weiss & Greene, 1992).

Rational decision-making procedures used in policy analysis are also essential in the design of a good program and a valid and reliable evaluation. The basic steps include formulating the problem, identifying salient factors and the relationships among them, building conceptual models of the problem, identifying appropriate alternative interventions, implementing the evaluation by collecting data on baseline conditions and the intervention process, interpreting findings, and comparing the effects of alternative strategies (see Table 18-1).

Social-Learning-Based Evaluations

Evaluations that are designed to promote social-learning approaches have their conceptual roots in educational, community, and organizational psychology. From this perspective, people confronted with new challenges try to set meaningful goals, map out plans of action, and take action in ways that they believe will help them attain their goals (Bandura, 1977). Self-assessments are an integral part of this complex, ongoing learning process. An individual's self-assessments indicate whether his or her personal efforts at each stage help achieve those goals or suggest ways of altering behavior so that success becomes more likely. When such efforts appear to be productive, they elicit feelings of self-efficacy and increase the likelihood that the person will persist in the face of obstacles (Bandura, 1986; Fetterman, 1996).

Change within organizations and communities involves a similar learning process. People with common interests learn together by gathering information for understanding the nature of their shared problems, identifying alternatives, taking action to remedy those problems, and assessing how well they succeeded. Where these processes are carried out effectively, collective self-evaluation can contribute greater cooperation between organizational units, more trust in the individual's ability to collaborate in problem solving, higher levels of participation, and a stronger sense of ownership among employees or individual citizens (Nelson, n.d.).

Pressures for Change in Evaluation Research

As with policy analysis and other social sciences, educational evaluation research prior to the 1970s reflected the prevailing experimentalism of the social science research paradigm. In the 1970s and 1980s, the civil rights and feminist movements gave rise to radical critiques of education and positivist social science research methods. Activists challenged the validity of these

Table 18-1. Stages of Rational Decision Making in Program Design and Evaluation

RATIONAL DECISION-MAKING PROCEDURES	PROGRAM DESIGN TASKS	EVALUATION TASKS
Problem formulation	Identify the stakeholders in the intervention and the evaluation. Clarify the objectives of the intervention. Specify the expected degree of impact. of the intervention.	Identify the stakeholders in the evaluation. Clarify the objectives of the evaluation. Clarify the purpose and scope of the evaluation.
Identifying salient factors	Identify conditions that the intervention is supposed to change. Identify mechanisms through which the intervention is supposed to achieve change.	Specify types of data to be collected. Identify valid and reliable measures for each factor.
Identifying alternative strategies	Review research and project literature on different approaches to the intervention.	Review research and project literature on different approaches to the evaluation. Specify the relationships between the evaluation and the program.
Model building	Select the appropriate intervention model. Specify the relationships among baseline conditions, program activities, and desired outcomes.	Identify potential interactions between variables.
Implementation	Develop program structure. Hire and train staff. Monitor provision of services.	Collect baseline data. Assign data collection responsibilities. Develop monitoring procedures. Train staff to do data collection.
Management	Adapt program procedures to changing conditions.	Fine-tune data collection procedures to changes in program operation.
Interpreting feedback	Interpret information from organizational and program operations.	Analyze process and outcome data. Relate evaluation findings to changing conditions within program or operating environment.
Comparison of outcomes between models	Identify community, program, and policy implications.	Compare intervention outcomes to baseline data.

learning and research models on the grounds that such methods submerged the perspectives of historically disenfranchised groups (Harding, 1993; Sayer, 1992). In addition, evaluation researchers began to point out that experimental models for evaluation were not providing the information needed by policymakers or program staff (Dugan, 1996; Usher, 1995).

Whereas evaluators continue to use conventional social science research methods, many researchers have begun to advocate alternative methods. Newer approaches take into account the ways both programs and their evaluations are implemented and sample a wider range of stakeholder viewpoints. Some evaluators now draw on the critical theories of Freire (1971) and newer theories of learning organizations (Chawla & Renesch, 1995). Evaluators who endorse this position believe that stakeholders' perspectives should not only be widely sampled, but that the evaluation itself constitutes an important opportunity for individual and collective learning and community mobilization (Fetterman et al., 1996; Kaplan & Norton, 1996). They argue that the evaluation process should be demystified and that stakeholders' experiences should be taken as a valid form of expertise. Furthermore, evaluations should be empowering by helping stakeholders develop a sense of ownership of programs and their evaluations by being included as active and ongoing participants in the evaluation process. In this way, they can learn how to design evaluations for themselves, collect and interpret data, and apply those findings to making the program more effective.

Each of the evaluation approaches described in this chapter has its particular strengths and limitations. In designing programs and choosing strategies with which to evaluate them, managers are challenged to find ways to approximate the methodological rigor offered by the rational decision-making model without losing the dynamic complexity revealed by process and participatory evaluations. Recognizing this reality, evaluation researchers have begun to investigate how these different research paradigms can be integrated to maximize their methodological strengths and minimize their weaknesses (Greene & Caracelli, 1997).

DIMENSIONS OF EVALUATION

Evaluations can be characterized along a number of dimensions (see Figure 18-1). These include the extent to which various stakeholders are involved; whether the focus of the evaluation is on process outcomes (or both); and whether an experimental, quasi-experimental, or nonexperimental design is used. The roles evaluators play in the evaluation process also vary on a continuum from independent third-party assessor to participant with a longer-term interest in the success of the program.

Figure 18-1. Dimensions of Evaluation Design

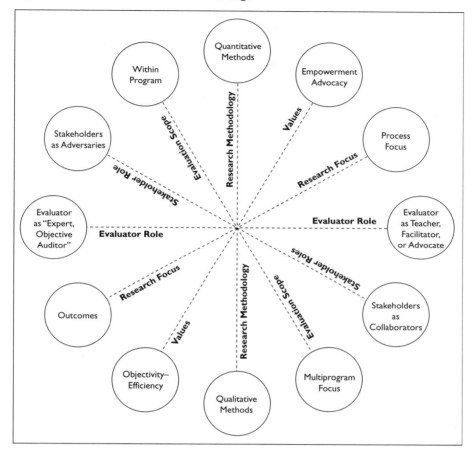

Stakeholder Involvement

Regardless of how they are carried out, evaluations of human services programs must be responsive to many societal pressures (Usher, Gibbs, & Wildfire, 1995). Policymakers and funding organizations are removed from the day-to-day operations of programs but are concerned with resource allocation issues. Program managers and front-line staff are much more in touch with how their programs function. Consumers and their families are directly or indirectly affected by how well programs are designed and implemented. Individual programs are nested within larger networks of interdependent community services, which must coordinate their efforts with one another to maximize their effectiveness (Center for the Study of Social Policy, 1996; Mulroy, 1997).

Each of these actors is a program stakeholder, motivated by different values and needing different kinds of information to perform their roles competently. Not surprisingly, the stakeholders who initiate an evaluation generally determine the purpose and scope of the evaluation. Thus, these initial decisions have multiple consequences. They affect the evaluation design, the role of evaluators, the framing of research questions, the implementation of the evaluation, and the interpretation and application of the evaluation findings.

Focus

Evaluation approaches can also be categorized according to the degree to which they focus on outcomes or process. Where key stakeholders—usually politicians and policymakers—are concerned with efficiency and cost effectiveness, evaluations are designed to measure program outcomes in ways that enable comparisons with other programs. If stakeholders' primary concern is program improvement, the evaluation measures aspects of both program implementation and outcomes. Some stakeholders are more concerned with governance issues—the extent to which administrators and staffs of various community services collaborated in creating and maintaining a social support network that maximized available resources (Center for the Study of Social Policy, 1996; Mulroy, 1997). If stakeholders are concerned with increasing organization or community capacity, the evaluation is designed not only to address program activities and outcomes, but also to train stakeholders to do their own evaluations and monitoring.

Designs

The constellation of stakeholders determines the focus of the evaluation and the evaluation design. Each design has advantages and disadvantages for increasing our understanding of programs. Because evaluations of community services must usually respond to the information needs of multiple stakeholder groups, program evaluators often accommodate them by using "mixed-method" evaluation designs that combine outcome and process evaluation strategies (Greene, 1997).

Evaluators' Roles

Evaluators are also stakeholders in evaluations because their professional reputations depend on whether their efforts produce reliable and valid results while satisfying other stakeholders' needs. Their roles depend on program structure and the type of evaluation. Evaluators may be employees working within the organization who are responsible for monitoring program operations along with their other duties. Alternatively, evaluators may be outside consultants with specific evaluation expertise whom the organization brings in solely to conduct the evaluation.

Depending on the evaluation design, evaluators' roles range from "program auditor" to "community facilitator." If the evaluation is based on an experimental, social science research paradigm, evaluators are expected to keep themselves separate from the program operations so they can maintain their objectivity. Evaluators in this kind of role are charged with judging the outcomes and counterbalancing the vested interests of program staff and management (Lowi, 1993; Usher, 1995). The more participatory evaluation models legitimize evaluators' roles as facilitators for organizational learning and as advocates. In these situations, evaluators may work with stakeholders to help them learn how to design and run their own evaluations and to use that information to make ongoing refinements in program operations (Usher, 1995). They may also draw on their expert status to help programs obtain needed resources (Fetterman, 1996).

RELIABILITY AND VALIDITY IN PROGRAM EVALUATION

Program evaluation is applied social science or behavioral research. Researchers must be able to justify how their research design and procedures produce reliable and valid findings. Reliability and validity have multiple meanings within the context of evaluation. One of the challenges evaluators face as researchers is to make these differences explicit and meaningful to the program stakeholders. If evaluators are unsuccessful in engaging stakeholders in the process, stakeholders are likely to be unwilling to invest the energy and attention needed to produce valid and useful evaluations.

For programs, reliability denotes the ability to produce consistent results using specified methods under a given range of conditions. Within social science research, reliability is also an index of generalizability—the degree to which a program design can be replicated in other sites with similar results. Program stakeholders differ in the importance they place on program generalizability, and the evaluation design reflects those priorities (Patton, 1990). To justify their conclusions, evaluators must also use reliable data collection strategies. If data collection methods are deemed reliable and significant differences in program outcomes are found over time, stakeholders can plausibly claim that the differences are attributable to the program or other factors and not to the ways in which the phenomena were measured (Frankfort-Nachmias & Nachmias, 1992). In evaluation research, concepts of reliability correspond to the type of evaluation design used.

Ideally, program services and the plans for delivering them are based on state-of-the-art knowledge. This knowledge can be derived from personal experience or experience reported by others. This knowledge base includes scientific knowledge about the problem the program is to address and the appropriate remedies. Programs may be more or less successful in applying this knowledge in the design of their services. The form of service delivery itself may enhance or obstruct the effectiveness of the service. Stakeholders want to know whether their programs are appropriate for meeting the needs of their intended recipients. The evaluators want to determine that too, but they have additional concerns. They need to ensure that programs have in fact been implemented as planned and to determine whether the evaluation procedures themselves have been carried out as intended.

If a program does not adhere to standards for reliability and validity, perceived benefits may not be attributable to program activities. If the evaluation procedures do not meet such standards, it is impossible to know whether the program was effective because it is impossible to know what was actually evaluated.

TYPES OF EVALUATION

Outcome Evaluations

Outcome evaluations emphasize results that can be assessed after a program cycle has been completed or the entire program has been terminated. This section compares three types of outcome evaluations: (1) experimental evaluations, (2) performance audits, and (3) decision-oriented or utilization-focused approaches (see Table 18-2).

Experimental Evaluations

Traditionally, outcome evaluations are most often done for distant stakeholders, usually under mandate from high-level policymakers. They usually incorporate research designs that reflect the assumptions and values of policy analysis and the rational decision-making model. This kind of evaluation uses the "gold standard" of research methodologies: experimental and quasi-experimental research designs (Usher, 1995; Weiss & Greene, 1992). For this type of research design, the goal is to establish that independent variables (such as program activities) and dependent variables (such as program outcomes) are causally related (Frankfort-Nachmias & Nachmias, 1992). To confirm this, researchers use strategies of comparison, manipulation, and control. Evaluators use various statistical techniques to assess the degree to which changes in program outcomes are related to provision of program services. Evaluators also seek to understand causal relationships by trying to control the internal and

Table 18-2. Outcome-Oriented Approaches to Program Evaluation

EVALUATION APPROACH	KEY STAKEHOLDERS	VALUES AND EVALUATION OUTCOMES PROMOTED	METHODS	TYPICAL QUESTIONS
Experimental evaluations	High-level policymakers and decision makers	Theoretical, causal understanding Efficiency Accountability	Experimentation Systems analysis Causal modeling Cost–benefit analysis	Are the desired outcomes attained? Are the outcomes attributable to the program? Is this program the most efficient alternative?
Performance audits	Program funders and program administrators	Efficiency Accountability Improved efficiency	Cost finding Process evaluation Output measurement	Has the program met or exceeded preset standards for performance?
Decision-oriented or utilization-focused approaches	Local decision makers and mid-level program managers	Practicality Pragmatism Program effectiveness Quality control Resource utilization	Case studies Interviews Systematic observation Document reviews	Which parts of the program work well? Which parts of the program need improvement? How effective is the program?

external conditions of the study systematically. In a laboratory setting, for example, researchers can use random assignment of participants into treatment and control groups to help rule out the possibility that factors other than the program caused the observed association between the "treatment" and specific outcomes. In classic experimental protocols, data are collected before the start of a program or program cycle and then again after a given program cycle has been completed.

In program evaluation, it is often impossible to impose the level of control required for experimental research designs. Pragmatic evaluators wishing to approximate the rigor of these designs may use quasi-experimental designs, which do not require randomization. Instead of randomized assignment and carefully matched control groups, researchers may use comparison groups that share critical characteristics. They may gather samples from various sites or make multiple observations of the same groups over time as supplementary data to support their conclusions about the extent and range of program effects (Frankfort-Nachmias & Nachmias, 1992).

Because outcome evaluations usually use only quantitative measures, they are somewhat simpler to conduct than process and participatory evaluations. The outcomes are also relatively easy to describe to policymakers. However, they may not produce valid information on which to base policy because they do not explicitly account for the normal dynamism within organizations. For example, program staff often view the evaluators as adversaries who threaten their ability to meet the needs of their clients and also their job security (Usher, 1995). As a result, they may not be committed to implementing new interventions or carrying out evaluation tasks as prescribed, thereby compromising the evaluation design to such an extent that it does not measure what was intended. In addition, key staff may leave the organization, experimental or control group participants may drop out, and organizational policy changes that occur during the course of an evaluation may threaten the validity of the findings (Lipsey, 1990).

Performance Audits

Performance audits are an outgrowth of performance contracting. In performance contracts, funders and program administrators negotiate performance contracts before the program begins. Such contracts specify the degree of change in specific conditions to be accomplished by the end of the funding cycle, the criteria to be used for measuring those changes, the means for monitoring them, and the incentives for meeting or not meeting these goals (Wedel, 1991). Here the funders are interested in knowing whether a program has met or exceeded pre-established standards of performance. The evaluator may be either a project or contract manager with specific responsibilities for program monitoring or an independent consultant brought in from outside. Performance contracts may be linked to linear or stepwise standards. When linear standards are used, incentives and penalties are keyed to incremental improvements. Performance contracts incorporating step-structure criteria reward or penalize programs on the basis of the proportion of overall change in the criteria over the course of a program cycle using some predetermined baseline (Wedel, 1991).

More generally, performance audits are used when decision makers want a "nonsympathetic" third-party review of program outcomes. They tend to be investigative in tone and assume an adversarial relationship between program evaluators and program managers and staff (Usher, 1995). Performance audits offer the same advantages and suffer the same limitations as outcome evaluations in general. Such evaluations can, however, be problematic for other reasons. Although the purpose of performance audits may be to promote efficiency, by presetting unit costs, the true cost of providing services may never be calculated. Performance audits are inflexible in that measurement of outcomes does not take into account the effects of changes within the organization or in the conditions within which the program operates (Wedel, 1991). From the standpoint of community governance, performance auditing may be self-defeating. Because the goal of performance contracting is to promote efficient use of resources, it spurs competition between providers to capture scarce resources rather than cooperation to create synergistic effects for communities as a whole (Nelson, n.d.).

Decision-Oriented or Utilization-Focused Approaches

Decision-oriented or utilization-focused approaches are designed to meet the needs of onsite program managers and local decision makers. Such evaluations are intended to determine which parts of a program work well and which need improvement (Weiss & Greene, 1992). Evaluators may be appointed from within the organization or brought in from outside, and they are expected to maintain a degree of objectivity. To collect data, these evaluators use administrative data, along with structured and unstructured surveys and questionnaires, interviews, and systematic observation.

Process-Oriented Evaluations

Process-oriented evaluations (also called "formative evaluations") are used to gain insight into the ways in which a specific program is experienced by staff and participants at a specific time under specific conditions (Weiss & Greene, 1992). These evaluations are intended to produce information that enables program managers to understand how a project's implementation is associated with stakeholders' feelings of satisfaction or frustration with the way services are delivered. Process-oriented evaluations are used to gain insight into the strengths and weaknesses of programs and to assess whether the program is working as planned (Patton, 1990). These evaluations use a variety of qualitative research methods, such as ethnographic and case studies, interviews with key informants, focus groups, and opinion surveys (Weiss & Greene, 1992). The evaluators are brought in from outside and are usually experts in these research methods.

In process-oriented evaluations, the evaluators themselves are data collection instruments. Their skills, sensitivity, and integrity largely determine whether such evaluations are considered reliable and valid (Patton, 1990). The validity of process-oriented evaluation findings can be challenged if the evaluators are unskilled in the systematic observation, in-depth interviewing, and survey design needed for this approach.

Participatory Evaluations

Participatory evaluations represent an important shift away from the deductive, researcher-centered approaches to more inductive, community-centered efforts (Langton & Taylor, 1992). Participatory evaluations also vary in approach and purpose. Some focus on remedying specific problems, whereas others explicitly aim to promote community empowerment through social criticism and long-term structural changes (see Table 18-3).

The following sections describe different participatory approaches to evaluation. A cross-cutting theme that has recently emerged and is compatible with all of these approaches, however, is the importance of strategic planning. More specifically, it is the recommendation that participants in an evaluation consciously and deliberately develop a "theory of change" to guide the development of new programs and policies (Connell & Kubisch, 1997). As the exercise later in this chapter illustrates, this demands a substantial level of commitment by participants and the self-discipline to think through the intentions and expected consequences of plans.

Action Research

Action research is similar to formative evaluation, but procedures are more informal. Where formative evaluation has a more restricted focus on a specific program, action research methods may be used to study and solve problems within a program, organization, or community (Patton, 1990). Where formative evaluations are usually done by expert evaluators, action research is often done by the people who are directly affected by the problems being studied. Community activists may use action research methods as a form of "rapid reconnaissance" to collect information quickly about a problem (Patton, 1990). This may involve content analysis of communication media, focus groups with stakeholders, interviews with key informants, and systematic observations.

As in all process evaluations, the skills of action researchers can affect the validity of the research findings. Because researchers are often not professionals and may have a vested interest in one outcome over another, they may not collect the range of information needed to present a balanced view of the situation. Action researchers may also be strongly partisan; thus, they may be unable to gain access to information and resources, which may prevent them from reaching accurate conclusions about problem conditions or the full range of possible solutions.

Cluster Evaluations

Cluster evaluations are a new form of participatory evaluation developed by the Kellogg Foundation to promote self-evaluation capacity across the programs it funds (Greene, 1997). Representatives from each project gather semi-annually for networking sessions. Cluster evaluations are founded on the idea

Table 18-3. Process-Oriented and Participatory Approaches to Program Evaluation

EVALUATION APPROACH	KEY STAKEHOLDERS	VALUES AND EVALUATION OUTCOMES PROMOTED	METHODS	TYPICAL QUESTIONS
Process or formative evaluation	Program directors, staff, and clients	Pluralism, understanding, diversity	Case studies, interviews, systematic observation, document reviews	How do various stakeholders experience the program?
Action research	Community activists; stakeholders who are directly affected by the problem under study	Pluralism, understanding, social change	Content analysis of reports in mass media, focus groups with stakeholders, interviews with key stakeholders, systematic observation	What are the needs within the system? What research needs to be done to improve understanding of the system? What interventions need to be developed to improve the system?
Cluster evaluation	Program funders, evaluators, program administrators, and staff	Pluralism, understanding, organizational learning, inclusion of multiple interests	Biannual networking conferences, focus groups	How do various programs respond to common problems? To what extent and in what ways do programs identify and address the needs of disenfranchised groups?
Empowerment evaluation	Disempowered groups (program clients and others), representatives of dominant system	Empowerment, social change	Stakeholder participation in the development and use of structured and unstructured surveys, questionnaires, systematic observation, historical analysis and social criticism	In what ways do the premises, goals, or activities of the program serve to maintain structural inequities in the distribution of power and resources?

of "open borders" in which the evaluation does not have to be protected from program activities to be considered valid. The purpose is to aid and support member projects in their evaluations and program development activities and to promote the expression "democratic pluralism." The foundation's intent is to ensure that the programs and evaluations that it funds take into account the interests of the least-enfranchised citizens. Kellogg staff help staff and evaluators of individual projects analyze their programs and evaluation implementation and give them feedback. Cluster evaluation feedback focuses on the degree to which the evaluations systematically include multiple interests.

The advantage of cluster evaluations is that they enable programs and evaluators to learn from each other about how to resolve common problems, such as how to engage stakeholders in the self-evaluation process or balance programmatic and materials development efforts. Cluster evaluators explicitly advocate empowerment values but avoid the charge of partisanship by promoting program staff and evaluator inquiries. Cluster evaluation discussions cover such topics as the role of expertise in evaluations, the appropriate balance of content and process, and definitions of the programs' and evaluations' stakeholders (Greene, 1997). Cluster evaluators may also help conference participants understand the range of their options within each dimension of an evaluation by developing typologies. The typology itself then is used as the basis of further discussion among participants.

The limitation of this approach is that funders, evaluators, and participants must be willing to think abstractly. Funders must value democratic pluralism and be interested in promoting and supporting organizational learning across projects. The funders must also have supported several similar projects to enable reasonable comparisons and to have a large enough sample. Cluster evaluators are necessarily distant from the ultimate consumers of program services. They must be informed enough about potentially disenfranchised groups and the conditions that contribute to disempowerment to be able to ask appropriate questions. In addition, program administrators must be willing to allow staff to take time out from their primary responsibilities to attend such conferences. Finally, program staff must be able to connect the rather abstract level of discussions about program evaluation to their own work as caregivers.

Self-Evaluations

Self-evaluations are specialized forms of participatory evaluation used within individual programs. The aim here is to help organizations integrate their management and evaluation procedures in such a way that "information about program performance feeds back into policy and program planning, [enabling] corrective action and quality improvement to become routine" (Usher, 1995, p. 62; see Table 18-4). Variants of such integrative approaches are

Table 18-4. Characteristics of Self-Evaluation

KEY STAKEHOLDERS	VALUES AND EVALUATION OUTCOMES PROMOTED	METHODS	TYPICAL QUESTIONS
Program funders	Community self-governance	Multimethod (quasi-experimental and qualitative methods)	Is the program serving the specified population?
Evaluators			
Program administrators, staff, and clients	Organizational learning	Surveys	To what extent is the program being implemented as planned?
Representatives from other community organizations	Enhanced capacity for self-evaluation	Questionnaires	How do various stakeholders experience the program?
	Implementation integrity	Record review	
	Program effectiveness	Focus groups	To what extent and in what ways is the program effective?
			To what extent is the program effectively coordinating its efforts with other community services?

also being promoted as complementary monitoring systems to conventional financial measures of productivity in for-profit corporations (Kaplan & Norton, 1996). In contrast to the adversarial relationships common in conventional evaluations, the self-evaluation approach is based on the assumption that stakeholders at different levels have a shared interest in making programs as effective as possible.

Instead of imposing a research design on the program, the evaluator acts as a consultant to work groups of managers, staff, and stakeholders to help them identify and articulate their program's theory of change (see the theory of change model in the exercise). Once they have developed their program models, staff members and the evaluator collaborate in developing evaluation designs and data collection procedures. If it does not exist already, the evaluator also assists the organization in developing the capacity to analyze and interpret the data that its staff members collect. The goal of this training is to help program managers and staff develop the skills to detect problems and make midcourse corrections. As program staff master these new skills, they become more comfortable taking the risks that come with innovation (Usher, 1995).

Figure 18-2 illustrates the basic structure of self-evaluation teams developed in the Family to Family child welfare reform initiative sponsored by the Annie E. Casey Foundation. At the center of these teams is a triumvirate of stakeholders within the child welfare agency who bring unique perspectives

Figure 18-2. Self-Evaluation Teams

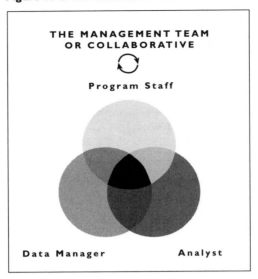

to the evaluation process but who often do not have a history of productive relationships. These three stakeholders include program staff, data managers, and analysts, positions usually found in child welfare agencies in large communities. Data managers are staff who oversee the operation and maintenance of information systems that support program operations and from which information about client characteristics and outcomes can be obtained. Analysts are staff who have the responsibility to meet state and federal reporting requirements, a set of responsibilities that often are a preoccupation that constrains their capacity to respond to information needs by managers, policymakers, and the public. The role of program staff is defined specifically—and pragmatically—as 15 percent of the time of at least one front-line supervisor or mid-level manager. Preferably, the person selected to play this role has demonstrated the ability to step back from the intensity of day-to-day, case-by-case activities and discern patterns in those activities.

The people in these roles bring unique perspectives. The reason program staff are engaged directly with families and children, for example, can be traced to their preference for this type of work rather than the somewhat impersonal involvement with hardware and data. Although their sensitivity to and regard for individual families and children are essential to the agency's effectiveness, it can be difficult for some to look beyond each client and to see what all the clients have in common. Just the opposite, however, can be true of data managers and analysts, who may ignore the uniqueness of individuals in their attempts to identify patterns across those individuals. Bringing them together, therefore, can help create a richer understanding of agency operations and impact.

Empowerment Evaluations

Empowerment evaluations aim to engage a wide range of stakeholders in the analysis of the role of programs within the larger social structure. Although empowerment evaluations seek to determine whether a program is effective, other goals also are considered important. These evaluations promote the learning that participants acquire in the process as much as the specific outcomes of the study. Stakeholders are taught to think critically in identifying key issues and different perspectives about how well a program addresses local needs. The goals of empowerment evaluations are ambitious: "to promote community-level collaboration, improve community climate, strengthen networks, promote positive identity and increase community assets" (Weiss & Greene, 1992, p. 141). This analysis lays the groundwork for community mobilization.

Ideally, empowerment evaluations increase the likelihood of precipitating institutional and policy changes. By participating on the evaluation team, members who historically have had little power establish relationships with others who are more powerful and influential. The evaluation team's decision-making process is intended to model standards of parity, justice, and caring. By collaborating in a joint effort with others who have historically been disempowered, stakeholders with power acquire insight from the historical perspective about social problems and are more motivated to support community activism (Weiss & Greene, 1992).

In empowerment evaluations, professional evaluators serve as teachers and facilitators. Their role is to help stakeholders acquire the skills they need to carry out an evaluation that produces valid and useful results. In essence, the evaluators teach stakeholders to use the rational decision-making model by following four basic procedures. First, the evaluator works with community members to establish a baseline against which future progress can be measured. Participants "take stock" by informally rating programs and their activities and learn about data collection by collecting information that would support their assessments of their programs. In the second step, participants engage in goal-setting exercises to develop a shared vision of what the program should be doing. After generating a list of goals, participants work to develop program models that specify clear causal connections between starting points, intermediate goals that are linked to routine program activities, and their global desired outcomes. In the process, participants learn how to use critical review and consensus-building processes in reducing and refining their goals to those that are most significant to the program's operation. In the final step, participants learn how to document program progress toward their

"Since that last interview only took nine minutes, your client-per-hour ratio increased to seven, which moves you up a notch to fourth fastest intake worker. However, I've noticed your effectiveness-per-client index has fallen."

goals. They identify the data they need, review existing data collection methods to see what data are already being collected, and (where necessary) develop new forms and methods for monitoring data collection (Fetterman, 1996).

Professional evaluators often take charge of the data analysis because program staff do not possess the skills or have the time to do this work. However, the results of such analyses are always given back to the participants, who are responsible for interpreting them and determining how this new information is used.

Although empowerment evaluations have the potential for revitalizing programs and communities, they are also more vulnerable to breakdown than more conventional forms of evaluation. They are more time consuming because they involve not only the evaluation but also a high degree of organizational and community learning. Differences in the individual skills and capacities of participants may cause some of them to feel frustrated and others intimidated. Because empowerment evaluations have explicitly political goals, they may break down if conflicts between stakeholders cause some to become alienated. Because empowerment evaluations compete for staff time and other program resources, the support of program leaders is essential. The evaluation can also break down if the leaders do not support the process by their withholding of resources or their unwillingness to make the changes endorsed by the evaluation participants.

CONCLUSION

Managers of nonprofits and public agencies and their staffs are more often the subjects (or victims) of evaluations than they are participants in the evaluation process (Terry, 1997). Conventional role definitions called for a clear separation of the roles of manager and evaluator, often to the point of adversarialism. However, two factors—more discretion in implementing policy accompanied by increased demands for accountability—are causing these roles to blur. Anticipating policymakers' concerns, more managers are trying to develop the capacity to provide answers before questions are asked. In addition, more managers recognize that they are managing learning organizations whose work entails a series of midcourse corrections that bring them ever closer to the outcomes they seek.

This conception of evaluation is gaining grudging acceptance among professional evaluators who traditionally adhered to a role more akin to that of the scientist than a vital participant in the public policy process. The changes in approach entail context and method as well as attitude. The new context is one in which evaluation is understood by policymakers and the public to be more than auditing and by evaluators to be more than detached, "objective" research. The changes also involve the enrichment of evaluation to encompass a wider range of methods and designs that collectively capture a more valid and reliable composite of what works and how.

Regardless of the type of nonprofit organization in which they work, the most effective managers have probably always understood the importance of evaluation and have incorporated it into their work. Recent political changes and emerging changes in the practice of program evaluation lend legitimacy to this dimension of human services management. By taking advantage of this opportunity, managers who develop their personal skills in evaluation and their organizations' capacity to conduct and use evaluations are likely to see substantial benefits as a result of the insights they acquire about their efficiency and effectiveness. Simply being able to produce valid and reliable information about program operations and impact helps build positive relationships with a wide range of organization stakeholders.

SELF-EVALUATION CASE STUDY:
SOBRIETY TREATMENT & RECOVERY TEAMS

NOTE: *START is funded entirely by the agency, with funding for technical assistance for the evaluation provided through the Annie E. Casey Foundation's Family to Family Initiative.*

In 1996, the County Department of Children and Family Services (DCFS) in a major midwestern city initiated the planning for Sobriety Treatment & Recovery Teams (START) in response to the growing number of children placed in foster care because their families were battling addictions. START's aim is to develop safe, nurturing, and stable living environments for children by helping their parents overcome drug addictions. The program began offering enhanced services in 1997.

The program takes into account that addicted mothers often have experienced repeated abuse and neglect themselves and are confronted with multiple family problems in addition to their addictions. These conditions increase the likelihood that these women will relapse and endanger their newborns and other children. In the past, problems have occurred because drug treatment providers and the DCFS have had differing—and often conflicting—priorities. Drug counselors focused on the addiction recovery needs of their clients, whereas DCFS workers had to devote their energies to keeping the children of those recovering mothers safe. Services to addicted clients were often fragmented as a result of poor communication between DCFS and drug treatment agencies and adversarial relationships between drug counselors and social workers. Clearly, no single city or county agency has adequate resources or expertise to meet the urgent and complex needs of addicted parents who have abused or neglected their children. To address this problem, START draws on a wide array of services and resources offered through nonprofit organizations and public agencies in the metropolitan area (North American Council on Adoptable Children, 1997).

START has four major goals:

1. to offer services that integrate the principles of 12-step recovery programs and family-centered social work practice
2. to improve the rates and proportions of DCFS clients entering and completing substance abuse treatment programs
3. to improve overall family functioning and reduce the risk to children who remain in the home with their addicted mothers
4. to reduce the time it takes to permanently place children who must be removed from their homes because of their mothers' addictions.

Participants

The participants are all mothers who live in the county who deliver their babies at five regional hospitals and test positively for drugs at the time of their deliveries. During the first 12 months of operation, DCFS will admit 150 clients in the treatment group who will receive enhanced services through START and 150 clients in the comparison group who will receive standard child welfare services.

Program Elements

To achieve project goals and to enhance standard DCFS services to addicted mothers, START added three program elements: (1) teaming MSWs with paraprofessional family advocates, (2) improving access to and coordination of services to clients' families, and (3) increasing the intensity of services. Each component is associated with specific, interrelated program activities and with activities that make up the other two components.

START Teams

Specialized Training

Before the program began, each START worker participated in an intensive training program. To compensate for their deficits in general work experience, family advocates were provided with job readiness training and core skills training in child welfare. Before the start of the program, both family advocates and social workers had completed the core skills training required by all DCFS caseworkers. They also participated in program-specific training sessions on the physiological and social–psychological aspects of addictions and their treatment. Team members also received team-building training to develop appropriate, mutual understandings about work roles and how they would share their responsibilities for clients. Teams also received cross–agency training with staff from participating substance abuse treatment providers.

Team Member Roles

START workers have frequent, ongoing personal contacts with their clients starting as soon as possible after clients are referred, while they are in treatment, and afterward for as long as they are in the program. In working with clients, team members draw on their formal training in addictions and child welfare and the advocates' personal experiences with child welfare clients and the addiction recovery process. The advocates' experiences provide clients with positive role models for recovery and help their social worker teammates interpret their clients' drug-related behavior more accurately.

Improved Services

Access to Drug Treatment

All hospitals in the county report perinatal mothers who show evidence of drug abuse to the DCFS child abuse hotline. Women with newborns referred to the hotline are treated as emergency cases. They are assessed by intake workers within 24 hours of the referral and referred to START within 72 hours. Within the first week, DCFS intake staff and START workers meet with the client. As soon as a client has recovered from the delivery, START workers arrange for her admission into the appropriate level of drug treatment and transport her to the first three sessions.

Interagency Service Coordination

Through cross-training sessions, START aims to improve service coordination by increasing DCFS staff and drug counselors' knowledge of each others' philosophies and treatment methods. START workers work with drug treatment providers in treatment settings and stay in frequent contact with their clients' substance abuse counselors while clients are in treatment. Drug treatment providers contact START promptly if a client relapses or stops attending treatment. The program uses a holistic approach to develop clients' service plans. In addition to drug treatment, clients may also receive other services, such as drug-free housing and job training. Other family members may receive family counseling, drug treatment, and parenting-skills training.

Increased Intensity of Services

DCFS services are enhanced through START because both team members work with each client for up to three years. START workers visit the client weekly and are available on an as-needed basis in emergencies. Frequent contacts between START and the drug treatment providers and between START workers and their clients make timely detection of client relapses more likely. Because relapse is a predictable part of the addictive disease course, clients who relapse are allowed to continue in the program, are encouraged to re-enter treatment, and are supported in their efforts to regain their sobriety. However, if a client is unable to stop using drugs, the DCFS can act more quickly to remove her children from the home and into foster care or adoption.

START PROGRAM SELF-EVALUATION

During 1996, DCFS staff developed a multilevel, interactive theory of change model as the basis for identifying causal relationships among initial conditions, program activities, and desired outcomes. The evaluation was designed to address the following questions:

1. Are program activities (client referrals, intake procedures, drug treatment, team building, case management, and coordinated services) being implemented as planned?
2. Are family-centered social work principles and practices and 12-step philosophies being integrated successfully?
3. To what extent does the program
   - reduce the risk for children who are not removed from their own homes when an addicted mother is present?
   - increase the rate and proportion of addicted mothers who enter and complete treatment?
   - reduce the time to permanent placement for children who must be removed from their homes and placed in out-of-home care because of an addicted mother?
4. To what extent is participation in START's intensive drug treatment and other support services related to changes in clients' families?

Evaluation Research Method

The evaluation incorporates a quasi-experimental design that compares START client outcomes to those of clients who received "standard" DCFS services in 1996. Guided by the evaluation consultants, DCFS managers and front-line workers and representatives from other participating agencies developed the theory of change model that described how they expected key elements of the new program to be different from standard agency practice and to contribute to the achievement of START goals. (The theory of change model presented here was developed by START staff and representatives from other participating agencies. Family to Family consultant Judy Wildfire created the model's graphic format.) As work on the project has progressed, this model has been refined to reflect changing conditions and staff understanding of program dynamics.

Based on this model, staff decided what information they would need to collect to obtain feedback about the impact of their efforts. They developed some measures for program indicators that used data that DCFS routinely collects. With technical assistance from evaluation consultants, DCFS staff also developed new data collection instruments to gather data that were not already being collected by the agency. After the program has been running for six months, the evaluation consultants will lead focus groups with managers, team members, clients, and representatives from the other participating agencies to collect their impressions of and reactions to the program implementation

Figure 18-3. START Program Stakeholders' Theory of Change and Evaluation Model

process. During this period, consultants also worked with DCFS managers to improve staff capacity to analyze and interpret the data collected for the project.

SKILLS-APPLICATION EXERCISE

Figure 18-3 and Table 18-5 describe a simple model of a theory of change in which sequences of intervention activities are assumed to lead to desired outcomes. Programs can be difficult to evaluate because their designs are underspecified (Connell & Kubisch, 1997). Often, client problems, precipitating conditions, and desired outcomes are known. However, the specific ways that program activities help consumers move from their initial problems to improved states may not have been clearly thought through. This exercise can help you articulate the theory that underlies an intervention, starting from its ultimate objectives and working backward. Each step in the theory of change is linked to a set of evaluation design questions to help you understand how you know what you know.

1. Think about the program in which you work directly or for which you have management responsibility. Review the questions in Table 18-5 and write brief answers to as many as you can. As you write, ask yourself
   - Which questions are hard to answer? Which are easy? Why?
   - For the questions that are difficult to answer, is there information available to answer that question? Why or why not?
   - Who can provide this missing information?
2. After you have answered the questions, diagram a theory of change model showing how the program works. (Your diagram will probably be much more complex than Figure 18-3, with multiple causes contributing to each program outcome. Review the theory of change developed for Project START in Figure 18-3.)
   - Where are the logical gaps?
   - Where do program activities conflict?
3. How does the organization analyze and use the information that is available to help staff improve their performance and improve overall program function?

Table 18-5. Theory of Change and Evaluation Model

STEP	PROGRAM CHARACTERISTICS	EVALUATION QUESTIONS
1. Long-term outcomes	What are the program's three major objectives? What knowledge base (theory, research, or professional experiences) have been used to select these objectives? What are the relationships among program outcomes?	How are these outcomes measured? When are they measured? How are data currently being analyzed?
2. Penultimate outcomes	How long can consumers remain in the program? How and when do program staff or consumers determine that consumers are approaching completion of the program? What does a consumer have to do to successfully complete the program? Identify program activities that are intended to most directly contribute to consumers achieving program goals. Describe how these program activities contribute to goal attainment. Describe how program activities enhance or interfere with each other.	How are consumers' participation levels documented? (What key aspects of consumer participation are currently not documented?) How does the organization assess consumers' satisfaction with services? What kind of follow-up does the organization do to determine the long-term effectiveness of the program? How is evaluation and client satisfaction survey data used within the organization to improve services?
3. Intermediate outcomes	How and when are program plans for individual participants or groups reassessed? What circumstances lead to changes in program plans? Who is involved in negotiating program plan changes? What criteria are used to decide which program services should be added or dropped at this stage? What combinations of activities appear to enhance or conflict with each other? In what ways? What circumstances lead to consumers being terminated or diverted from the program?	How and when are changes in program plans documented? How are program interactions documented? How and when are revised program plans reassessed for appropriateness and effectiveness?

Table continues

Table 18-5 (continued)

STEP	PROGRAM CHARACTERISTICS	EVALUATION QUESTIONS
3. Intermediate objectives (continued)	*Organizational learning*	
	What organizational structures and processes interfere with effective delivery of services to consumers? (When, how often, and under what circumstances do these problems occur? How are they resolved?)	How are problems with organizational structures and processes documented?
		How are the resolutions of organizational conflicts documented?
	How is knowledge acquired from organizational learning fed back to program managers and staff?	
4. Early outcomes	*Participant entry*	
	What must a person do to be considered a participant in the program?	How are these behaviors documented? (What key behaviors are not currently documented?)
	When must these requirements be completed?	
	What are staff responsibilities when enrolling a new participant?	How are staff actions documented?
	When must these procedures be completed?	
	Early-stage program management	
	When are program plans established?	How are these procedures documented? (What key procedures are not currently documented?)
	Who is involved in program-planning negotiations?	
	What criteria (if any) are used to individualize program plans?	How are program plans documented?
	How are decisions made about sequencing of program activities?	How is client feedback solicited and incorporated in program plans?
	What staff are involved in implementing program plans?	How is the implementation of program plans monitored?
	When and how often are program plans reviewed by supervisors?	
	What criteria are used to determine appropriateness and adequacy of plans at this stage?	
	When and how is feedback given to staff members?	

Table continues

Table 18-5 (continued)

STEP	PROGRAM CHARACTERISTICS	EVALUATION QUESTIONS
5. Initial conditions	*Key demographic and problem characteristics*	
	What are baseline levels of consumer characteristics or problematic conditions?	How are these characteristics measured?
		How often are these characteristics measured?
		When were they last measured?
	Predisposing and precipitating environmental conditions	
	What are baseline levels of these factors–conditions?	How are these factors measured?
	How are changes in environmental conditions fed back into program planning and program staff?	How often are these baseline factors measured? (What factors have not been measured?)
		When were baseline factors last measured?
	Stakeholders	
	Who are the key stakeholders for the project?	How are contacts with stakeholders documented?
	How are these defined?	
	What kind of information does each stakeholder need?	
	How will they use program–client information?	
	When do they need the information?	

REFERENCES

Bandura, A. (1977). *Social learning theory*. Englewood Cliffs, NJ: Prentice Hall.

Bandura, A. (1986). *Social foundations of thought and action*. Englewood Cliffs, NJ: Prentice Hall.

Center for the Study of Social Policy. (1996). *Toward new forms of local governance: A progress report from the field*. Washington, DC: Author.

Chawla, S., & Renesch, J. (Eds.). (1995). *Learning organizations: Developing cultures for tomorrow's work place*. Portland, OR: Productivity Press.

Connell, J., & Kubisch, A. (1997, January). *Applying a theory of change approach to the evaluation of comprehensive community initiatives: Progress, prospects and problems*. Paper presented at the Aspen Institute Roundtable on Comprehensive Community Initiatives for Children and Familes, Aspen, CO.

Dugan, M. A. (1996). Participatory and empowerment evaluation: Lessons learned in training and technical assistance. In D. M. Fetterman, S. J. Kaftarian, & A. Wandersman (Eds.), *Empowerment evaluation: Knowledge and tools for self-assessment and accountability* (pp. 277–301). Newbury Park, CA: Sage Publications.

Durning, D. (1993). Participatory policy analysis in a social service agency: A case study. *Journal of Policy Analysis and Management, 12*, 297–322.

Edwards, R. L., Cooke, P. W., & Reid, P. N. (1996). Social work management in an era of diminishing federal responsibility. *Social Work, 41*, 468–479.

Fetterman, D. M. (1996). Empowerment evaluation: An introduction to theory and practice. In D. M. Fetterman, S. J. Kaftarian, & A. Wandersman (Eds.), *Empowerment evaluation: Knowledge and tools for self-assessment and accountability* (pp. 3–46). Newbury Park, CA: Sage Publications.

Fetterman, D. M., Kaftarian, S. J., & Wandersman, A. (Eds.). (1996). *Empowerment evaluation: Knowledge and tools for self-assessment and accountability.* Newbury Park, CA: Sage Publications.

Frankfort-Nachmias, C., & Nachmias, D. (1992). *Research methods in the social sciences* (4th ed.). Harrisburg, PA: St. Martin's Press.

Freire, P. (1971). *Pedagogy of the oppressed.* New York: HarperCollins.

Greene, J. C. (1997). Evaluation as advocacy. *Evaluation Practice, 18*(1), 25–36.

Greene, J. C., & Caracelli, V. J. (1997, Summer). Defining and describing the paradigm issue in mixed-method evaluation. *New Directions for Evaluation: Advances in Mixed-Method Evaluation, 74*, 5–17.

Hall, R. H. (1991). *Organizations: Structures, processes, and outcomes.* Englewood Cliffs, NJ: Prentice Hall.

Harding, S. (1993). Rethinking standpoint epistemology: What is strong objectivity? In L. Alcoff & E. Potter (Eds.), *Feminist epistemologies* (pp. 49–82). Boston: Routledge & Kegan Paul.

Kaplan, R. S., & Norton, D. P. (1996). Using the Balanced Scorecard as a strategic management system. *Harvard Business Review, 8*(1–2), 75–85.

Langton, P. A., & Taylor, E. G. (1992). Applying a participatory research model to alcohol prevention research in ethnic communities. In P. A. Langton (Ed.), *The challenge of participatory research: Preventing alcohol-related problems in ethnic communities* (pp. 1–20). Washington, DC: U.S. Department of Health and Human Services.

Levitan, S. (1992). *Evaluation of federal social programs: An uncertain impact* (Occasional paper 1992-2): Washington, DC: George Washington University, Center for Social Policy Studies.

Lipsey, M. W. (1990). *Design sensitivity: Statistical power for experimental research.* Newbury Park, CA: Sage Publications.

Lowi, T. J. (1993). Legitimizing public administration: A disturbed dissent. *Public Administration Review, 53*, 261–264.

Loyacono, L. L. (1995). The arts: Singing the blues. *State Legislatures, 21*, 24–27.

Mulroy, E. A. (1997). Building a neighborhood network: Interorganizational collaboration to prevent child abuse and neglect. *Social Work, 42*, 255–264.

Nelson, D. (1994, September). *Keynote address.* Reforming Systems, Reforming Evaluation Conference, sponsored by the Annie E. Casey Foundation, Baltimore.

Nelson, G. M. (n.d.). *Self-governing communities and families: Engaging the community voice in the process of change*: Unpublished manuscript.

North American Council on Adoptable Children. (1997, April). *Shortening children's stays: Innovative permanency planning programs.* St. Paul: Author:

Patton, M. Q. (Ed.). (1990). *Qualitative evaluation and research methods.* Newbury Park, CA: Sage Publications.

Quade, E. S. (1979). *Analysis for public decision.* New York: Elsevier.

Quinn, R. E. (1988). *Beyond rational management: Mastering the paradoxes and competing demands of high performance*. San Francisco: Jossey-Bass.

Sayer, A. (1992). *Method in social science: A realist approach* (2nd ed.). Boston: Routledge & Kegan Paul.

Schorr, L. B. (1997). *Common purpose: Strengthening families and neighborhoods to rebuild America*. New York: Doubleday.

Terry, L. D. (1997). Public administration and the theater metaphor: The public administrator as villain, hero, and innocent victim. *Public Administration Review, 57*(1), 53–59.

Usher, C. L. (1995). Improving evaluability through self-evaluation. *Evaluation Practice, 16*(1), 59–68.

Usher, C. L. (in press). Managing care across systems to improve outcomes for families and communities. *Journal of Behavioral Health Service Research, 25*(2).

Usher, C. L., Gibbs, D. A., & Wildfire, J. B. (1995). A framework for planning, implementing and evaluating child welfare reforms. *Child Welfare, 74*, 859–876.

Walters, J. (1994). TQM: Surviving the cynics. *Governing, 8*, 40–45.

Wedel, K. R. (1991). Designing and implementing performance contracting. In R. L. Edwards & J. A. Yankey (Eds.), *Skills for effective human services management* (pp. 335–351). Washington, DC: NASW Press.

Weiss, H. B., & Greene, J. C. (1992). An empowerment partnership for family support and education programs and evaluations. *Family Science Review, 5*(1–2), 131–148.

Wildavsky, A. (1979). *Speaking truth to power: The art and craft of policy analysis*. Boston: Little, Brown.

INTERNET RESOURCES

Although the addresses of Web sites and listservs are subject to change without notice, the information about how to access online information about evaluation and evaluation research listed here should be fairly stable because the listservs and Web sites are sponsored by well-established charitable foundations, government organizations, and national associations.

Foundations Supporting Self-Evaluation and Empowerment Evaluation in the Human Services

Annie E. Casey Foundation   www.aecf.org/
M. Clark Foundation   fdncenter.org/grantmaker/emclark/index.html
W. K Kellogg Foundation   www.vision.agri.umn.edu/capacity.html

Other Important Web Sites

Alliance for Redesigning
    Government   www.clearlake.ibm.com/Alliance

American Society for Public Administration	www.unomaha.edu/~himbergr/aspa.html
Council of State Governments	www.cst.org
Electronic College of Process Innovation	www.dtic.mil/c3i/bprcd/
Learning Organization	world.std.com/~lo
Pro Futura Professional Business Management	www.lia.co.za/users/johannah/noframe.htm
Society for Applied Sociology	www.Indiana.edu/~appsoc/
U.S. Department of Health and Human Services	www.os.dhhs.gov/search/prog_eval.html

Electronic Discussion Groups (Listservs)

There are still no standard procedures for subscribing to listservs. The directions below specify the e-mail address of the host computer and the required format of the "subscribe" command. In all cases, the subject line is always left blank, and the subscribe command is typed into the message section of the e-mail window. Where there are a number of related listservs on the same host, type in the name of the specific listserv to which you want to subscribe. In place of the words "YourFirstName YourLastName," type in your own name. Web site and listserv addresses and commands are case sensitive; upper-case and lowercase letters must be used as shown in the command.

AEA Collaborative, Participatory, and Empowerment Topical Interest Group

To subscribe: send an e-mail message to MAJORDOMO@LISTS. STANFORD.EDU
In message section, type: SUBSCRIBE EMPOWERMENT-EVALUATION@lists.stanford.edu

American Educational Research Association

AERA has several listservs including two general lists, 12 division lists, and several Special Interest Group lists. Information about these lists can be found on the AERA Web site at www.ed.asu.edu/aera.
To subscribe: send an e-mail message to LISTSERV@ASU>EDU
In message section, type: SUBSCRIBE ListservName YourFirstName YourLastName

American Evaluation Association

To subscribe: send an e-mail message to LISTSERV@UA1VM.UA.EDU
In message section, type: SUBSCRIBE EVALTALK YourFirstName YourLastName

National Institute of Public Administration

This is a a list for evaluators of government programs and others interested in public-sector evaluation.

To subscribe: send an e-mail message to LISTSERV@JARING.MY

In message section, type: SUBSCRIBE GOVTEVAL YourFirstName
YourLastName

Society for Applied Sociology

To subscribe: send an e-mail message to MAJORDOMO@INDIANA.EDU

In message section, type: SUBSCRIBE APPSOC YourFirstName
YourLastName

CHAPTER 19

Managing Risk in Nonprofit Settings

Paul A. Kurzman

> *The life of the law has not been logic: it has been experience; the felt necessities of the time, the prevalent moral and political theories, intuitions of public policy, avowed or unconscious, even the prejudices which judges share with others, have a good deal more to do than syllogism in determining the rules by which we should be governed.*
>
> — Justice Oliver Wendell Holmes, Jr.

For nonprofit managers few topics cause more concern than the issue of risk management. This concern is well founded given the increase in litigation against nonprofit organizations and their boards and staff. Much of the current vulnerability results from changes in the practices and funding of organizations. Human services agencies, for example, no longer are seen merely as compassionate caretakers but as professional service providers. Youth recreation programs, senior citizens' outings, crafts projects, and remedial reading programs have been supplemented (if not supplanted) by sophisticated employment, child development, group home, employee assistance, and family treatment programs. Similarly, voluntary charitable contributions to fund programs in nonprofit organizations (through theater benefits, bequests, thrift shops, community foundations, and United Way contributions) have, in many cases, given way to major contracts and fee-for-service arrangements with governmental agencies, which now provide the bulk of the income. Human services agencies are no longer playing "sandlot ball"; they are playing in the "big leagues" and have correspondingly big risks to manage (Bernstein, 1981; Kurzman, 1995).

As nonprofit organizations come of age, they find that maturity involves new risks and responsibilities. This is true for such disparate entities as museums, hospitals, camps, research institutes, public television stations, zoos, libraries, orchestras, philanthropic foundations, colleges, churches, civic associations, historical societies, technology institutes, private schools, nursing homes, missionary societies, fraternal lodges, community improvement districts, literary guilds, botanical gardens, university presses, and animal welfare societies. Using social work and social agencies as a template for discussion, we may view the nature and complexity of the change for nonprofit organizations more broadly.

LEGAL ENVIRONMENT

In tandem with rapid social change has come the recognition of social work as a full-fledged mental health profession. Social workers are, by far, the largest professional group today in the human services arena. However, 25 years ago, in 1973, only 11 states provided for the legal regulation of social work practice; in 1998, all 50 states do. Similarly, professional social workers enjoy the status of qualified providers of mental health services under state insurance laws in 32 states today, whereas such vendorship status for social work did not exist in a single state 25 years ago (American Association of State Social Work Boards, 1996). With licensure and vendorship have come the authority to be direct and independent providers of clinical treatment services, generally without referral from or supervision by psychologists or physicians. Increasingly, clinical social workers make the diagnoses, provide the treatment, authenticate clients' claim forms, and authorize third-party reimbursements, not only with private insurance carriers, but with the Civilian Health and Medical Program of the Uniformed Services and Medicare. Today, social workers serve as expert witnesses in courts of law, as mental health managed care experts for major health insurance carriers, and as framers of clinical service regulations in the departments of both state and federal governments.

As lawyers have noted, "professionals are held to a higher standard of behavior in their professional capacities than that of the general population" (Watkins & Watkins, 1989, p. 36). Hence, the recent recognition of social work's autonomous professional stature by the government, insurance companies, courts of law, and the public has helped create new forms of exposure and greater risk in practice. Some service settings, of course, involve inherently higher levels of potential peril than do others. Nonprofit organizations with foster care, adoption, day care, debt management, family planning, protective services, group home, camping, residential treatment, and sexual dysfunction programs, for example, place practitioners and managers at particularly high levels of risk. Even the public sector of social work practice is no longer protected. As Besharov (1985) noted: "Courts have all but abolished the doctrines of sovereign, governmental, and public official's immunity, so that it has become easier to bring tort suits against public social service agencies and their employees. Similarly, the abolition of the doctrine of charitable immunity has exposed private agencies and their employees to greater liability" (p. 13).

Today, nonprofit managers also must "look within" to managing their risks as employers in a competitive and heterogeneous world. For example, do women have access to senior positions in the same way men traditionally have? Are people of color well represented on staff, not just at the clerical or custodial level but in professional, supervisory, and managerial positions? Are appropriate accommodations made for people with disabilities, both as staff and as clients, in a barrier-free environment? Are ageist and homophobic biases toward colleagues and clients dealt with promptly, honestly, and openly? Many of these issues are dealt with, in part, when a union represents staff or when strong organizations are present in the broader community to ensure nondiscrimination and the ongoing accountability of organizations to their consumers of service—but increasingly, such intermediaries are not at hand.

The foregoing realities would be cause enough for concern if professionals were well prepared for risk management issues in their graduate education; however, many are not (Barker, 1984; Besharov, 1985; Schroeder, 1995). Professional codes of ethics are rarely mentioned in the curriculum; moreover, the legal dimension of ethical issues in practice receives scant attention in higher education curricula, despite the guidelines of accrediting bodies. Hence, managers may have little preparation for this critical dimension of their professional responsibility. This situation is certainly no better with respect to members of other disciplines who are involved in nonprofit organizations. Indeed, managers may be skilled supervisors, wise administrators, and even creative fundraisers, but managing the institution's legal obligations and vulnerability is an area for which they are apt to be unprepared and unqualified. Moreover, because staff are likely to perceive themselves as "good-doers" and "do-gooders," risk management may seem an oxymoron (Barton & Sanborn, 1978; Everstine & Everstine, 1986).

COMPETING VALUES

As Quinn and Rohrbaugh (1981) suggested, competing values underpin any assessment of an organization's effectiveness. Organizations that follow an "open systems" model, for example, may value behaviors and outcomes that would be perceived as less important to leaders who pursue a "rational goal" model. Simply put, "the Competing Values Approach suggests that the selection of various criteria of effectiveness reflects competing value choices" (Edwards, 1987, p. 5). As a manager, should one emphasize chance taking, creativity, and innovation, or rules and regulations that may reduce risk, exposure, and potential organizational jeopardy, from without and within? Does promoting innovation and decision making at the level closest to the client enhance the organization's posture, or place its stability (in an unstable world) at too great a risk (Kurzman, 1977)?

To many observers, the term "risk management" connotes caution, collaboration, and consultation. Professionals, who are trained to have expertise in autonomous practice, may perceive such an agenda as a series of illegitimate boundaries circumscribing their judgment, discretion, and freedom to maintain service-centered interventions. Too much management of risk indeed may inhibit the freedom one wishes to promote to keep the organization at "the cutting edge"—competitive and therefore stable in an ever-changing external world.

As Lewin and Cartwright (1964) noted, a dynamic field of forces conditions and constrains managers' decisions. In fact, recognition of and a healthy respect for the inevitable competing values just noted can lead managers to a different use of self that may strike a proper balance among the several forces over time. A competing values approach gives recognition to this reality and provides a useful framework for analysis and conceptualization. The approach both highlights elements and values that are often overlooked (such as risk management activity) and encourages the manager to place the need for action in this arena in a broader perspective that may condition implementation. Quinn and Rohrbaugh's (1981) perspective can prod the nonprofit manager to initiate instrumental activities toward the legitimate protection of the organization, its staff, and those whom it serves without placing an inappropriate or exclusionary value on this activity over others. In Simon's (1961) terms, an acknowledgment of competing values can lead to the development of a "satisficing" model of management that recognizes legitimate contending interests among the field of forces, without and within.

RISKS

As the references to this chapter indicate, many books have addressed the vulnerabilities and the liabilities inherent in professional practice. However, less emphasis has been placed on the nonprofit agency per se and on the role of the executive or manager in establishing and managing risk management activities. This section examines the major risks that require management and the complexity of the competing values that must be squarely addressed.

Six risks in prototypical human services practice are most frequently noted. If these risks are not understood and approached from a preventive posture, they most likely result in litigation or claims of unethical practice. (Note:

Although the following is addressed primarily to the human services, with social workers as one example, it is also applicable to other professionals in similar voluntary, charitable, nonprofit organizations.)

Best known perhaps may be the employee's and organization's duty to warn if the client discloses an intent to harm himself or herself or others. Codified in what has become known as the *Tarasoff* decision, a ruling by the California Supreme Court in 1976 imposed on therapists the duty to "exercise reasonable care" in the protection of potential victims from the violent acts of clients (Weil & Sanchez, 1983). The court concluded that therapists have "an affirmative duty to warn and protect" when they determine, through appropriate standards of their profession, that their clients present a serious danger of violence to a particular person or persons (*Tarasoff v. Board of Regents of the University of California*, 1976). Although the *Tarasoff* case was decided by a state court and thus technically may be of limited jurisdictional value, few cases have had as far-reaching an effect (Hull & Holmes, 1989). Several landmark decisions in subsequent years affirmed the *Tarasoff* principle and extended its intent to cover nonlicensed "mental health counselors" and licensed mental health providers (*Hedlund v. Superior Court of Orange County*, 1983; *Jablonski v. U.S.*, 1983; *Peck v. Counseling Service of Addison County*, 1985). In the *Tarasoff* decision, the court said, in part,

> When a therapist determines, or pursuant to the standards of his profession should determine, that his [or her] patient presents a serious danger of violence to another, he [or she] incurs an obligation to use reasonable care to protect the intended victim against such danger. The discharge of this duty may require the therapist to take one or more of various steps, depending on the nature of the case. Thus it may call for him [or her] to warn the intended victim or others likely to appraise the victim of the danger, to notify the police, or to take whatever other steps are reasonably necessary under the circumstances.

A second area of risk to human services organizations comes ironically from the duty to keep confidential all material that is shared with them and their practitioners in the course of a professional relationship. Section 1.07(c) of the *NASW Code of Ethics* (NASW, 1996), for example, states, "Social workers should protect the confidentiality of all information obtained in the course of professional service. . ." (p. 10). However, confidentiality is not absolute, which is why the sentence continues, "except for compelling professional reasons" (see also Promislo, 1979).

What the *Tarasoff* decision did was to delineate one such "compelling professional reason" and to clarify that the word "should" may imply an obligation to act and disclose. In the words of the *Tarasoff* decision: "The protective privilege ends where the public peril begins."

Indeed, the concept of client confidentiality is governed for social workers in law in 44 states as "privileged communication." The state statutes provide

*"According to the **Tarasoff** decision, I'm obligated to warn the people below of your intention to jump on them."*

protection for service recipients similar to the protection they enjoy in the context of their relationships with attorneys, members of the clergy, and physicians (Knapp & Van de Creek, 1987). However, almost all such statutes make exceptions to privilege when such disclosure is necessary to avert serious foreseeable and imminent harm to self or other identifiable people or to prevent the abuse or neglect of children. In fact, most states today have a specific law that mandates professionals to report known or suspected cases of child abuse and would define nonreporting as a *prima facie* case of unprofessional conduct.

A third professional obligation involves the duty to ensure continuity of service to people under care. The expectation is that the institution does not abandon or neglect a client who needs immediate care or currently is under its care without making reasonable arrangements for the continuity of service. Such a duty obligates the organization to uncooperative and "undesirable" clients, whose hostility and initial unresponsiveness may indeed be a symptom of their need and their disorder. Being able to demonstrate outreach, empathy, flexibility, and appropriate referral to an alternate provider may be essential (Meyer, Landis, & Hays, 1988; Salzman & Proch, 1990). Similarly, the duty adequately to record services provided is incumbent on all providers and practitioners (Schrier, 1980). As social workers and other human services providers achieve the status and recognition of vendors, accurate and timely recording becomes essential to ensure that both institutions and clients are properly protected for the receipt of third-party payments. The failure to support a diagnosis from the American Psychiatric Association's (1994) *Diagnostic and Statistical Manual of Mental Disorders* (4th ed.), commonly known as DSM-IV, in recording that has been provided to an insurance carrier to justify a fee payment may be defined as an act of fraud within state statutes. In addition, many states that license professional practitioners define the failure to provide adequate recording of services and to retain such records for a specific number of years as grounds for charges of professional misconduct.

Practitioners also have a duty to diagnose and treat their clients properly. This is a major issue for organizations that have weak procedures for supervisory review and few standards to support interprofessional consultation and referral (Corey, Corey, & Callanan, 1993; Reamer, 1989). The failure to refer a client to a physician to rule out biological, organic, or genetic conditions that may trigger psychological symptoms is perhaps the largest arena of risk. Alexander (1983) noted that half the claims for erroneous diagnoses made under an Insurance Trust's professional liability insurance program were based on a charge that the clients' problems were actually medical, not psychological. In addition, organizations need to provide for consultation in psychosocial areas for which individual providers may still be poorly trained, such as learning disabilities, eating disorders, and substance abuse.

The expectation that practitioners reach an appropriate DSM-IV diagnosis also implies that this correct assessment is recorded on insurance forms to Medicaid, Medicare, and private insurance carriers such as Blue Cross/Blue Shield. Because social workers and other human services providers are often recognized as eligible vendors of psychotherapeutic treatment, care must be taken that errors in diagnosis, whether intentional or inadvertent, are not recorded. Research (Kutchins & Kirk, 1987) has shown that service recipients may place pressure on providers to report less severe diagnoses than are indicated because of their fear of the potential adverse effects of labeling. Staff may conversely feel pressure to increase the severity of the diagnosis falsely or to exaggerate symptoms so the consumer can qualify for third-party payments.

Finally, a risk to practice is inherent in the duty to avoid sexual impropriety. Sexual acts performed under the guise of therapy are not permitted between clients and staff (Schultz, 1982). Virtually all the codes governing the professional conduct of social workers, for example, in the 50 states (and three jurisdictions) that regulate their practice make this prohibition explicit. Moreover, section 1.09(a) of the *NASW Code of Ethics* (NASW, 1996) makes no exceptions to its unequivocal statement: "Social workers should under no circumstances engage in sexual activities or sexual contact with current clients" (p. 13). Such activity cannot be defended in the guise of "supporting the transference" or helping to "overcome sexual inhibition or dysfunction." Given the position of trust that the employing organization shares with its practitioners, courts may view employers as having culpability as well. The potential perils here are even greater than with the risks previously described, because most insurance policies exclude intentional wrongdoing, such as sexual involvement with clients. Managers and supervisors, moreover, generally are viewed in the role of *respondeat superior* and share vicarious liability for such tortuous acts committed by those under their supervision or in their employ (Watkins & Watkins, 1989).

I highlighted these most serious risks and duties to demonstrate that great caution and sound judgment are needed by those who lead nonprofit service organizations today. The litigious environment in which professionals currently practice makes it imperative that managers reduce their organization's exposures while preserving a spirit of flexibility and innovation. Procedures have to be put in place because good intentions provide insufficient protection. In addition to the possibility of government-sponsored criminal actions against nonprofit employers and their practitioners, civil actions by consumers are becoming more common and more successful. The defense against torts, such as the negligence of employers and the malpractice of individuals, requires as careful thought as preparation of the budget and staffing of the board of trustees do. These exposures are shared by all nonprofit organizations, including churches, libraries, schools, civic associations, hospitals, museums, and cultural organizations.

RECOMMENDED RESPONSES

Four major recommendations flow from this discussion. They reflect a focus on the competing values that are intrinsic to the issues at hand and therefore deal with process and goals, the maintenance of and competition among systems, planning and training, and the internal and external loci of organizational concern.

Insurance Protection

No nonprofit entity can afford to be without adequate forms of insurance. Such coverage should include

- premises liability, covering all sites at which services may be delivered
- professional liability, including the activities of all paid staff, volunteers, and consultants
- coverage of officers and directors, to shield members of the board of trustees from individual and collective personal liability in the performance of their fiduciary duties
- vehicular insurance, generally at a level higher than the mandated state minimum
- bonding for all officers and staff who have the authority to sign contracts or manage the institution's income and assets.

Such casualty policies should cover the organization and key participants for most losses and damages, including negligence, provided that one cannot prove nonfeasance or malfeasance (Angell & Pfaffle, 1988). In addition, insurance generally provides for the funding of the potentially expensive legal defense against charges that may be brought, regardless of the outcome. Without adequate insurance, winning a case in court may actually be a pyrrhic victory (Jones & Alcabes, 1989). Out-of-pocket legal fees and court costs may be so high that, in effect, one "loses" even when one wins. In summary, it is essential for the organization to obtain insurance coverage that is commensurate with the organizational scope and program complexity of its services (Tremper, 1989).

Legal Counsel

Every nonprofit organization should establish legal counsel in the same way it sets up an ongoing relationship with an accountant or program consultant. One should not wait until a crisis occurs and then select an attorney under pressure. Most managers try to ensure that one or more attorneys serve on their advisory board or board of directors, so they can get the frequent informal advice they may need on such issues as reviewing a lease, framing an amendment to the bylaws, or signing a governmental contract, usually on a *pro bono* basis. However, an independent counsel often is warranted. First, some legal opinions may involve a potential conflict of interest for a board member because the questions involve actions by the board itself or one of its members. Second, the legal issues may be outside the board member's legal specialization and expertise. Third, the individual (or organization) that is taking legal action may be a client of the board member's firm.

Whether done by a board member or an external counsel, new legal agreements and contracts should be fully reviewed before they are signed. Given the principle of *respondeat superior* noted earlier, it also is important for an attorney to ensure that insurance covers those people, for example, who are agents of the facility's service (under the supervision of organizational employees), such as student interns, Volunteers in Service to America workers, community volunteers, and trainees (Cohen & Marino, 1982). On a proactive basis, an attorney should regularly explore the major federal, state, and local statutes (and evolving case law) that govern the organization, its funding, and its services.

Staff Training

The best way to avoid trouble is to prevent it from occurring. Professionals know the value of education and prevention, often deploying these skills on behalf of customers and clients with remarkable creativity and success. As managers, however, they often forget to apply what works in their own practice to the organizations for which they now are responsible.

In addition to ongoing service-centered training activities that may accompany monthly administrative meetings or periodic case conferences, it may be wise to institute quarterly half-day sessions for formal administrative training. Such sessions not only provide line staff with the information they need for advancement into administrative positions, but they also send the message that organizational issues are everyone's concern (Besharov & Besharov, 1987; Sharwell, 1982). Experts can be invited to speak, or staff with special expertise can lead the sessions. From a risk management perspective, among the important items to cover may include

- state laws governing the requirements and procedures for reporting known or suspected cases of child abuse or neglect
- principles that are embodied in the *Tarasoff* decision with regard to the "duty to protect" when there is serious potential danger by a client to self or to others
- current federal and state regulations on record keeping and maintenance
- statues on privileged communication governing the several mental health professions and the specific principles of confidentiality embodied in the professions' ethical codes
- the proper completion of insurance forms for third-party reimbursement, including the appropriate use of the several axes of the DSM-IV
- additional training for proper differential diagnoses in areas in which many professionals may be poorly trained, such as learning disabilities, organic pathology, psychopharmacology, and chemical dependence
- relevant state rules and standards of professional conduct for the licensed professions, as appropriate, including nursing, social work, nutrition, audiology, architecture, accounting, and engineering.

Special emphasis must be given to the need to train staff to avoid even the appearance of sexual impropriety. Occasionally, it may be appropriate, for example, for a therapist to hug clients momentarily to console them; to stroke their wrists briefly during a moment of stress; or to compliment clients on their dress or appearance if this is a new sign of strength and self-esteem. It would be naive, however, not to understand that there is a thin line that would be easy for staff to cross. Moreover, one must remember the clinical dictum, especially in working in the context of a helping relationship with troubled clients, that "perception is reality." The alarming rise in charges of professional misconduct that have been brought before disciplinary committees of licensing boards and committees of inquiry in various professional associations in the past few years (charging service providers with both heterosexual and homosexual sexual misconduct) must be understood and underscored. As was noted, such charges against social workers, for example, have become so prevalent in recent years that a cap has been placed on professional liability insurance coverage when a sexual impropriety by a practitioner has been documented (Besharov, 1985).

Furthermore, managers should note that this issue is not profession specific. An American Psychological Association study showed that during a 10-year period, 45 percent of all malpractice awards through its professional liability coverage dealt with therapist–patient intimacy ("Therapist–Patient Sexual Intimacy," 1988). Bringing in a member of an appropriate professional association's committee on inquiry to discuss the respective provisions of the *NASW Code of Ethics* (NASW, 1996) in this area is warranted. In addition, it may be wise to invite a member of the disciplinary panel of relevant state licensing boards to speak about standards for licensure and case law experience regarding sexual impropriety. Training staff members to avoid giving even the possible suggestion of improper behavior in their speech, conduct, and presentation of self is crucial to limiting a facility's exposure. If such a transgression occurs, the staff person should be quickly identified as "an impaired professional" and referred for appropriate help, and the consumer's needs and rights must be served and protected.

Internal Audit

All nonprofit organizations conduct a fiscal audit each year, if only because it is required by funding bodies and by the Internal Revenue Service as a condition for maintaining their tax-exempt status. However, most managers do not retain outside experts to conduct a periodic program and management audit to ensure that risks are being properly managed. An external and board auditor and a senior member of the managerial staff should review the following items:

- Are the organization's governmental licenses and accreditations in order?
- Are all eligible professional staff currently licensed and registered for practice?
- Are provisions for emergency actions (fire drills, the reporting of theft, the involuntary hospitalization of clients, the safety of staff, and responding to accidents) well known and regularly updated?
- Have premiums for all forms of casualty insurance coverage been paid?
- Are procedures for the management of records being properly followed?
- Are governmental vouchers and records of insurance reimbursements being maintained in keeping with contractual requirements?
- Are supervisory evaluations being conducted and reviewed in a timely fashion?

A biennial internal management audit of the appropriateness of such standard operating procedures and the staff's adherence to their provisions is a preventive risk management activity that may pay big dividends for the organization, the staff, and those they serve.

CONCLUSION

New opportunities have brought new risks. As professionals who often are managing regulated organizations in the context of a litigious society, nonprofit managers can no longer consider risk management a luxury. The demands of clients, funding sources, and the standards of the professions suggest that managing risks is part of the prudent manager's responsibility for implementing a strategy of primary and secondary prevention. That is, risk management is better conceptualized as a proactive strategy of affirmation than as a reactive response to a crisis. Managers who organically build in this function as a normative component to their administrative role and function should not find this activity any more burdensome than hiring staff and balancing the budget. Although managers have to respond to many competing values as they control and adapt to their environment, the growth and stability of organizations are dependent on the managers' competent performance of risk management functions. Nonprofit service organizations have legitimate "survival needs" because they must coexist with internal and external forces that constantly impinge on them. In a sense, they are social organisms that reflect the legitimate competing values to which they must respond. In this context, they must manage risks to thrive and survive, often in turbulent times, because consumers—often with few options in life—depend on them.

SKILLS-APPLICATION EXERCISES

- You are the manager of a hospital-based employee assistance program (EAP) that provides free and confidential professional mental health and substance abuse services to all hospital employees and their families. An emergency room nurse voluntarily comes to the EAP to see a counselor on your staff about her cocaine and alcohol addiction, which she says "seems to be getting worse." Because she is exceedingly good at what she does and generally careful about when she "snorts" and drinks, her addiction has not been detected by supervisors or peers. She wants help for her problem, but only if she can stay on her job and only if the EAP promises her confidentiality. Provided that the EAP staff make these two promises, she indicates she will do whatever they recommend, including coming in for daily EAP sessions, gradually eliminating her use of alcohol and cocaine, and joining Alcoholics Anonymous and Cocaine Anonymous in the community. She reminds your staff person that she is a voluntary self-referral and of the EAP's long-standing and well-known promise of confidentiality (Kurzman, 1988). Without revealing the client's identity, your EAP counselor wants to know whether you permit him to honor the client's requests. What do you do, and why?

- Your private community college has received a letter from a prominent negligence attorney alleging that a male faculty member at the college made explicit verbal and physical advances to a female student after evening classes and during advising sessions held in his office. It is said that the student, in the context of a relationship of unequal power, was told that her course grade and letter of recommendation for senior college depended on her willingness to become sexually intimate with the faculty member. The attorney says these advances made her physically ill and unable to function at her well-paid job as an executive secretary, because she could no longer concentrate at work. She further claims, through her attorney, that your faculty member's actions alienated the affection of her husband, a prominent physician, who wants a divorce. The client's attorney wants to meet with you to explore a $1 million settlement, in lieu of a protracted, public, and potentially more costly outcome of litigation against you, the faculty member, and the college. As the provost, would you meet with the client's attorney? What are your short- and long-range plans of action?

- You are the new executive vice-president of a center for the performing arts that has a symphony orchestra, theater repertory, opera company, music conservatory, experimental drama workshop, modern dance ensemble, and a ballet. You have several state-of-the-art facilities, many prominent performers, and a large number of performance support personnel. Your center receives income not only through sales and subscriptions but also from government arts and humanities grants, rental agreements, teaching and training contracts, corporate sponsorships, foundation grants, and an endowment. You have a diverse professional, paraprofessional, and support staff and the immediate aid of three experienced deputies (for program, development, and administration). What is your plan of action, during your first year, to assess the adequacy and sufficiency of your organization's risk management policies and procedures?

REFERENCES

Alexander, C. A. (1983, November). *Professional liability insurance: Jeopardy and ethics.* Paper presented at the Professional Symposium of the National Association of Social Workers, Washington, DC.

American Association of State Social Work Boards. (1996). *Social work laws and board regulations: A state comparison study.* Culpeper, VA: Author.

American Psychiatric Association. (1994). *Diagnostic and statistical manual of mental disorders* (4th ed.). Washington, DC: Author.

Angell, F. J., & Pfaffle, A. E. (1988). *The whole field of insurance and risk management* (3rd ed.). Mt. Vernon, NY: Chase Communications.

Barker, R. L. (1984). The *Tarasoff* paradox: Confidentiality and the duty to warn. *Social Thought, 10*(4), 3–12.

Barton, W. E., & Sanborn, C. J. (Eds.). (1978). *Law and the mental health professions.* New York: International University Press.

Bernstein, B. E. (1981). Malpractice: Future shock of the 1980s. *Social Casework, 62,* 175–181.

Besharov, D. J. (1985). *The vulnerable social worker.* Silver Spring, MD: National Association of Social Workers.

Besharov, D. J., & Besharov, S. H. (1987). Teaching about liability. *Social Work, 32,* 517–522.

Cohen, R. J., & Marino, W. E. (1982). *Legal guidebook in mental health.* New York: Free Press.

Corey, G., Corey, M., & Callanan, P. (1993). *Ethics in the helping professions* (4th ed.). Pacific Grove, CA: Brooks/Cole.

Edwards, R. L. (1987). The competing values approach as an integrating framework for the management curriculum. *Administration in Social Work, 11,* 1–13.

Everstine, L., & Everstine, D. S. (1986). *Psychotherapy and the law.* Orlando, FL: Grune & Stratton.

Hedlund v. Superior Court of Orange County, 34 Ca. 3d 695 (1983).

Hull, L., & Holmes, G. (1989). Legal analysis and public agencies: The therapist's duty to warn. *New England Journal of Human Services, 9*(2), 31–34.

Jablonski v. U.S., 712 F. 2nd 391 (1983).

Jones, J. A., & Alcabes, A. (1989). Clients don't sue: The invulnerable social worker. *Social Casework, 70,* 414–420.

Knapp, S., & Van de Creek, L. (1987). *Privileged communication for mental health professionals.* New York: Van Nostrand Reinhold.

Kurzman, P. A. (1977). Rules and regulations in large-scale organizations: A theoretical approach to the problem. *Administration in Social Work, 1,* 421–431.

Kurzman, P. A. (1988). The ethical base for social work in the workplace. In G. M. Gould & M. L. Smith (Eds.), *Social work in the workplace* (pp. 16–27). New York: Springer.

Kurzman, P. A. (1995). Professional liability and malpractice. In R. L. Edwards (Ed.-in-Chief), *Encyclopedia of social work* (19th ed., Vol. 3, pp. 1921–1927). Washington, DC: NASW Press.

Kutchins, H., & Kirk, S. A. (1987). DSM-III and social work malpractice. *Social Work, 32,* 205–211.

Lewin, K., & Cartwright, D. (1964). *Field theory in social science.* New York: Harper & Row.

Meyer, R. G., Landis, E. R., & Hays, J. R. (1988). *Law for the psychotherapist.* New York: W. W. Norton.

National Association of Social Workers. (1996). *NASW code of ethics.* Washington, DC: Author.

Peck v. Counseling Service of Addison County, 499 A-422, VT (1985).

Promislo, E. (1979). Confidentiality and privileged communication. *Social Work, 24,* 10–13.

Quinn, R. E., & Rohrbaugh, J. (1981). A competing values approach to organizational effectiveness. *Public Productivity Review, 5,* 122–140.

Reamer, F. G. (1989). Liability issues in social work supervision. *Social Work, 34,* 445–448.

Salzman, A., & Proch, K. (1990). *Law in social work practice.* Chicago: Nelson-Hall.

Schrier, C. (1980). Guidelines for record-keeping under privacy and open-access laws. *Social Work, 25,* 452–457.

Schroeder, L. O. (1995). *The legal environment of social work* (rev. ed.). Washington, DC: NASW Press.

Schultz, B. (1982). *Legal liability in psychotherapy: A practitioner's guide to risk management.* San Francisco: Jossey-Bass.

Sharwell, G. R. (1982). Avoiding legal liability in the practice of school social work. *Social Work in Education, 5,* 17–25.

Simon, H. A. (1961). *Administrative behavior* (2nd ed.). New York: Macmillan.

Tarasoff v. Board of Regents of the University of California, 17 Cal. 3d 425, 551, p 2d 344 (1976).

Therapist–patient sexual intimacy. (1988, September–October). *EAP Digest,* p. 13.

Tremper, C. R. (1989). *Reconsidering legal liability and insurance for nonprofit organizations.* Lincoln, NE: Law College Education Services.

Watkins, S. A., & Watkins, J. C. (1989). Negligent endangerment: Malpractice in the clinical context. *Journal of Independent Social Work, 3*(3), 35–50.

Weil, M., & Sanchez, E. (1983). The impact of the *Tarasoff* decision on clinical social work practice. *Social Service Review, 57,* 112–124.

PART FIVE

DIRECTING

SKILLS

DIRECTING SKILLS

Managerial directing skills encompass the roles of producer and director. Competencies for the producer role include personal productivity, motivating others, time management, and stress management. Competencies for the director role include taking initiative, goal setting, assigning and guiding the work of others, and effective delegating.

Thomas P. Holland, in chapter 20, stresses the importance of the manager's role in strengthening the performance of the organization's board. He suggests that creating, nurturing, and renewing the board is basic to an organization's survival and effectiveness. Holland considers the basic functions of a nonprofit board, suggests criteria for selecting board members, and identifies characteristics of effective boards. He also discusses the role of the chief executive in relation to the board and suggests a number of specific steps managers can take to enhance board performance.

In chapter 21, Douglas C. Eadie discusses the field of strategic planning and management, suggesting that the central issue for nonprofit organizations is maintaining a dynamic balance between their internal and external environments. He argues that managers need to engage in strategic issue management and delineates specific steps in the process. Eadie believes that the enhancement of the relative position of an organization to its external environment is a key function of nonprofit managers.

Laurie N. DiPadova and Sue R. Faerman discuss the management of time in chapter 22. They stress the competencies of personal productivity, goal setting, taking initiative, delegating, and managing stress. They believe that the effective management of time is a personal responsibility and can be learned. Further, they suggest that managers can increase their ability to accomplish more in less time by working smarter, not harder. To support their view, they explore some of the myths of time management and present detailed techniques to enable managers to improve their time management skills.

In chapter 23, John A. Yankey, Barbara Wester, and David Campbell point out that organizational merger has become an increasingly important response of nonprofit organizations to changing environmental conditions. They define merger as a form or organizational restructuring and explore reasons for the increase in mergers among nonprofits.

In chapter 24, John A. Yankey suggests that nonprofit organizations have increasingly needed the services of consultants. He identifies reasons nonprofits use consultants, as well as why consulting relationships sometimes fail, and provides guidelines that nonprofit managers can use to help them select and contract with consultants. Yankey concludes with recommendations for making consultation engagements more productive.

CHAPTER 20

Strengthening Board Performance

Thomas P. Holland

The competing values framework suggests that managers must be adept at performing many roles more or less simultaneously (see chapter 1). Some of these roles involve attending to the organization's external environment and providing appropriate structure. Given that nonprofit organizations are established to accomplish societal objectives, managers must be aware of environmental trends affecting the organization and its users, patrons, or clients. As a manager, you must be concerned about the process of establishing organizational goals, ensuring organizational continuity and goodwill, and stimulating the individual and collective achievement of staff and volunteers. The governing board is a nonprofit organization's most important volunteer entity. Having an effective, supportive, and involved governing board is essential for an organization's long-term success.

The governing board carries out a range of vital functions for any non-profit organization. Its members—sometimes called "trustees," "overseers," or "directors"—are people in whom power is entrusted by the community to act as fiduciaries and to guide their organizations with caring, skill, and integrity. They represent the voice of society and are expected to act on behalf of the interests of the community, constituents, and sponsors. Creating, nurturing, and renewing this core group of leaders are basic requisites for an organization's survival and effectiveness.

BASIC FUNCTIONS OF THE BOARD

The board has a wide range of functions and responsibilities. As summarized by Houle (1989), these include the following:

- formulating and sustaining the mission of the organization, making sure that every component of the organization is consistent with the mission and is focused on accomplishing it

- representing the interests of those sponsors whose resources allow the organization to pursue its mission, while balancing those interests and the needs of the intended beneficiaries of the services
- translating values into policies that serve to guide the operations of the organization, providing the top-level manager (hereinafter referred to as the chief executive officer, or CEO) and staff with rules to govern operations and clarifying the latitude allowable for action
- selecting, guiding, overseeing, and evaluating the organization's CEO
- obtaining, allocating, and monitoring the use of the organization's resources
- reporting to the public and sponsors about the organization's activities and use of resources
- working with the CEO to develop long-range plans and to revise them periodically
- ensuring that all legal and ethical responsibilities of the organization are being fulfilled
- assuring that the organization's goals and objectives are being achieved as efficiently and effectively as possible
- setting aside time periodically to assess its own performance and composition.

In summary, the board is the focus of power and legitimacy of the organization. It brings together representatives of the major stakeholders in the organization and seeks to synthesize their values and concerns into guiding principles for mobilizing and using resources. It is the arena within which all the competing values, interests, and perspectives are articulated, examined, and resolved into a single direction for the future of the organization. The responsibility for implementing the policy directives of the board falls on the CEO.

Boards have multiple responsibilities—so many, in fact, that they usually create a variety of committees to which specific tasks are delegated (such as financial planning, nominating and evaluating the executive, fundraising, buildings and grounds, personnel, and services). These work groups develop specific plans and recommendations for consideration by the full board at its regular meetings, and they may be charged with responsibilities for overseeing implementation of recommendations approved by the board.

In addition to regular committees, some boards also create special ancillary structures or advisory groups to provide the board and CEO with particular resources or forms of assistance. For example, a need for specialized expertise in some program or service area (such as accessibility by people with special needs or analysis of legislative bills) may prompt the board to establish an advisory group composed of leading experts in the relevant area and possibly also including some of the organization's senior staff. Such groups may work closely with the board's own committees and assist with their efforts to provide recommendations to the full board, or they may link with the CEO or other management staff, who in turn present the group's recommendations to the board.

Fundraising is another area in which boards may involve others selectively. Some boards create an honorary trusteeship status for people whose major role is limited to making financial contributions or providing access to others who can make such contributions. Through its capital campaign committee or its fundraising committee, the board can link with these individuals and draw on their specialized resources to advance its overall plans. (See chapter 4 for a more complete discussion of fundraising.)

CRITERIA FOR SELECTING MEMBERS

The board is composed of leaders who are committed to carrying out their responsibilities so that the organization thrives. For most nonprofit organizations, selecting these members is the responsibility of the board itself, carried out by its committee on nominations. The goal is to have a cohesive group of hard-working, resourceful, creative, and dedicated trustees who work together effectively to mobilize concerted action across the community or region on behalf of the constituencies the organization intends to serve. The board should be large enough to allow it to carry out its duties, yet small enough to be a cohesive working group. It should contain that blend of diverse characteristics and skills required to carry out the organization's mission.

Numerous criteria should be considered in identifying potential board candidates. The following are some of the most important attributes of a good board candidate:

- An interest in learning about and working on the issues of primary concern to the organization. The person should be interested in and committed to the organization's specific programs or services. Boards have also found it helpful to include among their membership some people with related areas of interest such as public policy, legislative processes, financial management, law, fundraising, and community relations.
- A reputation as an opinion leader, having prestige and esteem in the broader community or region. This should include the ability and willingness to open doors to others needed by the organization.
- The ability to contribute money to the organization or to provide access to others who can provide funds, including key individuals, corporations, and foundations.

- The ability to identify the major issues facing the organization, to focus clearly on the tasks facing the board, and to work effectively with the group to achieve its goals.
- The interpersonal skills and sensitivities necessary to develop, nurture, and sustain communications within the board and between the board and various outside groups.
- A leadership role with a specific constituency that is important to the organization, defined perhaps in terms of age, geographic area, gender, race, profession, or other relevant characteristics.
- Willingness to make one's skills, talents, and time available to the organization. Without this quality, any other characteristics are of limited value to the organization.

CHARACTERISTICS OF EFFECTIVE BOARDS

In addition to being composed of individuals with desirable characteristics, strong boards also have several distinguishing features relating to the whole group. Researchers (Chait, Holland, & Taylor, 1993; Holland, Chait, & Taylor, 1989) found that effective boards differ from ineffective ones in the following ways.

The Contextual Dimension

Effective boards understand and take into account the culture and norms of the organizations they govern. They adapt to the distinctive characteristics and culture of the organization and its staff. Relying on the organization's mission, values, and traditions to guide their decisions, they act so as to exemplify and reinforce its core values and commitments. They cultivate this competence in various ways:

- Orientations include explicit introduction to the organization's values, norms, and traditions.
- Former members, administrators, and "living legends" are invited to convey the organization's history.
- Current leaders discuss the concepts of shared governance, collegiality, and consensus.
- Leaders review the organization's hallmark characteristics and basic values that set it apart from competitors.
- They resocialize members to the board's role and the organizations's values through readings, stories, pledges, and other practices.
- They are explicitly conscious of their actions and decisions as statements of values.

The Educational Dimension

Effective boards take the necessary steps to ensure that their members are knowledgeable about the organization; the profession; and the board's own roles, responsibilities, and performance. They consciously create opportunities for board education and development. They regularly seek information and feedback on the board's own performance. They pause periodically for self-reflection, to assess strengths and limitations, and to examine and learn from the board's mistakes.

Board members learn how to improve their performance through educational programs and retreats, where matters of substance and process are examined. They make use of introspection on the board's internal operations and the ways it carries out business. They reflect on the lessons that can be learned from their own experiences and mistakes. Other ways that these boards strengthen this educational competency include the following:

- setting aside some time at each meeting for a "seminar" or workshop to learn about an important matter of substance or process or to discuss a common reading
- conducting extended retreats every year or two for similiar purposes and for analyzing the board's operations and its mistakes
- asking members and senior staff to report briefly on the best ideas they heard at a recent conference or meeting
- meeting periodically with "role counterparts" from comparable organizations
- rotating committee assignments, so members come to know many aspects of the organization.
- establishing internal feedback mechanisms such as evaluative comments from members at the end of each meeting, seeking feedback from senior staff and outside observers, and conducting annual surveys of members on individual and collective performance.

The Interpersonal Dimension

Effective boards nurture the development of their members as a working group, attend to the board's collective welfare, and foster a sense of cohesiveness. They create a sense of inclusiveness among all members, with equal access to information and equal opportunity to participate and influence decisions. They develop goals for the group, and they recognize group achievements. They identify and cultivate leadership within the board. Board members develop this competence in many ways:

- They create a sense of inclusiveness through events that enable members to become better acquainted with one another, distributing annual notebooks with up-to-date biographical sketches of each member, build-ing some "slack time" into the schedule for informal interaction, and shar-ing information widely and communicating regularly.

- They communicate group norms and standards by pairing newcomers with a mentor or coach and by being sure that everyone understands the informal "rules of the game."
- They cultivate the notion of the board as a group by establishing and pub-licizing group goals for the board itself.
- They ensure that the board has strong leadership by systematically groom-ing its future leaders and encouraging individual growth in skills and con-tributions to the group.

The Analytical Dimension

Effective boards recognize the complexities and subtleties of issues and accept ambiguity and uncertainty as healthy preconditions for critical discussions. They approach matters from a broad institutional outlook, and they critical-ly dissect and examine all aspects of multifaceted issues. They raise doubts, explore tradeoffs, and encourage expressions of differences of opinion. This competence is cultivated by

- fostering cognitive complexity by using multiple frames of reference to analyze issues and events
- seeking concrete and even contradictory information on ambiguous matters
- asking a few members to be critical evaluators or "devil's advocates," exploring the downside of recommendations and worst-case scenarios
- developing contingency and crisis plans
- asking members to assume the perspective of key constituencies by role-playing
- brainstorming alternative views of issues
- consulting outsiders and seeking different viewpoints
- reinforcing and rewarding constructive criticism.

The Political Dimension

Effective boards accept as a primary responsibility the need to develop and maintain healthy relationships among major constituencies. They respect the integrity of the governance process and the legitimate roles and responsibili-ties of other stakeholders. They consult often and communicate directly with key constituencies, and they attempt to minimize conflict and win–lose situ-ations. Board members nurture this competence by

- broadening channels of communication by distributing profiles of board members and annual board reports, inviting staff and consumers to serve on board committees, inviting outside leaders to address the board periodically, visiting with staff, and establishing multiconstituency task forces
- working closely with the CEO to develop and maintain processes that enable board members to communicate directly with stakeholders
- monitoring the health of relationships and morale in the organization
- keeping options open and avoiding win–lose polarizations
- being sensitive to the legitimate roles and responsibilities of all stakeholders
- protecting the integrity of the governance process.

The Strategic Dimension

Effective boards help the organization envision a direction and shape a strategy for the future. They cultivate and concentrate on processes that sharpen organizational priorities. They organize themselves and conduct their business in light of the organization's strategic priorities. They anticipate potential problems and act before issues become crises. They cultivate this competence in the following ways:

- They focus attention on strategic issues by asking the CEO to present an annual update on organizational priorities and strategy, establishing board priorities and work plans, and developing an annual agenda for the board and its committees.
- They structure their meetings to concentrate on strategic priorities by prioritizing items on the agenda, providing overviews of the major topics and linkages among committee agendas, and providing a preface to each major policy issue to place it in a larger context.
- They reinforce attention on priorities by providing key questions for discussion in advance of meetings, displaying prominently the annual or continuous agenda, reserving time at each meeting for the CEO to discuss future issues, and making use of a "consent agenda."
- They develop a board information system that is strategic, normative, selective, and graphic.
- They monitor the use of board time and attention.

Such behaviors enable a board to add value to the organization by taking actions and reaching decisions that enhance the organization's long-term vitality and quality. Effective boards intentionally cultivate these skills and apply them in a number of ways.

HOW BOARDS ADD VALUE TO ORGANIZATIONS

The skills and practices of high-performing boards serve as examples for other boards to consider. Although not every practice may be transferrable, boards that want to improve their effectiveness can draw selectively on the lessons offered by their high-performing counterparts and adapt them locally (Chait, Holland, & Taylor, 1996; Holland, Ritvo, & Kovner, 1997).

One basic way effective boards add value to their organizations is by helping executives determine what matters most. Working closely with the CEO, such a board identifies and examines the most significant issues facing the organization and influencing its future. Not every matter is equally important and not all issues can be addressed, so relative priorities must be set. The board concentrates its attention on identifying and addressing such matters.

Boards add value by creating opportunities for CEOs to think aloud about questions and concerns well before it is necessary to come to conclusions or make recommendations. However, boards do not add much value through listening passively to voluminous reports. If they are to help as sounding boards for executives, time must be available for candid discussion of embryonic ideas, ambiguous issues, and unclear challenges in the road ahead. Through such unstructured discussions, boards can help CEOs frame the issues and reflect on the values, alternative directions, and tradeoffs that may eventually lead to a recommendation. Such exploratory discussions allow members' wisdom and counsel to contribute to the definition of issues the organization must face in the future.

Effective boards encourage experimentation, trying out new approaches and alternative ways of dealing with issues. The seeds of change can come from insightful questions that help others "get outside the box" of old assumptions and patterns. Raising critical questions and challenging assumptions can stimulate new ideas and creative alternatives for the future of the organization (Pound, 1993).

Another way that effective boards apply their skills and add value to organizations is by actively monitoring their own progress and assessing their performance. Most boards are given reams of data on inputs, numbers of clients or patrons served, and costs of various programs. Less attention is given to the impacts or results of those activities. Part of the problem is lack of agreement on what would serve as appropriate indicators of effectiveness. Many trustees are unsure how to go about measuring performance or results of the organization's activities.

Strong boards have developed sets of specific performance indicators that enable them to monitor performance. These "dashboards" of indicators of key aspects of performance include periodic information on such areas as number of clients completing recommended services, costs per contact and per program, staff assessments of outcomes, and client satisfaction.

Such indicators are especially important as a component of the organization's strategic plan. Each goal in that plan should have accompanying indicators that allow the board to monitor progress toward its accomplishment. For example, if the plan calls for improvements in the quality of services or staff morale, the board and staff should work together to identify appropriate ways to measure the results of efforts intended to achieve those goals. These indicators should provide the board with means to assess progress, to see whether midcourse corrections are needed, and to draw conclusions about the effects of changes.

Most importantly, effective boards model the behaviors they desire in others (Holland, 1997a). Boards are appropriately seen as the leaders of the organization, and their decisions are subjected to critical scrutiny by all constituencies. Boards appropriately are concerned about the quality, costs, productivity, and innovation of staff; however, many boards are hesitant to apply the same expectations to themselves. Boards that call for accountability of staff have far greater credibility if they "walk the talk" and show by example how quality improvements are made.

Board members cannot be both leaders of change for the organization and followers of the status quo. If they want staff to identify and implement changes that reduce costs and increase productivity, then they should demonstrate that they have defined their own productivity, measured it carefully, and made changes that increase the value they add to the organization. Such efforts put the board's own actions in line with its policies for the whole organization and demonstrate commitment to them for others to observe and follow.

CONDITIONS FOR SUCCESSFUL BOARD DEVELOPMENT

In considering efforts to improve board performance, many obstacles should be anticipated and faced, including ambiguous expectations of boards, weak accountability, unclear returns on the investments of time for development, and members' discomforts over giving up familiar patterns and practicing new ones. Overcoming these barriers requires the concerted and sustained attention of the board. For these efforts to be successful, several conditions must be met.

For improvement to take place, a board must be ready for change and accept the importance of attending to and improving its own performance. Board development cannot be imposed on members or the top-level management. The CEO, the chairperson, and a substantial number of board leaders must have concerns about the board's performance and want to work on improving it. These leaders must initiate the process with enthusiasm and clear commitment to working with the board to bring about changes. Many of the members must come to share these concerns in the context of loyalty to the organization and its mission.

Development of improved performance must be carried out as the board works on its business items rather that doing the business and then doing "development." Distinguishing board development from the "real" work of the board is a false dichotomy. The processes of learning how to work together more effectively should be embedded within the efforts to carry out the instrumental expectations of the board. Learning involves looking at tasks the board carries out and identifying ways that enable the group to work better and produce more useful results.

Next, the focus of development efforts should be on changing a board's behavior rather than changing attitudes or personalities. Exhortations and prescriptions do not work nearly as well as changes in routines, procedures, or structures for doing work together. Members begin to think differently and act differently as a result of such practical steps as bringing thoughtful questions to the board, providing relevant and focused information on the issue, dividing members into small groups to brainstorm alternative solutions and formulate recommendations, and encouraging critical and analytical thinking about issues before the group.

Development activities should be individually tailored to the specific needs and concerns of the board. Although a retreat approach is often useful in getting started, development activities should be built into the board's ongoing agenda and ways of doing business rather than being treated as a separate activity. This is due to the instrumental expectation of many members, who tend to see the board's effectiveness primarily as a means to advance the organization's performance rather than seeing board development as an end in itself.

The best approaches link process and substance. For example, asking the board to set goals for itself or to formulate indicators to monitor its performance sets in motion a process that builds cohesion and educates participants while also generating substantive products.

Board development is an extensive, long-term process, not a quick fix. To sustain the process, some of the board members must be "product champions" for the board and its performance, just as some advocate balanced budgets or client satisfaction. The pressures of business as usual are strong, and without continuing attention to how well the board is performing, it settles back into comfortable ways of working that may not match the needs of a changing organization or environment.

INITIATING ATTENTION TO THE BOARD'S PERFORMANCE

Boards can make productive use of recent successes or problems as occasions to reflect on what happened and how the board contributed to the results. Positive or negative situations provide opportunities for the board to consider how it has performed during the time leading up to this point and to think about how it wants to perform in dealing with them in the future. They invite members to look beyond mere reaction to external events and to consider ways the board might carry out its business more intentionally in the future so as to provide more effective leadership. Whatever the issue, the board can ask itself how it has contributed to the successes and problems in the area and what lessons it should take from the experiences to become more effective in the future.

Even when it is not facing critical turning points, the board can periodically ask its CEO to talk about some of the major challenges coming in the months ahead or to describe the organizational issues that keep him or her awake at night. The group can then discuss how it has contributed to the organization's readiness to deal with these matters and how it could prepare itself to provide stronger leadership on them in the future.

The board should include in its agenda some time at each meeting for candid, off-the-record talk with the CEO about the most complex or troublesome issues coming in the months or years ahead. Then it should explore ways the board could become a stronger partner with the CEO in working on those issues. Thus, the board makes use of work on substantive challenges to the organization as opportunities to learn how to improve its own performance.

Another opportunity for examination of the board's own performance is in discussions of how the organization deals with accountability for its use of resources. Most boards expect the CEO to report on how staff are being held accountable, and many boards specify expectations of the executive and criteria for assessing that person's performance. Fewer boards, however, apply the same principles to themselves and have clear evidence of how the board itself is being accountable for its use of time and resources.

Developing means for demonstrating the board's own accountability is crucial for modeling the behaviors it expects of others in the organization. Initiating such a process begins with recognizing that the board has a duty of accountability for its responsibilities and then engaging in candid discussions of how well it is carrying out this obligation. Useful questions for group discussion include the following:

- How is this board adding value to the organization, beyond the contributions of staff and administration?

- What steps should the board take to improve its performance and increase the value it adds to the organization?
- What criteria or indicators are appropriate for monitoring and demonstrating the board's improving performance?

Rather than approaching this matter in terms of forced compliance with external rules or avoidance of public embarrassment, it is more productive to approach accountability as a matter of mutual expectations and shared commitments among members. Conversations about goals and promises to one another about steps the board will take together to attain them serves to build a climate of responsibility and mutual commitment to one another. Such commitments guide behavior more powerfully than external rules or threats (Fry, 1995). Intentional examination of the board's commitments and the ways it ensures that they are carried out sets the stage for further steps to strengthen individual and group performance.

Boards can take advantage of a wide variety of opportunities to look at their own performance and the value thay have been adding to the organization. Efforts to look at this area are prompted by participants' desires to increase the value the board adds to the organization and to maximize its contributions to the organization's accomplishment of its mission. However they are expressed, members' concerns provide vital signals that it is time to begin involving others in reflections on the group's work together. As one experienced board leader advised, "Don't hesitate to ask yourself and others, 'Is this board truly adding as much value to this organization as it could? Could we do better?'" Raising such questions may seem like small beginnings, but numerous boards have found that they are vital first steps toward important changes.

Although every member of the board should be concerned about how well the group is doing its job, it is important that these concerns move from individuals and come to be shared and owned by the full group. The board's leaders are vital to this step, and it usually falls to them to initiate open attention to the board's performance. Anyone can propose a discussion of how the board is working, but the positive response and commitment of the CEO and board chair are essential to the success of efforts to bring issues before the whole group.

The best orchestra or sports team steps back from each performance and reviews how well it did and where changes could be made to improve future work. High-performing groups take time for practice and for reviewing their performance, thus learning and growing together as a team (Senge, 1994). Boards can learn from such examples. As the leader of one strong board noted, "After we've finished working a particularly difficult problem, we try to take some time to reflect together on what we can learn from what we've just come through." Boards that take time to examine and reflect together on their own performance can identify useful lessons that will guide them into increased effectiveness as leaders.

USING ASSESSMENTS TO IDENTIFY TARGETS FOR CHANGE

Initial discussions about board performance can be carried to an important next step by getting more extensive information from all participants regarding their views of the board's work, areas warranting attention, and suggestions for change. It is useful to broaden the inquiry so participants can find out if their concerns are things that more than just a few want to work on. An assessment of the full board supports this step. As one experienced member emphasized,

> Any board interested in improving should get going with an evaluation of its strengths and weaknesses. It should ask a whole series of tough questions about what's working well and what isn't. You can't just depend on a few insiders to run things. You're ALL the *owners* of the institution and all responsible for finding ways that enable you to help it work better.

In addition to gathering information for everyone to examine, a crucial function of board assessment is that it serves to spread responsibility for findings and conclusions across the whole group, thus building shared ownership of conclusions and consensus for taking steps of change. In the words of one board chairperson, "The most important result of starting to evaluate our work as a board was that the group began to think about itself purposively and to ask questions about how we could do our work better in the future. It got all of us going with taking responsibility for improving the quality of our own work."

The various approaches to board assessment may be divided into two areas of focus: group performance and individual performance. A few approaches link these domains. Many boards have made use of one or more assessment methods to identify aspects of board performance that members see as needing improvement. They can choose from numerous resources and approaches in such efforts, and many national associations have developed board assessment tools. The various approaches include self-evaluations, constituency surveys, third-party reviews, internal reviews by an ad hoc or standing committee on trusteeship, reflective discussion of critical incidents, and feedback at the conclusion of meetings.

One comprehensive board self-assessment package is offered by the National Center for Nonprofit Boards (Slesinger, 1991); another approach is based on the six competencies of effective boards (Holland, 1991). Other approaches range from brief evaluations at the end of meetings to bringing in outside evaluators to interview and summarize the views of board members, staff, consumers, and sponsors. Each approach to board assessment has strengths and limitations. They vary in time and resources required and in vulnerability to bias. A board should begin by experimenting with whatever approach to assessment seems comfortable and appropriate and then evaluating the usefulness of the results. It should revise and expand the steps in ways that the group finds helpful and comprehensible. At some point, the group should invite in some outsiders who bring objectivity and experience with other boards for comparisons and for innovative ideas.

RETREATS AS A MEANS TO WORK ON BOARD PERFORMANCE

Many boards have found that retreats are powerful tools for stimulating and extending board growth. A retreat is typically a one- to three-day special meeting, held off-site and away from wherever the group usually meets. Retreats allow a group to devote extended time to working on a major issue, such as developing or updating its strategic plan, gaining a better understanding of the external environment, clarifying its mission, evaluating a possible new market, or solving some problem. In this section, we consider their use specifically for working on improvements in the board's own performance.

A board development retreat is an investment in the future of the board and the organization it governs. It provides an opportunity to step back from routine business agendas for an in-depth look at the future and the board's role in it. A retreat can be a major boost to the board's efforts to make more effective and efficient use of the time that it gives to the organization (Holland, 1997b; Savage, 1995).

Boards have found that their retreats served several important purposes:

- strengthening performance through a review of governance processes and the board's roles and responsibilities
- assessing the board's contributions to the organization and identifying ways it can add greater value
- establishing priorities for the board and identifying strategies and actions to achieve them
- enhancing collegiality and working relationships among board members and between board and staff
- determining next steps in board development and in the implementation of overall action plans.

A board may use numerous resources in planning and conducting its retreat. The National Center for Nonprofit Boards in Washington, DC, publishes useful resource materials on board development and maintains lists of consultants and facilitators in many regions of the country. Similar resources are available through the national associations of many other organizations.

A retreat can generate a great deal of enthusiasm among participants. However, a board can lose momentum when it returns to its regular meeting schedule and reverts to familiar old patterns. Likewise, turnover in membership introduces newcomers who are unacquainted with the board's efforts to change behavior and improve performance. Agenda items that are scheduled almost automatically demand attention, and promises made at a retreat may be forgotten like last year's New Year's resolutions. Therefore, it is essential to have explicit methods for reminding everyone of the agreements and changes identified at the retreat and regular evidence of how those resolutions are being implemented. The underlying goal is to build habits of reflection and learning into the group's culture, so that both newcomers and old-timers are socialized into effective patterns of behavior.

ONGOING BOARD EDUCATION

Incorporating educational activities into board meetings is a vital practice for making ongoing improvements in the board's performance. Boards should be models of "learning organizations" (Senge, 1994). The assembled intellectual abilities of members are extended by acquiring new knowledge and skills as a group and by identifying and developing improved ways to carry out their work.

Rather than simply relying on past knowledge and skill as sufficient, effective boards acknowledge their need to learn and take responsibility for continuing to expand their competencies. They identify topics and issues to examine, develop appropriate programs and resources, and encourage all members to participate in ongoing educational sessions. Effective boards encourage ongoing education among their members by bringing in special speakers, holding miniseminars and study groups, visiting other boards, attending conferences on governance, and rotating committee assignments (Taylor, Chait, & Holland, 1996).

It is especially important to have thorough orientation programs for incoming members. New members should be enabled to get off to a good start by means of receiving clear expectations for board membership, extensive orientation to the board's roles and responsibilities, and information about the organization. Assigning an experienced member as a mentor for a newcomer is another useful practice that provides both with a greater awareness of board performance. Outside speakers and mentors from other boards are useful resources to help a board learn. Many national and regional associations can recommend knowledgeable leaders who can serve such educational or consultative roles, and some boards also recruit resource people from similar organizations in their region. Any board can make occasional use of outside consultants, mentors, or evaluators to help the group gain independent perspectives on its performance, identify issues needing its attention, and learn about best practices of other boards.

Better boards enlarge this process of education by assisting every member to develop learning plans that enable him or her to make greater contributions to the group in the following year. This process may be as simple as rotating committee assignments or as extensive as sending members to conferences on governance and bringing in speakers on topics of interest to members. Some boards establish procedures for all their members to set individual performance goals and to obtain feedback on their progress. They make use of feedback to coach members in improving their contributions to the group's overall effectiveness. They use coaching sessions and mentors for underperformers and term limits to ease out chronic poor performers. In these ways boards can use individual and group goals as well as monitoring and feedback to sustain attention on improved performance.

RESTRUCTURING MEETING TIME AND COMMITTEE WORK

An important approach to improving performance is to restructure the board's use of committees and meeting time to emphasize its strategic priorities (Carver, 1990). Careful use of the scarce resource of meeting time is a concern of many members, and many sense that agendas pack too many issues into limited meeting time. Meeting agendas should be designed so that they sustain focus on the few, most important issues of strategy and policy. Preparation for making changes in the agenda may begin with having a member simply monitor the amount of time the board spends on each issue in a meeting and rate its relevance to the board's priorities. The board can discuss the feedback and consider the relationship between its priorities and its actual use of time.

Better use of meeting time can result from setting clear priorities for the board's attention and leaving nonessential items for individual review. Strong boards limit the agenda of meetings to a few, top-priority matters, rather than trying to cover the waterfront. They cluster routine reports and nonexceptional motions that require board approval into a "consent agenda" to be voted on in one action rather than separately. Any member can request that an item be separated out for discussion, thus protecting the board's ultimate right to examine any issue. However, the practice allows the board to concentrate most of its attention on those matters of highest priority to the organization and avoid getting bogged down in operational details.

Restructuring how the board organizes and charges its committees is another way to improve performance. Instead of committees that mirror management divisions (such as personnel, programs, finances), boards should let form follow function. The strategic priorities provide the point of departure, from which work group assignments and meeting agendas are derived. Board committees should be constructed to focus members' efforts on each of the board's goals, and each committee should be dissolved when a goal is attained.

Rather than using board meeting time to hear routine reports from every committee, the board can structure its meetings to focus on one or two goals or priorities at each meeting, with discussions led by those groups that have carried out the background preparation. Leaders should make sure that every report begins with a clear statement of the question being presented to the board and how the issue is linked with a goal or priority of the board.

For changes to outlast individuals and become embedded in the board's culture, there must be some "champions" for the group's performance, in the same manner that a finance committee or buildings and grounds committee carries its portfolio. To build in advocacy for the board itself, members can assign to a group the task of keeping the board reminded of its commitments, monitoring its performance, and periodically recommending actions that will strengthen meeting processes. Strong boards have their committee on nominations or some other permanent group take the responsibilities for developing and implementing steps for monitoring board meetings, soliciting participants' assessments and recommendations for improvement, and arranging for periodic board education sessions and retreats on issues of interest.

Many of these boards expand the duties of the nominating committee to include carrying out periodic assessments of individual and group performance. This group makes use of findings to coach members in expanding their leadership contributions to the board, to identify people to nominate for additional terms, to identify skills needed in new members, and to plan regular educational sessions in areas in which the board needed improvement.

The committee's experience in carrying out these tasks is applicable in its nominations of future members. It broadens the scope of characteristics sought in new members to include skills in working with groups, linkages to key constituencies, ability to contribute new perspectives to examining issues, and a track record of making positive contributions to group communication and learning.

Boards that restructure their meeting agendas and committees can then monitor the usefulness of those changes by evaluating their meetings, including plenary sessions as well as committee meetings, getting feedback and suggestions to improve future meetings. Brief assessment forms, followed by discussion of participants' concerns and recommendations, can lead to more productive and satisfying meetings.

BUILDING GROUP COHESION AND TEAMWORK

The instrumental orientation of many members makes structural changes more attractive than efforts directed explicitly at relationships, processes, or communications. However, the most effective boards take careful steps to transform an assembly of talented individuals into a well-integrated group.

Many board members are comfortable providing individual expertise or advice to the CEO, whereas others see their service taking place on a committee related to their area of interest. The most effective boards go beyond these efforts and also emphasize the whole group as the decision-making unit. A cohesive board makes better decisions than individuals do, yet it draws on members' multiple perspectives to avoid the traps of "group think."

Transforming an assembly of skilled individuals into a well-integrated team is a long and difficult process. It requires taking critical issues to the group for deliberation and taking the time necessary to hear the views of each participant, rather than relying on a few leaders to predigest issues and present foregone conclusions. It requires that the issues taken to the board are vital to the future of the organization, not window dressing. It requires making sure that everyone has equal access to information about the issues and the organization. It requires taking time for members to get to know one another beyond the formal setting of the boardroom. Strong boards pay careful attention to communications among members, to nurturing and sustaining inclusive relationships and a sense of mutual responsibility for the board's success. They are aware that silent members may have some important concerns that the board needs to hear. Social events and informal time for conversations are important means to build trusting relationships.

The most effective steps for building group cohesion are ones that closely link instrumental and relational components and allow members to deal with the latter by means of overt attention to the former. For example, working to formulate goals for the board itself is a good means for building group cohesion while also serving to focus the board's use of time and energy. Goals for the board should be distinct from but lead to the overall goals it has for the organization. They identify specifically what the board will do to maximize its contributions to the attainment of the organization's strategic goals.

The board identifies its goals, which should be kept in everyone's awareness by posting them in conspicuous places and by repeating them in meetings and at the beginning of reports. Keeping the board's own goals paramount in meetings by means of the agenda plan and the focus of each report or discussion keeps everyone clear about the purpose and direction of each step. It also allows the board to monitor and evaluate its own progress toward its goals.

Formulating specific goals for the board also helps the process of clarifying expectations of the board as a group and of individual members, officers, committees, and senior staff. It is important to make sure that each participant understands what is expected of him or her and how those expectations contribute to achieving the overall goals. Setting goals for the board as a whole and periodically reviewing progress toward them serve to maintain the board's attention to its own performance and how it adds value to the organization. The board should monitor indicators of its performance regularly and make sure that each member has this information. Sharing this information with outsiders and inviting their assessments of progress further sharpens accountability for performance.

Throughout these steps, an underlying concern is to develop a stronger sense of inclusiveness and cohesiveness among board members as a group. This requires paying careful attention to communications among members and intentionally nurturing and sustaining inclusive relationships. These processes should begin at recruitment and orientation, be carried forward by all leaders, and be reinforced at social times and retreats. Strong boards are careful to schedule social time and informal interaction for their members. They celebrate members' accomplishments, have meals together before or after meetings, take breaks for refreshments, make regular use of name tags, and participate as a group in social events sponsored by the organization.

ROLE OF THE CEO

The CEO plays a central role in creating and sustaining an effective board. He or she most often initiates attention to the board's performance and advocates for improvements. No longer content with the cynical old advice to "keep them in the dark so they'll leave you alone," good executives realize that their boards can be their best partners in creating a strong organization. They invest time in examining the group's performance and educating members in leadership skills.

If boards are to improve, the CEO must be committed to leading efforts to learn better ways of working together and take the initiative in raising members' sights and expectations of themselves. Working closely with the chairperson of the board, the CEO raises performance questions with the group and helps members consider new approaches to its work. The CEO describes approaches to governance that raise aspirations and prepare the group for making changes in its own patterns. He or she helps the group focus its attention on those aspects that warrant attention and then identify specific steps for change. The CEO raises group expectations and aspirations by initiating questions about group performance, suggesting alternative approaches to dealing with issues, and offering new possibilities for improving group effectiveness.

By opening up discussion about the board's performance, the CEO demonstrates that it is appropriate to direct attention to the board's own work and to explore ways of improving it. Rather than avoiding discontents or treating problems as occasions for blaming someone, effective CEOs turn problems into occasions for the group to learn more effective ways of carrying out its work. Discontents are moved from back channels to the forefront of everyone's attention, and the group is invited to take on responsibilities for identifying solutions to problems and better ways to deal with issues. The CEO models the desired behavior of respectful listening and constructive use of feedback to improve the quality of work, inviting others to join in similar steps. In so doing, he or she confirms that everyone in the leadership group is committed to doing their jobs more effectively, not just avoiding criticisms, blaming others, or settling for business as usual.

Effective CEOs expect and tolerate some anxiety that comes with questioning old assumptions and relinquishing familiar practices for the unknown. Their persistence in seeking improvements, even when solutions may not yet be apparent, encourages experimentation with new approaches to dealing with tasks and invites others to try out alternatives without fear of being blamed for mistakes along the way. Reflecting on experiences together, identifying areas to change, and trying out new approaches are difficult but crucial steps in learning for anyone in the organization, including the board. CEOs recognize and celebrate incremental steps toward goals of improved board performance, thus establishing it as a model for others in the organization.

CONCLUSION

By working intentionally on its own performance, a board makes some fundamental changes in the ways it uses its time and energy, not just engaging in a temporary quick fix that solves immediate problems. Attention to how it is carrying out its work becomes part of the agenda rather than something separate from and independent of ongoing tasks and responsibilities (Holland, Leslie, & Holzhalb, 1993). The board makes fundamental changes in its culture, reinventing and rejuvenating itself. It incorporates into its basic sense of responsibility a continuing concern with improving the quality of its performance, rather than seeing it as something separate or occasional. Leaders can reinforce this understanding by pausing occasionally during discussions or at the conclusion of a major agenda item to invite reflection on how the group dealt with the issue and what could be done to improve the process next time. Such reflective practices become part of the group's culture.

Time and intentional work are essential for such changes to become integrated into the board's culture. To ensure that lessons are learned and used, boards have found that they must allow enough time to address their concerns and explore alternatives fully. This cannot be accomplished at one meeting; rather, some attention should be devoted to reflection on the group's work performance on a regular basis. The group should build into its expectations that time is allocated to discuss how it dealt with key agenda items as well as to work on the tasks themselves. Even a few minutes per meeting on such reflections can lead to greater board efficiency and effectiveness. It can also ensure that minor irritants do not mushroom into major problems.

Taking time to reflect on how the board has used its time and attention, particularly after dealing with a difficult issue, enhances the group's ownership of its own processes and performance. Such discussions should take place at the conclusion of each meeting and allow members to share perceptions of performance and consider ways to improve future meetings.

Effective boards attend to how they work together as well as to what they do. Members take responsibility for initiating discussions of ways the group carries out its work and seek ways to improve performance. They take advantage of breaks or turning points in the organization's experience to draw attention to the board's role in leadership and change. They test out their perceptions with others and identify shared concerns of the group. They move ahead by means of assessments of group performance to identify specific issues and goals for change. They lay the foundation for ongoing work by means of retreats and careful follow-up. They reinforce and institutionalize changes by means of in-meeting discussions of feedback on performance and educational sessions that contribute to strengthening the board's effectiveness.

These efforts bridge the gap between learning and doing, integrating reflection with work. They help the group to develop a culture of active responsibility for making ongoing, self-directed improvements in its own performance. By taking consistent initiatives to improve their work together, boards set the example for others and show how to add greater value to their organizations. However, boards rarely are able to initiate such activities by themselves; they generally require strong leadership and direction from their CEO. The payoff can be substantial.

As one senior chairperson summarized his group's experience:

> Our board members' sense of the importance of working on our own performance went from zero to extremely high. I've had a lot of experience as a

member of several national corporate boards and initially was impatient with more time spent on this area. But now it has become a basic part of the way this board works. . . . To come through all the changes this organization faced, you really have to become a *team* with many skilled players. . . . We started off with some retreats and had some speakers who really opened my eyes. . . . Now board development is fully owned by this board, and one of our members arranges for us to work together on some topic for about an hour at every meeting. We're all committed to moving ahead with our own education as a board so we will be more effective leaders of this organization in the future.

SKILLS-APPLICATION EXERCISES

Metropolitan Family Services Board

Beth Jefferson, CEO of the Metropolitan Family Services Center, and Frank Watson, chair of its board, were talking over lunch about how the board was performing and possible ways it might be improved. "I think we're going to face increased pressure from managed care and from other service providers coming into our area," Beth reflected. "I think we should get the board to work on doing a better job so we can survive in the years ahead."

"But we already have a fine board," Frank responded. "Our members have their hands full with overseeing all we do now. All the committees are working hard, and most of our members have many years of experience in their roles. They've all done good work, so I don't see why you think we need to change."

"Well, perhaps we're victims of our own past success," said Beth. "There's no doubt that our committee structure and our membership have served us well in the past, and I don't mean to be critical, it's just that things are changing from how they were even a few years ago. The population we serve is getting younger, poorer, and more troubled. I doubt that many on our board know much about our current clients. If we're going to understand our community and the people we're supposed to be serving, we need some new blood."

"But we'd be losing a lot of wisdom and experience by changing membership just for the sake of change," replied Frank. "After all, these folks have come through many years with the center and know it inside and out. They trust you and each other, and they work together well. I just don't see how changing the people will accomplish what you seem to want. It certainly will cause a lot of disruption. There's lots to lose and little to gain, as I see it."

"It's certainly true that our board members have been helpful," Beth acknowledged. "But they seldom dig in and help improve recommendations that I bring to the table. They're willing to listen and raise a few questions, but the weight is all on me to come up with the ideas and the plans. They're passive reactors, not real leaders. I don't think most of them are actively in touch with much of the community. As a matter of fact, I fear that this group really has no clear goals or criteria for evaluating the quality of anything, other than how comfortable they feel about where I'm taking them. That may have been acceptable in the past, but I want some bright and capable partners who can really contribute to our understanding of trends and political issues, people who can actively chart a course into the future. Maybe we could start by suggesting term limits and then talk about what characteristics we'd like to see in new nominees. Perhaps we could plan some new education sessions for the board on changes in the community."

"I'm afraid many of our members would view your efforts to change the board as a power grab," Frank replied. "A few may be willing to retire, but most are just pleased with the way things are going and would resist change. I doubt they'd understand what you're trying to do. You know the old saying, 'If it ain't broke, then don't fix it.' Why not just leave well enough alone?"

Discussion Questions

- What are some of this board's strengths, and what are some of its weaknesses? How would you rate it on each of the characteristics of effective boards presented in this chapter?

- What opportunities and constraints confront Beth in moving foward on her goals for the board? How could she take advantage of the opportunities, build on strengths, and overcome weaknesses?

- What should be Beth's short-range and long-range objectives? What resources could she draw on for each?

- How would you describe the relationship between Beth and Frank? What important steps should each take to work together more effectively?

- Develop an action plan for Beth, identifying important steps and resources.

- What criteria should she use to monitor progress toward her objectives?

WESTSIDE COMMUNITY CENTER

The slow-moving traffic drew little attention from Wilma Jefferson this afternoon. She was headed for Westside's quarterly board meeting and was decidedly uncomfortable about what lay ahead. "Why do I keep on doing this when it's so frustrating?" Wilma grumbled to herself.

Four years earlier, Wilma had been flattered by Executive Director Don Carlisle's call asking her to serve on the board. She was sure that the request had been linked to her family's ownership of one of the largest manufacturing corporations in the city, but the prospect of helping improve the quality of what was already a top-notch community center had caught her interest. She'd like to feel that she was a part of such an effort to "ratchet up Westside," as Don had put it, so she had agreed to this venture onto a nonprofit board.

Over her first year on the Westside board, Wilma had kept a low profile as she watched how this group conducted its business. The organization's budget had been balanced every year, membership and participation were growing, and programs were good in quality. Everyone on the board and the management team seemed quite contented with how things were going for the organization. Although fund accounting still struck her as a curious way of financial management, Wilma really enjoyed the occasional talks by senior members of the staff at board meetings.

The four meetings a year were efficient, usually starting with committee meetings in the afternoon, followed by a social dinner sometimes including a staff "show and tell," after which the board met as a whole from 7 P.M. until about 10 P.M. to hear and discuss committee reports. Some of the committee reports were thorough; others seemed vague and pointless. Neither sort evoked much response from anyone in the meetings, and Wilma wondered if others found these sessions as tedious and boring as she did. Only occasionally were there recommended actions that were not routine and, for all intents and purposes, predetermined. "Surely," Wilma mused to herself, "there's more to being a board member than approving contracts with suppliers, building renovation projects, and joint activities with other organizations in the city. The only real discussion each year was about setting membership fees and staff salaries."

When Wilma joined the board, she had acquiesced to the request that she serve on the fundraising campaign committee. Soon, however, she became dismayed at the confusion in signals from the CEO and the committee chairman. She made several calls to friends and opened some doors that led to other contributions; however, the campaign ended far short of its goal. It seemed to have concluded with a whimper, not a bang. Even more curiously, from Wilma's perspective, the board had never addressed the lingering dissatisfactions from that experience. Two years later, Don was pushing hard for the board to start yet another campaign, this time with an even higher goal.

One evening after the end of that last campaign, Wilma and several other members of the board had talked in the parking lot after a board meeting about what might have gone wrong. Part of the problem seemed to have been that there was no clear strategic plan for the organization, a point another member brought up at the next board meeting.

Don had really gone to work on that challenge and done a fine job with it. Over the next nine months, a series of planning meetings included many of the board members and a number of staff and community leaders. The plan that emerged was saluted by everyone—staff as well as the board—as excellent, distinctive, and comprehensive. There was a sense that the document, although ambitious and a bit ambiguous in places, had instilled in Westside a new sense of purpose and overall direction.

Why, then, Wilma wondered, was she still uncomfortable? The strategic plan was unquestionably good, just what the organization needed. However, the subsequent board meetings seemed to have continued with business as usual, with only occasional references to the plan. It didn't appear to have had any evident effect on either the substance or the processes of meetings.

At the most recent meeting, Don had pushed hard for the board to authorize the new campaign. Backed by the board chair, Don called for volunteers to form a campaign committee. However, few members had responded. The "usual suspects" had raised their hands but with little evident enthusiasm. The spark just did not seem to be there for anyone in the room.

During a break in the meeting, Arnold Moore, the chair of the committee on programs and services, had commented to Wilma and a few others gathered around the coffee urn that there seemed to be a lethargy in the room. Everyone, including Wilma, had nodded in agreement, but no one raised the issue once the meeting resumed. Apparently nobody wanted to seem like a wet blanket, Wilma surmised, especially without some specific reason or recommendation about how to improve things.

After that meeting, Wilma had tried to engage Don in some conversation about her unease, but somehow the response seemed to miss the point. "I'm not sure that our board members see how we fit into the plan," she said to him. "Isn't the board itself one of the organization's strategic assets that should be included in our thinking somehow? Shouldn't life on the board be different now that we actually have a strategic plan?"

"Certainly the board is central to the plan," insisted Don. "Its job now is just to roll up its sleeves and get to work raising the money so Westside can achieve the goals detailed in the plan. We're all counting on the board this time, Wilma, to make sure that we reach our target. And frankly, I see you as a key player."

"Get on board or get out of the way," Wilma thought as she drove to the next board meeting. That was a motto that Wilma had often heard among her own company's senior staff when a new venture was getting started, and now she was hearing it at Westside. Why did it seem so irritating now? "Maybe it's just me," Wilma mused as she pulled into the parking lot. "Am I just getting too old for all this? Should I just get out of the way, resign this volunteer position, and take that long-overdue vacation?"

The meeting was just getting underway when Wilma walked into the conference room. "Welcome, ladies and gentlemen," boomed the chairman. "We have a full agenda this evening, so I hope you are prepared to work a little later than usual. In addition to all our usual committee reports, we have two bids for renovations to review, a proposal for some changes in programs and in membership regulations, plus several budgetary adjustments. Then I'd like for us to get back to preparations for the campaign and see what we need to do to get that project launched. Any questions before we dig in?"

By the time the meeting ended, Wilma was exasperated by what she regarded to be an endless stream of trivia and minutae. On her way out to the parking lot, she walked with Freddie Ackerman, assistant director of Westside, and said, "Freddie, you know this organization and this board better than I do. Am I crazy to think that the board should be dealing regularly with crucial issues like strengthening our competitive advantage, monitoring the quality of our programs, improving our market share, and controlling costs? It seems like our leaders steer clear of issues like that in favor of discussions of program regulations and rehabbing the physical plant. Those things may be important to somebody, but frankly they just sap my energy. Furthermore, I just don't think the board's heart will be in another campaign now. So, I have two questions for you: First, am I correct in my perceptions about what a board should be and what this one is? And second, if I am, what should be done to change things? I really hope you can help me out, because frankly, I've about had it."

Discussion Questions

- Why do board members sometimes raise questions and offer comments outside the board room that they wouldn't make inside the board room? What, if anything, should a chief executive or a board chairperson do about this?

- If you were Freddie, how would you answer Wilma's two questions?

- Why do some boards have difficulty in keeping focused on strategy instead of operations?

- What, if anything, should this board do differently? What should the executive director do? What should Freddie do? What should the board chairperson do? What should Wilma do?

- What goals should this board set for itself (as distinct from goals it has for the organization)? How should it go about that process?

- How could this board know if and when it was improving its performance? What would be some useful indicators for it to monitor?

- What are the implications for such issues for the development of effective trustees and volunteers for a nonprofit organization?

Group Discussion

Executive Director Don Carlisle has called together the Executive Committee of the Westside board and made the following request: "Please help me come up with a plan that will significantly improve the value added to this organization from our board members. I am particularly concerned that we make effective use of these folks in our upcoming campaign. Our plan should include specific objectives, a credible approach, assignable tasks, observable outcomes, and minimal expenses." Your assignment is to develop and present the key features of such a plan, including your recommendations and the reasoning that supports each of them.

REFERENCES

Carver, J. (1990). *Boards that make a difference*. San Francisco: Jossey-Bass.

Chait, R. P., Holland, T. P., & Taylor, B. E. (1993). *The effective board of trustees*. Phoenix: Oryx Press.

Chait, R. P., Holland, T. P., & Taylor, B. E. (1996). *Improving the performance of governing boards*. Phoenix: Oryx Press.

Fry, R. E. (1995). Accountability in organizational life: Problem or opportunity for nonprofits? *Nonprofit Management and Leadership*, 6(2), 181–195.

Holland, T. P. (1991). Self-assessment by nonprofit boards. *Nonprofit Management and Leadership*, 2(1), 25–36.

Holland, T. P. (1997a). Board self-assessment: A model of accountability. *Not-for-Profit CEO Monthly Letter*, 4(1), 5–9.

Holland, T. P. (1997b). Setting the stage: Planning board retreats. *Board Member*, 6(4), 10–11.

Holland, T. P., Chait, R. P., & Taylor, B. E. (1989). Board effectiveness: Identifying and measuring trustee competencies. *Journal of Research in Higher Education*, 30, 451–469.

Holland, T. P., Leslie, D., & Holzhalb, C. (1993). Culture and change in nonprofit boards. *Nonprofit Management and Leadership*, 4, 141–155.

Holland, T. P., Ritvo, R. A., & Kovner, A. R. (1997). *Improving board effectiveness: Practical lessons for nonprofit healthcare organizations*. Chicago: American Hospital.

Houle, C. O. (1989). *Governing boards: Their nature and nurture*. San Francisco: Jossey-Bass.

Pound, J. (1993, March–April). The promise of the governed corporation. *Harvard Business Review*, pp. 89–98.

Savage, T. J. (1995). *Seven steps to a more effective board*. Rockville, MD: Cheswick Center.

Senge, P. (1994). *The fifth discipline: The art and practice of the learning organization*. New York: Doubleday.

Slesinger, L. H. (1991). *Self-assessment for nonprofit boards*. Washington, DC: National Center for Nonprofit Boards.

Taylor, B. E., Chait, R. P., & Holland, T. P. (1996). The new work of the nonprofit board. *Harvard Business Review*, 74(5), 36–46.

ADDITIONAL READING

Association for Governing Boards of Universities and Colleges. (1986). *Self-study criteria for governing boards of independent colleges and universities.* Washington, DC: Author.

Bowen, W. G. (1994). *Inside the boardroom.* New York: John Wiley & Sons.

Chait, R. P. (1994). *The new activism of corporate boards and the implications for campus governance.* Washington, DC: Association of Governing Boards of Universities and Colleges.

Drucker, P. F. (1990). Lessons for successful nonprofit governance. *Nonprofit Management and Leadership, 1*(1), 7–14.

Eadie, D. C. (1994). *Boards that work: A practical guide for building effective association boards.* Washington, DC: American Society of Association Executives.

Eadie, D. C. (1997). *Changing by design: A practical approach to leading innovation in nonprofit organizations.* San Francisco: Jossey-Bass.

Eadie, D. C., & Edwards, R. L. (1993). Board leadership by design. *Nonprofit World, 11*(2), 12–15.

Herman, R. D., & Van Til, J. (1989). *Nonprofit boards of directors: Analyses and applications.* New Brunswick, NJ: Transaction.

Holland, T. P. (1996). *How to build a more effective board.* Washington, DC: National Center for Nonprofit Boards.

Schein, E. H. (1993). How can organizations learn faster? The challenge of entering the green room. *Sloan Management Review, 34*(2), 85–92.

Smith, D. H. (1995). *Entrusted: The moral responsibilities of trusteeship.* Bloomington: Indiana University Press.

Zander, A. (1993). *Making boards effective: The dynamics of governing boards.* San Francisco: Jossey-Bass.

CHAPTER 21

Planning and Managing Strategically

Douglas C. Eadie

S trategic planning and management processes have been widely used in the for-profit sector for the past quarter-century, and their application is now spreading rapidly in the nonprofit arena. Sound reasons support the growing use of these processes in nonprofit organizations:

- Nonprofit managers work in a complex and rapidly changing environment that places a premium on flexibility, adaptability, and the conscious management of change—in missions, strategic directions, plans, and programs. Strategic planning and management processes focus on the management of change, whereas traditional long-range planning approaches have basically projected current activities into the future, on the assumption of continuing environmental stability.
- Competition among nonprofit, public, and for-profit organizations is increasing in many fields—from education and training to health and human services—and organizations that can plan and manage strategically are far better equipped to survive and flourish.

Strategic planning and management techniques are quickly becoming a staple in the nonprofit manager's cupboard. However, discussing them is far easier than putting them to practical use in the near term, with concrete results and at an affordable cost. The popular adage "no pain, no gain" is all too true in applying strategic techniques. Not only are these technically demanding, their application inevitably involves significant costs, most notably in the time of board members and managers. No simple cookbook can be followed to plan and manage strategically. Rather, a broad logic and methodology must be adapted to the specific needs, circumstances, capabilities, and personnel of particular organizations.

The history of planning in nonprofit and public organizations is replete with tales of woe, as elaborate, ambitious planning processes have not achieved the expected results or have even broken down midstream. This chapter prepares you to venture confidently onto the complex, shifting, and occasionally even treacherous terrain of strategic management, to recognize certain guide-posts, to spot and avoid certain pitfalls, and ultimately to find a path that leads to successful application.

I begin this chapter by describing the rapidly changing field of strategic planning and management, with special attention to a variation on the theme that is proving especially useful in the nonprofit sector: strategic issue management. I describe the process of designing applications to fit particular organizations and then address two special issues: (1) the role of the nonprofit board in strategic planning and management and (2) the tie between strategic management and the annual operational planning and budget preparation process. Finally, a practical exercise provides an opportunity to try some of the techniques.

LOGIC AND METHODOLOGY

Strategic management is a balancing act among competing values; its primary purpose is to maintain a dynamic balance between an organization (its mission, goals, plans, and resources) and its external environment. The balance is maintained by ensuring that the organization's scarce resources are invested to take maximum feasible advantage of opportunities (for new or additional revenues, new patrons or clients, or new products or services) and to deal effectively with challenges (the decline or disappearance of a major source of revenue or the appearance of a significant competitor) (Eadie, 1997a).

Strategic planning and management is a relatively new and rapidly developing field, especially in the nonprofit sector, where its presence is just now being felt (Bryson, 1989; Bryson & Roering, 1987; Eadie, 1989, 1997a; Olsen & Eadie, 1982). One of the most important innovations in the field in recent years has been the rejection of the notion that the primary product of this process is a weighty, comprehensive plan that encompasses all of an organization's activities. It is now widely accepted that the real product is organizational change in response to environmental change, not the elaborate codification and projection into the future of current programs and functions. Indeed, experience has shown that, in a time of often dizzying environmental change, the production of massive documents may be a harmful waste of time.

The term "strategic management," which is now used far more widely than "strategic planning," developed in response to the early overemphasis on the production of documents at the expense of attention to actual change. Strategic management encompasses both the formulation and implementation of strategies and is best seen as an ongoing process (Bryson, 1989; Eadie, 1989; Edwards & Eadie, 1994; Tichy, 1983).

Another major current in the field is the attention paid to the collective involvement of people in fashioning and implementing strategies (Robinson & Eadie, 1986). Strategies are implemented by people, not computers, forms, procedures, or six-pound documents. Now that people are recognized as being important for the formulation of successful strategies, developing the human resource and building strong teams are rightly seen as critical to the success of strategic management (Gluck, 1985; Nutt & Backoff, 1987).

There are strategies, and *there are strategies*. A community may stage participatory meetings that result in a vision and a set of broad directions for development—a kind of global strategy far removed from detailed action planning. A nonprofit organization may develop such a global strategy as well. However, the community or the nonprofit organization may also formulate detailed action strategies (specific change targets, or initiatives, along with implementation plans) to address particular issues that have been identified. These are also strategies. To narrow the focus even further, a particular division or department in a nonprofit organization may produce its own strategies, including both a global strategy and detailed action strategies.

The point is that saying that an organization is engaging in strategic management means nothing until the kind of strategy being produced is known. As is explored later, until an organization knows the kind of strategy it wants to produce, it cannot determine the specifics of the process required to produce it.

STRATEGIC ISSUE MANAGEMENT

"Strategic issue management" is increasingly used to describe an entire process that begins with the development of a global strategy and ends with the generation of detailed action strategies. As is demonstrated, the focus on strategic issues safeguards against using the process merely to describe and codify what an organization is already doing. Therefore, strategic issue management has sometimes been called "management by selection" (Eadie, 1986, 1987; Eadie & Steinbacher, 1985).

The principal elements in the process are the clarification of values and vision, external and internal environmental scanning, the identification and selection of strategic issues, and the formulation and implementation of strategies. The following discussion addresses both the content involved in each element and the process used to generate it, drawing on real-life examples.

Clarification of Values and Vision

Values are the most cherished principles—the "golden rules"—that guide an organization's planning and management activities. A *vision* is a word picture of an organization's desired impact on or contribution to its community or service area and of the organization's role in the community (O'Toole, 1995).

The clarification of values and vision provides the strategic issue management process with a kind of "natural law": a strategic backdrop for scanning the environment, selecting the issues, and gaining information about the strategies. Without this backdrop, the strategic management process would be like an automobile engine without a driver or a steering wheel: undirected motion and energy.

Meeting with the executive director and members of the management team, the board of the Glen Retirement System in Shreveport, Louisiana, fashioned a statement of values (Eadie, 1997b) that included the following points:

- We believe in the value of elderly people as contributors, using their gifts to enrich the lives of the people around them.
- We believe in the independence, dignity, and security of elderly people.
- We believe in health care of the highest quality.
- We believe in meeting individual needs and in personal growth.
- We believe in professionalism, competence, attention to detail, and accountability.
- We believe in responding promptly and positively to complaints.

At a two-day retreat, the board and staff of Dobama Theater in Cleveland envisioned the following effects of its efforts in the community (Eadie, 1994b):

- Theater audiences will increase.
- A growing number of youths will become involved in theater.
- New financial resources will be attracted.
- Audience attention spans will lengthen.
- Dobama will be more widely recognized—locally, regionally, and nationally.
- Dobama will be sought after as a collaborator.
- New works will be commissioned.

Statements of values and vision are often fashioned in intensive, facilitated work sessions involving board members and top managers. Certainly, something this important to the long-term success of an organization should not merely be delegated to staff and then passively reviewed by a board. The board and staff of the National Parks and Conservation Association (Eadie, 1995), for example, developed detailed impact and role statements as part of a vision statement, which was refined by staff and the board's planning committee and eventually adopted by the full board.

External Environmental Scanning

In light of its vision and mission, what information must a nonprofit organization have about the world in which it works to spot issues and formulate effective strategies? The environmental scan answers this question. The vision and mission provide the boundaries that keep the scan from being an overwhelming task.

Developing the Content

Whether the scan is prepared by a staff task force and then reviewed in an intensive board–staff work session or is developed in a work session, it is necessary to identify the national, state, regional, and local trends and conditions that must be understood to fashion a strategy. The board and management team of the Health Industry Distributors Association (Eadie, 1994c) were interested in the following:

- new health care technologies
- emerging international markets
- restructuring of the health care system in the United States, such as managed care and consolidation
- government funding and attempts to influence and regulate health care
- changing demographics.

Analysis of Stakeholders

In the quest for statistics, it is all too easy to forget that an organization's environment also consists of other entities that significantly influence or have the potential to influence its vision, mission, and strategies. These influential organizations are often loosely known as "stakeholders," and understanding them is a critical part of the external environmental scan.

Stakeholders may be understood both in terms of organizational characteristics and actual and potential relationships with the organization. Organizational characteristics include vision, mission, priorities, plans, resources, style of operating, track record, and (perhaps most important) perceptions of the organization. Vis-à-vis the organization, a stakeholder may be a cooperator, a partner in a joint venture, a provider of resources, a provider of legitimacy (blessing the organization's endeavors), a wielder of authority, a competitor, a paying customer, or a client. For example, the board and staff of the Glen Retirement System identified as key stakeholders the Louisiana Nursing Home Association, local hospitals, the local Council on Aging, and higher education institutions, among others (Eadie, 1997b). Each stakeholder relationship was assessed. To take the Council on Aging as an example, the Glen Retirement System hoped to obtain client referrals, information on trends, and networking opportunities. In return, it expected to "pay" the council with political support, transportation, food service, and communication on its activities. The relationship was assessed as "generally positive."

Customers and Clients

When analyzing stakeholders, nonprofit organizations must distinguish between paying customers and clients, because the two groups involve different relationships that require special management. Clients of a battered women's shelter or rape crisis center, for example, do not directly buy the services they receive (although, indirectly, they may pay through taxes), but funders, such as the state department of welfare, the county commissioners, and the local United Way are direct customers with considerable power over the mission, plans, and programs of the organization. The point is that the service delivered to the client is only one kind of product; other kinds may be delivered to the paying customers.

Internal Environmental Scanning

The foundation for identifying strategic issues is fully in place when an organization leaves its external environment and looks inward. The internal environmental scan basically involves assessing organizational strengths and weaknesses in terms of human, financial, technological, and political resources, and organizational performance in its major programs and businesses. For example, during their two-day work session, the Glen Retirement System board and staff assessed the performance of each major site and then identified strengths and weaknesses in board leadership, management, finances, and organizational image and clout (Eadie, 1997b). With regard to the board's leadership, they identified strengths as "talent; level of involvement; commitment and enthusiasm; teamwork; strong staff support; being manageable in size; and successful fund raising" (p. 38). The weaknesses they saw included "lack of diversity in membership; too little contact with staff; limited use of standing committees; lack of a strong board role in strategic planning; and the absence of a systematic approach to board member capacity building" (p. 40).

Identification and Selection of Strategic Issues

What Are Strategic Issues?

Strategic issues may be thought of as major "change challenges"—opportunities and problems that appear to demand an organizational response, so a successful balance can be maintained between the organization's internal and external environments. Opportunities are principally avenues to organizational growth—delivery of new services or products—through tapping new

*"The strategic plan says we facilitate the timely flow of interdepartmental and exter-
nal communications. So try not to think of yourself as 'just a mailroom clerk.'"*

sources of revenue and through addressing new needs (these avenues of
growth, or levers, are intertwined and are never mutually exclusive). Problems
are conditions, events, or trends that threaten to reduce an organization's
resources and its program competitive position (including its reputation and
political clout).

No scientific test can determine whether an issue is truly strategic or
merely operational. Certainly, in the course of an organization's annual operational planning and budget preparation process, many issues arise that relate
to refining and adjusting operating programs, and they can involve major
expenditures (such as instituting a new computer registration system in a
recreational department). However, some issues always rise above others in
terms of the stakes involved (both benefits and costs) and their complexity.

It is worth noting that because strategic issues often cut across organizational functions and departments, they require organization-wide attention;
similarly because they sometimes transcend organizations, they require that
different organizations cooperate in addressing them. Moreover, issues may
relate to administrative or managerial concerns and to the content of programs and services.

Some Examples

In their two-day work session, the board and staff of the National Parks and Conservation Association identified the following strategic issues: the need to tap more fully the tremendous resources brought to the organization by its board members; the absence of an ongoing strategic management capability that provides for a proactive leadership role for the board; the need to strengthen image and public relations; the need to provide opportunities for member involvement; the need to strengthen retention of younger members; and the reality of a Congress that is more hostile to environmental concerns (Eadie, 1995).

The members of the Organizational Structure Task Force of the American Health Information Management Association (AHIMA) met for two days in Chicago and identified the following as key issues facing the association: an organizational structure "that is baroque in its complexity, that is too vaguely defined, that is tremendously time-intensive . . . and that too often leads to adversarial interaction"; "uncertainty about who the primary customer is: members at the local level or highly active members climbing the volunteer 'career ladder'"; a House of Delegates that "tends to operate as a quasi-legislative body that is competitive with the AHIMA Board of Directors, causing considerable tension and confusion among AHIMA members"; and various task forces and committees that mix operating and governing responsibilities that are "only vaguely tied into mainstream AHIMA planning and management processes," and that "chew up far too much volunteer time" (Eadie, 1997c, pp. 5–6).

Selection of Issues

As a preface to the selection of strategic issues, keep in mind that any organization's resources in time, energy, dollars, political capital, and so forth are not only finite, they are usually stretched to the limit in the nonprofit sector. Therefore, it is highly unlikely that many strategic issues can be addressed effectively at any one time. Selectivity is thus more than a virtue; it is a necessity.

One cannot choose in a simple or scientific way which issues to address in the short term through the formulation of strategies. Some believe that a highly effective approach is to analyze issues in two ways:

1. Evaluate the potential cost that the organization might bear if it does not move forward now in addressing a particular issue, considering both direct costs (dollars, lost credibility, human pain and suffering, and so on) and lost benefits (lost revenue from a grant not obtained).
2. Assess the organization's ability to have a positive impact on an issue within the resource constraints. For example, a school district may think more

than twice about taking the lead in addressing the drug dependence of students because of the complexity of the issue and the substantial costs involved in addressing it comprehensively.

The ultimate decision on which issues to tackle in the short term will depend, then, on a rough cost–benefit analysis. The objective is a set of issues that promises the most potential benefit (and avoided costs) for the price in time, dollars, and political capital.

Formulation and Implementation of Strategies

When the strategic issues to be addressed have been selected, task forces often are appointed to fashion action strategies to address them. A staff steering committee, comprising senior managers, may be used to review the work of the strategy formulation task forces, and the board ultimately reviews and approves the task force's recommendations. The steps involved in formulating strategies are as follows:

- Get a firm grasp on an issue by breaking it into its various subissues. This step inevitably involves the task force doing a more detailed, second-stage scan of an issue than was possible when it identified and selected the issues.
- Determine which subissue to tackle.
- Brainstorm action initiatives to address each of the subissues and to select the initiatives that appear to yield the most benefit for the cost, within acceptable resource limits.
- Fashion detailed implementation plans that set forth a schedule of events, specify who is accountable for what action, and detail the costs involved.

Implementation involves three key issues: (1) the organization's commitment, (2) the allocation of resources, and (3) the implementation structure and process. Commitment means that, at the very least, the policy body, the chief executive officer, and senior managers are committed to the results anticipated from implementing proposed strategies, to the roles that must be played to implement these strategies, and to the costs that must be incurred. The wider the ownership is felt for an organization's strategy, the more likely the strategy is to be fully implemented. This fact argues for widespread participation in strategy formulation task forces as a vehicle for building ownership; another vehicle is effective internal communication.

Financial resources can be explicitly allocated to implement strategies through the annual operational planning and budget preparation process by ensuring that the work of the task forces feeds into the budgetary decision-making process in a timely fashion. Another approach is to allocate dollars from a contingency fund established to finance innovation and change.

Finally, a structure and managerial process is required to ensure the full and timely implementation of the strategy. This process may include a steering committee of senior managers that meets once a month, a technical coordinating committee that provides detailed guidance, implementation task forces that provide hands-on management of the implementation process, a high-level staff person to coordinate the whole effort, and a system for regularly reporting progress and resolving problems (Kanter, 1989).

DESIGN APPLICATIONS

Experience with unsuccessful planning processes has at best made many managers of nonprofit organizations skeptical of planning initiatives: at worst, it has bred cynicism. Processes have collapsed midstream because organizations have lacked either the capability or the commitment required to implement them. Some organizations have faithfully gone through all the steps in their planning processes, only to find that the results were not worth the effort (witness the many shelves groaning under the weight of never-consulted, dust-covered tomes).

The purpose of design is to ensure that an organization achieves precisely what it wants through its planning process and at a cost that it can afford. Through design, the outcomes or products to be generated are identified, the process and structure required to produce the outcomes are developed, and the resources required to implement the process are specified. Armed with a sound design, an organization can move forward with confidence to implement the techniques of strategic issue management, knowing that it can implement a process to produce the outcomes it wants.

The design process is a prelude to applying strategic issue management that is typically initiated by the chief executive officer and preferably involves both board members and senior staff. In one or more intensive work sessions, process outcomes are identified, and the process and structure of strategic issue management are worked out. The resources (time, consulting fees, and so on) that are required to implement the process should also be spelled out. The design should be described in a document that is formally reviewed and accepted by the board, the chief executive, and senior managers.

A Word on Outcomes

There are two primary categories of outcomes in the strategic management process: (1) those that relate directly to the kinds of strategies that are generated and (2) those that are process-related spinoffs. For example, an organization that is facing a fiscal crisis may decide in the design process to deal during the first cycle of strategic issue management with only one issue—the enhancement of revenue—and to make the primary outcome of the first-year planning effort a detailed action strategy to deal with that overriding issue. Another organization may determine that during its first cycle, its whole focus is the generation—in a concentrated work session of the board and top management staff—of a vision for the organization and a set of broad strategic directions. A third organization may decide to engage in the full-blown process, from environmental scanning through the identification of issues to the selection of issues to the formulation of strategies for action.

The foregoing are direct, content-related outcomes. In addition, organizations can identify some less direct—but not necessarily less important—outcomes. For example, building a team of managers may be an important outcome of the process, as may strengthening the leadership role of the board. Another outcome may be to increase the staff's morale or to strengthen the public's understanding of the organization's mission and goals. All these outcomes—direct and indirect—drive the development of the process and structure of strategic issue management.

Also driving this development are what may be called "rules of the game." For example, an organization may specify in its design that any strategies that its task forces recommends during the first cycle must be achievable within current resource limits or specify precisely how the additional required resources are to be obtained. An organization may specify in its design that a highly controversial matter not be raised during the process (for example, the distribution of syringes to addicts as a tactic to prevent AIDS). The point is to ensure through these rules that the strategic ship does not hit an iceberg that could have been avoided through forethought.

A Word on Process and Structure

Designing the process and structure to achieve the identified outcomes involves determining what should be done, when it should be done, and by whom it should be done. This determination will be driven by the identified outcomes, the rules of the game, and the organization's capability. It is important not to underestimate the potential for any process to collapse midstream if it is not carefully designed. The strategic management effort, no matter how modest or elaborate, will not be an established organizational routine during the first one or two cycles; it will always be threatened by the press of day-to-day events and loyalties to established organizational units (in contrast to ad hoc task forces).

Examples of structure are a board task force to formulate a statement of vision; a staff task force on environmental scanning; a two-day work session of the board and staff to review and confirm the statement of vision, discuss the environmental scan, and identify strategic issues; and the use of task forces to formulate strategies.

The Organization's Capability

Whether an organization is able to carry out a design successfully depends on its capability. Although organizational capability is a nebulous concept, practical experience suggests that the following factors should be explicitly considered.

First, the commitment of the board and chief executive officer to the process is central, in terms both of the outcomes to be generated and the costs that are incurred in going through it. The board's and chief executive's participation in developing the design and reviewing and approving it help ensure this commitment. The commitment of the organization's senior managers also is critical to the success of the design.

Second, people make or break strategic management processes, so understanding the human resource dimension is critical to developing a sound design. Obviously, skills and experience deserve consideration. A staff that has never participated in strategic planning and management activities is less capable than one that has. Also important is the organization's internal climate. Skepticism of planning on the basis of negative experiences or a general malaise related to working conditions definitely lessens the staff's capability to engage in strategic management activities.

Third, time and attention are also important aspects of organizational capability. An organization that is severely understaffed is hard pressed to devote time to strategic management. Similarly, one that is grappling with one or more crises, such as a looming budget deficit or an audit uncovering irregularities, is less able to devote attention to strategic issue management.

Finally, money is always an important aspect of capability. Doing strategic issue management costs money—for work session space, the production of materials, and external technical assistance.

Following the inexorable rule that the strategic management process and the organization's capability must match, an organization can always reduce its expectations of outcomes and the demands of the process or spread a process out over a longer period. Keep in mind, however, that systematically strengthening capability may be part of the strategic management design. For example, funding from foundations may supplement the organization's budget. Orientation and training sessions may enhance skills while reducing skepticism. Participation in shaping the design may counter low morale.

BOARDS AND BUDGETS

Board Leadership

The boards of many nonprofit organizations are highly frustrated at what they rightly consider to be their vaguely defined, often obviously unimportant roles (Carver, 1990; Eadie, 1994a). It is common to see the "illusion of control" that comes from two equally unimportant and unproductive kinds of board work: (1) paying inordinate attention to the review of trivial details, such as detailed reports of payments to vendors, and (2) thumbing through finished documents, such as a completed, bound budget, and asking random questions.

The process of strategic issue management provides ample opportunity for a board to be fully engaged in carrying out important leadership responsibilities: in defining outcomes of the process and confirming the design, in formulating statements of vision and mission, in reviewing the environmental scans and identifying strategic issues, in selecting the issues to be addressed, and in reviewing the strategic actions that are recommended to address the selected issues.

A particularly effective device is to stage an intensive one-and-one-half- to two-day work session involving the board, staff, and key "outside" stakeholders. The Dobama Theater, Glen Retirement System, and AHIMA, for example, all held sessions that focused during the first day on organizational strategy. Using breakout groups, they clarified values, vision, and mission; assessed the external and internal environments; identified strategic issues; and brainstormed possible change initiatives to address the issues. The second day was devoted to assessing the performance of the governing board and discussing possible enhancements in board role, structure, and processes. In every case, the staff comprising the management team in follow-up sessions analyzed the issues and possible initiatives and recommended action to the board's planning committee.

Such board–staff work sessions are likely to be successful if the outcome agenda is agreed to in advance, a comfortable off-site location is used, preparation is meticulous, and adequate time is allowed. Professional facilitation can also help, particularly when highly complex and possibly emotional or controversial issues are being addressed.

Budget Connection

An explicit connection is needed between any strategic issue management effort and the annual operational planning and budget preparation process.

Two obvious connections are these:

1. scheduling the formulation of statements of vision and mission, the environmental scan, and identification of issues so they can be factored into the budgets of operating units (strategic input helps guide preparations of the budget at the operating-unit level, where trends, conditions, and issues are, indeed, pertinent in shaping budgets)
2. ensuring that the recommendations of strategy formulation task forces include detailed cost estimates and that the cost estimates are considered part of the decision-making process on the budget.

CONCLUSION

This chapter has traced the rapid development of strategic management in the nonprofit sector, from the original notion of heavily documented comprehensive planning to the more action-oriented process of strategic issue management. Strategic management enables an organization to respond effectively to challenges—significant opportunities and major constraints or problems—in its environment. The key elements of the process are the clarification of vision and values, an external and internal scanning, the identification and selection of issues, and the formulation and implementation of strategies.

The chapter examined the design process, through which an organization ensures that it achieves what it wants from the application of strategic management at a cost that it can afford. The design spells out the outcomes or products that the strategic management application generates and details the structure and process required to achieve the outcomes. As part of the design process, an organization explicitly determines that it has the capability to implement the process or it builds the requisite capability.

SKILLS-APPLICATION EXERCISE

- If the organization you work in has a vision and a mission, describe them. If not, create a statement of vision and mission for your organization.

- What is your personal vision, in terms of career aspirations and personal lifestyle? Scan your environment externally and internally, and identify any strategic issues you face in light of your vision. Formulate broad strategies to address those issues.

- Make a list of stakeholders of the immediate organizational unit in which you work and of the organization in which your unit fits. Analyze each stakeholder's characteristics and the relationships (actual and potential) that your unit and organization may have or build with each stakeholder.

- You also have stakeholders with whom you must deal in your career and personally. Name a few of the most important and analyze their characteristics and the nature of your relationships with each. Fashion stakeholder management strategies to ensure that the working relationships are effective.

- Scan the external and internal environments of the organization you work in to identify major trends and conditions and assess the organization's resources and strengths and weaknesses.

- On the basis of this scan, identify some strategic issues that your organization may need to address and evaluate the potential costs (direct or in lost benefits) of not addressing each issue.

- Select one or two of what appear to be the most critical issues and brainstorm possible initiatives to address them. Identify for each initiative the anticipated impact on the issue and the costs (time, money, political capital) that may be anticipated in implementing it.

- Your organization is considering undergoing a process of strategic issue management. Assess your organization's capability to undertake such an ambitious project, paying special attention to the barriers that may be faced.

REFERENCES

Bryson, J. M. (1989). *Strategic planning for public and nonprofit organizations.* San Francisco: Jossey-Bass.

Bryson, J. M., & Roering, W. D. (1987). Applying private-sector strategic planning in the public sector. *Journal of the American Planning Association, 53,* 9–22.

Carver, J. (1990). *Boards that make a difference.* San Francisco: Jossey-Bass.

Eadie, D. C. (1986). *Strategic issue management: Improving the council–manager relationship.* Washington, DC: International City Management Association.

Eadie, D. C. (1987). Strategic issue management: Building an organization's capability. *Economic Development Commentary, 11,* 18–21.

Eadie, D. C. (1989). Building the capacity for strategic management. In J. L. Perry (Ed.), *Handbook of public administration* (pp. 162–175). San Francisco: Jossey-Bass.

Eadie, D. C. (1994a). *Boards that work: A practical guide for building effective association boards.* Washington, DC: American Society of Association Executives.

Eadie, D. C. (1994b). *Report to the Dobama Theater Board and CEO.* Cleveland: Strategic Development Consulting.

Eadie, D. C. (1994c). *Report to the Health Information Management Association.* Cleveland: Strategic Development Consulting.

Eadie, D. C. (1995). *Report to the National Parks and Conservation Association*. Cleveland: Strategic Development Consulting.

Eadie, D. C. (1997a). *Changing by design: A practical approach to leading innovation in nonprofit organizations*. San Francisco: Jossey-Bass.

Eadie, D. C. (1997b). *Report to the Glen Retirement System*. Cleveland: Strategic Development Consulting.

Eadie, D. C. (1997c). *Report to the Organizational Structure Task Force, American Health Information Management Association*. Cleveland: Strategic Development Consulting.

Eadie, D. C., & Steinbacher, R. (1985). Strategic agenda management: A marriage of organizational development and strategic planning. *Public Administration Review, 45,* 424–430.

Edwards, R. L., & Eadie, D. C. (1994). Meeting the change challenge: Managing growth in the nonprofit and public human services sectors. *Administration in Social Work, 18,* 107–123.

Gluck, F. W. (1985). A fresh look at strategic management. *Journal of Business Strategy, 6,* 4–21.

Kanter, R. M. (1989). *When giants learn to dance*. New York: Simon & Schuster.

Nutt, P. C., & Backoff, R. W. (1987). A strategic management process for public sector organizations. *Journal of the American Planning Association, 53,* 44–57.

Olsen, J. B., & Eadie, D. C. (1982). *The game plan: Governance with foresight*. Washington, DC: Council of State Planning and Policy Agencies.

O'Toole, J. (1995). *Leading change: Overcoming the ideology of comfort and tyranny of custom*. San Francisco: Jossey-Bass.

Robinson, R. V., & Eadie, D. C. (1986). *Building the senior management team through team issue management*. Washington, DC: International City Management Association.

Tichy, N. M. (1983). *Managing strategic change*. New York: John Wiley & Sons.

CHAPTER 22

Managing Time

Laurie N. DiPadova and Sue R. Faerman

As a manager in a nonprofit organization, one of the roles you must play is that of a producer; you must be task oriented and able to focus on the work at hand. To be a successful manager, you must invest a great deal of energy in your work, and you must be able to handle a heavy, complex workload. Unless you have good time management skills, you may feel overwhelmed by the competing demands on your time, and your productivity may suffer as a result.

Few people in today's society feel free from time pressures. Managers, office workers, homemakers, and students frequently report that they need more time or feel stressed because they do not have enough hours in the day to accomplish all of the things that must get done. Such images of needing more time or not having enough time develop from thinking of time as linear, such that one cannot recover time that has passed or save time for use in the future. Instead, people think about each moment in time as existing only for that moment and become frustrated when they have not stuffed all that they can into each of those moments. Unfortunately, this view of time creates the potential for developing time management approaches and techniques that focus solely on efficient use of time, without attention to issues of whether time is being spent effectively (Whetten & Cameron, 1995). Thus, you may efficiently add more activities into your day but find that, in the long run, these are not the activities that are most appropriate for helping you reach your most important goals.

We approach the topic of time management from the perspective that it is important to pay attention to both effective and efficient use of time. We recognize that, in fact, there may not be enough hours in the day to do all of the activities you would like to or feel that you must do, and so we attempt to help you think about how you might manage your time by choosing activities that allow you to feel the greatest sense of accomplishment. We also recognize that not all techniques of time management work well for all people

(McGee-Cooper & Trammell, 1994). For some of you reading this chapter, efficient time management might mean working on one project at a time, starting at the beginning and working through until it is done. For others, it might mean working on several projects at once, so that you can temporarily switch from one project to another if you get stuck on a problem or begin to feel bored. Finally, we recognize that time management is not just a work-related skill; it is a life skill. Indeed, we begin with a brief discussion of how your approach to time management can affect various areas of your life, including your physical and mental health, and suggest that as you read through the entire chapter, you should think about how the ideas presented here pertain to your life in general, not just your life at work.

TIME MANAGEMENT IS MORE THAN MANAGING TIME

Research over the past few decades has indicated that our concern with the passage of time and our sense of urgency can result in greater, rather than reduced, levels of stress. Stress, in turn, has been linked to a vast array of illnesses, including tension headaches, various forms of heart disease, cancer, ulcers, and even arthritis (Dossey, 1982; McGee-Cooper & Trammell, 1994). Indeed, Larry Dossey developed the term *hurry sickness* to describe the condition of people who experience an elevated sense of time urgency and whose lives are driven by goals, objectives, and deadlines. Of course, managers as well as many other people are constantly faced with deadlines and time-related goals, and so it is not surprising that managers identify time management problems as their greatest source of stress (Mintzberg, 1980; Whetten & Cameron, 1995). The flip side of this coin is that one can take a first step in reducing the stress that accompanies the time pressures of meeting goals and deadlines by improving one's ability to manage time, assuming that the emphasis is on developing effective, as well as efficient, time management approaches.

You are probably aware of the abundant sources of sound advice for managing time. Seminars and workshops for improving time practices abound for virtually everyone—employees, college students, homemakers, children, and volunteers. Informative books on the subject can be found in any bookstore (see, for example, Knaus, 1979; Lakein, 1973; Mackenzie, 1972; McGee-Cooper & Trammell, 1994; Smith, 1994; Winston, 1983). Given the universally acknowledged problem of time management and the extensive resources available to individuals, it is ironic that many individuals still experience considerable stress because of too little time. The question is, Why do so many people feel that they have trouble managing their time? One reason may be that because everyone has the same 24 hours to manage, there may be a tendency to compare oneself unfavorably with other people who appear well organized and accomplished. In doing so, individuals neglect to give themselves credit for what they are doing well. The unfortunate inclination to focus on shortcomings without acknowledging strengths simply fosters discouragement, which may in turn inhibit the energy needed to make necessary changes.

Second, as noted in the introduction, feverishly embarking on strict schedules, carefully monitoring each conversation, and accounting for minutes wasted does not necessarily mean that you focus on the most important activities. Moreover, as we demonstrate later in this chapter, working constantly, with no time for breaks or relaxation, can make it more difficult for you to work productively. Thus, paradoxically, the result is often a reduction of productive time.

Finally, time management problems may sometimes be a manifestation of unresolved deeper concerns in a person's life. Individuals may budget their time as they would their money, without understanding why their time management problems are so persistent. Rather than approaching time as a resource to be budgeted and accounted for, the perspective we take is to focus on managing oneself in relation to time (Mackenzie, 1972). Self-management includes managing our schedules, calendars, and everything from paper to attitudes to relationships. It involves being just as aware of where you are going as you are of how fast you are getting there (Covey, Merrill, & Merrill, 1994).

In trying to develop one's time management skills, it is important to understand how one's assumptions about time influence how one uses time. Below we present some of the underlying assumptions of this chapter. We suggest that as you read through the chapter, you should try to become more aware of the assumptions you make about time and your personal use of time. For example, do you assume that you cannot work on a large project unless you have a large block of available time? That scheduling time with employees is more important than scheduling time for yourself? That developing and using solid time management skills require you to limit your creativity or spontaneity?

In this chapter, time management is discussed as a personal responsibility. People make decisions in life for which they must bear direct consequences. Other people cannot be blamed for one's frustration. Hence, each person must examine his or her own situation and explore what actions can be taken to change it.

Second, improving time management skills means increasing the ability to accomplish more in less time by working smarter, not harder. Planning does not waste time; it focuses efforts. The time spent planning ultimately yields greater productivity.

Third, time management is a learned skill. People are not born good time managers. Their current practices are a result of learning. Sometimes poor time management behaviors result from faulty beliefs and attitudes. When individuals correct misperceptions, they are better able to unlearn what they no longer need and to learn new techniques.

Fourth, time management for managers differs from time management for nonmanagers. Although everyone can benefit from basic time management methods, the supervisory role of managers suggests unique time management opportunities, challenges, and techniques. For example, managers can delegate work tasks to their employees, but they are faced with more interruptions and distractions that can interfere with their time management efforts.

Finally, time management is very individualized. Individuals cannot look at what others do as an accurate gauge of personal progress. Everyone approaches his or her work and personal responsibilities in a somewhat different manner. As a result, this chapter offers some suggestions to consider, not rules by which to abide.

The next section presents the organizational context of time management for managers. The sections that follow focus on individual issues and techniques for time management within organizations. In particular, we explore time management techniques that have proven helpful for managers.

ORGANIZATIONAL CONTEXT OF TIME MANAGEMENT ISSUES

Managers and their employees operate within the setting of formal organizations. Within these organizations, many structures and processes affect how individuals manage their time. Some enhance how people use their time, whereas others create time management problems.

Several organizational structures and processes create paradoxes for managers. For example, many forces in organizations operate to control and standardize people, yet the organizations—as well as the people—often need individuals to contribute their unique skills, perspectives, and creativity. Trying to balance these two forces can lead managers to communicate with mixed messages and conflicting expectations. A second example arises when managers need to accomplish their tasks, yet at the same time need to be available to respond to interruptions from others. Handling interruptions is sometimes seen as a time waster, but it is actually part of the manager's job description. A final example occurs when individuals are promoted to managerial positions without appropriate management education and development opportunities. Often, in public and nonprofit organizations, professional employees are promoted from within the ranks of the organization to a managerial position on the basis of their ability to excel in the professional position. Conflict arises as the professional-turned-manager tries to continue to spend time engaged in nonmanagerial activities. Moreover, in small, nonprofit organizations, everyone may occasionally get involved in some activity to meet a pressing deadline. In developing effective time management skills, the manager must constantly make decisions about time use on the basis of what is the most important use of his or her time.

In addition to the paradoxes created by organizational structures and processes, individuals bring into the organization false beliefs or myths about how to manage their time. The combination of myths and paradoxes can create additional problems for managers. Recognizing and confronting these myths is particularly important, not only for your own time management efforts but to enhance your ability to assist employees. Here we specify six myths of time management. You can probably think of others. As you examine this list, consider the extent to which you subscribe to each.

- *Myth 1: Being busy means being productive.* This myth is especially harmful because it encourages us to look at activity rather than at the quality of work being produced. The truth is, the active person may be disorganized, inefficient, or ineffective and, as noted earlier, the efficient time manager is not always the effective time manager.
- *Myth 2: Work must be completed before there is time for fun or relaxation.* Research has shown that relaxation and renewal are vital to effective time and stress management (McGee-Cooper & Trammell, 1994; Metcalf & Felible, 1992). When individuals do not consciously save time for rest or relaxation, they risk becoming overwhelmed or unable to focus. Even a 15-minute break, during which you are doing a completely different activity, can increase your energy and allow you to work more productively. The expression "you cannot pour from an empty vessel" provides an appropriate metaphor for describing the importance of making sure that managing one's time includes making time for personal renewal.
- *Myth 3: Only upper management can make the most important decisions.* In reality, decisions should often be made at the lowest possible level in the organization, because people lower in the hierarchy have greater familiarity with the circumstances. Belief in this myth often causes time to be wasted because decisions at lower levels generally require less time than decisions at upper levels.
- *Myth 4: The more information you have, the better your decisions will be.* More information is often better than less information, but obtaining it may require more time. Thus, although it may be wise to defer some decisions pending availability of information, it is often not possible to have all of the information or to know with certainty each consequence of various courses of action. This myth is particularly destructive when managers and employees use it to procrastinate.

- *Myth 5: The quicker things are done, the better.* Our debunking of Myth 4 suggests that sometimes it is more important to make a decision or to act than to wait for additional information. However, hastening a decision without the critical facts or initiating action prematurely without taking the time to elicit input from key people can spell disaster. People who "do not have the time to plan" often subscribe to this myth.
- *Myth 6: It takes too much time to delegate.* Although the skills of effective delegation may require time to learn and apply, delegation saves time and empowers employees. This myth is deceptive because refusal to delegate locks managers into the mentality of always having too much to do.

As is readily apparent, accepting these myths hinders the pursuit of positive courses of thinking and action. In camouflaging the truth, myths make it more difficult to take corrective action. The first step in time management is to recognize and reject these myths as a basis for action.

Furthermore, managers and employees need to recognize that they control the bulk of their time. The extent of control is related to the level of initiative one takes (Oncken, 1984). For example, if your style is low initiative—waiting to be directed in each step of a given assignment—your supervisor may ask you to report more frequently so that your progress can be monitored. In this situation, your time is being controlled by your supervisor. Conversely, if you take the initiative and act on your own, your supervisor is more likely to give you greater freedom to control your own time. As a manager, you can train and encourage your staff to control their time by providing opportunities for them to act independently rather than requiring continual direction from you.

INDIVIDUAL ISSUES IN TIME MANAGEMENT

We began this chapter by distinguishing between notions of efficiency and effectiveness in time management. Here we expand on this issue, focusing on personal issues that may keep individuals from using their time effectively. Before we examine these issues, however, it might be useful to clarify further the meanings of and differences between effective and efficient time management. One of the best ways to distinguish between these terms is to think about the difference between prioritizing your activities on the basis of urgency and prioritizing your activities on the basis of importance.

Time Management Matrix

In their book *First Things First*, Covey and associates (1994) presented a time management matrix. The matrix is divided into two dimensions—importance

"Pencil me in at 7:00 for 15 minutes of coloring and storytelling."

and urgency—and includes four quadrants: (1) important and urgent, (2) important but not urgent, (3) urgent but not important, and (4) neither important nor urgent. Quadrant I (important and urgent) includes crises, pressing problems, and projects with deadlines. You could also include crises with close friends, relatives, or coworkers in this quadrant. Quadrant II (important but not urgent) includes long-term planning and prioritizing, professional development, relationship building, taking care of your physical and mental health, and working on long-term projects that do not have imminent deadlines. Covey et al. referred to this as the "quadrant of quality," because it is the quadrant that contains activities that are related to long-term goals and personal growth and development. You should expect to spend most of your time in these two quadrants. The balance between these two quadrants is crucial; the more time you spend in Quadrant II, the less time you may need to spend dealing with crises and problems in Quadrant I.

Quadrant III includes those items that are urgent but not important, such as telephone calls, mail, meetings, and drop-in visitors. This is where you spend a lot of time meeting other people's expectations and demands rather than your own. Finally, Quadrant IV includes those items that are neither important nor urgent. These are the real time wasters—junk mail, busywork, and some "escape" activities that do not help to re-energize you. When people are overwhelmed with the amount or nature of work in Quadrants I and II, they often procrastinate by dealing first with items in Quadrants III and IV, where there may be more safety.

Procrastination

You should ask yourself, Are you among the many who consider themselves to be procrastinators? Do you find yourself putting off necessary tasks and consequently elevating your levels of guilt, frustration, and stress? Do you engage in this behavior on a regular basis? If so, the remainder of this section may help you understand why you procrastinate. Even if you do not procrastinate, you may find this section useful in dealing with others who do.

From time to time, everyone puts things off. As was noted in discussing Myths 4 and 5, sometimes it is helpful to postpone things; other times it is self-defeating. The key is being able to determine when is it beneficial and when is it indicative of a harmful habit. It may be functional at times to put off a task until more information is available or to defer making assignments on a project until your employees draw their current activities to a conclusion. Delaying things may be as functional as not turning the car off the road before one reaches the driveway. Procrastination develops when tasks are habitually postponed until the last minute, causing considerable suffering and anxiety in the interim. As Knaus (1979) put it, many who procrastinate "place themselves on psychological trial daily" (p. 107).

It is important to note that procrastination is not the result of laziness, irresponsibility, or the lack of discipline. Such beliefs merely add to procrastinators' tendencies to denigrate themselves, feeding their self-defeating behaviors. Consequently, traditional admonitions to "just do it" are consistently ineffectual in dealing with procrastinating behaviors. Rather, it is important to understand the underlying reasons that lead you to procrastinate.

Psychological Functions of Procrastination

Even when procrastination appears to be harmful and problematic, it often meets a person's psychological needs. Individuals procrastinate to avoid inner conflicts and to protect self-esteem (Burka & Yuen, 1983). For example, procrastinating important tasks may reflect a basic fear of not performing perfectly. Individuals also tend to procrastinate when they wish to avoid a task they consider unpleasant or distasteful. Keep in mind that procrastinating would not be so consistently used if it did not serve a purpose.

Understanding the needs that are met by procrastination is the first step in changing this behavior. If you procrastinate, you should ask yourself, What do

I get out of it? Why do I put off things that should not be delayed? Burka and Yuen (1983) identified a number of beliefs and attitudes associated with procrastination, which they referred to as the "Procrastinator's Code":

> I must be perfect.
> Everything I do should go easily and without effort.
> It's safer to do nothing than to take a risk and fail.
> I should have no limitations.
> If it's not done right, it's not worth doing at all.
> I must avoid being challenged.
> If I succeed, someone will get hurt.
> If I do well this time, I must *always* do well.
> Following someone else's rules means I'm giving in and I'm not in control.
> I can't afford to let go of anything or anyone.
> If I expose my real self, people won't like me.
> There is a right answer, and I'll wait until I find it. (p. 16)

Do any of the above statements reflect your view of yourself? Can you identify ways in which you have received any of these messages in your life? Do any of the people with whom you work seem to operate under these premises? If so, you should recognize that these beliefs are self-defeating and that procrastination is not the best way of dealing with them.

It is important to understand that procrastination is a learned behavior, and as such it can be unlearned and replaced. Breaking the procrastination habit involves identifying those inner conflicts and relearning more positive and less self-defeating ways of dealing with them.

Procrastination in the Organizational Setting

Tendencies to procrastinate may accelerate in the organizational setting. Although procrastinators often experience their lives as out of control, they tend to use procrastinating behaviors as a way of asserting a measure of control in life. Important tasks and projects are more likely to be carefully examined and critiqued by others. By working on tasks that fall into Quadrants III and IV, people may feel that they are exerting greater control over their destiny, because they are reducing the chance that their work is seen by others. Similarly, when individuals find it difficult to be open with their supervisors about what they can do or feel comfortable doing, they may put off the task rather than engage in a difficult conversation. If you find that you procrastinate more at work than in other areas of your life, you may wish to explore the extent to which you feel a lack of control over your work tasks and environment and whether you feel you have the ability to discuss work practices with others, particularly your supervisor.

Paradoxically, procrastination is a prescription for loss of control rather than gain of control. First, freedom is lost when tasks hang over your head, taking up energy and providing cause for worry. Waiting until the last minute also means that the deadline—not you—determines your schedule. Furthermore, if procrastination is carried to an extreme and poor work performance results in disciplinary action, demotion, or dismissal, the guilt and anxiety of having been poorly evaluated are sure to create a downward spiral.

Breaking the procrastination habit is difficult because it meets psychological needs. Although it is hard to do, progress can be made. Consider the following steps:

- Write a time management matrix for yourself. Ask how much time do I spend each day in Quadrants I and II? How much time do I spend in Quadrants III and IV?
- Identify those activities in Quadrants I and II that you tend to avoid. Think about why these are activities you would prefer to avoid.
- Analyze your situation to see if you accept any beliefs listed in the Procrastinator's Code. If so, understanding that these beliefs are false and then correcting them is a first step in changing procrastinating behaviors.
- Examine each faulty belief. For example, if you wrote "I must be perfect," examine that statement critically. Ask yourself, Why must I be perfect? Was I taught that I had to be perfect to be loved? What is the worst thing that can happen if I am not perfect?
- Think about what you know that contradicts the belief. Write it down. For example, write why perfection is a totally unreasonable expectation to hold of any human being. Write why self-improvement is reasonable.
- Instead of trying to achieve perfection (or any other faulty belief), direct your energies toward accepting yourself as a person of worth. Refuse to see yourself as lazy or undisciplined, and insist on viewing procrastination as a signal to investigate your assumptions about yourself. Many find that exploring these assumptions serves as the beginning of a meaningful self-improvement journey.
- Decide which activities in Quadrant IV should be reduced to make more time for activities from Quadrant II. Think about whether some of the activities you put in Quadrant III really belong in Quadrant IV, and repeat this step.

Of course, not all procrastination can be assumed to be a function of subconscious psychological dynamics. Often those who procrastinate simply have not learned some basic time management techniques.

TIME MANAGEMENT TECHNIQUES

Like many people, you have probably decided that your management of time may need some adjustment and fine-tuning. This section offers several time management techniques to assist you in deciding what changes to make in your life. Before going further, however, you need to understand how *not* to approach these techniques. Do not assume that these techniques will help you become the perfect time manager. All of these suggestions probably are not appropriate for you. All probably are not applicable to your situation now, although you may find other suggestions more helpful later in your career. In addition, many time management techniques tend to focus on those that encourage you to be logical and orderly. Research on brain hemisphericity—the tendency to rely on cognitive processes that occur on one side of the brain—has shown that people do not work equally well with these techniques (Springer & Deutsch, 1981). Indeed, this research has found that those whose left brain dominates their cognitive processes (sometimes referred to as "convergent thinkers") work well with techniques that are logical and orderly, whereas those whose right brain dominates their cognitive processes (sometimes referred to as "divergent thinkers") tend to need techniques that allow them to be more intuitive and visual in their organization (McGee-Cooper & Trammell, 1994).

The following collection of techniques may be helpful. Although it is not an exhaustive list, it does cover two important areas for managers: (1) organizing yourself and (2) helping others be organized. As you review this section, you may think of additional techniques that you need to implement. The references at the end of this chapter can help you pursue these topics further. It is important to assess your situation, decide what to do next, and begin.

Organize Yourself

Organizing the Day

Keep a calendar. Combine all of your appointments on one calendar: office appointments, social engagements, volunteer obligations, personal and medical appointments, trips, and so on. Keeping a separate calendar for work is less practical and often results in making several appointments for the same time period. Although your life takes place in multiple settings, it is only one life and needs one comprehensive calendar. Keep this calendar with you at all times, and refer to it. Having appointments written down not only diminishes the chances of forgotten obligations, but it frees your mind of details. Rather than trying to remember the dozen appointments you have, all you have to remember is two things: (1) check your calendar and (2) keep it current. Note that if you find calendars too constraining, you might find that writing your appointments with colored pens or pencils makes your calendar more enjoyable to look at and less constraining.

Write everything down. In a notebook or a part of your calendar, keep a master list of things to do as they occur to you. Jot down everything: work-related assignments, letters to write, appointments to schedule, arrangements to make, store items to pick up, and so on. Do not worry about organizing at this point. Just focus on having one place to write down everything. The value of putting things in writing cannot be overstated; as with calendar appointments, writing down your tasks relieves you of having to mentally keep track of things that you are afraid of forgetting.

Take time once a day to plan. Imagine taking an extended travel vacation without bothering to plan it. You would return frustrated because the weeks had gone by without your seeing everything that you had expected to see. Imagine the same trip with planned airline flights, hotel accommodations, and lists of sights to see. In which situation would you be getting the most out of your time?

Planning is simpler than it may appear when you use the master list as the raw material. Take a few minutes every day to review your master list and decide when you need to do what. From the master list, compile a to-do list of things to be done that day. Decide what items you can delegate to someone else. It is all right for the master list to be messy and marked up; it is for your use only. Remember that it is simply a tool for putting on paper everything you have in your mind that you have to do.

Set priorities among the items on your daily to-do list. Do not expect to accomplish everything on your list. Consider where you would place the items on your time management matrix and determine which are the most important. You may further distinguish the importance of the items using the ABC method: A items are the most important, B items are moderately important, and C items are the least important. The C items may be the easiest to do, but resolve to tackle the A items first. Again, if you focus on getting the Cs out of the way first, most of your life may be spent on lower-priority items rather than on what you regard as important (Covey et al., 1994; Lakein, 1973).

Next, decide what goes on your calendar, and transfer items from your to-do list onto your calendar. We are not suggesting that you place everything on your calendar, but some things do need to be scheduled. For instance, if you need to make an airline reservation by a certain date to qualify for a discounted fare, schedule that in. The financial savings can be substantial. In addition, if you are working on a large project, you should feel free to schedule time on your calendar to work on this project, as if it were an appointment. Moreover, if you are working on a large project, make sure to schedule some time intervals for short breaks, so that you can renew yourself and continue to work on the project in the most productive manner. If someone tries to schedule an appointment with you during those times, ask yourself whether the other person's needs are as important as your Quadrant I and II items.

Some people prefer to use the end of the day to review their day's activities and plan for the next day. Others prefer to start each day with a brief planning session. Regardless of when you schedule your planning session, make your calendar and master list an integral part of your day. Do not forget to take pleasure in marking off the things you have accomplished.

Analyze your master list on a regular basis. If you find that some items on your list just are not getting done, ask yourself, Why am I putting this off? Do I really have to do it? Do I resent having to do it? Did I overextend myself and try to do too much? If I do not act on this at all, what happens? What are my options? Make your master list a learning tool as well as a planning tool.

Organizing at Work

Reduce the information overload. Have on hand two file folders; label one "Action" and the other "To File." If you tend to be right-brain dominant, you might think about using colored files to make them easier to identify on your desk. Divide all incoming papers into two groups: (1) those that take more than five minutes to read, and (2) those that take less. Sort the papers using the toss, refer, act, and file (TRAF) system (Winston, 1983):

- Most of the paper and mail you receive takes less than five minutes to read. Resolve to handle these pieces of paper only once. *Toss* ads, seminar notices, FYI weekly reports, and other disposable papers. Freely use the "quick toss" method of paper management. *Refer* papers to other people (colleagues, staff, and others) for action, review, or response. *Act* on papers that require your personal attention; place in an "action" folder for completion. *File* papers. Write on the document the name of the file into which it should go and a discard date. Place in a "to file" folder for filing later.
- Place papers that take five minutes or more to read in the action folder.
- Schedule time for acting on the papers that are in the action folder.

Set up a tickler file system. Winston (1983) also recommended the following system: Number file folders from 1 to 31 (indicating the day of the month) and take 13 folders and label them for each month of the year, as well as one labeled "next month." Simply put the papers that need action this month into the numbered file according the date that you have to respond. Place papers for next month in the next-month file. Use the rest of the months' files in like manner. During the last week of each month, file the contents of the next-month file into the current month's numbered file, and place the contents of the following month into the next-month file. You can use these files as reminders of action you have to take, as well as for knowing where to find some of the current papers you need.

Handle telephone calls efficiently. Treat telephone calls as meetings. Plan for the calls ahead of time. When possible, have a prearranged written agenda in hand. At the same time, when holding a scheduled meeting with someone in your office, treat unexpected telephone calls as interruptions. Respect the time of the person in your office by telling the caller that you will call back.

Design your workspace. Have your work area laid out in such a way as to minimize unnecessary movement. You do not necessarily need to have a clean desk, but you need to feel comfortable with how things are arranged and be able to locate what you need fairly easily. Keep supplies and materials that you use frequently in a designated place or near your desk. When you need uninterrupted time, keep your door shut. Have the file folders and a wastebasket in easy reach for "TRAFing" your papers.

Schedule interruptions. Restrict your open-door policy to certain periods unless something critical happens. Restrict telephone conversations. To the extent possible, answer and make calls during certain periods only. In some cases you can have messages taken that you can answer later.

Answer mail quickly. When possible, write a response on the letter or memo, photocopy for your files, and return the original.

Delegate papers and assignments when possible and appropriate. Delegation is not only an important management competency (Quinn, Faerman, Thompson, & McGrath, 1996), it is also a proven time management technique. Delegation saves time and indicates respect for the person who is given the responsibility of completing the task. Consider the nature of the task and the needs and abilities of the individual before delegating. Be certain to communicate your expectations clearly and offer to assist the person in the delegated task, if necessary.

Do not accept upward delegation from employees. Be aware of who owns the problem. If you are not careful, you might find yourself working for employees by taking on assignments they give. This can be remedied in part by insisting that when they bring you a problem, they also offer a solution.

Tackle your "Overwhelming A." The focus of this group of strategies is coping with tasks you find overwhelming and difficult. Usually these tasks are important (labeled "A" on your to-do list), large, complex, of long duration, and appear to be difficult. Many times they are tasks that have not been tackled previously. Lakein (1973) termed this type of task an "Overwhelming A." The following suggestions draw on Lakein's work:

- *Identify your Overwhelming A.* Choose a task that you have difficulty with because of its size, complexity, or expected duration (or all three).
- *Assess the appropriateness of the Overwhelming A.* Be sure that you should embark on this task. If you have designated it as something you should do but find yourself continually resisting it, perhaps it is not right for you. It may be too overwhelming. Ask yourself, Is it realistic? For example, if you

are applying for a grant with which you have little or no prior experience, you might want to ask for help from someone who has prior experience in this area. Listen to your intuition. Once you decide on an Overwhelming A, proceed with the following steps, keeping in mind that if you find you are being unrealistic, you can always reassess your choice.

- *Divide and conquer.* Take a few minutes to write out the components of the task. Break it down to the smallest parts possible.
- *Use the Swiss cheese method.* Take five to 10 minutes to work on the first part of the task. This part may be as simple as making a telephone call to request needed information. Use five- to 10-minute breaks to punch holes in your Overwhelming A. Notice the sense of personal energy you receive after using the first five to 10 minutes.
- *Refuse to underestimate the usefulness of small spans of time.* Recognize that a lot can be accomplished in these five- to 10-minute periods. You can use them to work on your Overwhelming A.
- *Create block time.* Schedule 30 minutes or more as protected block time to work on your high-priority items. As noted above, if you are working on a large project, you should feel free to schedule time on your calendar to work on these projects and consider this time as important as a scheduled meeting. Know your most productive times of the day and create block time during those periods.

A final principle of effective time management: When you have five or 10 minutes, ask yourself, "What is the best use of my time right now?"

Help Others to be Organized

As a manager you are responsible for helping staff members organize their time. First, you influence how their time is organized when you schedule meetings, set expectations, and give assignments. In addition, your employees may look to you for indications of how they should manage themselves with respect to time. The following are suggestions especially for managers in the organizational setting.

Manage your meetings carefully. Meetings take up a large percentage of a manager's office time. Managers report that almost 60 percent of their time is spent in scheduled meetings and 10 percent in unscheduled meetings (Mintzberg, 1980). The management of meetings, then, is a crucial aspect of managing your and your employees' time. Proven meeting management techniques include the following (Quinn et al., 1996):

- *Set a time limit for your scheduled meetings.* Setting a time limit creates the expectation of having to finish the business at hand within designated time limits.

- *Hold meetings only when needed.* Feel free to cancel meetings if there is no pressing issue to discuss. Doing so may improve the quality of the meetings that are held.
- *Prepare an agenda for the meeting.* Using clear objectives of the meeting and inviting only those who need to attend, prepare an accurate agenda for the meeting. Distribute the agenda beforehand, and follow it during the meeting. An agenda helps participants to be prepared; it also clarifies what needs to be accomplished during that time. In developing the agenda, consulting with participants beforehand further enhances their participation.
- *Start meetings on time.* Beginning meetings on time not only models an expectation that schedules will be kept, but it also shows respect for the time of the individuals who made the effort to arrive at the appointed time.
- *Prepare minutes promptly, and follow up on the issues of the meeting.* Distribute the minutes in a timely manner, and check on any assignments that have been made. Doing so helps people recognize that most of the work takes place outside of meetings, not in the meetings.
- *Hold routine meetings at the end of the day.* Energy and creativity are usually low toward the end of the work day, and quitting time helps enforce the meeting's timely finish.
- *Stand up during short unscheduled meetings.* Standing helps ensure the brevity of the meeting. Be aware that sitting down may signal a longer meeting than necessary.

Model sound time management practices for your staff. Make certain that your employees know that you use a calendar, master list, and to-do list to help you keep track of your projects and other activities. Suggest that they do the same. Find ways to let them know that your time—and their time—is important.

Communicate carefully. Practice reflective listening skills. Make sure that your messages are clear to your staff. Clear communication is your responsibility.

Help employees establish priorities for their work. Explain the time management matrix to employees, and help them understand the reasons for prioritizing on the basis of importance rather than urgency. Help them develop strategies to ensure that they are focused on activities in Quadrants I and II. You may also need to clarify expectations regarding specific assignments. For example, if you have given an employee three assignments, be sure to indicate which aspects of those assignments have the highest priority.

Allow your employees to say no to you. Good time managers are aware if they have too much to do. Recognize that saying no to a supervisor is awkward at times. As a manager, encourage your employees to evaluate their time critically and to let you know if they feel overloaded. This promotes discussion and saves you time and difficulty later.

Take advantage of opportunities for staff development and training. Enhance your time management skills and those of your staff. Good training is a sound investment in performance and productivity.

CONCLUSION

We have explored the organizational setting of time management challenges for managers and some issues that vary across individuals. We presented suggestions for improving your use of time, several of which bear repeating. First, you constantly make decisions regarding the best way to use your time. Important issues to consider now may not be significant later. Be aware that time management is a dynamic process. It requires reassessment as situations change. Such changes are not cause for discouragement. Be realistic and recognize that the demands of changing situations require you (and your plans) to be flexible.

Second, remember that implementing new techniques is not easy. It may be more difficult at first, but eventually the techniques you choose become a matter of habit. Finally, be assured that you are probably a better time manager than you give yourself credit for. Be generous with yourself—give yourself credit for your time management strengths. In so doing, you empower yourself to make the changes you desire.

ANALYSIS EXERCISES

The Case of Frank Franklin

Adapted from training materials for Getting Work Done through Others: The Supervisor's Main Job. *Albany, NY: Advanced Human Resources Development Program, New York State Governor's Office of Employee Relations and the Civil Service Employees Association, Inc., 1987.*

Frank is the director of the Education and Outreach Unit at a regional office of a national nonprofit agency involved with health care research and education. Monday morning, Frank reported to the office promptly at 8:00 A.M. After washing out his cup, Frank poured himself fresh coffee and walked over to Bonnie's desk. The previous week she had attended a seminar on the use of distance-learning technologies, and Frank wanted to know what she had learned and if she thought that distance learning was a direction the agency should seriously consider. He also needed to tell Bonnie about a few issues that had arisen while she had been out and to give her information she had asked him to obtain for a report that she was writing for him.

Leaving Bonnie, Frank stopped by the washroom and headed back to his desk. There he found a memo from the director of the Fiscal Planning and Budget Unit detailing new policies from the national office concerning reimbursement of travel when employees take vacation days before or after work-related conferences. Basically the policy stated that employees who arrive in the conference city two or more days ahead of the conference or leave two or more days after are reimbursed for meals and lodging during the actual conference days and do not receive reimbursement for any travel days. Frank was surprised by the news and went to ask Ralph, another unit director, if he had read the memo. Although Ralph was a good colleague and would always help out if you were in a tough spot, he did have a reputation for talking; once he started it was hard to get him to stop. Around 9:30, Frank finally indicated that he had some important work and would have to return to his desk. In fact, Frank needed to get started on a new grant proposal that was due in two weeks. The regional director had said that she wanted to see a first draft by the end of the week.

When Frank got back to his office, Bonnie was waiting to talk to him. Some pages were missing from the information he had obtained for her. She wanted him to track them down.

At 10:00 the regional director telephoned and asked Frank to find a report detailing program expenditures over the past three years. She also expressed her concerns over the new travel reimbursement policy and discussed (at length) the absurdity of the policy given its low potential for saving money or improving the agency's image with any of the funding agencies and its likely negative impact on employee morale. Clint, the administrative assistant, would usually be the one to locate the report, but he was upstairs attending a meeting of the employee assistance program's peer counselors. Frank decided to locate the report himself. However, trying to understand Clint's filing system confused him, and after 20 minutes he decided to wait until Clint returned to the office. It was now almost 11:00, and there was not enough time to begin working on the grant proposal before Frank's 11:30 lunch meeting. Frank cleaned up his desk instead, preparing himself for an efficient afternoon.

Returning to work at 1:00, Frank quickly glanced over the agency newsletter and then noticed that the Monthly Activities Reporting Form had arrived while he had been at lunch. He decided to start filling it out. He had considered working on the grant proposal but decided to give himself an hour to work on the monthly report, assuming that he would have from 2:00 to 4:30 to work on the proposal. It was 1:30 before Frank remembered to ask Clint to find the report that the director had requested.

About 15 minutes later, Clint returned with two reports. One listed program expenditures over the past two years, and the other listed program expenditures over the past five years. There was no three-year report, and Clint said that he was pretty sure that there never had been one. Frank asked him to look one more time.

At 2:00 Clint returned and this time insisted that there was no three-year report. Frank called the regional director to ask which report she wanted, but her secretary said that she was upstairs at a meeting and it was not clear when she would return. Frank left a message and told Clint to return to his other work.

Frank went back to his desk, returned two telephone calls, and decided to work a little longer on the monthly report. It was only the 20th of the month, but Frank had not gotten as far as he had expected in the hour he had promised himself.

When he next looked at his watch, he noticed that it was almost 3:00. Now there surely was not enough time to work on the grant proposal before the end of the day. A project like writing a grant proposal is best accomplished when a large block of time is available. Frank knew that by the time he had gathered up all the materials he needed to work on the proposal, it would be just about time to put them away. Frank decided that he would see what other tasks he had on his to-do list and plan to work on the proposal the next day.

Discussion Questions

1. What are some of the problems Frank has in managing his time? Which myths of time management has he bought into? What other difficulties does Frank have in getting his work done? If his productivity today is typical, what will happen to his levels of stress and frustration in the coming months?

2. What behaviors should Frank change to improve his use of time? What techniques would he find particularly useful?

3. What specific time management issues does Frank have in dealing with his employees? His peers? His supervisor? What can he do to gain more control of his time?

4. How often have you found yourself in Frank's situation? What has your analysis of Frank told you about yourself?

When Do You Procrastinate?

Adapted from Knaus, W. J. (1979). Do It Now *(pp. 10–13). Englewood Cliffs, NJ: Prentice Hall.*

Listed below are 12 common behaviors and feelings. Review this list and, in each case, identify examples in your own life that reflect or refute this type of behavior or thinking. After reviewing the items, respond to the questions that follow.

Example

Problem	Evidence
1. I delay until the 11th hour before beginning important projects.	Reports often started near deadline; taxes paid late; usually make travel arrangements just before deadline

Please complete the inventory with a view toward presenting a fair picture of yourself.

Problem	Evidence
1. I delay until the 11th hour before beginning important projects.	
2. I remain angry for long periods of time contemplating how I will take revenge on an adversary.	
3. I feel overwhelmed.	
4. I do not return telephone calls.	
5. I show up late for appointments.	
6. I collect materials to use on a project and then delay doing the project.	
7. I avoid situations in which I believe I won't be successful.	
8. I delay sending out correspondence.	
9. I feel as though there is just one crisis after another in my life.	
10. I tell myself that tomorrow I'll begin.	
11. I feel that I lack drive or energy.	
12. I often agree to do things I don't really want to do because I have a hard time saying no.	

Discussion Questions

1. What are the ways in which you procrastinate most frequently? Do you see patterns in your procrastinating?

2. When you find yourself procrastinating, what are the excuses you give yourself (and others) for this behavior? How can you become more aware of when you are procrastinating, as opposed to having a legitimate reason for delaying doing something?

3. In what areas do you not have a problem with procrastination? What can you learn about yourself from these areas that can help you with areas where procrastination is a problem?

SKILLS-APPLICATION EXERCISES

The following are two skills-application exercises. The first exercise gives you the opportunity to look at some of your general problems in time management; the second helps you plan to improve your time management skills on a specific project on which you are currently (or will soon be) working.

How Well Am I Using My Time?

In responding to the following questions, you should identify some of your own time management problems and find ways to improve your use of time.

1. Think about how you managed your time last week. Remember, be generous with yourself and give yourself credit for positive accomplishments. Identify specific problems that you had in accomplishing some task or tasks. The rest of this exercise focuses on the problems.

2. What are some of the problems you have in managing your time? Which myths of time management have you accepted? What other difficulties did you have in getting your work done?

3. What time management techniques could improve your use of time? What steps do you need to take adopt them?

4. What specific time management issues do you have in dealing with your employees? Your peers? Your supervisor? What can you do to change the situation?

5. Choose one or two specific situations in which you find yourself procrastinating. Identify several ways in which you can change your behavior in this situation. Now identify what you can do the next time you find yourself in this situation. For each situation, think about what might happen to prevent you from changing your behavior. What can you do now to decrease the chances of that happening?

Overcoming Your "Overwhelming A"

Identify a project on which you are currently (or will soon be) working that is highly important and that you find overwhelming or difficult to think about. Respond to the following questions and statements in terms of this project.

1. Think about the ways that this project seems overwhelming to you. How have you reacted to these feelings? How have these feelings affected your ability to make progress on this project? How can you use Lakein's (1973) approach to help you accomplish this project?

2. Is this project appropriate for you? Do you have the correct skills to be carrying out this project? Is this the correct time for you to be embarking on this project? Are there other reasons that this may not be the right project for you? If you decide it is inappropriate, decide what steps you need to take to discontinue working on the project. If you decide it is appropriate, continue responding to the questions and statements that follow.

3. What are the component parts or tasks of this project? Try to break the project into the smallest tasks possible.

4. Think about the time required to complete the various tasks. Divide your list among tasks that will take only five to 10 minutes to complete, tasks that may take up to one hour to complete, and tasks that will take more than one hour.

5. Identify several tasks that will take only five to 10 minutes to complete, and schedule time to complete a few of them.

6. Identify the tasks that require a block of time to complete, and schedule time to complete the first one or two of them. In scheduling blocks of time, remember to consider what time of day you work best.

7. Identify what you need to do to remind yourself to return to the list of five- to 10-minute tasks, when this time is available.

8. Finally, schedule some time in the next week or two when you can review your progress. Be proud of what you have accomplished. Review what remains to be done, and plan for the next period of time.

REFERENCES

Burka, J. B., & Yuen, L. M. (1983). *Procrastination: Why you do it, what you can do about it.* Reading, MA: Addison-Wesley.

Covey, S. R., Merrill, A. R., & Merrill, R. R. (1994). *First things first: To live, to love, to learn, to leave a legacy.* New York: Simon & Schuster.

Dossey, L. (1982). *Space, time and medicine.* Boulder, CO: Shambhala Publications.

Knaus, W. J. (1979). *Do it now: How to stop procrastinating.* Englewood Cliffs, NJ: Prentice Hall.

Lakein, A. (1973). *How to get control of your time and your life.* New York: New American Library.

Mackenzie, R. A. (1972). *The time trap: How to get more done in less time.* New York: McGraw-Hill.

McGee-Cooper, A., & Trammell, D. (1994). *Time management for unmanageable people.* New York: Bantam Books.

Metcalf, C. W., & Felible, R. (1992). *Lighten up: Survival skills for people under pressure.* Reading, MA: Addison-Wesley.

Mintzberg, H. (1980). *The nature of managerial work.* Englewood Cliffs, NJ: Prentice Hall.

Oncken, W., Jr. (1984). *Managing management time.* Englewood Cliffs, NJ: Prentice Hall.

Quinn, R. E., Faerman, S. R., Thompson, M. P., & McGrath, M. R. (1996). *Becoming a master manager: A competency framework* (2nd ed.). New York: John Wiley & Sons.

Smith, H. W. (1994). *The 10 natural laws of successful time and life management: Proven strategies for increased productivity and inner peace.* New York: Warner Books.

Springer, S., & Deutsch, G. (1981). *Left brain, right brain.* San Francisco: W. H. Freeman.

Whetten, D. A., & Cameron, K. S. (1995). *Developing management skills* (3rd ed.). New York: HarperCollins.

Winston, S. (1983). *The organized executive: New ways to manage time, paper, and people.* New York: W. W. Norton.

CHAPTER 23

Managing Mergers and Consolidations

John A. Yankey, Barbara Wester, and David Campbell

The merger of organizations historically has occurred primarily in the business sector. However, in recent years there has been a proliferation of merger activity in the nonprofit community. As a restructuring strategy, the merger has become an increasingly important vehicle for nonprofit organizations in dealing with changing environmental conditions. This chapter explores six theoretical perspectives to explain why organizations come together, or merge. These perspectives suggest conditions that lead organizations to consider merger and, as such, provide leaders in nonprofit organizations with tools for assessing the appropriateness of merger as a strategy for restructuring.

DEFINITION OF MERGER

Merger is a form of restructuring whereby one or more organizations is completely absorbed by another organization whose corporate existence is preserved. The body being absorbed dissolves and loses its corporate existence (Yankey & Singer, 1991). The American Hospital Association (1989) defined *merger* as a statutorily defined corporate transaction, in which two similar corporations come together permanently, leaving a single survivor corporation. Assets do not have to be transferred, because this happens by operation of law, and the surviving corporation owns all the assets and liabilities of both parties.

NOTE: Darlyne Bailey, dean of the Mandel School of Applied Social Sciences at Case Western Reserve University, and research associate Kelly McNally-Koney have done extensive work in adapting the perspectives on collaboration identified in this chapter to address conditions in nonprofit organizations. In our discussion of nonprofit mergers as a particular form of collaboration, we have borrowed from their adaptation and express our appreciation to them for their contribution to our effort.

REASONS FOR MERGER

Several reasons that contribute to a nonprofit organization's decision to merge have been identified (Grahm, 1986; Greater New York Fund/United Way, 1981; Plimpton, 1989; Yankey & Singer, 1991):

- greater organizational efficiency and cost reduction through economies of scale, such as combined management functions and physical facilities, reduced staffing levels, increased technology, and increased purchasing power
- increased effectiveness of client services (two organizations combined may provide a more comprehensive array of services in a single setting)
- greater financial stability through such factors as an increased or more reliable base of funding
- greater organizational stability through a partner that has strong leadership and management
- increased market power by gaining control over pricing of services
- increased geographic market share resulting in greater access to both the population served and more funders
- enhanced community image and credibility by absorbing an agency or program with a poor reputation into an agency with a good reputation
- increased power and prestige for the organization, executives, and board members
- reduced competitive fundraising by combined resources.

Although these reasons may appear situation specific, they may be generalized to other settings. Indeed, the six merger perspectives that follow provide order to these reasons and theoretical structure to thinking about the conditions that lead nonprofit organizations to merge.

CONDITIONS LEADING TO NONPROFITS COMING TOGETHER

Why do organizations merge? Some researchers have argued that environmental conditions lead organizations to pursue collaborative strategies including merger (Emery & Trist, 1965; Gray, 1985; Wood & Gray, 1991). Wood and Gray described how those conditions inform the merger process. They identified six theoretical perspectives as collaborative strategies addressing environmental conditions and complex problems that lead organizations to come together: (1) resource dependence, (2) institutional or negotiated order, (3) microeconomics, (4) political, (5) strategic management–social ecology, and (6) corporate social performance–institutional economics.

Resource Dependence Perspective

The resource dependence perspective suggests that organizations need resources such as infrastructure (administrative capacity), funding stability, and technology (management information systems, financial management systems) to accomplish goals, if not simply to survive. Organizations unable to access resources on their own look to agents in the environment for those resources to "secure organizational survival" (Galaskiewicz, 1985, p. 282). If funding stability is critical to an organization's survival and that stability cannot be accomplished by that organization alone, it looks to other organizations to provide that stability.

A turbulent environment in which the resource dependence perspective has explanatory power is one in which an organization lacks resources, and this deficiency places the organization's mission in jeopardy. The serious absence of resources leads organizations to consider dramatic strategies, such as merger, to ensure the continuation of their mission. The pooling of resources through merger strengthens that mission for the future.

What would a merger look like that came about because each partner needed resources that could be provided by the other? O'Brien and Collier (1991) presented a resource dependence case study involving the merger of two Portland, Oregon, social services agencies: a long-established, traditional family services organization and a relatively young grassroots organization. In this case, the family services agency provided several key resources critical to the success of the grassroots organization. First, the grassroots agency lacked the administrative capacity to manage the service provided; administration was provided through an advisory council and not professional staff. Second, the agency suffered from a lack of income to support program operations. The authors described income flow as "erratic" and the agency as struggling with "chronic financial problems." In contrast, the family services agency identified growth as a critical strategic imperative. Growth, seen as increased service volume, was a needed resource for the family services agency. The importance of growth was further described as extending "operations into a new geographical area of the community" (p. 23).

Conditions of resource need defined the coming together of these two agencies. Merger worked as a strategy because each of the partners in the merger brought a resource the other needed. The grassroots organization brought the increase in business and geographic expansion desired by the family services agency. The family services agency brought the administrative support and stable finances needed by the grassroots agency. The resolution of each agency's resource needs through merger responds to the turbulence in the environment and positions the new agency for future growth.

Managers who consider the future in terms of the organization's dependence on resources might ask these questions:

- What are the critical resources the organization needs to survive?
- How critical are these resources? Today? Over the long term?
- Is there an organization from which I can acquire those resources without sacrificing those things that are most important (mission, values, strategic direction)?
- What is the possible range of places from which my organization can acquire needed resources?

Institutional or Negotiated-Order Perspective

The institutional or negotiated-order perspective identifies the role institutional legitimacy plays in defining organizational success and, consequently, organizational behavior. That is, the greater an organization's perceived legitimacy in its environment, the greater the organization's success. As such, if "legitimacy is the primary resource sought or at risk" (Wood & Gray, 1991, p. 157), an organization pursues strategies that bolster its institutional legitimacy. Such strategies could include merger or other kinds of collaboration. The process by which institutional legitimacy (or other environmentally defined problems) is accomplished is through a negotiated strategy with community partners.

A turbulent environment in which the institutional perspective has explanatory power is one in which the criteria by which social legitimacy is measured changes dramatically. For example, when funders change expectations for funded agencies, the institutional credibility of each funded agency is placed at risk. In such situations, organizations may pursue collaborative strategies that rebuild their credibility and meet the new funding requirements. In such situations, the environment forces organizations to look outside themselves for solutions that enable them to be successful over the long term. Mergers may result from organizational realization that institutional legitimacy is a requirement for survival and may not be accomplished without merger. The merger creates a new order that responds to the environment. That new order is a negotiated one.

What would a merger look like that came about because of each partner's need for institutional legitimacy? Legitimacy is conferred by institutions. With nonprofits, their funders, both public and private, frequently are the legitimacy-conferring institutions. Changes in the expectations of funders can destabilize the environment within which nonprofit organizations operate altering funder–organization relationships that have been in place. Imagine a case in which a public funder of mental health services changes the administrative reporting requirements for funded agencies. The changes involve adding new administrative functions that provide information that analyzes and describes the service provided by funded agencies. The new administrative services require infrastructure that many of the small, currently funded agencies lack. However, without the capacity to meet the new administrative requirements, funded agencies lose the legitimacy they have established with the funder.

What options do small agencies have in this case? One option might be for two or more of the smaller agencies to consider merger. How would merger increase institutional legitimacy? The combining of two (or more) similar agencies could accomplish economies of scale (efficiencies), which could be reallocated to create the administrative capacities needed to be competitive. With increased administrative capacity, the new organizations formed from the merger would be able to maintain the reputation each agency held with the funder previously and enhance institutional legitimacy through the demonstration of new capacity to meet the funders' administrative requirements.

Managers who consider the organization's future in terms of its legitimacy might ask these questions:

- What are the institutional requirements for long-term success (as defined by key funders or other stakeholders)?
- What are the other sources in the community from which the organization can acquire those institutional requirements?
- Do those organizations share the organization's mission and values?
- What organizations are perceived favorably by institutional forces?
- Are funders directing me to any particular organization or kind of organization?

Microeconomics Perspective

The microeconomics perspective emphasizes accomplishment of economies of scale that may not be accomplished by one organization alone. A turbulent environment in which the microeconomics perspective has strong explanatory power is one in which funder expectations of an organization dramatically increase such that infrastructure becomes critical to success. In such a situation, a small organization would view its lack of infrastructure as inhibiting and would consider merger with another organization as a strategy to make management more efficient. Through meeting funder requirements that would be too costly to develop on its own, merger is viewed as a strategy that can eliminate inefficiency and accomplish long-term organizational success. What would a merger look like that came about because of a need for efficiency? It is not difficult to apply the case study associated with institutional legitimacy to the microeconomic perspective. Imagine that the same funder of mental health services adjusted its provider expectations so that more serious volume was expected at a lower reimbursement rate. How would agencies in an environment made turbulent by that reality respond?

One could easily imagine merger. Perhaps in this situation larger agencies might merge with smaller agencies, rather than small agencies merging with each other as described in the institutional perspective. The difference is that the environment presents a problem that requires as a solution sufficient efficiency so that service can be provided at a lower reimbursement rate without operating at a deficit. How would efficiency be accomplished? To operate a balanced budget and provide more for less requires significant increase in service volume. Merger is an important, and perhaps the only, strategy to increase service volume. The small agency, with its limited base, could not compete without a dramatic increase in volume. A large agency with a significant base on which to build could accomplish the needed volume by adding the service provided by the smaller agency. Merger would force administrative efficiencies within the two agencies (shared functions would be eliminated in the merger) and would provide the capacity to increase volume to remain competitive with the new reimbursement rates. A turbulent interorganizational environment defined by inefficiency could lead to merger as a key survival strategy.

Managers who consider the organization's future in terms of economies of scale may ask these questions:

- Where are the functional areas in which my operation is least efficient? Administration? Direct service? Support? Fundraising?
- What are the inefficient areas that have been identified for me by funders or other key community stakeholders?
- Are there organizations that share my organization's mission from which I can gain needed efficiencies?
- Are those organizations weak in places that my organization is strong?

Political Perspective

The political perspective emphasizes the acquisition and maintenance of power as the reason organizations come together. Organizations can increase their power through shared access to resources and the withholding of needed resources from other organizations. The perspective is relational, explaining both how and why organizations come together.

A turbulent environment in which the political perspective has explanatory power is one in which many active interests vie for predominance. The forces with sufficient power dominate discussions regarding resource use and

"It isn't your 'desire' to buy Park Place or Boardwalk that concerns me. . . .
It's your 'motivation.'"

establish rules that enable the accomplishment of goals they support. As policymakers develop new requirements, previous certainties are made uncertain, and organizational futures become unclear. In such situations, organizations that share a common interest in a particular outcome may pursue
various forms of working together, including merger. From the political perspective, mergers may guarantee an outcome that saves the interest of the
merging organizations at the expense of other organizations in the sector.

What would a merger look like that resulted from power dynamics defined
by a political perspective? Consider the environmental realities defined in the
examples for microeconomic and institutional or negotiated-order perspectives. A public funder of mental health services informs a community of 30
funded agencies (large and small) that it is changing its expectations to
include additional administrative requirements and increased service volume
at lower reimbursement rates. These new realities reflect a turbulent environment indeed for those funded agencies.

One can easily imagine power dynamics forcing merger between funded
agencies. In the context described, small agencies, lacking in administrative
capacity, do not have resources to create that capacity. In addition, the limited agency size does not allow the generation of sufficient service volume to
break even with the new reimbursement rate. Given the new requirements,
that agency is in a politically weak position. In contrast, the agency that is the
largest provider of mental health services in the community with a well-
developed administrative infrastructure has the capacity to meet the new
administrative requirements. Service volume could be increased through

merger. The large agency has a variety of merger strategies it can pursue, which leverage its position of power. The large agency may seek to force small agencies to merge on the basis of the latter's long-term inability to compete. Another option might be to pursue merger with medium-sized or other agencies as a strategy that isolates smaller agencies, vulnerable to defunding because they lack capacity. Should this happen, the larger agency can leverage its political advantage to assume the lost business of the smaller agency. Political explanations of merger ultimately allow organizations in positions of power to use that power to their advantage in response to the turbulence affecting the interorganizational environment.

Managers who consider the organization's future in terms of maximizing power may ask these questions:

- What kinds of organizations can maximize the organization's power in the community?
- If my organization lacks power, what like-minded organization can benefit from linkage with my organization (and increase its power and standing in the community)?
- What is required for organizations to have power in the future?
- How can that power be achieved?
- What organizations are well positioned to have power in the future?

Strategic Management–Social Ecology

The strategic management–social ecology perspective emphasizes collaborative action as a means "to support the positive gains of competitive advantage" (Wood & Gray, 1991, p. 156) not only by providing access to resources, but also by strengthening the collaborating organizations in the marketplace.

A turbulent environment in which the strategic management–social ecology perspective has explanatory power is one in which organizations must respond to the requirements of their environment to increase their competitive advantage. For example, funders may move from funding stand-alone services to integrated services or continuum of care. That movement is turbulent by definition because it creates problems for organizations that may not be solved by any organization alone. A long-term strategy would be to achieve competitive advantage through merger with an organization that provides complementary services or establishes the continuum of care required by funders.

What would a merger look like that could be explained in terms of the strategic management perspective? Return once again to the situation of agencies funded to provide mental health services. If the changed expectations of that funder are modified once again, the strategic management perspective provides an explanation for merger between organizations. In this case, assume that the funder of mental health services has changed requirements to include not only additional administrative infrastructure, but also the capacity to provide a broad range of community mental health services. The strategic management perspective emphasizes maximizing strategic advantage. In an environment made turbulent by the requirements identified above, the way to maximize strategic advantage is to identify a strategy that enables an agency both to meet the additional administrative requirements and to provide a broad range of services. Two medium-sized agencies would merge for strategic advantage if together they could meet these requirements. A merger would occur if the service complement created by the merger reflected the needed broad range of services and if the coming together of the two agencies allowed reallocation of resources to create needed administrative infrastructure. A strategic management explanation of merger allows organizations to see and seize advantage in turbulence. That advantage is accomplished through merger.

Managers who consider the organization's future in terms of strategic advantage may ask these questions:

- What are the requirements of the competitive organization of the future?
- Does my organization have the capacity to achieve competitive advantage on its own, as presently configured?
- If not, what mission-compatible organization can most enhance my organization's competitive advantage?

Corporate Social Performance–Institutional Economics

The corporate social performance–institutional economics perspective emphasizes an organization's role and responsibility in solving social problems. It describes how responsibility and risk are shared among the various players who have a stake in the issue or problem.

A turbulent environment in which the corporate social performance–institutional economics perspective has strong explanatory power is one in which a new phenomenon emerges. In such a situation, the community would look to the nonprofit sector to address the problem. Examples of such phenomena would include the emergence of youth gangs or new forms of drug use. The emergence of HIV/AIDS in the early 1980s is also a good example. Addressing such problems often requires the coming together of service providers that have expertise in areas related to the new phenomenon. Successful development of a solution to that problem may best be accomplished through the merger of the related organizations.

What would a merger look like that was explainable in terms of the social performance perspective? We may expand on the reference above to services to people affected by HIV/AIDS. In the early 1980s, when AIDS was first identified and diagnosed, an AIDS-specific service infrastructure did not exist. The community looked to the nonprofit sector to develop a response to the social services needs of those affected by the illness. One immediate response was the proliferation of grassroots organizations that addressed different aspects of the social services needs presented by people affected by HIV/AIDS: prevention, housing, counseling, nursing care, and so on. The service infrastructure that developed was fragmented, and AIDS services were provided for different purposes in different organizations throughout the community. A social services delivery structure was needed to offer services that reflected the community goal of an HIV/AIDS service infrastructure. Community pressure could lead providers of different HIV/AIDS services to merge to accomplish that goal.

Managers who consider the organization's future in terms of better solving a community problem may ask these questions:

• What does the community need to solve this problem?
• How can my organization add value in solving this (new) community problem?

CONCLUSION

The six perspectives discussed in this chapter explain reasons for organizations coming together and, at the same time, provide tools for developing those relationships. Given an understanding of the environment and an organization's strategic direction, potential merger relationships may be identified. As an organization approaches a potential relationship with another organization (either as initiator or reactor), knowledge of the environment and organizational need may determine which (or what combination) of explanatory perspectives is operative. For example, knowledge that the funding environment is shifting from one that encourages many community service providers to one that supports a few corporate service providers may lead a small organization supported by that funder to understand its position in terms of political theory. On receiving an inquiry regarding merger from a larger provider, the smaller provider is likely to see power dynamics as operative and look to political theory for guidance regarding how to maximize that organization's position given environmental conditions. Other situations could be explained in terms of negotiated order or pure resource dependence, each of which would lend itself to a particular set of merger development strategies.

Understanding the reasons that lead organizations to come together is a critical element in strategic planning (see chapter 21). Effective nonprofit leaders must have the capacity to identify through strategic planning processes those issues that challenge their organization's long-term success. Nonprofit organizations face many potential challenges today, including insufficient resources, lack of institutional credibility, and inefficiency in operations. Leaders experiencing or anticipating these challenges in their organizations must be aware of merger as a tool to address those challenges.

Merger is a wise strategy when the management problem presented, given all other considerations, may best be addressed by the coming together of two or more organizations. The explanations provided by the theories described in this chapter provide a framework for how merger may address certain kinds of management problems effectively.

SKILLS-APPLICATION EXERCISE

Identify a nonprofit organization you are involved with and develop answers to the following questions:

- What impact would increased power have on my organization? What are my options for increasing my power? If merger is an option, what characteristics in a merger partner should I identify to increase my power in the community?

- What resources does my organization lack? How important are these resources to my long-term survival? What is the possible range of places from which I can acquire these needed resources?

- What is required of my organization to be competitive in the future? Can my organization meet those requirements on its own? Do we have a defined strategy? Is it cost-effective? What are my strategic options?

- How do key funders and other stakeholders view my organization? Are we perceived as having credibility? What do they require for the long-term success of the organization? What characteristics in a merger partner should I identify to increase my credibility and legitimacy with funders and stakeholders?

- What are the potential changes in community values that may affect my organization? What might the community ask of my organization to meet these changes in values?

- In what functional areas is my organization least efficient? What are the inefficient areas that have been identified for me by funders or other stakeholders? What characteristics in a merger partner should I identify to increase my organization's efficiency?

REFERENCES

American Hospital Association. (1989). *Merger guidelines/checklist*. Chicago: Author.

Emery, F., & Trist, E. (1965). The causal texture of organizational environments. *Human Relations, 18*, 21–32.

Galaskiewicz, J. (1985). Interorganizational relations. *Annual Review of Sociology, 11*, 281–304.

Grahm, J. (1986). Not for profit hospitals may benefit from merger, acquisition strategies. *Modern Health Care, 16*(17), 108–110.

Gray, B. (1985). Conditions facilitating interorganizational collaboration. *Human Relations, 38*, 911–936.

Greater New York Fund/United Way. (1981). *Merger: Another path ahead*. New York: Author.

O'Brien, J., & Collier, P. (1991). Merger problems for human service agencies: A case study. *Administration in Social Work, 15*(3), 19–31.

Plimpton, G. C. (1989). Keys to formulating a successful business combination. *Topics in Health Care Financing, 15*(4), 18–25.

Wood, D., & Gray, B. (1991). Toward a comprehensive theory of collaboration. *Journal of Applied Behavioral Science, 27*, 139–162.

Yankey, J. A., & Singer, M. L. (1991). Managing mergers and consolidations. In R. L. Edwards & J. A. Yankey (Eds.), *Skills for effective human services management* (pp. 352–364). Washington, DC: NASW Press.

CHAPTER 24

Selecting and Using Consultants

John A. Yankey

he seemingly age-old jokes describing a consultant as "someone who borrows your watch to tell you what time it is" or "somebody with a brief case a few miles from home" too frequently describe how the leadership of nonprofit organizations view consultants. Other often-expressed opinions about consultants include "she didn't tell me anything I didn't already know," "he told me what to do but not how I should do it," and "the consultant didn't do any of the work himself." Notwithstanding such negative (if not hostile) views, the explosive growth in the nonprofit sector over the past decade has increased the demand for consultancy services. Although empirical documentation of the magnitude of this increase is limited, much anecdotal evidence suggests the number of consulting opportunities has grown dramatically. The need for consultants' services has been fueled not only by growth of the sector, but also by the increasingly complex and ever-changing environment in which nonprofits function.

DEFINITIONS OF CONSULTANTS AND CONSULTING

The *Random House Dictionary* (Flexner, 1988, p. 289) defined *consulting* as "employed in giving professional advice, either to the public or to those practicing the profession" and defined a *consultant* as "a person who consults someone or something . . . a person who gives professional or expert advice." According to Shulman (1995), *consulting* is "an interaction between two or more people in which the consultant's special competence in a particular area is used to help the consultee with a current work problem" (p. 2377). Block (1981) defined *consultant* as "a person in a position to have some influence over an individual, group, or an organization, but who has no direct power to make changes or implement programs." Block made the important distinction that the consultant ceases to act as a consultant when he or she takes direct control over an action; rather, the consultant has begun to act as a manager if or when he or she begins to take direct control. This distinction is an important one because it underscores the necessity for nonprofits to analyze carefully why consultants may or should be hired to address organizational issues. As a first step toward having an effective consultancy experience, nonprofit leaders should be quite clear as to why they want to hire a consultant.

WHY HIRE A CONSULTANT?

Nonprofit organizations hire consultants for a variety of reasons:

- to provide expertise or information not currently possessed
- to identify and define organizational problems
- to solve organizational problems
- to provide an independent perspective that is regarded as legitimate to those individuals and organizations involved
- to offer services cutting across multiple professional disciplines
- to learn about similar situations or efforts elsewhere
- to assist in effecting organizational change
- to develop organizations' capacities to resolve similar issues in the future
- to serve as a mentor to volunteer leaders or professional managers.

Nonprofit organizations may use consultants in situations in which they have sufficient expertise to do what the consultants are being engaged to do. In some instances, the nonprofits cannot afford the disruption that would occur were employees with the expertise deployed to do the required work. In other instances, the urgency of the task requires the use of a consultant. Some nonprofits view it as cost-effective to engage consultants on a time-limited basis rather than establishing a permanent position. Finally, some consultants are engaged to do the "dirty work" of effecting changes when leaders in the organization cannot or do not want to undertake the necessary steps to achieve such change. This often places the consultant in the role of the "hatchet person" (Davis, 1983; Turner, 1982). Although serious questions may be raised about the appropriateness of using consultants for these latter two reasons, a listing of reasons is incomplete without their inclusion.

Nonprofit leaders must be very clear about the reasons they want to engage consultants. With clarity, all parties are likely to be satisfied with the consulting experience. Turner (1982) suggested that "as managers understand the broader range of purposes that excellent consulting can help achieve, they will select consultants more wisely and expect more of value from them. And as clients learn how to address new needs, good consultants learn how to address them" (p. 129).

IDENTIFYING AND SELECTING A CONSULTANT

After nonprofit leaders have clearly identified the reasons for a consultation engagement, they are confronted with the significant challenge of identifying and selecting the appropriate consultant. In many communities, no common repository of information about individual consultants or consulting firms is available to nonprofit organizations. Frequently, identification of consultants results from lay and professional leadership's personal relationships with or knowledge of particular individuals or firms. Such personal relationships and knowledge are not inappropriate, but neither are they usually sufficient to provide organizations with a range of consulting options. Consequently, many nonprofits use a request-for-proposal (RFP) approach to increase their options. The RFP details the work to be done, required or preferred qualifications and experiences of the consultant being sought, procedures for submitting a proposal, and the approximate amount of funding available for the consultation. This approach usually generates a list of interested consultants from which nonprofit organizations can make an appropriate selection.

These two approaches—personal relationships with consultants and issuance of an RFP—are the most frequent approaches for identifying consultants. Additional approaches include the following:

- A systematic search can be undertaken with other area nonprofits to identify consultants with whom those organizations may have had satisfactory consultations.
- Funders, especially foundation officers, represent an especially good source of information regarding available consultants.
- Local colleges and universities frequently have faculty and staff engaged in consultation. For example, contact with business, organizational development, social work, and public administration schools can identify a number of consultants.
- A management assistance program or management support center can either provide consultation or identify consultants appropriate to a nonprofit organization's needs.
- Federated planning and funding bodies, with their broad local or national networks, represent a significant source of information about available consultants.
- Many professional associations now compile lists of consultants as a service to their membership.
- An increasing number of Internet sites provide information on consultancy services, including individual consultants creating their own Web sites and promoting themselves through listservs.

Once identified, the task of selecting the consultant most appropriate to an organization's needs becomes pivotal. Bruner (1993) pointed out that whether nonprofit organizations simply employ the consultant without competitive bidding or use a formal review and selection process, specific steps are involved:

- A statement outlining the nature, scope, and purpose of the consultation engagement should be prepared before contacting prospective consultants.
- Two or more consultants whose general qualifications suggest their ability to meet the organization's needs should be interviewed.
- A preliminary check of references should be made.
- Preliminary discussions should be conducted with all potential consultants to determine their approach to the required work. A brief, written proposal should be submitted by each consultant to explain his or her plans.
- Organizational leadership should study these proposals in terms of the approach, benefits and costs, experience, and qualifications of the consultant and (if a firm) the qualifications of the personnel who actually will be working on the project.
- The references of the consultants to be interviewed should be checked in depth.

Bruner suggested that the following questions be considered when making in-depth reference checks and a final selection:

- What was the nature and scope of the previous work done by the consultant?
- Did the consultant demonstrate professional competence, objectivity, and integrity?
- How constructively did the consultant work with the organization's personnel?
- Did the consultant adhere to time lines?
- Was the completed work on schedule and at the quality level anticipated?
- Did the consultant have a generally "objective" approach to the required work?
- Did the consultant demonstrate an understanding and appreciation for the various disciplines or professions within the organization?
- Was the consultant able to communicate effectively with those involved in the consultation engagement?
- Were the consultant's recommendations practical and sufficient to the organization's needs?
- What is the overall assessment of the value of the consulting engagement?
- Would the organization use the consultant again if a need arose for his or her kind of professional service?

As indicated, these questions can be used as guidelines in conducting in-depth reference checks and serve as points of discussion in interviews with potential consultants. In addition, interviews should be structured to obtain a sense of the candidate's honesty about capabilities, compatibility with the organization, beliefs and values regarding organizational development, personality fit, motivations, ethics, and appreciation for confidentiality.

ESTABLISHING FEE ARRANGEMENTS

Both the nonprofit organization and the consultant have a number of decisions to make in establishing fee arrangements. Tepper (1993) listed questions that consultants consider in determining their fees:

- How long will the project take, and how profitable will it be?
- Will additional help be required, or can I do all the work myself?
- If additional personnel are required, how many and at what cost?
- What will the expenses be?
- Will the organization pay for the expenses, or do I absorb them as part of my fee structure?
- If the organization pays expenses, will all expenditures require preapproval, or just those above a particular amount?
- How should the fee structure take into account the unexpected?
- How stable is the organization, and what is the vulnerability factor should a change in leadership occur?
- Is this project likely to lead to other consulting engagements with this organization?

The hiring manager also must consider these questions before signing the consultation agreement or contract. Moreover, the manager must select the basis and method for fee payment from among four options: venture marketing, hourly rate, fixed rate, and retainer.

Venture Marketing

In the venture-marketing approach, payment is structured in direct relationship to goal achievement. Rather than paying a specified fixed fee, the organization pays a percentage of gain pegged to accomplishment of established goals (such as gains achieved through an increase in productivity or a decrease in absenteeism). This method requires the consultant to assume a significant amount of risk-taking in the consultation engagement. The nonprofit organization does not have to pay a fee unless certain outcomes are obtained, and it does not have to pay up front. The major risk for the nonprofit organization is an error in its selection of a consultant. Thus, the leadership must be exceptionally careful to select consultants who can enthusiastically and energetically engage in this entrepreneurial approach. The selection of an unsuitable consultant may not cost much in hard cash, but it may lead to very unhappy outcomes for all parties and represent indirect losses as a result of limited return on the investment of time and effort by management, staff, lay leaders, and other volunteers. It should be noted that the venture-marketing approach may be considered an inappropriate, if not unethical, arrangement for compensating consultants in certain areas of nonprofit functioning, such as fundraising.

Hourly Rate

In the hourly rate method, the organization agrees to pay the consultant an amount for each hour of project work. This method is generally held in some disfavor by both nonprofits and consultants. For nonprofits, the negatives are that they are billed on an hourly basis (or a fraction thereof) and thus may be reluctant to use the consultant as frequently as needed, they may not receive adequate attention from the consultant if he or she is on retainer for a number of clients, and they could be taken advantage of by a consultant who needs to generate income. For the consultant, the method makes record keeping difficult and requires much more explanation in regard to carrying out specific tasks.

The hourly rate charged by consultants varies widely throughout the United States. Generally, rates range between $50 and $200 per hour. The rate usually is related to the scope of work to be done, the amount of funds nonprofits have available for the consultation engagement, consultants' educational and experiential backgrounds, and traditional market factors (such as the number of available consultants from which to choose). Consulting fees among nonprofit subsectors may differ (for example, fees in the health subsector are frequently higher than in social services). Some consultants may reduce their fees if they are committed to the cause of a particular nonprofit organization or view their consultative services as a community service.

Fixed Rate

The fixed-price arrangement is the preferred method among most nonprofit organizations. In this arrangement, the consultant enters into an agreement whereby he or she conducts the engagement for a specified amount, and the organization pays on a regular monthly basis (or some other mutually defined payment schedule). This method involves extensive delineation of the consultation "deliverables" and a specified time line for tasks and processes to be completed. It allows nonprofits to be more effective in seeking competitive bids and do some "comparison shopping" in their selection of consultants. If the consultation work extends beyond the agreed-on time frame in the contract, the consultant assumes the cost of such extension by doing the work without additional compensation. On the other hand, nonprofit organizations may be required to make a partial payment before receiving all the deliverables.

Retainer

In the retainer arrangement, the consultant is paid a fixed amount according to a mutually agreed-on payment schedule. In this approach, nonprofits have more strongly guaranteed access to the consultant's expertise and time. Usually, consultants are considered to be "on call" and to be available to respond to a variety of organizational issues as they arise. This consultation and payment arrangement frequently is established on a longer-term basis (usually annually). For nonprofits, the retainer approach is based on the notion that it provides them with guaranteed, timely expertise to address multiple issues, some of which may not be well defined. In this regard, the retainer is different from the typical fixed-price arrangement, which is very project specific. This arrangement carries with it the strong expectation by the nonprofit organization that the consultant will give it priority attention. Consultants obviously appreciate the guaranteed income generated through the retainer arrangement. However, they cannot afford to leave their consulting relationships totally open and fluid. Thus, most expect nonprofit organizations to define their overall consultative needs and to specify the minimum number of hours of services to be provided in a particular time frame.

DEVELOPING AN AGREEMENT OR CONTRACT

Whatever the fee structure and payment arrangements established, both nonprofits and consultants have reasons to commit in writing their expectations of the engagement. Both agreements and contracts are used to capture and formalize these expectations. Which of these is used relates to the mandates and policies of the specific nonprofit organization. In practice, both have the same aim. As Tepper (1993) stated, "The cardinal rule is to be as specific as possible. Put everything into writing. There is less room for confusion and questions. The client and consultant know exactly what is expected. The specific agreement frequently helps avoid differences between client and consultant, while the general one fosters it" (p. 125).

Although agreements and contracts have the same objective of specificity in the consultation engagement, nonprofits tend to use the agreement approach when given a choice. This approach seems to be less intimidating to nonprofit managers and suggests an environment for a cooperative or collaborative working relationship rather than one governed by more formal, legalistic stipulations.

Given that agreements and contracts are mutually beneficial to nonprofits and consultants, these documents should include items of mutual interest, such as the fee structure and payment schedule. Block (1981) identified other ingredients as being boundaries of the analysis–project work, objectives of the project, types of information sought, consultant roles in the project, products to be delivered, support and involvement by the client, time schedule, and confidentiality expectations or mandates.

Even if agreements or contracts are not required, such documents are part of the consulting business. It behooves nonprofit organizations to use these documents in working with their consultants. Many nonprofit organizations and consultants have developed standard formats for use in their consultation engagements. If standard forms do not exist in a particular situation, the ingredients suggested by Block constitute an excellent framework within which to develop such agreements or contracts.

MAPPING THE CONSULTATION PROCESS

The consultation process can be defined and understood on two levels. The first level is an overview of the entire process, constituted by the following phases:

1. securing the engagement
   • precontracting
   • contracting
2. conducting the engagement
   • data or information collection
   • data analysis
3. action planning
   • presenting findings from data analysis
   • formalizing recommendations
4. evaluating the consultation engagement
5. terminating the consultation services.

The second level of mapping is at the diagnostic level. Block (1981) provided a model for this mapping:

1. Client gives the consultant a presenting problem.
2. Consultant begins to refine or redefine the problem.
3. Consultant's goal is to develop a clear picture of what is causing and maintaining the problem. Included in this picture is a description of technical or business problems the client wishes to resolve and a description of how problems are managed (such as attitudes of people, managers' styles, politics of situation).

4. Both of these descriptions lead to recommendations to resolve technical and managerial problems.

As the consulting process unfolds, the consultant may assume various roles. These roles are a learner who attempts to understand and appreciate the organization, an instructor who provides the client with new insights, an investigator who seeks to discover the reasons for the client's problems, a monitor who observes the client system from multiple levels or vantage points, and a change agent who advocates for action to address the identified problems. Consultants assume these roles with varying frequency and intensity as dictated by the circumstances of a given consulting engagement. Establishing appropriate role relationships is critical to success in any consulting engagement. Consultants and nonprofit organizations share responsibility for developing role relationships and, usually, both must assume some portion of blame when consulting engagements go off course.

WHY DO CONSULTING ENGAGEMENTS FAIL?

A range of factors may cause consulting engagements to be unsuccessful, and both client organizations and consultants usually must share the responsibility. The following factors are attributable to client organizations:

- Clients did not properly screen prospective consultants, leading to the employment of those who are not a good fit with the organizations. Too frequently, selections are based on personal relationships, or references are not thoroughly checked.
- Clients did not clarify their goals and objectives. In some instances, clients did not explain the organizational culture or inform consultants about all the motivations for and anticipated resistances to the consultation.
- Clients did not adequately inform all employees and lay leaders about mutually agreed-on goals and objectives for consultation engagements and the roles the consultants are likely to assume.
- Clients may not consider the problems to be urgent or may not agree with the problem definitions.
- Clients are unwilling to relinquish control sufficiently to allow consultants access to needed information.
- Top management may not allocate resources to implement consultants' recommendations. Too often, clients do not adequately inform consultants about the human and financial resource limitations, thereby creating an environment wherein consultants tailor solutions that are deemed impractical.

"Terry is our so-called motivation consultant."

Such shortcomings are sufficient to derail consulting relationships. Consultants may contribute to unsuccessful engagements in the following ways:

- They may inadequately specify the roles they will assume in the engagement and not gain agreement with clients regarding such roles.
- They may not identify the true problems. Sometimes, they too readily adopt clients' diagnoses or focus on symptoms rather than the real problems.
- They may promise too much too soon. Many problems initially look easier to resolve then they really are, and consultants may fall into the trap of oversimplifying problem definition and resolution. Later, when the problems are more fully understood by consultants, clients already may have been misinformed and misled by earlier promises.
- They may not adapt to the individuality of clients and their organizations. Thus, consultants use experiences that are not applicable to the client's

organizational culture and state of readiness to respond positively to recommendations.
- They may have access to sufficient data and people, yet offer impractical or nonfeasible recommendations for solving problems. Although consultants frequently like to suggest optimal solutions, sometimes these are not the best solutions.
- They may accept engagements that are beyond their competencies. Driven by financial or other motivations, consultants are not totally honest with clients and accept engagements wherein they use trial-and-error problem-solving approaches, a luxury clients can ill afford.

Both consultants and nonprofit organizations can contribute to outcomes that are less than satisfactory for all involved. However, consultants can be exceedingly valuable to nonprofit organizations when both parties assume responsibility for making the engagement work.

MAKING CONSULTATION MORE PRODUCTIVE

Nonprofits should pursue specific steps to maximize the benefits from a consultation engagement. Lant (1997) and Bruner (1993) offered a number of ideas for enhancing the productivity of consulting relationships. Both begin with the assumption that consultants, when selected and used wisely, can be most helpful to nonprofit organizations. A blending of their views results in the following considerations for getting the most from organizational consultancies.

Get agreement on the problems within the organization. Prior to seeking assistance from a consultant, the organization should identify very clearly the problems for which it seeks help. In so doing, the client determines the type of consultant it requires, defines the consultation focus, avoids unrealistic expectations regarding consultancy outcomes, and diminishes dissatisfactions that may arise. Furthermore, agreement on the problems should more adequately prepare organizations to listen to consultants' recommendations.

Get agreement on the objectives and methods of the consultation. The organization and the consultant should agree on the outcomes sought and the methods for achieving them. This agreement should be in writing, either as a formal or informal contract. Achieving this agreement provides an opportunity to review alternatives, determines precisely which tasks will be done by the consultant and which will be undertaken by the organization, details the necessary resources (such as personnel, equipment, and expenses), and delineates the time lines within which the consultation will occur. The agreement provides a comprehensive framework for the organization to evaluate the consultant's performance throughout the process.

Commit the organization to work with the consultant. Many consultancies are not as productive as they could be because organizations are unwilling to follow through on the established agreement. Sometimes this is a result of employees not knowing the purpose, objectives, methods, and time lines of the consultancy. Consequently, consultants encounter needless resistance as they begin to interact at different levels of the organization. It is imperative for organizational leaders to communicate with their employees prior to their contact with the consultant. Beyond this initial provision of information, it is the ongoing responsibility of an organization's lay and professional leadership to encourage, support, and cajole (if necessary) open and energetic involvement of employees in the consultancy process. Such involvement not only leads to a better set of recommendations put forward by consultants, but also should contribute to a greater sense of ownership of and willingness to implement them.

Establish explicit expectations for the consulting process to be interactive. Frequent exchanges between organizational leadership and the consultant are critical. This interaction can, in some instances, be done through telephone contact and written reports. However, most consulting relationships are made more productive as a result of regularly held meetings. As Lant (1997) put it,

> One of the avoidable problems in a client–consultant relationship is that the parties fail to meet often enough and don't have meetings that are properly structured for success. Obviously different kinds of consulting relationships demand more or less frequent meetings, but all demand meetings that are tightly structured and focused on achieving the objective. (p. 36)

An interactive consulting process affords multiple opportunities for effective consultants to present findings, ideas, and issues that may be unpalatable to organizational leadership. However, for organizations to achieve the best possible return on their investment in consultative services, organizational leadership should encourage their consultants to tell the whole truth. Truly ethical consultants who care more about being effective than being popular welcome such encouragement, and all parties will consider the engagement more productive. The truth may not be pleasant to hear, but organizational leadership should never become angry with consultants for providing honest professional assessments. For consultants to do less would, indeed, diminish the full value of the consulting engagement.

Do not become overly dependent on consultants. An interactive consulting process helps an organization develop the capacity not to hire consultants to do similar things in the future. Organizations should strive to reach the stage where no consultant is deemed indispensable. When a consultant has been engaged to carry out tasks that are likely to be required again in the future, it behooves that organization—if at all feasible—to build in some additional time in the engagement to allow selected staff to learn the knowledge and skills necessary to do those tasks. Many consultants greatly enjoy teaching and mentoring. It can be a rewarding experience for all parties, and an organization gains longer-term returns on its investment for the consultancy. Although organizations may use consultants even if they have resident knowledge and skills to carry out required tasks, building organizational capacity is nonetheless a beneficial aspect of making consultation engagements more productive.

Evaluate the consulting relationship to find out what went right and wrong. All consulting relationships do come to an end. It is important to conduct an evaluation that focuses on both the things that went well and those that did not. This evaluation should be integrated into the ongoing consulting process and should not be delayed until the consultation is concluding. A more formal evaluation should be conducted at the end of the consultancy, including input from a variety of people affected by the engagement. The evaluation should tease out why the consulting relationship worked and why it did not. Answers to the "why" questions enable organizations to strengthen their future consulting relationships. If this evaluation is to be maximally helpful, consultants should be engaged in an honest discussion of the organization's attitudes and behaviors in carrying out its responsibilities in the consulting relationship. Although this includes some highly subjective exchange, the consultant's views and opinions are a part of what organizations have paid for and deserve to receive.

As Lant (1997) noted, too many consultation engagements with nonprofits do not conclude happily; neither client organizations nor consultants accomplish the outcomes sought. However, if organizations give serious attention to the foregoing considerations, they can enhance the consulting relationship for all parties.

CONSIDERING ETHICS

Most consultants present themselves and behave in a highly ethical manner. Unfortunately, a nonprofit organization need only have one bad experience with an unethical consultant to view other consultants negatively. There are no foolproof ways of identifying and screening out consultants who may be ethically challenged, but some signals can alert organizational leaders to possible ethical flaws.

Pfeiffer and Jones (1977) presented an overview of signals for which to be alert. The first indication comes in consultants' establishment of their professional expertise and qualifications. It is incumbent on consultants, if potential client organizations have an inaccurate perception of their qualifications, to correct both explicit and implicit misrepresentations. Understandably, consultants do not want to focus too much attention on their limitations. They do, however, have an ethical obligation to present themselves honestly and help potential client organizations understand the special knowledge and skills they can bring to addressing the organization's needs. If they are unable to correct any misperceptions about what they bring to the table, even after they have been given an opportunity to do so, potential client organizations should proceed with great caution.

A second indication relates to consultants' health status. This is especially important in situations in which a consultant operates as a one-person firm. Ethical consultants are straightforward regarding their health status, knowing they lack backup if their physical or emotional health interrupts their work. If they suspect that their health status may interfere with providing the best possible consultative services, ethical consultants seek postponement of the consultation engagement or request they be dropped completely from consideration. Consulting can be very demanding work, requiring enormous energy for both analytical tasks and interpersonal relationship development. If consultants are not in good physical or emotional health, they cannot provide their best effort. Client organizations have a right to know (and consultants have a responsibility to indicate) whether health factors are likely to affect the consulting relationship. Obviously, this is not always easy for consultants, especially if they work alone, and consulting fees are their primary or only source of income.

A third indication relates to consultants' making inappropriate promises regarding what they can achieve. Good consultants are cautious about what they promise as a consequence of their services. In reality, consultants cannot guarantee particular kinds of outcomes. They can promise to be interactive, to be sensitive to the needs of those affected by the consultation, to be resourceful, to work diligently, and to be open to various ideas. However, ethical consultants understand that client organizations may be unable or unwilling to carry out specific recommendations leading to outcomes and, thus, they do not make promises about such outcomes. Clearly, this can be a considerable dilemma for consultants. They must promote or market their skills but not in a blatant, overpromising manner. Simply put, consultants cannot promise what will happen as a result of their efforts, and nonprofit organizations should be wary of those who make such promises.

A fourth indication—and a clear one—relates to any breach of confidentiality. Ethically behaving consultants will keep information confidential if they agreed to do so. If this commitment cannot be made, consultants should not allow client organizations to provide them with confidential data. This is especially true regarding information whose disclosure could contribute to resolution of issues on which the consultation is focused. Consultants can easily find themselves conflicted by having a great deal of confidential data that cannot be disclosed. In some instances, consultants attempt to obtain permission to use the data but keep the sources anonymous. Sometimes this can help resolve the confidentiality dilemmas. In the selection of consultants by nonprofit organizations, attention should be given—in reference checks and in straightforward discussions with consultants—to how they have dealt with confidential information in the past and the extent to which they view confidentiality as among the significant issues in the consulting relationship. If references suggest that a particular consultant had violated confidentiality in previous engagements, nonprofits would be wise to avoid contracting with that individual. Likewise, nonprofits should be equally cautious of contracting with consultants who do not appreciate the potential dilemmas presented when dealing with confidential data. This lack of insight can prove detrimental to achieving mutual satisfaction. Both will conclude that the final work products from the consultation engagement were not optimal.

Finally, nonprofit organizations should be wary of those consultants who publicly criticize other consultants. Even when knowing about or having heard things that are troublesome, ethical consultants either speak positively about other consultants or decline the opportunity to comment. Furthermore, ethical consultants do not direct negative or mixed messages to colleagues or the general public through nonverbal communication. If nonprofit organizations have concerns about consultants they are considering engaging or have already engaged, they should check with former client organizations or directly confront consultants with their concerns. Nonprofits should not seek to gain information about one consultant from another consultant. Ethically behaving consultants do not divulge this information. Doing so is a signal for nonprofits to avoid hiring them.

SOME FINAL THOUGHTS

The concepts discussed in this chapter provide nonprofit organizations with a pathway to more effective consultant relationships and engagements. Jokes about consultants are not likely to subside, but nonprofit leaders can become more effective in selecting and using them. No insurmountable obstacles preclude consulting relationships from being win–win situations for both nonprofit organizations and consultants. Lant (1997) succinctly made this point:

> Too many consulting relationships end unhappily: the client doesn't achieve the result he thought he should have, and all the consultant gets is his check. This is wrong. Clients should get the results they bargained for, consultants should not only get paid but should get a constant stream of referrals from satisfied clients. If both clients and consultants insist upon and follow these simple steps, they will both get what they want out of the relationship. Which is just the way it should be. (p. 36)

Selecting and using consultants effectively is like most other aspects of non-profit management and leadership. It is a matter of thinking through issues and using common sense. Following the tips in this chapter could prevent non-profits from being in unpleasant, unproductive consultative engagements.

SKILLS-APPLICATION EXERCISE

You are the chief executive officer of Arts R Us, an arts organization that has an important social services component related to teaching art appreciation to inner-city children. The organization has been in existence for 35 years but has never had a business plan or strategic plan to guide it. During each of the past three years, Arts R Us has ended with a financial deficit. Two funders—one corporate and the other a community foundation—have determined that they can no longer make grants to Arts R Us unless they are shown a business plan and strategic plan. The two funders have each committed $10,000 to Arts R Us to engage a consultant to develop these plans.

The organization has never used a consultant previously. The board of trustees requested that you develop and present to them a plan to identify and select a consultant. Please develop a proposed plan (maximum of five pages) for board consideration. The plan should address, at a minimum, the following areas:

- consultant's qualifications (required and preferred)

- methods for identifying potential consultants

- ingredients for an RFP

- process for selecting the consultant

- fee amount and payment arrangements

- deliverables and time lines.

REFERENCES

Block, P. (1981). *Flawless consulting*. San Francisco: Jossey-Bass.

Bruner, C. (1993). *So you think you need some help? Making effective use of technical assistance*. New York: Columbia University, National Center for Service Integration.

Davis, B. (1983, March–April). How and why to hire a consultant. *Grantsmanship Center News*, pp. 27–34.

Flexner, S. B. (Ed.). (1988). *The Random House collegiate dictionary* (rev. ed.). New York: Random House.

Lant, J. (1977). Why consulting relationships fail. *Contributions, 11*(2), 32–36.

Pfeiffer, J., & Jones, J. (1977). Ethical considerations in consulting. In J. Jones & J. Pfeiffer (Eds.), *The 1977 annual handbook for group facilitation* (pp. 217–224). San Diego: University Associates.

Shulman, L. (1995). Supervision and consultation. In R. L. Edwards (Ed.-in-Chief), *Encyclopedia of social work* (19th ed., Vol. 3, pp. 2373–2379). Washington, DC: NASW Press.

Tepper, R. (1993). *The consultant's proposal, fee, and contract problem-solver.* New York: John Wiley & Sons.

Turner, A. (1982, September–October). Consulting is more than giving advice. *Harvard Business Review*, pp. 120–129.

PART SIX

LEADERSHIP FOR
QUALITY AND
INNOVATION

LEADERSHIP FOR
QUALITY AND INNOVATION

As discussed in chapter 1 and elsewhere throughout this book, managers must function in an atmosphere of competing values, in which they are required to use various sets of skills and perform many different roles, often more or less simultaneously. In the day-to-day world of the nonprofit manager, it is easy to get bogged down with the work at hand and lose of sight of the reason for it all. Periodically, it may be important for mangers to pause to ask themselves, and to engage others in their organizations in discussion on, such questions as "Why?" "So what?" and "What difference does it make?" The answers to these questions should have something to do with your organization's mission and with the people you serve.

In the final chapter in this book, Frank Hawkins and John Gunther consider the issue of service quality. They give particular attention to managerial effectiveness and suggest that total quality management (TQM) is an approach organizations can take to help them achieve the goal of continuous quality improvement. In the present climate of increasing calls for accountability, quality assurance measures assume greater significance than ever before. Hawkins and Gunther argue that TQM is a tool for improving service quality that can be applied in the nonprofit sector but that requires that nonprofit mangers draw on the various sets of skills identified in competing values framework.

CHAPTER 25

Managing for Quality

Frank Hawkins and John Gunther

The context of nonprofit human services organizations is constantly changing, in both the public and private sectors. However, as Weiner (1990) pointed out, the purpose of human services management remains constant: "The purpose of human services management . . . is to create and maintain an environment of societal community services that are responsive to people, individually and in groups, as they strive to improve the quality of their lives. This is the distinctive role of the human services manager" (p. x).

The distinctive purpose of human services management translates differently for managers in various places across a spectrum of human services provision. Managers in both nonprofit and public organizations have used various managerial skills and structures that have their origins in business organizations. Three of these are Program Evaluation Review Technique (PERT), Program Planning Budgeting Systems (PPBS), and Management By Objectives (MBO). PERT is a planning technique first used by the Special Projects Office of the U.S. Navy to develop and plan a guidance system for the Polaris missile (Carlisle, 1979). This technique is used in situations involving complex, multilevel tasks in which clarifying timelines in relation to the completion of specific tasks is important. Tasks and completion of dates are presented in a PERT chart to show the relationships and sequence of key tasks.

PPBS was introduced to the federal government in the 1960s by President Lyndon Johnson and was intended to bring rationality to the management planning process. This system of management gives special attention to analysis, planning, the study of alternatives, and the measurement of outcomes. Management components included clarity of objectives, specification of program structure and strategic choices, program, and financial plans involving the allocation of resources. Excessive paperwork and insufficient financial resources and expertise may explain the limited use and effectiveness of this program (Abels & Murphy, 1981).

MBO is perhaps the most dominant paradigm in recent years. First referenced in the work of Drucker (1954), it was later developed by Odiorne (1965) as a novel approach to managerial leadership. This management approach incorporates the notion of intentionality and places a high value on envisioning intended objectives or results as the first step in accomplishing the organization's overall purpose or mission. This forward-looking mindset is operationalized throughout the organization in the form of specific verifiable objectives that serve as benchmarks against which organizational units and individuals measure their success. It is essentially a method of evaluation and accountability.

Although these approaches to management problem solving possess strengths, they do not correct many of the fundamental issues that Hasenfeld and English (1974) recognized over two decades ago as shortcomings in human services organizations.

1. The failure of HSOs [human services organizations] to respond to the populations they claim to serve . . . ;
2. The service techniques employed in such organizations are inconsistent and ill-organized, failing to demonstrate their effectiveness . . . ;
3. The mechanisms these organizations develop to transact and work with their clients are dehumanizing, degrading, and insensitive to their individual attributes and needs;
4. [HSOs] are ill-managed, wasteful and inefficient, thus consuming an ever increasing share of public and private resources. (pp. 3-4)

It may be argued that the fundamental problem with nonprofit organizations is the presence of a domesticated service delivery ideology that is, in large measure, indifferent to the financial realities of a competitive marketplace, where survival depends on the ability to make a profit. Survival in the world of nonprofit organizations finds its roots in the goodwill, generosity, and commitment of stakeholders whose motivations cannot be understood simply against the backdrop of a profit-and-loss statement. However, the realities of deficit control, downsizing and restructuring in all sectors of the community, increased competition for scarce dollars, and demands for increased accountability make nonprofit organizations vulnerable. Public goodwill and a record of service are not sufficient to ensure long-term survival in the present human services marketplace. More highly educated and discriminating consumers demand higher levels of accountability and return on investment, whether the investment takes the form of tax dollars and public expenditure or charitable givings and support of initiatives in the nonprofit sector.

Related to these issues is another area of major concern: Nonprofit organizations have given little attention to issues related to service quality. Quality assurance programs illustrate some of the early attempts to address quality, particularly in the public and health care sectors of the community. Coulton (1991) viewed the development of some early quality assurance initiatives as growing out of the regulatory requirements of the social security acts of the 1970s. Here the emphasis was on evaluating and monitoring services. In addition, the Joint Commission on the Accreditation of Health Care Organizations played a major role in the development of standards for the purposes of quality assurance and accreditation in the health care field (Lehmann 1987, 1989).

Although quality assurance programs have contributed to an understanding of the importance of quality in the delivery of social services, they have not addressed the more fundamental question of how to move organizations beyond a concern with minimum acceptable standards. Galea-Curmi and Hawkins (1996) pointed to quality assurance's focus on outcome measures rather than the work processes that lead to these outcomes: "While the value of quality assurance measures and programs in establishing the thresholds of acceptability is recognized, such measures and programs continue to be limited in their ability to improve quality beyond minimum thresholds" (pp. 163–164).

TOTAL QUALITY MANAGEMENT

Background

A recent development has been the emergence of total quality management (TQM), a holistic management paradigm that sees PPBS, PERT, MBO, and quality assurance as inadequate to meet the current challenges of the human services marketplace, with its rising costs, increased competition for scarce resources, and broader expectations of customers. TQM is a new approach to management, one that challenges many traditional notions of how work is best performed. TQM views the problems of management as rooted in a preoccupation with productivity, coupled with a lack of attention to the work processes that define and operationalize an organization's mandate to serve the community. TQM sets aside traditional approaches to management and gives top priority to quality. The preoccupation with quality is the defining characteristic of this approach. It is an organizing and synergistic theme that calls for the total transformation of an organization's culture and work processes—in other words, changing the way work is carried out.

TQM finds its origins in the work of several management theorists. Three of them—Philip Crosby, W. Edwards Deming, and Joseph Juran—are considered leaders in the field and merit attention. Philip Crosby obtained his

Table 25-1. Comparison of Key TQM Tenets Identified by Crosby, Deming, and Juran

CROSBY	DEMING	JURAN
Obtain management commitment	Create constancy of purpose Adopt the new philosophy Do not judge on price tag alone	Raise awareness of need for improvement
Form quality improvement teams Establish quality council Establish zero-defects program Raise awareness of the cost of defects Identify barriers to error-free work	Remove barriers between staff areas and departments Remove systems of mass inspection Remove barriers to pride in workmanship	Organize to reach goals
Measure for quality Establish cost of quality evaluation		Keep score
Take corrective action	Take action to transform the organization	Implement project to solve problems
Implement supervisor training	Institute education and training (retraining) Institute leadership	Provide training
Establish goals with employees	Eliminate slogans, targets Eliminate numerical quotas	Set goals
Recognize performance	Drive out fear	Recognize performance Communicate results
Promote continuous improvement	Improve constantly	Improve yearly

initial quality management experience with the International Telephone and Telegraph Company and later distilled his ideas in the book *Quality Is Free* (1980), in which he focused on the importance of management commitment to quality, the cost of poor quality, and the strategies necessary to implement TQM. W. Edwards Deming, a statistician who worked for Western Electric's Hawthorne Plant of Technology in Boston, established himself as a quality expert as a result of his influential work with Japanese government and industry leaders following World War II. Joseph Juran, like Deming, worked for Western Electric in Chicago and was invited by Japan to lecture industry leaders on quality management. Although these management specialists gained their expertise and experience in manufacturing and business organizations, they believed that the tenets of a quality management approach were equally relevant and applicable to nonprofit human services organizations (Crosby, 1980, 1984; Deming, 1986, Juran, 1989). Table 25-1 outlines the key tenets of TQM as developed by these three theorists. A review of the seminal ideas of each reveals some interesting similarities.

Each theorist emphasized the importance of a consciousness-raising process, which begins with an understanding of the costs associated with poor quality, management's commitment to quality, and the need to organize for change. Education and training are given a high priority for all employees. Management problem solving is viewed as a team effort and part of a continuous cycle of improvement. These and other writers have contributed to our knowledge of TQM and its relevance to nonprofit human services organizations. A model for the successful implementation of TQM is described in relation to several key processes involved in the transformation from a traditional managerial approach to a quality management system.

Key Processes and Skills

TQM is gaining prominence in the human services management literature (Edwards, Cooke, & Reid, 1996; Gummer & McCallion, 1995; Gunther & Hawkins, 1996; Martin, 1993). This development is not an accident. As noted earlier, TQM has been credited with bringing Japan out of its postwar economic crisis (Deming, 1986; Walton, 1986) and has actively demonstrated quality effectiveness in several public and nonprofit human services organizations (for example, Breen et al., 1996; Comstock & Price, 1996; Hassen, 1993; Henderson, 1996; Henry, Wedel, & Czypinski, 1996).

TQM has been defined as "a set of process practices that emphasize continuous quality improvement. Customer focus, fact-based decision making and team work serve as the cornerstones for effective quality practice" (Gunther & Hawkins, 1996, p. 221). Embedded in this definition is a core philosophy that stresses a commitment to customers and the importance of continuous quality improvement. *Continuous quality improvement* refers to the ongoing activities that monitor organizational processes to ensure quality and customer satisfaction. *Customers* are defined as all the recipients of services or products associated with a TQM system.

There are three classes of customers in TQM: external, internal, and ultimate. External customers include individuals and systems that are recipients, funders, and legal or accreditation regulators of an organization. Internal customers are generally employed by an organization (for salary or voluntary) and engage in the delivery of services and service products. Ultimate customers are considered to be the community or society as a whole. Figure 25-1 outlines the structural features of a TQM system.

The most important tenet of this model is commitment to customer service, and this is the starting point for the implementation of a quality program. Some managers may assume a commitment to customer service, but

Figure 25-1. TQM Flow Chart

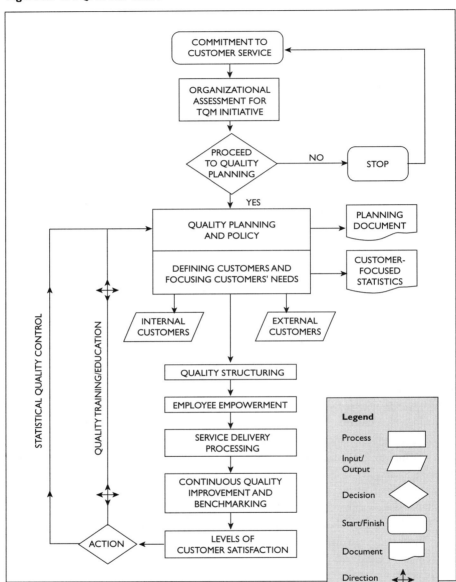

SOURCE: Gunther, J., & Hawkins, F. (1996). *Total quality management in human service organizations* (p. 20). New York: Springer. Copyright 1996 by Springer Publishing Company, Inc. Used by permission.

this is not always the case. An organization's readiness to implement TQM may be determined by a number of strategies, such as meetings with staff or use of an outside consultant. This ultimately involves a judgment (assessment) of the organization's readiness to commit considerable resources of time and energy to improve customer services. Commitment to customer service and organizational assessment are intended to move the organization forward to the important decision of whether to implement TQM. Such a decision should not be taken lightly, because TQM is not a quick fix. The decision to adopt TQM involves quality planning, which introduces the next phase of the model.

Quality planning and policy involves, in essence, the process of defining where the organization is now, where it wants to go, and how it wants to get there. The first part of this process has been partially addressed in the first step, the assessment phase, which has provided a picture of the organization in the present. The second step, quality planning, involves the development of policy documents to guide the TQM initiative. This may begin with the development of a vision statement, a synthesis of the ideas that best capture what the organization wants to become. The articulation of quality objectives is part of the planning process and a clear statement of how these objectives are to be achieved.

These steps or phases of TQM are not mutually exclusive but rather should be seen as a series of overlapping processes. Note the two vertical lines in the left margin of Figure 25-1 referring to statistical quality control and quality education and training. The planning documents for quality acknowledge the need for valid information related to customer needs and services. The collection and analysis of this information (statistical quality control) is important in all phases of this model. Facts must inform all decisions if they are truly to be made in the interest of improving service quality to customers. Thus, defining customers and customer-focused statistics are viewed as integral parts of the process of planning and policy. Similarly, education and training is not only part of policy and planning; it also is part of the other phases of the model as well.

Quality structuring in this model draws attention to the need to redesign the organization in a manner that is congruent with the process-oriented focus of TQM. Understanding how work is done and how decisions are made is important. Traditional ways of doing work are examined from the perspective of how processes can be improved. In TQM, the traditional top-down hierarchical models give way to much flatter–horizontal structures with communication and work relationships being informed by the nature of the task at hand and a common commitment to quality improvement.

Another facet of the model, employee empowerment, gives credence to the tenet of commitment to customer service. Employees as internal customers of the organization are both recipients and providers of service and thus play a critical role in developing a quality organization. Shared decision making and team development coalesce as part of a new organizational culture that places high value on employee participation, constructive feedback, and reward. The final two phases of the model, service delivery processing and continuous quality improvement and benchmarking, underline the importance that is given to understanding what is meant by quality and how this must be subject to continuous examination and review.

Service delivery processing within the context of TQM brings the processes of service delivery under constant scrutiny in the continuous quest for quality improvement. This is a never-ending cycle in which rapidly changing circumstances and needs make today's solutions part of tomorrow's problems. Organizations committed to the realization of quality in all facets of their operations must be receptive to continuous change. Benchmarking provides a means of achieving service excellence through the active pursuit of best practices, both within one's own organization and elsewhere. It gives meaning to the phrase "continuous quality improvement" in underlining the value of searching out and striving toward "best practice." The final phase of the model is identified in terms of an outcome, that is, levels of customer satisfaction. Customer-focused statistics provide evidence that the system works according to expectations or alternatively, that changes are necessary. Thus, the cycle of continuous quality begins again.

Customer satisfaction processes are monitored through quantitative and qualitative tools. The primary tools are statistical in nature and are generally referred to as the "magnificent seven." Hassen (1993) noted that statistical tools are used to help internal customers understand processes as they are currently used or administered and to identify and measure the variation in processes so that continuous improvements can be made to attain consistently high-quality services and products (see Figure 25-2).

Flow charts are used to analyze the steps involved in work processes within the organization. They give clarity to the chain of events involved in key activities and serve as a planning tool in implementing quality improvements. For example, the processing of applications for enrollment in a personal development program may be improved by the recognition that no screening is done at the beginning of the review process. As a consequence, incomplete applications cause delays and rework, which can be solved by modest changes in the sequence of steps.

The cause-and-effect chart is frequently referred to as a "fishbone diagram" because of its shape. A fishbone diagram is intended to assess the root causes of a problem or serve as a planning tool to accomplish a goal or objective. The problem (effect) or desired outcome is normally placed on the right of the diagram. The causal or contributing factors are linked by arrows to a central arrow that points to the right, the problem. Causal factors are normally categorized under headings such as personnel, methodology, resources,

Figure 25-2. The Magnificent Seven:
Tools and Methods of Continuous Quality Improvement

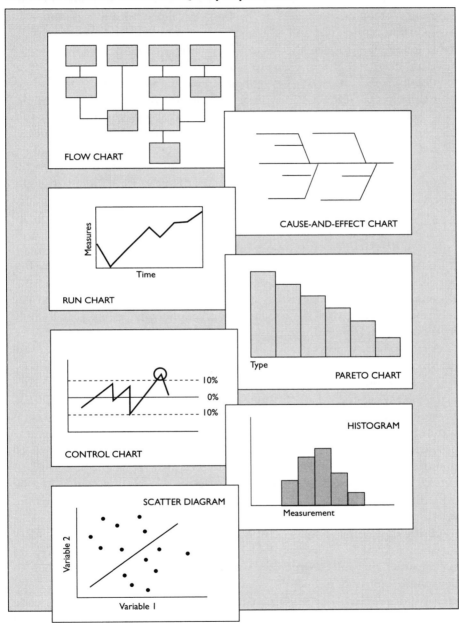

SOURCE: Hassen, P. (1993). *RX for hospitals* (p. 5). Toronto: Stoddart. Copyright 1993 by Stoddart Publishing Co. Reprinted by permission.

and equipment. This pictorial display identifies all the factors (possible causes) of a problem and is intended to promote a greater understanding of its eti-
ology, as a stepping stone toward finding a quality resolution. A nonprofit
organization can use this tool to analyze the reasons behind a decline in charitable givings and to plan an effective fundraising initiative.

A run chart is useful in TQM to plot changes that take place over time or
to identify trends in certain key activities. For example, it can chart changes
over time in the number and type of referrals or shifts in supporter population and the magnitude of contributions. Alternatively, the Pareto chart is
used to identify the most important or critical problems in a work process
related to a quality improvement initiative. It is used as a means of ranking
problems or their causes, from the most frequently occurring causes to the
least frequent, ranked in descending order, from left to right, on a bar graph.
The value of this chart is derived from the Pareto principle that asserts that
80 percent of difficulties occurring in organizations are caused by only 20
percent of the problems (key variables). The latter, sometimes referred to as
"the vital few," become very important in planning for quality improvement.
It underlines the importance of a strategic investment of resources in carefully selected areas, with an expectation of optimal results. For example, personal contacts by the manager with key supporters or selected employees may
solve most of the problems associated with morale and support, something
that a raft of memos and reports may never do.

A control chart shows process performance in relation to specified control
limits, referred to as "upper control limits" (UCL) and "lower control limits"
(LCL). Variation within UCL and LCL is viewed as normal within a particular system depending on statistics that have been gathered over time.
Variation outside UCL and LCL occurs when a system or process is seen as
out of control and needing corrective intervention. Statistical data over time
provide a useful monitoring device to determine when events appear to be
unusual (brought about by special causes or factors) or when variation is as
expected (within specified limits) and the result of common causes. Among
other things, this quality tool can be used to track data related to absenteeism
in relation to critical events in an organization.

Histograms or bar graphs identify the frequency and distribution of key
variables that have been identified in a quality improvement initiative. As
noted earlier, they are incorporated into the construction of a Pareto chart to
determine the most frequently occuring factors in relation to a particular
concern or problem. The histogram can be used to display the frequency and
nature of complaints related to various processes (for example, the allocation
of seats at a local symphony) and as an agenda-building strategy in the establishment of quality improvement projects.

A scatter diagram illustrates pictorially the relationship between two
process characteristics in TQM. Plotting information on a graph in relation

to key variables, such as length of waiting time and perception of quality service, may reveal important relationships between variables. A clustering of points on the diagram shows that these variables are related, whereas a randomly scattered pattern reveals that there is no relationship. This type of graphic representation provides decision makers with important information about the organization and the operation of key variables in relation to quality processes.

Implementation

Quality improvement teams provide the framework within which process analysis and decision making are carried out in the interest of enhanced customer services. Teamwork is achieved in TQM when individuals recognize that it is in their and the organization's interest to meet or exceed customer expectations, thus establishing a network of mutual interdependencies and common purpose.

Effectively implementing TQM requires a culture of quality. A quality culture is seen as being in sharp contrast to the traditional organizational culture of productivity found in many organizations of today, both nonprofit organizations and business. It should be noted that the TQM model does not ignore or sacrifice productivity. However, in TQM there is a substantive shift in emphasis, a shift that values the processes that lead to quality services. In the MBO framework, this system is a failure. Of the leading theorists on quality, Deming was most critical of MBO. He believed that MBO "must be abolished" and replaced with a management system that gives less attention to productivity and results and focuses more on sources of improvement (Deming, 1986). Juran (1988, 1989) was less critical, viewing MBO as acceptable provided that the focus was on quality objectives, change, and breakthrough quality initiatives. Crosby (1980) saw MBO as compatible with TQM provided that the emphasis was on quality objectives such as "zero defects" and quality improvement processes. Neither Juran nor Crosby saw a productivity- or results-driven paradigm as adequate to meet the rising expectations of customers for quality services. How are these paradigms different in their influence on key organizational processes? Table 25-2 outlines the distinguishing features of a "culture of quality" as represented by TQM and a "culture of productivity" as represented by traditional management practice.

An organizational culture of quality gives priority to customers and their definitions of quality. This is different than the results–productivity orientation, which follows the rules of the market and frequently views more as better and quotas as the order of the day. Organizational structures are different in a quality culture. Traditional vertical structures are replaced by organizations that are more horizontal (that is, fewer middle managers). Work groups or project teams replace the more traditional, segmented departmental struc-

Table 25-2. Characteristics of the Cultures of Quality and Productivity

CULTURE OF QUALITY	CULTURE OF PRODUCTIVITY
Focus on quality	Focus on productivity
Customer focus	Market focus
Horizontal organizational structures that are integrated and aligned	Vertical organizational structures that are segmented and centralized
Process monitoring	Outcome monitoring
Statistically based decision making	Vertical and rational sequences of decision making
Creative thinking	Regimented thinking
Continuous quality improvement	Outcome- or results-oriented management
Top management participation, commitment, and action	Top management support for operations
Collective orientation	Individual orientation
Teamwork performance	Individual performance
Innovation (individual–organization)	Organizational conformity
Change process	Change individual

SOURCE: Gunther, J., & Hawkins, F. (1996). *Total quality management in human service organizations* (p. 15). New York: Springer. Copyright 1996 by Springer Publishing Company, Inc. Used by permission.

tures, with work processes concerned with quality rather than quantity of output. Centralized decison making is replaced with processes more closely aligned and responsive to the customer's needs, with actions guided by facts or statistics rather than the formalities of red tape and bureaucratic protocols.

Quality cultures bring management and workers together in a spirit of teamwork, where a collectivist orientation values cooperation and shared responsibility, unlike the individualist orientation of a productivity culture. In the latter, results are measured by individual performance. In a culture of productivity, outcomes are viewed from the perspective of team performance. Change within the paradigm of quality is a continuous process, with a high value placed on innovation and creativity. In a productivity orientation, problems are considered to reside in the employee, and solutions are sought in strategies designed to change the individual. Quality cultures view problems from a systems perspective: How do work processes influence outcomes, and how can work processes be changed in the interest of quality improvement? These questions are answered by monitoring processes, in the interest of better understanding and enhancing service outcomes.

The philosophical principles of TQM underline the importance of managerial commitment to customers and responsiveness to their ever-changing expectations in terms of service quality. Supporting these principles and developing an organizational culture of quality require a set of managerial skills. The roles and skills embedded in the competing values model, when aligned with TQM's continuous quality improvment tools, present a powerful foundation from which to build a culture of service quality. The ultimate purpose of TQM in organizational processes is to achieve the goals of quality, productivity, efficiency, effectiveness, workplace satisfaction, and ultimately an enhanced quality of living, both in the workplace and in the community.

COMPETING VALUES FRAMEWORK AND TQM ROLES AND COMPETENCIES

The issue of quality is a central concern in the development of managerial skills. To date, however, quality management as an integrated system has not been organized from the perspective of a competing values framework and the associated skills that nonprofit managers need to create and maintain a quality service delivery system.

Quinn (1988) developed a useful heuristic framework to explain and organize a spectrum of managerial effectiveness skills. Figure 25-3 presents the competing values framework within which requisite management skills are conceptualized. Edwards and Austin (1991) have operationalized the four levels of skills involved in this framework:

> The competing values model is an analytic framework built around two dimensions representing competing orientations or "values" in the organizational context. These dimensions are flexibility–control and internal–external. The combination of these two dimensions distinguishes four sectors of organizational activity, each of which embodies distinctive criteria of organizational effectiveness. . . . For an organization to perform well with respect to the various criteria of effectiveness, managers must use the following different and sometimes conflicting sets of skills: boundary spanning skills, human relations skills, coordinating skills and directing skills. (pp. 8–9)

The complexity of modern organizations makes great demands on the technical, human relations, and conceptual skills of the manager. This is just as true for the chief executive officer (CEO) of a large organization with hundreds of employees as it is for the small nonprofit organization with few employees. Although CEOs of large organizations have more people to whom they can delegate responsibilities, they are still ultimately responsible for ensuring that the mission of the organization is being realized in the multitudinous tasks and activities that represent the work of the organization. The same is true for CEOs of smaller organizations. The competing values

Figure 25-3. Competing Values Framework of Leadership Roles

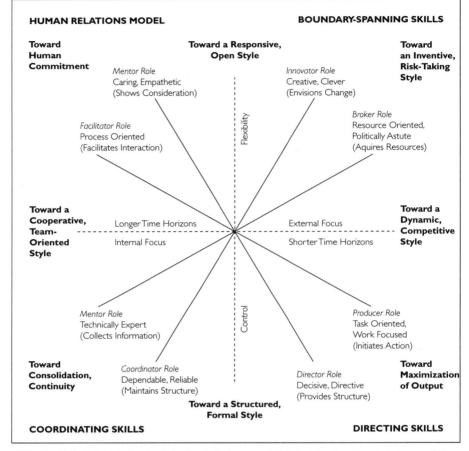

framework provides a useful paradigm from which to organize and conceptualize the nature of the various competing and conflicting demands that managers face in carrying out their responsibilities in a competent manner. The realities of the workplace are represented in this framework by competing values, an understandable tension between the need for flexibility on the one hand and the need for control on the other. At the same time there are the demands of the internal environment, the organization itself, and the external demands coming from the community. An effective organization may be seen as one that simultaneously manages these varying demands as they are operationalized in four sectors of organizational activity.

Four skills sets (boundary spanning, human relations, coordinating, and directing) correspond to four pairs of leadership roles that fall within different sectors of the values framework. These leadership roles incorporate various internal–external and flexibility–control functions within the skills sets. Thus, the framework serves as a useful heuristic tool to expand and deepen one's understanding of management. For example, boundary-spanning skills are particularly important in assuming the role of broker or innovator. Managers may not be equally competent or skilled in all four skills sets, but depending on the circumstances and situation, they may be called on to assume each of these roles at various times.

Austin (1988) viewed the competing values framework as providing two important criteria in measuring organizational outcomes: (1) the quality of services and (2) organizational continuity (survival). If nonprofit organizations are to survive, they cannot ignore the demands for quality in every facet of their operations. Customers' rising expectations for quality services, increased public concern for fiscal accountability (in all sectors of the service community), and heightened competition for scarce resources make "business as usual" no longer a viable option for managers of nonprofits.

The competing values framework draws attention to the inherent complexity and tension of the managerial world of nonprofits where frequently there are no easy right answers; rather, there are choices between two or more competing "good options" representing conflicting values. This reality makes the interface between TQM and the competing values framework important. The four quadrants of the competing values framework take on special meaning when viewed through the lens of total quality and the challenges associated with commitment to customer service. The framework is a template for the various managerial skills and roles necessary to achieve organizational effectiveness (Edwards, Faerman, & McGrath, 1986; Quinn & Rohrbaugh, 1983). Integrated with TQM, the competing values framework presents an opportunity to deepen and expand one's understanding of continuous quality improvement and organizational effectiveness.

Coordinating Skills

Quinn (1988) noted that coordinating skills encompass the roles of monitor and coordinator. Edwards and Yankey (1991) stated that "competencies for the role of monitor include receiving and organizing information, evaluating routine information and responding to routine information. Competencies for the role of coordinator include planning, organizing and controlling" (p. 219).

The traditional function of monitoring developed mainly out of concern for productivity. Within TQM, however, the coordinating function (monitor and coordinator roles) may be operationalized through three important processes: statistical quality control (SQC), quality planning (QP), and activity-based costing (ABC). These management tools are used to promote continuous quality improvement, assess progress toward quality goals, and determine customer satisfaction. Each management tool is explained, with an illustration of its application to the nonprofit sector.

To achieve continuous improvement, managers must engage in monitoring the information that is intrinsic to SQC. SQC involves the collection and analysis of data acquired about various organizational processes. Gunther and Hawkins (1996) noted that through the processes of SQC, managers are able to provide information and data for managerial analysis to improve the reliability of service, while minimizing service variations in human services organizations. Activities related to SQC cross a spectrum of data collection and analysis processes, ranging from customer satisfaction surveys to the application of statistical tests to data sets, such as showing the relationship between charitable givings and various fundraising initiatives. SQC involves the collection of information in the interest of promoting quality improvements.

Nonprofit managers make numerous decisions each day. To be effective as monitors and coordinators of information and resources, managers must have access to valid and meaningful information and not rely on intuition or hearsay. For example, explaining a decrease in membership subscriptions to this year's community concert series is both difficult and meaningless if it is not presented within the context of relevant and valid information. SQC places a high value on the systematic collection of and review of relevant information related to quality improvement initiatives. Decisions based on facts rather than intuition can mean savings amounting to thousands of dollars for a board of directors deciding to invest in a major capital works project such as the construction of a local civic center. If an appropriate financial plan (with valid cost information) is not in place, excellent ideas may become mired in errors related to mismanagement.

The role of coordinator takes on special meaning in TQM. Specifically, the competencies related to planning, organizing, and controlling now have as their primary focus a customer orientation that emphasizes quality. First and foremost, QP is a process designed to meet the quality needs of customers. Juran (1988) has developed a road map that outlines the components of quality planning as both a sequence of steps and a set of activities (see Figure 25-4). He stated that "each step is an activity whose output becomes an input into the next step in the sequence" (p. 6.3).

Before discussing Juran's QP road map, it is important to recognize the relationship between planning and organizing. Within the TQM paradigm,

Figure 25-4. The Quality Planning Road Map

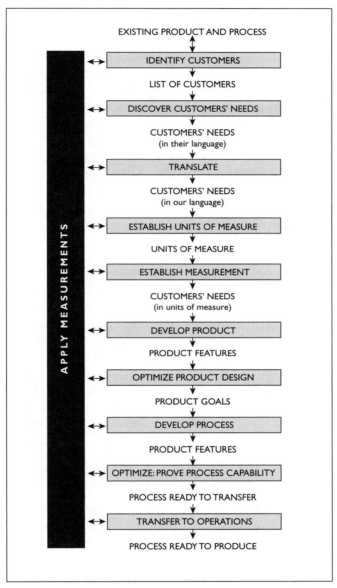

SOURCE: Juran, J. M., & Gryna, F. M. (1988). *Juran's quality control handbook*. New York: McGraw-Hill. Reprinted by permission of McGraw-Hill Companies.

the development of quality policies and goals usually involves groups of committed policy makers or planners (such as a board of directors), whereby organizing activities (new structures) are put in place to address quality problems. This may involve the formation of a quality council or a quality project planning group to oversee the implementation of a quality initiative. Quality goals, developed under the umbrella of a quality council or planning group, represent a set of expectations regarding future accomplishments and a basis from which to measure progress. Although this may seem similar to MBO, it is qualitatively different in that quality goals are the product of cooperation and team initiative and provide a structure within which accomplishments can be assessed and from which new learning and continuous improvement efforts can be promoted. It also provides a framework within which quality policies can be developed. Policies are essentially guides to organizational action. As such, it is imperative that quality managers be involved in the identification of quality needs and the planning–development of requisite programs and policies.

The Juran QP road map (Figure 25-4) may be used as a guide in the planning process. Some of these steps are familiar because they overlap with the first phase of the TQM model presented earlier in this chapter. The most important feature of the road map—apply measurements—is noted in the left margin. Thus, it incorporates the SQC process discussed earlier, drawing attention to the importance of fact-based decision making. The planning process begins with customers: Who are they, and what are their needs? For the nonprofit manager of a community planning research organization, the customers may encompass hundreds of people both internal and external to the organization. Careful planning means being clear about who these customers are and the nature of their respective needs. The needs of wealthy benefactors are quite different than the needs of a group of volunteer fundraisers. Nevertheless, both groups are important to the organization, and both require the services of a manager who has internalized both skills sets— boundary spanning and coordinating.

The next phase of Juran's planning map draws attention to the importance of language in understanding and interpreting customer needs. The understanding of customers' needs, expressed in their language, is important in TQM because it validates the commitment that has been made to customers to provide quality services. While a translation process is necessary, in terms of organizational processing, it is grounded in an understanding of the customer's needs. For example, a group that conducts research to understand and meet the needs of poor people finds variation in the meanings ascribed to the word "poor" when moving across diverse cultural groups. Units of measure have to accommodate these differences if they are to have validity in the planning process. Framing information related to poverty is different in a lobbying initiative directed to members of the local legislature than it is for a group of new immigrants trying to access community resources or a church group wanting to start a day care center for children of poor people.

The product and process features of the planning can be meaningfully understood only within the context of what is intended, that is, the goals of the initiative. If the purpose is to influence legislative action, the product may be a policy paper, and the relevant processes may encompass a range of lobbying activities such as letter writing, strategic meetings, telephone calls, and information gathering. If the purpose is the establishment of a downtown day care facility in partnership with a group of churches, the product and processes are different.

The final phase of the planning process involves "design features" of the new service (what services are provided, to whom, under what circumstances, and how) and "process features" related to how stakeholders work together. Stakeholders include everyone who has a real or potential interest in the organization's current or future activities. A range of decisions are involved and may include issues related to the facility's financing, fundraising, staffing, quality standards, constituency representation, leadership, and governance, to name but a few. These and other decisions are informed by facts related to relevant information gathering and analysis. Proving or establishing process capability and the transfer of operations is demonstrated in the coordination of resources and the compilation of information related to "readiness" to begin. This means that the decision makers are confident in their judgments, having based their decisions on valid information and carefully weighed the alternatives. Thus, the results of planning are ready to be put to the test, meeting the needs of customers.

A third process under the coordinating function, ABC is related to the earlier discussion regarding SQC and QP, because accountability in decision making finds tangible meaning in questions related to the cost of quality and the cost of service provision. ABC is intended to introduce control functions, different than the function of flexibility as articulated within the competing values framework. Under the coordinating role, costing becomes a central function, relevant to all dimensions of organizational activity. This is particularly relevant today, in a climate of fiscal cost consciousness and shrinking budgets. Managers in the nonprofit sector find ABC to be a valuable tool in answering questions related to the cost of such processes as recruitment, fundraising, contract negotiations, skills development, training, proposal development, budgeting, marketing, public relations, planning, brokering, mentoring, negotiating, delegating, monitoring, lobbying, and teambuilding. These processes—a sampling of those found within any nonprofit organization—are listed to highlight the difference between ABC and other more traditional accounting systems. The latter are outcome oriented, whereas ABC is process or activity oriented. An astute manager, operating from a quality paradigm, is concerned with the nature and outcome of all of the activities (processes) taking place under the mandate of the organization. The coordinating function of the managerial role is enhanced when activities and associated costs can be integrated with quality planning.

The ABC system provides a breakdown of the costs of all work processes associated with the provision of a particular customer service. It is also an important tool in understanding the cost and nature of poor quality. The work processes associated with having to go back and redo poor work represent an added cost, a cost that concerns the quality-conscious manager. ABC contributes to a deepened understanding of the true nature of quality in service provision. Thus, attention shifts to the question of what processes led to this outcome (a satisfied or dissatisfied customer). Forrest (1996) noted the value of ABC in providing an operational understanding of activities as follows:

1. It identifies key activities and resources consumed:
   - What do people do?
   - What resources are consumed and how?
   - Establish appropriated nonfunctional activity work drivers.
2. It establishes inputs to and from each activity:
   - Inputs to one activity may be outputs from another.
   - Understand the interactive relationships among activities.
3. It documents activity work flow using activity work flow diagrams:
   - Create a network of interrelated activities.
   - Identify any multistage activity relationships.
   - Graphically represent business process. (p. 308)

The quality parameters of a customer focus and continuous quality improvement give focus to the importance of coordinating skills within the context of the key roles and competencies of the competing values framework. Within this context, the tools of SQC, QP, and ABC have been discussed and viewed as particularly relevant to the role of management in the nonprofit sector of human services.

Directing Skills

Quinn (1988) identified the roles of producer and director as encompassing directing skills. Edwards and Yankey (1991) noted that "competencies for the producer role include personal productivity, motivating others, time management and stress management. Competencies for the director role include initiative taking, goal setting and effective delegating" (p. 283).

One of the key manager roles in TQM is that of producer. However, as previously noted, this role is embedded in a TQM team approach to quality initiatives and improvement. The manager is seen as assuming a leadership position in the production of services while setting a tone of cooperation and support in the motivation of team members. Included in production is the design of a support system through which quality outcomes are realized. The production of quality services is operationalized through key processes in critical areas of the organization's operations. As noted earlier, understanding the nature of work activities (processes) is central to an in-depth understanding of the nature of quality outcomes.

Kessler (1995) has listed the key areas necessary to address productivity in a TQM system:

- Research and development
- Design of new products and services
- Management of supplier quality
- Improvement of products and services
- Betterment of the improvement process
- Management of the quality of key support services, such as purchasing, sales, accounting, legal, finance and so on. (p.119)

Related to productivity is the issue of employee motivation. Motivation is a key ingredient in promoting and maintaining an organizational climate conducive to the attainment of quality in all spheres of service. A central task of the TQM manager is to set a tone of achievement. Management accomplishes this task by planning and developing short-term goals that are rigorous in terms of quality, yet achievable. It is also important that constructive feedback be provided to employees in support of an environment that sustains quality. In summary, a quality manager is always driven by the question, How can we make a better quality product or service for our customers? In a fully developed organizational culture of quality, the question is asked by all employees at all levels.

The notion of "high achievement" is important to the accomplishment of quality goals. Factors that play a role in high performance and productivity include the integration of tasks with organizational objectives and the willing investment of resources in support of this initiative. Other factors include a work environment that supports optimal input by employees and work structures that integrate formal and informal processes with production technology.

Effective delegating is another critical skill in TQM. The key to effective delegating is the ability to assign tasks to the right person who has the skills and is ready to engage in a specific quality task. Thompson (1995) regarded effective delegation as including four steps: preparation, delegation, monitoring, and evaluation. In many respects this follows the plan, do, check, act (PDCA) cycle popularized by Deming in his work in Japan. This process improvement tool, sometimes referred to as the "Deming cycle," draws attention to the importance of planning as the first step in a four-step quality improvement cycle. The other steps are implementing the change, evaluating the results, and acting on the findings to either stabilize the results or begin the PDCA cycle again to plan an alternative strategy (Baker, 1988).

Effective delegating involves a planning process in deciding who may be the right person to do the job. Some nonprofit managers find it difficult to assign tasks to others, and as a consequence they suffer from work overload and unnecessary stress. Part of the planning process involves letting go and empowering others to get on with the job, unencumbered by the insecurities of managers constantly looking over their shoulders. The actual task of delegating includes clarification of the nature of the task, the goals and expected outcomes, the timelines, the structure of reporting, and the method of evaluation. Also important is the nature of the support system that is in place, such as the availability of regular supervision or consultation and the nature and extent of resources that are provided to do the job. Perhaps nothing is more frustrating to an employee or work group than a manager who delegates responsibilities without providing the requisite resources or authority to do the job effectively.

The final two steps in the delegation process are monitoring to see how work is being done and evaluating. As noted above, this should not involve looking over the shoulder. Rather, it should follow an agreed-on protocol that clarifies how progress is assessed. This may involve meetings, regular reporting (verbal or in writing), or systematic and planned observation. Feedback is part of the monitoring process to support quality progress or, if the situation is not working as planned, moving from the act phase back to the planning phase of the cycle.

As noted earlier, expert consultation, information, and support must be available to team members when delegated a particular task. Delegation is not an abdication of responsibility; rather, it is the assumption of responsibility in the interest of getting the job done in an effective and efficient manner. Perhaps the chief reason for delegating is that quality objectives are always more easily achieved by sharing tasks and working cooperatively through teams.

The new generation of nonprofit managers must come to grips with the ever-changing demands of their customer base. In this regard, directing skills of the future must be sensitive to the new realities of process management sequences embodied within TQM. The new realities include a more highly educated, sophisticated, and discriminating customer population; a higher level of cost and quality consciousness; a more competitive human services marketplace (where value is measured in both cost and quality); and more pressing demands for higher levels of accountability. Each of these new realities affects the work of the organization and translates into management process sequences. In other words, changes in one sphere of the organization's activities have a ripple effect and play out in other areas. Higher levels of service accountability may translate in recruitment activities that bring strategically placed individuals to the board of directors or the consulting team. In some instances this may be a person with powerful connections in the community; in other instances it may be a person with specialized knowledge, such as grant writing or government lobbying skills. Directing skills make it incumbent on managers to incorporate the continuous quality improvement cycle in the organizational culture to meet and even exceed customer expectations.

Boundary-Spanning Skills

The effective management of change is an important facet of both TQM and the competing values framework. This competency is essential to managers whose work involves the use of boundary-spanning and innovator skills. Boundary-spanning activities bring TQM managers into the political and funding environments that comprise the organization's external customer base. Brager and Holloway (1978) characterized this environment in the following terms:

> An organization's environment is that wide arena beyond the organization's boundaries that includes such societal features as economic structures and conditions as well as power arrangements and social climate. Within this general environment are groups, organized and unorganized, some in direct contact with the organization and others not, many of which overlap and shift as they attempt to alter or to accommodate broad social conditions. (p. 39)

Engaging politically with the organizations's external environment means that the nonprofit manager may have to take a proactive stance to change "the distribution of sentiment (values, norms, and beliefs) within a community and the respective power resources of its members" (Brager & Holloway, 1978, pp. 50–51). The key point here is that the manager considers the dual dimensions of sentiment and power in developing an effective change strategy. Sentiments encompass the norms and belief system of the community and play an important part in the social, economic, and political life of citizens. Sentiments play a part in shaping the power structure, that is, who occupies positions of power and how that power is exercised and in what areas of community life. In a conservative rural community the church may play an important part in the life of the community. The wise nonprofit manager is sensitive to this reality in planning to work with community leaders or to implement a change strategy that depends on citizen support and understanding.

From a political framework it is apparent that different interests compete for scarce resources (Bolman & Deal, 1993). Within TQM attempts are made to develop horizontal relationships with external customers (for example, funders and vendors) so that long-term customer relationships can be developed. Nevertheless, competition does arise for scarce resources, and the skills needed to influence power brokers become critical. For the nonprofit manager the power brokers can include a range of people, depending on the sphere of influence that is relevant to the situation. It may be the local politician, the minister, a powerful union leader, a community elder, or a sports leader. Probably one of the most important areas of power and influence falls within the political arena, where local politicians play a key role. One of the important skills in this area is lobbying. Hrebenar and Scott (1982) characterized lobbying as "purposeful communication with a public official with the intention of influencing a decision that an official may make on a specific matter" (p. 399).

Boundary-spanning skills are becoming an ever more important facet of managerial responsibilities in today's rapidly changing world. Particularly in light of the decline of a publicly supported welfare state, the nonprofit manager must become increasingly sensitive to the needs of customers (or potential customers) in this type of external environment. An important feature of this is an increase in government "contract for service" opportunities where nonprofit managers can play a key role in addressing gaps in services. The privatization of governmental services presents another fundamental challenge to nonprofits. This adaptation to the external environment requires that nonprofit human services managers be comfortable with change and the political nuances that are inevitably involved. TQM presents an approach to planned change that accommodates the competing values inherent in human services management while being sensitive to and understanding of the value of self-determination for the organization's internal and external customers.

Human Relations Skills

Quinn (1988) identified the roles of group facilitator and mentor as critical in deploying human relations skills. Edwards and Yankey (1991) noted that "competencies for the mentor role include an understanding of self and others, interpersonal communication skills and development of subordinates. Competencies for the group facilitator role include team building, participatory decision making and conflict management" (p. 115).

Mentoring within the context of human services organizations can be considered a process wherein an individual or team selects a trusted individual to teach and give guidance in navigating the various organizational systems of the workplace. This process incorporates skills related to role modeling and training.

Inherent in effective mentoring is the ability to communicate performance expectations to the person being mentored. Communication about team and individual performance is essential to the TQM process. Communication within a mentorship relationship should be anchored in developmental terms. In addition, in the achievement-oriented culture of TQM, communication about performance is a necessary condition to sustain achievement motivation. Communicating about an individual's team performance can be an arduous task. Thompson (1995) acknowledged this reality: "Communicating about good performance is surprisingly difficult, perhaps because we believe that we should only speak up when someone does something wrong, fearful that anything we say will jeopardize the status quo. . . . Communicating about poor performance is also difficult. It means giving someone bad news" (pp. 124–125).

Previously, the point was made that the mentoring process should be developmental in nature. This type of personal–professional development should take place within the context of a plan, involving both career and performance objectives. It should be noted that peer mentoring is another process used in TQM organizations to promote self-improvement.

The group facilitator role is another facet of successful TQM initiatives. The development of teams is a medium for the empowerment of the organization's internal and external customer base. If teams are to be truly empowered, their members must be free from fear and experience a sense of safety—a freedom to speak and act. Deming (1986) believed that without safety, no quality initiative can be undertaken: "No one can put forth [his or her] best effort unless [he or she] feels secure. . . . Secure means without fear, not afraid to express ideas and not afraid to ask questions" (p. 50).

Given the importance of teams in a TQM initiative, it becomes necessary for the manager to develop group facilitation skills that emphasize a customer focus and the strengths and contribution that group members can bring to the continuous quality improvement cycle. Katzenbach and Smith (1993) suggested eight common approaches to the facilitation of high performance teams:

1. Establish urgency and direction;
2. Select members based on skills and skill potential, not personalities;
3. Pay particular attention to first meetings and actions;
4. Set some clear rules of behaviour;
5. Set and seize upon a few immediate performance oriented tasks and goals;
6. Challenge the group regularly with fresh ideas and information;
7. Spend lots of time together;
8. Exploit the power of positive feedback, recognition and regard.
(pp. 119–127)

Within the processes noted above, the manager–facilitator should also have good interpersonal skills that allow him or her to interact with all constituents, within and outside the organization, for the purposes of conflict resolution, change management, and problem solving. The manager should also be familiar with the structures, processes, and services within the organization and have a value-laden commitment to and understanding of the technical knowledge base of TQM.

People and systems constitute the customer base of TQM. Therefore, the manager in a TQM organization must possess excellent human relations skills. Indeed, the proliferation of TQM's philosophy and practices in nonprofit organizations can largely be attributed to management's realization that the ability to work effectively with people is at the core of maintaining a customer-oriented focus. In supporting this focus the TQM manager engages in both mentor and group facilitator roles. These roles allow managers to respond to the contingencies confronting the organization in the quest for quality and opportunities for continuous quality improvement.

CONCLUSION

The rapid pace of policy change and devolution in nonprofit organizations in the past decade has led to a contingency-based situational approach to nonprofit management. Indeed, governmental policy has traditionally set the parameters for the allocation and provision of resources in the nonprofit sector of the community. Increasingly, however, nonprofits are being asked to develop delivery systems that are less dependent on public resources. The pattern of operating in an environment of scarce resources was highlighted almost two decades ago by Gates (1980):

> Many observers contend that resource scarcity will be a permanent and pervasive fact of life for the foreseeable future . . . the surplus that has enabled a capitalist state to nurture and maintain the nonprofit sector is over. As this reality has become more apparent, so has the need to develop alternative views of organizational and administrative behavior that see decline and change not as an anomaly but as a normal condition of organizational life. (pp. 285–286)

The patterns noted by Gates have now evolved to the point at which the nonprofit human services industry is being questioned in terms of its relevance. This current reality is also characterized by frequent and pressing demands for greater accountability, especially in situations in which traditional public services are being privatized. Managers in the 21st century, faced with the rapid change of social policy mandates and the challenge of creating effective, efficient, and quality-based delivery systems, are being called on to create organizational systems that are flexible and responsive to their environmental contexts and at the same time are expected and to sustain administrative control in the goals, structure, and internal processes of their organizations. In responding to this new ecology of uncertainty, with shifting administrative mandates and changes in community expectations, nonprofit managers are creating new systems of management, such as TQM, and at the same time are developing an appreciation of the competing values framework that profiles the skills needed to effectively operationalize this quality paradigm. The integration of these two systems provides both a foundation and a framework for the achievement of greater organizational efficiency, effectiveness, and quality.

Earlier discussion in this chapter focused on TQM as a management system that emphasizes the importance of continuous quality improvement and responsiveness to customers. Current reports provide evidence of the effectiveness of TQM within the context of nonprofit organizations (Henry et al., 1996). However, TQM has also been profiled as a passing fad and even a management failure. Some of the concerns about TQM's lack of success have been cogently articulated by Brown, Hitchcock, and Willard (1994):

> Much has been written recently about the failures of total quality management (TQM), as if this is just another management fad in decline, following in the grand tradition of quality of work life programs, quality circles, and the like. When they read about these problems, managers shake their heads, sighing, and then go in search of the next panacea, this time with a little less enthusiasm. Many try not to smirk too openly, as if they always knew they could out-wait this "program" as they have successfully withstood a barrage of previous management initiatives. And those in our workforce who invested their spirits and energy in TQM efforts are reminded of just how powerless they are. We believe that this perspective is seriously flawed. After all, how can you dispute the need to delight customers and produce high-quality products and services? As an organizational philosophy, total quality management is even more critical now than it was just 10 years ago. If there has been a failure, it is not one of philosophy; it is one of implementation. And if we allow management to go in search of a replacement, we only enable them to avoid facing their own failures, thus perpetuating the search for the silver bullet. (p. v)

Although the data are mixed, several reports on TQM acknowledge that the system works when it is fully implemented in nonprofit organizations. However, failures in the system, as has been pointed out, seem to occur at the level of implementation. Here the explanatory variables include inadequate support (lack of top management commitment and resources), unrealistic expectations regarding the time frame for results, and inadequate preparation and training. The philosophical tenets of TQM, which promote an organizational culture of quality and place a high value on serving the needs of the organization's customer base, seem to be unquestioned. If nonprofit managers accept the "culture of quality" premises embedded in TQM and are truly committed to customers, then they are challenged to develop the requisite skills to bring this management system into operation—in other words, to give it life.

The competing values framework as presented by Quinn (1988) and Edwards and Yankey (1991) is complementary to the TQM model and presents the roles and associated skills that managers in nonprofits need to build an effective TQM system. Effective implementation of a TQM system occurs when TQM principles guide decision making at all levels, and they are integrated into all phases of the organization's work activity and key processes as part of a continuous quality improvement process.

The competing values framework's greatest value lies in its comprehensiveness in addressing the skills needed in confronting the daily complexities of work in a nonprofit organization. Intrinsically, the model as explicated in this chapter profiles the human relations, open systems, goal-oriented, and internal process management skills needed by nonprofit managers to work effectively in today's human services marketplace. The framework also profiles external foci that a nonprofit organization must have, not just to survive, but to prosper and develop. The management roles and skills presented in this chapter give credence to a contingency approach to management, that is, the competing values framework and its integration with a quality management system. TQM gives new meaning to customers and their central place in an organizational culture of quality. These two systems, when merged, clearly challenge traditional notions about management and present a new and innovative approach to the "management of complexity," a most relevant and contemporary concern for nonprofit organizations.

SKILLS-APPLICATION EXERCISE

Assume that you have just been appointed CEO for the Johnstown Mental Health Center (JMHC). JMHC has not been successful in its latest accreditation initiative and is looking to you to implement a management system that is both responsive to the center's employees and community needs. Given this situation, complete the following tasks:

1. Using Gunther and Hawkins's (1996) TQM flow chart, how would you explain to your board of directors the merit of adopting that system?

2. Select an activity that you view as important in linking the needs of JMHC with the resources of the community, and explain how it may be congruent or in conflict with the needs of other sectors of JMHC or the community.

3. What TQM steps or tools would you use to coordinate and direct initiatives within the JMHC to achieve customer (internal and external) satisfaction?

4. In what quadrant of the competing values framework would you place the following TQM activities: conducting a customer satisfaction survey; fundraising; developing a grant proposal; team building; counseling a troubled employee; setting up a citizen advisory council? Explain your choices.

REFERENCES

Abels, P., & Murphy, M. (1981). *Administration in the human services: A normative systems approach.* Englewood Cliffs, NJ.: Prentice Hall.

Austin, D. M. (1988). *The political economy of human service organizations.* Greenwich, CT: JAI Press.

Baker, E. M. (1988). Managing human performance. In J. M. Juran & F. M. Gryna (Eds.). *Juran's quality control handbook* (4th ed.). New York: McGraw-Hill.

Bolman, L., & Deal, T. (1993). *Reframing organizations.* San Francisco: Jossey-Bass.

Brager, G., & Holloway, S. (1978). *Changing human service organizations: Politics and practice.* New York: Free Press.

Breen, S., Cazenavel, L., Dodge, B. C., Kliebart, K., McDaniel, S. K., Moore, P. K., & Reck, M. (1996). Total quality management for the developmentally disabled. In J. Gunther & F. Hawkins (Eds.), *Total quality management in human service organizations* (pp. 136–148). New York: Springer.

Brown, M. G., Hitchcock, D. E., & Willard, M. L. (1994). *Why TQM fails and what to do about it.* New York: Irwin Professional.

Carlisle, H. (1979). *Management essentials: Concepts and applications.* Chicago: Science Research Associates.

Comstock, C., & Price, S. B. (1996). Hillside children's center. In J. Gunther & F. Hawkins (Eds.), *Total quality management in human service organizations.* (pp. 123–135). New York: Springer.

Coulton, C. J. (1991). Developing and implementing quality assurance programs. In R. L. Edwards & J. A. Yankey (Eds.), *Skills for effective human services management* (pp. 251–266). Washington, DC: NASW Press.

Crosby, P. (1980). *Quality is free: The art of making quality certain:* New York: McGraw-Hill.

Crosby, P. (1984). *Quality without tears.* New York: McGraw-Hill.

Deming, W. E. (1986). *Out of the crisis.* Cambridge, MA: Massachusetts Institute of Technology, Center for Advanced Engineering Study.

Drucker, P. (1954). *Practice of management.* New York: Harper.

Edwards, R. L. (1987). The competing values approach as an integrating framework for the management curriculum. *Administration in Social Work, 11*(1), 1–13.

Edwards, R. L., & Austin, D. M. (1991). Managing effectively in an environment of competing values. In R. L. Edwards & J. A. Yankey (Eds.), *Skills for effective human services management* (pp. 5–22) Washington, DC: NASW Press.

Edwards, R. L., Cooke, P. W., & Reid, P. N. (1996). Social work management in an era of diminishing responsibility. *Social Work, 41,* 468–479.

Edwards, R. L., Faerman, S. R., & McGrath, M. R. (1986). The competing values approach to organizational effectiveness: A tool for agency administrators. *Administration in Social Work*, *10*(4), 1–14.

Edwards, R. L., & Yankey, J. A. (Eds). (1991). *Skills for effective human services management*. Washington, DC: NASW Press.

Forrest, E. (1996). *Activity based management*. New York: McGraw-Hill.

Galea-Curmi, E., & Hawkins, F. (1996). Benchmarking. In J. Gunther & F. Hawkins (Eds.), *Total quality management in human services organizations* (pp. 163–181). New York: Springer.

Gates, B. L. (1980). *Social program administration*. Englewood Cliffs, NJ: Prentice Hall.

Gummer, B., & McCallion, P. (Eds). (1995). *Total quality management in the social services*. Albany, NY: Rockefeller College of Public Affairs and Policy.

Gunther, J., & Hawkins, F. (Eds). (1996). *Total quality management in human service organizations*. New York: Springer.

Hasenfeld, Y., & English, R. (1974). *Human service organizations*. Ann Arbor: University of Michigan Press.

Hassen, P. (1993). *RX for hospitals*. Toronto: Stoddart.

Henderson, P. A. (1996). Freeport Hospital Health Care Village. In J. Gunther & F. Hawkins (Eds.), *Total quality management in human service organizations* (pp. 75–88). New York: Springer.

Henry, G., Wedel, K. R., & Czypinski, K. S. (1996). "Quality Oklahoma" and the Oklahoma Department of Human Services. In J. Gunther & F. Hawkins (Eds.), *Total quality management in human service organizations* (pp. 89–102). New York: Springer.

Hrebenar, R. J., & Scott, R. K. (1982). *Interest group politics in America*. Englewood Cliffs, NJ: Prentice Hall.

Juran, J. M. (1988). Company wide planning for quality. In J. M. Juran & F. M. Gryna (Eds.), *Juran's quality control handbook* (pp. 6.3–6.5). New York: McGraw-Hill.

Juran, J. M. (1989). *Juran on leadership for quality: An executive handbook*. New York: Free Press.

Katzenbach, J. R., & Smith, D. K. (1993). *The wisdom of teams*. New York: Harper-Collins.

Kessler, S. (1995). *Total quality service*. Milwaukee: ASQC Press.

Lehmann, R. (1987). Joint commission sets agenda for change. *Quality Review Bulletin, 12*, 72–75.

Lehmann, R. (1989). Forum on clinical indicator development: A discussion on the use and development of indicators. *Quality Review Bulletin, 15*, 223–227.

Martin, L. (1993). *Total quality management in human service organizations*. Newbury Park, CA: Sage Publications.

Odiorne, G. (1965). *Management by objectives: A system of managerial leadership*. Belmont, CA: Pitman.

Quinn, R. E. (1988). *Beyond rational management: Mastering the paradoxes and competing demands of high performance*. San Francisco: Jossey-Bass.

Quinn, R. E., & Rohrbaugh, J. A. (1983). A spatial model of effectiveness: Toward a competing values approach to organizational analysis. *Management Science, 29*, 363–377.

Thompson, B. L. (1995). *The new managers handbook*. Burr Ridge, IL: Irwin Professional.

Walton, M. (1986). *The Deming management method*. New York: Putman.

Weiner, M. E. (1990). *Human services management*. Belmont, CA: Wadsworth.

A Sampling of Web Sites Related to Nonprofit Management

Compiled by Jeffrey A. Edwards

The Internet has been called the "information superhighway." A collection of computer networks that has been growing at an incredible rate, the Internet via the World Wide Web makes it possible for nonprofit managers to access up-to-date information about many topics, ranging from government policy to information about foundations and corporations. Numerous Web sites are of value to those involved in nonprofit management, and new sites are created every day.

A wealth of information can be obtained from a range of government, for-profit, and nonprofit organizations. Nonprofit managers often find that the Internet can help them locate possible funding sources and compile information they need for funding proposals. Managers may also find that is useful to get current updates on legislation and governmental policy initiatives.

Given that new sites are rapidly being added to the Web, it is impossible to print an up-to-date, authoritative list of addresses. The following list of Web addresses is a starting point for nonprofit managers who want to access online resources.

ORGANIZATIONS

AccessPoint
www.accesspt.com
This site provides information about consulting and Web site development and technical assistance to nonprofits and individuals seeking to make an impact using Internet technology.

American Association of Fund-Raising Counsel
25 West 43rd Street, Suite 820
New York, NY 10036
212-354-5799
www.oramgroup.com/aafrc.html

This site is currently under construction. The association represents professional fundraising firms who help nonprofits plan and manage fundraising campaigns. It also publishes *Giving USA* on an annual basis, as well as the bimonthly newsletter *The Fund Raising Review*.

Center for Community Change
1000 Wisconsin Avenue, NW
Washington, DC 20007
202-342-0519
www.pratt.edu/picced/resource/ccc.html

This organization provides resources to nonprofits assisting low-income populations and helps racial and ethnic groups with planning, organizational, and fundraising issues.

Council on Foundations
1828 L Street, NW
Washington, DC 20036
202-466-6512
www.cof.org

The Council on Foundations is a nonprofit membership association of grantmaking foundations and corporations. The council's mission is to promote responsible and effective philanthropy. Members of the council include nearly 1,500 independent, operating, family, community, public, and company-sponsored foundations; corporate giving programs; and foundations in other countries.

Donors Forum of Chicago
Metro Chicago Information Center
University of Illinois–Chicago
www.uic.edu/~mhurst/donors

This site provides access to the 1994 Donors Forum Philanthropic Database, a foundation grants database made possible by the Donors Forum of Chicago, the Metro Chicago Information Center, and the University of Illinois–Chicago Great Cities Program. The database is searchable by foundation, benefactor type, grant purpose, support type, and recipient.

The Foundation Center
79 Fifth Avenue
New York, NY 10003-3076
212-620-4230
www.fdncenter.org

The Foundation Center is an independent nonprofit information clearinghouse established to foster public understanding of the foundation field by collecting, organizing, analyzing, and disseminating information on foundations, corporate giving, and related subjects. The center operates libraries at five locations, including national collections at its national office in New York City and at its field office in Washington, DC, and regional collections at its offices in Atlanta, Cleveland, and San Francisco. Center libraries provide access to a unique collection of materials on philanthropy and are open to the public free of charge.

The Grantsmanship Center
1125 West Sixth Street, 5th Floor
Los Angeles, CA 90017
213-482-9860
www.tgci.com

The Grantsmanship Center is a training organization that conducts workshops nationwide on grantwriting, program management, fundraising, and other issues that affect the nonprofit sector.

GuideStar
Philanthropic Research, Inc.
1126 Professional Drive
Williamsburg, VA 23185
757-229-4631
www.guidestar.org

This site provides information on more than 600,000 American charities and nonprofit organizations, including up-to-date news on philanthropy and resources for donors and volunteers. The entire database is searchable by keyword.

Impact Online
Impact Online, Inc.
715 Colorado Avenue, Suite 4
Palo Alto, CA 94303
www.webcom.com/~iol

Impact Online is a nonprofit corporation whose mission is to facilitate and increase community involvement via the Internet. It seeks to collaborate with and complement existing organizations and build community resources to get more people involved in volunteering and fundraising.

Independent Sector
1828 L Street, NW
Washington, DC 20036
202-223-8100
www.indepsec.org

Independent Sector is a national coalition of nonprofit organizations, foundations, and corporate giving programs working to encourage philanthropy, volunteering, nonprofit initiatives, and citizen action that help better serve people and communities. The organization is involved in advocacy, research, and leadership development activities.

Information for Nonprofits
Evergreen State Society
1122 Pike Street, No. 444
Seattle, WA 98122-3934
206-329-5640
www.eskimo.com/~pbarber

This site includes a listing of useful resources and frequently asked questions that concern issues in the nonprofit sector. Discussion areas include how to start nonprofit organizations, how to raise funds for them, and how to effectively use the Internet.

Internet Nonprofit Center
www.nonprofits.org

The site has four areas: (1) The library is a repository for publications, information, and data about nonprofit organizations and the nonprofit sector, generally by sources other than nonprofits themselves; (2) the gallery includes information drawn directly from nonprofits themselves, and nonprofits may use this space to post their own brochures, annual reports, and home pages; (3) the parlor is a chat area with bulletin board to share information and ask questions; and (4) the heliport has links to additional resources of special interest to donors and volunteers.

National Center for Nonprofit Boards
2000 L Street, NW, Suite 510
Washington, DC 20036-4907
1-800-883-6262
www.ncnb.org:7002/1

The center serves as a resource to members of nonprofit boards. It publishes *Fund Raising and the Nonprofit Board Member.*

National Committee for Responsive Philanthropy
2001 S Street, NW, Suite 620
Washington, DC 20009
202-387-9177
www.primenet.com/~ncrp/index/html

This organization is committed to making philanthropy more responsive to socially, economically, and politically disenfranchised people and to the dynamic needs of increasingly diverse communities nationwide. The committee's programs aim to maximize the financial capacities of organizations that seek justice for these populations.

Non-Profit Cyber-Accountability

www.bway.net/~hbograd/cyb-acc.html

Home of the Cyber-Accountability listserv, this site provides a discussion area concerning the impact that the Internet and technology have on the nonprofit world, and it provides links to other nonprofit-focused Web sites. Information in this site is compiled by the National Accountability Research Project at the Nonprofit Coordinating Committee in New York.

Nonprofit Partners Virtual Bookstore

Nonprofit Partners
4502 Groveland Road
P.O. Box 18937
University Heights, OH 44118
1-800-860-4490
www.nonprofitpartners.com

Nonprofit Partners was founded to help improve the results achieved by nonprofit organizations by providing a one-stop source for the most useful publications and training tools. The company offers books and CD-ROMs on nonprofit development, grant writing, management, marketing, leadership, and consulting.

Nonprofit Resources Catalogue

www.clark.net/pub/pwalker

This site catalogs Internet sites that could benefit nonprofits and those interested in a wide variety of issues. There is an emphasis on metalinks to other catalogs in a particular subject area.

The Urban Institute

2100 M Street, NW
Washington, DC 20037
www.urban.org/index.htm

The Urban Institute's objectives are to sharpen thinking about society's social and economic problems and efforts to solve them, improve government decisions and their implementation, and increase citizens' awareness about important public choices. This site provides up-to-date information on institute activities and research centers and also provides information about the Center on Nonprofits and the National Center on Charitable Statistics.

Periodical Publications

The Chronicle of Philanthropy
1255 23th Street, NW
Washington, DC 20037
1-800-842-7817
www.philanthropy.com
Published biweekly by the Chronicle of Philanthropy

Foundation News & Commentary
1828 L Street, NW
Washington, DC 20036
202-466-6512
www.cof.org
Published bimonthly by the Council on Foundations

Grassroots Fundraising Journal
P.O. Box 11607
Berkeley, CA 94712
510-704-8714
emf.net/~cheetham/ggrral-1.html
Published bimonthly

Nonprofit and Voluntary Sector Quarterly
350 Sansome Street
San Francisco, CA 94104-1342
1-800-956-7739
jbp.com/index2.html
Published quarterly by Jossey-Bass Publishers

Nonprofit Management and Leadership
350 Sansome Street
San Francisco, CA 94104-1342
1-800-956-7739
jbp.com/index2.html
Published quarterly by Jossey-Bass Publishers

Nonprofit Research News
1333 New Hampshire Avenue, NW, Suite 1070
Washington, DC 20036
202-736-5800
www.aspeninst.org/index.html
Published quarterly by the Aspen Institute

Nonprofit World

6314 Odana Road, Suite 1
Madison, WI 53719
608-274-9777
www.cpn.org/sections/affiliates/society-nonprofitorgs.html
Published bimonthly by the Society for Nonprofit Organizations

Philanthropic Digest

414 Plaza Drive, Suite 209
Westmont, IL 60559
708-655-0177
weber.u.washington.edu/~dlamb/apra/APRA.html
Published monthly by the American Prospect Research Association

Philanthropy Journal Online

5 West Hargett Street, Suite 805
Raleigh, NC 27601
www.philanthropy-journal.org

Published monthly by the Philanthropy Journal of North Carolina; provides a searchable version of the publication, as well numerous links to other nonprofit Web sites

Index

Group cohesion, 442–443
Group facilitators
competencies for, 153, 155
goals of, 12–13
managers as, 12
Group-think decisions, 159
Groupware, 329–330
Gunther, J., 540

H

Hasenfeld, Y., 526
Hawkins, Frank, 523, 527, 540
Hawthorne Western Electric Studies, 186, 528
Health care market, 115
Health Industry Distributors Association, 457
Heath, P. P., 325
Hedlund v. Superior Court of Orange County, 410
Henry, Christine E., 25
Herzberg, F., 188
Hierarchy of needs, 188
Hirschhorn, L., 291
Histograms, 533, 534
HIV/AIDS, 500, 501
Holland, Thomas P., 423
Holloway, S., 547
Holmes, Oliver Wendell, Jr., 406
Houle, C. O., 425
Hourly rates, 509
Huberman, J., 273
Human relations skills
in competing values model, 12–13, 538
management level and, 7–8
total quality management and, 548–550
Human resources management, 363–364
Hurry sickness, 470

I

Implementation, 40–42
Independent foundations, 48
Independent Sector (Washington, DC), 110
Individuals with disabilities, 178–179. *See also* Americans with Disabilities Act (ADA)

Information technology, 325. *See also* Computers
Information technology management
assessment and, 331–332
budget plans and, 335–338
hardware and software purchasing and, 335
maintaining and upgrading, 338–339
personnel and, 332–333
strategic plans and, 332
training and, 333–335, 338
Innovation
barriers to, 28–30
competencies for, 25
creativity and, 31, 38–39
leadership through, 37–48
managers and, 11
planning and, 39–40
Institutional or negotiated-order perspective, of mergers, 495–496
Institutional theory, 211
Insurance, for nonprofit organizations, 413–414
Internal control, 361–362
Internal Revenue Service (IRS), 85
International City Management Association, 83
International Telephone and Telegraph Company, 528
Internet. *See also* Electronic mail (e-mail); World Wide Web (WWW)
description of, 330–331
program evaluation information on, 403–406
Interpersonal skills, 7–8
Interviews
dismissal, 273–275
employment, 164–169. *See also* Employment interviews
with media, 105–106
Inventory, 356

J

Jablonski v. U.S., 410
Janz, T., 168
Job classification, 173–174
Job descriptions, 156–157

The Editors

Richard L. Edwards, PhD, ACSW, is dean and professor at the School of Social Work, University of North Carolina at Chapel Hill, where he provided the leadership to develop an interdisciplinary certificate program in nonprofit leadership and teaches courses on fundraising and nonprofit management. He has worked in nonprofit and public organizations as a supervisor and manager and serves on the boards of directors of several nonprofits. In addition, he frequently consults with nonprofit organizations. A frequent contributor to the management literature, he is senior author of *Building a Strong Foundation: Fundraising for Nonprofits* and editor-in-chief of the *Encyclopedia of Social Work—19th Edition*. He is a former president of the National Association of Social Workers.

John A. Yankey, PhD, ACSW, is the Leonard W. Mayo Professor at the Mandel School of Applied Social Sciences and Director of Community Services for the Mandel Center for Nonprofit Organizations, Case Western Reserve University, in Cleveland. He teaches fundraising, strategic planning, and legislative and political processes. He also serves as a consultant to a wide range of nonprofit organizations throughout the United States. He is a co-author of *Building a Strong Foundation: Fundraising for Nonprofits* and is a frequent contributor to the management literature.

Mary A. Altpeter, MSW, MA, ACSW, is associate director for operations of the Institute on Aging and adjunct lecturer in the Department of Health Behavior and Health Education at the School of Public Health, University of North Carolina at Chapel Hill. She has extensive experience as a trainer, grant writer, and manager. She has been a consultant to a variety of nonprofit and public organizations and is a proposal reviewer for several national foundations.

The Contributors

David M. Austin, PhD, ACSW, is the Bert Kruger Smith Centennial Professor in the School of Social Work at the University of Texas at Austin. He is a member of the board of directors of the Institute for the Advancement of Social Work Research and has many years of experience in community organization and social planning, as well as a distinguished career in university teaching and research. He is a frequent contributor to the professional literature.

Darlyne Bailey, PhD, is dean of the Mandel School of Applied Social Sciences, Case Western Reserve University in Cleveland. She has a secondary appointment in the Weatherhead School of Management and is a faculty associate with the Mandel Center for Nonprofit Organizations. She has worked in the nonprofit human services arena for more than a decade and currently serves on several nonprofit boards of trustees.

Richard E. Baznik, BA, is vice president for public affairs at Case Western Reserve University in Cleveland, where he is responsible for government relations and other communication and marketing activities, as well as having oversight of strategic planning for the university. He has served as trustee or board member for nonprofit organizations in the arts, health care, and primary and secondary education.

Elizabeth A. S. Benefield, BA, is a consultant to nonprofit organizations on issues related to fundraising and marketing. She was formerly the assistant dean for development and external affairs at the School of Social Work, University of North Carolina at Chapel Hill. She is coauthor of *Building a Strong Foundation: Fundraising for Nonprofits.*

Andrew Broughton, PhD, is a senior research associate in the School of Social Work at the University of North Carolina at Chapel Hill, where he is responsible for designing and delivering training courses in technology and helping nonprofit organization personnel use modern computer technology, such as local area networks, database systems, and the World Wide Web.

David Campbell, MAR, is vice president of the Center for Families and Children in Cleveland, a multiservice nonprofit organization that was formed by a merger in 1970 and has grown by merger since then. He is a doctoral candidate at Case Western Reserve University, studying organizational restructuring in the social services delivery system.

Roslyn H. Chernesky, PhD, is professor at the Fordham University Graduate School of Social Service in New York, where she chairs the Administration Concentration. She publishes and teaches on administration, organizational theory, program development, and service delivery. She has written extensively on women and management.

Todd Cohen, BA, is publisher and editor of the *Philanthropy Journal of North Carolina.* He also writes a weekly column on philanthropy in the Business Section of the *News and Observer,* a major daily newspaper published in Raleigh, North Carolina.

Laurie N. DiPadova, PhD, is chief program manager at the Center for Public Policy and Administration, University of Utah, Salt Lake City. Her articles have appeared in numerous journals. She authored a chapter in and wrote the *Instructional Guide* for the management text *Becoming a Master Manager: A Competency Framework.*

Douglas C. Eadie, MS, is founder and president of two firms based in Cleveland—Doug Eadie Presents! and Strategic Development Consulting, Inc. He writes, speaks, and consults in three areas: innovation and change leadership, chief executive leadership, and board capacity building. He is the author of nine books, including *Changing By Design* and *Boards That Work,* and his articles and chapters have appeared in numerous books and journals.

Jeffrey A. Edwards, BA, is prospect research analyst in the Office of Development, University of North Carolina at Chapel Hill. He is a coauthor of *Building a Strong Foundation: Fundraising for Nonprofits.*

Sue R. Faerman, PhD, is associate professor at the Nelson A. Rockefeller College of Public Affairs and Policy, University at Albany, State University of New York. Her major teaching and research interests are in the areas of management and organization development. She is also interested in conflict management, particularly how conflict can be used to generate more creative organizational outcomes. A frequent contributor to the management literature, she is coauthor of *Becoming a Master Manager: A Competency Framework* and *Supervising New York State: A Framework for Excellence,* as well as a number of articles that focus on the evaluation of management development programs.

Peter Ben Friedman, JD, is professor of lawyering skills at Case Western Reserve University School of Law. After 12 years of practice as a commercial litigator, he now teaches a first-year course in research, analysis, and writing; an upper-level course in pretrial practice; and American contract law to foreign students enrolled in Case Western's LLM program in International Legal Studies. In addition, he has taught continuing legal education courses on contract remedies to Ohio judges and magistrates.

Ronald K. Green, JD, ACSW, is professor and chair, Department of Social Work, Winthrop University, Rock Hill, South Carolina. He has more than 20 years of experience in negotiating the provision of contract services among university-based training and technical assistance units, nonprofit organizations, and public social services agencies. He teaches social policy and human services management courses. He also served on numerous nonprofit boards and currently chairs the Public Policy Committee for the National Association of Staff Development and Training, an affiliate of the American Public Welfare Association.

John Gunther, PhD, is professor and director of the School of Social Work at Southwest Missouri State University in Springfield. He is an active member of the American Society of Quality Control and has served as a consultant and trainer for Total Quality Management in both the United States and Canada. He is coauthor of *Total Quality Management in Human Service Organizations* and *Making TQM Work: Quality Tools for Human Services.* His articles have appeared in a number of journals.

Frank Hawkins, PhD, is professor and chair of the Doctoral Studies Program in Social Work at Memorial University in St. John's, Newfoundland, Canada. He is a former director of the School of Social Work at Memorial University and former president of the Canadian Association of Schools of Social Work. He is a frequent contributor to the literature and is coauthor of several books, including *Total Quality Management in Human Service Organizations* and *Making TQM Work: Quality Tools for Human Services.* He serves as a management consultant and trainer in Canada, the United States, Great Britain, and Japan.

Christine E. Henry, MNO, is director of the William J. and Dorothy K. O'Neill Foundation in Cleveland. She has worked in community education, hospital administration, and nonprofit public relations and volunteer management. Her current affiliations include Grantmakers Forum in Cleveland, the Council on Foundations, and numerous volunteer activities. Her areas of teaching include sociology and proposal writing.

Thomas P. Holland, PhD, is professor and director of the Institute for Nonprofit Organizations and director of the School of Social Work's Center for Social Services Research and Development, University of Georgia, Athens. He has published extensively on nonprofit management and governance. Recent publications include *Improving Board Effectiveness: Practical Lessons for Nonprofit Health Care Organizations* and *How to Build a More Effective Board.* His chapters and articles have appeared in numerous books and journals, including *The Harvard Business Review.* He consults with executives and nonprofit boards across the United States.

Mary Kay Kantz, JD, is professor of lawyering skills at Case Western Reserve University School of Law. Her areas of teaching include legal research, analysis and writing, persuasive public speaking, and appellate advocacy.

Paul A. Kurzman, PhD, ACSW, is professor at the Hunter College School of Social Work and the Graduate Center of the City University of New York, where he specializes in organizational theory, risk management, and occupational social work practice. He has been an administrator of public and private human services agencies and is author or editor of six books and numerous articles in human services journals. He contributed "Professional Liability and Malpractice" to the 19th edition of *The Encyclopedia of Social Work.*

Daniel A. Lebold, MSW, is assistant dean for administration and coordinator of the Nonprofit Leadership Certificate Program at the University of North Carolina at Chapel Hill School of Social Work. He has more than 15 years of board experience in nonprofit organizations and continues to serve as a board member and consultant to several nonprofits.

Andrea Meier, EdM, is a doctoral candidate in the School of Social Work at the University of North Carolina at Chapel Hill. Before beginning her doctoral studies, she worked as a substance abuse counselor and supervisor, as the founding director of a statewide training program on substance abuse issues for professional caregivers in Massachusetts, and as an organizational consultant. Currently, she has been involved in providing technical assistance on self-evaluation for programs in several states. Her research and publication activities have focused on program evaluation, as well as on professional stress management and on the role of telephone, computer, and Internet technologies in social interventions.

Kathryn Mercer, PhD, JD, MSSA, is professor of lawyering skills at Case Western Reserve University School of Law. She is a trainer for social workers in the child welfare field and teaches interdisciplinary courses on law and social work and alternative dispute resolution to students of law, social work, and business. Other teaching areas include family law; lawyering skills; and legal research, analysis, and writing. Her research has focused on child custody standards.

Kenneth I. Millar, PhD, is dean of the School of Social Work at Louisiana State University, Baton Rouge. His areas of specialization include performance evaluation, leadership, and legislative issues, particularly those affecting children and families. He is chair of the Legislative Affairs Committee of the National Association of Deans and Directors of Schools of Social Work. The coauthor of *Performance Appraisal in the Human Services,* he serves on the boards of directors of several nonprofit organizations in Baton Rouge.

Peter J. Pecora, PhD, is manager of research with the Casey Family Program and associate professor at the School of Social Work, University of Washington, in Seattle. He is a frequent contributor to the literature, and his chapters and articles have appeared in numerous books and journals.

Emily D. Pelton, MPA, is director of government relations for Case Western Reserve University in Cleveland. She has worked as a policy analyst on a wide range of federal science and technology issues in the White House Office of Science and Technology Policy, as well as the Office of Management and Budget. Before joining Case Western Reserve University, she was assistant to the executive director of the American Institute of Physics, a nonprofit industry association. She has also served as a board member of a nonprofit organization in Arlington, Virginia, that provides assistance to homeless families and victims of domestic violence.

Robert F. Rivas, PhD, ACSW, is professor of social work at Siena College in Loundonville, New York. He has experience in organizations dealing with families and children, as well as in residential treatment centers for children. His research and public actions have focused on management, social work education, and group work. He is coauthor of *Introduction to Group Work Practice* and *Case Studies in Generalist Practice.*

James L. Strachan, PhD, CMA, CCA, CCP, has been a member of the Mandel Center's Faculty of Case Western Reserve University since the center's inception. He earned his PhD at the University of Texas at Austin and his MS and BS degrees at Southern Illinois University. He is the coauthor of the article "Crime Doesn't Pay (If You Are Accused)" and the book *How to Get into the Right Business School.* He has won several teaching awards.

John E. Tropman, PhD, is professor at the School of Social Work and the School of Business at the University of Michigan in Ann Arbor. He also teaches courses in the University of Michigan Progam in Nonprofit Executive Leadership. He has authored and edited a number of books, including *Entrepreneurial Systems for the 1990s, Strategies of Community Organization,*

Tactics of Community Organization, Meetings: How to Make Them Work for You, and *Making Meetings Work: Achieving High Quality Decisions in Groups and Teams.* He provides consultation and training to nonprofit organizations across the United States.

Charles L. Usher, PhD, is the Wallace H. Kuralt Professor of Public Welfare Policy and Administration in the School of Social Work at the University of North Carolina at Chapel Hill. He was formerly the director of the Center for Policy Studies at the Research Triangle Institute. He is currently directing evaluation activities in several systems change initiatives sponsored by national foundations. He also manages a program sponsored by the Annie E. Casey Foundation that seeks to identify and provide apprenticeship opportunities for consultants who can assist foundation grantees to develop their capacity for self-evaluation.

Barbara Wester, MNO, is president of Sententia, Inc., a nonprofit management consulting firm based in Cleveland. She previously spent 10 years in new market development for a for-profit corporation both in the United States and Southeast Asia.

Laura I. Zimmerman, PhD, is a clinical associate professor in the School of Social Work at the University of North Carolina at Chapel Hill. She directs the school's Computing and Information Technology Unit and its Human Services Smart Agency. The latter entity is dedicated to the improvement of computer use and knowledge in the human services. She serves on nonprofit agency boards and frequently consults with nonprofit organizations about computing and technology.

Skills for Effective Management of Nonprofit Organizations

Cover and text designed by Naylor Design, Inc.
Text composed by Maben Publications, Inc.
Type set in Bembo and Gil Sans
Printed and bound by Boyd Printing Company